Striking Change

The Great Artistic Collaboration of Theodore Roosevelt and Augustus Saint-Gaudens

Michael F. Moran

Atlanta, Georgia

Striking Change

The Great Artistic Collaboration of Theodore Roosevelt and Augustus Saint-Gaudens

www.whitmanbooks.com

© 2008 Whitman Publishing, LLC
3101 Clairmont Road · Suite C · Atlanta GA 30329

All rights reserved, including duplication of any kind and storage in electronic or visual retrieval systems. Permission is granted for writers to use a reasonable number of brief excerpts and quotations in printed reviews and articles, provided credit is given to the title of the work and the author. Written permission from the publisher is required for other uses of text, illustrations, and other content, including in books and electronic or other media.

Correspondence concerning this book may be directed to the publisher, at the address above.

ISBN: 0794823564
Printed in China

For a complete catalog of numismatic reference books, supplies, and storage products, visit Whitman Publishing online at www.whitmanbooks.com.

Contents

List of Illustrations iv
Foreword by Henry J. Duffy x
About the Author xii
Acknowledgments and Dedication xiii
Introduction by Q. David Bowers xv

Prologue: "All Ye Need to Know" 1

Part I: A Most Unique Cast of Characters

1. New York City 13
2. Making Their Way 25
3. Gilder's Dream 43
4. A Mountain of Labor 53

Part II: "Fair Enough"

5. The World's Columbian Exposition 71
6. Ladies Rebuffed 87
7. Thacher's Gambit 101
8. Embarrassment Enough for All 113
9. Aftermath 137

Part III: On the National Stage

10. A Sherman Connection 151
11. In Search of an Angel 157
12. Edith 169
13. Homeless 177
14. The Confident Years 193

Part IV: The "Pet Crime"

15. The Stage Is Set 215
16. A Medal for Edith 221
17. An Unwanted Headache 235
18. Engagement 255
19. An End of Sorts 277

Part V: Carry a Big Stick — Cast a Long Shadow

20. A Cameo in Gold 299
21. A Man for the Occasion 305
22. The Last Words 323
23. A Requiem for Gus 331
24. The Legacy 339

Postscript

25. Striking Change 363

Resources

Endnotes 371
Bibliography 421
Index 427

Illustrations

1. Augustus Saint-Gaudens in 1865. Photo courtesy of Dartmouth College Rauner Special Collections Library. 19
2. Theodore Roosevelt, brother Elliott, and sister Corrine, in 1873. Photo courtesy of Theodore Roosevelt Collection, Harvard College Library. 19
3. The Lincoln funeral procession approaching Union Square, New York City. Photo courtesy of Theodore Roosevelt Collection, Harvard College Library. 20
4. Augustus Saint-Gaudens as a student. Photo courtesy of Dartmouth College Rauner Special Collections Library. 27
5. Charles Follen McKim, bas-relief by Saint-Gaudens, 1878. Photo courtesy of Saint-Gaudens National Historic Site, Cornish, New Hampshire. 28
6. Augusta Homer at the time of her engagement. Photo courtesy of Dartmouth College Rauner Special Collections Library. 31
7.–8. Bas-reliefs by Saint-Gaudens: the Richard Watson Gilder family, 1879, and the angel from an early Shaw Memorial model. Photos courtesy of Saint-Gaudens National Historic Site, Cornish, New Hampshire. 32
9. Monument to Admiral David G. Farragut, by Saint-Gaudens, 1881. Photo courtesy of Dartmouth College Rauner Special Collections Library. 35
10. Theodore Roosevelt with Alice Lee in 1879. Photo courtesy of Theodore Roosevelt Collection, Harvard College Library. 36
11. Liberty Seated coinage design. Photo courtesy of Whitman Publishing, LLC. 45
12. Horatio Burchard Mint director medal. Photo courtesy of National Numismatic Collection, Smithsonian Institution. 45
13. Morgan silver dollar. Author's collection. 46
14. James P. Kimball Mint director medal. Photo courtesy of National Numismatic Collection, Smithsonian Institution. 46
15.–16. George Washington Inauguration Centennial medal: official badge, author's collection; mold for an early version, photo courtesy of Saint-Gaudens National Historic Site, Cornish, New Hampshire. 51
17. George Washington Inauguration Centennial commemorative medal. Author's collection. 52
18. Charles Barber, U.S. Mint engraver. Photo courtesy of Heritage Auction Galleries. 55
19. 1883 "racketeer nickel." Author's collection. 55
20. Edward O. Leech, U.S. Mint director. Author's collection. 56
21. Joseph Francis medal. Author's collection. 63
22.–24. Charles Barber designs for the subsidiary silver coins: first design and subsequent revision, photos courtesy of the National Numismatic Collection, Smithsonian Institution; accepted final design, author's collection. 64
25. Daniel H. Burnham. Photo courtesy of Library of Congress. 73
26. The World's Columbian Exposition Court of Honor. Photo courtesy of Chicago Public Library, Special Collections and Preservation Division. 74
27. James Ellsworth, chairman of the Committee on Liberal Arts for the Exposition Company. Photo courtesy of Chicago Public Library, Special Collections and Preservation Division. 77
28. Christopher Columbus portrait, by Lorenzo Lotto. Photo from *Numismatic Art in America*, 2nd ed., by Cornelius Vermeule (Whitman Publishing, 2007). 78
29.–31. World's Columbian Exposition designs: sketch for half dollar by Charles Barber, photo courtesy of Chicago Public Library, James Ellsworth Collection; directorate badge by Olin Warner, photo courtesy of National Numismatic Collection, Smithsonian Institution; Proof Columbian half dollar, author's collection. 85

Illustrations

32. Bertha Honoré Palmer, chair of the Board of Lady Managers of the World's Columbian Exposition. Photo courtesy of Chicago Public Library, Special Collections and Preservation Division. 89

33. Caroline Peddle, artist, in 1894. Photo courtesy of Swope Art Museum, Terre Haute, Indiana. Gift from Barbara, Carlotta, and Ellen Hayes in memory of the Peddle sisters. 90

34. Sketch of the proposed Isabella quarter, by Caroline Peddle. Photo courtesy of U.S. National Archives and Records Administration, College Park, Maryland. 95

35. John G. Carlisle, secretary of the Treasury. Photo courtesy of U.S. Treasury Department. 96

36. 1893 Isabella quarter dollar, Proof. Author's collection. 96

The first color section appears after page 96.

37. "Brooklyn Heights, Opposite the City of New York," 1854. Photo from *Gleason's Pictorial Drawing-Room Companion* (1854). C1

38. "View in Wall Street from Corner of Broad," 1867. Photo from *Thirty Years' Progress of the United States* (1867). C1

39. Frederick's Photographic Temple of Art, circa 1850. Photo courtesy of Bibliothèque Nationale de France, Paris. C1

40. Abraham Lincoln, Bureau of Engraving and Printing vignette. Photo from *Obsolete Paper Money Issued by Banks in the United States*, by Q. David Bowers (Whitman Publishing, 2006). C2

41. Series of 1923 $5 Silver Certificate. Photo from *A Guide Book of United States Paper Money*, 2nd edition, by Arthur L. and Ira S. Friedberg (Whitman Publishing, 2007). C2

42. Abraham Lincoln plaque, by Victor David Brenner. Photo courtesy of Stack's Rare Coins. C2

43. Lincoln presidential medal, by George Morgan. Photo from *Numismatic Art in America*. C2

44. Theodore Roosevelt and siblings in Dresden in 1873. Photo courtesy of Theodore Roosevelt Collection, Harvard College Library. C3

45. Current coins of the mid-19th century. Photos from *A Guide Book of United States Coins*, 61st ed., by R.S. Yeoman, edited by Kenneth Bressett (Whitman Publishing, 2007). C4

46. Admiral David G. Farragut, by Mathew Brady, 1863. Photo courtesy of U.S. National Archives and Records Administration, College Park, Maryland. C5

47.–48. Farragut postage stamps: 32¢ stamp photo courtesy of H.E. Harris & Co; 3¢ stamp photo from *100 Greatest American Stamps*, by Donald Sundman and Janet Klug (Whitman Publishing, 2008). C5

49. Series of 1890 $100 Treasury Note. Photo from *A Guide Book of United States Paper Money*. C5

50. Steel storage vault of the Philadelphia Mint, circa 1880. Photo from *History of the United States Mint and Its Coinage*, by David W. Lange (Whitman Publishing, 2005). C6

51. Morgan silver dollar. Photo from *A Guide Book of United States Coins*. C6

52. Rutherford B. Hayes, medal by George Morgan. Photo from *Numismatic Art in America*. C6

53. 1883 "Without Cents" Liberty Head nickel. Photo from *A Guide Book of United States Coins*. C7

54. 1883 "racketeer nickel." Author's collection. C7

55. 1890 "With Cents" Liberty Head nickel. Photo from *A Guide Book of Shield and Liberty Head Nickels*, by Q. David Bowers (Whitman Publishing, 2006). C7

56.–57. Columbus-related postage stamps. Photos from *100 Greatest American Stamps*. C8

58.–59. Tickets and souvenir postcard from the World's Columbian Exposition, 1893. Photos from *100 Greatest American Stamps*. C9

60. Olin Warner's director badge for the World's Columbian Exposition. Photo courtesy of National Numismatic Collection, Smithsonian Institution. C10

v

61. Columbian half dollar, Proof. Author's collection. C10

62. World's Columbian Exposition exhibitor's certificate, designed by Will Low. Photo courtesy of Mystic Stamp Co. C11

63. *Central Pavilion, Horticultural Hall*, by L. Marold. *World's Columbian Exposition: Art and Architecture*, by William Walton (Philadelphia, 1893). Photo courtesy of Mystic Stamp Co. C12

64.–65. Views from the art gallery at the World's Columbian Exposition. *World's Columbian Exposition: Art and Architecture*. Photos courtesy of Mystic Stamp Co. C13

66.–67. Prussian 5-mark coin, 1888, and Austrian 2-gulden commemorative, 1879. Photos from *A Guide Book of Modern World Coins*, 14th ed., by R.S. Yeoman (Whitman Publishing, 2008). C13

68. *The Golden Door*, by Felicien de Myrbach. *World's Columbian Exposition: Art and Architecture*. Photo courtesy of Mystic Stamp Co. C14

69. World's Columbian Exposition award medal, by Saint-Gaudens. Author's collection. C14

70.–72. Images of the U.S. Mint in the 19th century from *History of the United States Mint and Its Coinage*. C15

73. Mint workers examining $100,000 face value in $20 gold coins, 1894. Photo from *A Guide Book of Double Eagle Gold Coins*, by Q. David Bowers (Whitman Publishing, 2004). C16

74. Liberty Head $20 gold piece. Photo from *A Guide Book of United States Coins*. C16

75.–76. Series of 1890 Treasury Notes. Photos from *100 Greatest American Currency Notes*. 99

77.–78. Anti-slavery tokens. Photos from *100 Greatest American Medals and Tokens*, by Katherine Jaeger and Q. David Bowers (Whitman Publishing, 2007). 99

79. John Boyd Thacher. Photo courtesy of New York State Library. 103

80. Edward Atkinson. Author's collection. 104

81. Augusta Homer, by Thomas Dewing, 1885. Photo courtesy of Saint-Gaudens National Historic Site, Cornish, New Hampshire. 111

82. Robert E. Preston medal. Photo courtesy of National Numismatic Collection, Smithsonian Institution. 115

83.–84. World's Columbian Exposition award medal by Saint-Gaudens: trial award medal cast in France with first or nude reverse. Photos courtesy of the American Numismatic Society. 116

85. Oliver C. Bosbyshell. Author's collection. 121

86. Page Belting Company facsimile of Saint-Gaudens's award-medal designs. Photo courtesy of Page Belting Company. 122

87.–89. World's Columbian Exposition award medal and alternate reverses. Author's collection. 129

90. Richard Watson Gilder, by Cecilia Beaux. Photo courtesy of National Portrait Gallery, Smithsonian Institution. 130

91. Augustus Saint-Gaudens in 1894. Photo courtesy of Dartmouth College Rauner Special Collections Library 141

92. Newspaper rendering of the "Pie Girl" incident. Author's collection. 142

93. 1900 commemorative Lafayette dollar. Photo from *A Guide Book of United States Coins*. 142

94. Elizabeth Sherman Cameron, by Fernand Paillet. Photo courtesy of the collection of the New-York Historical Society. 153

95. Ordination announcement for Tom Sherman, by Saint-Gaudens. Photo courtesy of University of Notre Dame Archive Sherman Family Papers. 153

96. Bust of General William T. Sherman, by Saint-Gaudens. Photo courtesy of the Metropolitan Museum of Art. Gift by subscription through the Saint-Gaudens Memorial Committee, 1912 (12.76-2). 153

Illustrations

97. Augustus Saint-Gaudens with Hettie Anderson, by Anders Zorn. Photo courtesy of Saint-Gaudens National Historic Site, Cornish, New Hampshire. 163

98. Monument to Colonel Robert G. Shaw, by Saint-Gaudens. Photo courtesy of Dartmouth College Rauner Special Collections Library. 163

99.–100. Roosevelt family portraits: the Roosevelt family in 1895 and Edith Kermit Roosevelt in 1900. Photos courtesy of Theodore Roosevelt Collection, Harvard College Library. 175

101. Theodore Roosevelt touring the Fine Arts Gallery at the Pan-American Exposition. Photo courtesy of Theodore Roosevelt Collection, Harvard College Library. 185

102.–103. Last working model for the Angel of Victory. Author's collection. 185

104. The Sherman Monument at its dedication in 1903. Photo courtesy of Dartmouth College Rauner Special Collections Library. 185

105. Charles Follen McKim. Author's collection. 195

106.–107. Views of Washington, DC: the National Mall at the time of the Senate Park Commission report, and the White House greenhouses. Photos courtesy of Library of Congress. 195

108.–109. East Wing of the White House, 1903: under construction and completed. Photos courtesy of Humphrey Engineering Center, Office of History, Ft. Belvoir. 205

110. Leslie Shaw. Photo courtesy of the U.S. Treasury Department. 207

111. *Head of Victory*, by Saint-Gaudens. Photo courtesy of the Metropolitan Museum of Art, Rogers fund, 1907 (07.90). 211

112.–113. Victory-Peace medal by Saint-Gaudens: plaster from original model; uniface medal, photo courtesy of the American Numismatic Society. 211

114. Theodore Roosevelt speaking at Arlington Cemetery, 1902. Photo courtesy of Whitman Publishing, LLC. 217

115. Liberty Head $20 gold piece. Author's collection. 217

116. Augustus Saint-Gaudens in 1905. Photo courtesy of Dartmouth College Rauner Special Collections Library. 218

117. Theodore Roosevelt, 1899. Photo courtesy of Whitman Publishing, LLC. 223

118. Official Roosevelt inaugural medal of 1905, by Charles Barber and George Morgan. Author's collection. 223

119. Adolph A. Weinman at work in his studio. Photo from *The Expert's Guide to Collecting and Investing in Rare Coins*, by Q. David Bowers (Whitman Publishing, 2005). 224

120. Wedding portrait of Henri Weil, 1900. Photo courtesy of Joseph Weil. 224

121. Theodore Roosevelt taking the oath of office, 1905. Photo courtesy of Theodore Roosevelt Collection, Harvard College Library. 229

122. Unofficial Roosevelt inaugural medal of 1905, by Saint-Gaudens and Weinman. Author's collection. 230

123. The Roosevelt family in 1903. Photo courtesy of Whitman Publishing, LLC. 230

124. The masque at Cornish, by Everett Shinn. Sketch courtesy of Dartmouth College Rauner Special Collections Library. 236–237

125. George E. Roberts, U.S. Mint director. Author's collection. 239

126. Harrison S. Morris, by Thomas Eakins. Photo courtesy of Pennsylvania Academy of the Fine Arts, Philadelphia. 240

127.–128. Franklin medal: plaster model by Louis Saint-Gaudens and reverse design sketch by Kenyon Cox. Photos courtesy of Saint-Gaudens National Historic Site, Cornish, New Hampshire. 245

129.–131. Franklin medal: original obverse, author's collection; cutout of original head, photo courtesy of Saint-Gaudens National Historic Site, Cornish, New Hampshire; approved obverse and reverse, author's collection. 246

Striking Change

132. Preliminary sketches for the design of the gold coins. Drawings courtesy of Dartmouth College Rauner Special Collections Library. Plasters courtesy of Saint-Gaudens National Historic Site, Cornish, New Hampshire. 258–259

133.–134. "Indian Princess" $1 gold piece and Flying Eagle cent. Author's collection. 265

135.–137. Saint-Gaudens coin designs: winged-Liberty obverse, Standing Eagle reverse, and Flying Eagle reverse. Photos courtesy of Saint-Gaudens National Historic Site, Cornish, New Hampshire. 266

138. Charles Barber's design for the $20 gold piece. Photo courtesy of National Numismatic Collection, Smithsonian Institution. 273

139.–140. Ultra High Relief models for the gold-coin design. Photos courtesy of Saint-Gaudens National Historic Site, Cornish, New Hampshire. 281

141.–142. Ultra High Relief $20 gold piece as struck and experimental small-size strike. Photos courtesy of the National Numismatic Collection, Smithsonian Institution. 281

143. George B. Cortelyou. Photo courtesy of U.S. Treasury Department. 282

144.–146. Models for the one-cent piece. Photos courtesy of Saint-Gaudens National Historic Site, Cornish, New Hampshire. 288

147. Indian Head pattern $20 gold piece. Photo courtesy of David Akers. 288

148. Obverse of the second model for the $20 gold piece. Photo courtesy of Saint-Gaudens National Historic Site, Cornish, New Hampshire. 288

149. John Landis. Photo courtesy of Heritage Auction Galleries. 289

150.–153. Saint-Gaudens $10 gold piece: striking from the first model, author's collection; as modified by Barber, photo courtesy of the National Numismatic Collection, Smithsonian Institution; final model by Hering, photo courtesy of Saint-Gaudens National Historic Site, Cornish, New Hampshire; striking from the official model, author's collection. 303

154. Theodore Roosevelt portrait plaque by James Earle Fraser. Author's collection. 309

155. Frank A. Leach, director of the U.S. Mint. Author's collection. 309

156.–158. Saint-Gaudens $20 gold piece: flat-rim High Relief from second model, author's collection; third model by Hering, photo courtesy of Saint-Gaudens National Historic Site, Cornish, New Hampshire; circulation strike, author's collection. 310

159.–160. $10 and $20 gold pieces modified for the mandated IN GOD WE TRUST motto. Author's collection. 327

161. Glenn Brown. Photo courtesy of U.S. Commission of Fine Arts. 330

162. Elihu Root, secretary of state. Photo courtesy of Library of Congress. 337

163. Indian Head $5 gold piece, by Bela Lyon Platt. Photo courtesy of National Numismatic Collection, Smithsonian Institution. 343

164. Lincoln cent, by Victor David Brenner. Author's collection. 343

165. James Earle Fraser in his studio. Photo courtesy of Whitman Publishing, LLC. 344

166. Teddy Roosevelt as the Rough Rider, by James Earle Fraser. Author's collection. 347

167.–170. Early 20th-century coin designs. Author's collection. 348

171.–172. MacNeil Standing Liberty quarter: original version, author's collection; 1917 modification, photo courtesy of the National Numismatic Collection, Smithsonian Institution. 349

173. High-relief Peace dollar of 1921, by Anthony de Francisci. Author's collection. 349

The second color section appears after page 352.

174.–175. Saint-Gaudens at work in his studio and on the Sherman Monument. Photos from *A Guide Book of Double Eagle Gold Coins.* C17

176. Unofficial Roosevelt inaugural medal of 1905, by Saint-Gaudens and Weinman. Author's collection. C18

Illustrations

177.–179. Ancient Greek distater, decadrachm, and tetradrachm. Photos from *Money of the World: Coins That Made History*, edited by Ira Goldberg and Larry Goldberg (Whitman Publishing, 2007). C18

180.–181. Franklin medal: original obverse and final approved version. Author's collection. C19

182. Lafayette commemorative dollar, by Charles Barber. Photo from *A Guide Book of United States Coins*. C20

183. Pattern $20 gold piece, 1906, by Charles Barber. Photo courtesy of National Numismatic Collection, Smithsonian Institution. C20

184.–185. Saint-Gaudens Indian Head $10 gold piece in Wire Rim and circulation-strike versions. Author's collection. C21

186. Ultra High Relief $20 gold piece, by Saint-Gaudens. Photo courtesy of National Numismatic Collection, Smithsonian Institution. C22

187.–188. Saint-Gaudens $20 gold piece in High Relief and circulation-strike versions. Author's collection. C23

189.–191. Fraser Buffalo nickel with original and modified reverses, author's collection; and Weinman Winged Liberty dime, photo courtesy of Matthew Moran. C24

192.–195. Commemorative coins of the 1915 Panama-Pacific Exposition. Photos from *A Guide Book of United States Coins*. C25

196.–197. MacNeil Standing Liberty quarter: original design, author's collection; modified 1917 design, photo courtesy of National Numismatic Collection, Smithsonian Institution. C26

198. Lincoln cent, by Victor David Brenner. Author's collection. C27

199. Walking Liberty half dollar, by Adolph Weinman. Photo courtesy of Whitman Publishing, LLC. C27

200. Indian Head $5 gold piece, by Bela Lyon Pratt. Author's collection. C28

201. High-relief 1921 Peace dollar, by Anthony de Francisci. Author's collection. C28

202.–203. Illinois Centennial and Oregon Trail commemorative half dollars. Photos courtesy of the National Numismatic Collection, Smithsonian Institution. C29

204. George Washington death bicentennial commemorative $5 gold piece, after Laura Gardin Fraser. Author's collection. C29

205. Augustus Saint-Gaudens, commemorative plaque by James Earle Fraser, 1934. Photo from *A Guide Book of Double Eagle Gold Coins*. C30

206. Theodore Roosevelt portrait by Gari Melchers, 1908. Photo courtesy of Freer Gallery of Art, Smithsonian Institution. Gift of Charles Lang Freer, F1908.17a. C31

207. Augusta Saint-Gaudens with the golden bowl, by Saint-Gaudens. Photo courtesy of Saint-Gaudens National Historic Site, Cornish, New Hampshire. C32

208. The golden bowl of the masque. Photo courtesy of Saint-Gaudens National Historic Site, Cornish, New Hampshire. 367

209.–210. Illinois Centennial and Oregon Trail commemorative half dollars. Photos courtesy of the National Numismatic Collection, Smithsonian Institution. 367

211. George Washington death bicentennial $5 gold piece. Author's collection. 367

212.–214. James Earle Fraser's Lincoln cent design: plaster model of obverse, photo courtesy of Fred Reed; sketch for reverse, photo courtesy of Fred Reed and the National Cowboy Hall of Fame and Western Heritage Center; plaster model of reverse, photo courtesy of Joe Lepczyk and Fred Reed. 367

Foreword

Augustus Saint-Gaudens

is a towering figure in 19th-century American art and culture. As an artist he changed the course of American art, introducing a classical simplicity that heralded the later developments of modern art. As a teacher he influenced the next generation of sculptors. As an organizer of associations and exhibitions he brought a new understanding of art to a wide audience. And as a city planner he played a significant role in creating the city of Washington, DC, as we know it today.

All of this is well known to art historians, but may not be as familiar in the specialized world of numismatics. It is for that reason that a new book about Saint-Gaudens and the creation of the 1907 gold coinage is not only valid, but welcome.

I met Mike Moran in 2003, in Colorado, at the American Numismatic Association, for the opening of an exciting exhibition of Saint-Gaudens's work. It was part of a five-year retrospective exhibition organized by the Trust for Museum Exhibitions, with the collaboration of the Saint-Gaudens National Historic Site. The exhibition was exciting because it was the first time that Saint-Gaudens's work was shown in the context of the American Numismatic Association Museum. The exhibition was shared with the Colorado Springs Fine Arts Center in a cooperative venture.

The year 2007 is the centennial year of Saint-Gaudens's death. The anniversary is being commemorated in many ways, including a feature-length film, exhibitions, and public programs. It is appropriate, then, that the book takes shape in this special year.

Mr. Moran has approached the subject with a fresh look, recounting the events surrounding Saint-Gaudens's design of the $20 and $10 gold coins, but also placing this accomplishment in the light of some other related work. The author's description of the World's Columbian Exposition medal, the Roosevelt special inaugural medal, and the Franklin medal is an added bonus for readers.

Readers will find the characters and events fascinating and indicative of the close-knit world of art and politics in the era of Theodore Roosevelt. A dynamic president, Roosevelt sought the design of new coinage as a small part of his administration's goal to revitalize American life. Along with the redesign of the city of Washington, DC, the renovation of the White House, and the building of other government buildings such as the Library of Congress, Roosevelt utilized the talents of Augustus Saint-Gaudens and his friends, including Charles Follen McKim, among others, to promote his dream for a new American nation.

Reading this book you will find yourself intrigued by the people and events described, and come to understand better the remarkable set of circumstances that came together at this moment in time. Perhaps at no other time could America's foremost sculptor partner with such a dynamic president to change the face of American coinage forever. The $20 and $10 gold coins are still considered the most vibrant and beautiful designs in the nation's coinage, telling of their era and the sense of promise envisioned by their remarkable designer.

Henry J. Duffy
Curator, Saint-Gaudens National Historic Site
Cornish, New Hampshire

About the Author

Michael F. Moran

has been a numismatist since childhood, when his grandfather got him started collecting Indian Head pennies. He fell in love with the art of Augustus Saint-Gaudens in 1960, and spent his summer lawn-mowing money on one of the artist's $20 gold pieces. Coincidentally, Theodore Roosevelt happened to be his favorite president. In these respects, this book has been a labor of love.

Mr. Moran holds a bachelor's degree in civil engineering and a master's in industrial administration from Purdue University. He has spent a business career in corporate mergers and acquisitions in the energy fields and now serves as a managing partner in several diverse businesses. He says only half jokingly that he learned to write by the seat of his pants, while providing economic justifications for major capital projects and acquisitions that he then presented for approval to his board of directors.

Since leaving his corporate career, Mr. Moran has turned to numismatic writing. He has written cover articles for *Numismatist* and recently received the American Numismatic Association's Heath Literary Award for his 2006 article about the survival of the San Francisco Mint during the earthquake of 1906. The thought of writing a detailed history of the collaboration between Saint-Gaudens and Roosevelt evolved as his research showed that what had been written before on the subject was incomplete and, worse, inaccurate. After five years of work and with the help of many new friends, Mr. Moran hopes that the reader will feel as he does about the exceptional men and women in this book who played a part in laying a firm foundation for the American culture of the 20th century.

The author lives in Lexington, Kentucky.

Acknowledgments and Dedication

No one writes a book worth reading by himself.

I tried it. I started out intending to focus on a part of the lives of two men whom I thought I knew thoroughly. It would be a book about numismatics and the famous interplay between Augustus Saint-Gaudens and Theodore Roosevelt. I quickly found that this story, which had been repeatedly told, was flawed by omissions and artificial time frames. It badly needed retelling on a broader stage.

The story of Saint-Gaudens and Roosevelt is just as much one of the awakening of America in the last two decades of the 19th century to the world of the arts. There were other players in this endeavor, such as Richard Watson Gilder and Charles Follen McKim. The fine hand of Edith Kermit Roosevelt was behind the scenes at every turn. The glory that was the World's Columbian Exposition announced America's potential. Yet the struggle of the Senate Park Commission to preserve the original L'Enfant plan for Washington, DC, warned of pitfalls. Against this backdrop Saint-Gaudens drew from his major monumental works to bring forth gold-coin designs that captured the essence of America. As beautiful as these designs were, they would have remained only designs without the determination of Theodore Roosevelt to bring them to reality on our $10 and $20 gold pieces. The new designs that subsequently appeared on all of our circulating coins were truly the fruits of their labor.

The work for this book started in the fall of 2002 in the South Carolina home of dear friends. I quickly turned to Sue Kohler at the Commission of Fine Arts for help. Research took me up and down the East Coast and to Chicago. Strangers went out of their way to help me. I have a newfound respect for the professionals who maintain the historical papers and records at the National Archives and Records Administration and at the various historical societies. Without them, ties to the richness of our past would be lost.

First and foremost I want to thank my sculpture editor, Dr. Michael Richman. He freely gave of his 35 years' knowledge of American sculpture. After four months of intense dialogue, we both came away with a new and better understanding of Saint-Gaudens. With Michael's guidance, I believe I have given the reader a unique insight into the evolutionary process leading to the gold-coin designs of 1907.

Richard Foster was invaluable for research at the New York Public Library. In Washington, Pam Scott took me under her wing. Will McFarland and the New England Historic Genealogical Society greatly assisted in Boston. Dr. Richard Mortara walked me through Saint-Gaudens's last horrific months. Wayne DeCesar patiently showed me the ropes at College Park. There is a special thanks to Barbara Gregory of the American Numismatic Association, who so long ago told me I really could write if I put my mind to it. Finally there is Jeff Garrett, a numismatist in every sense of the word.

I want to thank my numismatic editors, D. Wayne Johnson and Katherine Jaeger. For French translation, which was invaluable in understanding the World's Fair award medal, Kristin Seymour was my go-to person.

I am greatly indebted to all the others who contributed, each just as important to me: Bill Allman, White House Historical Association; Louisa Bann, Tiffany & Company; Bill Boehm, New Mexico State University; Q. David Bowers; U.S. Senator Jim Bunning; Roger Burdette; Judy Burgess; Francis Campbell, American Numismatic Society; Mark Coen, Page Belting Company; Jane Colvard, American Numismatic Association; Wallace Dailey, Houghton Library; Matthew Dibiase, Philadelphia Archives; Henry Duffy, National Park Service; Eric Esau, Dartmouth College Library; Connie Gordon, Chicago Public Library; Elaine Grublin, Kim Nusco, and Peter Drummey, Massachusetts Historical Society; George Gurney, Smithsonian Institution; Nancy Hadley, American Institute of Architects; Sarah Hutt, Boston Art Commission; Kevin Knoot, University of Iowa; C.J. Moore; Jennifer Nace, Syracuse University; Barbara Natanson, Library of Congress; Roger Natte, Fort Dodge Public Library; Annalee Pauls, Princeton University; Lisa Petrulis, Swope Museum; Becki Plunkett, State Historical Society of Iowa; Sally Pore, Concord Public Library; Susan Procell, American Numismatic Association; Michelle Rothenberger, Syracuse University; Warren Stone; Kristen Swett, City of Boston Archives; Arline and Rita Tehan; Tony Terranova; Thayer Tolles, Metropolitan Museum of Art; Ruth Wellner, New England Historic Genealogical Society; Helen Weltin, New York State Library; Jim Witham, Lexington Public Library; and Mary Woolever, Ryerson & Burnham Library.

For illustrations I am indebted to Nan Card, Kevin Cawley, Richard Doty, Mary Edwards, Lizanne Garrett, Lee Glazer, Cory Grace, Robert Hoge, Jim Hughes, Barbara Katu, Cheryl Leibold, Itty Mathew, Tom Mulvaney, Fred Reed, Jill Reichenbach, Jay Satterfield, Stack's Rare Coins, Elena Stolyarik, Joseph Weil, Teresa Yoder, and Julie Zeftel. Also, Greg Rohan, Mark VanWinkle, and Lucas Garritson of Heritage helped me in a real pinch.

To Dee Dee
The love of my life

Introduction

To the numismatist, or coin collector,

Augustus Saint-Gaudens stands high as the creator of what many believe to be America's most beautiful circulating coin—the double eagle or $20 gold piece dated MCMVII (1907), produced in sculptured relief, a brilliant work of art. In the same year the artist's $10 gold eagle made an appearance: a different design, with Miss Liberty in an Indian headdress, with a stalwart eagle on the reverse. This, too, has been a favorite. By 1907, which also was the year of Saint-Gaudens's passing, he had been accomplished in medallic art for many years, with achievements including a memorable medal for the 100th anniversary in 1889 of George Washington's first inauguration, and one side of a controversial award medal intended for the World's Columbian Exposition in 1893, and more.

Today, American numismatists regularly honor Saint-Gaudens. He is discussed in extensive comments in auction and sale catalogs. There have been several fine books relating to double eagles and gold coins, and various exhibits, such as one mounted a few years ago at the headquarters of the American Numismatic Association in Colorado Springs, and another at the Federal Reserve Bank in New York City in 2007.

Separately, without a great deal of overlap, admirers and students of art recognize Saint-Gaudens for his sculptures, some of heroic proportions, such as the Shaw Memorial in Boston across the street from the State House, and the Sherman Victory group on a pedestal at the Grand Army Plaza at the southeast corner of New York's Central Park, right across from the famous Plaza Hotel. (The goddess in that group, variously known as *Victory* or *Fame*, was the inspiration for the aforementioned MCMVII $20 gold coin.)

A third emphasis is the Saint-Gaudens National Historic Site itself, in Cornish, New Hampshire, a magnet for thousands of visitors annually, who come from all over the nation—and, indeed, the world—to see where the artist lived, visit his studio, and view many of his sculptured works. Although his passing was more than a century ago, on August 3, 1907, in many ways Saint-Gaudens lives today. His art, numismatic as well as sculptural, is timeless.

In the present volume, Michael F. Moran combines the biography of the artist, the story of his sculptures, and the development of coins and medals into a single volume that tells about everything one might want to know concerning how these were produced, plus many facts, anecdotes, and interesting side trips to areas one might not have imagined.

Among the multiple attractions of the present book, the illustrations are beyond superb—more than have ever appeared in any other numismatically oriented reference on this artist.

The text is particularly valuable in showcasing the sculptor's activities with important numismatic projects beyond the famous 1907 coinage. While the story of the coins has been told in depth in several places, including in *Renaissance of American Coinage 1906–1908* (Burdette, 2007) and *United States Gold Coins: An Illustrated History* (Bowers, 1982), treatment of the important medals has ranged from scarcely anything, to light sketches. *Striking Change* ends that.

Further, the author gives a comprehensive look at the design competition for new United States coins in 1891. This involved quite a bit of effort at the time, but ultimately ended as a non-event, as outside artists consulted in the competition did not seem to have created motifs that anyone liked—and Chief Engraver Charles E. Barber of the United States Mint ended up creating new motifs for the dime, quarter, and half dollar. We learn then, and also later, that in many ways Saint-Gaudens was an idealist, desiring artistic high-relief, sculptured-effect coins as objects of art, in a world of mechanical coin production in which high-speed presses needed to stamp these things out like so many tokens, without being able to have the designs in high relief.

The World's Columbian Exposition in 1893 forms a focus for another adventure with Saint-Gaudens, who was involved in designing the fair's award medal. The ensuing events, brought on in part by Saint-Gaudens's towering ego, turned into a fiasco and marked a low point in his professional career. The end result, much to the sculptor's disgust, was a medal with his obverse muled to a reverse designed by Chief Engraver Barber. The resulting ill will on the part of both men was still raw more than a decade later, when Saint-Gaudens undertook President Theodore Roosevelt's commission to redesign the American coinage.

As is already well known to many readers, but which is amplified in fascinating detail in *Striking Change*, the numismatic high point of Saint-Gaudens's career occurred in 1905, when Roosevelt met with the sculptor, later corresponding in detail, encouraging him to redesign all United States coins from the cent to the $20 gold piece. This relationship had its own set of complications, again resulting in confrontations and clashes with Chief Engraver Barber. The president of the United States took the side of Saint-Gaudens, ignoring the highest engraving position in the government mint—this certainly being an interesting footnote in political as well as numismatic history. All the details are played out in Moran's text, with the result that anyone interested in Saint-Gaudens, or who owns one of the coins, will be greatly enriched by reading through the following pages, savoring all of the details.

Every good novel, at least, should have a hero and a villain; in the present saga, Augustus Saint-Gaudens fills the first role and Chief Engraver Charles Barber, to perhaps oversimplify, the second. As to "love interests," another element of novels and film, Saint-Gaudens had a way with women, as the text notes. President Theodore ("Teddy") Roosevelt and his influential wife Edith earn their share of the limelight as well.

Although the historical and numismatic narrative and details are the main focus of this book, it is entertaining as well. The net result is a "good read," in modern parlance—a book that will inform as well as delight. It certainly will be a welcome addition to the literature currently available on Augustus Saint-Gaudens, without question the most famous artist ever to be associated with American coins and medals.

My congratulations to Michael Moran for a job well done.

Q. David Bowers
Wolfeboro, New Hampshire

Prologue

"ALL YE NEED TO KNOW"

Prologue

"All Ye Need to Know"

Seated three places to the left of William Eames, the president of the American Institute of Architects, Augustus Saint-Gaudens surveyed the dignitaries assembled for this annual dinner of the association. He had been looking forward to this event with great anticipation, even if he did have to "utter ten of his classic words."[1] It was a Wednesday night, January 11, 1905, in Washington, DC.

To arrive for this meeting Gus had traveled from his home and studio in Cornish, New Hampshire, first to his old haunt, New York City. There he had had dinner with Helena and Richard Watson Gilder.[2] Gilder was the publisher of the immensely influential magazine the *Century*, which showcased the American arts and literature. More important, he and Gus had been friends for what seemed like forever. Gilder at critical times had been both the sculptor's mentor and his cheerleader. On those public occasions when Gus lost his temper—which could be volcanic—it was Gilder who reined him in. From New York City, a special train had brought Saint-Gaudens down to Washington that morning.[3] Accompanying him had been, among others, Henry James, the noted literary figure, and Elihu Root, the former secretary of war and a strong supporter of the arts.

The place was the old Arlington House, now the Arlington Hotel. It was the best hotel in Washington, located at an angle to Lafayette Square.[4] St. John's Episcopal Church was across the street, and the White House was just a short walk through Lafayette Park. They were gathered in the Dining Hall.

For the occasion, Frank Millet had been called upon to decorate the banquet hall. He covered the walls with unbleached, pleated cotton gauze to give the room a warm, soft, creamy background. Large branches of palms at intervals along the walls and flowers at the tables gave needed color. Festoons of green had been added as well, to emphasize the architectural lines of the room. The high table at which Gus enjoyed a prominent position stretched to three sides of the hall to accommodate the 75 dignitaries.[5]

Although it was part of the annual meeting of the American Institute of Architects, the dinner had taken on a much deeper meaning. First and foremost, it was an occasion to further cement the work of the Senate Park Commission. This commission had recommended the restoration of the L'Enfant vision for Washington, DC. With the rapid post–Civil War expansion, the city's development had badly strayed from the original plan that Pierre L'Enfant had made for George Washington and Thomas Jefferson. Acceptance of the Senate Park Commission's 1902 report had not

3

been universal. This evening would help official Washington to refocus on its crucial recommendations concerning the Mall. Also, the meeting was to promote Congress's chartering of the American Academy in Rome. This school was conceived as a place where Americans could learn and create the arts in a classical setting. Joe Cannon, Speaker of the House of Representatives, had kept the authorizing legislation bottled up in the House. Finally, the meeting was a quiet affirmation of the successful renovation of the White House, which stood for all to see.

Gus had been associated in varying degrees in all three projects. His role this night was to speak to the assemblage on behalf of sculptors. Also, with the French ambassador Jules Jusserand present, it would be a proper occasion to wear his little red button as an officer of the French Legion of Honor.[6]

Seated at the table directly across from Gus at the open side of the room was his old friend Charles Follen McKim, or, as Gus affectionately called him, "Charles the Charmer." They had met some 30 years before in search of ice cream in New York City.[7] Gus was the aspiring young sculptor, just returned from Paris and Rome. Charles was the young architect launching a career that would establish McKim, Mead, and White as one of the premier architectural firms in America. Their professions would have arguably drawn them together anyway, but their mutual love of ice cream seemed more fitting. The sculptor had an incurable sweet tooth and a very vivid imagination. To Saint-Gaudens, paradise must surely have golden streets of taffy and white walls of ice cream.[8]

McKim had been deeply involved in each of the three projects being honored at this dinner. He had been a driving force for the American Academy in Rome from its very inception in the days of the Chicago World's Fair. He had personally overseen the renovation of the White House. Of the most importance, he had deeply immersed himself in the work of the Senate Park Commission. This group had been charged with development of the park system within the District of Columbia. More specifically, they were to address the locations of future public buildings and memorials to ensure an orderly development consistent with the original L'Enfant city plan.[9] Upon securing his appointment to this commission, McKim had insisted that Saint-Gaudens be added as the fourth member. The commission's report, amplified by an exhibit at the Corcoran Gallery of Art, had been presented to the president, first lady, and members of the executive and legislative branches of government on a cold January day in 1902.[10]

For McKim, this night was the fulfillment of long years of hard work furthering the arts in America. Yet he would play no role in the evening's proceedings; he had real trouble with public speaking.[11] Seated with him at his table, dubbed the "pilot house," was Glenn Brown, who as secretary of the American Institute of Architects ran the organization's daily affairs. Brown had labored behind the scenes with both the Senate Park Commission and the White House renovation. At this moment, McKim was on pins and needles, and Brown would be his solace if the evening took a turn for the worse. McKim had devoted seven months to the arrangements, and getting the dignitaries to commit had been like herding cats. Everyone called it "McKim's Dinner."[12]

At this same table sat McKim's partner Stanford White, with his signature mustache and close-cropped hair. It was White who had provided the pedestal mountings for many of Gus's commissions, such as his statue of Admiral Farragut. The two men had pioneered the concept in America that sculpture and architecture should be equals in good monument design.

There was another side to "Stanny." Through the late 1880s and into the '90s, Gus and Stanny had partied together in New York City at all the exclusive gentlemen's clubs. Gus preferred to keep his personal life private, and Stanny's name tended to show up in the public domain a little too much. Since Gus's return from Paris in 1900, the two had worked together less frequently. It was not Stanny but McKim who had done the pedestal for Gus's equestrian Sherman Monument and its Angel of Victory, which now graced the southeast entrance to Central Park. Still, Gus and Stanny remained close friends.

Seated directly on Gus's right at the head table was John Hay. McKim had had Gus write to Hay urging his attendance.[13] This was the same John Hay who had been Abraham Lincoln's personal secretary, and later secretary of state under William McKinley. Now he was secretary of state under Theodore Roosevelt. Gus had just finished a bust of Hay. Together the two of them had conspired to surprise their mutual friend, Henry Adams, the eminent historian. Adams was famous in Washington society for his breakfast salons, at which Hay and Saint-Gaudens were regular attendees. Henry was also noted for his prickly personality; he would not sit for either painter or sculptor. He did and spoke as he pleased. The preceding year, Gus, at Hay's instigation, had done a medallion caricature of Adams. It consisted of a profile of his famously bald head, a body of porcupine quills, and the wings of an angel. Gus called it *Porcupinus Angelicus*. It captured Adams perfectly. Hay sent it to Adams in Paris by courier, under diplomatic seal.[14] Adams loved it. In spite of their radically different backgrounds, he and Saint-Gaudens were good friends.

To the other side of William Eames sat Elihu Root, recently resigned from the Roosevelt administration. From his position as secretary of war with authority over the public buildings and grounds of Washington, he had been essential to the Senate Park Commission plan as well as the White House renovation. Root had the respect of all the artists gathered for this occasion.

At one flanking wing of the head table sat Gus's fellow sculptor and good friend Daniel Chester French. French was now president of the National Sculpture Society, an organization Gus had helped to found; he shared Gus's support of the American Academy in Rome. Saint-Gaudens had strong emotions when it came to the Rome academy.

> If but one man in a country, a commanding figure, a man inspired by the breath of genius, is the result of this foundation or is even fostered or helped in the slightest degree by it, it will have been worth all the money devoted to its foundation and maintenance.[15]

Other dignitaries deserved honorable mention. J.P. Morgan and Henry Walters had each given $100,000 to help endow the Academy. Whitelaw Reid, newly minted American representative to the Court of Saint James, had opened the doors for Saint-Gaudens to do a bust of General William Tecumseh Sherman, which, after the general's death, became the equestrian monument. At McKim's table was James

Ellsworth, who had done battle with the United States Mint to dictate the design of the commemorative half dollar at the World's Columbian Exposition in 1892 and 1893. From that experience Ellsworth had come away bruised.

The evening was passing pleasantly. McKim was a connoisseur of both music and food, demanding the best.[16] A double quintet provided the music. Their selections ranged across the popular tunes of the day. No real theme was obvious to Gus, with the selections ranging from Schubert's "March Militaire" to "Old Folks at Home." The menu was heavy with local specialties washed down with champagne and a good 16-year-old Pommard.[17]

When the first lady, Edith Roosevelt, entered the dining room with her party and made her way to her special box, a quartet of male voices sang "Hail to the Fairest." The president of the Institute then gave one of the many toasts of the evening: "To the gracious lady whose presence is inspiration, because her thought is ever on the things that are true."[18]

Gus liked Edith Roosevelt and she liked him. When Edith called upon McKim to renovate and redecorate the White House in 1902, he had been quick to bring Gus on board as an informal advisor.[19] The first lady had grown to trust Saint-Gaudens's judgment in artistic matters. Yet when she felt strongly on a point, she could stand her ground with "Charles the Charmer." In this capacity, Edith's work with the renovation had been particularly valuable. Saint-Gaudens, McKim, and the others had developed a respect for this lady. That they chose this toast to her was no trivial decision. The toast alluded directly to a passage from Keats:

> Beauty is truth, truth beauty—that is all
> Ye know on earth, and all ye need to know.

When the meal was completed, the time for speeches began. Now McKim's concerns came to the forefront. Just before Christmas he had asked Gus to drop John La Farge a note. La Farge had been instrumental in giving Saint-Gaudens work when he first returned to the United States. Through the years Saint-Gaudens and La Farge had remained close. McKim wanted Gus to remind La Farge of the dinner and that both Hay and Root considered La Farge's presence to be a central feature. He also took the time to ask about Gus's speech. He knew Gus hated speeches, but it was most important that he, like La Farge, speak at the dinner. One paragraph was sufficient, he assured Gus, and all of his friends would be there around him.[20] However, McKim soon had a larger problem: he had scheduled the dinner the preceding October after clearing the date with President Roosevelt's calendar; on January 3, just eight days before the dinner, he learned that certain prominent members of government, including Joe Cannon, would be unable to attend due to a conflicting dinner at the White House scheduled by the president![21] McKim had really scrambled over that one. Now the president would arrive after his White House dinner to deliver his address to the gathering. He was late. The program would go on with the other speakers until he arrived.

The president of the Institute opened with a short welcome; he was recovering from surgery undergone two days before. Still, he had refused to relinquish his duty of presiding at this dinner. As a result, McKim made the program as foolproof as possible.[22] With Roosevelt missing, the program moved next to Nicholas Murray Butler, president of Columbia University.

Butler strongly asserted that art was a mode of expression of human feeling and human aspiration.[23] Much was owed to the many civilizations for the development of art and architecture. However, behind all of these lay the eternal wellsprings that were fed by the genius of Greece and Rome. "It was given to them to create the highest standards of excellence alike in architecture, in sculpture and in letters, and to those standards it has been the effort of all intelligence ever since to conform."[24] This embrace of the classical was the defining concept of the times, for American art and for Saint-Gaudens.

Just as the French ambassador was preparing to speak, the notes of the national anthem rang out. The president had arrived and was proceeding to the podium. He had McKim to thank for this appearance. Upon seeing the entire event fall apart because of the scheduling conflict, McKim had written to Roosevelt's personal secretary, William S. Loeb. McKim pleaded in the name of Republican justice that those summoned to the conflicting dinner at the White House be allowed to attend. With the topics at hand for the dinner, there were certainly enough reasons for Roosevelt to adjust his schedule sufficiently to deliver a speech to the group assembled.

McKim left nothing to chance. At the end of the letter, he stated that a box was being improvised for a few ladies. It was a first for the staid Arlington Hotel. Theodore's two sisters, Corrine and Anna (or "Bamie," as she was known to friends and family), were planning to attend. Then McKim applied the coup de grace. He was proposing to place the box at the disposal of the first lady and had written her to this effect.[25] Theodore was had, and he knew it. Under the circumstances, Edith would attend and expect him to perform likewise. McKim's role as decorator of the White House had given him a unique vantage point to see how decisions were made within the first family. On January 9 McKim learned that he had carried the day. Roosevelt and his guests would come after their dinner at the White House.[26]

It was not one of Theodore Roosevelt's better speeches. The house organ of the AIA called it a "felicitous little address."[27] Nevertheless Theodore had points to make, and he made them in words anyone could understand. He defined a "real American" as a man whose belief in and work for his country was not merely for the America of today but for the America of the future. He went on to say, "We owe that beauty, we owe the elevation of thought, of mind and soul that come with association and belief in it to the fact that there were a sufficient number of men in the spirit . . . of doing work not for the sake of the time, but for the sake of the work itself."

Theodore clearly placed Augustus Saint-Gaudens within that select group of men. "There are things in a nation's life more important than beauty, but beauty is very important," he declared. "And in this nation of ours, while there is much in which we have succeeded marvelously, I do not think that, if we looked dispassionately, we will say that beauty has been exactly a strong point." More importantly, Theodore went on record supporting the Senate Park Commission.[28] That one pronouncement was an important victory for McKim and Saint-Gaudens. The president was refocused on its goals, from which he had wavered the preceding year.

Roosevelt left the dinner early. He certainly supported the worthy artistic endeavors being celebrated that evening, but he believed they impacted relatively few of his countrymen. He had in mind a pet project—or "pet crime," as he liked to call it. This project would bring the work of artists to the common man across the country. Theodore Roosevelt thought the designs on American circulating coinage were awful and should be improved. He intended to recruit Saint-Gaudens as his partner in this endeavor. With presidential backing, Roosevelt no doubt believed this task easily accomplished once he had the sculptor on board to provide new designs.

With the president finished, the speaking sequence should have returned to the French ambassador. However, toastmaster Eames, confused by the interruption, became lost in the progression. Jusserand turned to John Hay and said, "Our chairman is a bit heavy." Never at a loss for words, Hay answered, "Yes, he lacks animation, but not spirit."[29] Everyone adjusted and the speeches continued.

Elihu Root made reference to the World's Columbian Exposition that took place in 1893: "The lesson of that Chicago Exposition has gone into every city, town, and hamlet of America. Chicago led our people out of the wilderness of the commonplace to new ideas of architectural beauty and nobility."[30] Supreme Court Justice John Marshall Harlan mused as to the reason why he was making a speech at this event. However, how could he refuse among the company of such men as the president, the secretary of state, Elihu Root, and last but not least, Augustus Saint-Gaudens?[31] Gus was a national celebrity of considerable note.

After La Farge came Saint-Gaudens. By now the toastmaster was beyond help. He had garbled the introduction that Saint-Gaudens had written for La Farge. La Farge had written one for Saint-Gaudens, and Eames garbled this one too. In a letter the next day to his wife, Augusta, Gus groused that the toastmaster was drunk.[32] Saint-Gaudens hated public speeches. Never at a loss for words among friends, he could never find words for public occasions. He appeared calm outwardly but admitted to his wife that he had been scared stiff.[33] He stood before the group, produced his carefully written notes, and commenced the longest speech of his career.

> Charles, the "Charmer," . . . has assured me that it is essential that I should speak tonight. This is as flattering as it is fallacious; for although I have doubts about many things in life, on one subject I have absolutely none; and that is the utterly hopeless and helpless limitations of my oratory. It is much more calculated to reduce listeners to tears than to contribute to their entertainment or instruction.
>
> You will understand why I refrain from expressing anything more than my great pleasure at learning of the munificent gifts to what we have so much at heart, the American Academy in Rome; and at being included in a company assembled to honor that which makes for the nobility and elevation of life—the love of beauty, character and dignity of surroundings, as much in the halls of law and government as in our homes, or wherever we live, move, and have our being.[34]

To his wife, he called it the best speech of the night because it was short. He also called it ten lines of oratorical idiocy, which it was not.[35] Throughout his life, this son of an immigrant with only a marginal formal education struggled with feelings of inferiority when surrounded by men of accomplishment. In spite of the accolades, he could never quite see himself as belonging within their circle.

Even "Uncle" Joe Cannon, both powerful and feared, addressed the group. He had opposed the plans for the improvement of Washington so vigorously that the architects gathered at the Arlington that night viewed him as a philistine. Yet it was McKim's practice to engage the opposition. Cannon readily admitted to the group that what he did not know about architecture would fill a library larger than J.P. Morgan's wealth could buy. He had previously opposed the charter for the school in Rome, feeling that it was only a matter of time until that organization would come to Congress, hat in hand, for monetary support.[36]

The speeches dragged on until past midnight. When it was over, McKim sat for two hours talking to Root and the others of the night's events. At 1:30 Gus rolled out with Henry James, John La Farge, and La Farge's Japanese valet. The four of them returned to Henry Adams's house squeezed into a cab built for two passengers.[37] All in all, the events set in motion by the dinner would have a profound impact on the nation's artistic future. Speaker of the House Cannon would withdraw his opposition to the bill for the incorporation of the American Academy. Roosevelt was back on board.[38] But for Gus the evening could not extend into the small hours of the morning. He, James, and La Farge would have breakfast with Henry Adams and his other salon regulars in the morning. Afterward, there would be the diplomatic reception and dinner at the White House.

Thus, the night ended. Energy had radiated from the young president. His enthusiasm was infectious to all those around him. He was fresh from a landslide election victory and he had much that he wanted to accomplish in the next four years. High on his list of priorities was using Saint-Gaudens as his partner to provide new designs for United States coinage—to place artistic excellence and beauty into the hands of all Americans.

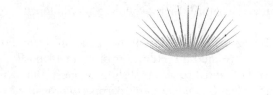

Part 1

A Most Unique Cast of Characters

Chapter 1

New York City

New York City and its environs were home for a good part of their lives for both Augustus Saint-Gaudens and Theodore Roosevelt. For Saint-Gaudens, life did not begin in this metropolis. Gus was born March 1, 1848, in Dublin, Ireland. He was the third of five boys born to Bernard and Mary McGuiness Saint-Gaudens. Only he and younger brothers Louis and Andrew would survive to adulthood. Their father Bernard was a shoemaker from Aspet, in the foothills of the French Pyrenees. In 1841 he had moved to Ireland to peddle his wares to various shoe shops, and it was at one of these that he met and fell in love with Mary McGuiness. Dublin at the time of the potato famine was a terrible place to raise a family. With thoughts of their two previous sons already deceased and revolutions wracking the Continent, the family pulled up stakes and immigrated to America just six months after Gus was born.

The Saint-Gaudens family did not come directly to New York. They departed from Liverpool, and at that time most British flag vessels made Boston their U.S. port of call. For Gus, surviving the journey at such a young age was no mean feat: one in ten of the Irish fleeing the potato famine perished on the journey to the United States.[1] The family's stay in Boston was brief, as the city was flooded with immigrants from Ireland. Prejudices had mounted against these destitute, often poorly educated people, and there was no employment for them. Bernard Saint-Gaudens left his little family behind and went to New York in search of a place to set up his cobbler's shop.

New York was better, although hardly ideal. The city was in the midst of an economic expansion of unprecedented proportions. The boom, which had started in 1845, propelled growth northward from the old city at the southern tip of Manhattan Island. Consequently there was space available for Bernard to rent in the older district. There, on Duane Street near City Hall, he set up his cobbler's shop and moved his family into its second-floor living quarters.[2]

Saint-Gaudens and his family were fortunate on two counts. First, they had arrived in New York in the earlier stages of the growing swell of immigration that would dwarf anything that Boston had experienced. Had they come much later, they would have experienced increasingly bleak prospects. (By the 1850s, artisans such as Bernard Saint-Gaudens would find only piecework, for miserable wages, and wives and children would be forced to find employment in order for the families to survive.) Second, Bernard Saint-Gaudens was a Frenchman. The wealthy of New York were crazy for anything French.[3] Bernard was quick to capitalize on this fad: the sign above his shop read "French Ladies Boots and Shoes." Soon he was drawing his customers from the city's moneyed elite, including Governor Edwin Morgan, journalist Horace Greeley, and some of the Astors and Belmonts.

Because Bernard was able to support his family adequately, they avoided the slums where most of the immigrant families would spend their first generation. Within the New York economic spectrum, the Saint-Gaudens family was lower middle class. Bernard was not always the most diligent businessman, taking time off for several French fraternal organizations.[4] Still, the family's circumstances were good enough for a boy of Gus's pluck to make a mark.

Gus's childhood could best be described as "rough and ready." He was gregarious, good-natured, and full of mischief. In his autobiography he would recall stretching strings in the evenings from porch stoops to wagons parked along the street in order to knock off men's hats. This prank was great fun until the occasional policeman walking his beat fell victim, forcing Gus and his friends to scatter.

He was also part of a group of boys who attached themselves to Fire-Engine Company number 40. Each volunteer fire company had its following of neighborhood boys who cheered the men in their competitions with other fire companies. In the midst of a vast city, these fire companies offered a sense of identity to the boys, who in turn felt duty bound to defend the turf upon which the fire company operated. Gus and his group could be counted upon to greet competing groups with a shower of rocks and stones. Gus had a pugnacious character and was right at home in this environment.[5] However, he regretted this association whenever he had to deliver shoes for his father to a customer in a competing fire company's territory, as he could count on a licking every time.

Public schools in New York had only recently been established when Gus came of age to attend. By this time the family had moved to Lispenard Street. Gus described himself as being overpowered with horror as he was dragged to the North Moore Street School. His teacher believed in liberal applications of corporal punishment and Gus got more than his fair share. In his memoirs, he recalled one particularly brutal incident.

> The boy by my side in the classroom whispered to me, "Say!" As I turned to him, his extended forefinger, which was meant to hit my nose, found itself at the level of my mouth. I bit it. He howled. I was "stood up" with my back to the class and my face against the blackboard, immediately behind the teacher who, turned toward the class, could not see me. To relieve the monotony of the view, I took the rubber [eraser], covered my features with white chalk, and grinned around at the class. The resulting uproar can be imagined. I was taken by the scruff of the neck and sent to the private classroom, where I had the honor of a solitary and tremendous caning on parts of my body other than my hands. The hatred and the feeling of injustice produced in me by this event were as profound as any that have occurred in later years.

Gus hated everything about the school except recess, when he could occasionally indulge in fights with the other boys.[6]

From very early youth, when he painted a dog's head on a sled and called it "Mastiff," Saint-Gaudens was artistically inclined. He drew at recess and on the fence behind his home, mixing his paints with saliva instead of water and getting sick to his stomach as a consequence. As his skills progressed, he began sketching the cobblers at work. One customer in particular, Dr. Cornelius Agnew, encouraged him to pursue a career in art.[7] Just as importantly, the customers noticed that Gus had a knack for arranging the shoe display in his father's store window.

The shoemaker's family continued to relocate: Bernard followed his wealthy clientele north as they distanced themselves from the disease and poverty of the teeming immigrant populations of the Bowery and Five Points. New York, now the preferred destination of refugees fleeing Europe, swelled in population almost 30% between 1855 and 1860.[8] While this growth fueled an economic boom, it also stretched what few government services existed to the breaking point.

The year 1860 found the Saint-Gaudens family making another move. In May, Bernard located his shoe shop at 268 Fourth Avenue,[9] just one door from the corner of 21st Street. The family took space above a nearby grocery store. For Gus, it was a dramatic change. The firehouse boys were left behind. So was the hated North Moore Street School. Gus was enrolled in the 20th Street School, where the environment was much different. The head of the school had authored a textbook on the history of the United States, and education took precedence over discipline and punishment.[10] Gus responded and for one glorious school year he immersed himself in his studies.

One block down and one block over from the Saint-Gaudens shoe shop lived the Theodore Roosevelts at 28 East 20th Street, between 4th Avenue and Broadway. Did young Theodore Jr.'s mother, the beautiful and stylish Southern belle, Mittie, and his two sisters ever patronize Bernard's little shop? Given the Roosevelts' social position, the probability is good.

Theodore Jr., or Teedie, as he was known as a child, was born October 27, 1858. In addition to his sisters, he also had a younger brother, Elliott. Theirs was one of the leading families of New York: Theodore's grandfather, Cornelius Van Schaack Roosevelt, was one of the wealthiest men in the city. Theodore Sr. (or Thee, as he was called within his family) was both a philanthropist and a junior partner in Roosevelt & Sons, an importer of plate glass.

The home on East 20th had been a wedding present for Thee and Mittie.[11] It was well located in an upper-class but not ostentatious neighborhood. Cornelius lived not far away in an exclusive enclave off Union Square. Those capitalizing most on the economic boom underway were building mansions on Fifth Avenue. Their main shopping thoroughfare was Broadway as it angled through the city. Development of this district had been spurred by the innovation of prefabricated iron building elements. Architectural pieces were cast, taken to building sites, and erected as storefronts. Plate glass was added, courtesy of Roosevelt & Sons. Goods were then heaped into the windows, to the delight of throngs of promenading window shoppers.[12]

There were means other than geography with which the wealthy separated themselves from the rest of the population. They had their clubs, among which the Century Club was one of the most prominent. Founded in 1847 by men such as Asher Durand and Samuel F.B. Morse, it had opened with the intent to bring together 100 gentlemen of talent and accomplishment from every field, with an emphasis on the fine arts. By 1857 it occupied a sumptuously appointed building just off Union Square on 15th Street. Now its membership composition had strayed away from its original precepts. Theodore Roosevelt Sr. became a member in 1864.[13] Membership was far beyond a man of Bernard Saint-Gaudens's means.

Even with these barriers, the elite felt swamped by the flood of immigrants, and moved on both religious and secular fronts to ease the burdens upon these poor and oppressed lest they seek the barricades as the radicals in Europe had in 1848. Charities were actively providing services that the city could not, such as assisting destitute children. The Children's Aid Society established by Theodore Roosevelt Sr. and two other philanthropists sought to place these "street urchins" with families outside the city in hopes that an improvement in their home environment would lead to productive lives.[14]

The industrialist Peter Cooper took a different approach. He had been a leader in establishing public schools in New York, and in 1848 was instrumental setting up evening classes in the schools. Then, in 1853, he founded Cooper Institute, later to become known as Cooper Union, which offered free education in the mechanical arts and sciences with an emphasis on practical education for working-class men and women. More importantly, the school would offer open-admission night classes to anyone, regardless of previous educational background.[15] When it opened its doors in 1859 it was a true lifeline for those who sought to better themselves.

That this kind of charity was a necessity was brought home to the upper classes during the Panic of 1857. As with so many economic downturns, this panic was driven by excessive speculation. Earnings from the railroads and manufacturing concerns had soared in the preceding years, with stock prices reflecting this newfound wealth. In 1857 the bubble began to burst when demand in Europe for American grain declined (amid a bumper crop in the Midwest) and railroad stock prices fell.[16]

In a seemingly unrelated event, the SS *Central America* sank in a hurricane off the North Carolina coast. Little known at the time was the fact that this ship was carrying substantial amounts of gold bullion and coins from the San Francisco Mint for delivery to the New York financial markets. Loss of this gold had the impact of a sudden monetary contraction. The New York financial institutions buckled and stock prices crumbled. Jobs were lost overnight. Immigrants suddenly found themselves destitute and starving through no fault of their own, due to a phenomenon they could not hope to understand.

In November, the unemployed rallied at City Hall to demand that the city provide jobs. On the third day rioting broke out, as some of the unemployed raided bakers' wagons and food shops. It took the police and armed militia to restore order.[17] The immigrant poor had made their point, however: in early 1858, the city hired men by the thousands to clear brush from the future location of Central Park.

Regardless of the motivation, Theodore Roosevelt Sr. derived pleasure from his philanthropic activities. He had no real aptitude for and took little interest in the family business. He was content to leave its management to his older brother, James

Alfred. Besides the Children's Aid Society, he was largely responsible for the News-boys' Lodging House. He certainly believed that decent society faced no greater threat than the existence of a class of vagabond ignorant ungovernable children.[18] He visited the lodging house every Sunday evening to talk with the boys, whom he knew by name, and offer them advice and help. Many times, young Theodore would accompany his father on these trips. Theodore Jr. came away from this experience recognizing that it was the right thing to ease the burdens of the less fortunate.

April 1861 burst upon the national consciousness with the opening shots of the American Civil War fired at Fort Sumter in Charleston Harbor. It was cataclysmic for 13-year-old Gus Saint-Gaudens for another reason: at about this time his father took him aside and said that school was over, that Gus must find a job. When he asked if there was anything that the boy might like to pursue, Gus responded that he would like to do something that would help him become an artist.[19] It was a fateful utterance. As luck would have it, his father was able to find him an apprentice position with a cameo cutter named Louis Avet, at a time when apprenticeships were virtually impossible to find in New York.

Louis Avet was a harsh taskmaster, although the life of an apprentice was no bed of roses in any case. There was little leisure time during the workday for the boy, but his North Moore Street experience helped him to endure. Saint-Gaudens described his years there as "miserable slavery." Avet provided minimal instruction, but Gus was quick to pick up the basics. The shop, just north of 11th Street on Broadway, was far enough from his family's apartment to require Gus to ride the horse cars either as a paying customer or, more often, by sneaking a ride on the back of the vehicle. From his window at his lathe he watched the regiments march down Broadway and off to war.[20] Soon afterward he also saw the amputees returning from the battlefield.

In September 1862, Bernard Saint-Gaudens took his son to Cooper Union to enroll him in a nighttime art class. That Gus was 14 and the minimum age of enrollment was 16 was not a problem: Bernard was providing shoes to the Cooper family, and Gus was easily able to demonstrate his innate drawing ability. So six nights every week Gus received instruction for an hour, staying often for another three hours honing his skills. It made for long days for the boy, but he was driven to live up to his self-perceived potential.[21]

Immediately after the Union's Gettysburg victory, the Civil War came home to Gus in a terrifying way. The Lincoln administration's new draft law was not popular in the city. Its provisions allowed the hiring of a substitute or paying a $300 commutation fee for each draft round. This practice was particularly loathsome to the working poor, who rejected the logic that businessmen were required to stay at home to supervise war production. Anxious that African Americans from the South would take their jobs, and squeezed by inflation and higher tariffs on imported goods as a result of the war, New Yorkers rioted on July 13, 1863. Gus could not understand when Avet uncharacteristically sent him home early that afternoon. He remembered what happened next.

I noticed the strange appearance of the absolutely deserted streets; no omnibuses on Broadway, which was always crowded at that hour, and not a soul, wagon, car, or anything that seemed alive on Third Avenue as I turned into it. A moment later men with guns, running in the distance, gave the only signs that the city was not dead. Then I vividly recollect my pounding upstairs, and my mother taking me wildly into her arms. She had been in a paroxysm of fear to what had become of me, the others of the brood already resting safe at home. Later on, as the storm lessened, it was strange to see two cannon posted in Twenty-First Street at the corner of Gramercy Park, pointing due east in the direction of the rioters.[22]

Fires and fighting went unchecked in the streets surrounding their little apartment for several days while the rioters focused their anger on the wealthy and African Americans. Even with troops brought in from the Army of the Potomac, it took the better part of a week to quell the riot.[23]

In 1864, Gus came to another crossroads. In a fit of rage, Avet fired him for forgetting to clean up the crumbs from his lunch under the workbench. Gus picked up his personal effects and went to the shoe shop. Avet was a craftsman, not an artist—and Gus wanted more. He found new employment with a shell-cameo cutter, Jules LeBrethon. The job felt like a comedown to Gus until he spied an unused stone-cameo machine in the shop. Avet had been one of the first in the country to use a stone cutter to produce cameos of malachite and amethyst, the very best of which he was able to sell to Tiffany's. LeBrethon could not use this device, but Gus was skilled on it. LeBrethon was as different in disposition from Avet as night from day. He taught Gus the basics of carving and gave him extra time for practice. This fundamental experience in small-scale, low-relief work was the beginning of Augustus Saint-Gaudens the sculptor.[24]

The war impacted the Roosevelt family on a different level. Mittie had brothers fighting for the Confederacy, but although Theodore Sr. was of the age to serve on active duty, when the time to enlist came, he hired a substitute. In later years he would admit to regrets over this decision, but in his social circle one did not fight in the war—just as one did not go into politics. When the draft riots hit New York, his family was comfortably vacationing at Long Branch, New Jersey.[25]

Having made the decision not to serve in the military, Theodore Sr. moved on in typically energetic Roosevelt fashion. He was instrumental in getting legislation passed that enabled soldiers to allot a portion of their pay for their families back home. He did not stop there. He served as an allotment commissioner for New York, visiting individual regiments in the field to explain the program and sign up the troops. In this capacity, he became good friends with Abraham Lincoln's private secretary, John Hay. Mrs. Lincoln herself succumbed to his charms, even taking him shopping with her (a dubious honor given her reputation as a spendthrift).

Roosevelt's work took him away from his family for the better part of two years. The tension arising from his wife's Southern sympathies was not easily addressed and

Augustus Saint-Gaudens in 1865. At the time this son of an immigrant French cobbler and his Irish wife was working days for Jules LeBrethon cutting cameos and at night studying sculpture at the National Academy of Design.

Theodore Roosevelt (far left) in Dresden in 1873. His brother, Elliott, is next to him, and their sister Corinne is second from right. "Teedie," as he was known in childhood, was born in 1858 to a prominent New York Knickerbocker family.

The Lincoln funeral procession approaching Union Square, New York City. Young Theodore and his brother, Elliott, are believed to be watching from the second-story window of the house on the left, belonging to their grandfather, Cornelius Van Shaack Roosevelt.

was in fact aggravated by these absences. It was during this difficult period that young Theodore came down with what would later be diagnosed as asthma. The attacks often came at night, when the boy would awaken gasping for breath. These episodes grew increasingly acute as time progressed, yet between them all would seem normal. For Theodore Jr. and his parents, the attacks were frightening. Even within the medical community of the time, precious little was known about the disease, and not knowing what brought on the attacks was maddening for both the boy and his parents. They were reduced to such actions as forcing Theodore Jr. to smoke a cigar or drink coffee to stop the attack.[26] Other times Theodore Sr. would take the boy for a night ride in the family carriage, driving at a rapid pace through the deserted streets, trying to force air into his lungs.[27]

On April 24, 1865, the body of the martyred Abraham Lincoln was brought to New York for a final farewell. The city shut down for the day while Lincoln lay in state at City Hall. With the day off, Gus went to pay his respects. Having seen the body once, he was so moved that he returned to the end of the line for a second viewing. The next day there would be a funeral procession through the city as the president's mortal remains continued their journey to Springfield, Illinois. Gus watched that procession from the rooftop of old Wallack's Theatre on Broome Street, deeply impressed by the solemnity of this final goodbye.[28]

The funeral car, drawn by 16 horses, progressed from its City Hall starting point up Broadway to 14th Street and across Union Square to the railroad depot.[29] As the procession approached Union Square, a photographer took a picture looking toward Cornelius Van Schaack Roosevelt's home. In the second-story window are two small boys, Theodore and Elliott. A little girl who was their constant playmate had been there a moment before. However, she began crying when an invalid regiment marched past the house in advance of the funeral car. For the boys, crying would just not do; Theodore locked her in the closet.[30] The occasion of this funeral was the first bond of common experience between Gus and Theodore. Both men would revere their memories of Lincoln throughout their lives.

Toward the end of the Civil War, Saint-Gaudens had taken a major step in his artistic career, transferring to the National Academy of Design. Still working by day for LeBrethon, Gus could walk to the Academy on 23rd Street at night. Here he received the benefit of instructors who taught art for art's own sake—not as a vocation, as practiced at the Cooper Institute. His instructors included Daniel Huntington, a prominent American painter.[31] At the Academy, Gus was able to expand his horizons beyond the technical and draftsman's training that he had received thus far.

At the beginning of 1867, Bernard Saint-Gaudens asked Gus if he would like to go to France to see the Paris Salon. It was a major financial sacrifice for the family, not only for the cost of the trip but also from the lost wages of Gus's work with LeBrethon. Clearly Gus at age 19 had won his father's admiration in his struggles to work during the day and attend school at night. However, there was only so much that the family could sacrifice. They sent him on his journey with only $100. LeBrethon augmented this amount with 100 gold francs. Gus traveled steerage class to Europe, suffering a horrible case of seasickness, and arrived in Paris with everything he owned in a carpetbag. He stayed temporarily with one of Bernard's brothers and immediately sought employment in cameo cutting.

Gus's original plan was to seek admission to the École des Beaux-Arts and remain in Paris for nine months to learn sculpture, having calculated that his money would be exhausted by then. He had no idea of what he was getting into. The École des Beaux-Arts was for Americans the most prestigious art school in the world, and he soon found that he must make application for admittance through the American minister. It took nine months before he was admitted. Broke, moving into increasingly smaller apartments, Augustus Saint-Gaudens now began his career.[32]

To young Theodore Roosevelt's parents, it was obvious by 1865 that something was wrong. His asthma attacks were showing no abatement and were taking a toll on the boy's physical development. While his body was weak, Theodore had a fine mind. He turned to books for solace, and reading became an avocation that would stay with him throughout his life. It seemed that he had an unquenchable thirst for knowledge. Natural history enthralled him, and he turned his bedroom into an embalming chamber for his collected specimens. In spite of the obvious drawbacks of such activity, his mother and father encouraged him, with Theodore Sr. going so far as to become one of the founders of the American Natural History Museum in New York City in 1871.

Theodore Jr. did not attend New York's public schools, being homeschooled, as were other boys of his class in the city. Aunt Annie Bullock, Mittie's sister, tutored the young Roosevelts and two of his sister's friends. Theodore excelled at reading and writing but not arithmetic. Aunt Annie also brought tales of Southern plantation life that whetted the boy's appetite for storytelling.[33]

Flush with the wartime profits of Roosevelt & Sons, on May 12, 1869, the Roosevelt family embarked upon a grand tour of Europe. It was the beginning of the Gilded Age, when continental tours were a must for the well-to-do. Theodore Jr. "cordially hated" the tour. His asthma attacks were frequent and severe, accompanied at times by diarrhea. The year-long tour included Paris and six weeks over Christmas in Rome, where there was a fashionable expatriate American community. It exposed young Theodore to European cultures and history.[34]

Upon the family's return home, 12-year-old Theodore experienced a growth spurt. Unfortunately his body added height but no mass, and his asthma seemed to get worse. It was at this time that Theodore Sr. challenged the boy to build his body in order to overcome the asthma. Outfitting a room in their home with exercise equipment, the father pushed the boy to work out constantly. With improving stamina, Theodore began venturing into the outdoors in pursuit of even more specimens for his bedroom natural history museum. Summer vacations now included hiking and mountain climbing in the Adirondacks. At 13, he acquired a rifle but found that he could not hit anything with it. After he was diagnosed as myopic,[35] glasses improved his aim and became part of the Roosevelt persona. Gradually his asthma lessened, but it did not go away. Throughout his life he put up a facade of strenuous activity that masked his poor health.

In this same time period, an experience brought home to Theodore that he was a weakling. He was traveling alone by stage when two boys spied him and commenced to pick on him. He described himself as a "predestined and foreordained victim." When he finally was forced to fight the two boys, he found that either one could handle him in a humiliating manner.[36] Upon returning home, he sought his father's permission to take up boxing. He said he was joining the "fellowship of doers."

In October 1872, the family embarked upon another European tour, which also included a journey up the Nile River. Here they ran into the young Henry Adams and his new bride, Marian (or Clover, as she was known to her friends), on their honeymoon. The trip ended with Theodore Jr. and his brother and younger sister spending the summer of 1873 with German families in Dresden. Here he received lessons in German grammar and culture.[37]

Upon his return to New York in October of that year, the decision was made that young Theodore would enter Harvard in the fall of 1876. His father had not attended college, and his younger brother would not have this opportunity. But in his battles with asthma, a bond had formed between his father and him: he was the anointed child. Yet Theodore did not feel he merited this position. Years later he would frankly discuss his perceptions of himself at this age.

> I was a rather sickly, rather timid little boy, very fond of desultory reading and of natural history, and not excelling in any form of sport. Owing to my asthma I was not able to go to school, and I was nervous and self-conscious, so that as far as I can remember my belief is that I was rather below than above my average playmate in point of leadership; though as I had an imaginative temperament this sometimes made up for my other short-comings. I had a very happy childhood, I am inclined to look back at it with some wonder that I should have come out of it as well as I have.[38]

The childhoods of Augustus Saint-Gaudens and Theodore Roosevelt could not have been more different. While each showed the grit and drive necessary to succeed, that they would become partners in an effort to put art into the hands of the common man seemed highly unlikely.

Chapter 2

Making Their Way

It was inevitable that the paths of Saint-Gaudens and Roosevelt would cross with that of Richard Watson Gilder as they advanced in their respective careers. The other person that both men in their own individual ways would come to trust was Charles Follen McKim.

Gilder's daughter described her father as instinctively peace loving, naturally of an optimistic and kindly disposition. He was repelled by any form of controversy, yet exhibited moral indignation as a compelling emotion. However, he never let himself be carried away by his feelings without a careful examination of the facts involved.[1] Here was a man who would serve both as a mentor to Augustus Saint-Gaudens and as a confidant to Theodore Roosevelt.

Born in February 1844, a young Gilder appeared on the New York scene in 1870 as the managing editor of *Scribner's Monthly* magazine. It was in these editorial offices that Gilder met his future wife, Helena de Kay. At that time Helena was studying art at Cooper Union. She brought to the future union knowledge of art and music.[2] With her strong appreciation of European literature, she and Gilder both complemented and reinforced one another. The couple were married in June 1874, when Gilder's career as an editor was beginning to show the potential to which it would ultimately rise.

It was a humble beginning for the newlyweds. There was no honeymoon. Their home on East 15th Street had originally been a stable. It was now transformed into a salon, although the double doors of the former entrance remained, and their furniture was secondhand.[3] In spite of these circumstances, Helena brought warmth to their little home. She also brought Gilder access to the artist community in New York. This little house, next door to the imposing Century Club, soon became a gathering place for the young artists and authors of the time. It wasn't just that the two were intimately associated with these professions; it was the offer of unquestioning friendship in a hospitable setting that drew others to them. On one side of the little path leading back to the studio was a garden. On balmy summer evenings the couple would throw open the stable doors to their guests.[4]

A salon of sorts soon developed, with the Gilders being "at home" on Friday nights to the artistic community. Just returned from studying in Paris, Will Low described the little house on 15th Street as an oasis in his desert home, for so New York appeared in comparison to the regions of flourishing art from whence he had come.

It was inevitable that Gus would find his way to the Gilder home upon his return from Europe in 1875. With the exception of one short visit, he had been gone from the United States for eight years, staying in Paris until the advent of the Franco-Prussian War in 1870 and then going to Rome. He returned to a changed America. Industrialization, jump-started by the Civil War, was in full swing. Enormous profits were to be had. The Civil War itself was now an event to be commemorated, at least in the North. Likewise Gus was changed. To be sure, he had received a solid training in Paris, but he was striving to break out and create a style of his own. There was a still more immediate priority, however: in Rome Gus had met a young art student from the Boston area, Augusta Homer, whom he wanted to marry. He had one problem—no money and no source of income with which to support a wife. He needed to establish himself as a sculptor in New York City before he could ask her to marry him. With unfailing optimism, Saint-Gaudens took a studio at the German Savings Bank Building at the corner of 14th Street and 4th Avenue.

Success remained elusive for Gus, but John La Farge gave a helping hand with small commissions when his needs were greatest. It was also La Farge who encouraged Saint-Gaudens to develop portraits in relief.[5]

The first real opportunity for Gus came with the Farragut commission, a possibility he had been vaguely aware of when he returned from Rome. Gus retained an unabated interest in the heroes of the Civil War from his early years. The Farragut Monument was something that he could put his heart into. Throughout the first part of 1876 the committee in charge of awarding the commission procrastinated. In June of that year, Saint-Gaudens submitted his proposal for the Farragut Monument. He actively sought the support of the established sculptor J.Q.A. Ward in his favor.[6] When the vote came in December 1876, the committee awarded the commission to Ward by one vote. Ward then generously stepped aside and used his influence in favor of Saint-Gaudens. Now Gus could move forward with his life.[7]

Charles McKim's first professional encounter with Augustus Saint-Gaudens came through the sculptor's work in 1876. McKim, along with his future architectural partner, Stanford White, would become quite close with Saint-Gaudens. Their minds worked alike: each had the artist's intuitive perception of beauty, a will to achieve that beauty, and an ability to convey the need for that beauty to the client. Years later, looking back, Gus would off-handedly describe McKim and White as "a couple of redheads who have been thoroughly mixed up in my life ever since."[8] Gus was a redhead himself, making the three men a striking presence.

McKim had entered Harvard in 1866 with the intention of becoming a mining engineer. However, he dropped out of school in favor of a career in architecture in 1867. Shortly thereafter he traveled to Paris and entered the École des Beaux-Arts. During this time he also visited England, Germany, and Northern Italy. With the outbreak of the Franco-Prussian War in 1870, he returned to New York and joined Henry Hobson Richardson's architectural firm. Richardson would impart to McKim his belief that architecture was one of the three fine arts, along with painting and sculpture, and must be practiced and appreciated as such.[9] For Charles McKim, this was a very orderly process in which to carry on into his chosen profession.

Augustus Saint-Gaudens as a student. He studied at the École des Beaux-Arts (for a young American artist, the most prestigious school in the world) starting in the late 1860s, and worked in Paris and Rome.

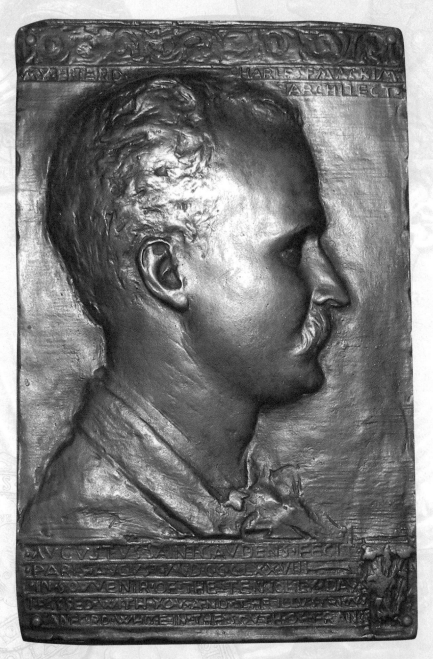

The bas-relief of Charles Follen McKim made by Saint-Gaudens in 1878. "Charles the Charmer" would become a trusted friend of both Roosevelt and Saint-Gaudens, and a champion of the latter's artistic career. (actual size 190.5 x 127 mm [7.5 x 5 inches])

In early 1872, Richardson participated in the design competition for Trinity Church in Boston. McKim prepared the drawings for the submission. When Richardson was notified of his selection, McKim resigned to set up his own firm. His office was just across the hall, however, and Richardson continued to throw work his way. The main beneficiary of the separation, surprisingly, was Stanford White. At 18, he stepped into McKim's shoes to play a major role in the Trinity Church project.[10]

As Saint-Gaudens returned from Europe, Trinity Church was nearing completion. Richardson had turned to John La Farge for the interior decoration. It was natural that La Farge would dole this work out to the returning European-trained artists, among them Kenyon Cox and Frank Millet. For an impecunious sculptor like Gus, this opportunity was too good to pass up. It also put him in closer proximity to his future wife, Augusta. So La Farge put Gus to work under his close supervision painting Saint Paul in Trinity Church during the fall and winter of 1876–1877. Intently watching the work from the back pews was the prematurely balding Harvard professor Henry Adams.[11]

As 1877 dawned, Gus had every reason to be optimistic. He had the Farragut Monument commission and would marry Augusta Homer in June. His mind was full of how he would achieve the potential for which he had trained in Paris and Rome.

In the interim, Richard Watson Gilder began to pressure Gus about breaking away from the National Academy of Design. Helena had been taking classes at the Academy. At the beginning of the 1875 class year, the Academy abruptly closed its school and terminated the professor. There was also dissatisfaction among the students with the rigidity of the curriculum and the restrictions on the use of the Academy's library. Helena had been part of the breakaway group who formed the Art Students League in reaction.[12]

Adding fuel to the fire, Gilder's friend, John La Farge, an academician himself, had become disenchanted with the control that the Academy exerted over exhibitors at its annual showings. Exhibitor selection and the placement of their work were determined by the artistic establishment, much to the frustration of the newly returned European-trained young artists. At first Gus was not interested in the conflict, although he knew that Europe was going through this same turmoil in Paris and Vienna. He had his Farragut commission, and marriage was in the immediate offing. He had also been asked to submit a sketch for the upcoming exhibit.

Then the Academy rejected his plaster from his days in Rome. Saint-Gaudens was furious: —first the Academy had asked him to participate and now they were rejecting his work. They claimed that there was just not room enough for his work, even though Gus knew very well that space was indeed available.[13] As he would do in other difficult times, he showed up on the Gilders' doorstep on June 1, 1877. It was noon and Richard Watson Gilder was home for lunch. He went to the gate to find Saint-Gaudens "as mad as hops" and ready to break from the Academy. That evening the Society of American Artists was formed in the Gilder home "on the wrath of Saint-Gaudens."[14]

Gus had little time to consider the full implications of his actions. He was married on June 4 in Boston and left for Paris from New York on June 6.[15] He had work to do. He would take an apartment and make his Farragut while living in Paris with his new bride. It would be the one romantic time this couple shared.

Prior to his departure for France, Stanford White had persistently asked Gus that he be allowed to do the pedestal for the Farragut. Saint-Gaudens kept putting him off. Then in March of 1878, Gus wrote to Stan that he needed help on the Farragut pedestal and asked him to come to Europe. Gus still remained vague about a commitment, but Stanny was looking for a reason to come to Paris.[16] As White prepared to leave, Charley McKim, newly separated from his wife, decided to join him.

The two architects arrived to a fully packed small apartment. Gus's brother, Louis, and another artist, Maitland Armstrong, were already there with the newlyweds.[17] What Gussie thought of having to share her husband in this arrangement can only be imagined. Needless to say, White and McKim did not move into the apartment.

Stanny and Charley wanted Gus to accompany them on a tour of the south of France, but he refused. It was a critical time: the Farragut Committee was coming to judge the progress of the statue, and Gus was nervous about their reaction to his work. He was not happy with the legs on Farragut. He was also apprehensive that the committee would be dissatisfied with his composition, as he was determined to break away from the regular conventional monument.[18] When McKim and White asked to be present while the work was reviewed, Saint-Gaudens refused.

At the review, the committee members professed themselves not entirely satisfied with the statue. Gus was in a quandary and still would not leave on holiday. He then asked some of the "boys," meaning fellow artists, over to view the work. They were not as tactful as the committee: their verdict was that Saint-Gaudens had given the Farragut his own legs. With this criticism, Gus removed the head and toppled the remaining work to the floor.[19] The legs would have to wait while Gus went to the south of France with McKim and White. Maitland Armstrong would later observe that alternate waves of exultation and despair would sweep over Saint-Gaudens as he worked.[20]

After six weeks, McKim returned to the States but White stayed on, rooming in Gus's studio. Now they had time to talk about the pedestal for the Farragut. Both wanted something radically new and different. It was not going to be a lifeless boxlike structure with moldings. The two men toured Italy and were influenced by the Renaissance statuary and benches. It then became an easy evolution to the radical idea of a semicircular bench ornamented with low-relief figures.

By 1879 Richard Watson Gilder, in what was to become the pattern of his life, had worked himself to exhaustion.[21] He had spent the better part of a decade building up *Scribner's Monthly* to a position of national prominence. Accompanied by his wife and son, he set sail for Europe in March. With Gus having urged them to visit, it was natural that their first stop was Paris.[22] Gilder found Gus well along on the Farragut; however, he was still struggling with the legs.

Gus took a look at Gilder and put him to work. It would always be a point of pride for Gilder that he had posed for Farragut's legs.[23] The work was consuming Saint-Gaudens. At times Gus would express befuddlement and disgust with the sculpture as he neared completion. He wrote to Gilder in London just after Christmas 1879 that his mind was awash in "arms with braid, coats, eagles, caps, legs, arms, heads, caps, eagles, caps and so on—nothing, nothing but that statue."[24]

Augusta Homer at the time of her engagement to Gus. He had fallen in love with the strong-willed, hearing-impaired young art student when they met in Rome. Upon his return and with no money to support a wife, Gus set up a studio in New York and set about gaining a commission that would launch his career and win her hand.

Saint-Gaudens bas-relief of Richard Watson Gilder with his wife, Helena, and son Rodman (1879). Gilder, the publisher of the immensely influential *Century* magazine, would over the years hold the role of friend, mentor, and cheerleader to Saint-Gaudens, and confidant to Theodore Roosevelt. (actual size 215.9 mm x 431.8 mm [8.5 x 17 inches])

A cutout of the angel, saved by Saint-Gaudens from an early Shaw Memorial model. The sources of the Shaw Committee's complaints are readily visible in this rendition.

There were other endeavors during this period in Paris. Saint-Gaudens chanced upon Henri Chapu's relief entitled *A Man With a Hat*. He was so taken by this work that he began to consider low reliefs. During gaps in his work, he started to develop his portrait relief skills using friends as his subjects. A particularly beautiful 8-1/2 by 17-inch bas-relief of the Gilder family showed his potential in this area.[25]

In August 1879 Saint-Gaudens made a decision about the pedestal: he wrote the committee that White would have full power over it.[26] The partnership that would serve the two men so well for more than a decade was formed. White had returned to New York, where McKim promptly asked him to fill a partnership vacancy at the firm. Thus was born McKim, Mead, and White, a partnership that would strongly influence American architecture for the next three decades. Saint-Gaudens made a caricature of the three partners, which depicts Mead struggling to fly two contrary kites marked "McKim" and "White." Mead later described his role by saying he "prevented his partners from making damned fools of themselves."[27]

Word began to leak out in 1880 that the Farragut was indeed going to be exceptional. Gus was besieged by American newspapers and magazines to grant an illustrated article. However, Saint-Gaudens, as was the practice for sculptors of that time, wanted no details of the monument to reach public awareness before the unveiling.[28]

As the Farragut progressed, Gussie looked at the work with pride. She had set up her paints and easel in the studio so that they could work side by side. The sword and the braid had been her contribution to the statue.[29] When Gus sent the plaster cast to the foundry for casting in bronze, there was no time to spare. Gussie was in her sixth month of pregnancy, and she wished for the child to be born in the States. The young couple set sail for Boston on July 3, 1880.[30] A son, Homer, was born to them on September 28.

As Saint-Gaudens returned to New York to prepare for the statue's unveiling, it was apparent to all that something entirely different had been created. The principles that would drive all of Saint-Gaudens's later creations were present. The Farragut was more than just a statue on a pedestal: the portrait figure and base were unified. Gus had originally wanted the memorial to be erected in Union Square, while Stan preferred Madison Square. Gus objected in vain, afraid that the reflected light of the morning sun from the windows of the nearby Fifth Avenue Hotel would detract from the setting.[31]

In his likeness of Farragut Saint-Gaudens used the modeling techniques he had learned in France. He turned Farragut's head slightly to the left with eyes glancing to the side. It was a portrait technique popularized by Houdon to give a sense of life to a sculpture. However, Gus did not stop there. He placed binoculars in Farragut's left hand. His right foot was advanced and the wind appeared to have tossed his uniform coat free of the upper part of his right leg, further enlivening the work. It is the admiral in command of the battle of Mobile Bay.

The completed work was a far cry from his original conception, which was to have been patterned after the François Rude statue of Marshall Ney in Paris. Farragut was to have had a sword upraised in one hand, commanding the action at hand. Once in Paris, Saint-Gaudens had realized the error of that composition. Farragut must have a gesture that "would give him the appearance of a grasp of the field of battle."[32]

White's pedestal consists of a classical exedra, or semicircular seat, elevated by three steps to a floor of pebbles representing a beach. After modeling the pedestal,

White agonized over whether to raise the broad pier at the center of the exedra upon which Saint-Gaudens's likeness of Farragut would stand. McKim finally settled the question by saying that White had a good work and should leave it alone.[33] On the flanking faces, Saint-Gaudens had modeled low-relief figures of Loyalty and Courage, two characteristics of Admiral Farragut's military career. Next to the figures were biographical inscriptions. The ends of the exedra were formed by the curving backs of dolphins. In the center pier, a sword cut down through waves. Saint-Gaudens used these waves and foam across the entire exedra to pull the various devices together and give them a sense of unity.[34]

The Farragut Monument was unveiled in Madison Square on Memorial Day 1881, to great fanfare. Dignitaries filled the platform. Much was said about the deeds of Farragut at Mobile Bay as Gus sat by, in dire fear of being asked to say a few words. He need not have worried; sculptors at that time were often overlooked in these ceremonies. At about this same time, Richard Watson Gilder gently took Saint-Gaudens aside and explained to him that the gentlemen of the press would be his best friends if he would let them, and that genius without publicity would simply not be recognized.[35] It was good advice, but Gus would struggle with it from time to time. As if to reinforce his advice, Gilder ran an article in *Scribner's Monthly* on Saint-Gaudens and the Farragut Monument. The article praised Saint-Gaudens for holding true to the essential spirit of the Greek taste but incorporating the influence of the Florentine Renaissance into his work. Then the article praised the decorative style of the lettering on the pedestal. It even went so far as to suggest that there were opportunities to employ this decorative style on American coinage.[36] It was Gilder's opening shot for improving the designs for United States coins.

This masterpiece was immediately and properly acclaimed. Saint-Gaudens had introduced the concept that the artist must consider not only the subject but also the surroundings within which his work would be viewed. Using a bench as part of the pedestal invited the viewer to participate, which was a novel concept for the time. In Saint-Gaudens's opinion, the artist must work with everything at hand. The acclaim for White, however, was not universal. Some thought the substructure inappropriate for its actual position and felt that it would have been better adapted to an angle of a building or a niche in some natural or artificial elevation.[37]

The Farragut Monument brought Saint-Gaudens instant celebrity. Work began to flow his way. In February, before the dedication and unveiling, H.H. Richardson had approached Saint-Gaudens about another Civil War–themed commission.[38] A friend and neighbor, Edward Atkinson, was treasurer of the Shaw Monument Fund in Boston. They were seeking a tablet in high relief to be mounted on the wall of the Massachusetts State House, honoring Colonel Robert G. Shaw, commander of the 54th Volunteer Infantry Regiment, one of the first African American regiments of the Civil War. Shaw and many of his men had fallen in the 1863 assault on Fort Wagner in South Carolina. Richardson pushed on the two parties through the summer and fall, showing Atkinson a photograph of the Farragut Monument to further promote Saint-Gaudens.[39]

Talks progressed until a letter agreement was reached in June 1882. Saint-Gaudens was to provide the Shaw Monument Committee with a model. If they accepted that model, a contract would be given to Saint-Gaudens without a competition. It would

Early photograph of the Farragut monument (1881). Its commission was awarded to Saint-Gaudens in late 1876, after it was declined in his favor by established artist J.Q.A. Ward. Admiral Farragut was one of Saint-Gaudens's many heroes from the American Civil War. The monument was unveiled on Memorial Day, 1881, to immediate acclaim, bringing national celebrity to its young sculptor.

Theodore Roosevelt with Alice Lee in 1879, one year before they were married. Rose Saltonstall, Alice's inseparable companion, appears to play the chaperone, seated between the young couple.

take almost a year for Saint-Gaudens to execute this model as he struggled to work out a combination of the real and the allegorical. His finished model included an equestrian figure with an angel overhead. Shaw's mother called the floating figure "a fat woman and nothing more."[40] The committee nevertheless acquiesced to Saint-Gaudens, although they asked that the allegorical figure be reduced in size and rendered subordinate to the rest of the work. The formal contract was signed in February 1884. Completion was stipulated in the contract for 1886.[41]

In addition to Saint-Gaudens's monumental works, now his bronze low-relief plaques and medallions were much sought after by both wealthy clients and his friends. With passing time, his skills with this medium sharpened and his fame spread. He had arrived. His workplace was a stopping point for those visiting New York to view his latest endeavor. When Clover Adams visited without Henry in 1883, she and a friend took in the sights at Saint-Gaudens's studio.[42]

Meanwhile, Richard Watson Gilder's career took another giant step forward. *Scribner's Monthly* severed its ties with Scribner and Company and re-formed itself under the name of *Century Illustrated Monthly Magazine*. With the death of one of the founding principals, Gilder found himself the managing editor in fact as well as title. The first issue of the newly named magazine came out in November 1881. It took its name from the Century Club next door to Gilder's home. He had been admitted to membership in 1880.[43]

Gilder saw in his position an opportunity: he was tireless in promoting American authors in his magazine, and he was just as strong in promoting the American arts. In this effort, Saint-Gaudens, as his favorite and good friend, was a direct beneficiary. Gilder used the magazine to promulgate his belief that truth and beauty were one. He insisted that the illustrations in the *Century*, under the supervision of Alexander Drake, be of the best quality.[44] Drake made the magazine a sort of illustrated textbook on the arts. He, like Helena Gilder and Saint-Gaudens, was an alumnus of Cooper Union.

Still, it was not enough for Gilder to give his readers pretty pictures. He sought ways and means to bring art directly into their daily lives.[45] His timing was right: the decade of the 1880s was the heyday of the family magazine, and Gilder made the *Century* number one. As a result he became a man who wielded great power and influence. His Friday-night salons took on added brilliance with Saint-Gaudens attending on a regular basis. In fact, some would have called it the "Gilder Age" of magazines.[46]

Richard Watson Gilder was 14 years senior to Theodore Roosevelt, so the bonds that tied them were of a different nature. In spite of the age gap, when the two men met in the summer of 1884, Gilder would have considered Roosevelt a kindred spirit full of potential.

There was much to like about Theodore Roosevelt. In spite of the premature death of his father in 1878, he was fully engaged in life. He graduated magna cum laude and Phi Beta Kappa from Harvard on June 30, 1880.[47] He had met Alice Lee while he was in school, and they married in the fall after his graduation. The newlyweds promptly moved into his family's home on West 57th Street, with Theodore assuming some of his father's old responsibilities.

That first winter back in New York, Roosevelt became interested in politics. His friends and acquaintances cautioned him that the political organizations were not

Striking Change

controlled by gentlemen. Roosevelt took the comment just the opposite of the way it was meant: he accepted it as a challenge to see if he could measure up in the rough-and-tumble world of politics. If these people were the ruling class of America, he proposed to be part of them.[48] In a backlash against the patronage system and machine politics after President Garfield's assassination, he found himself nominated and subsequently elected to the New York State Assembly.

The next three years were a whirlwind of activity. After a brief period of disbelief from fellow legislators over the dude from the city, Roosevelt's rise in the New York legislature was meteoric. He immediately allied himself with independent Republicans in the Assembly. His activity as a moral force of individual honor and political honesty made for good press in the New York City newspapers.[49] He did not have to be told by a Richard Watson Gilder that reporters could be his best friend; he knew that fact instinctively. He more than survived his first encounter with "the ruling class"—he held his own in the process, successfully pursuing a case of judicial corruption.

The year 1883 brought his reelection and selection as the Republican minority leader in the Assembly. Reform politics had brought a Democrat, Grover Cleveland, to the governor's chair. Cleveland and Roosevelt both wanted civil service reform in New York State after it had been implemented at the national level. A coalition of sorts was formed that successfully pushed this legislation through the Assembly.[50] When the bill became law, Grover Cleveland gained national stature.

The year 1884 dawned full of promise for Theodore Roosevelt: he was campaigning for Speaker of the Assembly, and Alice was due to deliver a child in February. On the political front, however, matters quickly deteriorated. He was outmaneuvered for Speaker and wound up majority leader instead.

Meanwhile Alice's pregnancy seemed to be progressing well. Theodore felt confident enough to leave for Albany on February 12. The next day, a baby girl, Alice, was born to the couple. Theodore was notified by telegram. Then the roof fell in with a second telegram: his mother and wife were dying in the same house at the same time. Mittie had typhoid fever and Alice was failing of unknown causes. Both women died on February 14, 1884, Valentine's Day. Later it would be apparent that Alice had been suffering from undiagnosed Bright's disease, a kidney ailment.[51] Theodore was devastated.

Roosevelt's career as a legislator was over. He was going to retreat to a ranch that he had purchased the preceding fall in the Dakota Territory; however, he had one piece of business remaining. Both Chester Arthur and James G. Blaine were seeking the Republican presidential nomination in 1884. Roosevelt wanted neither man. He successfully set out to avenge his defeat for the position of Speaker by the Republican machine by preventing them from capturing the New York delegates-at-large for President Arthur. He was successful, attracting the attention of Henry Cabot Lodge from Massachusetts. Both men were uncommitted delegates to the Republican National Convention who were seeking to nominate a Reform candidate. It was logical that a friendship would develop. Lodge suggested that they visit Washington to interview Senator George Edmonds, who was campaigning in opposition to Arthur and Blaine. Roosevelt wanted Lodge to stay over in New York as his guest. Lodge agreed.[52]

If Roosevelt and Lodge were seeking an alternative to Arthur and Blaine, whom they believed to be creatures of machine politics, who better to visit during Lodge's stopover than Richard Watson Gilder. The *Century*'s associate editor, Robert Underwood Johnson, described the meeting. Roosevelt was full of humorous anecdotes from the New York Assembly. The stories proved so good that Gilder suggested that he pull them together for an article in the *Century*. Theodore easily won over Gilder and Johnson with his humor and democratic spirit. Johnson noted how attractive Roosevelt's spirit was when one met him face to face.[53]

Perhaps there was another reason that Roosevelt was attracted to Gilder: Gilder had served. He was a member of the Pennsylvania militia called up during the crisis surrounding Gettysburg. He was 19 years old at the time. Granted, Gilder saw virtually no action; still, he had been there. Tragically Gilder had lost his father during the war. The elder Gilder was a chaplain serving with the Army of the Potomac, who contracted smallpox in 1864 and died.[54] Roosevelt would deeply respect this service to the country.

Roosevelt and Lodge went down in defeat at the Republican convention. Blaine carried the day. Both men, though much conflicted, gave their grudging support to the nominee. To bolt the party would have been ruinous for either young man. After the convention Roosevelt left his little daughter, Alice, in the care of his sister, Bamie, and went into self-imposed semi-exile at his ranch in the Dakota Territory. However, Gilder had no such constraints. He gave his support to Grover Cleveland in what turned out to be a close friendship that lasted until Cleveland's death. On June 10, 1884, Gilder took time to write Theodore Roosevelt concerning his support of Blaine.

> The paper has conflicting accounts as to your intentions with regard to the Blaine & Logan outrage. Personally, I have too small an acquaintance with you to venture to advise or exhort—but as one who has had unbounded admiration for and faith in your career will you let me make an earnest and [illegible] hope that today's news [in the *Tribune*] is untrue and that the enormous body of genuine though independent Republicans in the state of New York will not have to lament a lost leader in this crisis.

Years later in 1898 Gilder penciled at the bottom of this letter that Roosevelt told him that this was the only remonstrance that made him feel badly.[55]

In spite of this difference of opinion, Gilder's regard for Roosevelt grew. In December 1885, Gilder nominated him for membership in the Authors Club of New York City.[56] Roosevelt had authored a definitive history of the naval war of 1812.

Just as Roosevelt included Gilder in his circle of friends, he should have made the acquaintance of Augustus Saint-Gaudens. Both Theodore and Gus were nominated for membership in the Century Club in 1884. For Theodore, acceptance was a foregone conclusion. His father had been a member, and he was well respected within the upper reaches of New York society. For Gus, it was another story altogether. He failed in his first attempt.[57] Daniel Huntington was president of the Century at the time. He had also been president of the National Academy at the time Gus instigated the breaking away of the Society of American Artists. Gus was rejected from the club and did not gain admission until 1886.[58]

Nor was all successful with Saint-Gaudens on other fronts. During the 1880s, his personal life began to come apart. Upon the couple's return to the States, Gussie, at her mother's insistence, remained at her family's home in Roxbury while Gus went on to New York to find an apartment and a studio. Waiting for the arrival of her firstborn, Gussie was encouraged by her mother to plan for extended convalescence.[59] After Homer's birth, Gussie remained bedfast for a month, as was the custom for the times. However, she did not start to move about freely for another 45 days, until mid-December.[60]

What Gus thought of this extended absence can be discerned from a comment in one of his letters to her. He spoke freely of the fine attributes of the New York artists' models compared to those of Paris.[61] Later, even when Gussie was in town, she was prone to periods of illness, and at these times she could be a real pill. One time her sister, Genie, came to nurse her. In his letter thanking Genie, Gus closed with one of his typical caricatures. He drew a woman of matronly Victorian proportions, under which he wrote, "Genie before she went to New York to care for her sick sister"; next to it he drew a figure in skin and bones, captioned "Genie after her sick sister got through with her"![62]

Then, to compound the situation, Gussie's father died on Christmas Day, 1880, after a very short illness. It was a blow to both Gus and Gussie. Mr. Homer had been most effective at managing the young couple's financial affairs. When payments on Gus's various commissions were slow in coming, it was Thomas Homer who sent the dunning letters.[63] Gussie would have to take over this role. While she could run a household and save money, she had no experience in managing finances. She now found herself in conflict with Gus, who refused to be concerned with financial matters.[64]

In 1886 Gus faced another problem: he had hardly started the Shaw Monument. Atkinson poured oil on the troubled waters, asking that Saint-Gaudens send photographs of another of his works to remind the committee members of what he could accomplish so that they would bear patiently with the sculptor.[65] After getting no results with this approach, Atkinson bluntly told Gus that he was the hyphen between the sculptor and the Shaw Monument Committee, who were much dissatisfied, considering the delays unreasonable. Shaw's mother wanted the memorial's proposed location moved from in front of the State House, no doubt fearing for its outcome. Atkinson pointed out that Gus had not met the terms of the contract and that he must be prepared to exhibit the model of his work to the committee in the very near future.[66] The Shaw promised to be a contentious commission.

A subtle shift in Gus's relationship with McKim occurred in 1887. The trustees of the Boston Public Library had decided upon Charles Follen McKim to design their new building. There would be no competition. By that point, McKim had the kind of stature within his profession, combined with the necessary social connections, to attract this sort of prestige commission. Samuel Abbot, a library trustee, came to McKim in New York to offer the commission on Saturday, March 19. The two men talked again the next day. After the second meeting, McKim insisted upon a long walk and talk with Saint-Gaudens and White.[67] Only then was he ready to take on the commission. A trend was established. Repeatedly, when McKim with his higher profile gained an assignment of national prominence, he sought Saint-Gaudens's counsel.

With troubles building at home, some time in the early 1880s Saint-Gaudens began an affair with one of his models, Davida Clark. She was in her early 20s, of Swedish origin, and quite beautiful. She would bear him a son named Louis, and Saint-Gaudens would maintain and support this second family for the rest of his life. Meanwhile Gussie's perceived and actual health problems put increasing strains upon their marriage. It seemed she was always traveling to seek cures at various health spas. Unquestionably real was the continued deterioration of her hearing. Tinnitus had developed to compound the problem. Socially the disease left her isolated.

It was into this unstable situation that Charles Follen McKim again stepped as a positive counterbalance, pulling Gus into his effort to establish an American School of Architecture in Rome. At the death of his second wife in 1887, her will endowed two architectural traveling fellowships, one at Columbia in McKim's name and one at Harvard in her name. As he worked with the country's leading architects on the World's Columbian Exposition he promoted his idea further.[68] An organizing dinner was arranged in McKim's home for May 23, 1894. Included in this exclusive gathering was the eminent architect Richard Morris Hunt. Also present were professors from the four American universities offering courses in architecture. McKim wanted Gus to join the meeting, believing sculpture went hand in hand with architecture. His invitation was curiously worded: "Come to dinner, even if you have to go away early."[69] Once involved, however, Gus stayed the course.

Again and again as the Rome school approached reality, McKim involved Gus. Using the same atelier system as the French, the school would serve as a postgraduate training center. It opened in 1895 with three students.[70] Almost immediately there was a push to add a school of sculpture to help establish the institution as an academy. The opportunity came when the Peabody Institute of Baltimore offered to devote some $100,000 bequeathed by the sculptor William Rinehart to establish the sculpture school.[71]

Gus then became involved in the preliminary details necessary for the school's startup. In this regard he was instrumental along with Daniel Chester French in insisting that the school offer a four-year curriculum.[72] As a result of his efforts he was elected to the Board of Trustees for sculpture. He was a major influence in awarding the first sculpture scholarship to Hermon A. MacNeil. It was a solid appointment: MacNeil, who had studied in Paris under Henri Chapu, would not disappoint.[73]

Thus both Saint-Gaudens and Roosevelt drew upon their friends in different ways as their careers advanced. It remained to be seen what they would accomplish once together.

Chapter 3

Gilder's Dream

To be sure, Richard Watson Gilder was not the first to view the designs on American coinage as not indicative of American art standards. As early as 1876, an article in the competing *Galaxy* magazine raised the issue:

> Why is it that we have the ugliest money of all civilized nations? For such undoubtedly our silver coinage is. The design is poor, commonplace, tasteless, characterless, and the execution is like thereunto. They have rather the appearance of tokens or mean medals. One reason for this is that the design is so inartistic and so insignificant. That young woman sitting on nothing in particular, wearing nothing to speak of, looking over her shoulder at nothing imaginable, and bearing in her left hand something that looks like a broomstick with a woolen nightcap on it—what is she doing there?[1]

The design in question was known as the Seated Liberty, modeled and engraved at the United States Mint by Christian Gobrecht after a drawing by Thomas Sully. Reflecting an English influence, it first appeared on the nation's circulating silver coins in 1837.

Perhaps Gilder was not the first to recognize that technological advances in the reducing lathe in Europe opened to sculptors and artists a world that had been the exclusive domain of mint engravers—the designing of coins and medals. He certainly would have been exposed to the latest developments in Europe from the returning artists attending his Friday-night salons. So it was in character that he would become a catalyst as managing editor of the *Century* to improve American coin designs and thereby put fine art in the hands of everyday people. As always it was his desire to try to work within the system.

The first step was a visit by Augustus Saint-Gaudens and Alexander Drake from the *Century* to the office of the Mint director in Washington. It was some time before 1885 that they met Horatio Burchard, who had been appointed director in 1879. Previously he had been a four-term congressman but had failed to gain re-nomination in 1878. The Mint position had then provided a satisfactory alternative.[2]

Saint-Gaudens and Drake found Burchard initially to be open-minded. They launched into a discussion of the aesthetic effect of fine coins upon the taste of the people. They displayed some beautiful Greek and Roman coins. Finally, to clinch their point, Gus pulled from his pocket a particularly rare Greek gold piece of exquisite

43

design. Burchard was not moved; he pulled from his pocket a silver dollar and said, "Now we think this is a very beautiful coin." The piece had been designed at the Mint in 1878 to replace the Seated Liberty style on only the silver dollar. It was really a pretty good work and a significant improvement. However, because of the awkward positioning of the eagle's head on the reverse, the coin was known derisively as a "Buzzard Dollar." At that point both men knew that they would get no further with this man.[3]

Gilder let the situation rest until 1887. By supporting Cleveland in 1884, Gilder gained a stronger position from which to influence affairs at the Mint. Cleveland appointed a new Mint director, James P. Kimball. With his scientific education, Kimball was a true outsider, coming neither from the political ranks nor from within the Mint bureaucracy.[4]

This time Gilder was ready and let fly with both barrels. In the March 1887 issue of the *Century*, an article by William J. Stillman on the coinage of the ancient Greeks made the point that the Greeks took coinage to be a favored vehicle for artistic expression. After a full survey of Greek coins, Stillman closed by stating that it would probably remain a dream for the United States, whose political existence so resembled old Greece, to employ its coinage as the Greeks did and emulate their beauty. Of all civilized nations, he asserted, the United States and its Mint mothered the most barbarous products.[5]

Gilder was not done. He editorialized in that same issue:

> Modern coinage must, of course, always conform to modern conditions of evenness and regularity. But living art—and to see that art is not yet dead, we need to look no further than to the work of French sculptors and to that of some that we have among ourselves—makes light of such restrictions. The Parthenon frieze proclaims for all time what can be done within fixed lines and in the extreme of low relief. It rests simply with the Treasury Department to consign to oblivion when it will our gawky fowls and disjointed goddesses. . . . The Administration which is the first to adopt this reform will win for itself high and deserved honor, and will at the same time give to the medalist's art an impetus greater than it has enjoyed since the day of its generous patrons of the Renaissance.[6]

The battle was now joined. Gilder never acted impetuously. Little did he realize that it would take 20 years and a power much stronger than the stroke of his pen for his labor to begin to bear fruit.

Gilder's pronouncements fell on fertile ground with Kimball in Washington. In the director's opinion, the artistic character of American coins was widely held in contempt. The country was not without a number of sculptors of great ability.[7] On April 6 he wrote Gilder that he was about to invite designs for all six of the non-gold circulating coins. He asked Gilder to provide him with a list of New York artists to whom he might send a circular letter announcing a competition. In particular, he wanted Saint-Gaudens's address.[8]

This action was all too quick. Gilder maintained a large inventory of articles from which to choose for each publication. This material could sometimes sit for months or even more than a year before it appeared in print, much to the frustration of the authors. Therefore, the timing for the publishing of these two commentaries was

The Seated Liberty coinage design that was so maligned in the 1870s and 1880s. The design had been around since 1837; it would survive through the criticism until being replaced by George Morgan's new dollar design in 1878, and Charles Barber's designs for the dime, quarter, and half dollar in 1892. (half dollar shown enlarged 2x)

Bureau of the Mint medal for Horatio Burchard, by Charles Barber. Burchard was a four-term congressman from Illinois before losing renomination in 1878; he was appointed director of the Mint in 1879. Discussing with Saint-Gaudens the aesthetics of coin design, Burchard was unmoved by a rare and exquisite ancient Greek gold piece. Gus knew at that point that the conversation would go nowhere. (shown enlarged 1.5x)

The "Bland" dollar, designed by George Morgan and introduced in 1878. Its nickname derived not from its design, but from the Bland-Allison Act of 1878, which authorized the resumption of silver dollar coinage. (shown enlarged 1.5x)

Bureau of the Mint medal for Director James P. Kimball, by Charles Barber. A metallurgist by education, Kimball was a government outsider, hailing from neither the political ranks nor the Mint's bureaucracy. He agreed with Richard Watson Gilder that the nation's coinage was held in contempt and needed improvement. In 1887 he asked Gilder for a list of recommended artists—with his eye cast in particular on Augustus Saint-Gaudens.

Gilder's Dream

Gilder's choosing. Kimball's prompt response would strongly indicate that the two moves were coordinated.

On April 2, Kimball had already drafted a circular to outside artists calling on them to submit proposed new designs, and the secretary of the Treasury had approved the draft three days later.[9] Each competing artist would be required to submit a plaster model no more than 2-1/2 inches in diameter for both the obverse and reverse of the coin being considered for change. The models should be free of all lettering, date, and denomination. The design should be low relief to minimize the excessive abrasion occurring in high-relief works. The designs must be submitted on or before June 1, 1887. The winning design would receive an award of $500. However, in a departure from standard artistic practices, the Mint reserved the right to combine designs from different artists.[10]

Matters were still on track when Kimball wrote Tiffany's on April 9 to see if any of their artists wanted to be considered, enclosing a circular in the process. Then things started to unravel. Justin S. Morrill, powerful chairman of the Senate Finance Committee, questioned Kimball's authority to initiate such sweeping changes.[11]

Morrill in a December 1883 speech had criticized the "absence of artistic perfection in the unattractive character of American coinage." However, the existing statutes of 1873 did not give the director of the Mint any discretion in regard to the designs of existing coins. The pieces must be struck from original dies already authorized. Only when new coins were to be authorized by Congress did the director of the Mint have the power to seek new designs, including the employment of outside artists.[12]

Kimball immediately was put on the defensive. He was admittedly acting on an ambiguous interpretation of Section 3510 of the Revised United States Statutes, under which the new silver dollar design had been brought forth in 1878, and likewise the new nickel design in 1883. If Morrill was right, these design changes had been illegal. Kimball had no choice but to call in the Treasury attorneys.[13]

It was a chastened Kimball who wrote Morrill on April 15. The first comptroller of the Treasury had decided that Kimball's interpretation of the statute in question had been "forced." Therefore Kimball was suspending the circular until further notice. The director made one last effort, asking the secretary of the Treasury to seek a second opinion from the attorney general. That finding only reinforced the Treasury's legal counsel.[14] Morrill was right: an act of Congress would be required to change designs.

Changing the statute was not going to be easy. Morrill's legislation in 1883 called for a study to be conducted on the issue of coin designs and results to be reported back to the Senate at the end of 1884.[15] While his bill passed the Senate, it died in the House.

Neither Kimball nor Gilder would give up. Kimball addressed the issue head-on in his annual report for the year ended June 30, 1887. Under the revised statutes, Kimball was without mandate to change U.S. coinage designs. A mechanism was needed that would allow design changes administratively. Kimball believed that a public competition would not be successful. Instead he was proposing that leading artists in their fields be engaged to provide new designs. Their work could then be judged by a jury appointed by the secretary of the Treasury. However, he cautioned that the high relief of the ancient coins was not practical and would not meet modern cost-efficient, high-volume minting requirements. Kimball also acknowledged that valid issues concerning changing the designs existed. Too-frequent changes would result in confusion among the public, which associated designs with the respective coin values.[16]

In 1888, editorials supporting legislative action to change the coin designs appeared in the *New York Times*, the *Evening Post*, the *Sun*, and the *Boston Globe*. These had been drawn from a pamphlet prepared by Kimball and forwarded to Gilder for distribution. Gilder provided extracts of the resulting editorials to Kimball and suggested they be published together to support the position for new designs. If the government would not cover the cost of this printing, Gilder volunteered to do it himself. In addition, he told Kimball that he was sending his pamphlet to a number of other papers. In total, supporting articles appeared in two magazines and 14 papers in New York, Boston, Washington, and St. Louis in April, May, and June of 1888.[17] One editorial went so far as to point out that America had at least one artist capable of providing acceptable new designs. The writer was Mariana Van Rensselaer, a good friend of Saint-Gaudens.[18] Gilder was doing what he did best, building up public opinion in support of change.

Kimball again addressed the issue in his annual report for 1888. He had drafted his proposed legislative amendment, and Morrill introduced it in the Senate.[19] A comparable bill was also introduced in the House. Changes for existing coins were to be no more frequent than every 25 years. The diameters of the existing coins were to be fixed as presently minted. Kimball was attempting to establish best practices for the Mint, legislatively. Also, in a backhanded acknowledgment that the current designs on the dollar and nickel had been implemented without proper authority, these two coins were exempted from the initial 25-year requirement.[20]

Progress was agonizingly slow, with the legislation bottled up in committee in 1888 and the 1889 rump session.[21] In fact, events not under the Mint director's control in the 50th Congress were conspiring against this legislation. Morrill was a Republican; the House was controlled by Democrats. The Speaker of the House, John G. Carlisle, was singlemindedly pursing administration policy to reform and lower tariffs on imported goods. By 1888 it had become a campaign issue. Carlisle attempted to control the situation by failing to recognize his opponents on the floor of the House when they wished to speak or introduce legislation. In doing so, he gained a deserved reputation for being tight-fisted with the federal purse strings.[22] In such a politically charged atmosphere, legislation to provide changes in coin designs did not stand a chance.

Gilder had another card up his sleeve. Efforts were under way to celebrate the 1889 centennial of the inauguration of George Washington. Plans called for the president of the United States to be rowed by barge from New Jersey, recreating Washington's journey to his inauguration in New York City. Gilder was deeply involved in the event, serving on several of the committees, including one for art. His avowed purpose was to bring into the celebration certain art features that would have permanent value.[23] Out of his efforts came Stanford White's temporary Washington Arch and Saint-Gaudens's centennial medal.

Gilder's Dream

The concept of a celebratory medal started innocently enough. At a meeting on November 30, 1888, a suggestion was made that the stationery of the Committee on Art and Exhibition be marked by some appropriate device. Alexander Drake and William Coffin, art critic for the *Sun*, were drafted to secure a design. The committee appropriated the princely sum of $50 for this effort. From this start, the idea expanded to include a commemorative medal, the design for which would also serve as the device appearing on the stationery. When Gilder was added to the subcommittee, Saint-Gaudens became the clear choice to do the work.[24]

In what would become a continuing problem for Gus, he simply had no time to do justice to the effort. However, Gilder prevailed. Gus relented, on one condition: he would design the medal and supervise its modeling, which would be done by his former assistant, Philip Martiny.[25] He would take no compensation.

Work initially progressed well. Saint-Gaudens began his research into the basic design. He approached Gilder about the fasces that he intended to use, a version that had first appeared in France some hundred years previously. The ancient versions were not nearly so ornamental. Gilder offered to put the *Century*'s dictionary department at his disposal for this work. The bust of Washington would come from a previous effort by Martiny.[26] Even so, there was little time to complete the work. The intent was that the official committee badges be miniatures of the medal. The design must thus be ready for the striking of the badges by March 1, 1889. The larger medal would be needed for the official opening of the exhibition accompanying the celebration on April 17.[27]

As the work hit full stride, Gilder wrote Kimball on February 13 to raise the possibility of having the Mint strike the badges.[28] Kimball answered that he could strike medals of a national character and he believed that this badge qualified. The work could be done out of pocket. However, in regard to the mechanical and artistic execution, Kimball was concerned that the work undertaken would not satisfy Saint-Gaudens. He recommended using a private establishment to give Saint-Gaudens more control. Then he went further. "I may also remark that the personal equation of such work in this case might be against the very best results as the personal disposition of the engravers at the Mint does not seem to be in favor of doing justice to designs prepared outside."[29] This statement was amazingly blunt. It was a fire bell in the night. Gilder promptly made the decision to allow Tiffany's to prepare the badges.

As the March deadline approached, problems began to develop. When William Coffin came by to check on progress, he saw that the casts had been thrown aside and Martiny was working at his easel on a new wax. Gus was caught up in what seemed a never-ending process of changes through trial and error. There were also changes in the arrangement of the inscriptions, because to Gus the inscriptions were an integral part of the composition.

Tiffany's began to pressure Martiny and Saint-Gaudens. The deadline came, and Gus made more changes that necessitated Martiny returning to his wax. Coffin came again to Martiny's studio to find the artist "mad all through." Martiny said he was "done out." Coffin then went to Gus for a long talk. The long and short of it was that Martiny made casts of his most recent wax and they were released for preparation of the badges the next day.[30]

Ultimately, Gorham cast the medal in Renaissance style. The design showed a number of characteristics that would carry over into Saint-Gaudens's future work. On the reverse, a magnificent eagle with wings spread bore a shield with the motto E PLURIBUS UNUM inscribed upon it. Held in the eagle's talons were an olive branch and arrows. To one side was the New Amsterdam coat of arms. Around the perimeter were 38 stars for the states of the Union.

The central device of the obverse was a profile half bust of Washington in Continental costume—a change from the norms of the time, which generally followed the Houdon work. The profile was in high relief in the style of the Italian quattrocento. Breaking the symmetry to the right of Washington's bust was the fasces. The Latin phrase PATER PATRIAE appeared but was not overbearing.[31] The centennial dates were in roman numerals. Most imaginative was the way Saint-Gaudens broke the inscriptions with the design motifs on the obverse and managed an unwieldy inscription on the reverse. When the medal was finally finished, it had Martiny's signature as well as Saint-Gaudens's. This was at Gus's insistence.[32]

At first glance this medal appeared very similar to the committee badge; however, subtle differences enhanced its overall effect. The bust of Washington had been softened. The inscriptions had been moved to improve balance and symmetry. The placement of the motto on the shield in the medal version was unique. These changes were from the hand of Saint-Gaudens, but they came at a price. Existing trial casts exhibit a different bust of Washington in comparison to the final medal. The forehead is higher. Facial features appear to have a different emphasis. Washington's coat is without buttonholes. The bands of the fasces are not split.[33] Saint-Gaudens had to see the changes with his practiced eye to judge their quality. It is obvious that Martiny's ordeal continued right up to the time of the celebration as Saint-Gaudens heedlessly strove for perfection.

These changes made a merely good medal into a great one. Gilder called the work a radical improvement upon medal work of the day in the United States. On the other hand, the badge did illustrate what could be accomplished on the small scale typical of coins. Gilder expanded upon this point, hoping that the medal in an indirect way would have an ultimate effect upon the coinage. In adherence to the committee's desire, the medals were widely distributed.[34]

The 50th Congress expired with the inauguration of Benjamin Harrison, a Republican. On February 24, 1890, the legislation was once again revived in the House. Finally, on October 3 of that year, Gilder received a note of thanks from the Treasury for his work on behalf of the new legislation permitting a change in coin designs, since Public Law 286 had been enacted on September 26. [35]

In the end Gilder had readied the stage for what Theodore Roosevelt would call his "pet crime." However, one needed to look only at the Mint culture in which Gilder's dream must come to fruition. Kimball's concern about the personalities in the Engraving Department was real. However, he had resigned with the exodus of Cleveland Democrats, and it would be up to a new Mint director to implement design changes.

Official badge of the George Washington Inauguration Centennial Celebration. Gilder sought to have this piece struck at the Mint. (shown enlarged 1.5x)

Mold from which an early version of the medal, without buttonholes, was cast.

51

George Washington Inauguration Centennial commemorative medal. (shown at .75x actual size)

52

Chapter 4

A Mountain of Labor

Charles Barber was born on November 16, 1840, into a family of London engravers. His father, William, immigrated to the United States with his family in 1852. Settling first in Boston, they moved on to Providence, Rhode Island, where William was hired as a die engraver for Gorham. Here he established a reputation for skill in the art of bronzing. This skill led to his appointment as an assistant engraver at the Philadelphia Mint in 1865.[1] When the chief engraver of long standing, James B. Longacre, died at the beginning of 1869, William was appointed to the vacated position. Soon after, Charles was hired by his father as assistant engraver.

The Mint organization in which Charles Barber apprenticed consisted of an administrative headquarters in Washington, DC, and actual mint operations in Philadelphia, San Francisco, New Orleans, and Carson City, supported by regional assay offices. The Philadelphia Mint was the main operation, while the other mints served as branches. Each mint and assay office was headed by a superintendent. They reported to the director of the Mint in Washington. The director in turn reported to the secretary of the Treasury. These posts were all political appointments. The chief engraver was in charge of preparation of all dies used at each of the mints for striking of the coinage. He was also called upon when new designs were required. He would compose the designs and oversee the models and reductions necessary to ultimately convert this work into the dies for producing coins. The chief engraver position was a political appointment reporting to the superintendent of the Philadelphia Mint. However, because of the skill required, the chief engraver's position was in effect a lifetime appointment.

The 1870s were a time of turmoil for the nation's monetary system. Silver was depreciating in value due to economic events in Europe and the discovery of large new minable deposits in the western United States.[2] In response, the Mint Act of 1873 increased the weight of the subsidiary silver coinage (the dime, quarter, and half dollar) in a futile effort to maintain intrinsic value. However, the same law discontinued the silver three-cent piece, half dime, and silver dollar, much to the silver lobby's distress. There were copper-nickel alternatives to both the three-cent piece and the half dime, and the dollar coin did not widely circulate.

There were complex financial and political issues as well, involving the continuance of the gold standard and the emergence of support for a bimetallic silver-and-gold standard. The Mint Act of 1873 had had the intended effect of placing the

53

United States more firmly on the gold standard. In 1878, with the passage of the Bland-Allison Act, the silver lobby gained the upper hand—the silver dollar was reinstated. However, the act went further by mandating substantial minimum monthly purchases of silver by the Mint for conversion into silver dollars, which in turn were used to back paper currency redeemable in silver. The act was both inflationary and a bonanza for Western silver producers.

At the same time, public dissatisfaction was mounting with the designs on the silver coinage. Up to the 1870s, the half dime, dime, quarter, half dollar, and dollar had all shared the same obverse design. With the exception of the half dollar, this Seated Liberty design had been modified in the early years of its use by the Mint engravers and had lost much of its distinctiveness. The Mint was not insensitive to these complaints; it just desired to keep the effort in-house. Annually, through the 1870s, numerous pattern pieces were struck testing new design concepts.

As a result of these pressures, the Mint director, Dr. Henry Linderman, sought to strengthen the engraving department staff. The existing staff with William Barber and his son, Charles, also included two additional assistants. Dr. Linderman turned to the deputy master of the Royal Mint in London, C.W. Fremantle, for a recommendation. In October 1876, a fifth, "special engraver" was added. He was George T. Morgan, who had previously been a Royal Mint employee.[3] Morgan immediately made his place within the United States Mint. His design was chosen over that of William Barber for the resumption of silver dollar coinage in 1878. During this period of feverish activity, Charles Barber was curiously out of the picture. He submitted no replacement designs for consideration on the subsidiary silver coinage. His work was in the backwaters of the Mint, designing special commemorative medals and helping his father. In fact he had almost been terminated at the time of Morgan's employment.[4]

This picture changed drastically when William Barber died on September 1, 1879, after receiving a chill at an Atlantic City seaside resort. There were immediate applicants for his position. As a result, the newly appointed Mint director, Horatio Burchard, informed the Philadelphia superintendent, A. Loudon Snowden, that he would ask Secretary of the Treasury John Sherman to postpone a decision on the replacement.[5]

Morgan appeared to have the upper hand initially in succeeding to the chief engraver's position.[6] He went so far as to have Fremantle write a letter of recommendation for him. Burchard told Fremantle that the appointment was not under his immediate control. It must be made by the president and confirmed by the Senate. However, it would be Burchard's great pleasure in presenting Fremantle's recommendation to the president.[7]

Seeking resolution, Burchard requested that Snowden come to Washington on Saturday or Saturday night, December 6.[8] Snowden was to bring examples of the work of the applicants for Secretary Sherman, to review. There was just one problem: Sherman did not know William Barber was dead. That Saturday found Burchard meekly informing the secretary.[9]

The decision was then made literally over cigars and brandy. President Rutherford B. Hayes nominated Charles Barber to take his father's position at the Mint and the Senate confirmed the appointment on January 20, 1880. Morgan was reduced to an assistant. Serving 37 years in this position, Charles Barber would outlast Mint

Born into a family of engravers, Charles Barber was hired by his father—chief engraver William Barber—to work at the U.S. Mint. In 1880 he would take the chief engraver position himself, serving for 37 years and outlasting several Mint directors, Treasury secretaries, and presidents.

Liberty Head nickel gold-plated to pass for a $5 gold piece; commonly called a "racketeer nickel." (shown enlarged 2x)

Mint Director Edward O. Leech. Like his predecessor, James Kimball, Leech sought to improve the nation's coinage designs, starting with the silver coins.

directors, secretaries of the Treasury, and even presidents. Upon his death, Morgan would finally succeed to the position of chief engraver.

Barber's first effort as engraver was to provide a new design for the nickel, which was assuming an important position in American commerce. It had been introduced in 1866 in an effort to retire the fractional currency printed during the Civil War to counteract the hoarding of minor silver coins. Its position within American commerce had been assured in 1873 with the discontinuance of the silver half dime.

For some time, Superintendent Snowden had sought to bring the same consistency of design to the minor coinage as was exhibited by the silver coinage. Considering that significant numbers of Americans could not read or write, Snowden believed the different designs now being employed were confusing. He had also recommended copper-nickel for all three coins, using size to differentiate value. By late 1881 he had decided to confine his initial efforts to the five-cent piece. Snowden was opinionated about what constituted a suitable replacement design. On the obverse there should be a head of Liberty. On the reverse he wanted a large roman numeral V surrounded by a wreath containing cotton, rice, tobacco, and wheat.[10]

Burchard concurred with this approach and directed Barber to prepare the design.[11] It was not a challenging assignment. With the design theme already set, Barber merely had to execute it. His Liberty was a Greco-Roman restyling of the fourth-century-B.C. Grecian bust on display at the Philadelphia Academy of the Fine Arts. He then drew from Morgan's dollar design by affixing several wheat ears and cotton bolls to Liberty's coronet. That part of the design was satisfactory, but hardly original. He followed Snowden's recommendations exactly on the reverse. His undoing was in the inscriptions: he failed to include the word "cents."

In 1882, the secretary of the Treasury, Charles Folger, made the decision to drop the concept of copper-nickel-based minor coins employing a unified design. He did, however, accept Barber's design as a replacement for the five-cent piece. The new nickels, with some modifications, were issued in 1883. Barber had to be satisfied as this design was his first work to enter general circulation.

Immediately counterfeiters began reeding the edges of the coins, gold plating them, and passing them off as $5 gold pieces that had nearly the exact same circumference. With great embarrassment, Barber was forced to rework the reverse design to add CENTS, to prevent their being passed off as gold pieces.

This first blunder was to stay with Barber. He became expert in the mechanics of his craft. He developed an eye for which artistic designs could be coined efficiently for general circulation. He also unfailingly learned the requirements of cost-efficient coin production. In so doing he became a staunch defender of the status quo.

The internal activity to develop new designs for the other coin denominations ground to a halt with a set of pattern coins developed by George Morgan in 1882. Whereas the father, with Morgan's help, had taken the initiative to develop new designs, the son showed no such inclination. As the issue of design changes wound through Congress in the late 1880s, Barber preferred to sit and wait. The little work that was done was in the area of experimental pieces rather than improvements in design.

This inactivity ended with enactment of the legislation in September 1890 that defined Treasury Department authority to change designs on circulating coins.

Striking Change

Heretofore, the Mint had evolved into a highly efficient manufacturing operation, minting more than 123 million coins in 1890. Of that total, 73 million were minor coins (pennies and nickels), all struck in Philadelphia. Dimes, quarters, and half dollars amounted to 11 million coins. Output of each denomination was demand-driven. The production of 38 million silver dollars, on the other hand, was legislatively derived; limited numbers of these coins circulated in the West and South, with the remainder going to the Treasury vaults to back up paper currency redeemable in silver. The gold coinage consisted of the $2.50, $5, $10, and $20 gold pieces, more familiarly called the quarter eagle, half eagle, eagle, and double eagle, respectively. The first three all had the same obverse and reverse designs that dated from 1838. The double eagle, which had its birth in the California gold rush, had a slightly different design. Production of gold coins languished in 1890, as it had for several years, as the United States seemed to be shifting toward a silver economy.[12]

Edward O. Leech succeeded Kimball as Mint director on October 16, 1890. He was a Columbia graduate who later obtained a law degree. Having joined the Bureau of the Mint in 1873, Leech was 38 when he assumed the director's position.[13] He had the self-assurance to make the coin-design changes. He would start with the subsidiary silver coins, which would both eliminate the disliked Seated Liberty design and be less disruptive of the Mint's manufacturing activities.

Furthermore Leech had in hand recommendations from Charles Barber should designs be sought from outside artists. Any designs should be models and not drawings. These models should be four to eight inches in diameter. They should be in low relief and include all inscriptions required by law. Barber had strongly opposed former director Kimball, who had advocated that the inscriptions were not necessary to judge the appropriateness of a design. In Barber's mind, it was absolutely important to judge the appropriateness of any design by how the inscriptions and date were placed within the design's field.[14]

Leech knew that he must rely heavily upon the New York artists in order to have a successful competition. He wired Andrew Mason, superintendent of the New York Assay Office, on April 2, 1891, for a list of the prominent artists to be considered for a planned competition. To get a better picture of this art community's reception to such a competition, Mason sent his assistant to interview the artists. First on his list was Augustus Saint-Gaudens.

Gus was honored to be considered, but he immediately stated that he would not be willing to enter such a competition—although he would be proud to be invited by the government to prepare designs. Mint personnel could not have been expected to know in advance Saint-Gaudens's aversion to competitions.[15] Gus did make several recommendations, suggesting that the competition be limited to qualified artists. If possible, they should be compensated. Saint-Gaudens even volunteered names of sculptors he thought might be interested. He described painters Will Low and Kenyon Cox as well qualified but requiring their designs to be modeled. In total his recommendations included all but two on the government's list.

J.Q.A. Ward and Will Low were also interviewed that day. Ward liked the idea of a competition, but was too busy with commissions already in hand. As the conversation progressed, however, he warmed somewhat to the idea of participating. Ward

58

agreed with Saint-Gaudens that a great deal of time and effort would be involved for the participants. He certainly did not want to see a commission go "to incompetent hands." He too provided names of potential contestants. However, he felt Saint-Gaudens and Olin Warner were the two most qualified.[16]

On April 3 Mason sent Leech ten names: Augustus Saint-Gaudens, J.Q.A. Ward, Daniel Chester French, Olin Warner, Herbert Adams, Charles H. Niehaus, Frederick MacMonnies, Kenyon Cox, Will Low, and H.S. Mowbray.[17]

Leech also sought input from Charles Barber, who responded supportively. He wanted the diameter specifications for each coin to be set forth as part of the process because a design might be suitable at one size and not at another. Barber did not believe that advertising in newspapers for designs would produce satisfactory results. Furthermore, he pointed out that compensation for any time expended in submitting the designs should be considered. He doubted whether any reputable artist would be willing to enter the contest if only the winner were to be compensated. Barber also provided potential names that included Saint-Gaudens, Ward, and Philip Martiny in New York.[18]

Leech wasted no time, setting the process in motion on April 4, 1891. A circular letter of invitation to compete in preparing the new coin designs was received by the New York artists on Mason's list. The proposal called for separate designs of the obverse and reverse of the dollar and obverses for the half dollar, quarter, and dime. The conditions were exacting. Completed plaster models, from four to eight inches in diameter, were to be submitted for judging no later than June 1. The models must be in low relief suitable for coinage and bear all the legally required inscriptions. The payment for each accepted model was $500.[19] Leech was, at this point, content with the reverse of the Seated Liberty design and wished only modifications at most to the eagle and shield. Leech followed with a press release setting forth this action and also stating that the motto IN GOD WE TRUST, though not required by law, would be retained.[20]

It had taken four years for James Kimball's visionary attempt for an outside competition for coin designs to be set into motion. Leech, ignoring a key recommendation of Charles Barber, would only compensate the successful design. While inadequately publicized and unknown to the New York artists, Leech also sent some 2,000 circulars throughout the country.[21] This action doomed the competition to failure.

The circular was greeted with consternation in New York. These artists wanted to contribute toward improving the designs on American coins but were unwilling to accept the burden of personal expense. It took some time for these sentiments to be communicated across the artistic community. Finally, on May 20, Saint-Gaudens, Adams, Niehaus, MacMonnies, Cox, Low, and Mowbray met at Daniel French's home to draft, sign, and publish a response to the circular.

> The undersigned, having been invited to prepare designs for a new coinage for the United States, beg respectfully to state that the conditions of the competition as given in the circular letter of invitation are such as to preclude the possibility of any good result from it. The time given for the preparation of designs is too short and the compensation altogether insufficient, while no assurance is given as to who will make the awards.

They beg to suggest the following terms of competition as such as they could accept:

> The awards to be made by a jury of competent artists of standing in the profession, to be chosen by vote of the competitors, by presidents of the great art institutions or otherwise.
>
> At least three months to be allowed for the production of sketch designs, and at least six months to be allowed for the production of completed models if these are to be insisted upon.
>
> One hundred dollars to be paid out to each artist competing for each sketch design submitted, or $500 to be paid to each artist competing for each completed model accepted.
>
> One thousand dollars in addition to the sum paid for competitive sketches for models finally accepted.
>
> The obverse and reverse of any coin to be designed by the same artist and the reverse of the present half-dollar, quarter-dollar and dime to be abandoned.[22]

In spite of these concerns, the men still wished to compete if the Mint would extend the deadline for the submission of proposals.[23]

It was reported in the New York papers that all of the artists, including Saint-Gaudens, signed the letter. Gus, however, had second thoughts. It was not that he disagreed with the conclusions of the group. He heartily concurred. It was that the response as drafted implied that he would compete if the terms were modified. As a result he took the time to write a letter of explanation to Leech. He was withdrawing.[24]

Leech could not understand why the artists had waited to respond until only 10 days before the close of the contest. He believed if he extended the deadline, he would be showing obvious favoritism to a select group of artists. That would not be fair to the others who had complied with the terms of the circular and already submitted their designs. As to the financial terms, no moneys had been appropriated for such payments. Here Leech was assuming that the New York artists were aware that he had issued a broad invitation. Leech regretted that these men found the conditions impossible for their participation. He did assure them on one point: a competent jury would be selected to judge the entries.[25]

On the margin of Saint-Gaudens's letter withdrawing his name from the competition are written in Leech's hand the names of Saint-Gaudens, Ward, and Gilder. This may have been Leech's first take at a jury to judge the designs. It would have been an excellent choice, had he stayed with it.

Leech regrettably changed his mind with only Saint-Gaudens surviving to make the final cut. Added were Charles Barber and Henry Mitchell.[26] Mitchell was a noted engraver of stamps and seals from Boston. He had engraved the dies for government-stamped envelopes in the late 1860s and designed medals for the Philadelphia Centennial Exposition in 1876.[27]

This final selection was tainted. Obviously Charles Barber had a vested interest in the outcome. So too did Henry Mitchell. He had been a member of the Assay Commission for 1890, indicating that the man had political connections. Also he had queried

Leech about the possibility of providing new designs as early as 1890.[28] Gus was the only committee member without a personal agenda. It is a shame that Gilder fell out of consideration. He had no agenda except the betterment of the nation's coin designs.

Gus walked into the June 3 meeting not knowing who else was going to be serving. Curiously, Leech had not informed him of the identity of the other participants. On the other hand, both Mitchell and Barber knew the makeup of the committee, and that information had been reported in the press. The submissions were disappointing, with Gus rejecting all out of hand.[29] He even confided to Leech that only four individuals were capable of doing such design work: three lived in France, and he was the fourth. Lest this statement be taken as self-serving, Saint-Gaudens stated that he had done a study of the subject prior to his attaining fame as a sculptor.[30]

Saint-Gaudens's statement could easily have been considered arrogant. However, the explanation lay in events that had transpired in 1890. His brother Louis, an artist in his own right, had executed a commission for the Mint honoring Joseph Francis for his contributions to the lifesaving service of the country. Upon his delivery of the medal in December 1889, the Treasury had insisted upon changes, particularly on the reverse, where the lifeboat was virtually redone. In addition, Charles Barber had been forced to do extensive retouching to compensate for the detail lost by the reducing lathe.[31] When the medal was struck in March 1890, Gus could not have overlooked the changes from Louis's original model. Thus, his statement to Leech was his way of not confronting the Mint directly.

When Leech in turn tried to constructively suggest to Charles Barber that he retain someone to assist him should this work now be done at the Mint, Barber bristled. He knew that Saint-Gaudens preferred a design from the ancient Greeks featuring high relief. He had an entirely different take on the prior year's experience with the lifesaving medal. It had taken 50 blows from the medal press to bring up the design details on this four-inch-diameter design. Allowing for the other steps in the process, including annealing after each strike, it had taken 25 hours to complete just one of these medals. From his craftsman's viewpoint, high relief would be impracticable for the Mint's equipment, geared to produce large volumes of general-circulation coins. In addition, high-relief coins would not stack, and would be easy prey for counterfeiters. He rebutted that he knew of no one who could even assist him in preparing acceptable designs.[32]

On that same day, the jury reported to the Treasury secretary that no design reviewed was acceptable. Leech's committee recommended that the services of one or more artists distinguished for work in designing and relief be engaged at a proper compensation to prepare new designs for consideration of the Treasury Department. Each of the committee members concurred and Leech signed off in a note at the margin.[33]

Leech had now put himself in a corner. In spite of his concurrence with his jury, he was unwilling to restart the competition in a manner that would permit New York artists to participate. His only option was to have the design work done internally at the Mint. On June 11 Leech instructed Barber to prepare sketches for the half dollar, quarter, and dime. He was content to leave the Morgan dollar, with its larger production requirements, in place for the time being. He was looking for one obverse design based upon the head of Liberty as depicted on the French five-franc piece. The design need not be an exact copy. For the reverse, Leech had no objection to the present eagle on the half dollar and quarter. If changed, he would want the shield either on the eagle's breast or in its talons. Leech strongly wanted the reverse of the dime retained. With the competition missteps, all Leech could hope for was that the Mint could provide the acceptable designs internally.[34]

Leech informed Mitchell of his decision. The man had written him after the judging, requesting that he be given an opportunity to try his hand at a design for the half dollar.[35] However, Leech did not share with Mitchell that he had been most specific in his instructions for the proposed designs to the engraver. He merely told Mitchell that if the designs requested proved unsatisfactory, he would look elsewhere.[36]

At the end of June, Saint-Gaudens had his say in *Harper's Weekly*.

> In this case a limited competition might be a better plan than that of depending on any single artist. . . . The coinage should be certainly in the hands of an artist capable of doing the work well, and the only means of getting such a one is through the offer of a proper reward. Every possible concession should be made, and no effort spared to reduce to a minimum the sacrificing of the artistic side of the work to mechanical necessities and technical requirements. The system of issues as well as the handling with facility of large sums of money in coins as in the banks of the nation, must be considered. A certain quality of relief, for example, may in some appreciable degree affect the exceeding rapidity with which coins are struck and which is of importance. None of the modern technical requirements can be disregarded, even the most remarkable—like that of the uniformity by which, I have understood, the banker is able to estimate vast amounts by trick of running the thumb-nail alongside a pile of coins. On both sides some concessions will be necessary. This makes the problem an interesting one for the artist to struggle with. Some of the French have struggled with it most successfully. In the present effort to secure models of artistic beauty for our coinage the government is deserving of praise rather than blame.[37]

Clearly Saint-Gaudens understood the impact of minting requirements upon potential coin designs. Would he have spoken differently had he known of Leech's decision to go in-house?

Leech went public with his decision to go with Charles Barber on July 20 in a brief report in the *Boston Transcript*.[38] His feelings were more fully quoted in the July issue of the *American Journal of Numismatics*.

> It is not likely that another competition will ever be tried for the production of designs for United States coins. The one just ended was too wretched a failure. The result is not very flattering to the boasted artistic development of this country, inasmuch as only two of three hundred suggestions submitted were good enough to receive honorable mention.
>
> It is realized that the money of a nation is expressive of its art culture. Therefore, lest posterity imagine the present generation to have been barbarous, it is desirable that our silver pieces should be as handsome as may be. I have told our engraver to prepare me a set of designs for the subsidiary coins to be submitted to Secretary (of the Treasury) Foster.

Joseph Francis medal, designed by Louis Saint-Gaudens and struck at the Philadelphia Mint in 1890. Augustus's influence in his brother's work is readily apparent in the relief and portrait of the obverse, the stars on the perimeter, and the arrangement of the inscriptions. (shown at .75x actual size)

Charles Barber's first attempt for the subsidiary silver coins redesign. (shown enlarged 1.75x)

Barber's subsequent revision for the new design, incorporating the clouds, oak wreath, and ribbon across the front of the eagle, but dropping the rays on the reverse and substituting the head of Liberty for the obverse. (shown enlarged 1.75x)

The accepted Barber design for the half dollar, which was modified slightly for the quarter. For the dime the Barber obverse was adopted while the former reverse, slightly modified, was retained, reflecting Mint Director Leech's desire. (shown enlarged 1.75x)

I do not see any prospect of getting our designs elsewhere in this country. We might get them in France. The French coin work is of the most artistic description. But the people of the United States would never forgive us if we went outside the country for our designs.[39]

Leech's comments could not have been overlooked by Saint-Gaudens. Sparks were flying. Richard Watson Gilder, after all of his efforts, wrote in frustration to the *New York Tribune*. Gilder protested against what he called the summary method by which the Mint was proposing to deal with a subject of highest importance. Gilder believed that Leech, by using Mint personnel in the redesign, was failing to avail himself of the best talent in the country. Gilder acknowledged that the design solicitation had been a failure. However, he questioned giving the Mint, in effect a manufacturing facility, artistic control of the redesign. In his opinion, the Mint director should have continued the process, perhaps by other means, within the artistic community until an acceptable solution was reached.[40]

By "other means," Gilder surely meant giving the commission to Saint-Gaudens. This letter was clipped and forwarded to the Mint director. Because the letter came from Gilder—who had worked so hard in support of the 1890 legislation—Leech had to respond.

On August 9 Leech's answer reached New York. The chief engraver at Philadelphia had prepared some new designs, which he had shown to both Leech and Henry Mitchell. Mitchell was decidedly pleased with them. Leech, however, did not give such an unqualified endorsement. He told Gilder that he had suggested modifications, which Barber carried out. However, he was still not entirely satisfied and expected that the changes would take some weeks more. The letter then took a defensive tone. Leech extolled Charles Barber's qualifications. In contrast, he stated, "artistic designs for coins, that would meet the ideas of an art critic like yourself, and artists generally, are not always adapted for practical coinage." He closed by saying that his objective was to improve the appearance of American coinage. If he could do this by staying within the Mint service, he saw no good reason to look beyond it.[41]

Leech's statement that he was reserving final judgment on Barber's new designs for the subsidiary silver coinage set the stage for a test of wills. The design first proposed by Barber for the half dollar ignored Leech's directions for the obverse. Its principal device was a standing female figure representing Columbia. In one hand was a liberty pole topped with the liberty cap, a theme identical to the Seated Liberty coins. In the background, behind Columbia, was an eagle with wings upraised, standing on a rock.[42] The bird appeared awkward. The complaints that appeared in *Galaxy* of a woman looking nowhere, wearing nothing in particular, and holding a broomstick topped by a woolen cap come immediately to mind. The reverse was no better. It consisted of the heraldic eagle from the Great Seal of the United States, downsized and surrounded by sun rays and an oversized wreath of oak leaves. The proportions were wrong and the elements impossibly crowded. It was a poor imitation of the heraldic eagle first used on the reverse of silver and gold coinage from 1796 to 1807.

Leech was not satisfied with the obverse and asked Barber to prepare a design along the lines he had originally suggested. On September 12 models were forwarded to Leech. Barber had performed as instructed. Liberty obviously had her origin from a composite of work emanating from France. For the reverse Barber still clung to his cluttered Great Seal design, although he was beginning to question the inclusion of the wreath.[43]

Leech had now immersed himself into the design process. He had submitted Barber's new design to the secretary of the Treasury and various friends in New York for criticism. On September 28 he wrote directly to Barber: Liberty's lips and chin seemed "rather voluptuous." On the reverse, the wreath seemed too heavy and there was too much filling up of the design. Leech directed Barber to prepare a new reverse omitting the wreath from the heraldic design. Once completed, Leech authorized trial patterns in silver with and without the wreath.[44]

Leech's criticisms were on target; Barber's effort was missing the mark. The engraver's reaction was quite defensive. In a long letter addressed to Philadelphia Mint superintendent Oliver Bosbyshell but meant for Leech, Barber stated that he was perfectly willing to make any changes in design, provided the suggested change was in his opinion a good one. However, he felt he must ask that criticisms come to a halt as he was well progressed in preparing the dies as instructed. Each change at this point would take him back to the starting point, with much time lost. He went on to give a tedious defense of the heraldic elements and his methodology for their incorporation in the reverse design based on the Great Seal. Barber was sorry to say but, as an artist, he begged to differ with the director.[45] Bosbyshell took this letter and attached one of his own in support.[46]

Barber's personality comes out clearly in this letter. Considering himself an artist, he totally ignored Leech's constructive criticism of the model for Liberty. He defended his interpretation of the Great Seal to a fault. In doing so, he was quite disdainful of his superior. Much to his detriment, this letter shows how Barber approached coin designs. He would look only to history as the source of his designs. The tone of the whole letter was testy.

An irritated Leech wasted no time in responding. He was going to have none of it.

Bosbyshell and Barber took direct hits from Leech over cutting off criticisms. Leech did not care how many dies were prepared. If a modification, however slight, improved the design in his opinion, that change would be made. It was his objective to get as nearly perfect a work as possible and he would do whatever it took to achieve that goal. After all, these designs could not be changed for 25 years. Then he laid down the law: any criticism given in the proper spirit and aiming to beautify American coinage should be cheerfully received and fairly considered.[47]

Leech left Barber no wiggle room. Barber would have to address the merits of Leech's criticisms; it was the only way to deal with the man. Leech also gave notice to Superintendent Bosbyshell to stop interfering. However, in his anger Leech failed to confront Barber on the principal issue of the rendering of Liberty on the obverse. If by throwing up objections to Leech's compositional issues with the reverse was a way to deflect criticism of the obverse and indirectly of his artistic ability, Charles Barber had carried the day.

On October 6 Bosbyshell was traveling and it fell to Acting Superintendent Cobb to transmit Barber's response to Leech's dressing down. Cobb stated in his letter that

Charles Barber had not intended to be captious and certainly did not intend to question Leech's prerogative to pass upon new designs for coinage.[48] It was hardly an apology, and raised the question of how Leech's criticisms would have been taken had he not been the director.

If Leech had been expecting to find an apology in the text of Barber's letter, there was none. What he got was more tedious recitation about the olive leaves, scroll, and star points within the design elements. The overall tone of the response remained argumentative.[49] Leech did back off in his next correspondence. He went to the Agriculture Department for an olive branch. The issue of the scroll the director took up with Secretary Foster.[50] He opted for six-pointed stars on the obverse and five-pointed stars on the reverse. Barber responded with three versions of the reverse, each incorporating clouds above the eagle. On October 31, Leech wired the Philadelphia superintendent to prepare dies using the third pattern.[51]

It did not end here. The clouds now became an issue. In the first week of November, two more variations were submitted.[52] Leech gathered these patterns and forwarded them to President Harrison. On November 6, 1891, the president and his cabinet reviewed Barber's work and chose the pattern without the clouds. On November 7 Leech ordered the adoption of this design, and the saga was over.[53] Barber then adapted the design to the smaller quarter dollar. Leech's preference for the existing reverse of the dime carried the day. Only the obverse was changed, to incorporate the new design on this coin.

"The mountain had labored and brought forth a mouse," declared *Harper's Weekly* when provided a photograph of the model for the new half dollar that November. Kenyon Cox was quoted as saying disdainfully: "Every time the government has anything to do in art matters it shows its utter incapacity to deal with such things. It [Barber's design] is beneath criticism. I think it disgraceful that this great country should have such a coin as this."

Another artist declared that the image of Liberty was evidently the work of an amateur who had mastered very few of the rudiments of modeling. He then went to the extreme saying that the head of Liberty appeared unintelligent and that the face suggested that of a disreputable woman just recovering from a prolonged debauch!

A "learned" numismatist, most likely a prominent New York coin dealer, commented only upon the promise of anonymity. He stated that his business relations with the Mint made it inexpedient for him to criticize the work of that department in his own name. He too was not favorable to the design. He called it inferior to the several pattern designs developed in the 1870s at the Mint but not adopted.[54]

The most lively criticism in the article was that of Saint-Gaudens. His attitude had significantly deteriorated since his last *Harper's* interview the preceding July. Gus injudiciously ranted:

> There are a hundred men who could have done a very much better job than this. This is inept; this looks like it had been designed by a young lady of sixteen, a miss who had taken only a few lessons in modeling. It is beneath criticism. I told Mr. Leech that if he invited several Frenchmen, whose names I would furnish, to give designs, he would be able to turn out a really "swell" coin. But it appears that was

not possible under the law. But under the law he could certainly have obtained something better than this. I then offered to give him the names of several Americans, either of whom if given a commission could have made a good design; but the suggestion was not acted upon. I am opposed to going to shops for artistic designs, but he could have done infinitely better by going to either of the great silversmith establishments for his designs. There are hundreds of artists in this country, any of whom, with the aid of a designer, could have made a very respectable coin, which this is not. Indeed, I cannot see that it is any improvement in any regard upon the old coins.[55]

Through this whole redesign process Barber came across as the consummate bureaucrat. He could be subservient when needed. However, it was a shoe that did not fit well. Once he had taken a position, he could also be extremely obstinate; his comments often came across as condescending. In retrospect, he was lucky that Edward Leech took such an active role in the process. Barber's initial work was unacceptable. Without Leech's guidance, the redesign effort would have failed. The coins themselves would never be popular. One positive was that Barber's design was physically durable. Over the years as these coins saw heavy circulation, the basic outline of the design's elements remained intact and identifiable.

Saint-Gaudens had been left at the starting gate. He had removed himself from consideration over his stated aversion to competitions. Leech had only himself to blame for the failed competition. Had he followed both Saint-Gaudens's and Barber's advice, matters would have turned out differently. Leech ignored the option of restarting the competition. His decision to turn to Barber was a natural one. Still, Saint-Gaudens must have harbored frustrations. His emotions were too intense in the *Harper's Weekly* interview. Gilder would have insisted that Saint-Gaudens temper those comments.

Part 2

"Fair Enough"

Chapter 5

The World's Columbian Exposition

It was called the "White City," opening in Chicago in May 1893. It didn't matter that this quadrocentennial celebration of Columbus's discovery of the New World came a year late. It mattered even less that the fair itself had little to do with Columbus. When it closed the following October, some 27 million visitors had admired its many exhibits. Given that the population of the young country in the 1890 census was just under 63 million, the Exposition was an unqualified success.

New York, Chicago, Washington, DC, and St. Louis all vied to host the fair. The field narrowed to Chicago and New York, and civic feelings were strong as New Yorkers and Chicagoans traded barbs. So much scorn was poured New York's way in the Chicago press that their journalistic counterparts in New York dubbed Chicago the "Windy City."[1] When the enabling federal legislation was signed into law in April 1890, Chicago had carried the day. Much work needed to be done in just three short years to the fair's opening date. Complicating matters, there were two competing management structures with overlapping authority.

The World's Columbian Exposition Company was formed by the leading citizens of Chicago to finance and build the fair. The enabling legislation set up a World's Columbian Commission that had responsibility for approving the plans and construction activities of the Company as well as oversight of the exhibits.[2] This commission was composed of two appointed members from each state, one Republican and one Democrat, plus at-large members. It was a political body. Committees under both organizations sprang up overnight like mushrooms, causing wholesale confusion as to who was acting under what authority. As construction expenditures skyrocketed, infighting between the two groups developed.

Much of the credit for meeting the opening-day deadline went to Daniel Burnham, who midway through the project became its construction czar. Burnham was a member and prime mover of the Board of Architects for the Exposition Company, which included most of the leading architectural firms in America. He was the ideal man for the job. He had a favorite saying: "Make no little plans; they have no magic to stir men's blood."[3] Concurrent with this appointment, the Columbian Commission under George Davis became subordinate to the Exposition Company.

71

In order to expedite construction and hold down costs, building exteriors were constructed of staff, a mixture of plaster of Paris and hemp. While efficient in purpose, this construction was certainly temporary in nature. Many of the structures burned in the months following the close of the fair.

The Exposition had many innovations as well as its share of the commonplace. There were some 65 thousand exhibits housed in the various buildings of the fair.[4] They included such items as a 22,000-pound block of Canadian cheese, which had required a collaboration of 10,000 cows and 27,000 gallons of milk. The interior of the Schlitz Brewery pavilion was in the shape of two immense beer casks. However, there was more to this fair than catchy gimmicks. The Page Belting Company displayed the largest conveyor belt in the world, 200 feet long, 8-1/2 feet wide, and weighing 5,176 pounds.[5] There was an entire hall of electricity, exposing fairgoers to the uses of an energy source just becoming available at affordable prices to Americans. As if to make that point, there was an 82-foot-tall tower within the hall strung with 18,000 lamps. In the U.S. Government building, the Mint mounted a display of a virtual operating facility although no legal-tender coins were allowed to be struck.[6]

The fair also offered an amusement section, known as the Midway Plaisance. Entertainment of this sort had never before made an appearance at a world's exposition. Included was George Washington Gale Ferris's magnificent giant wheel, with gondolas taking riders up 25 stories. This never-before-seen structure was Chicago's answer to Gustave Eiffel's tower at the Paris Exposition of 1889.

The fair became a showcase for American technology. It was a precursor for the American mass culture that would grow to dominate the world of the 20th century.

For buildings and decorations, the organizers of the fair sought to bring together the best minds in America in each of their respective fields. Augustus Saint-Gaudens remarked at one of the first planning conferences that the fair had brought together "the greatest meeting of artists since the fifteenth century."[7] The nation had previously experienced nothing approaching this concentration of artistic talent. The buildings and, more importantly, the fair itself embodied the Beaux-Arts tenets of scale, harmony, and ensemble.

Henry Adams visited the fair in its second week with his friends Elizabeth and Don Cameron, arriving in the senator's Pullman car. That there were uncompleted exhibits and landscape work remaining to be done bothered the usually persnickety Adams not in the least. Afterward he wrote, "If the people of the Northwest actually knew what was good when they saw it, they would someday talk about Hunt and Richardson, La Farge and Saint-Gaudens, Burnham and McKim and Stanford White when their politicians and millionaires were otherwise forgotten."[8] After visiting the fair and continuing west, Katherine Lee Bates penned "America the Beautiful." She drew from her Chicago experience to make reference in the song to gleaming alabaster cities.[9]

For an artist of Saint-Gaudens's stature and reputation, involvement in the fair was a foregone conclusion. He would be working with his close friend, Charles Follen McKim. All wanted Saint-Gaudens's unfailing critical eye. Burnham also wanted Gus to commit to a major piece for the Exposition. Gus declined. Burnham had to settle for an oversight role for Saint-Gaudens. The July 1891 contract stipulated that Saint-Gaudens would be paid $6,000, the going rate of Exposition Company managers,

Daniel H. Burnham, the construction czar of the World's Columbian Exposition. His motto was "Make no little plans; they have no magic to stir men's blood."

The exposition's Court of Honor as seen looking toward the Administration Building from the Statue of the Republic. This view shows the Grand Basin and the dramatic grouping of the main buildings of the fair.

including Burnham.[10] His duties, however, would be very specific and limited. He would direct the execution for the two great sculptural centerpieces in the Court of Honor at the fair.[11] Daniel Chester French, a colleague and a friend, was given the principal piece, the Statue of the Republic. Willie MacMonnies, a former assistant, was given the balancing but smaller Columbian Fountain.

Still Burnham pressed Saint-Gaudens for a statue of Columbus, standing in front of the Administration Building. Gus balked. Finally a compromise was agreed to that satisfied Burnham. He would have his assistant, the 25-year-old Mary Lawrence, prepare the model under his direct supervision. She had been a favorite when she studied under him at the Art Students League.[12]

Gus throughout the period made multiple visits to Chicago in the company of McKim and White. It was a heady time for him, working with the other architects and artists but with no real responsibility, no schedules to keep and no deadlines to meet.

For those in charge of paying for this fair, it was not so heady a time. By May 1892 it was apparent that the Exposition Company was in need of additional funds beyond moneys raised in its stock subscription and bonds issued by the City of Chicago to complete construction. Construction budgets for the fair had been inadequate. The Exposition Company now sought an appropriation of $5 million from the national government. Support in the Senate was offset by stiff resistance in the House; an outright appropriation proved impossible. Then a compromise was struck: five million dollars' worth of souvenir half dollars would be authorized instead.

Never before had the United States struck a legal-tender coin designed for a specific occasion. Bullion was to be provided from obsolete and underweight silver coins removed from circulation as a result of the nation's monetary restructuring of 1873. For the government, the only cash cost of this action would be for melting and recoining.

Still there was resistance in the House. That body was in a foul temper. They had received a formal report in May accusing the World's Columbian Commission of paying exorbitant salaries. They immediately mandated that the director general, George Davis, and other officers of the Commission take a pay cut. With adjournment nearing and the heat of the summer pressing, a compromise was reached. The authorization was cut back to $2.5 million.[13]

Fair officials easily saw the way to recoup their lost appropriation by selling these souvenir half dollars for $1. They reasoned that 10 to 15 million fairgoers would want one; hence a premium could be supported. Reflecting this heady optimism, a New York newspaper stated, "Chicago got 2-1/2 million dollars for the Fair from the meanest House of Representatives that ever met but is going to blow that sum from its inexhaustible supply of that article and make it five million dollars. That town beats the world."[14] Cooler heads, notably the Chicago financier Lyman Gage, doubted the magnitude of the markup. A few thousand might be sold at that price but the remainder would be left in the hands of fair officials.[15]

For the Exposition Company, time was of the essence. There was a desire to have some coins dated 1892. The more pressing concern was to have coins available as soon as possible to help fund construction, which was now starved for cash. Word from the Mint was that preparation of the designs and dies would take at least five months.[16] It went without saying that the coins were going to have to be sold at a premium. Using in part the promise of future sales from the coins, the Exposition Company proceeded to float their own bonds. Public acceptance of these coins was going to be critical in the coming months.

Some preliminary design work had anticipated the legislation. As early as January 1892, James Ellsworth, chairman of the Committee on Liberal Arts for the Exposition Company and a noted numismatist, had contacted Olin Warner, whom Frank Millet, as director of decorations, had recommended for the possible design work.[17]

In April, Mint Director Leech had endorsed the idea of issuing souvenir half dollars. The obverse might bear a head of Columbus and the reverse an appropriate inscription.[18] The following month William Eleroy Curtis, who was in charge of the Commission's Latin America Department, had a conference with Leech about the coin's design. Leech wanted to leave it largely up to the Exposition people. Curtis suggested a bust of Columbus for the obverse and an outline of the Administration Building for the reverse. Alternately the newspapers were reporting a proposal for the reverse of a sketch of the Columbus landing or "something typifying scenes incident to the cause of the Exposition." Curtis wrote James Ellsworth of this meeting and suggested that the Executive Committee of the Exposition Company get the design process under control.[19]

Just who was this William Eleroy Curtis? He was an author and journalist of some note and Washington correspondent for the *Chicago Record*. More importantly, he was a special U.S. commissioner to the Central and Latin American republics. He was director of the Bureau of American Republics for the State Department and special envoy to the queen regent of Spain and Pope Leo XIII for Spain's celebration of Columbus's discovery of the New World.[20]

Leech must have wondered why someone with these credentials was bothering himself over the souvenir coin design. There was a subplot at work. Curtis had helped Ellsworth in 1891 to acquire the Lorenzo Lotto period portrait of a learned man, thought to be Christopher Columbus. Ellsworth wanted his Lotto portrait on the souvenir half dollar.

Curtis was a smooth operator who would not hesitate to give his opinion when he thought it was needed. He also knew Richard Watson Gilder and was intimate with Alexander Drake. In this capacity he would have been well aware of the entrenched interests at the U.S. Mint. Thus his advice for Ellsworth to preempt the Mint came from lessons learned in 1891 and earlier.[21]

More suggestions were forthcoming. Lyman Gage, the former president of the Exposition Company, asked Daniel Burnham to become involved. Burnham went to several eminent artists who recommended Philip Martiny, Saint-Gaudens's collaborator on the George Washington Inaugural Centennial medal, to execute the souvenir coin's design. Gus's invisible hand was evident here. Burnham went so far as to write Martiny to determine if he would do the work, to which Martiny readily consented. Burnham then communicated his actions to Ellsworth on June 13.[22]

Ellsworth moved. Curtis feared the Mint would involve a number of artists with the work, jeopardizing the chances that the Lotto portrait would be the basis for the coin design.[23] He gained the endorsement of the Columbian Commission's Committee on Design for his portrait—however, an unforeseen complication arose. William

STEFFENS, CHICAGO.

James Ellsworth was chairman of the Committee on Liberal Arts for the Exposition Company, and a noted numismatist. He wanted the commemorative Columbian half dollar to feature the portrait of Columbus painted by Lorenzo Lotto—which he happened to own.

Lorenzo Lotto's portrait of Christopher Columbus.

T. Baker, president of the Exposition Company, forwarded to Leech a photograph of a different frontal portrait of Columbus and a drawing of the Administration Building for consideration for the proposed coin.[24]

After consulting with Barber, Leech replied to Baker that a frontal portrait design would be unacceptable. Barber must have a profile portrait to model the obverse.[25] As the souvenir half dollar was to be for general circulation, it must meet all the criteria for such a coin.

Now everyone had a dilemma: how best to portray on the souvenir coin a man in profile whose physical appearance was open to interpretation. The ever-nimble Curtis solved the problem. He had the Lorenzo Lotto painting in his possession, so he had the Committee on Design direct him to hire Ulric Stonewall Jackson Dunbar, a minor sculptor in Washington, DC, to create a portrait bust based upon the Lotto portrait.[26]

That this action met the approval of the Treasury Department became apparent from a Washington-dateline story on August 6. It announced the passage of the enabling legislation and that the designs for the half dollar had been selected and would bear a likeness of Columbus provided by Dunbar on the obverse and the Administration Building of the Exposition on the reverse. Two months would be required to complete the engraving of the dies. Curtis had indeed conveyed Dunbar's work to Leech on August 4.[27] He must have been congratulating himself on how he had outmaneuvered the Mint—however, his elation was premature.

Problems popped up immediately. The department heads within the fair did not like the reverse. They rightly noted that after the fair closed, the reverse design would represent nothing. They instead petitioned to have the names of the 15 great departments of the Exposition substituted for the Administration Building.[28]

On August 15, Charles Barber volunteered his proposed design. Robert E. Preston, acting Mint director in Leech's absence, sent Barber's sketches to Director General Davis for his review. The obverse showed Columbus, based on the Lotto portrait, in profile, while the reverse depicted an image of the Western Hemisphere with a caravel in the background.[29] Barber had wisely ignored using a building profile or inscriptions. The two continents were flanked by the numbers 14 and 92. Preston asked Davis to provide suggestions that he might think proper. However, he closed by saying that Davis would be afforded an opportunity to consult with the Mint before the designs were finalized.[30]

Davis balked. He had not liked Baker's version.[31] Davis provided the crude Mint sketches to Ellsworth who in turn showed them to artists working at the Exposition. This group drafted a protest calling the design proposal absolutely inartistic, unsuited to purpose and unworthy of the country and the occasion. Among the signers were Daniel Chester French, Philip Martiny, and Olin Warner. Even worse, the press said Barber's Columbus looked like a namby-pamby, smooth-faced, long-haired professor instead of the ruler of the sea. There was no sternness apparent in the lines of the face in the sketch.[32]

James Ellsworth lost his temper, no doubt stung by the crass criticism of the Columbus sketch in the newspapers. Worse, a controversy appeared to flare over whether his Lotto portrait was even an accurate depiction of Columbus. Ellsworth promptly withdrew permission to use the Lotto for the souvenir coin's obverse design.[33]

Leech, who had been on vacation, waded into this mess on August 26. Accommodatingly, he wrote that the sketches were still based on the original Lotto portrait but he was enclosing, as an alternative, a woodcut magazine illustration of a Columbus medal by Enrique Lopez-Lorensis, prepared in Madrid for that country's celebration. Facing the requirement that a large number of pieces be coined by year's end, Leech closed by begging for prompt action on the part of the Exposition managers.[34]

A key point was left unsaid by the Mint. The bust by Dunbar had been sent to Barber on August 4 with instructions that he prepare profile sketches for the World's Fair people to consider. Barber subsequently requested a photograph of the Lotto portrait of Columbus from the Bureau of Printing and Engraving, which was preparing a postage stamp from the same. This was promptly done and Barber completed the assignment the following day. Barber had ignored the Dunbar bust and prepared his own sketch. Thus Leech in his communication to Davis was forced to avoid all reference to the Dunbar work.[35]

As if the situation were not complicated enough, Frank Millet took it upon himself to approach Olin Warner once again about designing the souvenir coin in early August. Warner got some wax and went to work. In a day he showed his sketch to Millet, who was greatly pleased. Warner then went to work to finish the design; however, the effort was pending James Ellsworth's approval. He was traveling so the effort was tentative.[36]

Warner's obverse consisted of a likeness of Columbus with a soft mariner's cap with fur flaps turned down. His long hair flowed over the fur collar of his mantle. The image was similar to a bust Warner had executed for the Long Island Historical Society. It was certainly not based on the Lotto portrait. The sketch contained the legends UNITED STATES OF AMERICA and COLUMBIAN HALF DOLLAR, with each separated from the other by a single star. The reverse featured a caravel symbolic of the *Santa Maria* above two globes representing the hemispheres without outlines of the appropriate continents. The numbers 14 and 92 flanked the two globes. The legends consisted of WORLD'S COLUMBIAN EXPOSITION and CHICAGO 1892.[37]

The whole affair then landed in the lap of the Finance Committee of the Columbian Exposition Company, of which Ellsworth was a member. The fair's art department had submitted a number of proposed designs to the committee that must have included Warner's work. Something was approved by the Finance Committee but they refused to release the details.[38] That there was an issue within the committee was demonstrated by James Ellsworth's wiring Leech on August 31 to ask if the head of Columbus from the Lotto portrait was acceptable to the Mint. Clearly Ellsworth had now regained control of his temper. Leech replied that the decision was in the hands of the World's Fair officials. Believing the fair executives needed more details of the Lopez-Lorensis medal, Leech requested that the secretary of state seek an example of the medal from the American embassy in Madrid.[39]

Faced with no consensus in the Finance Committee,[40] its chairman, Ferdinand W. Peck, forwarded to Leech only Warner's sketch for the reverse of the coin. This package landed on Leech's desk early in September. A September 3 story with a Washington dateline claimed a radical change had been made in the souvenir coin's designs: the Lotto likeness would be replaced with a profile from a medal struck in Spain. For a reverse, a representation of the "Western Continent" instead of the Administration

The World's Columbian Exposition

Building would be used. A building would not make a good showing.[41] Those were Barber's words. This story was at odds with the Finance Committee with respect to the reverse.

Leech went to Philadelphia on September 5 and 6 to confer with his people before replying on the 9th.[42] He mentioned that Barber was going to move forward with a model of the head of Columbus. Corrections could be made to the head when the Spanish medal was received. Leech then countered that the officers of the Mint did not think the proposed reverse would show well as a coin. Barber was proposing an alternative that consisted only of the Western Hemisphere nestled in a half wreath of oak leaves.[43] Indeed, the Mint had leaked their opposition to the reverse chosen by the Finance Committee to the newspapers. Leech returned sketches of the first alternative with modifications to the inscriptions that the director felt appropriate and the alternative as prepared by Barber. To better illustrate his point, he included a bronze medal showing the North American continent in the style of the first sketch. Also he enclosed a crude lead impression to demonstrate the second sketch by Barber.[44]

Meanwhile Warner, with his souvenir coin sketches completed, started work on the directory badge for the dedication ceremonies scheduled for October. Ellsworth's influence is apparent on this second version in that Warner's depiction of Columbus is more nearly in line with the Lotto portrait in which the navigator is without a cap and has his hair shorn at the ears. The badge had only the words CHRISTOPHER COLUMBUS and the designer's initials. The bust of Columbus, done in high relief, extended to the lower rim of the badge, adding a sense of animation to the design. This work was finished early in September and was immediately seen as a possible alternative to Warner's proposed obverse for the souvenir half dollar.[45]

Perceiving an impasse, George Davis determined that a face-to-face meeting with the Mint would be necessary to resolve the design so that a coin bearing the date 1892 could be issued. Besides, the Exposition Company badly needed the sales from this half dollar. The meeting was set for September 17 at Leech's office in Washington. The Mint director urgently requested that Barber be present.[46] It was a clash of wills. Davis wanted to use Warner's reverse design in conformance with the Finance Committee's wishes. He most likely also broached the subject of Warner's badge design as an alternative for the obverse of the souvenir coin. Barber pushed for a design that would show the coin well in low relief. Davis lacked the technical expertise to argue about the requirements for low relief. No decision was reached. On the 21st Leech authorized Barber to travel to Chicago to consult further with Davis.[47]

The meeting took place between Barber and the Finance Committee on September 23.[48] Barber brought with him struck metal designs of the portrait provided by Baker and his version of the Lotto. Barber favored the Lotto version. In the only indication of the committee's position, the news release the next day noted there would be a slight alteration removing the cap from the Lotto head.[49] It was a roundabout way of saying that Warner's second or Lotto version of Columbus would be used instead of his first.

By the 28th, Leech summarized what had been agreed to in a letter to Davis. Barber had just brought him the proposed designs for the slightly altered obverse and reverse of the coin based upon Warner's work, using the Lotto portrait for the likeness of Columbus. Ellsworth had carried the day. Leech found the selections fitting and the designs handsome. The Mint director was willing to let matters move forward from there.[50] However, with the inscriptions unsettled, it was yet to be determined whether this design would be successful.

What had caused Barber to capitulate in Chicago? Many World's Fair artists had come out in favor of the Warner designs for the obverse and reverse of the souvenir coin.[51] As a member of the Finance Committee, Ellsworth was present and determined that Warner's badge design using the Lotto portrait be chosen. He had lined up expert support for the Lotto portrait and was prepared to take the matter back to Washington.[52] Charles Barber was no match for such determination.

Barber, his pique showing, wrote Ellsworth on September 29, petulantly asking that a letter be provided authorizing the use of the Lotto head and the caravel and globes for the coin.[53] He made no reference to the fact that these were Olin Warner's designs. On the next day, there appeared in the *New York Times* quotes from the chief engraver objecting to Warner's designs for the souvenir half dollar. Artistically there were too many objects in the reverse field. When the model was reduced to the size of the coin, the results would be unsatisfactory. The relief of the coin was also too high. The coin presses would not be able to strike off the pieces rapidly, and the finished coins would not stack well. The designer had forgotten that this piece was to be a coin for circulation and not a medal.[54] On the surface, it appeared to be gross insubordination. That Barber got away with it indicated that he had solid support within the Mint's bureaucracy.

Warner's obverse showing Columbus with strong facial features was a handsome design, unlike anything that had been produced to date at the Mint. Barber was faced with two difficulties. First, Warner's final obverse design did not have the proper inscriptions.[55] It was the same issue that Barber had raised in 1887. A design without the necessary inscriptions could cause problems. In this case Warner's positioning of Columbus left little rim for the inscriptions. Barber was faced with either coming up with a unique approach to incorporate inscriptions or making a major modification to provide necessary background space. Second, the details of the head and face were strongly emphasized, in a pronounced but tolerable high relief and slightly off center. Metal flow problems would arise during the striking, causing an uneven rim. The coins would not stack as a result.

Barber also had an issue with the reverse. Warner's model of the ship was lacking in details. He immediately asked Ellsworth for a photograph of the caravel at the Exposition in order to fine-tune this design.[56] He feared that people would look at the caravel and then compare the reverse of the coin to the ship. If the likeness were not perfect, his work would be subjected to criticism. Ellsworth sent photos but they were lacking in sufficient detail. He relayed back to Ellsworth that he would use what material he had.[57] He then turned the reverse over to the assistant engraver, George Morgan, thereby avoiding the risk of any future criticisms directed at him.

By the 17th of October, Barber had dies in the preliminary stages of preparation. He wrote a chatty letter to Ellsworth, wishing that the man had taken the time on his recent trip to New York to stop in Philadelphia to review progress on the coin. Barber graciously thanked Ellsworth for the invitation to attend dedication ceremonies but said that he lacked the time for a week or more of pleasure. Barber had now come to realize that Ellsworth's main concern had been in the selection of the Lotto portrait.

On the 31st Barber again wrote to Ellsworth. Leech had just seen a preliminary strike and expected the souvenir half dollars to be the best-looking coins struck by an American mint.[58] Barber would be most happy to see Ellsworth in Philadelphia but would not expect him to come for the sole purpose of seeing the coins. After all, he would be able to send him the finished products in November.

Barber had provided Bosbyshell with cardboard impressions that the superintendent had in turn forwarded to Ellsworth. However, no metal strikes had been created. Work remained to be done on the master die itself on the hair of Columbus.[59]

In 1891 when the circulating subsidiary silver coins had been redesigned, Leech had micro-managed the project, much to Barber's chagrin. This time, Leech did not intervene. The models had been agreed to and only the issue of engraving remained. Barber maintained good communications with Ellsworth, and Leech stayed out of the process. While no trial strikes were forthcoming in October, Leech was expecting no difficulties.

Leech was scheduled to leave the country for an extended period to attend an international monetary conference in Brussels on November 9. He planned his departure believing that the project was under control. He went so far as to inform Director General Davis that striking of the souvenir half dollars would begin about the middle of the month. He aggressively predicted that some two million of the coins would be struck before the end of the year. The dies would have to be completed and the production slotted into the Mint's schedule. Bosbyshell had Leech's personal instructions to facilitate in every way the wishes of the officers of the Exposition. Leech had also told Bosbyshell to forward to Brussels a few of the first coins struck, but not to distribute any coins until authorized by the secretary of the Treasury.[60]

On November 8, something unforeseeable happened. Grover Cleveland defeated Benjamin Harrison—and Leech became a lame duck.

On November 11, Barber wrote Ellsworth. He had just supplied him with impressions of the coins. Ellsworth was pleased although he really had no choice, given the time constraints. Barber told Ellsworth that he was providing the Philadelphia superintendent with his plaster model. The work was rough because he preferred to do his finish work in the steel die; it was as his father had done it. While others relied upon a better model and allowed the reducing lathe to make the necessary cuts in the master die, he had clung to the old ways. He might have added that this skill was necessary because the Mint's reducing lathe was not capable of making exact, extremely detailed cuts. Barber expected to have working dies ready in a week; and striking of the souvenir coins could begin immediately.[61]

What had Barber done to the obverse? He had materially altered Warner's model. He had shrunken Warner's portrait of Columbus and moved it to the center of the coin. This action allowed the addition of the inscriptions UNITED STATES OF AMERICA and COLUMBIAN HALF DOLLAR. These inscriptions were unimaginatively placed around the head of Columbus. In addition the coin was done in low relief. What had been a unique work by Warner was now uninspiring to say the least. The strength and subtlety of Warner's modeling were compromised in the smaller bust, low relief, and fastidious attention to detail.[62] The crowning insult was that Barber

83

and Morgan inserted their initials into the obverse and reverse of Warner's designs. The reality was that Warner's handsome design had been badly diluted.

Minting of the souvenir coins commenced on Saturday, November 19. Ellsworth was present. A million of the half dollars were planned to be struck in November and December—far below Leech's estimate.[63] At Barber's suggestion and then Bosbyshell's, 100 were to be struck in Proof. Proof coins are made from specially selected dies that are polished with a diamond compound and polishing rouge. Their planchets (the metal blanks from which they are struck) are likewise polished to yield, after striking, specimen coins exhibiting sharp details and a mirror-like finish.[64] These coins would be minted separately from the production run but after the coining process had started, because certain pieces in the emission sequence were already spoken for. Ever the numismatist, Ellsworth was pleased by this proposal and immediately made plans for an exclusive distribution to prominent World's Fair participants. High on the list were the railroad executives on whom he had pushed the most recent bond issue so necessary to keep the fair finances liquid.[65]

It was a major undertaking for the Mint. The first coins arrived in Chicago on December 19, to great fanfare. Fifty thousand coins came in five stout oaken kegs, five bags of 2,000 coins each per keg. Each keg weighed over 400 pounds.[66] It was front-page news in the *Chicago Daily Tribune*. Every detail from the opening of the wooden kegs to the distribution of the coins was described.

Buried near the end of the article were several critical assessments. Opinions were somewhat negative although good points were noted. Almost to a person, the interviewees wished for higher relief. One noted the lack of detail in the hair of Columbus. There was some disagreement over the selection of the Lotto portrait as the basis for the coin. Ominously, one individual called the design weak and predicted that sales of the coin would be poor. These comments should have been taken in stride compared to the great enthusiasm of the common people at the celebratory event. A premium of 25¢ to 50¢ over the dollar asking price quickly developed.[67]

Ellsworth clipped this article and sent it to both Barber and Warner. Immediately, Barber poured out his invective against the criticisms contained at the end of the article. In a five-page letter, Barber replied to Ellsworth on December 22, addressing each and every negative point. Much of his rebuttal was a justification for low relief. It took nerve on Barber's part, when addressing criticism that the hemispheres on the coin's reverse should be in higher relief, to fall back upon Warner's wish that the globes be in low relief. Barber ended by suggesting that the newspapers of Chicago should restrict their publishing of "opinions of people who display a deplorable amount of ignorance and likewise seem inclined to say 'Stinking Fish.'" The papers would be much better off trying to promote sales in support of the Exposition.[68] The Christmas spirit eluded Charles Barber that year.

Warner's response to Ellsworth, without understanding the reasons behind Barber's alterations, was one of resignation. He had seen the process in 1891 that resulted in a very ordinary new design for the circulating subsidiary silver coinage. He told Ellsworth, "I have not seen the souvenir coin yet but I'll wager it doesn't look like the model."[69]

Charles Barber's sketch for the souvenir half dollar. It retains his version of the "Lotto Head" so vilified in the Chicago newspapers, in combination with the hemisphere reverse.

The directorate badge, by Olin Warner, that served as the basis for the obverse design of the World's Columbian Exposition half dollar.

One of the Proof Columbian half dollars that James Ellsworth intended for gifts. These were impounded by the Exposition Company president. (shown enlarged 2x)

85

The New Year found Barber in no better frame of mind. By now, the New York papers had picked up the criticisms of the Columbian half dollar. The *American Journal of Numismatics* called the coin a great artistic disappointment and a lost opportunity. The article called into question the need for low relief. It dismissed the supposed requirement that these coins meet the standards of circulating coins. They were commemorative coins designed to be a souvenir.[70]

This time Barber was upset with the "New York artists." He found it strange that they would abuse the work of one of their own and then hold the Mint answerable for what they condemned.[71] The hypersensitive Barber was now more than willing to share credit with Warner.

Barber wasn't the only one upset. Harlow Higinbotham, the current president of the Exposition Company, after first agreeing to let Ellsworth handle the distribution of the special Proof strikes, had expropriated the coins for his own use. The man proposed to share them with Ellsworth, but that put Ellsworth in an untenable position of having to decide which people got the promised Proof strikes and which did not.[72] He was an unhappy man.

Leech returning from his trip abroad was upset with Bosbyshell. No coins had been provided for his review in Brussels. In a polite but firm letter, Leech pointed out that his instructions had been ignored.[73] Bosbyshell in explanation pleaded that he had been complying with the wishes of the World's Fair officials as allowed in Leech's instructions. Leech wasn't buying that excuse.

On a more serious note, sales of the souvenir half dollar had slumped. By February, the newness of the souvenir coins had worn off and the problem was serious enough to affect fair finances. To generate quick cash some two million of the half dollars were turned over to Chicago-area banks to be held as part of their legal reserve requirements. The banks in turn advanced face value for the coins to the Exposition Company. It was a desperate but successful move to generate enough cash to keep going until the fair opened and revenues began to flow in May.[74]

In March, to add insult to injury, Congress, seeing the sluggish coin sales, unfairly expropriated 1,141,760 of the souvenir half dollars to pay the estimated costs of the Columbian Commission for judging and making awards to the exhibitors at the fair. If the Exposition Company would agree to fund this expense, then the coins would be released. Tempers flared and the Exposition Company refused to make the necessary appropriation, leaving the government with the coins. They went so far as to call this action a breach of faith by the federal government.[75]

Chapter 6

Ladies Rebuffed

Watching the struggle of the Columbian half dollar authorization in Congress in the summer of 1892, the Exposition's Board of Lady Managers decided to postpone their funding effort to the next session of Congress.[1] The chairperson of the Lady Managers was Bertha Honoré Palmer, a headstrong lady not to be trifled with. Congress promptly responded, authorizing a souvenir quarter dollar on March 3, 1893, as a form of funding a $10,000 appropriation. Congress was getting amenable to this method of funding a worthy cause while putting the burden on the recipient organization to generate the revenues. Total mintage of this second commemorative coin was to be limited to 40,000 pieces.

As with the half dollar, the devices and designs for the coin were to be prescribed by the director of the Mint with the approval of the secretary of the Treasury. Palmer was annoyed by this requirement. She had not been impressed by the Mint's souvenir half dollar and wished the ladies "to have credit of being the authors of the first really beautiful and artistic coin that has ever been issued by the government of the United States." To achieve this goal, Palmer had done her homework. She asked for a design concept from Kenyon Cox.[2] She also sought a woman to design the coin, consistent with the Board of Lady Managers' desire to showcase the abilities and progress of women.

It was natural that she turned to Sara Hallowell for advice. Sara was extremely knowledgeable in the fine arts. She was helping the Palmers amass a significant collection of impressionistic art, and also serving as secretary to the fair's director of fine arts. Many rightly thought that had she been a male, the directorship would have been hers.[3]

The assignment would be difficult, requiring the ability to work quickly, with great feeling and exquisite delicacy.[4] Sara turned to Augustus Saint-Gaudens. She knew Gus gave women in his sculpture class equal treatment with their male counterparts, and Gus thought highly of Sara, calling her "all right down to the ground." A decision would have to be made immediately. Mary Lawrence was already committed, so Gus recommended another of his former students.[5]

Leech, now nearing the end of his Mint service, contacted Palmer on March 14. Having learned from his previous experience with the World's Fair managers, he was the perfect diplomat. He asked Bertha Palmer if any work had started on the designs. He was quite willing to conform to the wishes of the ladies. He even offered to send Charles Barber to Chicago.[6] However, there was more at work here behind the scenes. He had received letters from Barber and Bosbyshell prompting him to take the initiative. His proposal to send the engraver to Chicago to meet with the ladies was at Barber's instigation.[7] Barber was making a concerted effort to keep this design process under his control.

Palmer was just as diplomatic in her reply. The Board of Lady Managers had decided what should be placed on the coin. They wished to commemorate the part played by Queen Isabella in the discovery of America and the action of Congress in creating the Board of Lady Managers. They were at the point of consulting with one or two friends to secure a highly artistic rendering of these concepts. It was their desire to have the coin available for the opening of the fair on May 1, 1893. Then Palmer very smoothly stated that she would be glad to have the Mint director come to Chicago to consult once the Board of Lady Managers had their suggestions. She closed with a masterstroke: would the Bureau wish to submit a design embodying the ideas that she had indicated for competition?[8] Bertha Palmer had every intention of controlling the process.

There was enough information in this short communication to signal to Leech that the women were trying to move forward without the Mint. He countered by suggesting that Palmer need only provide a rough sketch of the design. Charles Barber would be able to then quickly translate that work into a suitable design. No sculptor or modeler would be necessary.[9]

Leech now had a new boss. John G. Carlisle was the new secretary of the Treasury. President Cleveland had come to respect and lean upon the former Speaker of the House for advice in financial matters. That he chose Carlisle for the position surprised no one; it was regarded as an excellent appointment. Carlisle hailed from Covington, Kentucky. He had been raised on a farm, with little formal education. As a young adult, he read for the law profession in the atmosphere of antebellum Kentucky. In spite of his Southern sympathies, he had remained neutral with his state in the Civil War and entered national politics during the Reconstruction period. He was a self-made man with strong rural roots that remained deep in his nature in spite of his years in Washington.

Bertha Palmer's next salvo was aimed directly at Carlisle. She called on Alan Durborow, a former Carlisle colleague. Durborow, a Chicagoan, was chairman of the House of Representatives Fair Committee. She wanted him to pay a visit to Secretary Carlisle and Director Leech. His charge was to broach the subject of a female designer with the two Treasury officials and secure their acceptance. He also carried a copy of a letter that she had sent to Carlisle setting forth her design proposal.[10]

In fact, Durborow had no choice but to be successful. Bertha Palmer had already settled on Saint-Gaudens's former student, Caroline Peddle. Caroline, or Carrie, as she was known to her friends, was raised in Terre Haute, Indiana, of a modest background. She had studied at Rose Polytechnic Institute in Terre Haute and the Pennsylvania Academy of the Fine Arts before moving on to the Art Students League in New York City. It was here that she drew the attention of Saint-Gaudens and made the acquaintance of Mary Lawrence.[11] She had just executed a commission for Tiffany's for exhibition at the World's Fair. For an inexperienced 23-year-old, she was gutsy and ready to take on a challenge of this magnitude.

Bertha Honoré Palmer, chair of the Board of Lady Managers of the World's Columbian Exposition. She worked in high circles to get what she wanted: a commemorative quarter honoring both Queen Isabella of Spain and the board itself.

Caroline Peddle in 1894. A former student of Saint-Gaudens, the self-assured 23-year-old was ready to take on the challenge of the Isabella quarter design—or so she thought.

In her charge to Peddle, Palmer was most explicit about the design motifs. The one side should have a figure of Isabella and on the other, in addition to the prescribed requirements, an inscription "Commemorative Coin Issued for the Board of Lady Managers of the World's Columbian Exposition by Act of Congress, 1492–1892." She included some engravings of Isabella for Peddle's guidance. By inference the ideas of Cox would have been included. Peddle would be free to arrange and choose the lettering for the inscription in such a manner as to "permit a most artistic appearance."[12] This long inscription was a terrible thing to force upon the young designer. There was little hope that the design could be executed with "great feeling and exquisite delicacy." However, there was another and much more serious problem: Palmer had failed to instruct Caroline Peddle that she should submit her sketches to the Board of Lady Managers for approval.

Carlisle and Leech had no real choice but to give in to Bertha Palmer. The secretary wrote her that the director of the Mint was willing to allow the modeling of the commemorative quarter by a woman and that the head of Isabella should appear on it.[13] The proposed design for the reverse was another matter altogether. Carlisle felt that the inscription was reminiscent of a tradesman's advertising token.[14] A different design would have to be formulated.

Leech now had to keep peace with his Philadelphia staff. On the 27th he sent a short note to Superintendent Bosbyshell. It was probable in his opinion that the Board of Lady Managers would have some sculptor model the obverse of the souvenir coin. However, Charles Barber should start work on some alternative designs for the reverse.[15]

Palmer informed Leech on the 28th of March that Caroline Peddle would be preparing the obverse and reverse models for the proposed souvenir coin. The Mint director politely agreed; however, there would be constraints. Instructions would be provided for Peddle. He confirmed that a head of Isabella would be an acceptable subject. He would have Barber prepare a suitable design for the reverse to be submitted to Bertha Palmer. Of course, no real progress could be made until the designs approved by the Board of Lady Managers had been prepared and submitted for review to the Mint hierarchy.[16]

Leech also wrote to Caroline Peddle that he had no objections to her doing the modeling but it would be necessary to secure his and Carlisle's approval. This request was in direct contradiction to Bertha Palmer's wishes. There was no objection to using the head of Isabella for the obverse, and that part of the work could proceed at once. The most onerous letter for Leech was the one to Bosbyshell explaining that Barber might not be doing the reverse after all.[17]

Meanwhile, on April 4, Bertha Palmer conceded that Carlisle's objections to the reverse might be valid. However, she insisted that "Board of Lady Managers" be retained in the final inscription. In place of the original inscription, she suggested a likeness of the Women's Building at the fair.[18] Palmer's entire effort was now focused on recognition for the Board of Lady Managers.

Once again events were unfolding rapidly. On April 3 Peddle had forwarded a design of the original inscription for the reverse that had been provided by Palmer to Leech. She felt it was cumbersome and required the entire reverse of the coin. She asked his help in shortening it. She had questions about the style of lettering and wondered if she could include the legend "Isabella" on the obverse.[19]

Peddle also opened a line of communication directly to Bosbyshell. He had previously provided her with the instructions for model preparation that Leech had promised.[20] She was proposing using a *figure* of the queen rather than a head in profile. Bertha Palmer had spoken of a figure of Isabella to Peddle. A rough sketch was included of the seated queen based upon one of the engravings provided by Palmer. Peddle believed the design more pleasing than a head unless it reduced poorly. She closed by asking that they telegraph their response.[21]

The sculptor was complying with Leech's instructions in good faith. That trust was not to be returned. Leech, upon viewing the awkward reverse, took action detrimental to Peddle: he immediately informed Bosbyshell that Barber should continue work on the reverse. It was not his intent to allow Peddle to *design* the reverse. That would be done by the Mint.[22]

On the day Caroline wrote this letter, Charles Barber submitted three alternative sketches of the reverse to Bosbyshell. Two of the three consisted only of inscriptions.[23] In Barber's opinion, it was most unsatisfactory to have to provide a design for the reverse without knowing the design and legends employed for the obverse.[24] It never entered Barber's head that Peddle should have an equal say in how the inscriptions should be divided.

The following day, Bosbyshell and Barber dismissed Peddle's obverse sketch. They felt the foreshortening of the legs of the seated figure would produce an unacceptable coin for circulating purposes. A profile head, in their opinion, would be more appropriate.[25] Both Leech and Secretary Carlisle rejected Peddle's obverse sketch as well. The secretary grumbled that he had given permission to Palmer only for a head of Isabella on the coin. Leech was leaving it to Bosbyshell to inform Caroline Peddle of this rejection.[26]

Peddle began to get a better picture of how this process was going to proceed the next day. Leech wrote that the reverse inscription was unacceptable. Carlisle was writing Palmer to that effect and changes would have to be made. Leech went on to say that he had asked Barber to prepare the reverse. Once completed, he would send it to Palmer for her review.[27] Peddle was now going to have her obverse muled with Barber's reverse without the benefit of seeing that reverse and knowing whether the two designs were compatible.

Adding to Caroline Peddle's frustration, Bertha Palmer both wired and wrote to her on April 6. She wanted to know what progress had been made on the coin. Palmer pointed out that the dies for the coin would require two months. In order to meet a June 1 release date, the designs were to be finished by April 1. Palmer had been counting on Peddle to meet that deadline. The design for the reverse had been changed. Possibly Peddle had not received an earlier letter setting forth this decision. In defense of the young sculptor, no record of such a letter appears in the letterbook meticulously kept for the chair of the Board of Lady Managers.

Palmer now wanted Peddle to use one of the drawings from the Women's Building as the central theme on the reverse. She would have written earlier but Saint-Gaudens had wired her that Peddle was preparing a status report. Palmer had intended to go into more detail in this letter but had not received the promised communication from Peddle. As a result of this breakdown, Palmer was sending Sara Hallowell to look into the matter. Now Caroline Peddle was getting it from all sides.[28]

April 7 brought the situation to a head. Caroline Peddle was unhappy. In a note to Leech, she threatened to quit working on the obverse model. She had been commissioned to do both sides of the coin. She had been complying with Bertha Palmer's instructions with her previous design for the reverse. She could not consent to having her work muled.[29]

Leech, already sensing that he was pushing too far with Peddle, took it upon himself to write to her that same day that the obverse design should be a head of Isabella with the inscriptions "United States of America" and "Columbian Quarter Dollar." A Mint designer would prepare a sketch of the reverse that Peddle would be free to model. As director of the Mint, he must prescribe the designs.[30] If that letter did not push her over the edge, then a second from Bosbyshell, as instructed by Leech, must have. He both enclosed a copy of Leech's letter and then added more design constraints of his own. The head of Isabella should be without a crown. In Bosbyshell's opinion, a crowned head on an American coin would be inappropriate. Also, Charles Barber was modeling the reverse and it would not be necessary for Peddle to remodel this work as suggested in Leech's letter.[31]

Leech immediately covered himself by wiring to Bertha Palmer.[32] Her reply the next day to Leech was conciliatory. Palmer regretted that she, Leech, and Peddle were at three points of a triangle instead of working together. She admitted to talking with Alan Durborow about Leech and learning of his distinguished service to the Mint. It was a flattering letter for a reason. The second half of the letter dealt solely with her advocacy for placing the inscription "Board of Lady Managers" or a representation of the Women's Building upon the reverse of the coin.[33] Ownership of the coin was Bertha Palmer's principal concern.

Caroline Peddle had had enough. On April 8, questioning the role of the engraver in dictating the designs for the coin, she resigned her commission.[34] Her frustration had lasted 11 days. Her mistake had been in innocently thinking that she could expedite her work by opening a line of communication with Bosbyshell. Everybody at the Mint from Charles Barber to Edward Leech already had their minds made up as to the obverse of the coin. Any deviation was going to be met with rejection.

Why had Leech allowed this direct communication with an outside party, in which his position was countermanded, to stand? The answer was simple. He knew that his stay at the helm of the Mint was virtually over. Within weeks he would leave for a banking job in New York. However, there was an added element to be considered. His son was employed at the Philadelphia Mint. Leech was not going to rock the boat at this point. Just as importantly, why had Bosbyshell done it? Certainly he and Barber had a common goal to defend the Mint's prerogative to choose the designs for United States coins. Still, Bosbyshell had developed a bad habit of interpreting instructions loosely and exercising his position as superintendent much too independently.

Unfortunately for the Board of Lady Managers, they could not disengage from either the Mint or Bertha Palmer. To make matters worse, Charles Barber rejected

Palmer's suggestion that the profile of the Women's Building appear on the reverse. If profiled in low relief, the building would appear as a mere streak across the coin.[35]

It fell to Leech to deliver the bad news to Bertha Palmer on April 10, informing her that the Mint would prepare the models in Caroline Peddle's place. Leech assured Palmer that the Board of Lady Managers would be pleased with the Mint's work.[36] He had a problem to address as well. He needed the model of Isabella from which Caroline Peddle was working. Anticipating resistance, he asked Palmer to request Caroline Peddle to forward it to Philadelphia.[37] That was going to be interesting, since Palmer was not communicating with Caroline Peddle.

Bertha Palmer was beside herself with anger, which spilled out in a letter to Saint-Gaudens. She considered it a "direct discourtesy" that Caroline Peddle had communicated directly with Treasury officials, thereby frustrating the plans of the Board of Lady Managers—and, more particularly, herself—for the souvenir quarter. Peddle had been engaged by the ladies and her communicating with Mint Director Leech was in very bad form and ill advised. In resigning the commission, Peddle had frustrated the Board of Lady Managers in their aim of having recognition given to women in every department of the Exposition. She wanted Saint-Gaudens to know that the whole matter had been arranged with great effort and that the ladies would have been able to take care of themselves as well as Peddle. Gus was a bit chagrined in his reply. He was very deferential to Bertha Palmer but he did not duck the issue. When Caroline Peddle told him that the reverse of the quarter was to be modeled by the incompetent designer at the Mint, he agreed with her that it would be dignified to refuse the commission.[38]

The issue of the reverse design selection remained open. There had been ongoing discussion in Philadelphia with Leech as to what was an original design. George Morgan had prepared a sketch of a kneeling woman in the act of winding flax with a distaff in hand, symbolizing patience. Leech thought that design, when paired with Isabella on the obverse, "too much woman" on the coin. He was still willing to consider it but he wanted an *original design* out of Barber as well. He suggested a handsome oak wreath as a suitable device for the reverse. He also pointedly said that the design did not necessarily have to conform to the ideas of the Lady Managers.[39]

Barber proceeded to dig his heels in to defend Morgan's design. Leech relented and authorized Barber to go forward with the modeling of Morgan's concept.[40] On the 11th and 12th Bosbyshell sent three new sketches for the proposed reverse to Leech. Barber had complied with Leech's instructions. However, his two alternatives hardly fell within the category of original designs. One contained the oak wreath surrounding a shield with a heraldic eagle superimposed. The second was of an eagle atop a shield surrounded by two laurel sprigs.[41]

Leech found himself boxed in by mediocre work, with time running out. On this same day, he wired Bertha Palmer that he had settled on a reverse emblematic of woman's work.[42] By default, George Morgan's kneeling woman design had carried the day. He then followed up with a letter to Palmer explaining that the depiction of the Women's Building would be unsuitable for coinage. The alternative reverse selected would give the ladies a much more appealing coin. He had even reviewed the situation with Alan Durborow. In closing, Leech mentioned that he still had not received

Caroline Peddle's sketch for the proposed commemorative quarter featuring a seated Isabella on the obverse and the unwieldy reverse inscription dictated by Bertha Palmer.

Former Speaker of the House John G. Carlisle was secretary of the Treasury during the design of the Columbian Exposition coins.

Proof Isabella quarter of the World's Columbian Exposition. The reverse was designed by George Morgan. Barber took credit for the obverse, although the extent of Peddle's contribution is open to conjecture. (shown enlarged 2x)

Various scenes from New York City, where Augustus Saint-Gaudens and Theodore Roosevelt both spent their youth.

Top: "Brooklyn Heights, Opposite the City of New York." (engraving from *Gleason's Pictorial Drawing-Room Companion* (1854))

Middle: "View in Wall Street from Corner of Broad." (engraving from *Thirty Years' Progress of the United States* (1867))

Right: Frederick's Photographic Temple of Art, New York City, circa 1850. Daguerrotype photography had been around for some ten years by the time Saint-Gaudens was born. (original in the Bibliotheque Nationale, Paris)

Abraham Lincoln's 1865 funeral procession in New York was an early bond of common experience between young Gus Saint-Gaudens and Teddy Roosevelt—though the boys didn't know it at the time. Both would grow up revering their memories of Lincoln.

The martyred president has long been memorialized in our nation's numismatic and medallic art. Shown here are a portrait from an 1876 Bureau of Engraving and Printing vignette book; a $5 Silver Certificate, Series of 1923 (called the "Porthole Note" for its round central frame); Victor David Brenner's plaque of 1907; and George Morgan's presidential medal.

Augustus Saint-Gaudens studied and worked in Paris and Rome in the late 1860s and 1870s. Meanwhile, in 1873, after a Roosevelt family tour of the Holy Land, 15-year-old Theodore, his younger brother Elliott, and their sister Corrine stayed the summer with a German family in Dresden. He is shown here (at left) during that stay, with Elliott (seated facing) and Corinne (second from right).

Current coins of the mid-19th century—what young Saint-Gaudens and Roosevelt and their parents might have found in their pocket change. With a purchasing power of 25 to 30 times its value today, this handful of coins would have meant much more than just pocket change to the late-19th-century American. (actual size)

David Glasgow Farragut was the senior officer of the United States Navy during the Civil War. His famous command from the Battle of Mobile Bay is remembered today, paraphrased as, "Damn the torpedoes, full speed ahead!" Farragut has been memorialized on U.S. Treasury notes and postage stamps. Through the late 1870s and early 1880, Augustus Saint-Gaudens turned his artistry to capturing the heroic admiral in bronze sculpture.

The Bland-Allison Act of February 28, 1878, brought back the silver dollar after a hiatus of several years. The act was passed despite the veto of President Rutherford B. Hayes, shown here on an official Mint medal by engraver George T. Morgan. It called for the Treasury to purchase $2 million to $4 million of silver at prevailing market prices every month, for coining into silver dollars. These coins, also designed by Morgan, were the backing for Silver Certificate notes that circulated among the public. So much silver was coined that the Philadelphia Mint built a steel vault for storage. (coin shown at 1.5x actual size)

In 1883 Charles Barber's Liberty Head nickel debuted. In a design faux pas, he had left the word CENTS out of the denomination. Some enterprising fraudsters gold-plated the new coins, which were roughly the size of a $5 gold piece, and tooled fake "reeding" onto their edges. They sought to take advantage of the public's unfamiliarity with the new coins by passing them as gold, for a hefty profit. These gilt shams earned the sobriquet of "racketeer nickels." Later in the year the word CENTS was worked into the design to thwart any such deceptions. (shown enlarged 2x)

This $4 postage stamp, issued at the time of the World's Columbian Exposition, features a portrait of Columbus based on Lorenzo Lotto's painting. Queen Isabella's portrait made this the first United States stamp to prominently bear the image of a historical woman.

Other stamps issued for the 400-year anniversary of Columbus's voyage.

Tickets from the World's Columbian Exposition, and an "Official Souvenir Postal Card."

Olin Warner's director badge for the World's Columbian Exposition, and the obverse of the commemorative half dollar engraved by Charles Barber. (Coin shown at 1.5x actual size)

Exhibitors at the World's Columbian Exposition received a beautifully engraved certificate designed by Will Low. Today these are treasured collectibles.

Central Pavilion, Horticultural Hall, painted by L. Marold, from *World's Columbian Exposition: Art and Architecture*, by William Walton, a limited-edition (500 copies) multi-volume study of the World's Fair and its exhibits.

Views from the Art Gallery, Room 34 (Germany) and Room 36 (Austria), at the World's Columbian Exposition. Inset: coins from each nation.

C13

The Golden Door, painted by Felicien de Myrbach, from *World's Columbian Exposition.* Inset: the Exposition award medal designed by Augustus Saint-Gaudens.

The U.S. Mint operated in its original 18th-century buildings for more than 40 years. In the 1830s a new structure was built to house all of the Mint's operations under one roof. The impressive Greek Revival building, pictured at top, was used through 1901. Middle: Workers in the melting and refining room. Bottom: Tourists viewing steam-powered presses in the coining room, circa 1885.

U.S. Mint workers examining $100,000 face value of newly minted $20 gold coins in the coiners' counting room of the Philadelphia Mint (January 1894). The Liberty Head design (shown inset at actual size) was minted from 1849, the year the denomination debuted, until 1907, when it was replaced by Saint-Gaudens's design. This particular image was prepared by the Treasury Department as a public-relations piece to instill confidence in the American public that the gold standard was not in danger.

the portrait of Queen Isabella used by Peddle. Again on the following day, he wired Bertha Palmer, requesting that she ask Caroline Peddle to forward the Isabella portrait. Peddle had only supplied her model.[43]

Meanwhile in Philadelphia, focus had shifted back to the obverse. With Peddle's model in hand, Bosbyshell thought the relief okay but crudely modeled. He felt the mantilla used ought to be lace. The top of the head appeared flat. All in all, there was insufficient detail, leaving too much for the engravers to interpret. Bosbyshell recommended turning to the curator for the University of Pennsylvania, who had just returned from Madrid with medals bearing the likeness of Isabella. He also mentioned that General O.O. Howard, who was writing a biography of the queen, could furnish engraved likenesses.[44]

On the 14th Leech forwarded Peddle's model to Palmer as well as Morgan's proposed reverse. He called the Peddle model crude and said that he and the secretary of the Treasury would not accept it. This gesture seemed aimed at foreclosing any claim for compensation that Peddle might file. He asked that Palmer authorize seeking another portrait source for Queen Isabella and to promptly approve the reverse model.[45] That approval was not forthcoming. The Board of Lady Managers queried if an effigy of a living person could be used. They also asked if, as an alternative to the building, its portal could be used. Leech countered that the reverse in hand was the one selected by the secretary of the Treasury and that he had instructed the engraver at the Mint to prepare the necessary dies.[46]

One final point remained to be resolved. Leech asked the women on April 21 to provide him with their desired inscriptions for the reverse. He had one caveat: they must omit any distinction of sex, which the secretary of the Treasury held improper on a coin of the United States.[47] For Victorian times, Carlisle's position, while strict, was not unusual. Still, there was no precedent for the secretary of the Treasury to insert himself so strongly into the process.

On the 22nd, Bosbyshell forwarded two completed obverse models to Leech, stating that their source was the Peddle photographs.[48] Given that Bosbyshell and Barber had attended the funeral of Bosbyshell's grandson the previous day, the completion time for these two models was uncharacteristically short. It begged the question as to whether Barber had actually relied upon Peddle's model to construct his own— and, if so, to what extent. Two days later, Leech sent the models of the head of Isabella to Palmer for her choice. One represented a frontal view of a mature queen, and the other a profile of a young queen. Both bore crowns. For the reverse, Secretary Carlisle relented to the inscription "Board of Lady Managers." Bertha Palmer had at least carried the issue most dear to her heart: the ladies would be represented on the coin. At their board meeting of May 5, the women chose the young head, and their ordeal was over.[49] So it was too for Edward Leech. He left Mint employment in mid-May to become a vice president of the National Union Bank in New York.

The Board of Lady Managers was outmaneuvered. Caroline Peddle was never given a fair shot. She deserved more credit than she received for the obverse design— which was none at all. The fault was Bertha Palmer's. She expended too much energy trying to direct the design content rather than overseeing the process. She would have been better served to have given Caroline Peddle a free hand while concentrating her efforts toward the Mint bureaucracy. Her failure to inform Caroline Peddle that all communications should first be with the Board of Lady Managers was fatal. The final design chosen for the reverse was simplistic at best. The women who composed the Board of Lady Managers were active in civic affairs and well educated on matters of art. To them, the selection of such a staid stereotype of womanhood for the reverse of the Columbian quarter was insulting. The *American Journal of Numismatics* agreed, saying it was mournfully suggestive of an old anti-slavery token.[50]

Winding up this affair, the Mint began striking these "showy quarters," to use Charles Barber's words, on June 13. The first 100 of these coins, plus the 400th, the 1,492nd, and the 1,892nd, were struck in Proof format.[51]

Nevertheless, the World's Columbian Exposition received great acclaim. Theodore Roosevelt arrived on May 11 for an 11-day visit. His sister Bamie was a member of the New York State Board of Lady Managers. He had taken a personal interest in the siting of the Boone and Crocket Club hunting camp exhibit for the fair. He had been instrumental in the founding of this organization several years before to study the natural history of animals and work for the preservation of American forest regions. This exhibit occupied a building formerly known as the "shack."[52]

From this structure on an island in the lagoon, Daniel Burnham had overseen the construction of the fair. It was also where McKim, Saint-Gaudens, and others gathered for long hours into the night discussing the arts and how to advance them in America. The American Academy in Rome had its genesis here. If anyone thought to contrast the two uses of this building at the time, they would have considered it ironic. However, with the passage of time, that comparison would prove to be anything but.

It was an ideal setting on the shores of Lake Michigan, yet not all was ideal in the world outside the gates of the fair. Carlisle had bigger problems in April than the design motif and legends for the Columbian quarter. The Republicans had badly mismanaged the American economy in their four years in power. In a misguided attempt to put the country firmly on the gold standard, they had passed the inflationary Sherman Silver Purchase Act of 1890, increasing monthly silver purchases by 50% and requiring that these purchases be financed through the issuance of currency redeemable in either gold or silver. With silver prices continuing to fall, all of these notes were going to be redeemed in gold. The intrinsic value of a silver dollar now stood at 48.8¢.[53] Counterfeiters had become brazen, making coins containing the same silver content as those of the federal government. Compounding matters, the Republicans had proceeded to deplete the Treasury through excessive spending and early redemption of government bonds.[54] Knowledgeable people were questioning the United States' ability to maintain the gold standard and business contracts began to contain gold clauses.

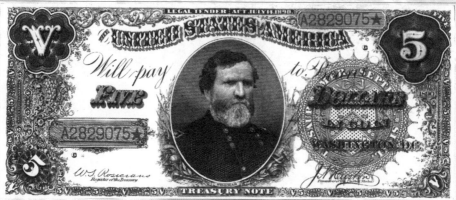

Under the Sherman Silver Purchase Act of 1890, the Treasury's monthly silver acquisitions served as the backing (along with gold) for paper currency "payable in coin." (shown reduced)

According to the *American Journal of Numismatics*, the reverse of the Isabella quarter (middle) resembled an anti-slavery token of the 1830s. (shown enlarged)

99

Carlisle walked into this potential time bomb without any practical experience. He haughtily canceled a dinner in New York City arranged to introduce him to the financiers on Wall Street shortly after Cleveland's inauguration.[55] Then as his plight became more apparent, he issued a statement on April 21, 1893, designed to assure the public that the Treasury would continue to redeem currency for gold upon demand. However, his statement was not unequivocal.[56] By the time he realized his error, it was too late. Fearing that the United States would go to a silver standard, in effect devaluing its currency, foreign capital began to leave the country. The American public was not far behind, withdrawing huge sums in gold coin from the banks. On May 4 a large unexpected bankruptcy set the stock market into a tailspin.[57] As the summer wore on, capital shrank and jobs began to disappear.

Chapter 7

Thacher's Gambit

As work progressed with the Exposition, Augustus Saint-Gaudens was confronted with another proposal. There would be an award medal presented to individual exhibitors for excellence in their respective fields. It had been authorized by that same Act of Congress on August 5, 1892, with $60,000 appropriated for the design, engraving of the dies, and striking of the medals under the supervision of the secretary of the Treasury.[1] Almost immediately, the Treasury secretary sought the advice of the Columbian Commission Awards Committee for input on appropriate designs and devices.[2]

The committee formed the Awards Subcommittee, led by John Boyd Thacher. With his background, he was comfortable in both corporate boardrooms and the smoke-filled back rooms of 19th-century American politics. In fact, as chairman of the executive committee within the Awards Committee, he held the power.[3] With responsibility for the appointment of exhibition judges as well as oversight of the exhibit awards, his influence really extended far beyond the confines of the committee.

Thacher wasted no time, contacting the Treasury Department on August 22 to set the process in motion. Secretary Charles Foster in turn laid the groundwork for the process in a communication to Director General Davis. Foster was reserving for the Mint the right to engage an artist. If the Awards Subcommittee desired, a competition could be conducted. He suggested considering Saint-Gaudens, Will Low, Henry Mitchell, and possibly the Mint's own Charles Barber.[4]

Here the matter stood. Three weeks later, Mint Director Leech prompted Thacher to make a decision. While the medal would be in high relief, the extensive inscriptions would prevent an elaborate display. Time was of the essence. While the design and the engraving work would be under Leech's control, the Mint lacked the capacity to strike the quantity of medals required. A contractor would be engaged, adding time to the whole process. Leech promised that if an outside designer were considered, he would seek to secure the best talent available. In early October, Charles Barber himself "consulted" with Thacher in order to instruct the Awards Subcommittee of the Mint's ability "in procuring a fine design."[5]

John Boyd Thacher had other ideas. The previous January he had been quoted firmly advocating a national competition. An enthusiasm would be generated that could not be duplicated by giving the work to a high-priced artist. Thacher wanted a medal that would last long after the fair closed; something that would go into museums all over the world.[6] Had the authorizing legislation been passed in a timely manner, his

101

approach would have been different. Now there was no time. He had to sacrifice a competition in return for the assurance that a competent designer would make what he hoped would be timeless art.

Thacher called for a meeting in Washington on October 5. He brought Alexander T. Britton from his committee. Representing the government were Leech and Assistant Secretary A.B. Nettleton. The gist of the meeting was that Saint-Gaudens would be invited to prepare the medal. Thacher would travel to Philadelphia within a couple of days for that "consultation" with Barber. However, for Thacher the only real question he wanted answered by Barber was the diameter to be used.[7]

The formal notifying letter from Thacher to Secretary Foster quickly followed. There was just not enough time to afford a competition so the Awards Subcommittee was asking the Treasury secretary to invite Saint-Gaudens to take the commission.[8] Foster complied although the letter was somewhat equivocal. At the suggestion of the Awards Subcommittee, the Treasury Department was requesting that Saint-Gaudens undertake the preparation of the designs for the award medal. His well-known reputation as a sculptor and worker in relief would commend his selection to the art world. Then came the details. The design was to be submitted in the form of a plaster model no more than three times the diameter of the proposed medal. That diameter had not yet been set but it would be either three or four inches. The dies would be engraved at Philadelphia for the use of a private contractor to strike the medals.[9]

There was one hitch: Gus turned them down. He forthrightly explained to Thacher that he had a problem. He needed to obtain permission from the Shaw Monument Committee before taking on any new commissions.[10] Leech then suggested to Thacher that he consider J.Q.A. Ward. However, Thacher would not budge even though he knew there were going to be difficulties. He told the press that the matter was in abeyance. He vaguely stated that he hoped to induce Saint-Gaudens to let the Exposition work take precedence over the less important commissions.[11] Then Thacher set out to gain permission of the Shaw Committee so that Gus could take on the award medal commission.

Securing permission from the Shaw officials was definitely not a foregone conclusion. Not only had Saint-Gaudens been unable to show any progress by the time this contract with the committee called for completion of the work in 1886; he had, by his own admission, now spent more time thinking about the commission than working on it. Two of the three committee members, Henry Lee and John Murray Forbes, were despairing if they would ever live to see completion of the work.[12] In addition, Forbes, in particular, had emotional ties to the Shaw. Mrs. Forbes had been with the colonel's wife and mother to receive his last salute as his regiment marched down Beacon Street to Boston's docks and ultimately to the ramparts of Fort Wagner in South Carolina.[13]

The situation was really much worse than Saint-Gaudens would admit. In January 1891 Gus had written Edward Atkinson, who served as spokesman for the committee with the outside world. He had an open space of time in front of him which he would devote to the Shaw. He had money enough to pay for the work. There was no reason for additional delay. Nine months would complete the model with another three months for the casting.[14] In June of that year Gus was contradicting himself and asking the committee for a cash advance. Atkinson obtained the committee's consent

John Boyd Thacher: writer, industrialist, historian, collector of books and autographs, former New York state senator, and ex-mayor of Albany. Thacher was quite comfortable in his leadership role in the Awards Committee of the World's Columbian Exposition.

Edward Atkinson, treasurer of the Shaw Monument Fund in Boston. He would find himself competing with other projects for Saint-Gaudens's time and attention. Yet he was the glue that kept this commission from flying apart.

although Forbes felt someone should be monitoring Saint-Gaudens's progress given all the delays.[15]

The real downfall for Saint-Gaudens came in a meeting with the committee in early December 1891. His work the preceding months had led to a much different composition than originally contemplated. Gus's problem was that as he progressed on the Shaw, so many more possibilities for composition presented themselves that in turn needed to be worked out.[16] It now was too large to go upon the State House wall, requiring Gus to seek a new location across the street on the edge of the Boston Common. Site preparation would be required. There was not money enough in the Shaw Memorial Fund, thus requiring an appropriation from the city. There were other issues for the committee. Forbes did not like the rendering of Colonel Shaw's horse. He liked the allegorical angel even less, calling it Cassandra-like and hoping that Gus's "better angel" would encourage the sculptor to improve it or leave it out.[17] Atkinson cautioned Saint-Gaudens to bring a good photograph of his work, as it now stood, for the meeting. He prompted Saint-Gaudens that it should show a new set of African Americans. Saint-Gaudens's earlier representations of the African American soldiers had not been realistic enough to suit Forbes. If the angel remained, it should be less prominent.[18]

Saint-Gaudens survived the meeting, with the committee agreeing to the site move. Atkinson immediately approached the mayor for an appropriation for a terrace to place the memorial opposite the State House. On December 24, with the city approval in hand, Atkinson now called Saint-Gaudens to account for all of his procrastinations and delays on the commission. The committee had a right to complain that Saint-Gaudens had put other work in front of the Shaw. Atkinson acknowledged that Saint-Gaudens had put much more work into this commission than originally expected. The artist was entitled to follow his own course in the matter of time up to a point; that point had been reached. The city's action had removed a financial burden that if strictly enforced was the obligation of the sculptor in this commission. If Saint-Gaudens needed additional money to finish this work, the committee would make such advances. They would much rather take this course than have Saint-Gaudens take on additional commissions of a potboiler nature to support his studio. Then Atkinson threw his spear. He believed that Saint-Gaudens was under an obligation to devote himself exclusively to this work. He likened it to the moral obligation of a businessman to not waive the terms of a contract for any reason, artistic or otherwise, except by consent of both parties.[19] It was this last statement that caused Saint-Gaudens to turn down Thacher.

Relations with the Shaw Committee showed no improvement with the new year. In early January, Augusta Saint-Gaudens wrote the committee to say that Gus's brother and father were gravely ill. As a result, the sculptor had neither the time nor thoughts for the Shaw.[20] Then the third member of the committee, M.P. Kennard, visited Saint-Gaudens's studio. The Shaw was dismantled. Gus was at work on a model for the equestrian statue of General Sherman. Frustrated, Kennard wondered if Saint-Gaudens was equal to the task. At Atkinson's query,[21] Augusta wrote defensively that Gus had indeed prepared the preliminary sketches in question to give the Sherman committee a conceptual idea of what he proposed to do, but that the project would have no impact upon the Shaw; however, Gus's brother Andrew had died and his father remained ill so the sculptor had been unable to focus on the Shaw.

Striking Change

In June 1892, the Shaw Committee was again optimistic. Atkinson had sent Saint-Gaudens four checks for $500 each to be cashed as certain completion goals were met. Their expectation remained that Saint-Gaudens's finishing was imminent. Matters seemed to progress toward completion, with the committee in early October considering inscriptions for the memorial.[22] Expectations were high that finally, after broken promises and delays, the end was near.

Thacher was going to have to bring his considerable skill to bear if Gus were to be released to design the award medal. Wasting no time, he wrote to John Murray Forbes. That was a mistake. Forbes was opposed but left it to Atkinson to deal with outside matters.[23] As October drew to a close with no reply from Forbes, Thacher began to grow testy. He sent first one personal agent and then another to Boston to ascertain the membership of the Shaw Committee and to interview those individuals in an attempt to sway the decision in his favor. He described himself to Edward Leech as firing hot shot into the Boston camp.[24] In the process Thacher learned that Kennard was the sub-treasurer for Boston. He immediately contacted Secretary Foster to apply pressure for Saint-Gaudens's temporary release. This Foster promptly did. There was even a letter from the sister of the late Colonel Shaw to the committee asking that Saint-Gaudens be released.[25] The letter disclaimed Saint-Gaudens as the source of the request, which left only Thacher.

By now the three members of the Shaw Monument Committee had begun to react. John Foord, secretary of the Awards Subcommittee, met with Atkinson on November 5. He had previously met in New York with Saint-Gaudens so he knew fully of Saint-Gaudens's desires on the subject.[26] Foord told Atkinson that if Gus did not take the medal commission, the alternative was obnoxious. It would take Saint-Gaudens about three weeks to complete the commission if he were to be released. Foord's approach was straightforward and favorably received by Atkinson.

Atkinson immediately followed up on November 9 with a query to Saint-Gaudens as to the sculptor's wishes. If the sculptor could give a certain specific timeframe there might be a chance that the committee would relent.[27] Saint-Gaudens was direct and to the point in his reply:

> In the matter of the medal I am much troubled. I only wish to do it to keep it out of the hands of the man at the mint who I am positively assured by Mr. Thacher and Mr. Ford [sic] will certainly do it if I don't. If I thought that it were at all possible that one of two or three other artists could obtain the work, I should certainly refuse to have anything to do with the matter. As that is not the case I should be glad to do it but it will take three months as it is a very serious matter. When I first considered the subject I thought six weeks would be the limit, but I had not given it serious enough consideration.[28]

Gus's opinion of Barber's abilities had clearly not changed since their encounter the previous year. His concern that the commission would go to Barber was no idle fear. Thacher restated his concerns in a letter to a third party. While he expected that Saint-Gaudens would make the medal he was not sure that he could control the process if Saint-Gaudens were prevented from accepting the commission.[29]

Meanwhile, Thacher was determined to have his way. On November 10 he went at Forbes again in a long letter. The Awards Subcommittee and the Treasury Department were united in their desire to have Saint-Gaudens do the awards medal. Optimistically, Thacher said it would take Gus only a few weeks. He appealed to Forbes's patriotism. The enterprise was of both national and international importance. Therefore it should not be looked at in the same vein as a private commission. Thacher also brought to bear the appeals of several distinguished individuals, including the vice president, for Saint-Gaudens's release. In a draft of this letter dated October 29, Thacher even went so far as to ask for a formal reply so that the public would know that the Subcommittee on Awards had done its duty.[30] In other words Thacher was threatening to go public to try to bring pressure. This was a tactic, even if only relayed verbally, that was not likely to sway Lee, Forbes, and Kennard. Thacher's letter in its watered-down final version still comes across as more of a strong-arm tactic. These men on the Shaw Committee were not about to be moved by such rhetoric. In fact Forbes, when he first learned of the proposal in October, had referred to Thacher and his committee as crazy folks.[31]

Still, it was an optimistic Thacher who told Director Leech in early November that everything pointed to success and that he was now arranging the terms of Saint-Gaudens's temporary release.[32] It was not to be. Atkinson and his colleagues had focused on the discrepancy between the estimates given by Foord and Saint-Gaudens for completion of the award medal. It only served to raise a red flag. Atkinson wrote Saint-Gaudens that three months was unacceptable. It would effectively delay completion of the Shaw by a year.[33]

On November 18, the committee unanimously rejected the request. To grant the release would show bad faith to the subscribers and to the City of Boston, which had committed to the site work. More importantly, some of the committee members still lacked faith in Saint-Gaudens's ability to complete the Shaw.[34] In their notification of this action to John Foord, the committee, wiser from the experience with Saint-Gaudens, pointed out the incapacity of artists to measure their own time. Clearly they were expecting Saint-Gaudens to take the full three months (if not longer) to complete the medal commission. They also made note that Saint-Gaudens had communicated that MacMonnies could do the work. Then, in a final bit of irony, they stated that Saint-Gaudens had promised once more "to finish" his work on the Shaw by the end of January 1893. Could not the work on the medal wait until afterward?[35]

This letter seemed to close the door finally and completely on the Awards Subcommittee. Then suddenly Thacher appeared to prevail. He told Gus on November 30 that the Treasury was treating his original rejection as withdrawn. The medal was his to design. Thacher hoped that the sculptor would have the work well in hand by the first of the coming year.[36] Clearly Thacher still believed in the three-week estimate. Saint-Gaudens's acceptance, reported in the newspapers on December 4, 1892, was greeted with much satisfaction. The medal would be distributed to exhibitors throughout the world. Thacher boasted in the newspapers that if Saint-Gaudens's work turned out well, the world would see that America could do quite as well as any other country if not distinctively better.[37]

Had anything happened to change the Shaw Committee's position? Thacher would not say. He shed some light on the situation in two letters written that December. He said his conscience was clear since he had exhausted every peaceful and considerate method before he had recourse to the last. He would not explain to the Awards Subcommittee on paper what he had done; however, he would explain in detail personally.[38]

The Shaw Committee had not changed their position and they knew what had happened. They first received word in mid-December that Saint-Gaudens was going to do the medal on the sly, in the evenings. He was, on the other hand, bound to work on the Shaw to catch up on his promises. Henry Lee believed that working evenings would impair Saint-Gaudens's energy during the day. The sculptor had contended in the past that he needed to think solely and continuously upon one design. If that was truly the case, he was being dishonest to the Shaw Committee to distract his mind by taking on the medal commission.[39] They were rightly upset and Atkinson went to New York to meet with the sculptor. Gus confessed. Thacher had represented to Saint-Gaudens that either he must do the medal or it would surely go to Barber. He had tried to arrange that the work be transferred to MacMonnies but this could not be done. To avoid an artistic catastrophe, Gus was going to do the medal on weekends and at night. His work on the Shaw would take place during the day when he could judge the effect of light upon his composition. Atkinson reluctantly accepted this explanation but he had great difficulty convincing the committee to accept his conclusion.[40]

This acquiescence came at a cost. The committee viewed Saint-Gaudens's actions as a breach of contract. Gus in turn spoke ill of what he perceived as their interference with his artistic prerogatives. He had his wife write Atkinson that he broke no promise by devoting time to the medal that would otherwise be spent at home or with friends.[41] Saint-Gaudens knew better. Thacher had used Gus's distaste for Barber's skills as an artist to strong-arm him when similar efforts with the Shaw Committee had failed. Had the commission money colored Saint-Gaudens's judgment?

Reflecting federal funding of the awards medal, the commission would be given by the secretary of the Treasury although the Awards Subcommittee would effectively administer the process. The sum involved for the commission, $5,000, was substantial for the times. Still, there was no contract. In effect, as long as there was no contract, there was no technical violation of the moral obligation to the Shaw. It was a handshake deal between Augustus Saint-Gaudens and John Boyd Thacher. Saint-Gaudens would uphold his part of the arrangement. On his side, Thacher must now keep his allies in line. Both Leech and Foster had been cooperative in the process. However, their positions were appointed and subject to the vagaries of politics.

Gus intimated to Thacher that his design for the award medal would be a departure from the usual form of allegory and would embody a great historical feature. Thacher crowed to Foster that Gus had the ambition to make this medal the chief work of his career.[42]

Work progressed during the early months of 1893. Saint-Gaudens wrote to his friend in Paris, Paul Bion, seeking representations of Columbus. He also assured the Shaw Committee that progress was occurring on that front as well. Only the allegorical angel remained.[43] Then there was dismay. Gus saw the final rendering of Warner's design for the Columbian half dollar. Forbes complained that the Shaw seemed to have gone to sleep, prompting another stern letter from Atkinson to Saint-Gaudens.[44] Finally the sculptor watched firsthand Caroline Peddle's sordid treatment by the Mint.

Within a week of Peddle's resignation, Gus began questioning John Boyd Thacher, first as to the validity of the agreement under which he was working, and second as to just exactly what work product he was to provide the Mint. Gus was first concerned about the money, not his artistic control. Despite any protestations that he always seemed to be making to the contrary, he needed the money. In an undated note to Gilder that year he described himself as being "bust absolutely" but hopeful of some large payments in the offing. Also Gussie was forced to ask her mother for a loan to tide the sculptor over.[45]

Because of the Shaw Monument Committee obligation, he was in a period where little or no payments from new commissions were flowing in to offset studio expenses while final payments from existing commissions including the Shaw were awaiting completion of the work. At the same time not only was Gus operating the largest sculpture studio in New York, he was also supporting two households in the city—his own and another for his mistress Davida Clark and their son. In addition he was maintaining a summer home in Cornish, New Hampshire. While cash income was being restricted, his cash outflow was hemorrhaging.

Gus now realized that his handshake agreement with Thacher left him exposed if there was a disagreement with the Mint, as he could now foresee. More specifically, Saint-Gaudens wanted the dies for the award medal cut outside of the Mint. That would eliminate interference in the artistic content of his work and hopefully avoid a conflict that would cause the government to walk away from the agreement. He was determined to avoid the fate of those who had gone before him. Yet he could ill afford to lose the payment.

As Saint-Gaudens was stewing over his predicament with the award medal, Atkinson again queried him about the Shaw. Completion seemed always to be one or two months away.[46] The medal work had left Forbes and Lee feeling hopeless about the statue. He reminded Gus that both men were old and had emotional ties to the project. Then Atkinson adroitly pointed out that Saint-Gaudens needed the goodwill of the committee. Additional contributions that would accrue to the benefit of the sculptor could be expected if death did not intervene. He closed by asking Saint-Gaudens to please write.[47]

Saint-Gaudens did not answer, leaving that for Gussie. She told Atkinson that Gus was so overwhelmed that he could not write. He had been sick and needed a rest. With his temperament, suggestions tended to hinder him. After living with the man for 15 years, she could say that it was absolutely useless to press him.[48] There was a problem with this letter: Gussie was writing in Gus's place because he was out of town dealing with the awards medal.

Thacher had set up a meeting in Washington at the end of April for Saint-Gaudens with Carlisle and Leech. He also wanted to know when the awards medal would be done. It was imperative that one side be done now. The man was beginning to better understand the Shaw Committee's exasperation. Thacher could not be present at the meeting but would send Britton—a politically connected Washington attorney, and well suited to this task. Thacher told Gus that he thought Leech to be in sympathy with Gus's desire and would help in the matter.[49] It was an optimistic assessment; Leech was a short-timer.

On the way to the meeting Saint-Gaudens stopped in Philadelphia at the Mint. He met with Charles Barber to review the Mint's methods of reducing models and preparing dies for medals. Gus revealed that the model was complete. However, it was between three and four feet in diameter, far larger than the Mint's requirement of no more than three times the diameter of the actual medal. The real question was, had he chosen this size deliberately to circumvent the Mint? Gus acknowledged that he knew of no reducing machine in America that could bring this model down to the size of the award medal. Coyly, he admitted thinking of shipping his oversized model to France. He went further in suggesting that it might be well to have the dies cut there too. It was very diplomatic of Gus, whose not-so-hidden agenda was to keep Barber at bay.[50]

Both sides now knew the issues for the meeting as Gus came to Washington. The decision-maker in the meeting was the acting secretary, Charles Hamlin, sitting in for Carlisle. The government stood firm. They certainly assured Saint-Gaudens that he would be paid the $5,000 in conformance with the understanding with the Awards Subcommittee. However, in a follow-up letter to Thacher, Hamlin reiterated the Treasury Department's original stipulation. Gus could not be paid until a plaster model had been submitted that conformed to Mint size requirements. He reminded Thacher that Gus was aware of this constraint, caused by the limitations of the reducing lathe that would be used to cut the dies from this model.[51] Thacher immediately wrote back saying that he would relay Hamlin's letter to Saint-Gaudens. More importantly, he stated that the subcommittee recommended the diameter of the medal be set at three and one-half inches. This recommendation really should have come as no surprise. During the previous November, Leech had agreed with Thacher that there should be no objection to that diameter as it seemed the proper size.[52]

From Gus's point of view, this letter fell far short of what he wanted. During the meeting he had forthrightly revealed that he had already sent his plaster models to Paris for reduction as well as to have the dies cut. The government had conceded the obvious. Gus could do whatever he wished in order to have the final model comply with the size restrictions. The reduction work could proceed in Paris but the dies would have to be cut in Philadelphia. Gus appealed again in a letter on May 12 to Hamlin to have the dies cut as well in Paris. Hamlin would concede nothing. He had gone over with Saint-Gaudens in the meeting the need to have the dies cut at the U.S. Mint. There was great anxiety on the part of officials connected with the Mint to have part of the work done at their facility. The liability of adverse criticism was too great if the dies were cut outside of the country. The reductions, once completed in Paris, must be delivered to the Mint as soon as practicable.[53]

Charles Barber's fine hand was all over this reply from Hamlin and Gus knew it. His temper flared in a letter to John Boyd Thacher on June 2.

> I am disgusted with this whole matter. In order to do this medal, after much solicitation I dropped important lucrative work for this Senate commission so that if possible something we need not be ashamed of should be awarded by the United

Augusta Homer Saint-Gaudens, from a portrait by Thomas Dewing in 1885.

States. Now, as what I wish seems to be an impossibility in making of the dies, I cannot be held responsible for them and if any liberties are taken with my work at the Mint such as have been taken with others I shall certainly publish it.[54]

Exasperated and not fully comprehending Gus's concern, Thacher wrote to Carlisle and enclosed the Saint-Gaudens letter. He professed ignorance of the vehemence of Saint-Gaudens's stance. He offered as an explanation that the Lord made artists differently from other men. Thacher hoped that Carlisle would placate Saint-Gaudens and have the dies cut in Kamchatka if that were the artist's desire. Thacher even threw out for consideration a compromise of having an outside party cut the dies under the direction of the Mint.[55]

Now Carlisle was involved. Leech was gone and Acting Mint Director Preston was forced to query him to confirm what had transpired in the April meeting.[56] Carlisle was not budging. It would be impossible to have the dies cut outside of the country. Popular prejudice was such and the possible misrepresentation of motives so great that it was necessary to have the work done here. Carlisle did, however, offer to Saint-Gaudens every assurance that the dies for the award medal would be a faithful reproduction of his design and that not the slightest deviation from the model would be made. Carlisle was confident that the work would be executed to Saint-Gaudens's entire satisfaction.[57]

Meanwhile on the Boston front, matters had deteriorated significantly over the summer of 1893. The Shaw Committee was now almost openly hostile in their dealings with Saint-Gaudens. They flatly stated that they felt aggrieved at his having accepted the award medal commission after having agreed to devote himself exclusively to the Shaw. They pressed continually for a status report on work accomplished and a commitment as to when his modeling would be finished.[58] Augusta wrote back that the work must be able to stand the test of time. Atkinson replied testily that his work would stand the test of time if speedily finished to the best of the artist's ability. If it were not finished promptly, Atkinson doubted if it would ever be put in place. Saint-Gaudens's reputation both as a man and as an artist was at stake. More calmly Atkinson asked that Saint-Gaudens defer the angel until the other parts of the work were complete.[59] Finally, in August, Saint-Gaudens told Atkinson that he was out of patience with the committee. Atkinson responded that Saint-Gaudens had brought this upon himself. Atkinson had stood between Saint-Gaudens and the committee as long as he could.[60]

Here matters stood as the World's Columbian Exposition, which had opened to such great acclaim and enthusiasm, drew to a close. Gus fumed over his relations with the Shaw Committee and waited for the return of his reductions from Paris. Barber stood ready to prepare the necessary dies. The award medal had an implied deadline that could not be denied. Just as importantly, the financial disaster known as the Panic of 1893 had set in and was showing no signs of abating.

Chapter 8

Embarrassment Enough for All

With the closing of the Exposition, one fact was clear. The souvenir commemorative coins struck at the Mint were a solid failure, or a "Stinking Fish," to use the unintentional words of Charles Barber. Newspapers derisively noted that the coin was the only half dollar ever minted worth 100¢. In a desperate promotion, Ferdinand Peck at the end of June 1893 had a pile of souvenir half dollars stacked to resemble the Washington Monument.[1] Charging the same $1 for the Columbian quarter made even less sense. The fact that the coins commemorated the popular World's Columbian Exposition was not enough to overcome their uninspired design.

The Mint coined 950,000 of the half dollars in 1892 and another 4,052,105 in 1893. Of the 1893 coins, 2,501,700 were melted. The Mint charged the Exposition a melting fee, which had to be forgiven by an Act of Congress. Also the Exposition Company continued to refuse to have anything to do with the coins withheld to fund the judging and award expenses of the Commission. Those 1,141,760 half dollars were simply released into circulation by the government starting in October 1894.[2] With no sustainable market premium, another 1,000,000 of the coins held by the Chicago banks also found their way into circulation. Sales to the public at the premium price had been a paltry 358,645 coins. The fate of the Columbian quarter was no better. The Mint struck 40,023 and melted 15,809. Additionally, Bertha Palmer and other Lady Managers purchased 10,000 of the quarters at face value.[3]

Now attention turned to Saint-Gaudens. Acting Mint Director Robert Preston wrote to John Boyd Thacher on September 1, 1893, asking if Saint-Gaudens could be hurried along. But Gus, with an agenda of his own, was still seeking to avoid working with Barber. Implementing Thacher's suggested compromise from June, he had approached Gorham and Tiffany's and each had agreed to engrave the dies and strike the medals within the congressional appropriation.[4]

By the end of October, Gus had delivered his models of the award medal to the Exposition committee.[5] Given that he had been working with Mary Lawrence, it comes as no surprise that the finished obverse, designed in high relief, bears a strong resemblance to her *Columbus*. His figure has the same emotional, upturned face. Saint-Gaudens was depicting a moment in history. He imparted fluidity into the figure of Columbus.

113

The explorer has placed his right foot upon a rock, and is three-quarters turned with arms outstretched. Contrasted to the high relief of Columbus, low-relief background figures stand in a boat with one holding a banner whipping in the wind. As Gus had promised, this work was a radical departure from the norm of a standard head-in-profile. In it, the story of Columbus's landing in the New World becomes real to the beholder.

For the reverse, Gus unexpectedly turned to classical Greek influences with a full frontal nude male youth. He stands holding wreaths in his left hand and a torch in his right while leaning against a large classical shield with the inscription E PLURIBUS UNUM and the image of a standing eagle.[6] This rendering is out of character with the obverse.

Now began the maneuvering as to who would cut the dies. The Awards Subcommittee asked on October 19 that Preston come to Chicago for consultation. They were not going to follow in the path of their predecessors with the commemorative coins. Preston, however, was unable to travel due to legislative matters and the preparation of his annual report.[7] In declining the committee's invitation, Preston reiterated that as soon as Saint-Gaudens delivered the models to Philadelphia, Charles Barber would begin preparation of the dies.[8]

Preston wrote Bosbyshell on October 25 asking that he instruct Barber to cut the dies following the models precisely, with all possible dispatch. He reminded the superintendent that Saint-Gaudens had wanted the dies cut in France. Preston wanted to give Saint-Gaudens no cause for complaint with the Engraving Department.[9]

The Awards Subcommittee supported Saint-Gaudens. The language in the authorizing act did not specifically direct that the dies be cut at the Mint. Potential bidders would be asked to provide the engraving work as part of a package bid.

November 4 found Preston writing to Saint-Gaudens asking for a brief description of the designs. He was receiving numerous requests for this information from the press. In accordance with Saint-Gaudens's request that the designs not be made public, he had declined to give out any description.[10]

Preston got more than he asked for: Saint-Gaudens sent the eight-inch models to Washington.[11] He also followed up with a description of the medal for public release, provided Thacher approved. In his words, on the obverse Columbus was represented stepping ashore in the New World with a gesture of thanks to God. The reverse depicted the Spirit of America as represented by a young man in full vigor of life.[12]

That description was not the one that appeared in the Washington papers on November 7. That storyline had the obverse being a bust of Columbus and the reverse, a chubby-faced boy, typical of youth and energy. The diameter of the medal was now supposedly set at three and one-half inches.[13] Preston sent the models to Philadelphia that same day.

Preston was still standing firm in support of Barber preparing the dies.[14] However, on the 8th Bosbyshell asked that work on the dies be put on hold. John Woodside, a Philadelphia businessman and the Awards Subcommittee's liaison to the Mint, had called on Bosbyshell. He reiterated the subcommittee's wish that the engraving be included in the bid package for the manufacturing of these medals. He argued that by combining these two processes, there would be no finding fault with the dies by the

Bureau of the Mint medal for Robert E. Preston, by Charles Barber. Preston took a personal interest in the design and production of the Columbian Exposition award medal. With Senate confirmation of his appointment as Mint director up in the air, he wanted nothing to go wrong.

One of the three trial award medals cast in France. It has a diameter of four inches (shown at .75x actual size). This piece was donated to the American Numismatic Society by a Saint-Gaudens relative. It has a paint mark on Columbus's left leg that would indicate that Saint-Gaudens intended to make a change. This is the same leg that critics later called "awkward." Intentional or otherwise, the hooded figure behind Columbus's left arm bears a striking resemblance to the profile of Saint-Gaudens.

World's Columbian Exposition award medal (first or nude reverse by Augustus Saint-Gaudens). (shown at .75x actual size)

116

party receiving the contract to prepare the medals. Furthermore, both Tiffany's and Gorham desired to submit bids on this basis. Bosbyshell, not wishing to unduly antagonize a politically connected World's Fair commissioner, now acknowledged the validity of Woodside's argument.[15] Just as likely, Barber, with the high-relief models now in hand, knew that his engraving skills would be put to the test.

At the end of the first week of November, the Cleveland administration nominated Preston to be director of the Mint pending Senate approval. The bureau had been almost six months without a leader. Preston, now living in a fishbowl, would not want anything controversial to arise.

On November 13, he wrote Saint-Gaudens and John Woodside acquiescing; no die cutting would be done in Philadelphia. He wanted Gus to supply him with a list of firms that could contractually carry out the combined work.[16] To Woodside, Preston was more specific: he was placing the matter of the medal entirely under their control. The Mint would not seek proposals by public invitation; they would simply send a circular letter to firms known to be capable of meeting the Mint's production standards. He did request that the Scovill Manufacturing Company, which had a complete metalworking plant capable of doing coining work, be included on the list of bidders.[17] By default, Gus had apparently carried the day.

The process sounded simple. Gus would supply a list and a circular would be prepared. The list was short, including only Tiffany's, Gorham, Scovill, and Krider. The award medal would by completed before the end of the year and Saint-Gaudens could move on. Concerns over Charles Barber were in the past. Woodside was to supply the specifications for Preston. What could be easier?

Wavering at placing the medal production in the hands of the Awards Subcommittee, Preston authorized Bosbyshell on November 22 to accompany Woodside on a visit to the manufacturing facilities of Tiffany's, Gorham, and Scovill.[18] Bosbyshell and Woodside visited Tiffany's plant in Newark, New Jersey, with Saint-Gaudens on Monday, November 27. When queried, the Tiffany's people were strongly in favor of having the dies made in the United States. Without Gus, the two men continued on to Gorham in Providence, Rhode Island. Here they learned that Gorham would prefer the dies to be made at the Mint, although they had a reducing lathe capable of doing the work. Gorham also preferred a three-inch diameter for the medal even though they had not seen the design. The trip ended in Waterbury, Connecticut, at Scovill.

At all three concerns, much time was spent discussing the process of adding the names of the awardees on individual medals. Saint-Gaudens's reverse had made no provision for the insert that was to bear the names. None of the three companies was particularly confident of how the process could be accomplished.[19] As well, there were issues concerning the composition of the names and the lettering style to be used.

The Gorham representative volunteered that Saint-Gaudens had offered to make the lettering for each award if he could receive a percentage of the whole contract. The Gorham people wanted to know if Saint-Gaudens had any right to demand such terms. Bosbyshell expressed no opinion. Given Gus's sculptural obligations, in particular his commitment to the Shaw Monument Committee, and the tedious nature of this work, his proposal to take it on was impossible. He must have needed the money desperately.

On November 29, the men returned to Tiffany's headquarters in New York City. Saint-Gaudens was again present, having received in the interim three cast bronzes from Paris. The medals were in the diameters of two, three, and four inches. Bosbyshell was astonished at their beauty. More discussion was advanced on the use of a panel upon which to insert the die that would impart the awardee names on the medal. Bosbyshell concluded that any of the three firms was capable of executing the contract, whether the medals be struck or cast. He then uncharacteristically went out on a limb, recommending that if the costs could be contained, a four-inch cast medal should be executed.[20]

December found Woodside asking Preston why there was a delay issuing the circular letter. Preston relayed that Secretary Carlisle had determined the specifications unsatisfactory given the unresolved size and the ambiguity over whether the medal would be struck or cast. Preston wanted Woodside to provide fuller specifications, which he promptly did.[21]

Meanwhile the issue of placement of award names continued to trouble the Mint. Bosbyshell asked Saint-Gaudens to come to Philadelphia. Gus could not, so Bosbyshell sent Barber to see the sculptor in New York.[22]

Still the process dragged. Now, Gus queried the acting director as to the status of the bids. Curiosity was intensifying over the designs. What Gus did not reveal to Preston was that even if the process was ready to move forward, he was not. He had carefully examined the four-inch cast piece and determined that Columbus's left leg must be modified:[23] it appeared to just dangle in the medal. Preston waited four days before answering him, and then said that only Gorham had submitted a bid to that point.[24] It was a very brief letter, addressing Gus's specific question and nothing more.

No additional bids had been received because the circular had not been issued. Preston was forthcoming as to why in a letter sent just after the New Year to C.P. Goss, head of Scovill. Goss had wanted to meet with Preston to discuss Scovill's bid. Preston related to Goss that he had delayed the circular while he investigated the possibility of striking the medals in aluminum. New technology had greatly reduced the cost of production for this metal. A great number of badges and medals had been struck in aluminum for the World's Columbian Exposition and were well received.[25] He had just learned that the delays would be great and that there was considerable opposition. Preston closed by saying that he would issue the circular calling for bids the following week.[26]

Meanwhile, the newspapers were more accurately reporting the obverse to be a representation of Columbus stepping ashore from a boat, surrounded by three companions, one holding a banner of Spain aloft. On the reverse Saint-Gaudens had supposedly replaced the typical female figure with that of a vigorous upright American male.[27] The elements of the design were clearly leaking into public awareness.

Then all hell broke loose on January 12. A crude likeness of Saint-Gaudens's design appeared in the newspapers. The depiction of the obverse was the least accurate. Christopher Columbus stood in a meaningless pose without banner or sword. The men in the background were supposedly representative of five different types of nations, all in contemporary clothing including derby hats. The reverse was much more accurate. The nude male was faithfully rendered although with a slight paunch.

All in all, it was an inept attempt to reproduce Saint-Gaudens's work. Nevertheless, a sudden firestorm over the issue of male nudity enveloped the sculptor. Augusta, in a letter to her brother Tom, gave some idea of what was happening:

> Of course you have heard of the great medal controversy. It's amazing, the excitement about it. The house has been besieged with reporters as well as the studio. One man came at 2 a.m. and was almost kicked out of the house by the irate sculptor, only as his feet were bare he thought it would hurt him more than the man's feelings.[28]

How did the medal design leak into the press? First of all, Robert Preston can be ruled out. He had nothing to gain and everything to lose. He would have done nothing to jeopardize his appointment as director that coincidentally was confirmed by the Senate on that same January 12.[29] His correspondence with Saint-Gaudens supports that he had honored the sculptor's request for secrecy. More importantly, the models were in Philadelphia, not Washington, where Preston had only a description of the medal's devices and inscriptions. The accuracy of the facsimiles printed in the newspapers could only have come from the original models. Erroneous later perceptions that the models were in Washington came from a quote of Saint-Gaudens's. In the heat of a newspaper interview, he stated that the original designs were at the "Mint in Washington."[30] He of course meant Philadelphia.

Part of the answer comes from a newspaper interview with the executive officers of Page Belting Company. They related that George F. Page, the company president, visited the Mint in Philadelphia on Saturday, December 8 and was shown the models of the medal by "officers of the Mint." Page apparently did have a letter of introduction from Senator Chandler of New Hampshire that he had presented to Robert Preston the previous summer. Preston in turn had given him permission to visit the Mint in Philadelphia.[31]

Seeing the models was not the primary purpose of his visit. With the financial panic of 1893 in full swing, Page was seeking business from the Mint. He examined the models in their presence and made a drawing from memory for use on an advertising circular.[32] This circular then found its way into the newspapers.

Page's motive very likely was driven by frustration. The medal had real commercial value. Page had put forth a substantial effort in his two Exposition exhibits. He was entitled to the two medals his company had been awarded and the business advantages that they would bring.[33] Also, reproducing medals won at trade expositions had been a common practice in Europe since the 1850s.

There has long been an understanding in the American numismatic community that Barber was the source of the leak. The facts just don't add up. Barber had no direct access to Page Belting. Motive for Barber was murky at best. Barber and Saint-Gaudens were at least maintaining a working relationship up to this point in the process. The two men met four days after Page visited the Mint. True, one cannot deny that Barber had custody of the models. Yet this fact only condemns him of allowing them to be seen. While Barber was a politically adept bureaucrat, he still considered himself a professional. He would not have knowingly disgraced the position of his father. So if it wasn't Preston or Barber, who initiated the leak of Saint-Gaudens's designs?

Oliver C. Bosbyshell entered the Mint service on May 4, 1869. This was the same period in which Charles Barber went to work for his father at the Mint. Bosbyshell, a Civil War veteran, worked his way through the ranks of the Mint, reaching assistant coiner in 1872, coiner in 1877, and superintendent in 1889. He was a lawyer by training and active in the Pennsylvania National Guard, being made a major in 1878 and achieving the rank of colonel in 1890.[34]

A long letter from Bosbyshell to James Ellsworth under the pretext of setting up the Mint exhibit at the fair on March 13, 1893, lays the foundation for the motive. In that letter Bosbyshell asked that Ellsworth put in a good word for him politically. He was in jeopardy. The superintendent's position at Philadelphia had no term of office. He was a Republican appointed by a Republican president and if Cleveland so desired, he could replace Bosbyshell.[35] There were grounds, however, for optimism. Cleveland was a strong civil service advocate who had replaced Leech with a career employee.

Coincidental to Preston's nomination for the director's position, Bosbyshell again wrote Ellsworth on November 3. He was still "doing business at the stand." However, "some little stir" was being made just that week. Any assistance that Ellsworth could give to help him retain his position would be felt with greater force at that time than at another time.[36] Clearly something about the appointment of Preston had Bosbyshell on edge. That he was willing to take questionable actions in this endeavor to save his job was also demonstrated in another letter to Ellsworth on November 13. The government was beginning to seek reimbursement for the cost of melting the surplus souvenir half dollars from the Exposition. Bosbyshell divulged to Ellsworth that the proposed fee for the melting was too high and that it could be negotiated downward. He offered his services to Ellsworth in proceeding further in this matter.[37]

When George Page showed up at the Philadelphia Mint to see the models of the award medal, Bosbyshell was not going to refuse the request. After all, he had made promises to others to secure photographs of the models at the appropriate time.[38] He had a history of interpreting his instructions loosely or to his benefit. To him, keeping the design secret meant no photographs. However, it did not prevent someone from viewing the designs. He was going to do all in his power to curry favor with Page and thereby hopefully gain another ally in his effort to retain his job. Bosbyshell and Page must have come to Barber and either coincidentally or specifically viewed the models. Bosbyshell had selfish motives. He was the culprit.

Ironically for Bosbyshell, Secretary Carlisle asked for his resignation on December 14. There were too many strikes against the man. The preceding September Carlisle had ordered all gold bullion at the Mint monetized in the effort to defend the gold standard. One vault at Philadelphia that had not been opened in six years was found to be short. An employee soon confessed to embezzlement.[39] Bosbyshell bore no blame in the theft but the timing of the discovery magnified the crime out of proportion. Also in the ensuing investigation, it was found that Bosbyshell had been lax in insisting upon bonds for his management people, as required by law. In addition, Preston had had to press the superintendent to make layoffs that fall. With the depression on, demand for coins had fallen. The government, facing declining tax receipts, was looking for any way to cut expenses. Bosbyshell was a lame duck when the controversy exploded over the nudity in Saint-Gaudens's design.

Oliver C. Bosbyshell. Enlisting as a private at the start of the Civil War, Bosbyshell distinguished himself and rose to the rank of major (and, later, colonel in the Pennsylvania National Guard). After the war he engaged in business, entered government service in Philadelphia, and was eventually appointed superintendent of the Philadelphia Mint.

Facsimile of Saint-Gaudens's designs, used by Page Belting Company on its advertising circular..

Nudes are rare in Saint-Gaudens's work. In 1891 he executed a stone likeness of Kenyon Cox's seal for the Boston Public Library that included two nude boys. This seal was to appear over the entrance to the new library building. It was not well received. Carved above the nudes was the library's motto, "Omnium Lux Civium" (The Light of All Citizens), and "Free to All." It was a real stretch, but people connected the phrase "Free to All" to the nude boys, and were offended. The controversy became known as the "boys without pants." It reached the public arena in February 1894 in the middle of the award-medal affair.[40] Saint-Gaudens was evidently trying to implant Greek ideals into American culture.

Gus should have backed off. No matter how meaningless the controversy over male nudity may have seemed to him, he should have recognized that he was pushing the limits of American public taste in the 1890s. The commission for the award medal was funded by the federal government and the medal itself would be struck under the authority of the secretary of the Treasury and the Mint. These institutions and individuals had to respond to the public.

Trouble was immediate in coming. The director general of the World's Columbian Commission learned of the controversy as it broke on January 12. Without having actually seen the medal or having a description of it, an embarrassed George Davis declared it an outrageous thing to be distributed among the exhibitors. It represented neither art nor science nor industry and appeared to be indecent.[41] Perhaps Davis was still feeling the sting of having been relegated to a secondary role at the fair by Burnham and the Exposition Company.

Then, having calmed down, Davis wrote to James Ellsworth on the 15th that he was only reacting to the caricature in the *Tribune*. However, he was afraid that if the medal were anything like the caricature, the general public would not regard it as up to Saint-Gaudens's standard. On the other hand, the general exhibitor would not care much about the depiction of Columbus or the "statue of a man."[42] However, by then the damage was done. The press and the public had seized upon Davis's original statements, which only served to inflame the situation.

Gus lashed out in anger. He explained his understanding of how the design had reached the public. He called the actions of Page Belting Company's representative disgusting, dishonorable, and dishonest. That was the expunged version printed in the *New York Tribune*. Gus actually called the Page Belting representative an "idiot" and a "New Hampshire ass."[43] He even used the term *theft* to describe the reproduction of his work by Page Belting. His temper had taken control. Subsequently cooler heads prevailed and he pledged not to publish anything concerning the controversy until the medal was issued. He considered a lawsuit and turned the matter over to the law firm of Evarts, Choate & Beaman. A letter claiming damages and criminal activity was sent to Page Belting. However, his attorney, Charles Beaman, explained that while the case was a good one in New York, Gus would have a hard time proving damages to a jury of New Hampshire farmers.[44]

Early on, William F. Vilas, chairman of the Senate Quadro-Centennial Committee with oversight for the fair, voiced his objection to the design. In a twist of fate, Senator Chandler had seen the Page Belting circular, found it objectionable, and brought it to Vilas's attention. Vilas asked that the models be brought to Washington

Striking Change

for an initial inspection by the committee on January 18.[45] Preston duly requested that the models be sent down from Philadelphia. Lame duck or not, Bosbyshell was not without an opinion in this matter. He suggested to Preston that if the senators or the secretary wished to throw out the Saint-Gaudens design, Will Low was already under contract to the Treasury Department as a designer and could provide a replacement design. Bosbyshell must not have known that Low, as a friend of Saint-Gaudens, would never touch such an assignment. Bosbyshell went on to suggest that if the decision were to retain the Saint-Gaudens design, then some sort of draping could be employed.[46]

When the models arrived, there was more in the box. Peter Krider of the medal firm in Philadelphia had provided 17 proposed designs for the award medal. He was offering them free of charge should the government decide to reject Saint-Gaudens's work. Krider's work was officially unsolicited. Clearly the award-medal design was a prized plum and the vultures were circling.[47]

The lack of a formal approval procedure for the award-medal design hurt Saint-Gaudens's case. Confusion reigned. The Committee on Awards stated that Assistant Treasury Secretary William Edmond Curtis had signed a letter of acceptance. Curtis rebutted that he never signed a letter, paper, or anything else authorizing the acceptance formally or otherwise. Curtis supposed that the Awards Committee accepted the design and in his opinion that was where the responsibility rested.[48]

There was precedent for Curtis's position. In the early spring of 1893, John Boyd Thacher had notified the secretary of the Treasury that the committee had approved the design for the award diploma that was to be presented to the exhibitors and requested payment to its designer, Will Low. This diploma was to be printed by the Bureau of Printing and Engraving under the authority of the secretary of the Treasury in the same type arrangement as the award medal.[49] The handshake agreement had come back to haunt Saint-Gaudens.

It seemed that the leadership of the Columbian Commission headed for cover. The *Chicago Tribune* reported on January 13 that "it is understood that Mr. Thacher has approved the design. In acceptance with his manner of doing business, he has not consulted the wishes of the Exposition officials, whose superiority he declines to recognize."[50]

The Quadro-Centennial Committee's objection to the award medal was conveyed by Treasury Secretary Carlisle to Saint-Gaudens on January 23. Carlisle noted that the design was unobjectionable as a work of art. However, it was not suited to the general distribution that would result from the awarding of more than 20,000 of the medals. He closed by asking that Saint-Gaudens submit a design that covered the figure's genitals. However, four days before he wrote Saint-Gaudens, Carlisle had a conversation with Vilas.[51] Here Carlisle was much more forthcoming. He was in agreement with the committee that the present design must be changed. Either a new design must be prepared or the existing one remodeled so that no "exhibition of vulgarity in art" appears. He was just as blunt in his correspondence to Thacher, also adding that he was directing that the design be changed.[52]

Clearly there was a difference between how Carlisle felt and what he had relayed to the sculptor. In being diplomatic with Saint-Gaudens, he had done the man a disservice. When queried by the press for a public response to Carlisle's request, Gus would not comment other than to say he was "tired of the whole thing."[53]

Carlisle's active role at this early stage is surprising when weighed against the economic crisis that was threatening to overtake the U.S. Treasury at that very moment. The gold drain that had started with the previous year's panic had continued through the fall. To maintain the gold standard, Carlisle, with questionable authority, on January 17 issued a circular that requested quotes on a bond issue of $50,000,000. Its validity in question, the bankers in New York sent a message that the "Blue Grass Secretary of the Treasury" needed to come to New York to allay fears.[54]

Meanwhile, in spite of public statements to the contrary, Saint-Gaudens had not given up. Gus wrote a letter of protest in response to Secretary Carlisle's notification. People's opinions as they now stood were formed from a rude picture that was published in violation of the rights of the government and Saint-Gaudens. The opinions of the Senate committee had been formed upon viewing the enlarged model. Gus was sending a three-inch model, the size now set for the medals themselves. He hoped that upon seeing the smaller scale that Carlisle and the committee would revise their opinion.

As an artist he protested against the proposed alteration. However, if the committee still wished a change, he preferred to submit a design rather than have someone else do it. Even at this early date, the sculptor was sensitive to the fact that a substitute reverse from the Mint was an option. Gus went on to state that he would, in self-defense, be bound to see that "the people" knew what the originally accepted design was, should an alternative reverse be used. At this stage Saint-Gaudens remained confident that the public would not object to the male nudity and that his reverse would compare favorably to any substitute coming out of the Mint. In closing, he reserved the right at some time to publish the correspondence between the two of them.[55]

Carlisle duly forwarded the model with the objectionable reverse to actual scale to the committee on the 27th, seeking their conclusions in writing. George Page was in Washington that day too, indicating that the committee made the effort to determine the circumstances of the unauthorized leak of the medal's design.[56] Gus felt confident that once the committee had a chance to review his work in proper scale, he would be vindicated. Newspaper reports were that unnamed senators on the committee had approached three noted artists about improving the design and none would have anything to do with such an effort. They believed the medal was a work of art and destined to rank among the most famous the world had ever seen. Saint-Gaudens probably believed that he had an advocate in one of the members of the committee, Don Cameron. The two men knew each other through their mutual association with Henry Adams. What he did not know was that Carlisle and Cameron were poker-playing buddies of long standing. There seemed but one voice from the committee, that of condemnation.[57]

On January 29, 1894, newspapers quoted Carlisle as saying that he had taken the position that since the government had paid Saint-Gaudens the $5,000 commission, his work was the property of the United States government to do with as it saw fit. Carlisle was reserving the right to have the design altered if he so chose, either by Saint-Gaudens or by someone else if the artist was unwilling. Those were ominous words from a man bearing tremendous stress over the rapidly deteriorating American economy.[58]

The Senate Quadro-Centennial Committee wasted no time. Upon a second review, committee members rejected the reverse of Saint-Gaudens's medal on February 1.[59] Gus had been overconfident to think that the political bosses in the Senate, epitomized by Don Cameron, would support his art over outraged public opinion.

In the press, Gus reassured Mint Director Preston that he would replace the offending reverse design if the Senate committee's objections continued. Preston relayed this information to Philadelphia and added that he was willing to give Saint-Gaudens a reasonable length of time to do so. He also instructed Barber to begin preparing the dies for the obverse of the medal.[60] Preston was regaining the initiative.

Privately Gus fought back. The possibility of a lawsuit was dropped. Page Belting Company had threatened to sue over Saint-Gaudens's libelous public statements calling the company a thief. One newspaper editorial called for him to simply release the actual medal designs and let them stand on their own merits. Instead, Saint-Gaudens sought to rally allies to his side. John Boyd Thacher and George Kunz of Tiffany's lobbied the National Sculpture Society.[61] On January 30, the executive committee of that organization, trying to protect their colleague, took a position:

> Resolved: That it is the opinion of the National Sculpture Society that the objections made by the Senate committee to the nude figure on the medal designed by Augustus Saint-Gaudens for the World's Columbian Exposition are unwarranted, and that said figure as presented in the medal is in every way unobjectionable.
> Resolved: That if changes in works of art are ordered, then such changes should be made under the immediate direction of the artist.

The full organization ratified the resolutions on February 12. The first resolution was obviously self-serving to Gus. The second resolution was an attempt to reserve the field to the sculptor. The specter of Charles Barber stepping forward to prepare an alternative reverse was troubling for Saint-Gaudens. Taken in total, these resolutions would have been easily perceived as home cooking. Gilder and his brother-in-law, Charles de Kay, were two of the organization's five officers.[62]

In addition, there was strong support, most likely at Gilder's prodding, from the *New York Tribune*. It was felt that if Saint-Gaudens had used a nude female figure instead of a male to represent America, there would have been no objections. After all, as the article stated, *America* as a word was feminine and use of a female figure was a more customary practice.[63] Still, there was no movement on the Senate committee's part to reconsider its actions.

Carlisle took his time communicating the official rejection of the reverse design to Saint-Gaudens. It came in a letter dated February 21 that enclosed a copy of the Senate committee resolution stating that the reverse *ought* to be changed.[64] That was different from Carlisle's original instruction that the offending parts of the nude be covered. He requested that in accordance with his earlier letter to Saint-Gaudens, the sculptor should submit a new design as soon as possible. However, there should be no additional expense to the government.[65]

Quietly, behind the scenes, Gilder urged Gus to amend and preserve the design.[66] Finally, on March 15, Saint-Gaudens relented. Working from the original instructions that Carlisle had communicated to him on January 25 and consistent with Gilder's

Embarrassment Enough for All

wise counsel, he submitted three modified reverse designs for this second version of the medal. In two, he strategically placed a ribbon over the offending anatomy. It was so suggestive as to not really help matters much. In the third version, he replaced the ribbon with a fig leaf. Following a suggestion from Gilder, he asked Carlisle to submit these alternatives and his original model to a committee composed of the heads of the principal art societies or men of recognized standing in these matters such as Ellsworth in Chicago.[67]

Carlisle had no intentions of following Saint-Gaudens's recommendation. He submitted the revisions to the Quadro-Centennial Committee.[68] Certain senators still opposed these alternatives. They then carefully pointed out that no formal meeting of the committee had taken place; their opinions were only of an advisory nature. Ultimately, authority rested with the secretary of the Treasury to accept or reject the work of Saint-Gaudens.[69]

With the committee having taken no position, Vilas and Carlisle talked the situation over. The senator told the secretary it was in his hands. Carlisle followed up, asking Vilas what character design the committee might consider appropriate that he could "cause to be prepared and submitted for inspection."[70]

At almost the same time, Carlisle fired a shot at Saint-Gaudens in the press, saying that if the sculptor did not provide another design, he would ask Barber to supply an acceptable reverse.[71] Carlisle's position was hardening. Moreover, he did just as he said he would. Barber quickly found himself in a difficult position of potential conflict but one that should not have surprised him. Years later, he confessed reluctance to undertaking the alternative reverse design, which he considered a no-win situation for himself.[72]

John Boyd Thacher attempted to support Saint-Gaudens by seeking a resolution of the full Senate instructing Carlisle to accept the original reverse design. Support was lacking. Saint-Gaudens's association with Thacher was in reality a liability. When Congress voted to impound the Columbian half dollars to fund the exhibit judging and awards, Thacher had been the one urging Carlisle to immediately take action. He then tried to placate matters by promising Ellsworth a say in the appointment of judges for the railroad exhibits, giving the financier a way to repay the railroads that had purchased bonds from him.[73] Thacher had tried to have it both ways. Further, seeing his unorthodox methods in determining the awards process, France and Norway had withdrawn their exhibits from the judging. From George Davis down, Thacher had alienated everybody.[74] He would be of no help now.

The one person who had the stature to help, Daniel Burnham, could not. Burnham had had a falling out with Secretary Carlisle. To quote the gentlemanly Richard Watson Gilder, Carlisle had responded to Burnham in such a manner as to cut off all future correspondence.[75] It was as if Carlisle were back in his position as Speaker of the House, refusing to recognize the opposition.

Saint-Gaudens heard nothing for three weeks. Finally on April 26, 1894, Preston notified Gus that Carlisle had formally rejected his alternate reverse designs. In political doublespeak, Carlisle felt that in view of the action taken by the Senate Quadro-Centennial Committee the modified nude would be subject to much the same criticism. Therefore Carlisle desired that Saint-Gaudens prepare a new design as soon as possible. The obverse design was acceptable. Preston wanted to assure Saint-Gaudens that the reproduction of his design by the Mint would be exact in every practical way.[76]

"Practical" was a far cry from the "faithful reproduction without the slightest deviation" that Carlisle had promised the preceding May. Not only had Gus lost the battle for the reverse design, he now knew that Charles Barber would be cutting the dies to his own satisfaction. For Gus this statement also meant that correcting the left leg of Columbus at this stage was out of the question. Receiving this letter, Gus most likely overlooked one more ominous fact. The letter had not come directly from Carlisle as the others had. Carlisle had ceased to communicate directly with Gus.

Finding an acceptable alternative was not that simple. Edward Leech had correctly observed that artistry would be limited on the medal by the need for the lengthy inscriptions. With no inscriptions on the obverse, the problem for the reverse was compounded. Also contributing to the difficulty were Gus's emotions. He had once described his life as "up and down, up and down." When he was discouraged, as in this case, it seemed he could get nothing done.[77]

There was another issue as well. Saint-Gaudens was again being pressed by the Shaw Committee. The preceding November, when the medal work seemed at a conclusion, Gus had traveled to Boston to quietly sit down with John Murray Forbes to resolve the bitter feelings. Forbes cynically felt that Saint-Gaudens had asked for the interview with him because the sculptor knew how soft a touch he was compared to Henry Lee, who wanted to scalp him. Forbes humored Saint-Gaudens, avoiding anything that would stir him up emotionally. Peace was made between the two men temporarily.[78]

As the medal controversy reached full stride in February, Atkinson told Saint-Gaudens that if he did not put aside all causes that seemed to crowd his time to finish the Shaw Memorial, he would be making the mistake of a lifetime. Days later Atkinson followed up asking specifically if the medal stink was distracting Saint-Gaudens. However, satisfactory progress made the committee feel at the end of March that Saint-Gaudens was at last approaching completion of his modeling work.[79] While they were wrong in that observation, there certainly was no doubt that Saint-Gaudens was now devoting some effort to the Shaw.

Meanwhile pressure mounted on Gus to take action on the award medal. John Woodside on behalf of the Awards Committee visited him in New York. At the beginning of May, Woodside thought he had the situation patched up, although still nothing happened.[80] At this point Gilder prodded. Throughout this tedious affair, Gilder had acted as a mentor to Gus. Now he was telling Saint-Gaudens to put the controversy behind him and make an acceptable reverse design.

Gus emphatically responded that he was going to do an alternative. However, he was going to confine this work to an inscription. He had no time for anything more. Obstinately he stated that the figure he had conceived was composed to be nude and he found it impossible to drape it without entirely destroying the composition.[81]

Gus's statement to Gilder was not a revelation; he had previously communicated in a letter begrudging the review process to Preston that he was commencing another model for the reverse. He already had a sketch, which he had shown to Stanford

One of the modified reverses submitted by Saint-Gaudens in March 1894.

The final rejected reverse from June 1894.

World's Columbian Exposition award medal (reverse by Charles Barber). The awardee for this particular medal was W.C. Blackfan, an Ohio farmer who developed a new strain of wheat.

Richard Watson Gilder, in a Cecilia Beaux portrait (1902–1903).

Embarrassment Enough for All

White. White called it a little too much like a tombstone and sent him two of his studies as alternatives. By now Gus had learned to take White's criticisms in stride, and he proceeded to implement his own design. Saint-Gaudens still wanted his next design submitted to a jury of "persons of standing" in the profession.[82] The nude would be entirely gone. Only a standing eagle surrounded by a wreath would remain. Of all the various reverse versions, this rendition was Saint-Gaudens's best by far. Preston, in a fit of optimism, told the press that the medal would be ready to strike six weeks after Saint-Gaudens had completed his latest design. Everything was in readiness for the obverse and there was a chance medals could be struck by July 1.[83]

Gilder's pressure, however, was not the real cause of Gus's capitulation. Saint-Gaudens's ego had gotten the better of him. In spite of the dangling left leg, the sculptor had allowed Paul Bion to submit on his behalf the award-medal design with the nude reverse to the Paris Salon for 1894. Approval from Paris would provide him with ammunition to resist changing the reverse. Bion attended the preview on April 29 to see how Gus's work was positioned. Bion was embarrassed for his American friend. The medal had been grouped with the work of some amateurs, and skied.[84] The French had just told Saint-Gaudens this medal was at best average. It was a stinging rebuke that cut to the quick.

With his eagle reverse model received by Preston by June 23, Saint-Gaudens included a bill for $1,000. He also reopened the issue of being involved with the inscriptions of the award winners and wished to know the firms that would be providing estimates for striking the medals so that he could make his "arrangements" with them.[85] Gus was unrealistically reaching, trying to regain control of the process. No doubt he had incurred legitimate additional expenses to comply with Carlisle's directives. Also his difficulties with the Shaw Committee were still pinching his cash flow. He revealed to Stanford White that he was short of cash. "Every blooming cent that I have has all poured out and I don't see how I am going to fix it," he lamented.[86]

Whether it was his financial condition or his pride that necessitated this billing is open to conjecture. Nevertheless, it was a big-time blunder. After Carlisle had stated that the work should be at no cost to the government, this action gave his opponents an easy opening. They no longer had to consider the merits of his art. They only had to point to the audacity of Saint-Gaudens to include a bill for his services. To a person of Carlisle's background and recalling his days in the House as guardian of the government's treasury, Saint-Gaudens's bill would have been an affront.

Preston presented the model to Carlisle on June 25.[87] Suddenly, on June 27, Gus received a rejection at the same time as the Mint announced that a reverse by Charles Barber had been adopted. True to form the rejection letter specifically pointed out that Saint-Gaudens's work was to be done at no additional expense. The Awards Committee had been completely cut out of the process. Saint-Gaudens had given Carlisle the opening and the Treasury secretary had leaped at the opportunity.

On the same day that Carlisle sent a rejection letter to Saint-Gaudens, he informed Barber of his selection of the engraver's reverse. Carlisle in his note to Barber said that to his mind Barber's design exhibited "considerable artistic taste."[88]

On the 29th Preston informed John Woodside that Barber would be doing the reverse. Preston assured Woodside that Barber would finish his work in the shortest

Striking Change

time consistent with good workmanship. The Mint director on June 28 returned to Barber an unspecified number of plaster models of which "No. 1" had been accepted by the secretary.[89]

The press reacted, proclaiming that Saint-Gaudens had been wronged by having his work combined with that of a vastly inferior designer. The government's dealings with Saint-Gaudens over the award-medal design had been disgraceful. However, this last action was of a coolness that took one's breath away.[90]

The redhead was beside himself with anger, going immediately to Gilder. A letter was composed to the secretary of the Treasury and sent on July 3. It was a measured response, typical of what Gilder would have counseled. Saint-Gaudens recapped the whole sordid affair, from the rejection of the first model after its unfortunate release into the public domain to the third version. He did exaggerate when he claimed that he took the commission only after urgings of others, through patriotic motives and to the detriment of his other commissions. He closed citing Preston's letter of May 18 stating that the Mint stood ready to engrave his last reverse once it was completed. In light of that communication, he considered the Mint's keeping him in ignorance that another design was being prepared concurrently in-house something less than discourteous. Against this lack of good faith on the part of the Mint he protested both for himself and on behalf of his fellow artists.[91]

In a note that same day, Saint-Gaudens updated Gilder.

> I have sent today the letter to Carlisle, and shall withhold the publication long enough to give him a reasonable time to reply.
>
> Of course my action will now be interpreted by men of the stamp that pervade Washington, as that of a person who wishes to retain the possibility of making the three or four thousand dollars still to be made on the reverse [awardee name inscriptions]. It is hardly necessary for me to tell you that that is not the case. I wish definitely to wash my hands of the infernal thing. If I was a calmer man I could go on; but I cannot sleep when I think of it all.
>
> My object in not stopping this thing at once is out of deference to your desire, and, stupid as it may seem, through the patriotic desire that the medal should not become the laughing stock of everyone. Feeling as I now do, and after the treatment I have received I should certainly not have taken even that into consideration were it not for your action and I wish it were ended. I fear more and more correspondence.[92]

To just what action of Gilder's was Saint-Gaudens referring? Gilder and his wife, Helena, were by now very good friends with President and Mrs. Cleveland. During February and March 1894 Richard Watson Gilder was a guest for extended stays at the White House.[93] He had every opportunity to discuss the award medal with the president. George Kunz, immediately after the National Sculpture Society resolutions were passed, had urged Gilder in the strongest terms to wire Cleveland to intercede. So had John Boyd Thacher. Leaks to the press indicate that Gilder had taken exactly this action.[94] Cleveland, however, was not supportive. The president would have been foolish to step into that public controversy. Besides, Carlisle had his confidence. All Gilder could have gotten from the president was time for an alternate reverse.

Even so, Gilder now came strongly to Saint-Gaudens's defense. He turned first to Assistant Treasury Secretary Curtis, a former New York attorney. Gilder admitted to being one of those who had pressed Saint-Gaudens to set aside important work to provide the last design. Now to have it replaced by one from a "vastly inferior hand making a hodgepodge of what promised to be a memorable piece of medal work" was an extraordinary proceeding. He felt the Treasury Department would be criticized for all time for this act by those both inside and outside the country who had knowledge of art. Gilder wanted to know if there were any unstated reasons for the rejection of the Saint-Gaudens's third reverse. He closed by offering his help.[95]

Gilder was not done with Curtis. He was bringing all of his public-relations skill to the forefront. Turning to the National Sculpture Society, he drafted a resolution of protest for the signature of the society's officers. He instructed the secretary of the organization to get what signatures he could of the officers, as time was critical. He wanted the resolution sent immediately to Curtis that the assistant secretary might give it Carlisle.[96]

Gilder was much blunter to Charles Miller, editor of the *New York Times*, whom he wrote asking that he support him in writing to Carlisle. He described Barber's work as always commonplace. He called the patching of Barber's reverse to the work of Saint-Gaudens a monstrosity.[97]

It was within this context of polite official exchanges and suppressed strong emotions that Gilder received Curtis's reply. He burned the letter. He told Curtis that he did not want to unduly draw him into the controversy. However, the usually judicious Gilder turned around and wrote a much stronger second letter to Curtis. From this letter, one point within Curtis's letter to Gilder can be concluded with confidence. Gilder was forced to defend Gus's action of sending a bill with his third reverse design for the $1,000. Carlisle had shown himself in the past to have a prickly personality, one that easily took offense. There was going to be no rectifying this mistake. Still, Gilder held nothing back in this second letter. The offending nude was entirely gone. Saint-Gaudens had carefully prepared this last design and it was astounding that it should be thrown aside for another seemingly made in competition to Saint-Gaudens's work. It was unfortunate that an artist of Saint-Gaudens's prominence should be treated with such indignity. Yet that was not what moved Gilder. It was that this country would do so gauche and inexcusable a thing as to cast aside the work of its most noted sculptor and patch on something from a man of no artistic reputation. Gilder noted that the secretary of the Treasury made no claim to being an expert on art matters. If possible, the man should be "saved from making so glaring an error as this." Gilder even went so far as to tell Curtis he could show his letter to Carlisle if it would do any good.[98] It wouldn't. Carlisle was not going to budge.

Gilder replied to Gus on the 28th. He had done all he could, with no results. Carlisle, as well as others in the government, was preoccupied with the ongoing labor strife, the potential for another run on the nation's gold reserves, and political divisions within and outside the Democratic Party. In very strong words for Richard Watson Gilder, he was sorry to say that the affair put the secretary of the Treasury to shame. However, they should not blame him; he had taken bad advice. In closing, Gilder said he had done his best to save Carlisle from a serious mistake.[99]

Gilder's insights into the state of the government most likely came from the burned letter of Curtis. This man wrote his mother almost daily. On July 7, in the middle of his correspondence with Gilder, Curtis had told his mother that Washington was very apprehensive about the ongoing railway strike that had its seeds in the Panic of 1893. At Carlisle's request, Curtis had had a meeting with Cleveland on July 6. Here he learned of the president's resolve to stand up to the lawlessness of the strikers if it took the entire army and militia.[100]

That would explain Curtis's state of mind. However, Carlisle had not hesitated to involve himself in the award-medal controversy in the past, no matter how serious other events might be. Curtis also saw Carlisle, who had taken to his bed ill, that same day. There is every indication from the fact that Curtis saved Gilder's correspondence in his personal papers that he considered the Saint-Gaudens matter important. In that case he must have broached the subject with Carlisle. Gilder's defense of Gus's billing for the extra work strongly indicated that Carlisle voiced this objection and dismissed the matter. Gilder was wrong in saying that Carlisle should not be blamed for the controversy. The secretary should have accepted Saint-Gaudens's eagle reverse and rejected his attached bill.

On July 30, having heard nothing but silence from Carlisle, Gus's patience was at an end. In a last note to Gilder, he stated that he was going to publish a letter of protest in the following days. In a sidebar, Gus wanted to know if Carlisle had been told that any issue of compensation could be put aside.[101] Gus was finally having second thoughts about billing the government for the last revision.

Still he felt the need to write one last letter to Carlisle. It took him three drafts before he could settle on his final version. In his first version he stated: "The intolerable, deplorable, vulgarity, hopeless, inane, offensive combination, absurd grotesque, patchwork that will be the result of your action, as well as the bad faith of your department leads me to give these letters to the public."

In the final version, Gus calmed down, but not totally. He coolly noted that his letter of July 3 had been ignored. His suggestion from March 15 that his work be submitted to a competent jury had been disregarded. He made his case for compensation for the third revision[102] but would now waive that charge. He noted that rejection of the eagle reverse could only have been on the basis that it was not acceptable as a work of art. The result of that rejection, in addition to the absurd stigma upon the first reverse, added the gratuitous insult that Saint-Gaudens was incapable of making a proper reverse for his own medal.

Saint-Gaudens went on to state that he had no one to blame but himself that he should for a second time suffer through the ignorance of Carlisle's people in art matters. With his continued compliance with requests for modifications of the award-medal reverse, he had at least expected courteous and honorable dealings from Carlisle and the Mint. He called the resulting medal a patchwork. He would concern himself no more with it. However, he could not suffer his work to be placed in combination with that of the character that defaced the United States currency (meaning the coinage) without making a public statement of facts.[103]

This letter seemingly fell on deaf ears. By this time, the Mint was advertising for bids to strike the award medal.

In reality Saint-Gaudens's protests and implied criticism of Barber had been heard at the Mint. In an interview with the New York *Sun*, Robert Preston gave the Mint's reply. The *Sun*'s reporter was doing a story on the proposed private competition to be held in New York the next spring for new designs for the silver dollar. The winning design would be made available to the Treasury Department at no cost. Preston would have considered Saint-Gaudens to be behind this effort and viewed it as meddling in the Mint's business. Associates of Gus including George Kunz, Olin Warner, Kenyon Cox, and Herbert Adams were leading the charge.

Preston condescendingly pointed out in the *Sun* interview that a design that appeared exquisite in black and white might be utterly unsuited for a medal. It took a peculiar skill for medal-designing work. Preston went on to say that Henry Mitchell in Boston and George Morgan at the Mint were quite capable. He named others but excluded all of the New York artists, including Saint-Gaudens. If Preston had stopped here, the snub could easily have been overlooked.

Preston proceeded to point out in his best bureaucratic manner that purchase of designs from outside artists would require a special appropriation from Congress. The secretary of the Treasury had no authority to go outside the Treasury Department for artists. He cited as an example a model submitted by a woman in New Orleans that he considered the finest that he had ever seen. However, he was going to have to return the model as he had no authority to buy it.

He then smoothly launched into the real point of his conversation.

> There is another plaster cast in Preston's office in which he finds a great deal of amusement. It is the substitute design for the obverse [the Mint considered the *reverse* of the medal as the obverse, because it included the name of the award winner] of the World's Fair medal sent in by St. Gaudens after the youth whom the Senate Committee called obscene had been rejected. Mr. St. Gaudens had received $5,000 for the rejected design, and when he was invited to send in a substitute for it he was advised that the department would not pay him any more money. He sent in a model with appropriate lettering covering all of the face except a little space at the top on which a very impertinent-looking eagle strutted on a wreath of laurel; and a panel below in which the name of the prize winner was to appear. The whole thing looks as if Mr. St. Gaudens had run it off in an idle hour. With this new effort came a modest bill for $1,000 which was promptly returned unpaid. And, by the way, it is not generally known that the President himself passed on Mr. St. Gaudens's first design. His criticism was not at all on the nudity of the figure. He remarked that the left leg of the young man looked as if it had been broken and set badly.[104]

With that last shot the interview ended. Preston had beaten Saint-Gaudens to the public podium.

Saint-Gaudens now hesitated about going public in his own defense. He enlisted the support of the artistic community in New York and had a proposed draft letter from James McNeill Whistler full of satirical jabs. As the interview with Preston was taking place, Gus was giving drafts of his proposed public protest to Stanford White for comment.[105] White urged him not to rely on Whistler's comments, and instead to take the best comments from himself and others and go forward. McKim drafted a modified reply. Mead was supportive. Three days after the *Sun* interview was published, White wanted to know if Gus had seen the "thing" in the newspaper. Again on August 27, White told Gus that he should not let this outrage pass without a protest.[106] Yet Saint-Gaudens never sent that letter. A draft survives in his personal papers and was published in his autobiography.[107] In reality the art community knew the circumstances and needed no public call from him to steer clear of the Mint.

Barber's reverse suffers in comparison to Saint-Gaudens's final eagle rendition. The inscription panel is centered in Barber's reverse design. Behind it is a redo of Morgan's replica of the *Santa Maria* used on the reverse of the commemorative half dollar. The ship sails over Greek waves and, above, partially nude Nikai record triumph over the globe by voice and by pen.[108]

Barber had gotten the better of Saint-Gaudens. Gus deserved the lion's share of the blame in this situation. His problem with the Shaw Committee, his lack of progress on that commission, and the resulting cash shortfalls all contributed indirectly to his downfall. His billing of an additional $1,000 when Carlisle had specified that all corrective actions be at no cost to the government can only be described as thoughtless. In the end, nobody could have been more frustrated than Richard Watson Gilder. With the rejection of Saint-Gaudens's work, he watched some 10 years of effort to secure acceptable designs for United States coinage go down the drain.

For Gus, the fiasco was at an end. For the Mint, problems were just beginning.

Chapter 9

Aftermath

It was a cold day in January 1895, as Mint Director Robert Preston sat at his desk going through his mail. There was a letter from his friend at Scovill Manufacturing Company, Charles Goss. He opened the letter to find just a short note along with an advertising circular. Goss thought that he would wish to *see the exact copy* of the Columbian award medal. The attached circular was the infamous one from Page Belting Company.[1] It was a very bad joke at Augustus Saint-Gaudens's expense.

For Preston, the award medal had been nothing but trouble from the minute the United States Mint had assumed responsibility for its completion. In spite of Preston's authorizing Barber in January 1894 to start on the obverse die, work was not complete in mid-July. Barber, at the beginning of that April, when his relations with Saint-Gaudens were still on a professional key, had queried the sculptor as to which company made the reductions of his models.[2] He may have wanted to compare his work with those cast medals from Paris. Barber, despite public statements to the contrary, must have been having difficulties with the dies for the high-relief obverse.

By mid-July 1894 Preston still had no photo or sketch that he could release for the medal's reverse design. He was answering inquiries that the medal would not be completed for probably three months. At the end of July, Preston asked Barber to draw up the specifications that would be included in the bid circular.[3]

In August, Preston was still informing exhibitors that the engraving of the dies was not completed. His circular calling for bids was published that month and all of the companies except Scovill complained that it would be impossible to bid without seeing the design or at least having a sketch.[4] Preston was now saying that the medal would be ready in four to five months from the end of August. Preston also returned the rejected reverse models from the multiple second and third versions to Saint-Gaudens.[5]

Now Preston ordered Barber to send photographs of the reverse model to the bidders with the understanding that each must return those photos with his submitted bid. Under no circumstances were the photographs to be exhibited or copied.[6] Charles Barber was extremely anxious that his reverse design not reach the public's hands. He knew his work would be instantly compared to that of Saint-Gaudens and the whole controversy reopened.

The contract was let to Scovill on September 7 with a low bid of $0.926 per medal. It should have come as no surprise to the other bidders. Scovill had been supplying the Mint with cent and nickel blanks since 1859.[7] They alone had actually received a bid

137

Striking Change

circular. Tiffany's, Gorham, and Krider had merely received letters calling their attention to the fact that the circular was being published. Now delivery of the medals was set for January 1, 1895. Then, with Scovill in the picture, Preston in November was saying that the medals would be delayed until June 1895.[8]

Preston's troubles were not over as he opened Goss's note at the beginning of 1895. There was the issue of placing the names of the individual awardees on the medals. Preston had requested the comprehensive list from John Boyd Thacher right after the contract had been awarded to Scovill. However, there was no such thing as one complete list. Partial lists had been coming in periodically and would continue into April before the Mint had a master list. As the names were being gathered, Scovill pointed out that special insert dies were going to have to be prepared bearing the names of each exhibitor. It would complicate the process and cost an additional $0.30 per medal.[9] Over the requirement for insert dies that should have been included in Scovill's bid, Preston was mute. His concern was how much longer this requirement would delay the issue of the medals. Goss guessed the medals now would be complete in July or August. In February Scovill raised another problem. Some of the foreign names were too long for the space allotted on the insert dies. Scovill felt uncomfortable using abbreviations on its own and wanted Preston's help.[10]

More difficulties of an entirely different nature arose in March. George Kunz, representing the American Numismatic and Archeological Society, wrote unofficially to invite Preston and the Mint to participate in an exhibit to be held in conjunction with the National Sculpture Society in New York in May. This exhibit would showcase the results of a call the two associations and others had issued the previous year for new designs for the silver dollar that had been the supposed subject of the *Sun's* interview with Preston. Kunz asked if Preston could provide a collection of typical United States coins, from the earliest designs, to exhibit with the proposed dollar designs. He also asked if the Mint would provide the obverse and reverse of the Saint-Gaudens award medal as well as the new Barber reverse.[11] Nothing good could possibly come out of this exhibit for the Mint.

In late April Kunz wrote Preston again, this time in his official capacity as secretary of the Joint Committee on the Improvement of United States Coinage, an ad hoc group formed from these two societies as well as the Architectural League, the Society of American Artists, the National Academy of Design, and the City College of New York. Representatives from these groups had met and were going to tender to Preston an official invitation to the opening ceremonies on May 6. There would be a dinner that night hosted by Kunz at his home. Kunz also took the opportunity to ask that Preston provide either electrotypes or models of the current dollar coin and to repeat his request for the World's Fair award medal. However, Preston would only allow the accepted designs for the fair award medal.[12] Even if he had wanted to comply with Kunz's request, he could not, having returned the rejected reverses to Saint-Gaudens.

Preston did not attend the opening. However, Saint-Gaudens was very much involved, serving on the jury of awards with Daniel French and Olin Warner. There was a first prize of $300 and a second prize of $200. Some 25 obverse and reverse designs were exhibited. It had been intended that the winning designs be made available to the United States government at the conclusion of the exhibit. However, the awards committee went to pains to point out that their awards, dictated by the terms of the competition, in no way committed the jury to an endorsement of the winning designs. In other words the competition was a bust. None of the prominent New York artists had submitted a design.[13]

There was another much more immediate concern for the Mint. This exhibit was the first opportunity for the public to see the combined designs of Saint-Gaudens and Barber for the World's Fair award medal. When the Mint could not provide the rejected designs of Saint-Gaudens, the sculptor took matters into his own hands. He made available his third design that dropped the nude theme entirely. When interviewed at the exhibition by the *New York Tribune*, Saint-Gaudens stated he was very much disgusted by his experience with the government. He could understand why some people objected to his first design with a nude figure although no person "of judgment in matters of art had any criticism on that account." He then draped the nude, which the government also rejected. Finally he prepared "a simple and typical" model. They rejected that one, too. Perhaps, he concluded, "they thought that whatever was plain and simple was not artistic."[14] Gus had at last gotten to the public podium.

That was not the only event on Saint-Gaudens's calendar that month. The evening of May 20 began innocently enough. There was to be a dinner given by Henry Poor, a Wall Street banker, in honor of John Cowdin's tenth wedding anniversary. Both conveniently and ominously, Mr. Cowdin's wife was away touring Europe. The list of invitees, 33 in all, was littered with the names of the leading clubmen of New York. Of course Stanford White and his two partners, McKim and Mead, were included. So was Saint-Gaudens. Even the young Bob Bacon, Theodore Roosevelt's Harvard classmate and future secretary of state, was included. That the party was being held at the studio of John Breese, a leading photographer, mattered not at all. Gus would not want to miss an evening with the boys.

Maybe a meal of 16 courses was a bit excessive. Champagne was the wine of choice for the evening. Maybe the fact that an alleged 144 bottles were consumed was a bit much. It was the 17th course that put the affair over the edge. As the men were lighting their cigars, there came a knock at the studio door. Six waiters entered carrying an enormous pie in the shape of a sphere. The headwaiter cut the crust with a silver knife. As if by magic, the pie parted and a great bevy of canaries flew into the room. But there was more. Out popped 16-year-old Susie Johnson in filmy black gauze and the likeness of a blackbird upon her head. That she wore nothing else was apparent to each of the guests. As she made her appearance all in the party broke out with "Sing a Song of Sixpence."

Gus might have escaped this little peccadillo except that details leaked into the press. On the day of reckoning, his likeness appeared in a ribald rendering on the front page of the second section of a Sunday edition of the *World*. The headline jumped from the page: The "Girl in the Pie" at the Three Thousand Five Hundred Dollar Dinner in Artist Breese's New York Studio. It was most embarrassing for Saint-Gaudens. Much was made of the girl's age and the fact that she had disappeared after the dinner. It was there for his friends and, worst of all, for Gussie to see. No one could ignore his indiscretion.[15] It was an epitome of the excesses of the Gilded Age.

Meanwhile, Charles Barber took the opportunity to visit the exhibit on the 13th of May. It was the professional thing to do. Barber left the exhibit an upset man. He had found none of the design proposals worthy of a second look. It was the manner in which the electrotypes of the award medal were displayed that angered him. The Mint had provided the electrotypes in a case for the exhibit. After receiving the case, someone reversed the Barber and Saint-Gaudens electrotypes. The problem's source stemmed from the Mint's treating the side with the awardee names, being Barber's design, as the obverse, while everyone else considered Saint-Gaudens's Columbus as the obverse. The result of the switch was that the Saint-Gaudens obverse was now displayed more prominently. In the course of making this change, the electrotypes had been mishandled in the remounting process.

In Barber's opinion, there had been "but one desire of those into whose hands the exhibit fell, namely to disgrace it."[16] He never mentioned Saint-Gaudens or the fact that Saint-Gaudens's third reverse was on display in his letter of complaint to George Kunz. From this point forward, Charles Barber would harbor much bitterness toward Saint-Gaudens for this public humiliation.

Seeing the exhibit was not the main purpose for Charles Barber to be traveling that third week of May. Scovill was having troubles with the edges of the dies turning or breaking for the award medal.[17] Barber visited their facilities in Waterbury and found the problem to be associated with the Saint-Gaudens model, as he expected. The obverse model had no rim, causing a weakness in the die at this point. Barber prepared another set of dies in which he essentially planed down or flattened the rim on the obverse. Barber was sure that his change would not mar the appearance of the medal and that no one except the designer would notice.

On this visit, Barber also checked on Scovill's progress toward completion of the medal contract. He noted that there still had been no decision on abbreviating those names that would not fit on the insert-die panels. He could see a serious delay on this account. Goss on behalf of Scovill was writing to Preston for help on the abbreviations again in early June. To compound matters, facsimiles of the award medal began appearing in the press. This award medal originally had great commercial value.[18] The continuing delays in its distribution only added to the frustrations of the exhibitors. As the fair receded in people's memory, the medal's value diminished commensurately.

September found Preston pressing for a completion date. Goss was backpedaling because now there was a problem with the bronzing. The different batches of sienna, a pigment used in the patina process, were not producing a consistent look across the medals. There was still no decision on the abbreviations. Scovill's staff was willing to try their hand at dealing with the different languages involved if the Mint would back them up. Goss also took the opportunity to remind Preston that each medal must be struck one more time after the bronzing. Two more trips to Waterbury were required of Charles Barber. Finally in mid-December the medals were ready for distribution.[19] Preston, however, insisted that Barber inspect them, so in the dead of winter Barber traveled to Waterbury and inspected 23,597 of the medals, all of which had had their award names individually placed on the reverse. Barber completed his assignment on January 11, 1896.[20]

Augustus Saint-Gaudens in 1894.

Newspaper rendering of the "Pie Girl" incident. Saint-Gaudens is at the far right. Stanford White is in the left foreground, and Charles McKim is at the left of the "Pie Girl."

Commemorative Lafayette dollar. Barber's bitter feelings toward Saint-Gaudens were still close to the surface as he prepared the design for this commemorative dollar. (shown enlarged 2x).

142

All was not perfection with this much-delayed medal. The *American Journal of Numismatics* noted the awkward position of Columbus's left leg, which Gus had allowed to fall by the wayside during the medal controversy. While the journal was pleased with the dignity of the figure of Columbus, they believed the overall effect hardly measured up to the high levels of other works by Saint-Gaudens.[21]

However, the Mint was not finished. Medals began to be returned from overseas because of misspellings. In January 1900 the director of the Mint was still requesting Scovill to replace several medals where names had been bungled.[22] The whole affair was anything but what was originally envisioned—a shining example of American medallic art.

The year 1896 was a national election year. The Democrats rallied to the banner of the Free Silver faction and marched off into the wilderness for the next 16 years. John G. Carlisle's political career was over. The people he had represented for a lifetime had deserted him. When he spoke in his hometown of Covington that October in defense of sound money, meaning the gold standard, he was pelted with rotten eggs, brickbats, and cigar stubs.[23] He could not go back to Kentucky politics. Instead he went to New York City and joined the law firm of his former assistant, William Edmond Curtis.

With the Republicans returning to power under William McKinley, Robert Preston was out as Mint director, returning to his old job within the Bureau. George E. Roberts assumed the post in February 1898. Prior to taking the reins at the Mint, he had been a newspaperman in Iowa. He had originally been brought to Washington by Lyman Gage, McKinley's secretary of the Treasury, for his ability to verbalize economic theory supporting the gold standard in easily understood terms. The director slot at the Mint was available, so here he went.[24] Actually, considering that the Mint was a major tool in the Treasury Department's nascent arsenal for fiscal policy, it was not such a bad appointment.

The first year of Roberts's term passed uneventfully. Then, with the coming U.S. participation in the Exposition Universelle or Paris Exposition of 1900, a grassroots movement was initiated to erect a statue to General Lafayette in Paris. This monument was to be America's reciprocal gift to France for Bartholdi's Statue of Liberty. Funding was to come from contributions from schoolchildren on October 19, 1898, the anniversary of the British surrender at Yorktown.[25]

The power behind this effort was Ferdinand Peck, the commissioner general of the United States delegation to the Paris Exposition. The man credited with the idea of the gift of the statue to France was Robert J. Thompson, a business associate of Peck's, who would serve as secretary of the newly formed Lafayette Memorial Commission. The Eastern press, perhaps still smarting over the ascendancy of Chicago in the nation's consciousness, called Thompson a pork packer, stenographer, and private secretary to Peck.[26]

That this memorial would involve the Mint came soon enough. It should have come as no surprise, given that Peck had served on the Finance Committee of the

World's Columbian Exposition Company in Chicago. In January 1899, the Lafayette Memorial Commission went to Congress to ask for supplemental funding of the project in the form of 100,000 souvenir half dollars to be sold for $1 apiece. In the face of the poor public acceptance of the Columbian half dollars and quarters, the mintage would be purposely held down for this third attempt at a souvenir coin, to give the perception of scarcity. At that point it was contemplated that the design would incorporate a miniature of the proposed Lafayette statue on one side and a symbol significant to the event with an appropriate inscription on the other side.[27]

It was another pyramid scheme sanctioned by the politicians. The government would supply about 50,000 ounces of silver at a cost of $25,000 to strike souvenir coins with a face value of $50,000. For budgetary purposes the government would appropriate $25,000 to cover the expense and record a credit to their operating budget of $50,000 in an anachronistic accounting practice called *seigniorage*. Any politician could do this math. Meanwhile the Lafayette Memorial Commission would attempt to sell these coins to the general public for $100,000. This proposal was a deal that Congress could not pass up, and they authorized the issue on March 3, 1899. In the final legislation, instead of half dollars, 50,000 circulating silver dollars would be struck and sold to the public for $2 apiece.[28]

While relatively new to the job, Roberts after several weeks of not hearing from the Lafayette Commission took the initiative, asking Charles Barber to prepare some preliminary sketches. As if on cue, Robert Thompson wrote the next day to state that they could not consider a design for the coin for another two to three weeks until they had selected a monument design.[29] They had good reason to request this delay. It was still their intent to incorporate the statue in some way upon the coin. Learning of this intent, Barber requested a drawing of the monument. Roberts also understood that the commission wanted the head of Lafayette on one side of the coin.[30]

On April 5 Roberts and Thompson met in Washington. They talked over various alternative designs. Roberts was in favor of a design using the heads of Washington and Lafayette in jugate on one side and the monument on the other. On the other hand Thompson related that Ferdinand Peck strongly wanted to include Lafayette's Prayer somewhere in the design. Quite possibly it was this desire that drove the move to the larger tondo of a dollar coin. Thompson was to meet with Barber to discuss the designs further.[31] It would be the first time a commemorative coin design would originate at the Mint.

This prayer inscription was unwieldy and would hurt the coin's appearance. Barber knew it and resisted it in his meeting with Thompson. The prayer was of a length to eliminate all possibilities for beauty and originality on the side of the coin on which it was to be employed. Thompson countered by asking if the size of the dollar coin could be increased. Ignoring the fact that the coin's diameter was fixed by statute, Barber rebutted this proposal by stating that the reduced thickness of the coin would leave less metal available to be moved. As a result, it would be impossible to obtain a suitable impression from the dies using one strike of the coin presses. The Mint was already pushed to the limits striking the dollar coin used for general circulation. This problem would especially be true if Roberts, as Barber expected, picked the jugate heads as one of the design motifs. This style required a greater relief for an effective appearance.[32]

Aftermath

What Barber should have addressed was the possibility of using the medal press to strike these coins for one or two blows to bring up a modest but necessary relief to better show the jugate heads. The time required on the medal press would not have been a factor in a limited issue such as the Lafayette dollar.

Thompson followed up the meeting sending a tentative sketch of the monument, but he also sent two more designs using only a standing figure of Lafayette, saying that the commission had not yet settled whether to use a statue or an equestrian group.[33] Everything was up in the air as Thompson departed Philadelphia to consult with Peck in New York.

Peck wanted the prayer. He had Thompson send Barber a sketch that included the prayer on one side adorned at the top by very small busts of Washington and Lafayette. On the reverse, the monument was flanked on either side by wording in the fields proclaiming the coin's origin and purpose. The commission believed the inclusion of the prayer would generate more interest for the general population.[34] Charles Barber rightly rebelled at this turn of events. This proposal had no artistic merit. The Mint would be striking an oddity for the sake of increasing sales. Surely something both artistic and interesting could be found that would generate the desired sales to the public.[35]

Barber had promised Thompson that he would prepare a sketch for the Lafayette Commission's review. On April 22, 1899, Roberts forwarded Barber's work, which certainly was no surprise to the Mint director. On the obverse were the jugate heads of Washington and Lafayette, and on the reverse a representation of the statue. Roberts went on to set forth the Mint's objections to including a prayer, using Barber's arguments, and stated that the coin would be of interest in Paris, which paid attention to art.[36]

By now Peck was in Paris, where the model sketches were forwarded for his review. Meanwhile Thompson optimistically told the Chicago press that he now expected the coins to be in circulation by July 1. Peck wired back that he favored the one put forth by Barber with Roberts's approval. Barber, upon learning that the design issue appeared to be settled, again requested a more elaborate and refined sketch of the monument and resolution of the date to be used.[37] That issue was driven by the commission's desire to market the coins as soon as possible but using the date of the completion and dedication of 1900.[38]

Meanwhile George Roberts found a work-around concerning the date. In an opinion from the solicitor of the Treasury, the law could be circumvented by having no date and incorporating 1900 into the dedication. The inscription prepared by Barber on the reverse of the coin would now read "Erected by the Youth of the United States in Honor of Lafayette, Paris 1900." Somewhat after the fact, Roberts then sought approval from Thompson for this finessed inscription.[39] That communication did nothing but reopen the whole subject of the designs.

Peck had not altered his opinion that the first sentence of Lafayette's Prayer was worthy of immortalization and would not materially detract from the beauty of the coin. He enclosed a sketch showing how it might be done with separate representations of the faces of Washington and Lafayette. He closed by asking that Roberts take up the matter with Lyman Gage.[40]

Barber harshly called the representations of the two men mere masks. They reminded him of the faces of comedy and tragedy. Washington and Lafayette were deserving of representations that gave dignity and grandeur to their likeness. Barber, however, left it up to Roberts to diplomatically convey the Mint's rejection of this proposal. That earned Charles Barber a trip to New York City to meet with Peck. Paul Wayland Bartlett, sculptor for the memorial, and an advisory group would be at the meeting. Roberts assured Barber that the artists with whom Peck was conferring would surely side with the engraver.[41]

Indeed Barber returned from the meeting feeling vindicated that the Mint would hear no more of the prayer. Peck now understood that space on the coin for decoration was really limited, given the desire to have the monument displayed. The commission now was asking that the monument be represented without the pedestal. As soon as Barber had a photograph from Bartlett, he would make more sketches. Peck also asked that Barber send his sketches directly to him, and said that he would forward them to Roberts. Peck left the meeting feeling that Barber was in concurrence with the commission.

Barber came away with another impression concerning the statue. There was real potential for delay well into 1900 if the depiction of the monument on the coin's reverse was to be accurate. Bartlett's work still must be submitted to a committee for approval.[42]

Now a certain amount of confusion spread among the parties. Peck telegraphed Barber that he understood Roberts had disapproved of the suggestions for changes to the design. He was confused, as Barber approved of them at the meeting. Peck reemphasized that he wanted the modified designs sent to Thompson. Barber then wrote to Roberts that he did not understand the origin of Peck's telegram. He had only indicated a willingness to make additional sketches of proposed modifications pending Roberts's approval. Later it turned out that the disapproval involved only the sketch including the prayer. However, adding to the uncertainty, Roberts was out of the office for a two-week period. The acting director bundled up Barber's rendering of only the Bartlett statue (eliminating the pedestal) and a copy of the telegram from Peck, and sent them to Thompson.[43]

Over the last week in June communications between Thompson, Peck, and Robert Preston as acting director resumed. The commission approved the last design of Barber's with the exception that they wanted the phrase "Lafayette Dollar" positioned directly under the jugate busts. Finally an exasperated Barber was writing to Washington wanting to know if the designs were approved or not. His answer from Preston was that the approval for the inscription positioning would have to await Roberts's return. Thompson then stirred the situation by asking that work now be expedited given that the Lafayette Commission had approved the designs for the coin. Preston, displaying his bureaucratic skills, in turn relayed Thompson's request to Barber and closed by saying that he thought it desirable to let the responsibility for the design rest with the commission.[44]

Accepting Preston's communication as authority, Barber wrote to Roberts stating he would begin die preparation as soon as he was provided a rendering of the equestrian statue.[45] That was July 6. For the next three months the record was completely silent. As he had done while preparing the dies for the World's Columbian Exposition award medal, Barber turned to his work without further comment.

Dialogue reopened in October. Thompson had seen a newspaper interview with George Roberts in which the director supposed that the Lafayette dollar would not be issued until the coming year. The secretary of the Lafayette Memorial Commission reacted instantly, having understood that the coin would be into their hands for distribution in time for the holidays.[46] Roberts in reply was forced to admit that he had disengaged himself from the project. He had learned of changes underway on the monument and had deduced that the coin would be delayed as well, given Barber's desire that the statue be accurately represented on the reverse. He had to admit that he had not conferred recently with Barber and that Thompson might be better informed than he as to where Barber stood with the engraving.[47] It was clear from this exchange that the commission wanted Barber to move forward regardless of what changes might happen at a later date to the monument.

On November 23, the first "specimen" coin was forwarded to Roberts from Philadelphia. Roberts duly sent it on to Ferdinand Peck. A very pleased Peck replied three days later. He had shown the coin to Frank Millet and A.C. Coolidge. Millet had charge of the decoration of the U.S. government's pavilion at the Exposition Universelle and was on the selection jury of the fine arts jury for the overall exposition as well. Just as important, he was a friend of Saint-Gaudens's. Millet pronounced the coin artistic and better in every way than the regular dollar coin. That statement was a bit unfair to the old "buzzard" dollar of George Morgan. The Treasury Department in releasing this statement to the press failed to realize the unstated critique embedded in Millet's praise.[48] The artistic bar for United States coin designs needed to be raised.

The commission requested a small ceremony with the press in attendance to celebrate the first strike. Roberts set the event in Philadelphia for December 14, the 100th anniversary of the death of George Washington. Fifty thousand of these dollar coins were minted that day. However, the event was all a show. The first striking, a Proof, had been sent to Roberts the day before. Ultimately, President McKinley would convey the coin to the Republic of France.[49]

In a final footnote, George Roberts agreed in December to make the dies for the Lafayette dollar available for exhibition in the government pavilion for the Exposition. Barber got wind of this action and, ever fearful of criticism, objected. George Roberts relented and ordered the destruction of dies with the completion of the authorized issue.[50]

Overall this issue was a modest commercial success, with sales amounting to 36,000 coins. The remaining 14,000 of the authorized issue ultimately were melted.[51] Subsequent critics would point out flaws in Barber's work. To insure that the design struck up well, Barber washed out much of the obverse relief, giving the busts a linear appearance. Barber could easily have experimented by striking a pattern of this design in the medal press using one or more blows. Had he done so, he would have advanced the Mint's knowledge of best practices. Instead, the engraver had sacrificed art to coin relief.

Critics also scored Barber for the lack of originality of the obverse composition. The final result is all too close to the medal by Peter Krider struck for the centennial of the battle of Yorktown in 1881. The reverse also suffered from the unwieldy inscription to avoid placing the date of 1899 on the coin. In retrospect that whole circumvention was really unnecessary since the coins did not reach the public's hands until after the New Year of 1900.[52]

Also, in a curious move, Barber gave credit to the sculptor by placing "Bartlett" on the base of the statue. Coming from the man who gave no credit to Olin Warner for his designs for the souvenir Columbian half dollar, the action raises the question as to why he would do so this time around.

Paul Bartlett's father, Truman, had known Saint-Gaudens since his student days in Paris. Over the years, as Saint-Gaudens's success increased, Truman Bartlett's attitude toward his fellow sculptor had soured considerably. By now the elder Bartlett, whose sculpture career had fizzled, was bitterly outspoken in his prejudice against Saint-Gaudens. Paul had provided some of his source material for allegations against Gus. In Truman Bartlett's mind, Saint-Gaudens had kept commissions from being awarded to Paul, and he believed that Paul had received the Lafayette equestrian in spite of Saint-Gaudens's efforts on his own behalf.[53] It can easily be inferred that when Paul Bartlett and Charles Barber came into contact at the New York meeting they would have shared their negative feelings toward Saint-Gaudens. Barber never revealed the reason for placing Bartlett's name on the base. However, it would be difficult not to take it as a barb aimed at Saint-Gaudens.

Part 3

On the National Stage

Chapter 10

A Sherman Connection

Gus had always admired William Tecumseh Sherman. "The general had remained in my eye as the typical American soldier ever since I had formed that idea of him during the Civil War."[1]

When Sherman moved to New York City in the fall of 1886, it was only natural that Gus would want very badly to have the general sit for him. He wasn't alone; any New York artist worth his salt wanted a shot at the general. Stanford White approached Sherman's daughter, Rachel, on his behalf. However, she wasn't the best go-between, being considered within the family as a spendthrift.[2] In typical fashion, the crusty old general would have none of it. He simply refused to be pestered by any more "damned sculptors."[3]

"Cump" Sherman was not the first from that family to come into Saint-Gaudens's life. That distinction belonged to the general's niece, Elizabeth. "Lizzie," as her friends called her, was a reigning beauty, well established in Washington society by the mid-1880s. Little is documented of this early relationship between Lizzie and Gus other than hearsay. Gus certainly was smitten by the woman. A friend once observed that she liked to flirt and tease, to kiss and cajole.[4] Gus at this early stage would have had little exposure to a woman of this social standing. Sherman family legend has Saint-Gaudens captivated by Lizzie.[5] Yet that was as far as the relationship went. Elizabeth was well aware of her position within society. There was an inner reserve and shield that was impenetrable to all, including Saint-Gaudens.

Her marriage had been arranged to the much older Don Cameron, heir to the Cameron political dynasty. Don was a widower with children close to Lizzie's age. Yet her most unusual conquest was Henry Adams. Adams had tired of university life at Harvard and moved to Washington to better observe the American political scene. He and his wife, Clover, had established a most unique salon in Washington that glittered with the luminaries of America. Lizzie was able to hold her own within this circle, increasingly attracting the attention of Henry. Their relationship flowered as the wrongness of her marriage to the gruff, hard-drinking Pennsylvania senator became more and more apparent to her.

A likely introduction to Gus may well have been through the Adamses. Henry had maintained his relationship with the sculptor from Trinity Church days through their mutual friend, John La Farge. Clover and Henry would stop in New York to dine with La Farge and Saint-Gaudens.[6] Lizzie as a friend would naturally have followed.

151

Lizzie Cameron was close to her "Uncle Cump." With her father's death in 1879, he had become a surrogate father to her.[7] Having failed once to get Sherman to sit for a portrait bust, it would not do for Gus to again use a woman in an approach. It also was not in his shy personality to approach the general directly. So, the rest of 1886 and most of 1887 passed without action.

Then Saint-Gaudens and White put their heads together for one last try. Sherman, since moving to New York, had been lionized by its high society. He rarely missed a theatrical opening.[8] Naturally White, although despairing of success, had one more connection that was worth a try. The architect was in the process of renovating the Villard house that had been purchased by Whitelaw Reid.

Reid, originally from rural Ohio, was an accomplished newspaperman. Using his wife's money, he had just acquired the *New York Tribune*, where he had been the long-time managing editor. He and the general had become close in New York in spite of Reid having crossed swords with Sherman as a war correspondent. At Shiloh, Reid had been quick to point out Sherman's and Grant's unpreparedness at the start of that battle.[9] Reid was agreeable to trying to arrange a sitting. First he approached Rachel, without success. Then, when the general paid Reid a visit in his home, the newspaper editor tackled him in person. In Reid's words, "He swore a little, but finally consented to give Saint-Gaudens the sittings."[10]

Gus was ecstatic over his success. The Sherman portrait bust would be a labor of love. That meant no money would change hands. He optimistically promised the general that he would complete his work with two sittings a week over one month. Starting on January 3, 1888, every Tuesday and Saturday promptly at 2:00 p.m. the general would appear at Saint-Gaudens's studio for a two-hour sitting. Sherman proved to be a good sitter, with one exception. He appeared uneasy when Gus would walk to one side or the other to study his profile. His eyes would follow the sculptor alertly. If Gus moved too far, his head turned too.[11] As progress was made, Gus grew optimistic over the results, saying, "I have not spoiled it yet thank God, in fact I'm sure it's better."[12]

January stretched into February with each session taking the full two hours. The general's patience was wearing thin. At one point Gus stepped over the line. He could not get General Sherman to button his coat and look his high rank. In exasperation, he turned to Sherman and said, "Look here, General! Where you see portraits of Bismarck, Von Moltke and other great generals, their coats are always buttoned up tight to the throat, and they look their rank. Do just for a short time, button yours up and set your tie straight so I can get it as it should be!" Gus had gone too far. Sherman fixed the sculptor with a hard stare and finally said, "Saint-Gaudens, I don't give a tinker's damn how men chose to wear their coats, but I want you to know that the General of the Armies of the United States of America will wear his coat any — way he pleases." Gus told years later of sweat breaking out all over his head. He was in jeopardy of "not getting the man," so necessary to the greatness of the piece.[13] Yet it was Gus's mistake and not Sherman's. If Gus had gotten the general to do as he asked, a masterpiece would have been spoiled.

Finally on March 6, after 18 sittings, the portrait was complete—but not without Sherman threatening to stop the sittings. He even insisted upon a "confidential presentation" when the work was done.[14] Though one month stretched into nine weeks,

Elizabeth Sherman Cameron, from a watercolor by Fernand Paillet (circa 1889). Augustus Saint-Gaudens was smitten with this reigning beauty of Washington high society, General William Tecumseh Sherman's niece.

The Saint-Gaudens ordination announcement for Tom Sherman.

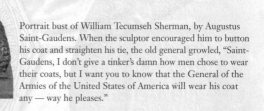

Portrait bust of William Tecumseh Sherman, by Augustus Saint-Gaudens. When the sculptor encouraged him to button his coat and straighten his tie, the old general growled, "Saint-Gaudens, I don't give a tinker's damn how men chose to wear their coats, but I want you to know that the General of the Armies of the United States of America will wear his coat any — way he pleases."

153

Gus was timely in this work. In the process, he had become even more attached to the general. Gus had had the rare benefit of seeing the real man without the trappings of fame. The sculptor felt confident enough of his relationship with Sherman to ask the general if he could introduce to him Robert Louis Stevenson, for whom Gus was doing a portrait medallion.

During these sittings, Sherman talked profusely about his war exploits. Gus was particularly impressed by the manner in which Sherman spoke, forcefully and directly to the point. He vividly remembered in later years a point the general made. During the Grand Review of the armies in Washington at the conclusion of the Civil War, the other commanders ordered their men to clean up before marching in review. Sherman refused, saying, "By no means. Let them be seen as they fought."[15] And so the general was seen in the finished work.

The bust is mounted upon a rectangular block that bears the inscriptions, which in turn rests upon a ribbon-bound pillow of laurel. The bust faces forward with the head slightly turned to the proper left. It is as if Sherman is watching as Saint-Gaudens walks around to get a better look at his profile. However, the masterstroke was simply that the general's uniform is unbuttoned at the throat and his string tie all over to one side of his carelessly turned-over collar.[16]

As his work drew to a close, Gus knew he wanted more. He had tried midway into the sittings to get the general to sit upon a horse. Sherman refused point-blank, saying he had gotten through doing that 20 years previously.[17] This time Gus did enlist Lizzie, who told Uncle Cump that the sculptor wanted him to sit upon a horse so that he would have an excellent likeness from which to do an equestrian statue some time in the future—that is, after the general's death. Sherman still refused, saying that no general ever had sat or would sit for an equestrian statue. More softly, he told Lizzie that he could not help but smile at her picture of him sitting upon Saint-Gaudens's hobbyhorse for an indefinite time for a statue that the sculptor would erect some 50 years hence. Saint-Gaudens had the bust, however, which was sufficient to complete a plaster cast that could be enlarged to life size after the model was gone.[18] There would be no more sittings.

Gus's association with the Sherman family did not end there. The contacts with Lizzie continued. Clover Adams, having struggled with mental depression most of her adult life, committed suicide in December 1885. In the aftermath, Henry and Lizzie drew closer. In the fall of 1886, with John La Farge's input, Henry commissioned Saint-Gaudens to do a memorial for his wife's grave.[19] In late fall 1888 Gus had at last started. As with his other commissions, this one progressed in fits and starts. In August 1890 Adams and La Farge left the country for the South Seas. As work neared completion, Lizzie became Gus's liaison, checking progress at the cemetery.[20] In March 1891, the memorial was put in place at the grave, with Stanford White contributing the accompanying stonework.

To Gus's disgust, Lizzie and Adams's personal secretary took photographs and sent them to Henry. Gus had wanted Henry to form his own first impression within the context of the memorial itself. He excused Lizzie from his rage with all of it falling on the head of the personal secretary. When Henry did return in February 1892, the work met his wholehearted approval.[21] It was a source of pride and satisfaction throughout the remainder of his years. It also cemented Saint-Gaudens as one of Henry Adams's intimate friends.

There was another connection to the family, through Lizzie Cameron as well. General Sherman's son, Tom, had become particularly fond of his first cousin. Their friendship had blossomed when Tom had been under a doctor's care with ear problems in Washington in early 1888. Lizzie had opened her home to him and offered to care for him while he was recovering.[22]

When Tom was ordained a Catholic priest on July 7, 1889, Saint-Gaudens produced an announcement for the event. The composition was centered upon an angel. While not signed, the work clearly came either from his hand or from his studio under his direction. The angel is straight from the Anna Maria Smith tomb in Newport, Rhode Island, signed by Louis Saint-Gaudens in 1887.[23] Most importantly, this work was the first in which Saint-Gaudens placed an angel in the context of the Sherman family. Whether it was conscious or subconscious, this association would sprout roots and take hold.

William Tecumseh Sherman died February 14, 1891, after a brief illness brought on by asthma.[24] Along with all of New York City and the nation as well, Gus was saddened by the great general's passing. Lizzie was devastated by his death. Charles Beaman, Gus's longtime friend, stepped in to arrange for the taking of the death mask. Saint-Gaudens would arrive at the family home the night of the 16th, accompanied by Daniel Chester French. Upon arriving, Saint-Gaudens broke down, leaving French to take the death mask.[25]

The citizens of New York wasted no time in forming a committee to erect a proper memorial to the general who had chosen their city as his final home. At once Saint-Gaudens wanted this commission. However, there were thoughts of having either a limited or an open competition. A competition would not do for Gus. If one were held, he would decline as he had others, regardless of how badly he wanted the opportunity. However, he preemptively sent a sketch model for consideration.

As March progressed, Gus was occupied with the placement of the memorial to Clover Adams. Sherman's niece thought the bronze at the gravesite "inexpressibly noble and beautiful."[26] It was within this context that Lizzie would find herself along with Tom Sherman, eldest surviving son of the general, in another memorial project.

On April 9, the committee met and announced their decision. They had considered both a limited and open competition. They dismissed an open competition because of the possibility of having someone other than an American create the work. Then they rejected a limited or invited competition as well. Saint-Gaudens was to receive the prize. They believed the circumstances were exceptional: Saint-Gaudens had recently completed a bust of the general, much to everyone's satisfaction; he had been the choice of the family to make the death mask; and most importantly, members of the family were very desirous that he be selected to design the statue. Gus was to provide both an equestrian bronze of Sherman and a figure of "Victory."[27]

There was only one hitch. In a letter agreement of May 21, 1891, Gus agreed to a completion date of May 1, 1894.[28] Saint-Gaudens had wanted this commission above all others. Now that he had it, he had to recognize that his plate was entirely too full. Most pressing, of course, was the Shaw, but there were others. The *Diana* was waiting to be installed atop the tower of Stanford White's Madison Square Garden. The Garfield Monument for Philadelphia, given to Gus in 1885, was not done. Work on the Peter Cooper Monument remained—one to which Gus had personal ties. The equestrian General Logan in Chicago was unfinished. These were just the major commissions.

It now becomes obvious why Gus was cool to the approach of the Mint at the beginning of that April concerning the redesign of the subsidiary silver coins. He could have circumvented their desire for a competition just as he had the Sherman Committee's. Now the motivation for Gus's withdrawal from all consideration in the coin design process a week after receiving the Sherman commission is obvious.

Gus immediately responded to the family's offer of help, saying, "I shall avail myself of all you can give me both as regards manner and dress as they will be of great value." Yet he put off signing the contract (which included an initial payment of $4,500) for almost a year until he completed a rough model.[29] This plaster was the one that the Shaw Monument Committee got wind of, aggravating an already deteriorating relationship with that group that in turn led to so much grief over the World's Columbian Exposition award medal.

Stanford White had once observed that "even with a contract and a time and price set, it was hard enough to get anything out of Saint-Gaudens."[30]

Chapter 11

In Search of an Angel

The Sherman matter sat and sat while Gus worked off his backlog of earlier commissions. There was one in particular that was eating him alive: he still did not have the Shaw completed. He had had troubles with the execution of this work, redoing the heads of the soldiers and struggling with the composition of the allegorical figure.[1] When he made temporary peace with John Murray Forbes in November 1893, this commission was in serious trouble.

The preceding September the committee had become concerned about the site for the memorial when Saint-Gaudens informed them of yet another delay. The City of Boston had now appropriated $19,500 for the preparation of a terrace upon which this bas-relief would be positioned. However, there was no formal arrangement between the parties. A change of city administrations coupled with Saint-Gaudens's continuing delays might result in the city using the terrace for something else. As a result Atkinson asked Saint-Gaudens as a man of honor to fix a date, certain without reservation, for completion of the monument. The committee was losing confidence in his ability to complete the commission and Atkinson had stood between the two parties as long as he could. Saint-Gaudens came back with a deadline of May 1894.[2]

Then the committee heard a rumor that Saint-Gaudens had taken down a large part of his work. He must better adapt it to McKim's architectural frame. In plain English, there were issues with the size and placement of the angel within the bas-relief. Atkinson at once queried Saint-Gaudens as to the status of the project. In February 1893 Saint-Gaudens had told them that all of the figures were completed in clay, and the larger part in plaster. The one exception was the low-relief allegorical figure floating over Colonel Shaw and the marching soldiers. It had not even been started.[3] Now in September 1893, the horse and rider were not complete. Work remained on the animal's tail and the frock of Shaw's coat. This portion was in plaster. Four of the 17 soldiers were complete in clay. The allegorical figure of the angel was completed in the small model and work was being done on its enlargement. He would have the work complete in two months.[4]

Forbes had been so worked up over this lack of real progress that he had proposed, only somewhat tongue in cheek, that they consider a new monument to Shaw by Daniel Chester French. He valued Saint-Gaudens's work very highly but confessed to deep shame for having the Shaw linger at a snail's pace without a protest that would have either given the committee a monument or left it free to seek another sculptor.[5]

Edward Atkinson, who had done so much to preserve the peace between the committee and Saint-Gaudens, gave in; this time he forwarded Forbes's letter to New York. He told the sculptor that the time for any further concessions or delays was gone. The committee had already yielded a great deal too much to Saint-Gaudens's reputation as an artist. Receiving this letter, Gus headed for Boston for that November meeting. Whatever was said in his meeting with Forbes brought peace, at least from this quarter, for the next 12 months.

The Shaw Committee sat on the sidelines as the award-medal drama played out in the spring and summer of 1894. By March, Gus still had not solved the dilemma of the angel. He sent two sketches to McKim, asking his opinion. After talking to his partners, McKim picked the angel conveying greater severity. Saint-Gaudens spent the summer at his second home in Cornish, while the Shaw relief sat in a studio in New York. In October Gus told Atkinson that he was back at work in New York and engaged in the final push to complete the memorial.[6] Finally, in December of that year, Forbes asked rhetorically what could they do about Saint-Gaudens—or should they drift a while further? Forbes called "the Saint" and his eternal angel's wing exasperating. Forbes never had good things to say about the allegorical angel. He then reminded himself that molasses catches more flies than vinegar.[7]

Meanwhile Saint-Gaudens knew he had to do something to break his logjam of work. If he did not get help, he would choke to death. He had cabled Phimister Proctor in rural France in 1894 to come help him with the Logan Monument. For a young sculptor such as Proctor, this invitation was more like a summons, coming from the likes of Augustus Saint-Gaudens. Gus sent the sculptor to Cornish for this work. As it neared completion he approached Proctor about coming to New York for the Sherman horse at a satellite studio.

Gus had done some very preliminary sketches and had some idea of what he wanted for the Sherman. Logan had been a flamboyant character and Gus had used a picturesque mount. That would not do for Sherman. Gus called the general a campaigner. His horse would have to be plain, a more serviceable mount. Saint-Gaudens and Proctor toured the horse shows looking for just the right horse to model. Finally they heard of a famous jumper on Long Island named Ontario. Proctor started the work immediately. The horse settled easily enough into the modeling routine. Proctor was always concerned lest the animal he was modeling spook and cause some damage to his work. Things went well enough until one day in the winter while Proctor and an assistant were working on modeling the horse's hindquarters. A potbellied stove was going in the studio to keep the place warm. All of a sudden Ontario seemed to jump in all four directions at once, kicking the assistant against the wall. Proctor immediately reached for the model to keep it out of danger. Luckily no one was hurt. Ontario in an idle moment had licked the red-hot stove!

In Search of an Angel

Proctor had helped with two of Saint-Gaudens's problems—however, not with the Shaw. Yet Gus was optimistic when Atkinson asked him for an update in April 1895. Saint-Gaudens would finish his work by the first of May. The allegorical figure of the angel was in place and requiring only a few final touches. The rest was done. He expected that the work could be put up in October.[8] Then in July Saint-Gaudens told Atkinson that he had just finished the angel. He was going away for a week. The work would be ready upon his return. He would then look it over one more time before having it cast in plaster.

There was now anticipation that Saint-Gaudens would request a draw against his contract. This advance would allow him to go abroad for the summer and rest while the statue was being cast in bronze.[9] These positive status reports seemed to lull the Shaw Committee to sleep. They should have known when progress did not develop that Gus, upon his return after a week's break, had embarked upon another round of changes on the angel. Upon seeing the enlarged flying figure, Gus had become convinced that it should be smaller.[10]

That was not the only absence from the studio. Saint-Gaudens was habitually absentminded about paying his assistants on a regular basis. One time during 1895 and 1896, he was gone for a much longer time than normal, leaving his assistants strapped for money. They solved the difficulty by pawning a gold medal that Saint-Gaudens kept in his desk. When he reappeared and paid them, they redeemed the pawned piece and replaced it, unbeknownst to Gus.[11]

Reality did not set in for the committee when the sculptor missed his October completion date. It hit the following May, in 1896, when Gus alerted the committee that a "construction difficulty" would prevent the Shaw from being put in the hands of the molder for a few weeks. The delay had nothing to do with the artistic portion of the work; however, it was inconveniencing him financially and he needed a bridge payment from the committee of $500 or $1,000.[12] That request got their attention.

Atkinson visited Saint-Gaudens's studio ten days later. The work was complete except for the allegorical angel. The figure was itself complete and was being molded in plaster. Unsaid was that virtually all work on the Shaw over the winter consisted of Saint-Gaudens tinkering with the angel in an attempt to get it right by trial and error. Still, Atkinson agreed that Saint-Gaudens's work was essentially done.[13]

Then the situation blew up in June. The artist had decided to again reconstruct the angel. Mrs. Shaw and the committee were upset that they were not being given any say in this matter.[14] After 15 years with Saint-Gaudens, Atkinson was exhausted and feeling he was at fault for not somehow forcing the Shaw to completion.

> We now are at the parting of ways. Your dissatisfaction with the present figure is with the size and not with the composition. The work is to be placed under great trees facing north, where it is not probable that one person in a hundred thousand would ever know the difference. You have given me your written and personal assurance that your part of the work was completed. On that assurance I was authorized to pay you the money lately paid you. Without it I was not. On that assurance I have given official information to the public, to the speaker of the [Massachusetts] House of Representatives, Mr. Von Meyer,[15] who procured the

appropriation from the city for the terrace, to the discontented subscribers, few in number [they were dying off], but now beginning to ask why the Committee permits such delay. I think you have no right either as artist, contractor or in your personal relation to myself to go back upon that assurance except on the alternative presented in my letter and on the assumption that that alternative will not delay the immediate molding of the work as it is, subject to a change in the mold if you get the new figure ready in time and if that figure is more satisfactory to yourself than the present one,—a very doubtful point in my mind.

Atkinson went on to say that should the statue not be erected the following May, he could not in good conscience continue to serve as treasurer of the fund. Given the delays he could only judge his own performance as incompetent and he must therefore cease to be involved with the commission.[16]

This letter received Saint-Gaudens's careful attention because the one person he could not afford to alienate was Atkinson. He replied that the angel was finished. He was entirely satisfied with it and was making no changes whatsoever. What he was doing to lengthen the figure was purely a mechanical process. The work would be ready next May. The lengthened figure was now being transferred to the big model. When it was pulled together, he would call the committee to visit and have photographs taken.[17]

Forbes was not pleased with Saint-Gaudens's response. In a letter to Atkinson he referred to Saint-Gaudens as "your Saint" and talked of the "cussed angel." Saint-Gaudens was demanding pay for clay when he should have long previously provided the bronze. Forbes closed by saying, "Brass is your Saint's proper metal and I should like to see a horse collar fastened around his neck."[18]

This time Saint-Gaudens delivered. The committee came together at his studio at 11:00 a.m. on September 3, 1896, to view the essentially completed work.[19] There would still be tinkering on the angel to the very end. A crisis was yet again brought under control.

Now with the sculptor's work nearly completed, Atkinson noted that there would be an excess in funds in the committee's bank account approximating $7,000 once all bills were paid. Saint-Gaudens was aware of this overage and expected that it would accrue to him.[20] While they had reason to be vexed at him for the many delays, Atkinson felt there was justification in granting the request because of the quality of the work. He noted that Saint-Gaudens had through the numerous delays become a contributor to the statue, which when measured in the money that he might have gained from other work not undertaken would have been more than double the whole fund.[21] This logic both placated the committee and provided a cover for outside questions.

The committee still proceeded cautiously. Contrary to general practice, they would pay the founder directly. They also insisted on a mortgage upon the work, in spite of existing insurance policies, to better cover their risks.[22]

Saint-Gaudens now returned to the Sherman Monument. For more than a year the sculpted horse had waited for his rider. Now the seed planted in the form of an angel at Tom Sherman's ordination sprang to life. This allegory, however, must represent the celebration of victory, and not death, as with the Shaw. No ordinary depiction of an angel would do. His thinking could have been influenced by the Nike of Paionios recently unearthed in Greece, or perhaps the Winged Victory of Samothrace, then on display at the Louvre. In any case, Gus's angel must reflect the general's relentless drive for victory. The likeness of Sherman would of course come from the bust completed almost ten years previously. Still, converting a portrait bust to a man on horseback would be no easy task, even for Augustus Saint-Gaudens.

For the figure of Sherman, he found an Italian peasant model who approximated the general's build and held his head in much the same manner as the general.[23] On February 17, 1897, Gus was writing Rose Nichols that he had the nude of Sherman done and the following week would put his clothes on him. He also wrote that he had had a go at the figure for the Angel of Victory the previous Sunday. The model was Harriette Eugenia Anderson. Hettie was an African American of light complexion from Columbia, South Carolina. The sculptor had first learned of her through Stanford White some two years previously. In Gus's opinion, she had the figure of a goddess.[24]

The Swedish painter Anders Zorn spent that day with Gus. They had known each other since the days of the World's Columbian Exposition. The man was quite well known for his etchings. As Gus worked, so did Zorn. It took Zorn about an hour etching directly on the copper to produce the scene of Gus seated with fatigue in his face while Hettie rested in the background, having just completed a modeling session.[25]

On May 30, 1897, the saga of the Shaw came to an end. The work was dedicated in Boston to great acclaim. The genius of Saint-Gaudens becomes apparent in this wonderful relief. However, his close friend of so many years, Paul Bion, had puzzled over the angel just before his death and wondered what it contributed to the work. It was one thing to use an angel in conjunction with a gravestone; it was quite another to incorporate it into a monumental work. Saint-Gaudens could be forgiven if this marriage of reality with the allegory needed some refinement. That was yet to come.

As Saint-Gaudens progressed on the Sherman Monument that year, he remained America's preeminent sculptor. However, his former comrades at the École des Beaux-Arts, judging his work from photographs, believed him over-praised and felt he would receive no such appreciation in France. Not the least of his considerations was the snubbing of his World's Columbian Exposition award medal in the Paris Salon of 1894. Gus felt he must face this criticism head-on. Thanks to the generosity of Atkinson, he had the windfall from the Shaw. He must go to France, exhibit a monumental work at the Paris Salon, and subject his creative ability to French critics. All of his friends in New York discouraged him from taking this action. Still, in justice to himself and his work he believed he had no choice. In November 1897 he, Gussie, and Homer arrived in Paris.[26] The figure of Sherman, the horse, and the angel went with him.

Gus was not alone in Paris. Lizzie came with Henry Adams discreetly at a distance. For her as with Gus, 1897 was a year of change. Don Cameron, having not stood for reelection to the Senate, wished no part of Washington and rented their home to the incoming vice president. Lizzie suddenly had no base of operations. She could go into self-exile with her husband or she could admit the marriage was a sham and leave. She had no grounds for divorce and Don was unwilling to grant one.[27] Lizzie chose trial separation and headed ultimately for Paris, far from the sharpness of gossiping Washington tongues.

Upon arriving, Saint-Gaudens endured the agony of finding suitable space for a studio. The task was made more complicated because of the space requirements for the equestrian Sherman. He also had other projects to consider, including the Boston Public Library groups. However, the Sherman came first of all. The New York committee had been upset about this seeming delay as the contractual completion date had long passed. Yet he felt they would be pleased with the final product. He found four connected studios on the Left Bank and proceeded to combine them into one large studio and a separate inner sanctum. While he was at it with the Sherman, days came and went rapidly because of his enthusiasm.[28] However, there was another reason for his unusual diligence on the Sherman: he intended to exhibit the completed work in the 1900 Exposition Universelle in Paris. Still he felt there would be no problem. He wrote Gussie on February 26, 1898, that the model—including the Angel of Victory—was entirely finished.[29] Of course Gus was not allowing for the endless refinements that he must work through.

Initially Gus had only one assistant in Paris. Subsequently he brought in Henry Hering, who had studied under his guidance for four years at the Art Students League. Louis Saint-Gaudens came and went.[30] In 1899, Gus would also add 23-year-old James Earle Fraser, who had won the prize in the 1898 Paris Salon for best work by an American. He was studying at the École des Beaux-Arts. Most important, Fraser had won the American Art Association's Wanamaker Prize, for which Gus had been a juror.[31] His winning exhibit had been a model of his Western-themed *End of the Trail.*

Fraser recalled later that Gus liked his Indian.[32] Several days afterward, a letter from Gus arrived, asking Fraser to bring his work to Gus's studio for a critique. An excited Fraser arrived eager for input from the famous sculptor. At the end of the session Saint-Gaudens ask Fraser to help him at the studio. Fraser accepted. He would study at the École in the mornings and work for Saint-Gaudens in the afternoons. The job consisted of making enlargements from the five-foot scale model of the Sherman that Gus worked with in his personal studio. Fraser's first task was Sherman's sword.[33]

Even with this help, conditions in the studio could be chaotic. An accident happened to the cast of one of the horse's hind legs. Gus was not concerned; he had a duplicate horse in Cornish. He sent a man back to retrieve the duplicate leg and oversee its packing. When the man returned three weeks later, Gus found that he had

The Shaw monument, honoring Colonel Robert Gould Shaw and the African-American 54th Massachusetts Volunteer Infantry. Even after the dedication in 1897, Saint-Gaudens retained a plaster model upon which he continued to make changes in the angel. This model is now on exhibit at the National Gallery of Art in Washington, DC.

Anders Zorn etching of Augustus Saint-Gaudens with Hettie Anderson while working on the model for the Angel of Victory in 1897.

brought the wrong hind leg. Later it would make a great story, but at the time it put gray hairs on his head.[34]

The angel underwent modifications. The head no longer resembled the bust he had made of Hettie Anderson. Gus was also struggling with drapery for the angel. The flow of this drapery was critical to the look and feeling that he wanted to achieve. He had four copies of the nude modeled by Miss Anderson upon which he arranged the drapery. He always considered arranging flowing draperies a complicated task. He used muslin calicoes that had a little starch in them. After wetting them, he would lay them over the casts, pinning them here and there to give the effect he desired. Once dried, he would go over it all with shellac using a very delicate brush, doing the hollows first to strengthen the rest as he proceeded. It was a matter of personal taste. He took four weeks with these models. One came out remarkably well, allowing Gus to proceed with a working model of the angel.[35]

As 1898 drew to a close, Gus was well along with the Sherman, writing confidently to Stanford White that the model was done. He was planning some travel as his assistants translated the model into plaster.[36] Then the same hind leg on the full-sized work of the horse plagued him again. Gus noticed that it looked out of proportion in relation to the rest of the animal. He discovered that the leg constantly sagged, and his assistants had been patching the resulting cracks without his knowledge. Over time, the leg had thus lengthened by three inches. A late Saturday afternoon found Gus frantically tearing through his studio looking for his original measurements for the horse.[37] His eye had finally caught the problem. Once past this hurdle, he began with some reluctance the process of pointing up the Sherman—however, he was not happy with the general's cloak. In November he had enlisted Gussie to make little cloaks to drape over small experimental models. He had learned that the simpler the cloak arrangement, the better. After resting, he stopped the process to have another go at the cloak. In frustration he described his trials with the cloak to Homer: "The Sherman after much turmoil will be ready for the salon. I've just remodeled the cloak over for the 10,000th time and today it seems beautiful. Tomorrow it will probably appear hellish and so things go." With the help of a manikin, he was finally able to satisfy himself with a much simpler arrangement for the offending garment.[38]

Gus's plan was to exhibit first at the 1899 Paris Salon. He intended to show Sherman on horseback in full size, accompanied by a small model including the Angel of Victory. This Salon would give him his first indication of how well he was progressing and perhaps how his work would be received by the Paris critics. If all went well, he would then exhibit the completed Sherman Monument at the Exposition Universelle in 1900.

If possible, Gus's personal life was even more chaotic than his studio life during this period. Gussie did not particularly like Paris the second time around. In the summer of 1898 she left for the spas. The following summer and fall she returned to Cornish in a visit prolonged by the death of her mother. Meanwhile, at some point in 1899 Gus brought his mistress Davida and their son Louis over. In a letter of exasperation he wrote that fall to his brother, Gus said that Gussie didn't like Paris and was coming back on November 1. Davida didn't like it either and wanted to leave. He called it a funny world.[39]

Depression now plagued the sculptor. In a letter to Gussie he complained of being so depressed and blue that he felt as he had only once before. He was suffering from a complete lack of ambition. He felt indifference about all that he had cared so much for before, and had a desire to be ended with life.[40] This letter was not the only documentation of Gus's depression. Henry Adams in his writings told of a time in Paris when Saint-Gaudens showed up at his doorstep to pour out his woes. In Adams's words, the sculptor was suffering from an oppression of life and dread of death. He complained of insomnia and depression. In typical Adams fashion, Henry flippantly replied that he never felt any other way and actually rather liked it.[41]

Counterbalancing the depression and perhaps as a result of it, there were periods of relaxation when Gus left the studio behind. His friendship and affection for Elizabeth Cameron continued. They exchanged mildly flirtatious notes concerning social engagements. Gus would dine with her to celebrate the Fourth of July in 1899. The sculptor wrote Rose Nichols of motoring with Adams through the French countryside.[42] On one such excursion, Saint-Gaudens and Adams went to the cathedral at Amiens. Gus was greatly moved by the play of light over the stone figures on the facade of the cathedral. Adams knew that Saint-Gaudens was going through some low times; however, he tended to dismiss Gus's condition as neurasthenic.[43]

The opening of the Salon for 1899 was scheduled for May 1. As April waned, the studio became a bedlam. Saint-Gaudens had 11 molders working night and day on the Sherman. Sometimes Gus would laugh, sometimes cry, and sometimes both during the process. He said there were times when he would rush into the street and howl.[44] Somehow he met the deadline.

Now, as the Sherman stood in the place of honor in the center of the garden at the Champ de Mars, Gus for the first time could feel cocky. Still he would come to the garden with his assistants for additional work from first light until the Salon opened at 10 in the morning. Henry Adams in his strolls stopped almost every day to admire the colossal work. Together with an exhibit of his other works from the Salon of 1898 that had achieved much critical acclaim, Gus was well on his way to achieving the recognition in France that he so earnestly sought.[45]

Next the work turned to the Exposition Universelle. As planned, Gussie returned in November only to find Gus still poking around on the Angel of Victory, which she had expected to have been long since completed. Henry Adams had observed that summer that Saint-Gaudens was spending all of his time getting ready to work and accomplishing nothing.[46] Gus had again struggled with the angel prior to the exhibition on the Champ de Mars. As the exhibition ended, the angel had acquired a free, forward-swinging gait and her features were youthful, soft, and sweet. Now in the late fall Gus had changed the model for the angel yet again. Gussie called it very stunning. Saint-Gaudens had pulled it all together. The angel grasped a palm leaf in her left hand. Her right hand was raised with authority, as if she were clearing away a path for horse and rider. Her gait remained, as before, bold and confident. Her head was crowned with laurel. The face had matured: she had a clear-eyed gaze, firm but rounded chin, and straight nose.[47]

Was it Lizzie? In Saint-Gaudens's autobiography, Homer Saint-Gaudens said of his father that in his ideal sculpture, little or no resemblance could be traced to a model. Saint-Gaudens was always quick to reject the least taint of what he called "personality" in such instances.[48] In general, that statement is true. Gus would tinker with his work until the likeness to the model was washed out and an idealized portrait emerged. However, there were exceptions. Characteristics of Davida Clark, a professional model, are clearly visible in his *Diana* and *Amor Caritas.*

Saint-Gaudens biographer Burke Wilkinson is clear that Lizzie did a quick one- or two-day sitting for Gus in New York and that this work was a basis for the head of the Angel of Victory.[49] That Lizzie would sit in this manner for Saint-Gaudens was not unusual. It was the practice for sculptors of the time to make sketches on the spur of the moment of a particular human feature of interest for future reference in their work. Daniel Chester French, for example, used this approach.

Other clues are revealed by Arline Tehan in her book *Henry Adams in Love.* Citing Sherman family legend and studio gossip, Tehan noted the similarity of the facial features of Lizzie to those of the angel. She also stated that Gus sent the Anders Zorn etching to Lizzie.[50] The innuendo is there. Lizzie would never have considered posing nude for the angel. The flirtatious banter that characterized their relationship in 1899 was her limit. Even in her first year of real separation from her husband and in the more permissive culture of France, posing was out of the question for Lizzie. Yet elements of her facial features and carriage can be found in the work.

Saint-Gaudens gave another clue. Some five years after his return to America, when he was in New York, Lizzie sent him a ticket to *Parsifal.* He responded that he had wanted to see this Wagnerian favorite of his but had lacked executive ability to acquire a ticket. "Now like a good angel you send me one."[51]

Tehan cites another revealing anecdote. In her final years, Lizzie lived with her son-in-law in England. A young Cambridge graduate student from America came to visit her. His father, an architect, had been a close confidant of Lizzie's in a friendship dating to 1903. The young man drove up to the old Georgian mansion that she called home. He "suddenly caught sight of her standing on the steps, her head thrown back, her arms outstretched and held slightly backward, looking for all the world like the Angel of Victory."[52] That young man was Burke Wilkinson.

There is one last piece of secondary evidence that comes directly from the Sherman family. In October 1902 Rachel Sherman, now Mrs. Paul Thorndike, wrote Saint-Gaudens after having seen the finished Sherman for the first time. She was deeply moved and wrote a long letter to the sculptor revealing her innermost emotions. Nothing of consequence appeared until the closing when Rachel, knowing of Gus's penchant for continual changes, added, "Please do not change the Victory. I shall never forget her face that morning [of the viewing]." Rachel had instantly recognized the resemblance.[53] So it was for some that Elizabeth Sherman Cameron became an "Angel of Victory."

More recognition now came Gus's way. At the end of 1899 he was elected a member of the Institut de France. Ferdinand Peck wrote asking him to mount a major exhibit of his works for the Exposition Universelle. The Luxembourg Museum asked to acquire examples of his work. A similar request came from Berlin. Gus was very much in demand.

In spite of this success, his depression persisted. Vacations to the south of France, Italy, and Spain failed to dispel the fatigue and illness. He let his innermost thoughts out in a frank letter to Helen Mears, a former student.

> It's dismal weather outside the entire winter has been awful, rain constantly now for almost three months just as it was two winters ago. Lately I've been having a return of neurasthenia and life has in a measure reverted to the sad tone of some time ago and it's a struggle to brace up. . . . I've been torn recently as to whether I should exhibit in 1900 or not, and I have about concluded not to, the wear and tear would be too great. . . . I'm beginning to think seriously of returning home now and do you know I'm feeling a vague shrinking from doing so, there is much that is a constant offense here, but on the other hand so much that is seductive to an artist that we have not at home that I fear I may be discontented in America. . . . My Victory is not quite finished. It has dragged from one week to another and now that I am at the end, I'm very tired of it. They will soon begin to enlarge it.[54]

March 1900 found Gus better. These mood swings seemed to be seasonal. His neurasthenia had returned but not like earlier attacks. The doctor blamed it on the stress of his work. More important, he was determined to exhibit the Sherman.[55] The Exposition Universelle or Paris Exposition of 1900 opened on April 14. These expositions were hosted by the French on 11-year cycles. The Sherman Monument was ready. Saint-Gaudens was again very cocky about the work, particularly with its Angel of Victory.[56] It received "special placement" among the sculptures in the Grand Palais. However, Gus was not happy with the overall presentation.

Such a collection of sculpture, rammed together ignominiously, had never been seen—nor ever can occur again. The space was so limited that in the foreign collection all statues were crowded pell-mell, helter-skelter, on top of one another, in a bewildering and phenomenal maze of extended and distorted arms, legs, faces, and torsos in every conceivable posture.[57]

Still the Sherman received high recognition, receiving a Grand Prix and a gold medal.

Gussie left Paris in June sharing in the glow of her husband's triumph but frustrated over his health. He seemed all used up. Gus was hoping to finish the Boston Public Library groups and follow, but that grand return was not to be. Now that the pressure of preparing for exhibition was at an end, Saint-Gaudens resolved to consult the doctors about the illness and the exhaustion that seemed to be his constant companions. He worried that he might have a heart condition.[58] The actual diagnosis left Gus in complete shock and denial: he had a tumor in the lower intestines and had to have it removed at once in a very serious operation. As bad as the diagnosis was, the prognosis was death. He was being struck down at the moment of his highest triumph.

The young Fraser recounted Saint-Gaudens's dreadful reaction to this tragic twist.

> I was working in the studio early one morning when he suddenly burst through the street door and went directly from our studio into his own. In a few minutes I heard the outside door in his studio slam. It was all so unusual that I was rather startled, but thought possibly he might have been in a hurry and got on with my work.

In about an hour and a half he came in again and said, "Fraser, come into my studio, I must tell you something." I went in and I noticed that his look was unusual and very excited, and he said. "I have just had the most extraordinary experience. You know I have never been ill in my life—as a matter of fact, I never thought of death, but it now appears that I am seriously ill and must go home for an operation. I am greatly worried and have been sleepless for many nights. Suddenly this morning, I decided that I would end it all, and when I came here I had definitely made up my mind to jump into the Seine. As I left here I practically ran down the Rue de Rennes toward the Seine. As I looked up at the buildings they all seemed to have written across the top a huge word in black letters—Death, Death, Death. This on all the buildings. You can readily understand my mental state. I ran—I was in so much of a hurry! I reached the river and went up on the bridge and as I looked over the water, I saw the Louvre in the bright morning sunlight, it seemed wonderfully beautiful, and suddenly everything was sufficient to me, the Louvre was wonderful—more remarkable than I had ever seen it before. Whether the running and hurrying had changed my mental attitude, I can't say—possibly it might have been the beauty of the Louvre's architecture or the sparkling water of the Seine—whatever it was, the weight and blackness suddenly lifted from my mind and I was happy and found myself whistling," and he still seemed excited and happy and I felt that he had passed a dreadful crisis and was safe for the time.[59]

Whatever the cause, the depression lifted as a veil, and Gus lost all desire to do away with himself. Yet he did nothing: he did not schedule the operation; he did not book passage back home. He was in this condition of mental paralysis when Stanford White discovered him, took matters in hand, and booked him passage back to the United States.[60]

Ill, Saint-Gaudens nevertheless returned to his homeland having achieved what he set out to do. In addition to the membership in the Institut de France, he had been made a corresponding member of the Société Nationale des Beaux-Arts. His highest honor came after his departure: he was created an officer of the Legion of Honor, with its little red lapel button.[61]

Just how good was the Sherman Monument? Yes, it had received a Grand Prix and a gold medal at the Paris Exposition. However, the Exposition had generated 42,790 awards in total. Included were 2,827 Grand Prix and 8,166 gold medals.[62] The Sherman awards were just two among many. One thing was for certain, however: the skying of his World's Fair award medal in 1894 was forgotten.

Chapter 12

Edith

Throughout this period of Saint-Gaudens's rise to national prominence, with its advances and setbacks, Theodore Roosevelt had labored within the political spectrum. However, to achieve the recognition and success he desired, there was a missing piece to the puzzle. He must fill the void in his life caused by the untimely death of his wife, Alice. What was more, this time around he must find more than a companion. To reach his full potential, he must have a partner.

The Roosevelts were going to Washington again: Theodore had lobbied successfully for a position of significance in the new McKinley administration. Even before the election in the summer of 1896, he had approached Mark Hanna, McKinley's political handler, seeking a Cabinet position.[1] There had been resistance, as Theodore's reforming nature caused hesitancy within the Republican political machine. Still, the position of assistant secretary of the Navy had been offered and Roosevelt had accepted. It was a long, sometimes uncertain, journey that had led husband and wife to this point.

They had been married for 10 years now. She had been the little girl that Theodore and his brother had shut in the closet for crying during the Lincoln funeral procession—Edith Kermit Carow, constant companion of the Roosevelt children as they grew up together in New York City. From early childhood, it had been apparent that Edith and Theodore had a special relationship. He was the love of her life—and yet it took a tragedy to bring the two of them together.

Edith was born of solid Knickerbocker stock in 1861, just short of three years junior to Theodore. It was through his sister Corinne that she met and took an instant liking to the asthmatic boy. Wanting to encourage these budding friendships, the Roosevelt family asked Edith to join their home-school kindergarten, being taught by Theodore's Aunt Anna.

Edith soon found herself swept up in the Roosevelt family activities. She and Theodore explored McGuffey readers together. (It was one of those readers that contained the phase about "speaking softly and carrying a big stick."[2]) The two children played house together. During their separations Edith and Theodore kept up a lively correspondence, although Theodore had trouble spelling her name. The Roosevelt children and their cousins took dancing classes with Edith. While there was much competition between the various Roosevelt cousins to be on Edith's dance card, Theodore usually won out.[3]

On the surface Edith's childhood appeared untroubled. However, all was not well within the Carow family. As the flush times of the Civil War were replaced by the tempestuous postwar economy, Edith's father struggled; his lack of business skills was compounded by a drinking problem. In spite of these difficulties, Edith was much closer to her father than she was to her mother and sister, Emily. Throughout this period, the Roosevelt household was a source of stability and a refuge from the troubles at home.

In 1871, Edith began her formal education at Miss Comstock's School, an exclusive private New York finishing school for girls. It was here that she developed a love of fine arts. She particularly enjoyed English literature and classical music, and attended Shakespeare matinees at the new Edwin Booth Theatre.

There were times when their bond became strained, such as Theodore's return from his second European trip. Her family could not afford the Grand European Tour. Yet, once back together, Theodore and Edith quickly became inseparable. She would travel to Tranquility, the Roosevelt home at Oyster Bay, to visit during the summers. All continued on an even keel as Theodore prepared to leave for Harvard in the summer of 1876.

That fall Edith, Corrine, and a friend busied themselves in Theodore's absence with a visit to the art exhibit at the National Academy of Design. Edith had developed an enjoyment for art and tried to make all the annual exhibits.[4] Ironically, this particular exhibit was one of the contributing factors to the establishment of the breakaway Society of American Artists.

The relationship took on a more serious tone when Theodore came home for Christmas. At a dinner party given for the young people by Aunt Anna, Theodore and Edith slipped upstairs together. Afterward, Theodore sang Edith's praises. Now references to Edith occasionally popped up in his letters home.[5] The following spring she joined the Roosevelt family on a visit to Theodore at Cambridge. The relationship was growing into something more than friendship. Several weeks later, Theodore wrote Corinne that he did not think he had ever seen Edith looking prettier. Edith's polite note to Theodore after the visit indicated that she too felt something more.[6] That summer there was another visit to Tranquility. Likewise Theodore, Corinne, and Elliott visited Edith at the New Jersey shore as they had in previous summers. Here Theodore's diary went silent on Edith. The following Christmas vacation was clouded by Theodore's father's illness and death some six weeks later. The spring and summer of 1878 found Theodore suffering a sense of loss over the death of his father.

The sharp pain began to dull in mid-summer, just in time for Edith's annual visit to Long Island. Then, after tea one afternoon, they went to the summerhouse. Neither one would ever reveal what happened that afternoon. The only thing known was that there was a quarrel. Years later, Theodore would only admit to a break in their very intimate relations. For her part, Edith would only say that Theodore had not been nice. Afterward, Theodore experienced an uncharacteristic rage. He practically rode his horse into the ground, and shot and killed a dog that irritated him. He went plinking with his rifle on Long Island Sound, shooting at anything that moved. Edith for the remainder of the visit kept her feelings to herself so that the family suspected nothing.[7] If a proposal had been tendered, it was an impetuous move on Theodore's part. He had two years remaining at Harvard, and Edith was only 17. It was too much, too soon, and Edith knew it. One thing was certain: the special relationship was over.

Still close to Corinne, Edith now had to watch as Theodore's courtship of Alice Lee in Boston unfolded. Edith was the first person outside of his family that he told when he and Alice became engaged in January 1880. The following October she gave a dinner party for Theodore in celebration of the upcoming wedding.[8] She attended the wedding in Brookline on October 27, Theodore's 22nd birthday. Throughout the occasion, she kept her innermost thoughts to herself. At the reception, she was constantly on the dance floor. The following December, Corinne debuted into New York society. For Edith, there would be no debut; the family simply had no money for such an affair. Still she found ways to maintain at least a friendship with Theodore, hosting a large party for him after his election to the New York Assembly.

Clearly, Edith continued to maintain an affection for Theodore. Alice and Edith, on the other hand, were not close. The new bride remarked to Corinne that Edith was the one person among Theodore's friends with whom she could not make any headway.[9] They oftentimes found themselves thrust together in Roosevelt family activities involving Corinne. However, Corinne's marriage to Douglas Robinson in April 1882 pushed Edith into the family background. Perhaps as a result, Edith turned more and more to Aunt Anna, her old kindergarten teacher. The two women took in art exhibitions and concerts together.[10]

The year 1883 was a difficult one for Edith. Her father died in March. Corinne was occupied with her marriage, and her ties to Theodore were tenuous at best. There was no one else with whom she was really close. At 22, she was fast becoming a spinster. The only realistic marriage prospect would have been a wealthy older man. For the intelligent and intellectual Edith, this prospect was no prospect at all. Then, on Valentine's Day 1884, matters changed in a way that Edith would never have wished— with the death of Theodore's wife and mother.

Crushed with grief, Theodore Roosevelt turned west for his solace. In the fall of 1884, he closed up his house in New York, put his sister Bamie in charge of baby Alice, and moved to his ranch.

The West made Theodore Roosevelt. Intellectually gifted, the man had made his way in politics without help from the family. However, there was an element missing. His days on the cattle ranch toughened the asthmatic young man physically. As he matched his ranch hands task for task, his body hardened. He gained their respect as he honed his leadership skills. No roadblocks were insurmountable. Whether it was calming cattle in the middle of a midnight thunderstorm or running thieves to ground in the dead of winter, Theodore found within himself the strength to persevere and succeed.

Theodore was careful during this period to keep up with New York politics. He found reasons to frequently return to New York City. Construction was underway on a house on Long Island at Oyster Bay. In spite of Alice's death, he intended to finish building this house and make it his home. However, there was one stipulation that he placed upon himself when he was back in the city—he told his sisters not to invite Edith to their homes when he was staying with them.[11] Theodore intended to be true to Alice even in death.

Striking Change

For 19 months Theodore stayed the course. In September 1885, he returned to New York for one of his visits. Some time shortly thereafter, Edith, visiting Bamie, was descending the front stairs to leave as Theodore came in the front door. Whether the meeting was accidental or contrived made little difference: they were a perfect match. Each had matured from that day in the summerhouse. They began to see each other, first in private and then gradually in public.

Within six weeks Theodore proposed, and Edith accepted. The engagement would by necessity be a long one; Theodore was concerned that it not appear too hasty following Alice's death. In addition, both had family responsibilities: Edith had her mother and sister to look after, and Theodore had to address the upbringing of little Alice. Moreover, there was the question of where the couple would settle. Living in the West was not a realistic option. The house at Oyster Bay, now named Sagamore Hill, posed a dilemma. Theodore had invested heavily in his cattle ranch. He could not afford both a town house in New York City and the home at Oyster Bay. There was also the overriding issue for him of whether to resume his political career or turn to writing.[12] The couple needed time to sort out these issues.

In the spring of 1886 Edith left with her mother and sister for Europe. Mother and sister had determined to set up housekeeping on the Continent, where living expenses were less than in New York. The plan was for Theodore to join Edith some time later that year and be wed in London. Meanwhile Theodore went west again. With cattle prices dropping precipitously, he made the decision to shut down his ranch and to consolidate his herds with those of his two ranching partners.

In October Theodore received a surprise Republican nomination for mayor of New York City. His prospects in a three-way race were slim. Still, if he turned down the nomination, he risked alienating the party bosses. He put up a valiant fight and, though he was soundly defeated, his reputation was enhanced within the press. Richard Watson Gilder for the first time in his life climbed to the speaker's platform to support Roosevelt. Even in defeat, Roosevelt's course in politics had been set.

Immediately after the election, Theodore and Bamie set sail to meet Edith in London. On the voyage over, they met Cecil Spring-Rice, third secretary at the British Legation in Washington and a regular at Henry Adams's salon. Spring-Rice had learned of the Roosevelts' being on board the steamer and had obtained letters of introduction. The chance encounter blossomed into a friendship, and Spring-Rice served as best man at Edith and Theodore's wedding on December 2, 1886.[13]

Through the winter of 1886–1887, Edith and Theodore blissfully honeymooned in Europe. They enjoyed a rare snowfall in Venice that February. However, their homecoming brought changed circumstances. First, Edith insisted that Alice be raised within their household. It became clear to Theodore's sisters that Edith was going to assume the major role in Theodore's life. The second circumstance was not of the newlyweds' making but of a much more drastic nature.

That winter was like no other in anyone's experience in the Dakota Territory. The range had already suffered from overgrazing. Now a fierce winter of staggering-cold temperatures descended across the land. Cattle froze or starved to death. When spring brought a snowmelt, ranchers could easily assess the damage: the range was littered with carcasses. Many ranchers were devastated, with whole fortunes disappearing.

Theodore, having rashly overinvested in the preceding years, now faced extremely reduced circumstances. Edith would be in charge of the finances. For a while the couple wondered if they could afford the upkeep of Sagamore Hill.[14] One fact was clear: Theodore must work to support his family. A political career would now help put food on the table.

There was just one problem with Roosevelt's desire to reenter politics. While Grover Cleveland was president, he would have to wait for the Republicans to recapture the presidency. In the meantime, literary pursuits kept him occupied and generated enough money for Edith to balance the family budget. That situation changed when Benjamin Harrison and the Republicans were victorious in the November 1888 election.

Henry Cabot Lodge now began to approach the party leaders to find a position for his friend Roosevelt, who, aggressive as ever, sought an assistant secretaryship. It was not forthcoming. Lodge began negotiating directly with a less-than-eager Harrison. Finally the position of civil service commissioner was offered. It promised to be a thankless and obscure job, and others had turned it down. Any decisions rendered in this position were bound to offend. Roosevelt took the job nevertheless and headed to Washington. Edith, pregnant with their second child, would remain at Sagamore Hill until the birth.

Theodore arrived in Washington on May 13, 1889, taking up residence with the Lodges. He assumed his office with his usual vigor. Civil service reform had had its birth in 1883 as an outgrowth of the Garfield assassination.[15] However, in the interim politicians had found many inventive ways to circumvent the laws. Theodore went after corruption like a whirlwind without regard to party affiliation. He quickly gained a national platform upon which to build his reputation as a reformer.

In October a second son was born. Edith was now ready to set up housekeeping in Washington. In late December she brought the family, along with Theodore's sister Bamie, to a small rental house in the northwest section of the city. She had arrived just in time for the 1890 social season. Now the city would be able to judge this woman who was the wife of Theodore Roosevelt. Edith was facing no small challenge. Her husband had made a name for himself in the short time he had been in the capital. There was a vital radiance about him for all to see. Edith was different; author Margaret Chanler described her as difficult to access. Praise could not reach or define her. Just as the camera would focus, she would step aside to avoid the click of the shutter. In most of her pictures she wore a hat that seemed to cast a shadow over her face, or she turned her head. She held to the belief that a lady's name should be in the newspaper only three times: at birth, marriage, and death. Yet she was a handsome woman. She could easily stand at Theodore's side in Washington society and project herself through him.[16]

In this new Washington environment, Edith blossomed. She found the conversations stimulating. At a party hosted by the vice president, Levi Morton, she was escorted to dinner by one of Washington's most powerful senators, James McMillan. Her own dinner parties were on a lesser scale but the guests no less important.[17] This was the couple that showed up on Henry Adams's doorstep.

Adams first hosted noonday breakfasts in 1887. With his wife's suicide now receding into the past, these salons filled his need for social interaction.[18] That the Roosevelts would join this exclusive gathering was only natural. Adams had been at Harvard while Theodore was an undergraduate. Cabot Lodge had been a graduate student with Adams and was a regular at the salon. John Hay was Henry's closest friend and next-door neighbor. Theodore was within familiar surroundings, while Edith was not.

To come to the Adams salon was one thing. To remain within this exclusive circle was another. If Adams found a guest uninteresting, he would make it perfectly clear that that individual was not welcome to return. Margaret Chanler experienced this cold shoulder for many years. Such was not the case with Theodore and Edith. Adams was fascinated by Theodore's vitality, so much the opposite of his retiring personality. Edith thrived in these surroundings and would develop a lifelong friendship with Henry.

Not just the salon was formidable. Adams lived in a Romanesque house designed by H.H. Richardson. Within were shelves of rare books, Japanese art, Chinese bronzes, English watercolors, and Italian drawings. Since Adams was short in stature, his chairs were low slung. Edith would find herself reclining in conversation with the salon regulars. She and Elizabeth Cameron took French lessons together. Some months later she knew that she had been accepted into Adams's inner circle when Henry sent her a copy of his *History of the United States 1801–1871* from a private printing just for friends. Adams also astutely observed how quietly Edith controlled the always-ebullient Theodore.[19]

Acceptance by Henry Adams made the Washington social season of 1890 a success for the Roosevelts. Theodore provided the entertainment as he expounded upon the pressing issues of the day and gave his opinions of how they should be addressed. Years later, Hay and Adams would look back wistfully to these times when they could still draw Theodore back when he went too far afield. If there could be such a thing as the education of Theodore Roosevelt in international issues of the day, Hay and Adams were the ideal instructors. His wife, on the other hand, would always be sweet little Edie.

With the onset of summer, Edith and the children returned to Sagamore Hill. It was the practice of official Washington to escape the summer heat whenever possible. Meanwhile, Theodore labored on at his civil service position, which gave him a unique insight into the federal bureaucracy. Not only did he learn its inner workings, but he also learned how to work the system to accomplish what needed doing.

Meanwhile in the spring of 1891, Augustus Saint-Gaudens was finishing the Adams memorial. He was in Washington at least twice. However, with Adams and John La Farge on a jaunt to the South Seas, it is doubtful that he met the Roosevelts.

Adams returned from his globetrotting in time for the 1892 social season. He had met Lizzie in Paris, where the potential for their relationship had fizzled. With this disappointment, he first laid eyes upon Saint-Gaudens's memorial. An impressed Adams said that the statue symbolized universality and anonymity. His name for it was "The Peace of God."[20] It was a strong endorsement for the artist. Throughout the spring of 1892, the Roosevelts frequently took dinner with Henry Adams.[21] There is no mention of Saint-Gaudens in Washington at this time; his focus was increasingly in Chicago at the World's Columbian Exposition.

In 1893 Grover Cleveland came back to the presidency. As a supporter of civil service reform, the president wanted Roosevelt to stay. Theodore was at least initially willing. In some ways he had a better relationship with Cleveland than he had had with

The Roosevelt family in 1895: Theodore, Archie, Ted, Alice, Kermit, Edith, and Ethel. The final addition to the family, Quentin, would be born November 19, 1897.

Edith Kermit Roosevelt in 1900. Known as the "goddess picture," this image provides a rare view of the "inner" Edith.

Harrison. In the spring of 1894, when the Gilders came to Washington, they secured an invitation to dinner for the Roosevelts with the president and first lady. When seated, Edith found herself honored to be at the president's right.[22]

The summer of 1894 again found the family at home at Sagamore Hill. Adams and Spring-Rice visited the Roosevelts there. Theodore balanced the demands of his job in Washington with his desire to spend as much of the summer as possible with his family. Here the reformers of New York City approached Theodore to run as their candidate for mayor. It was an opportunity that Theodore wanted, but Edith was of another opinion. She liked Washington. However, there was another and more serious concern: economic conditions were tight, and the civil service job offered a secure source of income. The mayor's job was subject to the electorate, and Edith did not want to take the risk. She prevailed upon Theodore to turn down the offer. It was the one time that their marriage became strained. Theodore promptly went west to struggle within himself over what he had done, bitterly second-guessing his decision.[23] Edith learned from the experience that there were lines within Theodore's life that were not to be crossed.

The reformers were victorious in New York City that fall. The new mayor offered Theodore the position of commissioner of street cleaning, but somehow dealing with horse manure did not appeal to Roosevelt; he turned the new mayor down. The next offer was for police commissioner. Believing that his work in Washington was nearing a conclusion, he accepted this position.[24] In the spring of 1895, Theodore came back to New York City.

Roosevelt threw himself into the new job with vigor and no fear of the political consequences of his actions as long as they were just and fair. Edith saw very little of him during this time. Her husband would go out on all-night patrols to assess the effectiveness of the police force. Often he would accompany Jacob Riis, the rising new-style reporter who sought to bring to public attention the squalid conditions of the working poor. It was here that Roosevelt gained an awareness of the hopelessness of lower-class Americans. He was able to put aside the prejudices of his father's generation against the lower classes.

Roosevelt's time in New York City added to his store of personal experiences. However, the arena was local and he soon grew restless for the national stage. The difficult economic times of 1893 and 1894 had been laid at the feet of the Democratic Party. Cleveland had served two terms and would retire in 1896. The timing was good for Theodore Roosevelt as he campaigned for William McKinley.

So now the family was returning to Washington. Edith was looking forward to getting back to her favorite city. Some members of the Adams salon had gone their separate ways: Elizabeth Cameron was in Europe, Cecil Spring-Rice had been posted to Germany, and John Hay had been appointed ambassador to the Court of Saint James. Henry Adams remained, though, and he was looking forward to seeing his sympathetic friend Edith.[25]

Chapter 13

Homeless

The weather smiled on Augustus Saint-Gaudens for his homecoming. Fresh southerly winds pushed white clouds across the blue skies, and temperatures hovered near 80 degrees. However, as he sailed into New York harbor on July 23, 1900, his arrival was nothing like what he had expected it to be.[1] He could not enjoy the Statue of Liberty or bask in the fact that he was a shining example of all that it symbolized. During the voyage he had suffered from mental and physical exhaustion. Augusta, alerted by an advance telegram, met him at the gangplank, steeled for the possibility of cancer.[2]

In 48 hours his wife had Gus checked into Massachusetts General Hospital. The operation to remove the tumor was performed on July 28 and pronounced a success. However, the prognosis confirmed their worst fears: the tumor was cancerous and the discovery had come late. Moreover, as part of the surgery, a colostomy was performed. At the beginning of the 20th century this procedure represented the cutting edge of medical science, but there were no antibiotics, and Gus's survival was no small feat. The attending doctors expected that another operation would be necessary in five to seven years.[3]

Most of August was spent recuperating at the hospital. Saint-Gaudens wrote Stanford White that he was as full of holes as porous plaster.[4] When sufficiently recovered, he journeyed to his summer home at Cornish, just across the Connecticut River from Windsor, Vermont.

October passed well enough, but November found Gus back in another Boston-area hospital, St. Margaret's, for a second surgery. Gussie tersely said that it was not a success. An attempt had been made to reconnect the colon and eliminate the need for the colostomy.[5] Afterward, Gus retired to Florida to recuperate before returning to Cornish in mid-December. The ordeal took its toll on Gussie as well. In the spring of 1901, saying she was miserable, she departed for the Azores for seven months.[6]

Now at home, Gus enjoyed the Cornish winter in a way he would never previously have contemplated. He jokingly described it as living near the North Pole.[7] Convinced that exercise was the key to his health, he took up skating, hockey, and tobogganing. He enjoyed going for sleigh rides in the brilliant winter sunlight. There would be no studio reopened in New York City; Cornish would become his year-round home and workplace. He would later say that he had worked too much during his life, and as a result he exhorted his assistants to play and not take things too seriously.[8]

With no more prospects of surgery, Gus began bravely to reclaim his life. He had his existing commissions to finish—the Robert Louis Stevenson plaque, the seated

177

Lincoln, the Phillips Brooks Monument, the Roswell Flower Monument, and the ever-present Boston Public Library groups, to name just the major ones. He issued calls to James Earle Fraser and Henry Hering to come and help.[9] However, first and foremost was the Sherman Monument. He had left behind his longtime molder and majordomo, Gaetan Ardisson, to oversee the bronze casting in Paris. However, Gus was not ready to let go of this work; there were still parts that did not satisfy him. The casting would now become complicated.

As he recuperated from his surgery, the America that Saint-Gaudens encountered was a different country than the one he had left in 1897. To begin with, the United States had fought and won a splendid little war with Spain in 1898 over Cuban independence. Noteworthy were the sea battles that projected American naval power around the globe. In the peace treaty Spain ceded the Philippine Islands and Puerto Rico to the United States. Like it or not—and there was spirited debate—the country had become an imperialist power. With the dawning of the 20th century the United States was now on the world stage, having equal footing with Britain, France, and Germany.

Embroiled in it all was Theodore Roosevelt. As assistant secretary of the Navy, he had been instrumental in positioning Admiral Dewey's Asiatic Squadron for a quick strike against the Spanish fleet in the Philippines.[10] With the declaration of war, he had resigned to assume a lieutenant colonelcy in a volunteer regiment that he was instrumental in raising, composed mostly of cowboys from the West and a few Eastern adventurers. They assumed the name of the Rough Riders and went on to capture the imagination of Americans with their participation in the assault of Kettle Hill and San Juan Heights in the campaign to take Santiago, Cuba. By then the commander of the Rough Riders, Theodore Roosevelt returned home a genuine American war hero. That a newspaper friend from his days as New York police commissioner, Richard Harding Davis, was a war correspondent had not hurt his situation. The Rough Riders had existed for a mere 131 days, but it was enough time to thrust Theodore Roosevelt into the consciousness of his countrymen.[11]

Back home, Roosevelt's luck was still holding. Scandal had discredited the Republican governor of New York, up for reelection in the fall of 1898. Roosevelt, with his reformist reputation, was a logical replacement. However, the state party boss, Senator Thomas Platt, regarded him as a bull in a china shop.[12] Nevertheless, facing certain defeat by the Democrats, Platt embraced him and Roosevelt became the Republican nominee. The campaign was short, and Theodore barely won. Still, the odds had been stacked against him, making his victory all the more impressive.

Two years later, Platt and the New York business community had had all the reform they could stomach. There was an out for the political boss. McKinley's vice president, Garret A. Hobart, in failing health, had died on November 21, 1899. McKinley had to choose a new running mate for the 1900 presidential election. Word began to leak to the press promoting Roosevelt for the vice presidential nomination.[13] As the months of 1900 progressed, Theodore fought against this move to nominate him. It was a do-nothing, dead-end job. He wanted another two-year term as governor of New York. However, politically he was muzzled lest he protest too vociferously. There were those of his supporters, including Cabot Lodge, who thought the vice presidency was a strong position from which to launch a campaign for president in 1904.[14] It was an ambivalent Roosevelt who attended the Republican National Convention that June in Philadelphia. McKinley stood neutral, and Roosevelt was swept to the nomination.

In spite of Roosevelt's being at the convention, there was still the formal custom of his meeting with the Notification Committee. It occurred on the piazza at Sagamore Hill. There was a crowd of some 200 to view the ceremonies. No family member was present, however. Publicity for a politician's family was not considered either necessary or nice. Their photographs were rarely permitted in the newspapers, and the idea of their talking to the press was absolutely beyond imagination. During the meeting Edith and her stepdaughter, Alice, remained in her sitting room with the window open so they could hear Theodore's acceptance speech. Alice observed that it was as if they were Oriental ladies behind a screen. To not be seen or heard in public was a protocol that Edith would not violate. She firmly believed that no lady should make herself conspicuous.[15]

Roosevelt went on to campaign vigorously. On Election Day, November 6, 1900, the ticket of McKinley-Roosevelt swamped the Democrats, led by the pro-silver William Jennings Bryan. As a parting gift after the election, some of his Albany staff gave him a sculpture of the *Puritan* by America's foremost sculptor, Augustus Saint-Gaudens. James Earle Fraser later described that work as "tense with religious fervor."[16]

Theodore Roosevelt was inaugurated as vice president on the gray, drizzling day of March 4, 1901. His first official act was to preside over the Senate, which remained in session until March 8. Then he returned to Oyster Bay. He made vague plans to resume the study of law when he returned to Washington in the fall for the reconvening of the Senate.[17] There would be a few ceremonial chores in between, such as opening the Pan-American Exposition in Buffalo in May. Boss Platt's strategy had worked: Theodore Roosevelt had been moved to the sidelines.

As the winter at Cornish progressed, Saint-Gaudens began to involve himself in his work. While he was recuperating in Florida, a large shed had been constructed under Fraser's supervision to house the plaster cast of the Sherman. It was not just any shed. From one side of the building Fraser constructed an extension that started at the eaves, telescoping down over a distance of 50 feet to a size six feet square. This modification would allow Saint-Gaudens to study the work both up close and from a distance. In addition, Fraser added a skylight and a turntable upon which to move the work.[18]

The young assistant's design was ideal to allow Gus to persist in tinkering with the work even though Ardisson was moving ahead with the bronze casting work in Paris. Saint-Gaudens intended to make changes and then forward them to the founders in France. In his new studio, sometimes seated at the end of the extension (which he called his "camera's eye") and sometimes close at the monument's foot, wrapped like an Eskimo, the sculptor spent days making modifications. The Angel of Victory still did not suit him.

Striking Change

At this point Alice Butler, a young Windsor girl, put in an appearance. She posed for him wearing cambric material draped and sewn into place to represent a classical Greek gown.[19] For once Saint-Gaudens had the time he wanted for changes, because there was serious indecision about where to erect the Sherman in New York City.

Gus had retained Charles McKim in mid-1897 to design the pedestal, and consequently the architect became point man in Gus's absence for siting the Sherman. It had been McKim's and Saint-Gaudens's hope to put the Sherman Monument in Central Park as Gus left for Paris.[20] McKim had prepared drawings for the pedestal in the late spring of 1899. When Gussie returned to Paris in November 1899, she brought these drawings for Gus to study. An initial approach to the outgoing city-reform administration had been made in late 1897 without success. Plans had been submitted but no action taken. The year 1898 brought the incoming Tammany administration, causing McKim a different problem. George Clausen, the Tammany man serving as president of the Parks Commission, ran the department with an iron fist. He was difficult to deal with, causing McKim to hesitate.[21] Now, with 1899 drawing to a close, the architect was optimistic. As Art Commission members, both he and Charles Barney, an investment banker, had developed friendly relations with the Tammany man. "Charles the Charmer" had also delegated to a fellow architect and former member of his firm, Tom Hastings, the task of lobbying Clausen. Hastings and Clausen were close associates. Still McKim had doubts. He could not speak for the Parks Board or the National Sculpture Society, which advised this group.[22]

Gus had been so positive about the proposed approach that he twice wrote Gussie before her arrival that fall telling her that all was on track. He had wanted Gussie to communicate to Rachel Thorndike that the situation was well in hand.[23] Now, after viewing the plans that Gussie had brought with her, Gus agreed in principle with the work but feared there would be serious objections due to the building out and transplanting necessary for its implementation. Speaking strictly as a sculptor, he wanted the statue set back slightly in the scheme.[24] There the matter stood at the dawning of the new century as McKim prepared to make a formal presentation.

McKim knew he was pushing the envelope with this proposal, and in spite of his careful preparations, problems arose, just as Saint-Gaudens had foreseen. In fact, there was downright controversy. McKim's plan called for placing the Sherman at the south end of the mall in Central Park. The mall begins just above the 65th Street traverse and runs about a half mile on a north-south diagonal. At this time, its entire length was planted with a double row of American elms, leaving a 35-foot walkway within. At the south end there was a large open space that commanded views down the center of the walkway as well as vistas to the right and left. It was the key point in the design of the south half of the park. Here was where McKim wanted the Sherman. He was planning to take a space some 600 feet square and construct an elaborate platform with steps leading up to the pedestal and its statue. In the process several trees would have to be removed. Such a plan, if executed, would present the Sherman most favorably—but it also would irreparably alter the original designs and concepts for this portion of the park.[25]

The Sherman Monument Committee was now chaired by William E. Dodge. The long-awaited meeting was held in April 1900 with Clausen. The commissioner was pleasantly disposed to the site proposed on the park's mall, but he had reservations. The plan had leaked into the public arena prior to the meeting, and the timing could not have been worse.

To begin with, at the end of March the Parks Commission had decided that all statuary, proposed as well as existing, must harmonize with the scenery of the parks. Clausen had argued that there was already too much statuary in the parks and that it was placed without regard to the best interests of art and landscape gardening. The adopted regulations were sweeping: no statue would be erected in any New York park where scenery was predominant. Statues could be placed as adjuncts of buildings, bridges, or viaducts to heighten and beautify the effect of the scenery. Only statues of great artistic beauty and of great national or universal interest could be placed in small parks or at the intersection of two or more avenues.[26]

Then, on April 10, the *New York Times* ran an inflammatory editorial. Without naming Saint-Gaudens or McKim specifically, the editorial called them artistic vandals. It asserted that the proposed placement of the equestrian statue would destroy the effect of the mall for no better reason than that it was the most conspicuous site that could be found for the monument. It was, asserted the author, the most serious disfigurement of the park ever proposed.[27]

Understandably, the Commission was now reluctant to place the statue in Central Park. Clausen's alternative proposal was to place the work north of Grant's tomb at a plaza then under construction that would overlook the Hudson River. That part of Riverside Drive was proving to be a popular carriage destination. In his opinion, it was the best site the Parks Department had. Dodge was agreeable, wanting to avoid a fight over the park location.[28]

It was a smooth denial of the Sherman Committee's request. The person behind it was Samuel Parsons. He was the widely respected landscape architect for the Parks Department. Having served in a variety of positions overseeing Central Park, Parsons was the last surviving link within the department to the original designers of the park, Frederic Law Olmsted and Calvert Vaux. The man was a skilled defender of Central Park, believing in the preservation of its natural beauty. In his almost 20 years of service, Parsons had stood fast against all manner of proposals for Central Park that he viewed as unacceptable to the original intent of the designers. His standard procedure was to speak first to the commissioners. If unsuccessful, he would then turn to anyone who would listen, including the editorial writers for the *Times* and the *Tribune*. McKim in developing his proposal for the mall had not consulted Parsons.[29]

After meeting with Clausen, Dodge opened correspondence with McKim. The site north of Grant's tomb had promise. McKim objected: the Sherman was made to face either south or west,[30] and Claremont Hill rose just to the south of the location, obstructing the natural light. Dodge told McKim that the city promised new levels in that area that would alleviate the problem. McKim, however, did not think anything short of total removal of the hill would result in a suitable setting.[31] Upon learning of the situation, Gus liked the site in general but deferred to McKim's concerns.

At this point, unhappy with the Parks Department alternative, McKim suggested placing the Sherman in front of Grant's tomb, on the south side. This proposal reached Gus just as the Exposition of 1900 was closing down. He was ecstatic over the possibility. However, he needed the approval of one man who just happened to be in

Paris at that moment, General Horace Porter, United States ambassador to France. Porter had been Grant's aide-de-camp in the Civil War and his personal secretary during his presidency. After Grant's death, the movement to erect a suitable tomb and memorial to him in New York City had faltered so badly that there had been talk of moving the body to Arlington National Cemetery. Porter stepped in as president of the Grant Memorial Association and raised the funds necessary. The tomb had been dedicated by President McKinley in 1897. By virtue of this accomplishment, Porter held sway in all matters affecting the Grant Memorial.

In Paris Gus hurried the plan for the Sherman over to Porter, only to be crushed by his immediate reaction. In fact, Porter had been aware for some time that a site near the Grant tomb was a possibility.[32] The monument, he asserted, would interfere with the view of the tomb. There would also be difficulty with the Grant trustees, because the site was a burial place and the Sherman would be distinctly out of context. Then Porter added that such a magnificent statue deserved the location on the plaza at 59th Street. The city had designated this site in 1891 as the future location of a memorial to the soldiers and sailors of the Civil War. Gus left the meeting disgusted. McKim's idea had been too good to be true.[33]

McKim did not trouble Gus again with the growing problem until December 1900, when he felt the sculptor was well enough to cope with the issues. During Gus's recuperation, the choice of available sites had narrowed. The proposed site north of Grant's tomb on the viaduct had been rejected, as relations between the families of Sherman and Grant were not good.[34] McKim had suffered on Gus's behalf "more talk, meetings and letter writing to no purpose than was ever heard of." An alternative at the south end of Riverside Drive was now under consideration. Dodge had also picked up on the site at 59th Street at the southeast corner of the park.[35]

On the last day of 1900, McKim met with Dr. and Mrs. Thorndike to review possible sites. Rachel was now involving herself.[36] Dr. Thorndike in turn saw Gus in Boston immediately after the meeting. They discussed another site at Park Avenue and 34th Street. Gus was willing to come to New York at a moment's notice if that would help resolve matters. He was still hoping for a September 1901 unveiling. However, Thorndike conveyed McKim's wishes to go slowly.[37]

February 1901 found McKim writing in frustration that another site between 72nd and 73rd Streets was being tossed about. In McKim's eyes the location was the only decent approach to Riverside Drive, and might meet Saint-Gaudens's requirements if the location had an acceptable setback from the surrounding buildings. McKim badly wanted Gus to come to New York, hoping that his presence might help to sort things out. Meanwhile, cooperation from the Parks Department was less than perfect. Six months later Stanford White was still trying to acquire a large survey map of Riverside Drive from the department to aid in the architectural firm's efforts.[38]

In March, William Coffin, who had helped to bring the Washington Inauguration Centennial medal to closure, began writing Saint-Gaudens in Cornish. He had seen Gus in Paris and gotten a commitment from the sculptor to exhibit a plaster of his Shaw Memorial and some lesser works at the upcoming Pan-American Exposition in Buffalo. This exposition was the first major American effort since Chicago, and hopes were high for its success. As director of the Exposition's Fine Arts Division, Coffin was determined to have the Sherman Monument. He was adamant, pestering Gus with letters almost daily throughout April. Gus was reluctant. The plaster cast of the Sherman had arrived damaged, and there were the never-ending modifications to be made. Coffin was persistent, offering to pay all the costs of mounting. Gus relented. He sent Hering to oversee the installation and patch up the damage.[39]

The opening of the Pan-American Exposition was set for May 20. Gus came to New York City well in advance of the opening in Buffalo. This would be the first American exhibition of his equestrian group. While the Sherman had met with much acclaim in Paris, Gus was anxious about its reception in America, especially now that its site was in question. He had already been to the fairgrounds to inspect the erected work. Coffin had been true to his word: the statue had a prime location in front of the Fine Arts Building, facing south. A fountain that was in the way had been removed. Although it faced the Fine Arts Building, Gus was content with the nearby lake as a backdrop. His only objection concerned the pedestal, which did not suit. As a result, Coffin had the offending surfaces hacked out and a new pedestal substituted.[40] Saint-Gaudens was being grandly treated in Buffalo.

On the appointed day, Vice President Theodore Roosevelt arose to do his duty in the opening ceremonies. He used the occasion to renew the principles of the Monroe Doctrine. He based his speech in part on six or seven quotations from those that Richard Watson Gilder had been asked to provide for the Exposition. The Exposition people had used the quotations to adorn the buildings of the fair. As Roosevelt spoke he made eye contact with Gilder, who was seated with Edith, and periodically moved toward Gilder to hurl one of the inscriptions directly at him. Everyone praised the inscriptions, which left Gilder saying that he had never had so much taffy.[41] Saint-Gaudens was there only to take a brief walk around the Sherman to see again how it appeared in the light. He was satisfied with the figure but still was not happy with the horse, which he thought looked as if it were trotting into a barn. After the speeches, there were tours and special activities arranged for the vice president's party. Edith was particularly taken by the Sherman, and the press hailed its arresting beauty.[42]

It was an interesting time for the otherwise bored vice president. On the way back home, Theodore, Alice, and Edith stopped at Geneseo to visit friends and go horse-back riding. Edith then wanted to spend some time in Albany. The afternoon of May 28 found the vice president traveling alone back to Oyster Bay.

On the train he happened upon Saint-Gaudens, who was traveling with Finley Peter Dunne. In their youth, their difference in social status had been like a divide running between the lives of Roosevelt and Saint-Gaudens that neither could nor would cross. Now the loquacious Theodore and the shy Gus, with Finley Peter Dunne thrown in for leavening, took lunch together.[43]

All three were master storytellers. Theodore tended to overuse the first person singular in his tales, but they did not lack in color. Dunne was a nationally syndicated political satirist. Gus was no slouch himself: he was noted for his vivid descriptions and scene setting. He was also a good listener. Of the three men, only Roosevelt recorded the chance meeting, and the account was scant in detail. He wrote his son that it was great fun meeting the two men and that he liked them both.[44]

At last, a friendship had formed between Roosevelt and Saint-Gaudens. For two decades their lives had been as different as their backgrounds. Still, there were common influences. They were friends of Richard Watson Gilder. They were routine members of Henry Adams's salon. They were both members of the Century Club. Yet Roosevelt was the patrician and the politician; Saint-Gaudens was the respected artist from a humble background.

Theodore wasted no time in cementing the bond. He wrote Saint-Gaudens on May 31 to invite the sculptor and his wife to come to Sagamore Hill as houseguests. But there was more.

> Probably you never will realize what a real comfort and source of pride you have been to me. I am very proud of America and very jealous of American achievement. It has been to me a source of real regret and concern to see how our writers have passed away and left no one to take up their plumes and as no amount of mere material achievement seems to me worth while, if taken purely by itself—I mean mere increase in wealth and industrial facilities—it is always a relief to think that there is one American in the prime of his powers who is leaving us the Lincoln, the Farragut, the Sherman, the monument to Shaw and so much else that represents a real addition to the national sum of permanent achievement.[45]

Roosevelt not only admired Saint-Gaudens's works; he had just critically identified the sculptor's very best public monuments. The seeds of what would become his "pet crime" had been sown.

Gus wasted no time either. He was at the same time writing Roosevelt for help with the siting of the Sherman in New York City. Given the relation of Sherman to Grant, he wanted it at the Grant site. It did not bother Gus that the Grant Memorial would be the grander of the two. He was confident that the Sherman would hold its own. Roosevelt agreed and wrote Secretary of War Elihu Root.

> I think that I have rarely seen a nobler monument than his Sherman. New York is thrice fortunate to have it, and it seems to me that it would be peculiarly appropriate to have it where Saint-Gaudens desires; that is, not far from Grant's tomb. The relationship between the two men was so close that this also would make it appropriate. Owing to the nature of the two monuments if either suffered it would be the Sherman, and Saint-Gaudens' confidence that this will not be the case seems to me to be sufficient guaranty of the appropriateness from the artistic standpoint.[46]

The subsequent note that Saint-Gaudens received from Roosevelt was disheartening, however. According to Roosevelt, Root believed that Horace Porter on behalf of the Grant Monument Association would object to the proposed site. Worse yet, Root understood that Dodge would not support locating the statue there either.[47] Roosevelt's letter offered no hope. But that wasn't exactly what Root had written to Roosevelt. Root had in fact said he believed that he could bring Porter around if Roosevelt could convince Dodge.[48] But Theodore wanted no part of a local political controversy; this was neither the time nor the place to spend political capital. He chose instead to close the door on Saint-Gaudens. Now the Sherman really had no home.

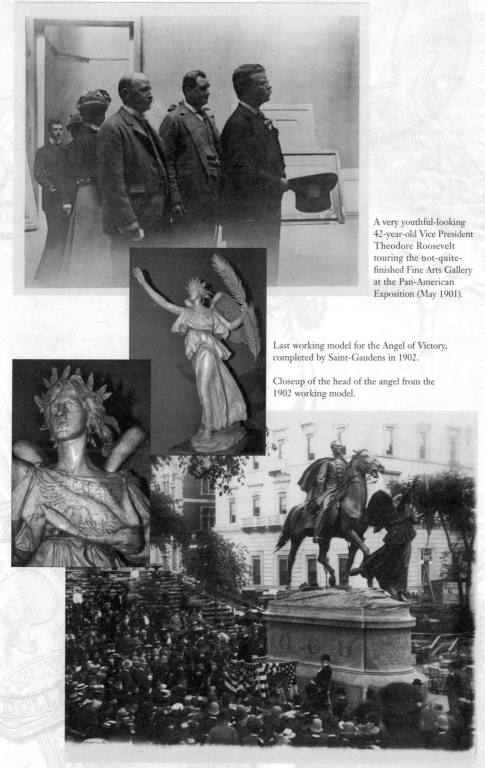

A very youthful-looking 42-year-old Vice President Theodore Roosevelt touring the not-quite-finished Fine Arts Gallery at the Pan-American Exposition (May 1901).

Last working model for the Angel of Victory, completed by Saint-Gaudens in 1902.

Closeup of the head of the angel from the 1902 working model.

The Sherman monument at the dedication in 1903.

185

Striking Change

Meanwhile, back at Cornish, Gus erected a third plaster of the Sherman in the shed. And still more changes were in store! He worked on the tail of the horse and added tiny angles and stiff marks of age to the animal that he felt increased its "nervous snap." Sherman's cloak and the mane of the horse received more work. To the discomfiture of Southerners, he added a pine bough beneath the horse's hooves to symbolize the destruction of Georgia.[49] However, all was not well that summer at Cornish. Gus called it his prolonged recovery. Henry Adams commented on his health during this period in a letter to Elizabeth Cameron: he looked wretched. Without knowing the cause, Adams suspected cancer. Saint-Gaudens had the look of it, the tone of it, and the melancholia.[50]

Theodore Roosevelt spent the summer at Oyster Bay with his family. Life had not been this peaceful for him since before the Spanish-American War. He took two trips west to Colorado and Minnesota. Little note was made that President McKinley would be touring the Pan-American Exposition during the waning days of summer. Theodore was in Vermont, a guest of the Vermont Fish and Game League, on September 6 when he learned the president had been shot by a young anarchist, Leon Czolgosz. The vice president rushed to McKinley's side. The president had a serious abdominal wound. However, he was so recovered that all thought it appropriate on September 10 that Roosevelt leave, projecting an air of confidence to the situation. Theodore gathered Edith and two of their children for a climbing expedition in the Adirondacks. On September 14 it happened: McKinley took a turn for the worse and died. Theodore Roosevelt became the 26th president of the United States.

Some two weeks later, Augustus Saint-Gaudens wrote to Will Low. Gus had had an awful time, he told Low, but he was out of it now, thanks in great measure to a change in his manner of existence: he stopped work at one o'clock and devoted the rest of the day to out-of-door things, golf, and walking.[51] It was as if everything was unchanged. Yet for this nation, everything had changed. Theodore Roosevelt was going to be an agent for change, and the United States would never be the same.

Still the Sherman siting remained unresolved. It was the kind of conflict that Gus detested. If there had been any doubt in Saint-Gaudens's mind about his work, the Pan-American Exposition removed it. Kenyon Cox called it one of the three greatest equestrian statues in the world. Herbert Adams said he had never been more moved by either painting or sculpture as he had been by the Sherman. In addition, the Exposition had awarded Saint-Gaudens an exclusive special medal of honor to be made by his respected assistant, James Earle Fraser.[52]

As 1902 dawned, McKim decided to make a major push to get the statue located in the Central Park mall despite the previous objections.[53] There were reasons to be optimistic: a change of administrations was once again underway in city government. The Tammany men had been voted out the previous November in favor of the reformers.

Likewise, McKim's term on the New York City Art Commission was expiring.[54] Perhaps a deal could be arranged in the twilight before the new administration took control.

This gambit opened with the Art Commission, which also included Daniel Chester French, passing a resolution favoring the location of the Sherman in the mall. It fell to Charles Barney, president of the Art Commission, to meet with his counterpart at the Park Commission. Barney acknowledged to Clausen that there were too many statues in Central Park but felt that a statue of this merit deserved an exception. The mall was the only formal arrangement in the park. At the north end, there was an object of interest, a flight of stairs leading to the reservoir. At the south end, there was nothing. The Sherman would provide a focal point. It would not interfere with the view, and it would provide a balancing object of interest at the south end. Barney argued that if Clausen approved this location he would go down as one of the very few commissioners that the public would remember positively.[55] Clausen was receptive, saying he wanted to do something good for Central Park and receive credit for it before it went to his successor.

The decision was quick in coming. Clausen had consulted with his fellow commissioners and "department experts in landscape and architectural art." They all agreed: a feature of this size and importance was not in the original plans for the park. The proposed location was intended as a viewpoint; a monument would detract from the effect and would be incongruous with the original plan. These words are so close to those contained in Samuel Parson's memoirs as to be almost certainly his. The mall site was vetoed.[56]

In March, with the new administration in place, McKim again attempted to achieve resolution of the location problem. Gus made one last appeal for the Central Park site. He wrote to Frederic Olmsted Jr., son of the Central Park designer, seeking his support. He was at his persuasive best, mentioning that the site had the support of the Art Commission, and offered to meet with Olmsted in Boston or New York to discuss his endorsement. That meeting took place in Boston in February. The landscape architect was only lukewarm toward the project and, most likely as a result of that meeting, the mall plans were modified.[57] The monument would be less obtrusive, and only two or four trees would have to be transplanted to facilitate its placement. The situating of the statue as now proposed would not interfere with the vistas and would provide the formal focal point that the southern end of the mall was lacking. Gus again told Rachel Thorndike, who had by now thrown up her hands in despair, that he was hopeful.[58]

A public hearing was called, and speeches were made by the West Side Association in support of a "Sherman Park." Dodge argued for the Grant site. McKim supported Dodge, saying that the site was central to New York and afforded a location allowing the Sherman to face south. Then old Samuel D. Babcock got up. He declared that it had been so long since he had first chaired the Sherman Committee that he could not remember all the various proceedings. However, he did remember that every proposed location had been refused by the Parks Department. In his opinion it was up to the Parks Department to find an acceptable spot.[59] It was a masterful move. Now the Parks Department was cornered. Parsons would have to compromise his principles and offer up a spot suitable for the Sherman.

Yet less than a week later McKim was writing to Dodge in exasperation. He had seen documents from the Grant Memorial Association. While their position was circumspect

Striking Change

with regard to the Sherman, McKim inferred that they were in opposition. The rond-point on 59th Street, what McKim called the "tulip bed site," was the only remaining location to be considered. Four days earlier he had sent photographs of this location to Olmsted by express mail.[60] Gus followed up with a letter to Olmsted, calling this site "most honorable and beautiful." However, he noted, the monument would be hidden by trees, and the circle within which it would be placed would have to be enlarged for proper pedestrian viewing. He closed by stating that he doubted that Willcox, the new president of the Parks Commission, would consent to these modifications. It was a backhanded way of lobbying Olmsted for his support. It was now up to Dodge and Saint-Gaudens to make a final determination.[61]

Dodge told Saint-Gaudens directly that both the Grant and Sherman families were opposed to the tomb site. In fact the real opposition was from the Sherman family. Rachel Thorndike was strongly against it. The mall site was now definitely out, leaving only one option.[62]

The decision was made. William R. Willcox consulted with Parsons and designated the tulip bed site for the Sherman. In a letter to Daniel French, Gus requested him to exert some influence on the Art Commission to extend the circle. The statue was best viewed from 65 feet away, and at the circle's present size one would have to step into the street to admire the Sherman. The sculptor went on to say that the grass plots should be eliminated and that there needed to be "some redisposition" of the trees surrounding the circle.[63] Samuel Parsons, who had had to compromise his principles to even approve this location, would oppose the cutting of any trees. Gus was exerting what leverage he could through French because the Art Commission had been newly empowered, being given charge of all works of art gifted to the city, as well as nebulous authority over structures erected.

The issue of the modifications to the 59th Street site continued to swirl around. Finally, on May 26, under the new strictures the proposed location was presented to the Art Commission for consideration. There was an attached approval from Parsons. There was also a memorandum from Saint-Gaudens and McKim, Mead and White agreeing not to make major alterations to the site at 59th Street. It was a rare capitulation for Augustus Saint-Gaudens and Charles Follen McKim.[64]

A committee was promptly formed within the Art Commission, with Daniel Chester French serving as its chairperson. At the June 26, 1902, meeting of the Board of Commissioners of the Parks Department, the minutes duly noted that the 59th Street location for the Sherman Monument had been approved by the Art Commission.[65] Sherman and the angel were no longer homeless.

Subsequently, Dodge sent Saint-Gaudens the extract of a letter to Horace Porter thanking him for his support before the Art Commission. It was too much for Gus. He had always considered Dodge much too political for his liking, and in his frustration Saint-Gaudens penciled at the bottom of the note that Dodge was a disagreeable man and no friend of his.[66] It was well that this fit of temper never saw the light of day.

As this mess was straightening out, the bronze pieces of the Sherman began to arrive from France. Gus erected them in a field near his house in Cornish, much to the amazement of the local farmers. He had always been very particular that his works have the right patina. Now he made an unusual decision, opting to gild the Sherman entirely.

188

In his typical laconic fashion, he said only that he was sick of seeing statues that looked like stovepipes.[67] Perhaps his real concern was that a bronze Sherman would not stand out sufficiently against the background streetscape at the 59th Street site.

There remained the issue of the pedestal. The base material specified was to be either Vermont green syenite or red Bay of Fundy granite. Naturally Parsons wanted the green syenite, which would harmonize better with the surrounding scenery. Ultimately Saint-Gaudens chose the red Bay of Fundy granite, since he believed red went better with the gilding.[68]

With the site and material settled, the height of the pedestal now had to be addressed. It was a wearying process. Gus wanted the statue near the ground; McKim desired it well raised on a high pedestal. An exasperated McKim, only somewhat exaggerating, related over lunch in Washington after a compromise had been reached that he had made about 1,500 studies for this base and was relieved that the matter was finally settled. McKim had not been at lunch more than a half hour when a telegram arrived. A curious expression came over his face as he read it: "Charles, that base is all wrong, Gus."[69]

Then other matters began to drag. The end of 1902 found McKim writing to Gus, pleading that he start on the inscriptions. The committee wanted an increase in the amount of the inscriptions. For Gus, less was always better. McKim told Saint-Gaudens to settle on the inscriptions with or without the sculptor's swear words. He needed resolution on this issue in order to have enough time to cast the lettering. Those days were not good ones for Gus. Son Homer's fiancée noted in January that Saint-Gaudens was in need of a doctor day and night.[70]

Finally, in March 1903, all was in readiness—with one exception: Gus could not abide the elm trees blocking the view. First he took a page from Parsons's book: an editorial appeared in the *New York Evening Post*. It acknowledged the special uniqueness of the trees but insisted that an exception should be made for the Sherman at the 59th Street site. It also rehashed the argument for the mall site, using words taken almost verbatim from an unsent letter of Saint-Gaudens's from the year before. Gus let the matter sit for a couple of weeks; then he wrote to Willcox to ask that he reconsider his decision and remove the trees.[71] The commissioner referred the matter to Parsons for study before lashing out in exasperation in a letter to Saint-Gaudens.

> When the question of locating the Sherman Monument was first brought to my attention, the one argument for placing it on the mall was that the trees were there, and the statue must have trees near it. When, however, I gave the hearing in the Chamber of Commerce, and Mr. McKim appeared, the only argument he made was that the statue should be placed three hundred feet in front of Grant's tomb. Here was a site where there were no trees, and you can appreciate how confused I am when the argument made in favor of the mall was that the statue must have trees, and later, Mr. McKim talked in favor of placing the statue at a point where there were no trees.
>
> Inasmuch as you enclosed the editorial from the Evening Post on the "sacredness of the Tree," I assume that this is a part of your letter and that you agree with its deductions. I entirely dissent from the views expressed in that editorial. A feeling exists among a good many people, that Central Park would be much improved

if a great deal of the statuary was replaced by trees, and personally I am not much impressed with the argument set forth in the editorial which you enclosed. We are all, of course, anxious to get the best possible setting for the Sherman Statue, but we must also remember that park features are entitled to consideration, and we must not forget that the parks are not made for statues but that the placing of statues within the parks is an incidental feature.[72]

This rebuttal was vintage Parsons. In fact, Willcox had come to respect Samuel Parsons very much.[73] The trees would stay.

The dedication for the Sherman was set for Decoration Day, May 30, 1903. Gaetan Ardisson was in charge of the erection process. Still Gus would not let go of the tree issue. They were big elms, each some 20 inches in diameter. He tried to get French involved, but French was now off the Art Commission. The preliminary feeling among the commissioners was that the trees were an issue between Saint-Gaudens and the Parks Department.[74] Direct measures were more successful: Ardisson was able to cut some of the offending tree branches from the scaffolding. Then Willcox began to have second thoughts himself and sent a work crew to trim more of the concealing limbs. Ardisson bribed the men with whiskey, and even more limbs came down.[75]

In a final indirect appeal nine days before the dedication, Gus wrote to his friend French of his willingness to give up the fight over the trees. French was not deaf to Saint-Gaudens's plight. A week previously he had taken it upon himself to again bring the matter of the trees to the attention of the Art Commission, giving the recommendation for their removal his forceful support.[76] Then suddenly Willcox resolved the situation. Still unwilling to order the trees down himself, he sought cover by asking the Art Commission to become involved. Two days before the dedication, the Municipal Art Commission ruled that two of the elm trees must come down: they would obstruct the view of the Sherman from Fifth Avenue. Phimister Proctor was now on the Art Commission and had chaired the committee looking into the situation. Once again several friends had come to Gus's rescue. There was just time enough to cut the trees down and not enough time for opposition to develop. Even so, when the act was reported in the newspapers, the reason given was that the trees would obstruct the view from the reviewers' stand.[77] No one wanted to admit publicly to cutting down trees for the sake of a memorial.

The day of the dedication finally arrived. The lowering skies and the constant threat of rain did not dampen the celebration. The festivities started at nine sharp as Regular Army soldiers followed by the New York National Guard stepped smartly off from Washington Arch in Washington Square. The men were 16 abreast, forming a solid phalanx from curb to curb. The pace was brisk, as the soldiers had to march 54 blocks in an hour and a half to reach the Sherman Monument at the entrance to Central Park.

At 42nd and Fifth, the veterans fell in behind the column.[78] First came the Loyal Legion, made up of former officers of the Union Army. Then came men from the various Grand Army of the Republic posts. While some marched well, these men mostly went at a slow gait, their ranks thinned by the ravages of time. Proudly they bore their tattered, war-torn battle flags. Slouch hats were doffed as the veterans marched the course.

At 10:20, with the parade column nearing the reviewing stand, the guns of the First Battery boomed, the sound magnified by the low-hanging clouds. William Tecumseh Sherman Thackara, the 17-year-old grandson of the general, pulled a cord. The veil of bunting that covered the monumental work came down—well, most of it came down. A swirl of wind caught part of the material on the spur of the general's boot and would not come loose. As the column of soldiers closed on the reviewing stand, at the side of the statue a city employee scrambled to bring a ladder to rectify the dignity of the situation. Meanwhile the Old Guard Band struck up "Marching Through Georgia." As if to make amends, they followed with "Dixie."

Finally freed of the bunting, the horse and rider of the Sherman Monument appeared. They seemed imbued with a spirit of restless advance, following the path where Victory pointed the way. Many in the crowd were familiar with the work in plaster, having seen it either in person or in pictures from the exhibition in Buffalo. However, they were not prepared for the stunning effect of the gilding.[79] They also had not seen the elegant pedestal. The bench for seating was brilliant. At its top, the pedestal became the rock upon which the horse stood.

As the old veterans and young soldiers passed by in review after the unveiling, Alice Roosevelt, escorted by Mr. and Mrs. Whitelaw Reid, cheered enthusiastically from a front-row seat. It took an hour and a half for the column to pass. Showers broke out intermittently and necessitated umbrellas at one point. Still the crowd's spirits remained undampened. Gus and Gussie were viewing the festivities from an inconspicuous spot. Gus had briefly inspected the statue the previous day.[80] How the veterans must have brought back memories for Saint-Gaudens, of watching from Louis Avet's cameo shop as these same men—young, then—marched off to a war from which so many would never return. As the old men went by, some struggling to keep pace, Saint-Gaudens could easily have been watching his own mortality pass. On this day, however, there would be little time for quiet moments filled with old memories for the sculptor. He and his wife were soon discovered and congratulations offered.

Rain or not, it was a grand day for speeches. Root was in from Washington for the principal address. In the preliminaries, Parks Commissioner Willcox, who had been so disdainful of the Sherman Monument, pledged to "at all times guard this statue with affectionate care."[81]

After the speeches, the politicians and generals adjourned with Gus to the nearby Metropolitan Club for a luncheon hosted by the Sherman Committee. Most of the men present were at best acquaintances of the sculptor. At least McKim was there to keep him company—and out of trouble, since Willcox was also at the luncheon. Among the politicians was none other than John G. Carlisle.[82] Carlisle's presence would not have overly upset Gus, however, since the sculptor had never really recognized Carlisle as his true adversary in the award-medal controversy from the World's Columbian Exposition. His animosity had always rested with the Mint's chief engraver, Charles Barber.

For Saint-Gaudens it was a grand day of achievement and recognition. He was an acknowledged leader of the American art establishment and a friend of the president and first lady. But why would Carlisle come to this event? Sherman had visited ruin upon his South. Still, this was a gathering of his fellow politicians. He was in his element. He had never recognized the travesty of his decision to mule Barber's work with that of Saint-Gaudens on the award medal. For John Carlisle, the occasion was one last fleeting recognition of what he had once been and of the power he had once wielded. His New York law practice, while taking on some high-profile cases, had never been monetarily rewarding. The self-styled defender of the workingman could never quite make himself into a corporate lawyer. Now he was without his two sons, who had died in early adulthood. His subsequent life had been in vivid contrast compared to the continuing success of Augustus Saint-Gaudens. One could even take some pity on the man.

That evening, there was a dinner given at Whitelaw Reid's home for the Sherman family and Mr. and Mrs. Saint-Gaudens. Reid felt it fitting that the affair ended where it had all begun, at his home.[83]

On the Fourth of July, 1903, Daniel Chester French sent his compliments to Saint-Gaudens.

> I told you the other day that I had something to say to you about the Sherman but I missed the opportunity and I have been trying for the last hour or so to write you what I feel. The result sounds so cheap and commonplace that I fear I must be content to express my approval with my congratulations and let it go at that.
>
> Yet I do want you to know how really and rarely great—I feel—I *know* the statue to be—great as few works of sculpture, ancient or modern are. Not only have you scored a great success, but the note you have struck is so entirely fresh that the statue stands in a class by itself. To say that it is better than this or next in rank to that is as idle as to compare a rose with an orange. It is one of the wonders of the world. Let that suffice![84]

It was the highest compliment a fellow sculptor can pay.

That following August, Saint-Gaudens received a letter from the president.

> Now to my mind your Sherman is the greatest statue of a commander in existence. But I can say with all sincerity that I know of no man, of course of no one living, who could have done it. To take grim, homely, old Sherman, the type and ideal of a democratic general, and put with him an allegorical figure such as you did, could result in but one of two ways—a ludicrous failure, or striking the very highest note of the sculptor's art. Thrice over for the good fortune of our countrymen, it was given to you to strike this highest note.[85]

Saint-Gaudens wrote back humbled.

> I don't know how to thank you for your more than kind words about the Sherman and my other work. And when I realize that you have taken the time to say this to me, amid the multitude of other things on your mind, it is a fact that touches me deeply and your letter will be set aside and treasured for those who come after me.[86]

Chapter 14

The Confident Years

There was more than just the Sherman project going on in Saint-Gaudens's life during the first years of the new century. Gus enjoyed that first winter of 1900–1901 in Cornish, but he wasn't prepared for the spring thaw. Early April snowmelts led to late-April flooding with the mud season reigning supreme. Wanting nothing to do with this kind of spring, Gus fled to Henry Adams's home. In fact, for Gus, spring with Henry Adams in Washington would become an annual event.[1] He could enjoy the comings and goings of the salon regulars. Henry was as acidic as ever. John Hay was secretary of state. Adams's drawing room was open to all yet closed to just a few of his truly close associates. He had endured the inauguration and would leave at the end of the month to join Lizzie Cameron in Paris.

Gus had a business reason to be in the capital that spring of 1901: He was sculpting a portrait of Assistant Secretary of State David Jayne Hill. While there, he received a note from Charles McKim saying the architect would be in town if Gus wanted to get together.[2] McKim's reason for coming to Washington was a meeting of the Senate Park Commission.

That whole affair had started the preceding year as efforts got underway to celebrate the centennial of the relocation of the nation's capital to Washington. To no one's surprise, organizers were calling for a restoration of the Mall. One of the issues impacting the Mall was a plan by the Pennsylvania Railroad to expand its 1872 station, at 6th Street, NW.[3] Included in the company's plans was an elevated railway to eliminate dangerous at-grade crossings along the southern approach to the station. Other proposals were put forth for consideration, including one by Colonel Theodore Bingham of the Army Corp of Engineers, head of the Office of Public Buildings and Grounds, to expand and substantially alter the White House (until 1901 officially known as the Executive Mansion).

Political heat developed, and a measure was introduced in the Senate that May, 1900, calling for a board of experts in architecture, landscape architecture, and sculpture to address the Mall, the White House, and other issues. It died in the House.

At this point Glenn Brown and the American Institute of Architects stepped in. Brown had for years advocated a planned approach to the placement of federal buildings in Washington. In the summer of 1895 he had participated with Gilder, McKim, Saint-Gaudens, and others in the formation of the Public Art League. While driven in no small part by the fiasco of Saint-Gaudens's World's Fair award medal, the league's stated goal was to encourage the acquisition of the best art possible for the government, be it statuary, paintings, building designs, or coin and medal motifs. Subsequently the

193

league had worked to establish a board of review to oversee these activities. While bills had been proposed in Congress, no legislation had passed.[4]

Now Brown tried another approach, proposing the Institute adopt as a theme for its annual meeting (to be held in Washington in December 1900) the unified and artistic development of the city.[5] The unbounded growth of the post–Civil War period had caused the city's development to stray far from L'Enfant's original plan. Most glaringly, the Washington Monument, which should have been located at the intersection of the Capitol axis and the White House axis, was not.[6]

At the architects' meeting, Frederic Law Olmsted Jr. presented an excellent paper. Without criticizing plans suggested earlier in the year, he set forth a proposal that would restore the park connection between the White House and the Capitol. He pointed out that the purpose of the Mall within that park connection should be to contribute to the grandeur and power that mark a seat of government of a great people. Overall, he called for a return to the L'Enfant plan.[7] Several days later a delegation from the Institute met with Senator James McMillan, chairman of the Senate Committee on the District of Columbia.

Early in his political career McMillan had served as chairman of the Detroit Park Commission. Just as important, he was powerful enough to take on Joe Cannon. Cannon, as chairman of the House Appropriations Committee, jealously defended the right of the House of Representatives to initiate appropriation bills. The dictatorial committee chairman strongly believed any activity even remotely associated with the fine arts would degenerate into a raid on the federal Treasury.[8] The senator introduced a resolution calling for a master development plan, which again failed in the House. Finally, in a backroom maneuver, McMillan gained approval for his committee to report to the full Senate plans for the development and improvement of the entire parks system of the District of Columbia. Thus the Senate Park Commission was born on March 19, 1901.[9]

McMillan wanted Daniel Burnham of Chicago Fair fame to head the Commission. Olmsted was the senator's logical choice for landscape architecture. McMillan's long-standing personal secretary, Charles Moore, would act as his liaison. Moore, Harvard educated, had come to Washington in 1889 as a newspaper correspondent. When McMillan came to Washington, Moore, a fellow Michigander, went to work for him. He was also a close friend of Glenn Brown's, and the two men often acted in concert when it came to the arts in Washington. Charles Moore knew the legislators and the legislative process inside out, and he had the trust of McMillan. It had been Moore who suggested Burnham to the senator.[10]

Burnham wanted McKim as the third member of the Commission. On the evening of March 21, 1901, the architect found McKim sitting with John La Farge in the Century Club in New York. The three men went to McKim's home and stayed up well past midnight talking of the possibilities. McKim's imagination was fired. The next day he accepted, recognizing that significant professional sacrifices would be required. However, the work was of such national character that it could not be declined.[11]

The opening meeting was April 6, 1901. McMillan laid down one condition for the Senate Park Commission: it must not interfere with the grant made by Congress the preceding year that would enable the Pennsylvania Railroad to expand their station

Architect Charles Follen McKim would engage Saint-Gaudens in the redesign and renovation of the White House, the restoration of the Mall, and the development of a master plan for Washington, DC.

(Left) The National Mall at the time of the Senate Park Commission report.

(Right) The White House greenhouses. "It was too good to believe," said Charles Follen McKim, "that those excrescences, the greenhouses, were to be abolished, or rather smashed."

opening into the Mall. The Commission met that day with Treasury Secretary Lyman Gage and Secretary of War Elihu Root. It was Root who held primary jurisdiction over much of the federal parklands, including most of the Mall. Then they adjourned to the White House to meet with President McKinley. The president heartily endorsed the work.[12] He was quite willing to let the process unfold under the auspices of the Senate Committee.

Much to the architects' relief, Bingham's renovation of the White House was taken off the table. Charles Moore had been confidentially told that Mrs. McKinley had served notice that she would have no hammering as long as she was in the White House.[13] With their marching orders, the Commission agreed to reconvene on April 18 in Washington. Thus, McKim's note to Gus was written in hopes of seeing him during a break in the work. There would be time enough for that, however, in New York. With Adams leaving for Paris, Gus was homeless. The widower McKim lived alone in New York except for occasional stays by his daughter.

On the first of June, 1901, McKim wrote to Burnham. Saint-Gaudens, prior to going to the Pan-American Exposition, had quite naturally used McKim's home as a base of operations. They had swapped stories and gossiped. More importantly, Gus had visited McKim's offices and seen the Washington plans. He had taken an active interest and given many valuable suggestions. Now McKim proposed adding him as the fourth member of the Senate Park Commission.

Burnham was more than happy to accommodate; he had wanted Saint-Gaudens from the beginning but was concerned over his ill health. Burnham went to Senator McMillan and it was done.[14] In a letter later that year, McKim shared his reasons for wanting Saint-Gaudens on the commission.

> As to Saint-Gaudens' relation to the Washington [sic] Park Commission, it is one of national appointment by Congress from which he could not be spared. Upon his judgement will largely depend the selection of sites, for such monuments as the Lincoln, Grant . . . and the solution of other problems not less essential to the work of the Commission. He has joined to the Commission because his authority would be accepted by the general public as more nearly final than that of any other man.[15]

McKim in particular began to devote full time to the Senate Park Commission report. The game plan was to finish by the end of the year, but there were problems to be addressed. The Victorian building housing the Smithsonian Institution on the south side of the Mall was at odds with the Beaux-Arts classicism to be incorporated into the master plan. Acknowledging the fact that razing the building was unlikely, the committee settled on the solution of using a screen of trees to mask its facades.[16]

A thornier question was the location for the Grant Memorial. In 1895 the Society of the Army of the Tennessee had called for a monument to their former commander. In April 1901 Grant's western army veterans secured congressional authority to build somewhere in Washington.[17] Now with the certainty that something would ultimately be built, the Commission felt pressure to recommend a suitable location. Burnham considered Grant the country's greatest 19th-century figure. First he and his colleagues proposed locating the memorial on the banks of the Potomac River. Yet there were others, including John Hay, who would take issue with that. Gradually through the adroit hand of Elihu Root, with John Hay in the background, the Senate Park Commission came around to the position that the spot at the west end of the Mall should be reserved for Abraham Lincoln.[18]

As the days fell away, the game plan remained to finish their work by the end of 1901. Two detailed models of the Mall area were being constructed as part of the formal presentation. This work would be augmented by numerous large-scale hand-colored drawings. One large drawing showed the city as it might become, including the proposed Arlington Bridge, and another showed it as it was. There were views from the Capitol to the proposed Arlington Bridge, toward the Capitol, and south from the White House. During the third week of November, Saint-Gaudens came to McKim's offices in New York to review the work. He strongly urged that the proposed Grant Memorial be placed at the foot of Capitol Hill, Washington's Place de la Concord. The conflict over placement of the memorials to Lincoln and Grant was now resolved. On the 21st of that month McKim forwarded three small-scale maps of the Mall plan to Senator McMillan. One copy was for the president.[19]

During December, work both advanced and stalled. There was to be a formal presentation of the plan by the Commission. The models would be set up in the hemicycle of the Corcoran Gallery so that they could be viewed both at eye level and from above. Illustrations would be mounted around outside walls. The problem was the models. The due date was pushed back from January 1 to the 15th. As late as December 28 the contractor for the models' construction was demanding an extension to February 1.[20] McKim refused.

As the due date drew closer, McKim came to Washington to oversee the final arrangements. It seemed that he spent his life on a stepladder for the three days prior to the opening, hanging and rehanging large photographs of the features of European cities that exemplified what they wished to emphasize in their plans. He overlooked not the slightest detail. Disliking the color of the walls in contrast to the drawings as well as the height of the ceiling, he draped unbleached cotton to give a false ceiling and to soften the contrast.[21] On the 14th he was up most of the night setting the exhibits. The two models, detailing the present and the proposed Mall, were the centerpiece. To further illustrate the plan, McKim had pressed into service artists from the leading illustrated magazines to create sweeping panoramas and eye-catching views that made the plans come to life. There was a huge exquisite bird's-eye view of the general plan and renderings of the key architectural centerpieces.[22]

McKim was leaving nothing to chance—yet the biggest coup had already been scored by Burnham. He had previously been retained by A.J. Cassatt, president of the Pennsylvania Railroad, to design the railway station that was to be rebuilt opening onto the Mall. Discussions had been ongoing between the two men with Cassatt intimating to Burnham that he had been retained to design a new station, not relocate it. While Burnham was in London during the Senate Park Commission whirlwind trip though Europe, he met again with Cassatt. Being Mary Cassatt's brother, the man was sympathetic to Burnham's cause. Still, he was a businessman first. He would not yield a position of value without receiving something in return. If the Senate would appropriate $1,500,000 to assist in tunneling under the Capitol Building, he would relocate the planned station to the north of the Mall. Learning of the proposal, Senator

McMillan put aside his previous strictures to the commission and pushed an appropriation forward.[23] Without the removal of the station, the Senate Park Commission's plans for the Mall would have failed.

On the morning of the 15th, McKim formally unveiled the plan to the Senate Committee on the District of Columbia. It was clear to all that the inspiration for this plan was the White City of the World's Columbian Exposition of 1893. The reception was positive. At noon the report was submitted to the full Senate. That afternoon a special presentation in the Corcoran Gallery was attended by the Congress, the Cabinet, and President and Mrs. Roosevelt.[24]

This president was going to take an active role in the process compared to the passive McKinley. Roosevelt took exception to the proposed gardens at the Washington Monument. McMillan immediately took him to a large rendering of the grounds so the president could grasp the full treatment of both the monument and the White House. Roosevelt became quite enthusiastic; McKim was out of the woods. John Hay, with an obvious concern for Lincoln, went straight to the proposed location of the Lincoln Memorial. He understood the significance of its axis with the Capitol and the Washington Monument and liked it. In Hay's opinion nothing should be near the Immortals.[25] This location did that for Lincoln.

Yet Hay and Henry Adams could not have been totally pleased with the plan. Their houses, along with all the others around Lafayette Square, were proposed to be replaced with executive office buildings. Henry as usual had a very original take.

> I have been out to my mansion at Rock Creek [Clover's gravesite], and have found it in good order for once, and ready for me to move in. I hardly know what still detains me; and the government seems to agree that I had better go, for the new plan of Burnham and St. Gaudens recommends turning Hay and me out of house and home into the cold. I am lucky to have a churchyard to shelter me, and out there I should have lots more visitors.[26]

The presentation was a success. Plans called for the complete exhibit to travel to New York, Chicago, and St. Louis. Yet it did not. The tour was canceled due to the back-door nature by which the work was authorized. Joe Cannon had been particularly offended by this affront. The exhibit would remain in Washington at the Library of Congress.[27] More importantly, the question of whether the Washington politicians would follow the plan remained unanswered.

If McKim on that day in January found the president and Mrs. Roosevelt difficult to read, matters were about to change. The White House was ill prepared to handle a young family with six children. The second floor of the mansion provided not only the office for the president but also his living quarters. Nevertheless, Edith made do as best she could with the cramped quarters. She appropriated the library as her personal office. It had a private door into Theodore's office. In this manner the two could consult

The Confident Years

between Theodore's meetings. Frequently the president had to appropriate the library for a conference or as a waiting room for special visitors. Edith would afterward say, tongue in cheek, that the windows had to be opened "to let out all the politicians!"[28]

Complicating matters was the accommodation of overnight visitors. The first of a steady stream was Richard Watson Gilder.[29] With only one room normally available for guests, Edith found herself in the awkward position of needing to know beforehand if a husband and wife shared the same bedroom. To top it all off, there were only two bathrooms on the second floor.[30]

With the opening of the 1902 social season, which ran from the New Year's Reception to Lent, Edith served notice that she would be a different first lady; she had a personal agenda before it became the accepted norm for the role. She would use the traditional first lady's weekly reception to promote the fine arts in the form of musicales. She did it after discussing its appropriateness as White House entertainment with Theodore.[31] She started simply, with light chamber music in the Green Room. Theodore was on hand to give autographed copies of his book, *The Rough Riders*, to departing guests.

As the season wound down, Edith stepped out in what would become her standard in the years to come. She invited the renowned pianist Ignace Paderewski to perform on the evening of April 3. Her guest list for the evening reflected the importance of the occasion; she invited, among others, Augustus Saint-Gaudens and his wife. Cecilia Beaux, who was at the White House putting the finishing touches on a portrait of Edith, sat next to the Saint-Gaudenses on the front row. Phimister Proctor and his wife were present.[32] The guests were received in the Green Room and then moved to the East Room, which had been converted into a music hall. The performance began at ten. A magnificent grand piano with a solid-gold-leaf cover had been wheeled between the double east doors. Afterward a light dinner was served where Theodore and Edith mingled freely with the guests. It was a brilliant evening for all.[33]

It was at this point that Saint-Gaudens found himself in the middle of a family disagreement. Gilder had written the president for permission to use Cecilia Beaux's portrait in the *Century* magazine. Normally such a request from Gilder would have been granted immediately, but Roosevelt delayed three days before answering. The truth was that the president did not like the portrait. Edith wanted Gus's opinion. He called it a masterpiece, and the painting stayed. Gilder got his permission.[34]

Edith's next effort started innocently enough. Some $16,000 had been appropriated by Congress for the routine upkeep of the White House. She was in a quandary as to how best to spend the money. Instinctively, she wanted to do right by the structure, so she turned to Charles Follen McKim.

McKim was not walking into this situation cold. When the Senate Park Commission briefly considered the White House, there had been disagreement. Burnham actually wanted to relocate the mansion. McKim felt that if it must be moved, it should be dismantled stone by stone. Roosevelt weighed in, telling Burnham and McKim that he regarded the White House as a historic landmark and would not listen to any proposition for its alteration. To change the character of the White House would be sacrilege. The Commission finally agreed that the White House should remain at its present location.[35]

Yet McKim was not prepared for what he saw on his walkthrough of April 15, 1902. He told Edith that the appropriation would not even pay for a proper cleaning of the mansion, much less repairs. After he left the White House, he went to see Charles Moore. The two men had become fast friends, and as McKim unburdened himself, Senator McMillan came from the Senate floor. There was a brief conversation. How much would it take, Moore wanted to know. McKim pulled a number out of the air—for starters, at least $100,000. There would need to be some accommodation for added office space that would cost another $10,000 to $15,000. With that McKim left for New York City feeling depressed and McMillan returned to the Senate.

When McKim arrived in New York there was a telegram awaiting him: McMillan had pressed the Senate Appropriations Committee to add $150,000 for repairs to the White House and another $15,000 for an office space. McKim was ecstatic, telling Moore it was a miracle. The only hesitancy was over the temporary office quarters to be added to the White House. McKim felt that a permanent separate building should be constructed as soon as possible. Burnham had warned him earlier that anything temporary in Washington would soon become permanent.[36]

Roosevelt was in New York the following weekend and he invited McKim to meet that Saturday. The president was aroused and understood that the renovation would be radical. He summoned McKim to his lunch table on the following Monday in Washington. He would make the White House available to him for an inspection on Tuesday, April 22. When McKim arrived, he had an opportunity to talk to Edith both days. Theodore and Edith wanted the White House returned to an 18th-century purity that had been lost through the many different occupants of the preceding century. Any expansion must be along the lines conceived by Thomas Jefferson, employing a colonnaded terrace.[37]

Charles Moore accompanied McKim on his Tuesday inspection. Both men were appalled at what they saw. Sanitary conditions were unspeakable. The place was infested with rats that provided the Roosevelt boys no end of entertainment. Of a more critical nature were severe structural problems and defective wiring. There were even signs still of the fire of 1814. Just as unsettling to McKim, the White House interior, under the supervision of Army engineers since 1867, was a hodgepodge of conflicting design schemes. The architect repaired to New York, knowing that he had his work cut out for him. The president had given him a deadline of four months. To make it happen, everything would have to fall into place.[38]

McKim's first act was to alert Gus. The architect was cheered that both the president and first lady took the high ground in regard to the renovation. He would have some preliminary sketches that Gus must look over before he presented them to the president.[39] McKim and Moore met with Gus in Washington on May 4, 1902. The three men talked and McKim sketched. Gus's eye was for the little details. He told McKim that the monumental iron vase painted white on the north porch of the White House must be abolished or he would leave the country! With this effort, McKim finished the preliminary plans and sent them to the White House.[40]

Edith immediately sent for Moore. It was a chilly day for May when she received him in the handsome second-floor oval library. A customary fire was burning in the fireplace. Moore shared his easy chair with young Archie Roosevelt and a collie. The informality of the setting belied the importance of the meeting. Edith was beginning to grasp the radical nature of the proposed changes. McKim was calling for an enlargement of the State Dining Room. Also, he was proposing that the conservatory be removed from the west terrace to make way for the new office quarters. Here he was facing some resistance from the president. The east terrace would be reconstructed on its original foundations. Construction would take place in phases as the appropriations became available. The first lady focused on the practical details, reviewing matters such as the bedroom configurations. Throughout the interview the president came in from time to time to ask questions about the plans or tell Edith of his next moves.[41]

Edith Roosevelt had a good sense of art and literature. Theodore observed that she was not only cultured but also scholarly. She knew instinctively what was right and appropriate. Roosevelt said that any time he went against Edith's advice he paid for it. Spur-of-the-moment decisions could get him into trouble. Edith, on the other hand, exhibited a judgment that was well weighed, free from impulse. As first lady, she perfected the art of invisible governance.[42] At nine each morning, immediately after breakfast, Edith set aside an hour to herself. Theodore always made it a point not to conduct official business at this time. They would walk the grounds, or sit in the second-floor library were the weather inclement, and talk of whatever was on their minds. Woe unto any staffer who was forced to interrupt them. In many respects they approached the presidency as a team. Others observed that Theodore, whom Edith adored, always was a little afraid of his "Edie."[43] Edith would manage the White House renovation.

Later that morning as Edith and Charles Moore were standing at the west end of the upper corridor looking through the window at the conservatories, Theodore came bounding up. "Smash the glasshouses!" the president exclaimed. Moore responded, "But Mr. McKim understands that you want to save the glasshouses." Roosevelt laughed, "When you come to know me better, you will understand that I sometimes speak before consulting the head of the house." With that he returned to his office. Edith then dryly said, "Tell Mr. McKim to make the new elevator door wide enough to admit a stretcher."[44]

Moore duly passed Edith's observations to McKim. McKim could not have been happier that Edith had roped Moore into her horizon. "It was too good to believe that those excrescences, the greenhouses were to be abolished, or rather smashed."[45]

On May 10 McKim got his specific orders from the president. Work was to begin in early June. The living quarters and temporary offices must be done by October 1 and the first-floor formal areas by December 1, when Congress reconvened. Roosevelt wanted no interference from the legislative branch of government. There was just one problem: the House of Representatives had yet to approve the needed appropriation. Someone had to go see Joe Cannon before the first hammer could be lifted. That someone was Charles Moore. He called it "confronting the lion."[46] Moore found the chairman in his domain in the rooms of the House Committee on Appropriations. Cannon's initial response was less than enthusiastic, expressing frustration that McMillan had stolen the show with the Senate Park Commission. Nevertheless the ice was soon broken. Cannon didn't care how much the renovation cost to put the

White House in proper shape. His only concern was that money requests not come dribbling in year after year—put the entire appropriation together immediately and Cannon would see that it got through the House.[47]

McKim got the phone call. His estimate had to be ready the next day with enough cushion to avoid going back to the well. The document arrived accordingly. However, electrical work had been omitted, as McKim wanted to add that later. The document would never do in that shape. The final estimate had pencil marks through line items as cushions were added. An estimate of electric expenses was thrown in. At the bottom of the page in pencil was the total: $369,050, a number well beyond everybody's expectations.[48] Moore went first to the White House, where he found the president about to be shaved. As Theodore was being lathered up, he told Moore to fire away. Moore told him the amount, and he practically jumped out of the barber's chair. Resignation then settled in. However, Roosevelt volunteered Moore for the assignment of telling Cannon of the higher amount. Several days later, Cannon's consent was relayed to Moore.[49]

All of this funding activity gave a false sense of finality. On a Sunday evening in May, Edith called Moore over to the White House to review the plans. He went to the library again, where she immediately quizzed him over the State Dining Room. By absorbing the west end of the adjoining corridor, the room was being expanded to handle 100 people. Quite often state functions exceeded the capacity of the room in its present size, requiring that the East Room be pressed. The president and the attorney general then entered the room, and Theodore in a businesslike manner began to go over the plans with a red pencil, starting with the basement. Edith reminded him that housekeeping was her province. He objected to the State Dining Room being enlarged in that it would disturb Edith's quarters upstairs. Edith countered that the State Dining Room needed to be enlarged. Theodore first argued the point and then gave up and left the room.[50]

As the time drew near for the work to start, Edith immersed herself more and more in the details. She wanted to see the plans for the wings as soon as they were ready. The freight elevator should be combined with the passenger elevator, which would free up space to enlarge the anteroom so that guests had a place to leave their coats while attending luncheons and small dinners. Also, McKim needed to add a small office for the usher, adjoining the hall.[51]

On the evening of Saturday, June 14, McKim met with Roosevelt for the final review. The temporary executive offices would take the place of the greenhouses on the west side of the mansion. Old prints and plans for the White House had been discovered in the Library of Congress that would enable McKim to return the building to its original design. The west portico would be restored to its intended original use through the removal of the greenhouses. The reconstruction of the east colonnade in combination with the west colonnade would relieve the main building of a number of office requirements. The work envisioned would put the building into the condition originally planned but never carried out. The only remaining problem was that construction of the east portico would require seven to eight months. However, it would not interfere with Roosevelt's deadline for use of the other portions of the White House.[52]

The appropriations bill was signed into law on June 20 and demolition began immediately.[53] Trouble was not far behind. The source was not unexpected: Colonel Theodore Bingham. In April he had approached his boss, Elihu Root. Bingham had been responsible for preparing a scheme for Potomac Park. Root noted that it bore no resemblance to the concepts for that area set out by the Senate Park Commission. Root handled the matter by asking Senator McMillan if the two plans could be reconciled. It was an adroit move on Root's part. He was very forthright with McMillan as to how he wanted the meeting to resolve the situation: "Of course, you understand correctly that I want to see every peg possible driven in to fasten the future development of the city down to the lines of the Commission's plans."[54] Root was a valuable ally.

Colonel Bingham then traveled to New York City to talk to Thomas Hastings at the beginning of June. His purpose was to convince Hastings that his designs for the wings to the White House were superior to McKim's. Hastings very strongly told him not to interfere. The profession had rejected Bingham's plans for the White House more than a year before. After the interview ended, Hastings promptly warned McKim. Not only did Hastings have strong professional ties to McKim, but his father had performed the ceremony at McKim's second marriage. McKim was shocked at Bingham's impudence. He suggested to Charles Moore that Root be made aware of what Bingham had done. He sarcastically told Moore that Bingham needed a broader field of action—there must be something waiting for him in the Philippines![55]

Armed with the knowledge that Bingham was not a friend, McKim then sought clarification on procedures to pay contractors. He knew that all payments had to be made through the Office of Public Buildings and Grounds. He wanted assurances from Roosevelt that would clarify his relationship with Bingham in this regard. If the work were to be done promptly, there could be no payment delays. Bingham was to merely process the payment certificates issued by McKim, Mead, and White. He wanted Bingham to have nothing to do with the work or have any authority to question amounts certified for payment. He warned Moore that only foresight in their dealings with Bingham could keep them clear of trouble.[56]

At this same time, McKim was fretting about the deadlines that Roosevelt had imposed. He had acquiesced originally because he knew to do otherwise would imperil the project. Now he was worried. It was more important that the public rooms be done right than to have the house ready for a reception that Theodore was determined to give that December. McKim decided to wait 30 days to see how the project was going. If delays looked imminent, McKim would enlist Edith's help.[57]

Colonel Bingham had a different solution for project delays. He proposed a $200 per day forfeiture from McKim, Mead, and White for each and every day that work was delayed beyond the agreed deadlines. McKim rejected this proposal out of hand.[58]

There was still more trouble with Bingham: the man would not give up his greenhouses. Flowers were his hobby, and he was resisting the demolition of the conservatories. Bingham took his case to the president, who consulted Edith. She recognized that flowers were needed to decorate the White House. Roosevelt ordered that the greenhouses must not be torn down unless provisions were made for their replacement.[59]

Striking Change

This time McKim went straight to Edith. He and Moore met with the first lady on July 2 at Oyster Bay. With the work in full swing at the White House, Edith had left Theodore in Washington. In what became known as the Treaty of Oyster Bay, Edith took the extraordinary step of exerting her authority in writing. The greenhouses were to be moved from their location on the west terrace and set up on the grounds in an unobtrusive location.[60]

Even the first lady could not carry the day with Bingham, however. The issue of a contract without forfeitures and prompt payment of the contractors remained unresolved. In addition, Bingham was proposing to apply purchases of items for the White House not included in the appropriation against the project. McKim could take no more and asked for a meeting with George Cortelyou, the president's secretary. That meeting was called for July 14 at Oyster Bay. William Mead accompanied McKim. When they arrived they found Root as well as Theodore and Edith. As they sat on the porch, the president sent for Cortelyou and dictated a letter. Every issue was firmly dealt with.[61]

McKim now retained Glenn Brown as his on-site representative. Brown's knowledge of both the politics and the construction requirements made him an excellent choice to manage a tight deadline.

Attention then shifted to interior decorating. Again Edith was very deferential to her husband in her communications with McKim, saying, "The president and I have consulted." Edith brought back the George Watts painting *Love and Life*, which had been banished from the White House for its nudity. For this first lady, nudity in art did not equate to crudity in art.[62]

McKim also learned that Edith would not back down once she had made up her mind.

Articles had begun to appear in the Washington papers critical of the renovation. McKim suspected Bingham was the source.[63] The national magazines had been clamoring for the opportunity to do articles on the White House. A positive article would counter the negative stories coming out of Washington. McKim turned to familiar ground: Richard Watson Gilder and the *Century*. Edith requested the galleys before the article was printed. McKim had assumed crimson draperies in the East Room. In handwriting that was clearly Edith's, *crimson* was crossed out on the galley and *yellow* inserted. There would be no appeal.[64]

It also was the end of Bingham. In March 1903, he was transferred. The colonel did not exit gracefully.[65] His departure was the subject of much speculation in the Washington papers. One political cartoon showed Belle Hagner, Edith's personal secretary, dragging Bingham by the ears from the White House grounds. In an unpublished autobiography, Hagner strongly denied any role in Bingham's departure. However, by implicating her, the newspapers could have been subtly pointing a finger at the first lady. In July 1904, Bingham was promoted to brigadier general and retired.[66]

Edith returned to the White House on schedule on October 1. She had every right to be satisfied with what she saw. Over the coming months, public opinion would gradually come to agree that the change was good. Others would share credit for the successful restoration. However, without Edith's steady hand, the outcome would have been in doubt. Margaret Chanler wrote that Theodore's sense of the arts was primitive, and that Edith's compass was safer to steer by.[67]

Construction and completed East Wing of the White House, 1903.

Saint-Gaudens appeared back on the Washington scene at the beginning of November. Actually, he was on his way to Hot Springs in Virginia when he stopped at the White House to give the finished product a quick inspection. It met with his approval.[68]

Some time later McKim attended a private dinner at the White House. Secretary of the Treasury Leslie Shaw and his wife were also in attendance. This couple lacked the social polish so necessary in Washington. Soon after their arrival from the Midwest, Mrs. Shaw was quoted as saying she was certain that she and Mrs. Root should be good friends; they were both so fleshy![69]

As the dinner progressed, Secretary Shaw began to belittle McKim's temporary office building for the president. Unable to suppress himself, McKim told Shaw that he was reminded of an afternoon in Paris when an American lady visited Saint-Gaudens's studio to see the Farragut Monument. Afterward, seeing Gus whistling, McKim observed that the woman must have liked the work. Gus replied that she did not. Had she liked it, the sculptor would have known it was bad. Shaw stiffened at this subtle rebuke before catching himself and joining in the laughter.[70] The normally smooth McKim had not been able to control himself. Shaw was a philistine. McKim may well have tarred himself and, inadvertently, Saint-Gaudens too.

In August 1903, when Gus responded to the president's glowing praise for his Sherman Monument, he also brought up the Senate Park Commission plan.

> I have been very apprehensive with regard to the disposition of the new public buildings proposed in Washington. It would be deplorable in the extreme if they were not placed according to some comprehensive plan, binding all the Public Buildings with some idea of unity and harmony. Even if the scheme suggested by the Commission of which I was a member was discarded, I can not express so strongly the hope that nothing will be done without first consulting professional men, not directly interested in any one building.[71]

These were strong words addressed to the president, and with good reason. The work of the Senate Park Commission had never been ratified and Gus was not about to let Theodore off the hook. It had lost its chief supporter when Senator McMillan died unexpectedly on August 11, 1902.

The first salvo against the plan had come from Shaw in the summer of 1903. Congress had appropriated moneys for a Hall of Records. Its proposed location was not in conformance with the Senate Park Commission plan for the Mall. Roosevelt asked Shaw to consult with Daniel Burnham.

The exchange quickly became testy. Burnham made the point that once a deviation for whatever reason was granted, each succeeding change would become that much easier to accomplish. To Roosevelt, Shaw called Burnham as impracticable as anyone he had ever run across.[72] The Treasury secretary argued in his reply to Burnham the practicalities of the issue. Congress had appropriated the moneys and directed the building be placed upon the proposed site. The building was needed and

Secretary of the Treasury Leslie Shaw, former governor of Iowa. In 1904 Theodore Roosevelt wrote to Shaw: "I think our coinage is artistically of atrocious hideousness. Would it be possible, without asking permission of Congress, to employ a man like Saint-Gaudens to give us a coinage that would have some beauty?"

it would be impractical for the president to veto the legislation just because it would not be in conformance with a plan for the Mall.[73] Shaw attached a letter from Roosevelt reiterating this point.

In the correspondence with Shaw, Burnham mentioned that the Agriculture Department building, then in the initial planning process, would cause more harm to the axis of the Mall than the Hall of Records. Now the secretary of Agriculture, James Wilson, was involved. Wilson had previously ducked Roosevelt's request that he consult with Burnham, reasoning that the location of the proposed Agriculture Department building was not yet determined. Wilson bristled, wanting to know just what kind of axis Burnham was referencing. Burnham was the consummate diplomat when he explained to Wilson the concepts behind the axis and the need for buildings lining the Mall to be centered on the same east-west line. He sent a map, with a copy to Roosevelt, to illustrate his points.[74]

Here matters rested until February 1904. Secretary Wilson and the 16 members of the House Committee on Agriculture asked to meet with Roosevelt. Because the Washington Monument had been erected south of the original L'Enfant axis, building space on this side of the Mall was constricted. Wilson wanted to shrink the width of the Mall from 900 to 600 feet to better accommodate his building. Roosevelt asked if the group was unanimous in this desire. They answered in the affirmative. He replied that the matter must then stand as requested.[75] This was one impetuous decision that Roosevelt would regret. It was also the genesis of the need for the American Institute of Architects dinner of January 11, 1905.

In later years, Glenn Brown, who became a one-man crusade for the Senate Park Commission plan, strongly believed that Joe Cannon, by then Speaker of the House, was behind this move to encroach upon the Mall. In fact Cannon had been heard to say he would rather see the Mall planted in oats than treated as an artistic composition. If the central axis were breached, the entire work of the Senate Park Commission would soon disappear to the back shelves of the Library of Congress.[76]

Learning of the president's decision, Brown alerted McKim.[77] McKim immediately wrote to Roosevelt.

> Knowing your deep interest in the right development of the Mall, and your desire that each step as time goes on, shall be wisely taken, but fearing . . . that action is about to be taken, which, once taken, will result to the injury of the development of the Mall as a whole, I venture to ask, in the name of the Park Commission, that before your authority is finally given to any change from the plans accompanying the report of the Commission, they may be heard, either officially or unofficially, as you may deem best.[78]

To help reinforce McKim's position, Saint-Gaudens likewise wrote Roosevelt requesting a hearing.[79] The president's reply to McKim was perplexing. Roosevelt stated that the architects of the Commission should have met with the House committee and must now appear at once before the Senate committee. If the Senate would support their position, Roosevelt would intervene. He then added that he personally had never felt any fondness for very broad straight malls. In frustration,

The Confident Years

McKim told Saint-Gaudens that Roosevelt's answer confirmed statements in the newspapers that he had already given his approval.[80]

Promptly the American Institute of Architects worked with Nevada senator Francis G. Newlands on a bill to prevent any building being erected within the approximately 900-foot width of the Mall. Upon learning that McKim had picked up the battle, Burnham wrote that behind the controversy was a very persistent effort by executive-branch officials to keep "intruders" out of their exclusive domains.[81] Burnham was soon called to testify before the Senate Committee on the District of Columbia. McKim, Olmsted, and Saint-Gaudens were there to hold his hand. Chairman Newlands then called upon McKim to opine on the narrowing of the Mall. The architect responded that even a one-foot reduction would be a fatal mistake. As a result the bill was reported favorably to the full Senate, where it passed without opposition. Roosevelt held to his word, ordering the building moved back to the site called for in the Senate Park Commission report.[82]

Subsequently, following McKim's advice, Roosevelt appointed a consultative board made up of the original Senate Park Commission and Bernard Green, superintendent of the Library of Congress, to advise government officials about siting new buildings. It was a stopgap measure in that it lacked congressional authority. It was, however, classic Roosevelt. The obtaining of House approval was problematic. In this manner the president circumvented established protocol and obtained what he wanted.

Roosevelt appeared to be on both sides of this issue; he should not have been. He could be forgiven. It was an election year and he badly wanted the presidency in his own right.

Meanwhile Saint-Gaudens continued to operate from Cornish. His life had settled into a routine around his persistent ill health. He took up landscape gardening and constructed a small golf course. Sculpture was no longer everything in his life. Next to opening up the daily mailbag, looking out the window in the morning was his first enjoyment of life.[83] In the west, Mount Ascutney loomed. From morning to evening, its colors were ever changing as the sun and clouds played upon its broad slopes.

Gus traveled when he could during these years. However, plans had to be tentative should a merciless attack of sciatica hold him down.[84] There were the juries to serve on in Washington for the McClellan and Grant memorials. There were numerous invitations for Gus and Gussie to White House egg rolls, teas, and family dinners. Edith was ever so unassuming, asking that the Saint-Gaudenses not break engagements to attend. Gus also worked with McKim in New York City, raising funds for the American Academy in Rome. There were dinners at the Century Club with Henry Walters, whose contribution would do so much to establish the legitimacy of the Academy.[85] Moreover he maintained his relationship with Davida Clark, whom he had set up in Darien, Connecticut.

A letter to Charles McKim on October 12, 1903, revealed much of Saint-Gaudens's life and mental state at that time. In this letter Gus said that he had not done a stroke of work in three months. It was the first time in six years that at some hour of the day he had not meditated suicide. For once he had loafed when he could have worked. He planned to resume his work when the coming winter weather drove him indoors.[86]

Yet work was accomplished during this period. Though Fraser had struck off on his own, Hering still worked at Cornish. There were others, including Frances Grimes, Gus's brother Louis, Elsie Ward, and young Barry Faulkner. Gus began to refine a second or youthful head from the Angel of Victory. It had been his favorite though he had opted for the more mature version in the Sherman composition. He again summoned Alice Butler from the village across the river to help him. He called this head the *Nikh-Eiphnh* (Nike-Eirene) in Greek or *Victory-Peace*.[87] The end result stood 8-1/4 inches high. A laurel crown is placed upon her hair, which is tied in the back. The effect is exquisite. In the fall of 1904 Gus had Barry Faulkner gilding and tinting bronze casts of this *Head of Victory*, which would go to Tiffany's. Some time later, perhaps as late as the following year, Saint-Gaudens also modeled a 9-3/4-inch relief patterned after the *Head of Victory*.[88] Clearly a design motif featuring this head was germinating in his mind. It had now evolved from a bronze head in the round to a plaster and possibly bronze relief.

As Indian summer settled into the mountains of western New Hampshire in 1904, Saint-Gaudens absented himself for New York. He had had to postpone the trip in September because of an attack of pain. Gus had begun to be more and more plagued by these attacks.[89] On the night of Friday, October 7, Barry Faulkner was the only male at the studio at Aspet (Gus's name for his home in Cornish). He and the "girls," as he called Frances Grimes and Elsie Ward, were boarding at a nearby farm. Augusta had taken the night watchman to drive her to dinner. The house servants, with the night off, were on an outing. Shortly after dinner, Frances stepped outside and saw a fire burning at Aspet. It was the studio. Virtually all was lost, including irreplaceable memorabilia and a lifetime of correspondence. Augusta stood upon a rise of ground watching the fire, silent and motionless.[90] Impeded by questionable health, Saint-Gaudens now faced the formidable task of starting over. He had no choice, for, as always, he had commissions to finish. He must rebuild.

That same fall, Theodore Roosevelt was also facing a momentous challenge—election to the presidency. By all measures his term since the McKinley assassination had been a tremendous success. Not the least of his accomplishments had been the vast broadening of the executive powers of the presidency. Just as importantly, he was open to progressive thoughts and ideas. Surprisingly, however, the president was never a newspaper reader. His staff would clip articles for his attention. Edith would then sift through these selections as well as read three or four newspapers herself and mark items she particularly wanted him to see.[91] Roosevelt also kept close touch with many of his progressively thinking friends from the New York and Boston areas.

Richard Watson Gilder was one whose mind Roosevelt frequently tapped. They would meet for lunch in New York. Other times it would be at the White House.

Head of Victory, by Augustus Saint-Gaudens.

First plaster from original clay model for Victory-Peace uniface medal. (actual size 234.95 mm [9.25 inches])

Victory-Peace uniface medal by Augustus Saint-Gaudens.

Gilder never shared the content of these conversations. However, he did give some insights as to their intensity. In February 1903 he had three meetings over two days with the president. He exclaimed that the last one got him up before breakfast. It was "an hour and a half of the President at the Breakfast Table! But 'twas immense fun." Gilder complained of being gouty afterward and said it was too much excitement. They had settled all things foreign and domestic. Anything left over they had settled since.[92] Gilder left one question unanswered concerning his talks with Roosevelt. For someone who had invested so much energy over the plight of U.S. coin designs, had he discussed this desire with Roosevelt?

As October drew to a close, Theodore Roosevelt stood in doubt as to whether he would be victorious in the election. He was about the only one in the country who entertained those doubts.

Part 4

"The Pet Crime"

Chapter 15

The Stage Is Set

Gus was looking forward to visiting the White House. The stress of the prior night's speech at the American Institute of Architects dinner was gone. Saint-Gaudens had grown close to the Roosevelts in recent years. During McKim's redecoration of the White House, he had come to appreciate Edith's quiet ways, and he was not immune to Theodore's rambunctious habits. Prior to 1901, Saint-Gaudens had observed Roosevelt's career through common friendships. For his part, Roosevelt was well aware of Saint-Gaudens's accomplishments. From the president Saint-Gaudens could expect the unexpected.

January 12, 1905, was the date of the Annual Diplomatic Reception. It was the highlight of the Washington social season. The diplomats appeared in full court dress. Their wives and daughters were attired in gowns carefully selected and ordered from abroad for the occasion.[1] More importantly, it was also the first diplomatic reception that Theodore Roosevelt would hold in his own right as president. Fresh from a landslide electoral triumph the preceding November, he was now free from the burden of following in the footsteps of the assassinated McKinley. He was intent upon setting his own agenda.

The day began pleasantly enough for Gus. He, Henry James, and John La Farge were all houseguests of Henry Adams. Along with Margaret and Winthrop Chanler, they would all gather for a quiet intimate luncheon. Mrs. Roosevelt had also sent word that she would be attending the little affair.[2]

The diplomatic reception was scheduled to begin at 8:45 that evening. Arrangements had been made down to the last detail. The White House steward's staff had been augmented by 42 men and women to handle the large crowd. In addition there would be 26 "footmen," as the police were described, inside the White House and 15 more on the grounds surrounding the house. Eight mounted men were available in hired livery uniforms to oversee the flow of carriage traffic. The public would enter the White House from the east colonnade. The south portico would be made available as a second entrance for the diplomatic corps, Cabinet, Supreme Court justices, and special guests, including Saint-Gaudens.[3] Gus would have cared little for this aspect of the evening. He had never been political but he would have enjoyed the pageantry unfolding around him.

At the stroke of nine, the president and his Cabinet entered the Blue Room. The ladies of the Cabinet took their respective positions to the right of the first lady. Edith,

215

quite naturally, was a center of attention; fluent in French, the diplomatic language, she was at ease in her setting. The newspapers the next day would say that her gown of soft yellow silk exemplified a return to the last century's fashions. The skirt was trimmed with streamers of dark brown and black velvet ribbon, to which were tied clusters of large flowers. Around her waist, white lace was festooned becomingly. All the ladies carried bouquets to eliminate shaking hands in the reception line. Only Roosevelt shook hands.

The diplomatic corps was received first. Its dean, the Russian ambassador, accompanied by his daughter, both wearing jeweled decorations recently sent by the czar, led the way. As the diplomats were greeted by the president, they quickly exited the Blue Room and promenaded the East Room and the corridor.

At 9:30 Roosevelt began to receive the other guests.[4] All told, between 2,200 and 2,300 guests were presented to the president. Afterward they were free to mingle. Ice water was the beverage of choice—that is, it was the only beverage offered. The affair was not all strict formality, though; a year later Gus would regale Will Low with humorous scenes from that evening, particularly of the Persian ambassador, whom he caricatured. The public reception ended promptly at 10:45.[5] Roosevelt had become quite adept at quickly moving the reception line forward. In Edith's opinion the reception had come off finely.

Now the first lady felt distinguished to be having supper with James, La Farge, and Saint-Gaudens, who were among the 100 select guests invited to stay for the affair. Saint-Gaudens found himself seated at the president's table. With him were Elihu Root and his wife, and Whitelaw Reid, among others. Gus was feeling cocky.[6] People in the United States might not recognize the red rosette of an officer in the Legion of Honor, but dinner at the president's table in the White House was recognition enough. It was a very high honor, and no accident. Edith always prepared the seating chart for Theodore's approval.[7]

An old friend was also among those attending. Elizabeth Sherman Cameron was seated at Edith's table. Gus had had lunch with Henry James and Lizzie the preceding November in New York.[8] On this evening they would have chatted lightly about the presentation of Wagner's *Parsifal*, being illegally staged for only the second time in America—Wagner in his will had forbidden the work to be performed except in his hometown of Bayreuth until 1914. Lizzie Cameron was using the diplomatic reception as a suitable debut for her daughter, Martha. She had pressed Henry Adams into service to ask Edith for the invitation.[9] Still estranged from her husband after eight years, this was the best that she could manage for her daughter. The papers the next day would barely take note of Lizzie's presence.

As he sat down to supper, Theodore Roosevelt had a specific project in mind for the sculptor. Perhaps it was only coincidence that Richard Watson Gilder had come to Washington seeking a few words with Roosevelt in early December. They had had lunch together on December 9.[10] Regardless, on December 27, 1904, Theodore had written Secretary of the Treasury Shaw, "I think our coinage is artistically of atrocious hideousness. Would it be possible, without asking permission of Congress, to employ a man like Saint-Gaudens to give us a coinage that would have some beauty?"[11]

President Theodore Roosevelt in a characteristically dramatic pose, addressing a Memorial Day audience at Arlington Cemetery (May 4, 1902).

Inset: the Liberty Head $20 gold piece, minted from 1849 to 1907. Roosevelt thought the eagle looked like a grilled squab. (shown enlarged 1.5x)

217

An aging Augustus Saint-Gaudens in 1905.

This note brought to light the 1890 amendment to the revised statutes allowing changes in a coin's design after that design had been employed at least 25 years. Theodore had what he needed. He could act through the secretary of the Treasury to change the designs immediately on the cent and the four gold coins then in circulation.[12]

Both Roosevelt and Saint-Gaudens admired the high-relief coins of ancient Greece. Why could not the United States produce a coin as beautiful as the Greeks? If Gus would design a modern version, Theodore would have the Mint produce it. Theodore made light, saying: "You know, Saint-Gaudens, this is my pet crime."[13]

Roosevelt particularly disliked the existing gold coins. He thought the eagle on the reverse looked like a grilled squab, and he didn't like grilled squabs. There was never enough there for a full-grown man to eat![14] Gus was taken aback. The president was asking him to become a partner in this adventure.

It had been some 20 years since Saint-Gaudens had first contemplated the American coinage designs. He had been young and naive at that time, thinking the task easily accomplished. His subsequent experiences had taught him otherwise. He later told Theodore that he had been "scared blue" at the possibility. Maybe so, but Gus had long wanted to see the designs on United States coins improved. He did not sidestep the president. The truth was that he still had one more demon to exorcise from the World's Fair award-medal fiasco.

In fact there was give and take in the conversation. Gus had come to the reception with an agenda of his own. He and his brother, Louis, were in the initial stages of undertaking a commission, at the request of John Hay, to prepare a medal honoring Benjamin Franklin in 1906. Adding to the significance of the occasion, one medal would be specially struck in gold for presentation to the French government. Inquiries to the Mint in Philadelphia had raised a roadblock regarding the time required to prepare the dies and strike the medal. Things had not changed at the Mint. Gus was straightforward in describing the problem and blamed the engraver, Charles Barber. In a letter to his brother Louis, he described the ensuing conversation: "Barber is an S.O.A.B. but I had a talk with the President who ordered Secretary Shaw in my presence to cut Barber's head off if he didn't do our bidding."

These were heady words coming from the mouth of the president. Still, Gus would have to weigh the president's desires that he undertake the coin design commission with other obligations. This time with Roosevelt was intense.[15]

Saint-Gaudens once remarked to La Farge that "life is a tug." He knew from experience that working with the Mint would be impossible. Individuals close to him had begged him to take no more commissions.[16] To accomplish this one task, the redesign of U.S. coinage, would be a race against time. Still, the president would be on his side.

Roosevelt strongly wanted Saint-Gaudens's commitment. He was master of the grand presidential gesture. His actions, while provocative within the context of their time, were carefully calculated. They would establish the power of the presidency and become standards for future American presidents. He was intent upon advancing the United States to a position of greatness on the world's stage. He was interested in more than just achieving military or diplomatic preeminence in this effort; he wanted the world to know that this country had arrived culturally. All too often during the second half of the 19th century, European critics had dismissed the United States as a backwater of commercialism. A gesture such as the World's Columbian Exposition was not enough.

His approach that evening to Saint-Gaudens was anything but casual. Theodore and Edith had choreographed the whole affair. A nation's coinage should convey a message to all who touched it. It would add to the beauty of living and therefore to the joy of life.[17] Gus was to be their partner in crime.

The stage was set. On January 13 the director of the Mint wrote to Saint-Gaudens. George Roberts was still at the helm, serving in his second five-year term. Throughout his Washington service, Roberts had continued to involve himself in economic matters outside his functions at the Mint. He was by now noted for his kindly ways and great consideration for those who reported to him.[18] For Charles Barber, Roberts was an ideal supervisor. He was an able administrator who did not overly interfere in the Mint's manufacturing work.

Roberts's letter, while polite, gave Gus little encouragement that much had changed.

> No designs have been prepared and nothing definite is in mind. The department is not even ready to give a commission but the counsel of such artists as yourself is desired. The Secretary of the Treasury would be pleased to hear from you with any suggestions that you might feel disposed to make, or if you chance to be in this city, would be pleased to have an interview with you.[19]

Gus must have doubted that Theodore's message was being received at the Mint. His reply was equally polite and noncommittal. He would give the subject some thought and would take great pleasure in assisting. He suggested that if Roberts desired, they could meet during his next trip to Washington.[20]

Secretary Shaw was to blame for this exchange of letters. Roberts had been unsure whether Shaw wished to consult with artists other than Saint-Gaudens. Clearly Shaw had not conveyed to Roberts the unique circumstances of Saint-Gaudens's participation. The Mint director was actually in full agreement with the president concerning the coin designs, thinking them artistically poor. He especially disliked the subsidiary silver coinage. However, those designs were fixed by law until 1916.[21]

On that same 13th of January, Gus took the train back to New York, undecided as to where the events of the last 24 hours were leading.

Chapter 16

A Medal for Edith

Throughout early January, preparation of the official inaugural medal had continued with little notice, driven by the March 4 inauguration. It was a repeat design from the presidential medal quickly prepared upon Roosevelt's ascension to office, with only the date being changed. The obverse likeness was a head in three-quarters profile. The work was a reasonable representation of Roosevelt but needed updating. The Inaugural Committee had not been happy with a recycled image of the president.[1] The Mint had let the project slide during November and December, thereby pre-empting the Inaugural Committee's ability to change the design. Also the Mint lacked the necessary equipment to strike 3,000 medals, so the work had been contracted to Joseph K. Davison's Sons of Philadelphia.[2] This medal seemed to be lurching toward the inauguration deadline as much from benign neglect as anything else.

Two days after the diplomatic reception, a letter arrived at the White House as if shot from a cannon. It was for Edith. Frank Millet, who had become close to the first lady, was addressing her in hopes of affecting a change. He had been stirred by a story on official medals issued by the Mint in the Sunday magazine section of the *New York Herald*. It was not that the official Roosevelt inaugural medal was declared ordinary; it was that it compared so poorly with the others highlighted in the article.[3]

> The [inaugural] medal . . . has no nobility about it; it does not satisfy any of the cannons [*sic*] of the medalists and it is commonplace (even worse) it is a libel.
>
> You are too familiar with this President's profile to need to have your attention called to its characters. You must have observed the nobility of the lines, the individual strength of the forms, the suggestive proportions. You know the ear, small, close to the head, refined but indicative of great strength, both physical and mental. The chin, the neck—in fact every point is his and his alone. To express this character, these characteristics, in a broad way, in a noble way is the task of a medalist, it is his duty.
>
> Cannot you bring it about that the President shall have a medal which will at least hold its own? Why can't he have a medal as Millard Fillmore, for example?

The Mint of late had allowed medal work to fall from a position of importance that Millet felt the art form deserved. To drive home the point, he enclosed eight 18th-century medals of American patriots from the French mint. The honor of the country demanded that the medals marking moments of history and individual distinction should always exhibit the highest state of perfection. Millet would leave that matter in Edith's hands. He would say no more.[4]

Millet had said enough—Edith's mind was made up. Now it was up to Theodore to implement the change. He moved quickly, requesting that an outside artist be employed by the Mint to provide a design for another inaugural medal. What he learned was both discouraging and consistent with what Millet had said. The director of the Mint readily admitted in a letter to Secretary Shaw that the medal work of the Mint was not up to the standards of the French or some of the other foreign mints. Efforts had been made over the previous three years to correct this deficiency through equipment upgrades. However, there were no funds to employ outside artists. If Roosevelt wanted a different inaugural medal, it would have to come through unofficial channels.[5]

Gus was due back in Washington for a meeting on the evening of January 16 with the president and the secretary of the Treasury. The sculptor had raised enough issues about dealing with the Mint to necessitate a second discussion. Roosevelt was still determined that Saint-Gaudens provide at least one design for the gold-coin series and made it clear to Shaw that Saint-Gaudens should have total artistic control of his design and its execution. He wanted no interference from the Mint.

Then Roosevelt raised a totally new issue. He wanted an unofficial inaugural medal. Saint-Gaudens hedged; there was so little time and so many hurdles. Roosevelt was adamant. He would give Saint-Gaudens, or whomever Saint-Gaudens and Millet chose, an absolutely free hand. In following up their meeting with a letter to the Treasury secretary, Roosevelt asked that his desires and concerns be communicated to the director of the Mint. To ensure that the president's concerns were heard, he freely lifted sections from Millet's letter in his communication with Shaw.[6]

There is a clear trail. Archie Roosevelt remembered seeing his father sitting with Oscar Strauss, a friend and later Cabinet member, who shared Theodore's love of Greek coins. The two men were talking while Saint-Gaudens sat nearby, intently sketching. Archie remembered it as a proposed design for the gold coins.[7] However, it was almost certainly the inaugural medal. As he sketched, the sculptor would have talked of the styles of Pisanello and Sperandio.

As Saint-Gaudens returned again to New York, his head must have been spinning from the onslaught of Theodore and Edith. While on the train, he sketched out a basic design for the inaugural medal.[8] When he arrived in the city, his angel, Elizabeth Cameron, had a ticket for him to *Parsifal*. He had not seen so much of Lizzie since the summer of '99 in Paris. On the appointed night, Gus was in a quandary as to which coat to wear. He easily sat through the long performance featuring Wagner's strong female character.

No doubt the "pet crime" was on his mind that night. The challenges that the Roosevelts had laid before him had made Gus ebullient.[9]

On the 17th, Theodore was pushing Gus to accept the commission to provide new designs for the gold coins and the one-cent piece. He asked Gus point blank if he would take on these designs, how much it would cost, and what Gus thought about having the Mint prepare the dies from his design. Roosevelt closed in typical manner by saying how delightful it had been to catch a glimpse of him at the supper the other evening.[10]

Official Roosevelt inaugural medal of 1905 (shown enlarged 1.5x), by Charles Barber and George Morgan. (photo portrait from 1899)

223

Adolph A. Weinman at work in his studio. A student of, and assistant to, Augustus Saint-Gaudens, Weinman would make his own mark on the nation's coinage as the designer of the Winged Liberty (or "Mercury") dime and the Liberty Walking half dollar.

Henri Weil, from his 1900 wedding picture. Weil, of Deitsch Bros. in New York City, was a Frenchman trained in Paris. He worked Deitsch's Janvier reducing machine, the first of its kind to be imported to America. He would play a significant role in translating the designs of Saint-Gaudens, Brenner, Fraser, and Weinman into reality.

On that same day, Roosevelt queried General John Wilson, chairman of the Citizens' Inaugural Committee, to determine if funding for a second medal could come from that source.

> It is out of the question for the ordinary government employee to design a medal which shall be worth preserving or which shall add to the stock of artistic achievement of the Nation.[11]

Wilson would do anything to avoid disappointing his president. However, funds were tight. There were legal ramifications since a contract had already been let for the striking of the official bronze medals. Roosevelt was not one to take "no" for an answer, and Wilson was certainly not going to say no to him.

On the 19th Wilson wrote Saint-Gaudens formally asking that he undertake the special inaugural medal. There would be two gold medals for the president and vice president. The inaugural committee members would receive silver medals and a limited edition of bronze medals would be made available to other privileged individuals. The medals would be 1-3/4 inches in diameter.[12] Wilson followed this letter with a telegram on the 20th alerting Saint-Gaudens of the request.

Had Gus waited for that letter to arrive, he might have hesitated about moving forward. It was everything that he abhorred. Funds would limit his artistic license. The diameter was entirely too small for his liking. The deadline was absolutely impossible for him to meet. But Gus did not wait; like Wilson, he was reluctant to say no to his president. Upon receiving the telegram, he immediately replied directly to Roosevelt.

> If the inauguration medal is to be ready by March the first there is not a moment to lose. I cannot do it but I have arranged with the man best fit to execute it in the country. He has a most artistic nature, extremely diffident but would do an admirable thing. He is also supple and takes suggestions intelligently. . . . He is so interested that he begged me to fix any price. I named $250. That is a low sum for such work.

Saint-Gaudens would confer with Millet. He would personally see to the medal's design. The sculptor he wanted to use was Adolph Weinman, who had been his assistant in 1895 and 1896. There was more: Gus supposed that the dies would be cut at the Mint; if not, Tiffany's and Gorham could do the work. Then he scribbled a quote from Tiffany's for making the dies and striking the medals. Gus was pushing to see how far the president would go in supporting him.[13] He also told Roosevelt that he would communicate in a couple of days on the coin project.

Obviously Saint-Gaudens had given the medal advance thought. He was optimistic about the deadline since the design, in his opinion, was nine-tenths of the battle. On the obverse would be Roosevelt's portrait. He intended keeping inscriptions in the simplest form to aid the dignity of the arrangement.[14]

On January 23 Gus had his answer. Roosevelt had shown his letter to General Wilson. Wilson was requesting that Weinman come to Washington to meet the president. Saint-Gaudens and Weinman would do the inaugural medal.[15] On the Washington trip, Weinman stopped in Philadelphia to meet with the officers of Joseph K.

Davison's Sons, who held the existing contract for the official medals. Weinman left the meeting believing there would be no trouble over a second medal.[16]

Work now began on two fronts. Weinman modeled the obverse bust of Roosevelt. Saint-Gaudens began maneuvering to obtain a medal with which he could be satisfied. He conveyed the quotes from Gorham and Tiffany's for striking the medal to the president, who in turn forwarded them to Wilson. On January 30 Wilson wrote Saint-Gaudens that both quotes were too high.[17] The general in turn covered himself, setting out in a letter to Roosevelt all the difficulties they might encounter.

Weinman countered Wilson's letter to Gus. He noted that Wilson had erred in his calculations and that the Tiffany's estimate was only $150 higher than Davison's Sons. Saint-Gaudens believed that improved quality would offset the increased price. The sculptor hoped that the higher Tiffany's price would not be a bar to getting the best medal possible.[18] What Weinman and Saint-Gaudens did not know was that Roosevelt in conveying the quotes to Wilson had been most persuasive: "I earnestly hope that Saint-Gaudens can be given absolutely what he wants in this matter; and, my dear General, I beg you to try to do it. Will you let me know?"[19] This was a game that Wilson could not win.

Here matters seemed to stop for about a week. Ominously, in late January, Gus had had another attack of pain. This one was severe, requiring morphine to get relief and laying him up in New York City.[20] This explains why Weinman, and not Saint-Gaudens, answered Wilson's complaints over the Tiffany's quote. By early February Gus was on the mend.

The next issue that Gus addressed was the adding of a phrase or motto specific to Roosevelt's presidency to the medal. The campaign motto for 1904 had been "A Square Deal for Every Man." Roosevelt objected to this motto as being too colloquial for a medal.[21] Gus came back with the Latin phrase "Aequum Cuique," meaning literally "to each what is equitable," or "The Right and Fear Not." On Tuesday, February 14, Roosevelt accepted "Aequum Cuique" as an excellent Latin rendering of his campaign slogan.[22]

With the inscriptions set, there was still time to make the March 4 deadline for the gold and silver medals. Weinman was prepared to put the finishing touches on the models with the intent of shipping them to Saint-Gaudens for review the following Friday. Tiffany's still had not formally heard from Wilson that they had been chosen to do the work. Weinman thought that a mere formality. Not a formality was Gus's desire to increase the diameter of the medal to at least 2-1/2 inches. Tiffany's told Weinman that there would be a substantial price adjustment for the increased metal required but that die cutting of course would remain the same regardless of the size.

Reflecting the importance of the issue, Gus first prepared a rough draft of a letter to the general. Finally, on Sunday the 19th, he formally communicated his true desires about the medal size. He wanted a three-inch-diameter medal, much larger than the "official" medals of recent inaugurations. Unsaid was that with the larger diameter, Saint-Gaudens would have the medals cast—always his preference. The additional cost would be $500; however, he felt it worthwhile. He suggested as a compromise that the silver medals might be made at a 2-1/2–inch diameter, however regrettable that would be. To sugarcoat this bitter pill, Gus held out hope, having now seen Weinman's model, that the gold medal could still be ready in time for the inauguration.[23]

Gus had great trepidation as to whether this proposal was going to fly. The following day, Weinman called on Henri Weil of Deitsch Bros. in New York City. Weil, a Frenchman trained in Paris, was working the firm's Janvier reducing machine, the first of its kind to be imported to America. Weinman was seeking from Weil a second bid for the making of the dies and striking of the Roosevelt medal. Clearly Gus was seeking a fallback position if the committee and, more importantly, Roosevelt rejected this latest cost escalation.

Weil could make the reductions at once. However, the model was 20 inches in diameter. There was a probability that Weil would have to make an intermediate reduction down to 10 inches in either plaster or paraffin and from that reduction cut the steel die in a second reduction. Next, Weinman went to Tiffany's to inquire as to whether they would insist upon putting their name on the medal and its presentation box. Then Weinman caught the ten o'clock train for Washington.

Arriving in the capital city, Weinman went directly to William Loeb. Saint-Gaudens had already written the president's secretary about increasing the size of the medal and Roosevelt had approved this request. Next Weinman went to see General Wilson. The sculptor pointed out that a three-inch diameter doubled the cost.

Wilson was simply amazed. At first he would not even entertain another appropriation from his inaugural committee. Finally he acquiesced. If Roosevelt wanted the larger diameter, he would go back to his committee. Now Weinman had to go back to Loeb. Did the president want to push ahead for the larger diameter? Loeb came back a few minutes later saying the president most certainly did. Weinman went back to Wilson, a man caught in the middle, who agreed to put the proposition to his committee at its next meeting on the 23rd.

Somewhere in this round robin, Weinman conveyed a possible compromise that Saint-Gaudens had held in reserve. Gus knew that bronze would cast better than silver and was suggesting the committee consider dropping the silver medals in favor of bronze, with a resulting cost savings.

Finally, while in Washington, Weinman tried to see the Mint director. It was late in the day and Roberts was gone. Weinman then tried his home but to no avail, necessitating a letter the next day. Saint-Gaudens's fallback plan should the inaugural committee balk at this latest change was to have the Mint strike the medal.[24] Gus was determined to complete the medal in the size he wished, even if it meant having to deal with the Mint. It was an exhausted Weinman that returned to New York that night.

On February 23, Gus learned that he had carried the day. Wilson's committee had accepted his recommendation for a diameter of three inches. There would be two gold medals and 120 bronze medals cast. With the monetary constraints, the entire issue would be severely limited and there would be no silver casts. Interestingly, the Mint director wrote to Weinman that same day saying that the hydraulic press at Philadelphia was adaptable to dies of any size, and that the Mint would strike the medal at cost.[25] That was useful future information for Gus. However, with the committee's acceptance of Saint-Gaudens's compromise, Tiffany's would do the work and any confrontation with Charles Barber would be avoided.

Striking Change

Now Gus began fine-tuning. The reverse design centered on an eagle but Gus wanted to see how it would look with a shield incorporated. It went without saying that making the March deadline was hopeless. On the day of the inauguration, Weinman was sending Saint-Gaudens a package containing models with four different arrangements for a shield on the reverse. Also, the models had been prepared assuming a diameter of 2-3/4 inches. Weinman still must make an adjustment in design scale on the final models, using a three-inch diameter. He believed that adjustment would give the appearance of a larger circle formed by the lettering on the obverse around the bust of Roosevelt.

In addition, Henri Weil was still in the picture. Weinman was going to meet with him the following Monday or Tuesday to get a price for a reduction of the medal's obverse. Saint-Gaudens at this point desired that his man, Ardisson, take on the eagle-side reduction. There would probably be a cost savings. Weinman also had a conflict: he had a commission to prepare the award medal for the 1904 St. Louis World's Fair. He was behind and one of the members of the awards committee had paid him a visit. He must devote some time to this work.[26]

At this point John Wilson re-entered the picture. With the inaugural festivities over, Wilson optimistically queried Tiffany's as to when the medals would be ready. The answer was jarring. They had no models from which to commence the casting and they had had no word from Weinman since their meeting the morning of February 20. They could give Wilson no definite date. Tiffany's immediately alerted Gus to the potential trouble. Gus promised Tiffany's that the models would be complete in ten days or a fortnight.[27] What he didn't address was the length of time necessary for the reduction of the models and whether or not he would be satisfied with those efforts. With no deadline, Gus was now going to be extremely particular about each step in the design and production process.

Gus's time assessment was optimistic, as he was not happy with any of Weinman's four versions of the eagle side with shield. Weinman had shipped another revised reverse the day before. The redo at a larger scale of the obverse was nearly done.

There remained the issue of the reductions once Gus had signed off on the models. Weinman wanted to use Weil at least for the portrait-side reduction because of the absolute accuracy of the Janvier machine and the neatness of its execution. Weil could also increase or reduce the relief at will. However, Weinman was happy with the relief as modeled. He liked how the larger, bolder lettering complemented the bust. Weil would require three days for the reduction, giving allowance for making an intermediate bronze cast.[28]

Gus wasn't happy. He fretted that the intermediate casting, if not well made, would detract from the finished paraffin reduction. He still wanted Ardisson to try his hand with the eagle-side reduction. He definitely wanted to see Weinman's last portrait-side model before it was released to Weil for reduction.

On Friday, March 10, the models were finished and shipped. There were still two versions of the eagle side, one with and one without the shield.[29] Weinman apologized that he had been delayed by his St. Louis work. Then, on that Saturday, Weinman looked over his work. He saw that he had omitted DC from the inscription WASHINGTON DC on the reverse. He was up until midnight correcting the mistake before expressing the models to Saint-Gaudens.[30]

President Theodore Roosevelt taking the oath of office for his "second" term, March 4, 1905. The oath is being administered by Chief Justice Melville W. Fuller (with his back to the camera).

Unofficial Roosevelt inaugural medal of 1905, by Augustus Saint-Gaudens and Adolph Weinman. The medal shown above (at .75x actual size) was given by Theodore to his son Archie (pictured in 1903, seated on Theodore's leg).

With this last effort, Gus approved the models, discarding the concept of an eagle with shield. There was one last hurdle before the models could go for reduction: it fell to Weinman to take the completed models to Washington to gain the president's approval. Years later Weinman related, "Teddy Roosevelt came in [at] about 80 miles an hour, said 'Bully, bully' and dashed out."[31]

Now the activity centered on Weil and Tiffany's. Gus was giving Weil little room for error, telling Tiffany's that his reductions would be ready in 10 to 14 days.[32] Weinman again queried Tiffany's concerning the imprinting of their name on the medal. Saint-Gaudens wanted the fields on the medal to be free of unnecessary lettering. It was agreed that the company's mark would appear on the edge of the medal and be no more than 1/4 inch in length. There was also the issue of the patina of the finished medals. Weinman asked that Tiffany's work directly with Saint-Gaudens on this matter.

Meanwhile, Weil called on Weinman on March 20 with the first paraffin reductions. They looked okay to Weinman but not perfect. There was a slight line 3/8 inch from the perimeter of the reduction. Weil said that the line could be taken out before the bronze medals were cast. Perhaps knowing that Saint-Gaudens would never approve this reduction, Weinman asked that Weil have a lead cast made for Gus. That lead cast would be ready in three days time, and a second reduction would be ready in two days. The next day Tiffany's suggested that the gold medals have a slight pinkish tint called a Burmese finish and the bronze medals have a slight gold tint.[33]

Somewhere in the middle of this process, Gus decided to change the lettering on the portrait side. That is why Weil told Weinman that a second reduction would be ready on the 22nd. Weil brought this reduction to Weinman on the 23rd. In an effort to save time, Weil had forgone making an intermediate bronze casting. The reduction turned out badly. The only thing Weinman could conclude from the work was that the new lettering harmonized better with the head. The process now would have to start over. Gus also at this point dropped Ardisson for the reverse. Weil now had both sides.[34]

On April 3, like a voice in the wilderness, General Wilson asked Weinman when the medals would be delivered. The reduction of the eagle side was done. Weil had promised the new reduction of the obverse the following day. With both reductions in hand, Weinman would then make plaster casts for Gus's review.[35] When the casts did not appear the next day in Cornish, Gus wired Weinman. By now Weinman must have understood that he was in the same position as Wilson: both men must please very difficult taskmasters. Weil brought the paraffin reductions a day late. The plaster casts turned out so poorly that Weinman sent the paraffin reductions themselves.[36]

For once Gus was pleased. He was ready to turn the reductions over to Tiffany's for casting.[37]

The paraffin reductions reached Tiffany's on April 10. The decision on the thickness of the medal had not been made. Tiffany's was proposing 1/8 inch. The first cast would be ready about the 18th. Here the record went silent for the remainder of April.

The mud season had hit Cornish and Saint-Gaudens had hit the road. McKim had put Gus to work raising money for the American Academy in Rome.[38] The Academy hosted a dinner at the University Club in New York City. The architect later told Burnham that he and Saint-Gaudens had partied "in real old Chicago style," not going to bed until three in the morning. Amid these comings and goings, Saint-Gaudens no doubt saw the first gold cast.

Gus was not happy with the Tiffany's work and rejected it. He went so far as to approach the Roman Bronze Works and they agreed to see what they could do in competition. On April 28 Weinman went to Tiffany's and found the man in charge of the project absent. He left a note saying that Saint-Gaudens was utterly discouraged with Tiffany's. Weinman revealed that another molder had been contacted about doing the work.[39] Tiffany's waited five days to respond, but they did not shrink from the implied displeasure of Saint-Gaudens. They were using their best molder on the project and felt their work to date as perfect as possible. They were pleased to hear that Saint-Gaudens was trying another foundry. They would await the result before attempting another medal of their own.[40]

On May 19, Tiffany's relented and sent two more gold casts to Weinman. They were not perfect, needing some manual chasing. Worse news for Saint-Gaudens was that the Roman Bronze Works was having difficulty with their casting.[41] Gus now had no choice but to be patient with Tiffany's. However, they were going to have to try a third time as he was still not happy.

Finally, at the end of the first week in June, Tiffany's delivered two more gold casts to Weinman. He rejected the first one as having a waxy appearance. However, the patina of the second was that of an old gold coin, which he found pleasing. Weinman thought the quality of the casts good. Gus would not accept his word and wanted the medals sent to Cornish.[42] With this last review, Gus signed off. He was ready for Tiffany's to complete its production run.

In this final version of the medal, the obverse featuring Roosevelt's bust was modeled in the Renaissance fashion. The pince-nez, being inconsistent with that style, was gone. While Roosevelt personally disliked having the glasses in any sculptured likeness, their absence seems to detract from the perception of the man and his personality.[43] The phrase AEQUUM CUIQUE appeared in the field to the right. Across the top perimeter of the obverse was the inscription THEODORE ROOSEVELT and in two rows along the bottom perimeter was PRESIDENT OF THE UNITED STATES OF AMERICA. The lettering worked well.

On the reverse, the rejected eagle from the World's Columbian Exposition award medal—although now unmistakably Weinman's—made its return. It stood purposefully upon a rock. Balanced across the field in the background was the motto E PLURIBUS UNUM. Along the top perimeter the inscription read WASHINGTON DC, with the inaugural date in roman numerals. Gus had kept the inscriptions minimal, as was his practice. In a nice touch, Saint-Gaudens's and Weinman's initials were superimposed on the reverse.

In its completed form, the medal displayed Saint-Gaudens's hand. By his own admission, he had subjected Weinman to "constant advisement and modification" during the modeling process. Weinman had willingly become Gus's modeling hands and Saint-Gaudens was appreciative. He considered Weinman one of the three or four top sculptors in the country.[44]

Of the 120 bronze medals cast, 82 went to the committee, 3 to government libraries in Washington, and 35 to Roosevelt for his distribution to close friends and

A Medal for Edith

family. Late in July, Saint-Gaudens realized that he was not going to receive any of the medals. Back to Wilson he went to get permission for five more to be struck for his personal use.[45]

Gus was never pleased with the gold casting. As the process came to an end, he sent the president a bronze medal instead for his review on July 6.

> As far as the actual casting in gold is concerned, I wish it were better, but it is impossible to have it executed in this country as it should be and as is done by workmen in their little shops in France. This is the best that can be produced in the United States.
>
> As to the designs, I am responsible for the composition and interpretation and supervised closely its execution by Mr. Weinman. He has done his work admirably, following my desires with great conscience. He deserves high credit and it is a pleasure for me to have our initials together on the work.
>
> I send you by this mail a bronze replica, which although precisely similar to the gold, has more vigor and character because of the better treatment of the metal.[46]

Glowingly, Theodore replied on the 8th.

> My dear fellow, I am very grateful to you, and I am very proud to have been able to associate you in some way with my administration. I like the medals immensely; but that goes without saying for the work is eminently characteristic of you.

Then he added handwritten notes on the letter of gratitude.

> Thank Heaven, we have at last some artistic work of permanent worth done for the government.
>
> I don't want to slop over; but I feel just as if we had suddenly imported a little of Greece of the 5th or 4th centuries B. C. into America; and am very proud and very grateful that I personally happen to be the beneficiary.
>
> I like the special bronze medal particularly.[47]

In a July 11 note to Lodge conveying an inaugural medal for his wife, Nannie, Theodore again praised Saint-Gaudens, saying that he was pleased.

> Edith makes believe that she thinks it is a good likeness of me, which I regard as most wifely on her part. But the eagle on the reverse I do approve and also the Latin rendering for "a square deal."[48]

For some reason, Theodore was ambivalent about his likeness on the medal. Edith, however, was not:

> Your medal lies before me as I write and I must say how very fine I think it and how happy I am in its possession. To me it is wonderfully good and I am indeed grateful that you were able to undertake the work—to me such an important one.

Gus was flustered by the emotions in the note. In his hand, written across it, was the notation: "Must I reply?"[49]

Frank Millet, who had started the whole affair, glowed, calling the medal a distinguished work of art. He gloated, saying, "doesn't it make that other one look like thirty

233

cents?" Later critics would say that Theodore's likeness on the obverse had been diminished in favor of the Renaissance style.[50] On the other hand, the eagle was superb. It had a future. Saint-Gaudens would see to that.

Gus now had no concerns about Roosevelt's ability to deliver on his promises. The president indeed wielded a big stick. With the conveyance of the bronze medal on July 6, Gus told Theodore that he was ready to take steps about the coinage designs. Accordingly he would write directly to the secretary of the Treasury.[51] The real question was whether the Mint bureaucracy was ready for Gus's drive for perfection in both design and die preparation.

Chapter 17

An Unwanted Headache

On the 10th of July 1905, Gus followed through on his promise to the president. He proposed to George Roberts that he would provide a design for the gold-coin series and the one-cent piece. His price would be $5,000—considerably less than his customary rate. If there were budgetary constraints, he would take less, since he had this project so much at heart. He did say that if additional models were required on the copper coinage, he would adjust his fee.

His closing was the most critical part. Fresh from his success of having the dies for his inaugural medal cut outside the Mint, he proposed the same approach for this project. He reasoned that the existing reducing lathe at the Mint required retouching the dies by hand, while a "modern" one would obviate the need, reducing and cutting the dies entirely, including the lettering. He absolutely did not want Charles Barber retouching his work.[1]

On the 29th of July, the Treasury secretary set forth the terms of the agreement. Shaw had no choice in the matter, knowing the president had this project greatly at heart.[2] Still, he pushed Gus to make concessions. A second design would be necessary for the cent so as not to cause confusion on the public's part because of its similarity in size to the smallest gold coin. In a bit of convoluted reasoning, the fee was to be held at $5,000. Shaw went on to quote the statutes regarding design requirements and inscriptions. He noted that the eagle should be omitted from the reverse of the cent. In a separate letter Roberts pointed out that the sculptor was to provide only models, no dies. Also, the rim on his models would have to be higher than the modeled portions to facilitate stacking of the coins.[3]

Gus, in typical fashion, was not off to a fast start on this project. To be sure, there were extenuating circumstances. The fire in his studio, which he referred to as "the hell at Windsor," had destroyed the seated Lincoln, Marcus Daly, and Charles Parnell monuments.[4] Reconstruction of the studio and rebuilding the three major works continued through the spring of 1905. In June his son, Homer, was married. Then on June 22 his friends in the Cornish art colony gave a masque on the property in his honor.

Sketch by Everett Shinn of the masque at Cornish. Gus and Gussie are in a chariot being pulled by the participants at the completion of the masque.

Sunday September the 30th, 1906

112 WAVERLY PLACE.

My dear Mr Saint Gaudens,

I greatly appreciate the beautiful token of your appreciation of our efforts in the "Masque".

Yours,
Everett Shinn

For the Mint during this period it was very much business as usual. Roberts sent Charles Barber to Europe in June to study modern minting practices. In his report to Roberts, Barber noted several pertinent issues. European mints matched the coin blanks to the diameter of the die, in direct opposition to the practice in the United States. The Europeans accomplished this adjustment by milling the coin blanks to achieve the correct diameter. In doing so, a ridge was formed around the rim of the coin. The face of the die was finished by hand and left almost flat. The raised rim then contributed to excess wear on the die itself, resulting in a much shorter useful life compared to that experienced in America.

Barber also noted that the Janvier reducing lathe was in use at the mints in France, Italy, Britain, and Austria. The lathe or pantograph, under the guidance of a skilled operator, could raise or lower relief, flip a design in contraposition to its pattern, or add a camber or basin to the background as often required for coin models. The French made some alterations to this lathe that they would not share. Barber was investigating this issue because the Mint had a contract in place to replace their existing Hill lathe. He suggested that, should the effort underway not prove satisfactory, consideration to purchasing a Janvier machine ought to be given.[5]

Roberts forwarded this report to Frank Leach, the superintendent at the San Francisco Mint. Leach and Roberts shared a common background in newspaper publishing. Leach was the senior superintendent in the Mint Service and Roberts valued his opinions.

Leach noted Barber's discussion of milling in Europe and that he might have taken the issue further. American practices called for "basining" the die. By that he meant that the face of the die was made to take on a slightly convex appearance by placing a camber in the engraver's model or pattern. In this manner the radius of the die was maintained and the need for milling the coin blanks eliminated. This added convexity also contributed to the die's prolonged life. It was a technical subject. However, it indirectly raised the issue of just what was a satisfactory coin relief. Leach implied that European reliefs were too low. What he could not say, though, was how much relief could be achieved. At some point too much relief would cause excess wear on the most convex portions of the die.[6]

On the Cornish front, coin matters continued to drift into the fall. Gus should have been further along with his work. He had Roosevelt's complete backing, so perceived issues with the Mint would have meant little to him. While he thought that his cancer was in remission, there were still health problems that would have contributed to the delay. He was suffering from night sweats, fever, and loss of appetite. He had progressed from codeine to morphine for his pain. X-ray treatment was also being continued.[7] His bowels required constant attention. He was on a specialized diet of sweets and coffee. Occasionally he was able to have his beloved ice cream. Clearly the man was sicker than even his friends knew. Golf in October and November was continuous, sometimes 18 holes on the little course he had

U.S. Mint Director George E. Roberts. When McKinley and the Republicans came to power, Robert Preston was out and Roberts—an Iowa newspaperman with a keen grasp of economic theory and the gold standard—was in.

Portrait of Harrison S. Morris, by Thomas Eakins (1896). Morris, a member and managing director of the Pennsylvania Academy of the Fine Arts, was de facto chair of the Franklin medal committee.

constructed at Aspet.[8] He was falling back upon vigorous exercise as a way to combat his pain.

Gus could no longer sidestep the issue when on November 6 President Roosevelt asked for an update. For reasons that the president could not suspect, Saint-Gaudens was now in a quandary. He must answer Roosevelt in a positive fashion yet postpone the project as much as he could. He was enmeshed in making the Franklin medal commemorating the 200th birthday of this great American on January 17, 1906. He had originally taken this work on behalf of his brother Louis.[9] The deadline was pressing and he could not concentrate on the gold coins' design until the Franklin medal was put to bed.

Saint-Gaudens had not intended for it to be this way but now he was distracted. When Weir Mitchell, the well-known Philadelphia physician, approached Gus for ideas on how a Franklin medal should be composed, Gus had not envisioned an active role. The whole affair had started in April 1903 when the American Philosophical Society set out to celebrate the upcoming bicentennial. One year later the society, at Mitchell's urging, decided to seek the enabling legislation for the issuance of a medal.[10]

However, getting Congress to enact the necessary appropriation was another matter altogether. With no one to delegate the chore to, Mitchell had to go to Washington to seek Joe Cannon's approval. The interview started off well enough, with Cannon giving Mitchell a "somewhat raw but hearty welcome." Cannon by now was a little deaf, requiring Mitchell to come into close proximity. Part of the ritual of an audience with the House Speaker required that Mitchell light up one of Cannon's long black cigars. Then Cannon threw an embracing arm around Mitchell's shoulder. As the two drew together, Mitchell watched in horror as the bright red tip of his cigar appeared destined to touch off the Speaker's celluloid collar. Only Cannon's relaxing the embrace at the last moment saved the situation. Afterward, with a $5,000 appropriation in hand, Mitchell would chuckle over the thought of what would have happened had Cannon held the embrace.[11] One gold medal was to be struck for presentation to the Republic of France and 150 bronze medals were to be made available to the United States government and the American Philosophical Society, of which Franklin was a moving spirit. The celebration was to be sponsored by the State Department. However, as if to ensure that proper attention be given to the event, the philosophical society had elected President Roosevelt a member that April.[12]

John Hay asked Gus to serve on the committee charged with overseeing the medal's preparation. Then, when Harrison Morris, a fellow member and managing director of the Pennsylvania Academy of the Fine Arts, asked Gus as chairman to convene the committee, Gus refused. Hay adroitly solved that dilemma by asking Morris to call the first meeting, thereby making him the de facto chairman.[13] Besides, Mitchell had an idea of how the medal should look. The head of Franklin would be on one side and on the other the Muse of History would record Franklin's accomplishments with dedicatory wreaths for Diplomacy, Science, and Philosophy. What could be simpler? Besides, this commission looked ideal for his brother, Louis.

Gus had through the years tried to take care of Louis by throwing commissions his way. It was not that Louis was a less-than-average sculptor; it was just the opposite. Gus felt that Louis was truly more of an artist than he. Studio assistants who worked with Louis at Cornish tended to agree. The problem was that while Louis could create, he could also be indolent and disliked the work of modeling. He was absolutely incapable of the final effort to get the work into marble or bronze. He was lacking in the necessary people skills: directing the workmen, conciliating the clients, and making the contracts.[14]

The project did not get off to a smooth start. Morris called for a meeting of the committee at the end of September 1904. At the last minute Gus had to cancel because of sciatica. The meeting was rescheduled to October 21.[15] Thus Gus was in New York for, among other things, this meeting on the Franklin medal when his studio burned. It was an ill omen.

Louis Saint-Gaudens was given the commission under Gus's oversight. A deadline of January 1, 1906, was set for distribution of the medal. In an unusual move the committee decided to ask Kenyon Cox for a design proposal.[16]

With the project being commissioned by the United States government, the committee assumed that the medal would be struck at the Philadelphia Mint. That November Harrison Morris wrote Hay asking that he ascertain how long the Mint would require for preparation of the dies. Receiving no reply, he wrote a second time.[17] Morris, who was living in Philadelphia, then took matters into his own hands and went directly to John Landis, the superintendent, and Charles Barber. He was met with "officialism and courtesy." Barber's reply of a six-month timetable set Gus off with the president at the dinner after the diplomatic reception at the beginning of 1905.[18]

In defense of Barber, the engraver had to allow for the probability of high relief that required more time and attention. Also, he had taken at least six months in 1894 to prepare the dies for the World's Fair award medal. That timeframe in the context of the Franklin commission was acceptable, if Saint-Gaudens was punctual. Within a month of that discussion, Saint-Gaudens in a letter to Mint Director Roberts very diplomatically pointed out that reducing machines were in existence that could complete a die in 60 hours without any retouching by hand. If it was decided to have the die for the Franklin medal cut elsewhere, could the medal press at the Mint still be used?[19]

In the interim Morris began pressing Louis Saint-Gaudens about the need for timeliness. Weir Mitchell had warned Morris that Gus could be slow to start. Obviously, Morris had taken this concern to heart and was going to push Louis. Morris attempted to interject himself into the design process; however, Louis and Gus turned this effort back. Cox came forth with a design proposal that pleased no one.[20] With the design seemingly at an impasse, Gus was pressed into duty. The obverse would be the head of Franklin patterned after the bust by Houdon. The reverse would follow Weir Mitchell's ideas with the exception that Gus would include male figures to represent the fields in which Franklin excelled. In a quaint touch, lightning came out of a cloud above the figures.[21]

On Inauguration Day 1905, Morris, at Gus's suggestion, was writing the State Department to inquire if the Franklin Committee must use the Mint to prepare the die for the medal. They received the reply that they wanted: there was nothing specific in the act requiring that the medal be struck at the Mint.[22] Gus was now free to solicit others while considering the Mint as a last resort. However, the money to pay for this outside work must come out of the appropriation. Now it was up to Louis to get the competing quotes, including from Deitsch Brothers, who were at that time cutting the die for the inaugural medal.[23]

Louis would be in charge of the Franklin medal while Gus concentrated on the Roosevelt medal. The bids came in, including one from the assistant engraver at the Mint, George Morgan, who would do the work for himself with no involvement of Barber. Morgan's work would be reduced in relief and not intaglio as the diesinkers in New York did.[24] In other words, he would be using the old Hill reducing machine at the Mint. Morgan believed that this approach yielded a better result than what could be achieved in New York. Gus reengaged at this point to recommend Deitsch Brothers. The Janvier quote from Paris was lower and their work would be superior, but the time involved for delivery was unacceptable. Morris accepted Gus's recommendation and on July 3, 1905, received State Department permission to proceed.[25] Henri Weil would again be working with Saint-Gaudens.

During July work on the Franklin medal seemed to take a step forward and a step backward. Louis finished the plaster reduction of the obverse and began work on a wax model of the reverse.[26] However, the obverse was now in Gus's hands. This model then sat in Gus's studio for ten days while he experimented with variations in the inscriptions. In Louis's words, Gus had taken an interest and it rested with him to say when the work was good enough to be called done.[27]

Was Louis expressing frustration or resignation? The answer was not forthcoming. A copy of the plaster obverse and photographs were promised to Morris but did not materialize. In the meantime Gus wrote Morris that his constant inquiries to Louis were upsetting his brother and interfering with the quality of his work. Future correspondence should be addressed to Gus.[28]

By August, Louis had neared completion of both models. Now it was time for Gus to take an active lead involving the actual striking process at the Mint. Saint-Gaudens went directly to Secretary Shaw. He wanted to know if there were any special requirements for a die from the outside to be compatible with the medal presses in Philadelphia, and how much time would be required to strike the medals. Charles Barber suggested it would be preferable if the diesinker were to visit the Mint.[29] Depending upon the relief of the design, it would require a month to strike the medals. Gus checked these answers against Weinman's experience with his St. Louis Fair award medal and found the length of time to be conservative. He then politely acknowledged their letters.[30]

In the meantime, Gus told Morris that a new composition for the head of Franklin had occurred to Louis and him. Fresh off his success with the Roosevelt inaugural medal, Gus wanted to give Franklin a Greek look. It would take a fortnight to complete. There would be no models as of the end of August for Morris to see.[31]

With Deitsch Brothers now came the tedious work in preparation for cutting the dies. Henri Weil told Gus that they could cut the dies with one reduction if the models were from 15 to 18 inches in diameter and assuming that the medal itself would be either 4 or 4-1/2 inches in diameter. If the models were larger, a double reduction would be required. In either case Weil would like to have bronze castings made from which to cut the die directly. Whether they would cut a die or a hub, Weil could not say until he had seen the models. Therefore Gus would have to send the plaster casts in both positive and negative.[32]

On September 13 Saint-Gaudens again promised Morris a photograph of the obverse. Now the issue of inscriptions that always seemed to be contentious with Gus came to a head. The celebration was being sponsored by the American Philosophical Society and Morris did not want to omit the organization's name. Louis's original model included the phrase "Founder of the Philosophical Society in Philadelphia."[33] That was too much for Gus. The committee decided to ask Weir Mitchell to supply the inscriptions. Mitchell submitted the issue to Elihu Root, who had taken Hay's place upon that man's death. All agreed to the omission of the unwieldy phrase as well as any mention of the Philosophical Society.[34]

Meanwhile Morris was waiting for the photograph that still had not come. There were tweaks being made to the model; Saint-Gaudens was not ready to let it go. Morris was beginning to get nervous, saying that the Philosophical Society was asking questions. Morris knew that Louis had wanted to finish the design and modeling work by the end of September. The deadline of January 1 was starting to loom. Weil was anxious as well, and ready to start.[35] Gus finally released the model for the obverse on October 11. Yet there was a change in the inscription even before it reached Weil: the chairman of the Franklin celebration insisted that Franklin was a "Diplomatist" and not just a plain ordinary "Diplomat."[36]

Morris now had to catch up to Saint-Gaudens. He would go to New York to see the obverse at Deitsch Brothers. There was the issue of approval of the two other committee members (Society president Edgar Smith of Pennsylvania University, and Charles McKim). Neither would be a problem, but Morris must observe formality. The design was also subject to the approval of the secretary of State and Morris wanted it done before the dies were cut. Saint-Gaudens agreed that as soon as he approved the Deitsch reduction, he would send a plaster copy to Secretary Root.[37]

At this point Weil had made decisions in his approach to cutting the die for the obverse. Gus was trying to achieve the look of a cast medal even though the law specified a struck medal. As a result the sculptor wanted a medal thickness of only 1/8 inch, requiring the additional step of cutting a hub. Weil was very concerned about the thinness of the resulting medal in relationship to its diameter. With so little metal available to move, any relief would be extremely difficult to strike. Intermediate bronze castings would also be necessary since the models were large enough to require a double reduction.[38]

Saint-Gaudens insisted upon inspecting not only the castings but also the paraffin reductions before allowing Weil to cut the die. With the added work, Deitsch Brothers now raised the issue of additional pay. Gus, admitting to acting as an intermediary for Louis, felt the overall charges too high. Still he acquiesced for the time being.[39]

Here matters stood at the beginning of November as the deadline began to press. Harrison Morris wrote wanting to know when the reverse model would be done. He asked if Shaw had ever replied to Saint-Gaudens as to how long the Mint

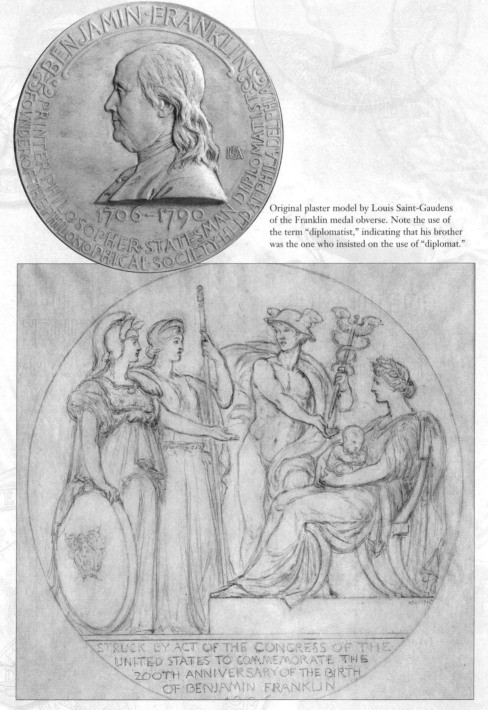

Original plaster model by Louis Saint-Gaudens of the Franklin medal obverse. Note the use of the term "diplomatist," indicating that his brother was the one who insisted on the use of "diplomat."

Kenyon Cox's original design proposal for the medal's reverse.

The original Franklin medal obverse with the laurel wreath. (.75x actual size)

Cutout of the original head, with the laurel wreath most likely done to facilitate the substitution of the former head without the wreath into the revised model.

Obverse and reverse of the Franklin medal as approved by Secretary of State Elihu Root. (shown at .6x actual size)

would take to strike the medals. Gus had not shared with Morris his obvious intent to cut the Mint entirely out of the process. By the 9th Gus had released the reverse model to Deitsch.[40] The design was as Saint-Gaudens had originally envisioned with the exception that the lightning was gone and another male figure had been added to represent Science.

Compounding the issue of the Franklin medal deadline, Gus was recuperating from a scare. He had been suffering from bad pain and an intermittent bowel blockage since the 1st of November. He had tried to play golf two days before and experienced a relapse requiring morphine. Still, he was on the mend, and golf in earnest resumed two days later. He even played in the snow.[41]

On November 11, Saint-Gaudens and Morris were exchanging letters. Morris had visited Deitsch Brothers to see the obverse model featuring the bust of Franklin. He called it "chastely beautiful and correct in every way to celebrate the large but simple character of the man." In an unusual move, the bust of Franklin in the Greek style was crowned with a laurel wreath skillfully set in low relief. Deitsch Brothers was aware that Saint-Gaudens had no intentions of using the Mint to strike the medals and told Morris as much. Morris related that he was glad that they would not have to use the Mint; Deitsch was doing better work. In a turn of phrase for the times, Morris said, "the Mint is incivility in the lump." He also told Gus that he would show the cast that the sculptor had just sent him to Weir Mitchell.

Morris brought up again the issue of gaining the approval of the secretary of state. Morris was concerned that the die work had proceeded without this necessary approval. Gus's rebuttal was to the effect that there was no time to spare. Submitting the models to Root was virtually a matter of form. If a problem developed, which it would not, Gus would pay from his own pocket the added expense of new dies.[42]

Morris felt it more correct for Saint-Gaudens to send the casts to Root. For a third time, on November 13, Morris asked Saint-Gaudens to seek the secretary of State's approval, though both thought it a mere formality.[43]

Also on November 13, a more contrite Saint-Gaudens admitted to feeling nervousness from all the postponements and dread of not getting the medal done on time. Everything should be submitted for review and changes accommodated if necessary.[44] Then, on November 14, in a response to Morris's letter of the previous day, Gus promised to send both models to Root as soon as the reverse was done, which would be in a few days. Gus preferred to do this himself rather than have Morris take on the burden. When the dies were complete, Gus also intended to finalize estimates from Deitsch Brothers, Tiffany's, Gorham, and the Mint to strike the medals. He volunteered that what Morgan had said earlier about the Deitsch reducing lathe was nonsense; it produced perfect reductions.[45]

Time now was becoming a major concern and work on the reduction of the reverse had only just started. To save time Gus asked Adolph Weinman to stand in for him to approve the bronze casting for the reverse when Weil had received it back from the foundry.[46] Morris again traveled to New York to check on the status of the reverse. He was pleased although not as much as he had been over the obverse. He also raised one troubling issue. He had shown the obverse to Weir Mitchell. The man had been concerned that the face was not altogether a likeness of Franklin. Morris had placed

Striking Change

his thumb over the wreath and noticed that the face at once became that of Franklin. Neither he nor Saint-Gaudens was troubled by that fact. Morris again pushed Gus to send both models to Root. He wanted nothing written about the medal until Root and the Philosophical Society had signed off. Again Gus asked Harrison Morris when the medal should be completed. He received the same answer as before: January 1, 1906.[47]

Up to this point, progress on the reverse side of the Franklin had been agonizingly slow. The original reduction from the large model had been done in four sections. Then, on December 4, Weinman rejected the intermediate bronze casting.[48]

In the meantime Saint-Gaudens pressed Tiffany's and Gorham for quotes on striking the medals.[49] He also had Weinman approach the Mint on this matter. Barber's answer was that the Mint's medal department was working overtime to fill current government orders. He had not the bronze on hand to strike so large an order and would not accept bronze from an outside source of an unknown mixture. As a result it would take three weeks. Their costs for striking the bronze medals were also well out of line compared to Tiffany's and Gorham.[50]

On December 19 Saint-Gaudens, in New York, could see a timetable to completion. George Kunz would be in charge at Tiffany's. Saint-Gaudens would leave the coloring of the gold and bronze medals in Weinman's hands. He knew just what Gus wanted: a medal that resembled the golden tint of the Roosevelt inaugural. Gus now addressed the need to get design approvals. However, he dumped it on Morris, sending the man plaster casts to show to "whoever is to see and approve of it." This information met Morris's approval. He did caution Saint-Gaudens that to his knowledge no arrangements had been finalized for presentation of the medal.[51]

Morris wrote Saint-Gaudens on the 23rd after having traveled to New York and calling on George Kunz, where he found Tiffany's feverishly at work. Now he had to talk to Saint-Gaudens about the deadlines. Morris again repeated that he was not aware of any plans for the conveyance of the gold medal in January. It had been the Philosophical Society that had insisted on this deadline. The celebration in which the medal would be the center attraction was not planned until April. There remained the issue of Root's approval. Morris had the casts in hand but was waiting to hear from Gus whether he wanted to send them off or if he wanted Morris to.[52] It seemed that neither man wanted the task of seeking Root's approval though Morris, unlike Gus, knew that it must be done. It was the Saturday before Christmas and this dictation sat until the following Tuesday.

Meanwhile Gus returned to Cornish on the 21st feeling the work was in hand.[53] He was dead wrong, as he found out on Christmas Day 1905. His son, Homer, had talked to Morris on the 22nd about doing an article on the Franklin medal. Morris told him that he could not allow publicity until the medal's release in April due to strictures placed upon it by the Philosophical Society.[54] Homer related this conversation to his father on Christmas Day and Gus instantly concluded that January 1 had never been a realistic completion date.

Now Gus was distressed and wrote Morris emotionally that he had worked under the impression from the beginning that the medal would be presented to the president of the Republic of France on January 16, Franklin's birthday.[55] Never had anyone told him otherwise. He had taken on the finish of this medal at a loss of both time and money. More importantly, he had allowed things on the reverse to go uncorrected. Now he would wire Kunz to stop everything. He wanted time to get a better reverse.[56]

At least that was what the final version of the letter said; in a scribbled draft Gus said something much different. He had let other projects slip or go unattended.[57] As always, the draft reflected his true sentiments. Number one on that list was that he had allowed himself to become distracted in regard to the president's coin-design commission. His desire to help Louis had forced a reordering of his priorities in a negative way.

Morris was mortified and chagrined by this letter. It was a shame that Saint-Gaudens found out about the deadlines from Homer. He told Gus frankly that the sculptor's letter made him feel forlorn. He did not know where Saint-Gaudens had gotten it into his head that the medal was to be presented January 16. The Philosophical Society had told Morris to keep the date confidential. A delegation of the Philosophical Society had met with Root but no arrangements had been finalized. A great deal remained to be done. Morris felt the reverse most acceptable but if Saint-Gaudens wanted it improved, so be it.[58]

In Gus's reply to Morris's conciliatory letter, he stated that he was sorry that he had pained Morris. He again asked Morris to handle conveying the plaster casts to Root.[59] Even so, Gus was not altogether sure that he had successfully dumped this chore off on Morris. Two days later he was asking Stanford White how he should address Root. Should he use "My dear Root," as Root did with him, or should he use "My dear Mr. Secretary"?[60] It is surprising that the always-reticent Saint-Gaudens would still stumble over this type of formality with someone as familiar as Elihu Root.

Saint-Gaudens proceeded to get a quote for cutting a new reverse die from Deitsch Brothers. After he saw the estimate of $345, he hesitated, telling Adolph Weinman to have Tiffany's proceed with the striking. He was overcoming a bout of pain that had taken a double dose of opium to subdue.[61]

On January 2, Saint-Gaudens received the Deitsch Brothers bill for their work preparing the first set of dies. It was $545. Gus was at a loss to understand how it could be that much.[62] Deitsch in turn was at a loss to understand Gus's frustration with their bill. Their thinking was that Saint-Gaudens was to provide his own bronze castings due to the requirement for a double reduction. Also, the workload increased beyond what was contemplated when hubs instead of dies had to be cut.[63]

Meanwhile Morris informed Gus that he had written to Root to seek the necessary approval. As soon as he heard from Root, he would forward his plaster casts to Washington. It would be nice to have a separate set of casts to send to Root if Gus could prepare them in the interim.[64]

Gus sat on the Deitsch Brothers letter of explanation for the bill for several days. Finally, on the 9th he sent a check but he made it clear he was not happy with the situation.[65] In the Deitsches' response, they said they felt badly about Gus's irritation although they had never had a complaint of this nature. They were sending him the finished dies. If he still felt a better reverse reduction could be done, they would recut the die for a trifling expense in an effort to placate him. Once the dies arrived it was obvious to Gus what he must do. He asked Deitsch for a quote on a new reverse die. They came in at $230 but asked that Gus prepare the model using "Keene cement" or very hard plaster.[66]

Now work on the Franklin stopped. No additional steps were taken to recut the Franklin reverse die. Tiffany's had received the first dies and were awaiting Weinman to call before starting work.[67] Morris wanted to know the whereabouts of the plaster casts for Root.

There was an explanation: Gus's health was ebbing. The doctors were recommending six meals a day to relieve him of his discomforts and to help him regain his strength.[68] Pain wracked Saint-Gaudens's body with morphine increasingly used to help him through the bad days. He needed medication to sleep at night. His increasing bowel irregularity was a symptom that a blockage was growing in his intestines. On the 15th of January Gus admitted, in the daily log he had been keeping of his pain and medication, to experiencing great depression and crying. He wrote to his doctor that day in despair.[69]

As January closed Gus began to feel better. A visit to Washington was in the works. En route he contacted Tiffany's for a quote on the Franklin reverse. The company would make a double reduction and cut the die for $100.[70] George Kunz wanted the business and he got it.

Upon Saint-Gaudens's return from Washington, he took time to write Harrison Morris that Tiffany's would do the new reverse reduction. There had been a "misunderstanding" at Cornish over the plaster casts for Root but he was now sending them. He sent the formal acceptance to Tiffany's on February 6.[71] Gus was back in the saddle at least temporarily, but an entire month had been lost on the Franklin medal.

Again the almost daily correspondence resumed on the Franklin medal. Morris had first written Elihu Root concerning approval of the models on December 29, 1905. This letter only surfaced on February 5. Panic set in. Herbert H.D. Peirce, third assistant secretary, needed the plasters for Root's approval at once.[72] Morris did not have the most recent reverse cast. Peirce had of course assured him it would be a mere formality as both Morris and Saint-Gaudens had expected. On February 10, Peirce, at Root's urgent request, was almost pleading for the casts. Gus, however, was of another mind. The cast of the reverse was unsatisfactory and he was making a new one. Finally, on the 15th Gus released the reverse.[73]

Meanwhile Morris sensed that the project was again slipping and wanted to know the latest schedule for completion. Gus told him Tiffany's would require three weeks to cut the die, three days to strike the gold medal, and ten days for the bronzes, leaving little time to spare.[74] Then real trouble started.

Elihu Root rejected the obverse of the medal. He didn't really reject it in the manner that John Carlisle had done in 1894; he was much more circumspect.

> I approve this design except that I am very doubtful as to the laurel wreath upon the head of Franklin. I question seriously whether that is not a mistake, whether, when viewed in connection with the venerable lines of Franklin's face and a knowledge of his character, essentially and pre-eminently a man of plain and rather homely common sense, the laurel wreath is not out of place. It seems to make him appear foolish.

... I have talked with the President and the French Ambassador and a number of others on the subject, and find a general agreement. Nevertheless, I make this comment with great diffidence. I should like to have it suggested to Mr. Saint-Gaudens.[75]

Morris was in a tizzy. He disagreed with Root, but he would leave Saint-Gaudens to mount any charge against the secretary. Fortunately there was still some time if Gus wished to make the change. He assumed that Root's interference would disconcert Gus. It was worse than that—Gus was now seriously sick and bedridden.[76]

Calmly Saint-Gaudens wrote to Morris that if Root, Roosevelt, and Jusserand preferred Franklin without the wreath, it was useless to try to persuade them otherwise. Root had been a champion of the Senate Park Commission plan. Gus respected this man and acquiesced. He had had his assistant Henry Hering talk with Kunz and Deitsch. Kunz's advice had been particularly valuable. The consensus was that a new obverse die could still be done in time.[77]

Events moved rapidly in Cornish and New York. Deitsch Brothers now dropped out.[78] On the 27th the new obverse model was shipped from Cornish. Gus's words to Kunz were the bare minimum: "Franklin now has a coat on." A surviving model fragment of the offending Franklin image points to the probability that it was cut out of the center of the working model and Louis's earlier profile dropped into its place. As if it needed saying, Gus pleaded, "Please *push* this as quickly as possible." The note was sent by Augusta's secretary, as Gus's condition had worsened. When Kunz replied that both dies would be ready by March 14, it was of little matter to Saint-Gaudens.[79]

Finally, on March 7, Gus could take it no longer. He left with Augusta for the Corey Hill Hospital in Brookline, Massachusetts.[80] Work on the medal would have to go on without him. On March 13 he was put under ether and an operation was performed on his artificial opening. While he was sedated, the doctors took the opportunity to examine his intestines. The prognosis was not good. Of the two doctors performing the surgery, one said the cancer would not return for five or six years; the other said it would return much sooner. Both men concurred that when the cancer returned it would be inoperable. The operation was taxing on both his body and his spirits. Gussie agonized over how much to tell her husband, and ultimately she decided to tell him that the doctors had found no recurrence of the tumor.[81]

Yet the Franklin medal would not leave the man alone. On March 16 and 17 there was correspondence. There was the issue of what quality gold content to use in the presentation piece. Gus wanted it simple, as with the Roosevelt medal. The patina for the gold medal would be at the discretion of Morris and Weinman.[82]

Then the seriousness of Saint-Gaudens's illness began to sink in to the outside world. After the surgery, Gus even wanted to hold Gussie's hand, something he had not previously done and which she found touching. Recovery from the operation was slow. Gus did not attempt to return to Cornish until March 28. In his later correspondence, he called it an "ugly time."[83]

Morris resumed his correspondence with Gus on April 4 after hearing from Homer that his father was better. While Morris preferred the figure with the wreath,

Striking Change

he had accepted the change. Kunz believed the medal in its final form the handsomest produced in America. The presentation medal was struck in Alaskan gold, giving it a greenish tint. The committee all approved of this look.[84] The bronze medals would be done in this manner also.

The sculptor immediately wrote to Tiffany's requesting a sample bronze medal done in this green tint.[85] Gus's desire to have the medal take on the look of the Roosevelt medal had been thrown to the wind in his absence.

Once again Root stepped into the process. He did not like the green tint of the Alaskan gold. He wanted the presentation medal restruck using 18-karat gold. The bronze medals likewise should reflect a natural "brown" tint.[86] This time Gus had no objections.

Now in a more relaxed manner, Gus wrote Morris that he agreed that the head with the wreath was better. Then, in a revealing comment, he said it was Louis's work. Saint-Gaudens's role had been to criticize Louis as he progressed. Gus's contribution had been the practical part of the medal production as Louis had "had to go west."[87] Right there Gus admitted that Louis had departed Cornish in either late summer or early fall, leaving Gus with all of the headaches. Gus also called Tiffany's die-cutting work infinitely better than Deitsch Brothers but infinitely worse than what could be obtained in France on the same machine.[88]

Tiffany's now took on Third Assistant Secretary Herbert Peirce. The end result was that the green tint would remain on the bronze medals but be reduced to about one-third in intensity. Peirce instructed that 100 of the bronze medals be delivered to the government for distribution and 50 shipped to the Philosophical Society. The dies must be broken up and all copies except those called for by statute destroyed.[89]

Finished bronze medals reached Gus on April 20. He was not feeling well that day and the medal was the last straw. He was keenly disappointed by the compromise patina. Tiffany's had had trouble maintaining its consistency across the medals. Yet he knew he must not be too tough on George Kunz; the man had moved mountains to get this medal completed on time.[90] Then, on the 21st, Saint-Gaudens received three or four medals with a patina that fairly pleased him.

Regardless of the patina problems, the medals were struck and the official presentation had occurred that day in Philadelphia. It went off without a hitch, with Root saying nice things.[91] But the focus of all in attendance, including the newspapers, was elsewhere. The world was still learning the horrible details of the San Francisco earthquake that had struck just two days prior. The celebration seemed a non-event.

Outstanding there still remained Peirce's request concerning the extra medals and the dies. Kunz would take no action on this matter until he had directions from Saint-Gaudens. The dies normally were defaced and given to a museum. In regard to the extra bronze medals that he had sent to Saint-Gaudens, Kunz felt they were the artist's proofs, to which Saint-Gaudens was entitled. Then he stated that the medal with the wreath of course does not concern this matter. In closing Kunz pointed out that Gus held title to the original obverse die and that he might want to retain it for some future use.[92]

Saint-Gaudens replied directly to Peirce. He had received several examples of the medal to determine the quality of the work and the patina. He regretted that his illness had prevented him from finishing the work. More to the point, Gus was puzzled in regard to the die for Franklin with the wreath. Did Peirce want it destroyed before other medals were struck from it? There were indeed three or four medals that Gus possessed of the version with the wreath that he would return to Peirce. Gus, however, argued against destroying the dies. He also had two lead first impressions that had been used to determine the character of the die cutting. He considered this work as a means to reaching an end and worth preserving.[93]

Optimistically Saint-Gaudens wrote Morris that he had no doubt that the State Department would let the sculptor have copies. As to the destruction of the lead impression and the trial medals with the laurel wreath, that decision rested with Root. Technically Gus felt he had a right to retain this work. However, morally he admitted that everything ought to go except the actual medal. He would feel uneasy retaining this work.[94]

There now were more dealings with Peirce. Saint-Gaudens wanted the entire $5,000 appropriation paid to his brother; he would then pay the expenses from the appropriation, leaving the excess to Louis. There had been no commission payable to the sculptor set in this appropriation and Gus by now was certainly wise to the ways of government. Peirce would not accept this approach.[95] The assistant secretary did relay that he had consulted with Root and that Gus could have a very limited edition of the Franklin obverse with the wreath, provided there was a blank reverse. Any lead impressions could be retained as long as the obverse and reverse were not married in a single piece. Other copies should be returned to him and he would forward them to Tiffany's for destruction.[96]

Gus took Peirce at his word and requested six copies of the Franklin medal with the wreath and a blank reverse. One he had sent directly to Harrison Morris as an expression of appreciation for all the work the man had contributed. The remaining five Tiffany's delivered directly to Saint-Gaudens.[97]

The issue of the disposition of the dies cropped up again. Peirce refused to process the payment vouchers until the dies were forwarded to the State Department. That action had its intended effect. Subsequently, a Senate bill was enacted allowing the Philosophical Society to have 200 additional medals struck at their expense. The dies would be sent to the Mint for the striking of these medals in February 1907.[98]

On May 26 Tiffany's again queried Gus in an attempt to wrap up the project. What did Saint-Gaudens want done with the rejected wreath die and the rejected wreath medal? Obviously the medals with the laurel-wreath head had reached Tiffany's for destruction. Saint-Gaudens's reply has not survived. However, at least one of these medals has survived and has appeared in numismatic auctions as recently as 2006.[99] George Kunz must have refused to comply with Peirce's instructions, and this unique design was preserved.

The Franklin medal was over! By pleading illness and retreating to California, Louis had left Gus in the lurch. The August letter to Morris asking that all communications come to Gus prevented Morris from learning of Louis's absence. Saint-Gaudens had turned to Frances Grimes and John Flanagan, another former assistant, in August, September, and October of 1905 to finish the modeling. Even with this help the strain on Gus had been too much. He confessed to Morris that the whole episode seemed interminable and he would hesitate a great deal before entering such an affair again.[100]

Late in the process, George Kunz offered Gus some unsolicited advice. The sculptor should have the entire decision in the final presentation of his work.[101] But that could not be. Gus knew from this experience that the politicians, even when his friends, could and would interfere in the design process.

It had been 16 months since Theodore and Gus had first discussed the gold coins' design. It had been nine months since the contract had been negotiated. Now the project must start in earnest.

Chapter 18

Engagement

Indeed the "pet crime," the collaboration of Theodore Roosevelt and Augustus Saint-Gaudens, had fallen by the wayside. By late summer of 1905 Gus had sketched some 70 eagles on tablets of clay. It was his practice to conceive his general scheme through countless models such as these. He lined up 25 small tablets at Aspet and sought critical comments from friends and guests. This work was an exercise in process only. He had also asked Henri Weil to quote a price for a reduction to 5-5/8 inches from a model of 33-3/4 inches.[1] He was looking to minimize the Mint's involvement in his design. Much remained to be accomplished.

Theodore Roosevelt's note on November 6, 1905, in the crush of the Franklin work, brought Gus back to life. It was chatty but there was no mistaking the underlying reason for the communication.

> How is the gold coinage getting along? I want to make a suggestion. It seems to me worthwhile to try for a really good coinage; though I suppose there will be some revolt about it! I was looking at some gold coins of Alexander the Great today, and I was struck by their high relief. Would it not be well to have our coins in high relief, and also to have the rims raised? The point of having the rims raised would be, of course, to protect the figure on the coin; and if we have the figures in high relief, like the figures on the old Greek coins, they will surely last longer. What do you think of this?[2]

Gus could put off the president no longer. Still he delayed until November 11 in drafting his answer.

> You have hit the nail on the head with regard to the coinage. Of course the great coins (and you might almost say the only coins) are the Greek ones you speak of, just as the great medals are those of Pisanello and Sperandio. Nothing would please me more than to make the attempt in the direction of the heads of Alexander, but the authorities on modern monetary requirements would, I fear, "throw fits," to speak emphatically, if the thing was done now. It would be great if it could be accomplished and I do not see what the objection would be if the edges were high enough to prevent rubbing. Perhaps an inquiry from you would not receive the antagonistic reply from those who have the say in such matters that would certainly be made to me.

255

Up to the present I have done no work on the actual models for the coins, but have made sketches, and the matter is constantly in my mind. I have about determined on the composition of one side, which would contain an eagle very much like the one I placed on our medal with a modification that would be advantageous. On the other side I would place a (possibly winged) figure of liberty striding energetically forward as if on a mountain top holding aloft on one arm a shield bearing the Stars and Stripes with the words Liberty marked across the field, in the other hand, perhaps, a flaming torch. The drapery would be flowing in the breeze. My idea is to make it a *living* thing and typical of progress.

Tell me frankly what you think of this and what your ideas may be. I remember you spoke of the head of an Indian. Of course that is always a superb thing to do, but would it be a sufficiently clear emblem of Liberty as required by law?[3]

The partnership was alive. While the Franklin work remained to be finished, Gus had completed multiple sketches developing his design, some of which still survive. For the obverse, Saint-Gaudens had started with a standing female figure for Liberty. Angel wings were optional. In one version, Liberty donned a blouse with the stars and stripes. In another version, there were shields in both hands. In one crude sketch Liberty had multiple hands as Saint-Gaudens looked at positioning. However, consistently through these trials Liberty was evolving to hold a torch in her right hand and a shield in her left. The shield in one example had "Liberty" and "Law" across the top, offset by vertical bars on the bottom. In another extreme, Gus positioned a small eagle with wings spread on top of the shield. He even put a fasces in the field reminiscent of the Washington inaugural medal. As the design matured, Liberty also took on more form, with hair gradually lengthening and finally blowing in the wind.

On the reverse the eagle was in almost every case standing. In one example, Saint-Gaudens deviated back to the classic heraldic eagle. In some sketches the eagle stood on a bundle of arrows. In others, the bird stood on a rock. In one sketch it held a shield. In most cases its wings were folded, but Gus also sketched them unfurled.

Throughout it is apparent that Saint-Gaudens was undecided about where to place the motto "E Pluribus Unum." It appeared on the rock upon which the eagle stood, and in the field of the reverse to the right of the eagle, surrounded by stars. In an unusual move, Saint-Gaudens even placed the motto on the edge, under the eagle or over Liberty's head, depending upon the viewer's perspective. Following Secretary Shaw's instructions, the sculptor excluded the motto "In God We Trust" from all the sketches.[4]

Now Gus was willing to declare a basic design to the president. At the same time, he was attempting to sidestep an issue. There was no sign of an Indian in this design. If Gus had hoped that the subtle objection in his letter would deter the president, he had underestimated the man. In closing he sent Roosevelt an old book on coins that he thought the president might find interesting.[5]

Responding much too quickly for Gus, Roosevelt told the sculptor on November 14 that he was summoning all the Mint people.

I am going to see if I cannot persuade them that coins of the Grecian type but with the raised rim will meet the commercial needs of the day. Of course, I want to avoid too heavy an outbreak of the mercantile classes, because after all it is they who do use the gold. If we can have an eagle like that on the Inaugural Medal, only raised, I should feel that we would be awfully fortunate. Don't you think that we might accomplish something by raising the figures more than at present but not as much as in the Greek coins? Probably the Greek coins would be so thick that modern banking houses, where they have to pile up gold, would simply be unable to do so. How would it do to have a design struck off in a tentative fashion—that is, to have a model made? I think your Liberty idea is all right. Is it possible to make a Liberty with that Indian feather head-dress? Would people refuse to regard it as a Liberty? The figure of Liberty as you suggest would be beautiful. If we get down to bed-rock facts would the feather head-dress be any more out of keeping with the rest of Liberty than the canonical Phrygian cap which never is worn and never has been worn by any free people in the world?[6]

Gus was stuck with the Indian headdress.

While Roosevelt did not want to unduly influence Saint-Gaudens, he had very specific thoughts. He considered the "Indian Princess" gold dollar coin that had been withdrawn from circulation in 1889 to be the best design to ever come from the Mint. He called the headdress on Liberty picturesque, typically American, and strikingly handsome.[7] The president was going to be hard to budge.

Roosevelt was now beginning to understand that commercial requirements were going to have to be balanced against the proposed high relief of the coins. He did not take an aggressive position in this regard at the meeting with the Mint. In attendance were both the director of the Mint and the engraver. Barber was instructed to bring with him examples of modern and European coinage.[8] Roberts and Barber left the meeting without understanding just how far Roosevelt would go to support Gus in his effort to push the relief issue to its limits.

On November 22 Gus got around to replying to Roosevelt. He had actually found time the two preceding days to do a little work on the gold-coin design, and felt enthusiastic. He would use the Indian headdress on Liberty. Now he needed Roosevelt's help with Treasury Secretary Shaw regarding the mottos. Gus closed with a handwritten note: "I think something between the high relief of the Greek coins and the extreme low relief of the modern work is possible, and as you suggest, I will make a model with that in view."[9]

In the follow-up letter that same day to Secretary Shaw, Gus wanted to add to the required inscription "Liberty" the term "Justice" or "Law." He also wanted to know if "In God We Trust" was required.[10] Shaw in his engagement letter had already covered the point of this religious motto. Saint-Gaudens was striving for as few inscriptions as possible. He was also conflicted about the idea of presenting one motto in Latin and another in English.

The laws regarding inscriptions on United States coins were clear, yet practices played a significant role. The original law of April 2, 1792, establishing the Mint and regulating coins, required a figure emblematic of liberty, the word "Liberty," and the date on one side of gold and silver coins. On the other side should appear a representation of an eagle, the denomination, and the inscription "United States of America."

Preliminary sketches for the

Liberty with coiled hair, no wings, and "union motif" shield.

Liberty with loosened hair blowing, wings, shield inscribed with LIBERTY and LAW, and fasces and LAW in field.

Liberty with coiled hair, no wings, fasces in field, and sun rising on her right.

Liberty with loosened hair blowing, no wings, shield inscribed with LIBERTY with eagle on top, and sun rising on Liberty's left.

design of the gold coins.

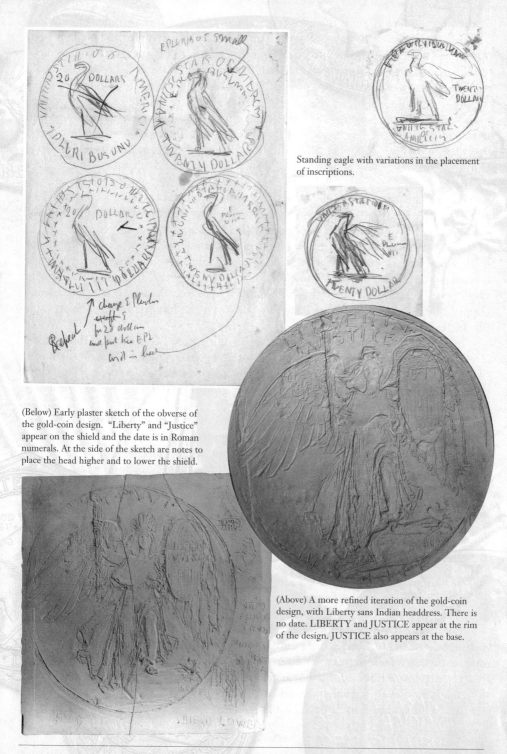

Standing eagle with variations in the placement of inscriptions.

(Below) Early plaster sketch of the obverse of the gold-coin design. "Liberty" and "Justice" appear on the shield and the date is in Roman numerals. At the side of the sketch are notes to place the head higher and to lower the shield.

(Above) A more refined iteration of the gold-coin design, with Liberty sans Indian headdress. There is no date. LIBERTY and JUSTICE appear at the rim of the design. JUSTICE also appears at the base.

259

Striking Change

In the first implementation of these requirements, the designs also incorporated 13 stars for the original 13 states. A figure emblematic of liberty in the past had been interpreted to be an allegorical female figure, although there was an alternate school of thought that the sitting president should be represented instead.

The motto "E Pluribus Unum" was introduced to United States gold and silver coinage with the adoption on the reverse of the Great Seal. Initially, stars were added to the designs as states were admitted to the Union, but this practice quickly proved unwieldy. In 1837, design requirements were reaffirmed by law with the exception that the eagle would no longer be required on silver coinage of a dime or less in value. With no legal mandate the motto "E Pluribus Unum" was dropped in designs after this date.

In 1864 the motto "In God We Trust" was incorporated on the two-cent piece by administrative action of the secretary of the Treasury. Reaction to the horror of the Civil War gave rise to appeals for a religious reference on American coinage, and in 1866 the motto was extended to each of the silver and gold coins required by law to incorporate the eagle on its reverse. In 1873 the statutes were again revised, giving the director of the Mint, with the approval of the secretary of the Treasury, the ability to require the inclusion of "In God We Trust." This law also exempted minor (meaning copper and nickel) subsidiary circulating coins from the requirement to use an eagle on the reverse.

In 1874, the statutes were changed for a third time. The motto "In God We Trust" would no longer be required on the nation's coinage, but in a switch, the motto "E Pluribus Unum" would be required on major silver and gold pieces. The Mint, however, made no effort to conform by changing the affected designs to include "E Pluribus Unum"; instead, "In God We Trust" remained. The situation became further confused when the new silver-coin designs of 1892 incorporated both mottos. At the time Saint-Gaudens undertook to redesign the gold coinage, the motto issues were thus murky, although "In God We Trust" was not required by law.

Stars for the original 13 states and stars for each state in the Union were not mandated by law. However, stars could be added to the background of any design without serious detriment to the overall result.

Roosevelt stepped in again on November 24. These letters were now flowing back and forth all too quickly for Gus, who was feeling the burden of the Franklin medal work. The president thought the design concepts for the obverse and reverse of the gold coins "first class." He liked the concept of adding the term "Justice." He was firm in his belief that Saint-Gaudens could be successful in obtaining some degree of high relief in his work that would meet modern commercial needs yet be worthy of a civilized people.[11]

Later that day Roosevelt followed up with a letter to Shaw supporting Saint-Gaudens's use of "Justice" as differentiating American liberty from that of the French during their revolution. Shaw countered by sending him a copy of the pertinent legislation that also addressed the motto "In God We Trust." On the 27th, a much more pragmatic Roosevelt scribbled a note back to Secretary Shaw, saying, "All right, put on 'Justice' in addition to 'Liberty' if St. Gaudens desires."[12]

The president's enthusiasm was beginning to waver. Adding the word "Justice" might stir up the conservative element in Congress, particularly Speaker Cannon. Consequently "Justice" faded from consideration. The motto "In God We Trust," on the other hand, lacked legislative authority. Roosevelt and Saint-Gaudens had no problem with its elimination.

Here the correspondence mercifully paused, allowing Saint-Gaudens to focus again on the Franklin medal. Upon his return to Cornish from New York on December 21, Gus found a letter written the day before, from Roosevelt. There was no hurry; Theodore was just curious how the coin project was getting along. Gus knew better. Believing the Franklin medal was firmly under control, he told Roosevelt on the 24th that a model of the Liberty side would probably be ready in a month.[13]

Saint-Gaudens had now decided on the design for the gold coins. For the reverse he intended using a standing Roman eagle as on the inaugural medal. He had always admired a flying eagle but had ruled it out. The reason was that on the obverse he was going to employ the figure of Liberty with outstretched wings, straight from his Angel of Victory. If he matched his obverse with the extended wings of a flying eagle, there would be, simply put, too many feathers.[14]

With the Christmas reprieve gained by the extended deadline for the Franklin medal, Saint-Gaudens switched his focus to implementing the obverse and reverse designs for the gold coins. He inquired of Adolph Weinman as to the possibility of persuading Hettie Anderson to come to Cornish for a couple or three days. His original plaster model for the Angel of Victory had been destroyed in the studio fire. Weinman forwarded this letter to Anderson, and Gus recalled in his earliest draft of his autobiography that upon her arrival, she was just as splendid as when he had first set eyes upon her.[15]

On the same January 2 that Saint-Gaudens first wrote Weinman, he also sent a letter to Secretary Shaw. In this letter he liberally invoked the name of the president.

> In my correspondence with Mr. Roosevelt in the matter of the coins, we concluded
> it would be well to try and make a coin with the design in higher relief than those
> now in use. Perhaps, as he suggested, a trial between the extreme high relief of the
> Greek coins and the very low relief of the modern ones might show that a higher
> relief is permissible in our currency than now prevails. I am working at this now
> and on reflection, I think it would be best to know at once if there are not some
> inflexible modern requirements that necessitate extreme flatness. If that is the case,
> it is useless to lose time on trials; also, to a certain degree, the relief determined on
> may modify the composition.[16]

He recognized that any work would entail the rim being as high as the highest point of the relief to facilitate stacking of the coins.[17] By the tenor of the final sentences of this letter, it is clear that Roosevelt and Saint-Gaudens were aware of the challenges ahead.

Shaw immediately ran to Roosevelt and the president in turn related the events of that meeting in a letter to Gus on January 6:

I have seen Shaw about the coinage and told him that it was my pet baby. We will try it anyway, so you go ahead. Shaw was really very nice about it. Of course he thinks I am a mere crack-brained lunatic on the subject, but he said with great kindness that there was always a certain number of gold coins that had to be stored up in vaults, and that there was no earthly objection to having those coins as artistic as the Greeks could desire. (I am paraphrasing his words of course.) I think it will seriously increase mortality among the employees of the mint at seeing such a desecration, but they will perish in a good cause![18]

This letter made it perfectly clear to Gus that without Theodore the redesign effort would be dead in the water. Shaw had offered a concession to Roosevelt. The Mint would strike a limited number of the coins but not for general commerce. Roosevelt was having none of it at that point.

With Roosevelt's letter in hand, on the 7th Saint-Gaudens again wrote Weinman asking for the loan of an Indian headdress. Weinman located the headdress and threw in some photographs of eagles for good measure, courtesy of John Flanagan.[19]

Ebulliently, Gus replied to the president on January 9:

All right, I shall proceed on the lines we have agreed on. The models are both well in hand, but I assure you I feel mighty cheeky so to speak, in attempting to line up with the Greek things. Well! Whatever I produce cannot be worse than the inanities now displayed on our coins and we will at least have made an attempt in the right direction, and serve the country by increasing the mortality at the mint. There is one gentleman there, however, who, when he sees what is coming, may have the "nervous prostitution" as termed by a native here, but killed, no. He has been in that institution since the foundation of the government and will be found standing in its ruins.[20]

Indeed the project was underway, with some hours each day being devoted to the "medal," as he sometimes called this project.[21] However, distractions remained with the Franklin medal.

It now fell to Shaw to set forth specifically the guidelines under which Saint-Gaudens would prepare trial high-relief designs. Director Roberts had written to Shaw on January 13 protesting in specific detail any design in high relief. He pointed out that the French government, which was the most responsive to the artistic community, struck general-circulation coins only in low relief. Roberts set forth two criteria that any design submitted by Saint-Gaudens must meet: the design must require only one blow of the coin press to permit cost-effective minting; also, the coin must not lose weight and therefore value through excessive wear and abrasion from circulation on its highest points. Finally, Roberts would extend an invitation to have Saint-Gaudens visit the Mint to carefully inspect the coinage operations.[22]

Shaw in his letter to Gus quoted Roberts's objections, but went on to note that he had submitted these points to Roosevelt, who sided with Saint-Gaudens. In accordance with the president's wishes, Shaw was authorizing Saint-Gaudens to proceed with the design proposed in his letter of January 2 and repeated the invitation to visit the Mint.[23]

In spite of the rough spell in mid-January, Gus decided to make a trip to Washington. However, no interim stop was made in Philadelphia to visit the Mint. Upon arriving in Washington, Saint-Gaudens visited Henry Adams. On February 1 he attended the congressional reception at the White House. Yet he could not deny the pain. The trip to Washington had sapped his strength. On the journey back to Cornish, he stopped first in New York City, where he was so sick he could not eat.[24]

Still, Gus took this time for a little personal touch. Since well before January, Edith Roosevelt had been immersed in planning for the White House wedding of Alice to Congressman Nicholas Longworth. The Saint-Gaudenses now sent as a wedding present a bronze of his *Head of Victory*. Knowing Edith's preference for the Sherman Monument, it was an easy choice for Gus and Gussie. They were not disappointed: Edith wrote promptly to say they were overcome by the gift.[25]

On February 15 Saint-Gaudens was again at work on the gold-coin design, writing to Adolph Weinman for some eagle or wild goose wing models that he believed either Weinman or Fraser possessed. It was at this point that Root objected to the Franklin wreath design and Gus's world began to fall apart. The hospital stay quickly followed. March and April would slide by with little being done on Roosevelt's project.

As springtime blossomed in Cornish, Saint-Gaudens began to feel better, but the pain was still too severe for travel. His morphine use became a real concern. Yet he was able to correspond with clients and to resume playing some golf.[26] McKim and White wanted to see him for just 24 hours for "auld lang syne." He wrote back jovially that he had been trying to get them to come up to Cornish for some 20 years. He put them off, however, saying that the mud season this spring was one of the worst and they should wait a couple of weeks.[27] White would not take "no" for an answer.

> Why do you explode so at the idea of Charlie and myself coming up to Windsor? If you think our desire came from any wish to see any damned fine spring or fine roads, you are not only mistaken but one of the most modest and unassuming men with so "beetly" brow, and so large a nose, "wot is." We were coming up to bow down before the sage and seer we admire and venerate so. Weather be damned, and roads too![28]

Gus was sicker than he wanted the world to know, and the trip never happened.

Work on the gold-coin design now resumed. He quickly finished the sketches that laid out the composition and arrangement of the design devices. In his weakened state, he delegated the modeling to Hering. Although he knew that Hering would be sadly at sea if left on his own, Saint-Gaudens considered him an admirable workman who could create excellently what was laid before him to do.[29] Just as Weinman had with the inaugural medal, Hering would, with Gus's much closer supervision, be able to skillfully translate Saint-Gaudens's penciled sketches into clay models.

Once again Gus seemed to cause a stir at the Treasury when he wrote Shaw on May 23 that the reverse was almost complete and the obverse was proceeding nicely. Now he was writing to ask permission to use roman numerals for the date. He also wanted to make a plaster cast of the existing $20 gold piece that would reveal precisely the relief presently being achieved.[30] By inference, Saint-Gaudens was going to adapt his design first to this largest of the gold coins. Shaw was against roman numerals but told Gus he would take it up with Roosevelt. On May 26, Theodore wrote Gus of his pleasure at the progress being made and enclosed a copy of a letter he had sent to Secretary Shaw supporting Gus. If Saint-Gaudens was clear that the effect would be better with roman numerals, Roosevelt was willing to give him his head about it.[31]

On May 29 an upbeat Gus wrote again to Theodore.

> The reverse is done. But before showing it to you I wish to have the reductions made at the different reliefs. They will take some time. The obverse I am hard at work on. Its completion will not be delayed long and your "pet crime" as you call it will be perpetrated as far as I am concerned.
>
> I have sent a practical man to Philadelphia to obtain all the details necessary for the carrying out of our scheme, but if you succeed in getting the best of the polite Mr. Barber down there, or the others in charge, you will have done a greater work than putting through the Panama Canal. Nevertheless, I shall stick at it, even unto death.[32]

Saint-Gaudens needed to make reductions from the model at different reliefs to compare against the current $20 gold coin. Henry Hering was the "practical man" sent to Philadelphia, armed with an innocent letter of introduction.[33]

Did Saint-Gaudens have a premonition about the gravity of his illness? Homer wrote his father-in-law that Gus was a very sick man. The doctors were no longer optimistic about his long-term prognosis. Homer was beginning to fear that his father would not survive to year's end. Will Low described him as ill beyond denial or concealment.[34]

The work at hand was now to finish the obverse design, which centered on the winged figure of the Angel of Victory standing with a foot firmly planted upon a rock. The sun rose on Liberty's right. In deference to the president, Liberty was adorned with a feather headdress.

Feeling that his design for the gold coins was to the point of fine-tuning, he shifted his creative work to the one-cent piece. He wrote to George Roberts on June 16—his first direct communication with the Mint since taking on the redesign commission—to ask if there would be a problem resurrecting a version of the flying-eagle design that had been used for a short period in the late 1850s on the newly created small-sized cent. Gus was now resurrecting what he had discarded for the reverse of the gold-coin design. Roberts wrote back that there was no problem using some form of the old design.[35] Roberts's position was open to question, however. Was the eagle, excluded by law from the reverse, a sufficient symbol emblematic of liberty for use on the obverse?

On June 22, Theodore, whether prompted or unprompted, wrote offering to help with the Mint personnel whenever Gus wished: "Don't forget to tell me when you want me to take up our brethren of the mint and grapple with them on the subject of the coins."[36]

If the president had missed the offhand comment about Gus's health in the previous letter, Gus's letter of June 28 from New York was much more direct. He was in the hands of the doctors until the beginning of August. Gus would let Roosevelt know when his presidential persuasion might be needed at the Mint. The project now loomed up like a specter to Saint-Gaudens, which would indicate that Hering's meeting in Philadelphia did not go well.[37]

While Gus was corresponding freely with the president on the subject of the designs, there was still the critical matter of who would engrave the dies—a question

Theodore Roosevelt's favorite coin design originating from the U.S. Mint: the $1 "Indian Princess" gold piece, discontinued in 1889. (shown enlarged 2x)

The Flying Eagle cent, from which Saint-Gaudens drew inspiration for his first design for the one-cent piece. (shown enlarged 2x)

Saint-Gaudens's final version of the winged-Liberty obverse for his gold-coin design, in the negative. The Indian headdress is in place and the shield has been replaced with an olive branch.

Standing Eagle reverse for the gold-coin design that was reduced in Paris.

The Flying Eagle design first proposed for the one-cent piece.

Engagement

that he was not ready to discuss directly with Roosevelt. In an undated note that summer, Gus asked Richard Watson Gilder to come see him. The standing-eagle side of the design was done and he wanted Gilder to help with having at least the dies cut abroad. "A word in someone's ear from you would settle it." Gilder that spring and summer was in particularly close contact with Roosevelt. The president had submitted an article for the *Century*.[38]

Preparatory to gaining that permission, Gus had sent the reverse model to France on June 10 to have reductions prepared at the three differing reliefs. Each reduction would have a diameter four times that of a $20 gold piece. Then a second set of reductions would be made taking the diameter down to actual coin size, allowing Gus to visually evaluate the design in its actual form at each relief. In an aside the French asked that should Saint-Gaudens send additional plaster models not to varnish or glaze them.[39]

At this point Saint-Gaudens was diverted by the firestorm that erupted over the sensational murder of Stanford White. The newspapers had a feeding frenzy when it was learned that the man who killed him was the husband of one of White's former intimates. Friends rose up in defense. McKim asked Gus to write publicly in White's defense. Both White's lawyer and his wife wanted Gus's support too. Gus agonized over what to say.[40] The work on the coin designs was left in the hands of Henry Hering, who maintained a studio in New York. Gus was shocked over the death of White. Finally, on August 6, he sent to *Collier's* the supporting letter that hit entirely too close to home.

> As the weeks pass the horror of the miserable taking-away of this big friend looms up more and more. It is unbelievable that we shall never see him again going about among us with his astonishing vitality, enthusiasm and force. In the thirty years that the friendship between him and me endured, his almost feminine tenderness to his friends in suffering and his generosity to those in trouble or want, stand out most prominently. That such a man should be taken away in such a manner in the full flush of his extraordinary power is pitiable beyond measure.[41]

Roosevelt wrote again July 30 to inquire as to what progress was being made. Unable to leave his room for days at a time and frustrated with the slowness of his recovery, Gus had Homer answer on August 2. Homer was not willing to discuss the cancer and told the president that Saint-Gaudens was sick with sciatica. Through the clear eyes of Homer's young wife, Cottie, the sculptor seemed to be dying by inches.[42]

Homer went on to say that the studio work was done. Experimental reductions were being carried out in Paris. It was the only place where the reductions could be given their proper relief. Homer expected the reductions for the reverse of the gold coins to be back by the end of the month. Then, if considered advisable, the model for the obverse in the studio could be sent to Paris where the dies could be properly made unless there was some difficulty with striking American coins with French dies. However, if the president wished, Homer could bring the models to Oyster Bay immediately for his review.[43]

The son had just waded into territory that the father had deftly avoided with the president. Gus's strategy to cut Barber out of the process was out in the open. It was

267

Striking Change

an unrealistic position. From the 1873 statutes, dies for circulating United States coins must be cut at the U.S. Mint, not in Paris.

First Roosevelt wrote back to Homer not to concern himself with the delay. It was a kinder and gentler Theodore, who was now aware that Saint-Gaudens was not well. He wished Gus a speedy recovery. The president would postpone action on the design effort until the following March, in 1907. The family's public denial of the seriousness of Gus's illness had had the unintended effect of misleading Theodore Roosevelt. In fact, they were also keeping the gravity of the situation from the sculptor himself for fear that he could not stand the shock.[44] Time was of the essence and neither the president nor Saint-Gaudens realized it.

When the reverse reductions returned from Paris, Homer met with the president, also bringing the plaster models for the obverse of the gold coin and both sides of the one-cent piece to a luncheon meeting at Oyster Bay on September 10. As his father's spokesman, young Homer bore a heavy responsibility. He was only three years out of Harvard, where he had struggled academically. In the short time since graduating, he had become disenchanted with his literary work in New York City.[45] Just the previous month, he had quit and moved to Cornish to work for his father with the goal of becoming a writer in the process. Present that day at the lunch were Paul Morton, former secretary of the Navy and now chairman of the Equitable Life Assurance Society, and Frank Higgins, governor of New York. Clearly Homer was a boy among men. There is no written record of what was said at this luncheon, but subsequent actions of the president give a clear indication.[46]

The letter the president wrote Shaw on September 11, 1906, was vintage Roosevelt.

> Now, a word as to my pet iniquity, the coinage, which I am getting Saint-Gaudens to start. I am afraid I shall have some difficulty with the Mint people, who are insisting that they can not make the coins as deep as they should be made. I enclose you a specimen, and I direct that Mr. Barber have the dies made as Saint-Gaudens, with my authority, presents them. Mr. Barber is quoted as saying that they could not cut them so deep as this. We then applied to Tiffany and Gorham, the two great silversmiths and jewelers of New York. Mr. Kunz of Tiffany, and Mr. Buck of Gorham's, at once stated that their houses could without difficulty at a single stroke make a cut as deep as this. Mr. Barber must at once get into communication with Tiffany and Gorham, unless he is prepared to make such a deep impression without such consultation. Will you find out from him how long it will take, when the full casts of the coins are furnished you by Saint-Gaudens, to get out the first of the new coins—that is, the twenty-dollar gold piece, which is the one I have most at heart? All I want to know from Mr. Barber is how long it will take to make them, and the cost, and if there is likely to be a long delay and seemingly too much expense I shall want him to communicate with Messrs. Buck and Kunz. But if he has to communicate with them I should regard it as rather a black eye for the Mint and a confession of inferiority on their part to Tiffany and Gorham. Will you communicate all this to the Mint people?[47]

Of singular significance in this letter was President Roosevelt's direct order to Charles Barber to have the dies made without modification.

268

This letter exploded with the impact of a bombshell at the Treasury. Shaw wanted Barber to proceed with the work at once. The engraver was rushed to Washington for a meeting on September 25. Roberts immediately afterward wrote to Shaw, who in turn forwarded the letter to Oyster Bay.[48] High relief remained an issue, needing a practical test to determine its feasibility. It would take six weeks to prepare the hubs and first two sets of dies. Everyone at the Mint would cooperate in this test. The Mint's coin presses and all their other equipment were modern and up to date, but those presses might not have the capability to strike the desired relief. Roberts went on to state that Mint personnel, meaning Barber, had recently toured the European mints and that those operations would face the same difficulty in striking high relief. If either Tiffany's or Gorham had developed coin presses better suited to high relief, Mint personnel would not hesitate in seeking their help.[49]

Maybe the coin presses were up to date, but the Hill reducing machine certainly was not, being almost 40 years old. This machine was slow and hard to operate, and skilled operators were becoming increasingly difficult to find.[50] It could not reduce a model larger than 5-3/8 inches in diameter for the purpose of producing the dies with which to strike a coin. In addition, the Mint's engravers used the Hill machine for reductions of the main design devices only, adding lettering, numbers, stars, and such in the master die with hand punches. Saint-Gaudens's plaster models were from 11 to 14 inches in diameter.

The Mint had contracted for a new electrically driven reducing lathe from the Keller Mechanical Engraving Company in May 1904, calling for delivery in nine months. However, four separate trials had been unsatisfactory, and Roberts canceled the contract in June 1906.[51]

Yet Barber was so focused when he saw Roberts's letter defending the Mint's coin presses to Shaw, he wrote saying that his only criticism would have been that the Mint director was too modest in allowing that Tiffany's and Gorham might have the equipment to succeed with high relief while the Mint did not.[52] The thought that he might have led his director astray about the capabilities of the Janvier reducing lathe never occurred to him.

Meanwhile Roosevelt forwarded Roberts's letter to Gus. He put the sculptor in a tight spot. Now that he had the Mint's attention, how soon could Saint-Gaudens get models to the Mint for a test?[53] Gus was in a quandary. While Roosevelt had come to his aid, his help came with a price tag. This request formally foreclosed the option of going outside of the Mint.

Saint-Gaudens now had to find another way to minimize Barber's work with his models. He had an answer. As part of the work on Roosevelt's inaugural medal in 1905, Gus had asked Henri Weil to prepare one additional reduction from his models that produced a relief one third as great.[54] He had wanted to see how a relief well below standard medal relief, but still greater than the flat coin relief, appeared. With the results of that experiment in hand, Gus's recommendation was obvious. The Janvier machine used by that company's American agent, Deitsch Brothers, would make accurate reductions, eliminating any need of retouching by Barber. An intermediate bronze casting would be required. More fully described, this bronze casting was an electrolytic cast or galvano that was highly accurate when properly executed. On

October 6, Homer Saint-Gaudens communicated the situation to Roosevelt. Gus was insisting upon "a machine as is to be had in Paris" and asking the president's help.[55]

Again Roosevelt came at the Mint.[56] Barber found himself writing the justification for the purchase of a new Janvier machine on October 8. He was forced to acknowledge that the Hill machine needed to be replaced and that the Janvier machine was in use at the leading mints in Europe. Barber had had discussions with Deitsch Brothers in the past and at that time they had been willing to give the Mint a machine at cost just to get an opportunity to show what it could do. Responding to Roosevelt's wish that the purchase be expedited, Roberts ordered Barber to travel to New York to inspect the Janvier machine at Deitsch Brothers.[57] That decision, however, had an unintended drawback: how well could Barber, a man comfortable in the old ways of engraving, adapt to this modern equipment?

Roberts immediately wrote Saint-Gaudens on the 10th to update him on the proposed purchase. Saint-Gaudens should forward the 5-3/8–inch model of the standing eagle to the Mint so that Charles Barber could take up work on this model.[58]

Gus now needed to update Roberts on the latest design changes. Roosevelt had taken a liking to Gus's flying-eagle design for the one-cent piece. The president most likely took the strict legal interpretation that its use on the one-cent piece was precluded by law. Wanting to preserve the design, he proposed using it for the reverse of the gold coins' design. The standing-eagle design was now orphaned.

Homer's luncheon meeting with the president was the only opportunity for this switch to have occurred. Thus the son, besides eliminating the option of using the Paris artisans, had ceded artistic oversight to the president. That was something that could not have pleased the father, and it explains why Homer never subsequently revealed the events of the September 10, 1906, meeting in any detail. Worse, with the flying eagle for the reverse, Saint-Gaudens's winged Liberty motif for the obverse would not work. The sculptor had rejected that pairing from the beginning. He must now start over on the obverse as well. In reality, the meeting between Homer and the president had now become a complete nightmare for Augustus Saint-Gaudens.

Saint-Gaudens had no option but to offer as an alternative that his 5-3/8–inch reduction of a standing-eagle reverse model be used for tests to determine if his relief was practical to strike. Meanwhile Saint-Gaudens would rework his designs in the larger-diameter models for the $20 gold piece. If the Mint received its new reducing machine promptly, reductions from these larger models could be made without sending them to Paris for an intermediate reduction to the smaller diameter required by the Hill machine.[59]

This setback could not have come at a more unfortunate time for Gus. He was laid up in bed, seeing no one and unable to visit the studio even for a short time. The treatments over the summer in combination with the surgery the preceding spring had been unable to stop the resurging cancer. In desperation Augusta turned to an experimental hypodermic treatment. While initial indications were that this radical approach had reduced the tumor drastically, the process itself had been extremely painful. Gussie described Gus's nervous system as a wreck. To allay his suspicions about the cancer, she had told him that he had been diagnosed with tuberculosis, which required this new treatment. To help with Gus's discomfort, a sleep aid, bromidia, was prescribed. Homer's mother-in-law, who was staying with the family at the time, feared that the dosage was particularly strong but did not want to cross Mrs. Saint-Gaudens.[60]

There was another burden on Augusta's shoulders that October: work at the studio without Gus's participation had slowed. The studio and its staff of assistants required $1,000 a week to run. If Gus could not resume his supervisory duties, Augusta was seriously considering layoffs. Over the years Gussie had grown to hate the staff. She saw Gus getting high prices for his work but spending it all on assistants. With the backlog of commissions, shuttering would be disastrous. For once, Augusta turned her back on her economizing ways, seeking instead a loan from one of Gus's clients.[61]

On November 6 George Roberts left for an extended trip to the West Coast. Roberts had written to Barber previously to expect models for the new design and to push them without delay. He failed to explain to Barber that the model in question was only for the standing-eagle reverse and that Barber's work would be "experimental."

On the day of Roberts's departure, Barber wrote in answer that Saint-Gaudens had supplied only the eagle side of the coin. He had completed his work from that model. He could do nothing more until he had the model for the other side. On the next day, the acting director wrote Barber suggesting that he inform Saint-Gaudens that he was waiting for the other model. This man was none other than Robert E. Preston, who had been around longer than Barber and was very much a part of the Mint bureaucracy. Neither of these two men was going to communicate directly with Saint-Gaudens. That task fell to Secretary Shaw, who queried Saint-Gaudens on November 10 as to the status of the model for the Liberty side of the $20 gold piece.[62]

Puzzled, Homer Saint-Gaudens replied on November 14 that the other models in the larger sizes were not ready due to his father's illness. He repeated that the reduction on which Barber had worked was experimental, to test their machinery. He also attached a copy of the October 10 letter of explanation to Director Roberts in support.[63]

Barber, seeing this correspondence, on November 20 rebutted that he stood ready to take the models chosen by the president in the 11- to 14-inch diameters and make the required reductions. He took issue with experimenting with a one-sided design that was not going to be used. The only experiment of any use would have to be made from designs ultimately to be struck.[64]

On November 21 Homer Saint-Gaudens wrote Secretary Shaw asking to see the tests of the standing-eagle reduction. His father desired "to see the result in order that he may model his final copy so that it will meet the demands of the machine."[65] The lead impression that Saint-Gaudens was requesting from this experimental die would allow the sculptor to see how accurately Barber translated the design motif from the larger model into a finished steel hub for die production. Saint-Gaudens would also be able to determine where additional sharpness of detail was needed to facilitate an acceptable hub.

This request landed on Barber's desk, much to his consternation. Barber's unofficial letter of protest went to Preston on November 26.

Striking Change

I cannot for the life of me see what Mr. Saint-Gaudens wants with the "result of the reduction" he now asks for, it in no way aids him in making his model, as we have told him, that if he will send us the models which he informs the department are from eleven to thirteen inch diameter, that we will take charge of the rest, and get dies made, he need not trouble his soul about our reducing machine, we will take all responsibility regarding the reductions, and know far better than he how to get the best effects.

He talks so much about experiments, it may be to him; but to us it is no experiment, as we are just as certain that the relief of his eagle will never coin, as we are certain that the Sun will rise each morning, and the only object in all this trouble and waste of money is to convince those who will be convinced in no other way, that to comply with the restrictions of law, and requirements of the civilized commercial world, you cannot depart from the experience of all nations namely, that to make coins of a given weight and fineness the operation of stamping the design on the piece of metal or planchet must be but one, and therefore the relief must be made to suit that operation, any repetition of the operation involves a number of others, and then both weight and fineness become an unknown quantity.

I think our friend is playing a game as he did when you and John G. [Carlisle] had to call him down, and that he is not anxious to show his hand, he possibly thought we would say we cannot coin your work and that would end the matter, but our willingness, nay more, our desire to let the work tell its own story has rather called his hand, and he is not prepared to show it, and therefore is sparring for wind, or time.

Barber also took the opportunity to complain about the reductions being made in Paris. He felt that if the reductions were made over there, dies also could easily have been made there. At some future date, impressions from the dies would most likely appear in the numismatic marketplace and the Mint would be blamed. Barber closed by saying he was simply desirous that Preston understand why nothing was being done at Philadelphia so that "when the patience of all folks in Washington is exhausted, the wrath shall not descend upon us."[66]

Barber's true feelings came out in this letter. He did not think that Saint-Gaudens had the technical expertise necessary to provide a satisfactory coin design. Barber had also concluded, based upon his recollection of events surrounding the Columbian award medal, that Saint-Gaudens would be unable to make workable designs for the gold coinage.

Did Barber have an ulterior motive for making these comments? Some time in 1906, he had set to work with George Morgan's help on a competing design for the $20 gold piece. His bad experience over the reducing lathe at the beginning of October would have provided the motivation to begin that alternate design. He had also queried George Roberts in early October as to the whereabouts of the Saint-Gaudens designs.[67] Allowing six weeks for completion of the work, his design would have been ready by the third week in November. With the exception of the motto E PLURIBUS UNUM in raised letters on the edge, his work plowed no new ground. The obverse bore a striking resemblance to his Liberty as depicted on the obverse of the subsidiary

272

Barber's design for the $20 gold piece that he quietly held in reserve should Saint-Gaudens's design prove unsatisfactory. (shown enlarged 2x)

silver coinage. The reverse resurrected his standing figure of Columbia that had been rejected early in the redesign process of 1891.[68] It would not do to bring this work out in competition with Saint-Gaudens. However, if Saint-Gaudens had no viable design, the way would be clear for Barber.

With George Roberts's return from the West Coast, affairs at the Mint resumed a more even keel. Roberts wrote a friendly letter on November 28 to George Kunz at Tiffany's to discuss the proposed high-relief coinage. He related that his people at the Mint did not believe that the desired relief could be struck by a single blow. Roberts had toured the Tiffany's and Gorham workshops, where striking high relief required multiple blows of a drop press without a collar. The process of finishing the edges with a file prohibited this approach for the Mint, which had to meet a legally set weight. Still, he wanted to see what could be done using a forming die to pre-strike each planchet before gaining the final impression from the regular die. He agreed with Kunz that the beauty of the resulting piece would be worth the slight additional expense. Roberts remained concerned about metal loss from abrasion and whether the Mint could maintain satisfactory execution of the design in the striking process when mass-producing the coins.[69]

Charles Barber had concerns of his own, which he voiced to Roberts at this point. While he would do everything on his part to demonstrate the possibility (or the contrary) of coining anything that Saint-Gaudens provided, he was pessimistic that the forming-die approach would work. Barber did not think that Kunz had an adequate understanding of Mint practices. He also raised the issue of whether the edge of the coin would be reeded, plain, or lettered. Barber then explained that he needed this information before making any dies, as the collar used for the edge treatment governed the size of the coin and the dies must fit the collar. A detailed question such as this could only have come from Barber's experience of applying edge lettering to his trial design.[70]

Finally the Mint forwarded to Saint-Gaudens a lead impression of the standing eagle. Little did Gus know how reluctantly the bureaucracy was providing this impression. The Philadelphia superintendent, John Landis, had written a long letter to Roberts setting forth pertinent regulations supporting his belief that he did not have the right to forward this lead impression.[71] He would provide the impression to Roberts, leaving it for the Mint director to forward to Saint-Gaudens. Roberts ignored this protest.

On December 8 Gus wrote to Roberts saying the models were ready. He asked if the Mint wanted the plaster models shellacked. Shellacking sealed the plaster surface, making it suitable for producing an intermediate bronze cast. The letter was signed by Augusta, as Saint-Gaudens was still not well.[72] Roberts forwarded Gus's letter to Philadelphia. He then went on to relate to Saint-Gaudens in detail the information he had gained by visiting the operations of Tiffany's and Gorham. Roberts was hopeful that a forming die to pre-strike each planchet would be successful. The Mint would work on the problem after receiving both the obverse and reverse models. He asked that Gus be patient as the Mint was attempting something that had not been done before.[73]

The forwarding of the Saint-Gaudens query on model preparation to Philadelphia gave Barber yet another opportunity, on December 12, to indirectly voice his criticisms of the sculptor. He returned again to the test of the standing eagle. He called the suggestion that an experiment be conducted on a discarded design "utterly useless." Metal flow on the surface of a planchet when struck by a die for a standing eagle would be entirely different from that of a flying eagle. This statement had to do with the differing locations of the high-relief points within the two designs. Therefore, until the Mint knew the actual design, the experiment would be "absolutely valueless and mere child's play." When models were in hand, he stated, he would do everything possible to make a success. The rest of the letter requested details about the lettering and stars that Saint-Gaudens wished to appear on the edge of the coin. Saint-Gaudens had been conflicted about where to place the motto "E Pluribus Unum." In the first version, it was on the rock upon which Liberty's left foot rested. He also struggled with the concept of sun rays on both sides of the design, leaving them off the obverse in the earlier version of this design. Now he had restored the sun rays and moved the motto to the coin's edge. The request concerning shellac application went unanswered.[74]

It was a different Barber that wrote to Roberts the preceding day. The Mint director had gotten a raise for the engraver through the House Appropriations Committee. If approved by Congress, it would be his first. He was filled with gratitude and gave "assurances that he stood ever ready and anxious to cooperate in any and every direction that tends to the good of the service to which we are engaged."[75]

Now the correspondence reopened between the president and Saint-Gaudens. Roosevelt's communications had reached a new urgency. Perhaps his frustration was building as the "pet crime" was approaching its second anniversary. His note was polite but adamant: when could he have the new models?[76]

For once, Saint-Gaudens was prepared. He shipped the large plasters to Roosevelt on December 14.[77]

Was the president satisfied? Gus began feeling some anxiety. On the 19th he followed with a letter. On the back of each model was inscribed the words "test model." He wanted the president to know that that was not the case. These models were the finished work.[78] What he really meant by the phrase *test model* was that the relief was set to the extreme. Depending upon the difficulty of this design to coin, he could back off the relief.

Saint-Gaudens sidestepped the president with this answer. His great strength as a sculptor was his unfailing eye. It was also his weakness, and contributed to many delays as he worked through concepts and changes. He had to see the executed result of each trial, not merely visualize it in his mind, to know if it was good.

This letter must have passed one in the mail from Roosevelt on December 20 that greatly eased Saint-Gaudens.

> These models are simply immense—if such a slang way of talking is permissible in reference to giving a modern nation one coinage at least which should be as good as the ancient Greeks. I have instructed the director of the Mint that these dies are to be reproduced just as quickly as possible and just as they are. It is simply splendid. I suppose I shall be impeached for it in Congress but I shall regard that as a very cheap payment![79]

For a second time Roosevelt was ordering Barber not to deviate from Saint-Gaudens's models. For Gus this letter was the nicest Christmas present that he could have gotten that year.

Roosevelt's reference to Congress had little to do with whether he had the authority to change the designs for gold coinage. He had that authority. It had to do with the growing testiness of his overall relations with Congress and the Senate in particular. He immediately sent the models to the director of the Mint. Roberts took the opportunity to personally deliver them to Philadelphia so that he could have another talk with Barber.[80] On Christmas Day 1906, the partners—one in Cornish, New Hampshire, and one in the White House—had every reason to be optimistic that the end of their project was now in sight.

Chapter 19

An End of Sorts

By late fall 1906, Henry Hering had returned to Cornish from his New York studio to rework the gold coins' designs for Saint-Gaudens.[1] Liberty, patterned after the Sherman Angel, had lost her wings and headdress. Desired by the president or not, the headdress was a distraction. In Liberty's right hand was a torch, a concept borrowed from the rejected reverse of Saint-Gaudens's World's Columbian Exposition award medal. In the left field was a silhouette of the United States Capitol, Saint-Gaudens's quiet salute to the ongoing efforts of the 1902 plan for the nation's capital. The much-simplified result was more compatible with the tondo for the largest of the gold coins under consideration—the one that so held Roosevelt's interest, the $20 gold piece. The reverse was the flying eagle originally intended for the one-cent piece. This was no ordinary eagle as had graced the old "white pennies." The wings of the Angel of Victory were gone from the obverse but not forgotten. They now graced a majestic eagle in full flight on the reverse.

Saint-Gaudens was always careful to sign his works, and discreetly placed his initials under the date. With his medals he had shared credit with Martiny, Weinman, and his brother Louis. That he did not do so this time with Hering is a clear indication that Saint-Gaudens had played a more active role in both composing the design and overseeing the modeling.

These were the models that Saint-Gaudens sent to Roosevelt just before Christmas 1906, which the president termed "immense," and that Roberts hand-carried to Philadelphia. The race was now on to prepare the dies and strike the gold coins before the cancer took Saint-Gaudens.

Roosevelt had qualms about the project and followed up the day after Christmas with a letter to Roberts.

> I suppose it is needless for me to write, but I do want to ask that you have special and peculiar care exercised in the cutting of that Saint-Gaudens coin. Won't you bring the die in for me to see, even before you send it to Saint-Gaudens? Of course the workmanship counts as much as the design in a case like this. I feel that we have a chance with this coin to make something as beautiful as the old Greek coinage. In confidence, I am not so sure how long I shall be permitted to keep such a coin in existence; but I want for once at least to have had this nation, the great republic of the West, with its extraordinary facility of industrial, commercial and mechanical

Striking Change

expression, do something in the way of artistic expression that shall rank with the best work of the kind that has ever been seen.[2]

The president acknowledged this model was not going to be practical for standard coinage. At the very least he feared his opponents would score this high-relief design for its additional cost to mint. Yet he very articulately set forth to Roberts his reasons for pressing ahead. He closed by cautioning the Mint director to keep the project absolutely confidential; he wanted no leaks.

In reply, Roberts thought the design beautiful and considered that its ultimate execution for general circulation would be a mark of distinction during his service at the Mint. Once the dies were complete, he would send them to Roosevelt for inspection prior to forwarding them to Saint-Gaudens. However, the Mint director still retained concerns whether the high-relief coins could be struck economically.

There was an unforeseen problem: the War Department was insisting that new coinage for the Philippines be given immediate attention. The rebel insurgency was winding down in the islands. It was important that the civilian government be firmly supported to cement American control of this former Spanish colony. An adequate supply of coinage as part of an overall economic stability was a necessity, and Roosevelt could not overrule his War Department. Making the dies for this Philippine issue, which had been requested by Secretary of War Taft on December 6, would require about six weeks.[3]

A more serious issue needed resolution, about making of the hubs for the Saint-Gaudens models. Roberts had not been happy with the length of the delay caused by the Philippines work and wanted to know why the use of the new reducing machine would not shorten the time required.[4] Barber had been forced to admit that he did not know how to use the Janvier reducing lathe. He complained that the person sent to Philadelphia to set up the machine and provide training had stayed for only a day and a half. Barber wanted Roberts to have the man return to conduct additional training and to make the paraffin reductions from the Saint-Gaudens's design for the $20 gold piece.[5] Barber did not want to work on the Saint-Gaudens models any more than Saint-Gaudens wanted him to.

Roberts approved Barber's request. Deitsch Brothers sent Henri Weil to the Mint from January 3 through the 8th. He made two full-sized plaster casts of the Saint-Gaudens models, paraffin reductions, and two plaster casts of these reductions. Barber was pleased as Weil displayed, in his opinion, an excellent knowledge of the machine and its capabilities.[6] Saint-Gaudens might have taken issue with Barber. Weil's work on the inaugural medal had been heavy in experimentation. Furthermore, Weil performed no work that would have demonstrated to Barber how to raise or lower the relief with the Janvier machine. Here Weil's work on the Saint-Gaudens models sat for the remainder of January.

As events unfolded in Philadelphia, Roberts turned for advice to Frank Leach in San Francisco, who had seen the standing-eagle design. In Leach's opinion, the standing eagle was not a faithful representation of the national bird since its legs were entirely too long. "This design inclines one to the impression of a crane in masquerade wearing pantaloons and a cutaway coat." Now seeing Saint-Gaudens's latest design with the flying eagle, Leach was pleased, yet he had his doubts about its popularity. Still, he would not speak for the public, as one never knew how these things might be received.

Design aside, Leach wanted to help in striking this high-relief coin. While Roberts was on the West Coast the preceding November, Leach had told Roberts that he thought he could put the planchets in optimum shape for striking high relief by manipulating the milling machine. Perhaps he had in mind the European practice. Upon receiving Roberts's latest letter, he had had the pressman make an experiment that confirmed it would be easier and less expensive than a forming die, though additional experiments would be necessary. The high-relief portion of the design must be contained within a certain radius of the center, away from the margin of the coin. When the dies were finalized, Leach wanted an opportunity to try his approach with the milling machine. He stood ready to help Roberts in any way.[7]

In what would become a routine, Roosevelt followed up in early February, having William Loeb ask for a progress report. Roberts replied that the dies were almost complete and asked if the president still wanted to see the Mint's work before the test striking. Curiously, Roberts also quoted in his letter the applicable statute regarding inscriptions required on the coins.[8] Someone must have been having some second thoughts about the omission of the motto "In God We Trust."

Meanwhile, Hering had drawn the difficult duty of dealing with Barber. He complained to Gus, "They take me for a kid. I can talk to these fellows about it but they are liable to run me down." He knew the model would meet resistance and had told Saint-Gaudens that it would not work. Gus had lightly responded that Hering could do as he pleased because "Teddy and I are behind you." When Hering wrote of this experience in 1949, the last year of his life, he recollected meeting George Roberts and Charles Barber in Philadelphia that week following Christmas 1906. He brought models with him that evidently had been cast after the first set sent to Roosevelt and now in Roberts's hands.

The tone of the meeting with Charles Barber had not dimmed in Hering's memory. When Barber saw the models, his ability to envision how a design would strike caused him to reject them out of hand. No modern mint could produce a coin for general circulation from these models with their extremely high relief. Hering informed Barber that he wanted to start from the highest relief possible and work backward, experimenting to find an acceptable level. Barber, after much discussion, acceded to Hering's request to prepare dies from this model.[9] He really had no choice.

At some point, Roberts had received the engraver's assurance that the Mint would cooperate fully. Hering got his two cents' worth in with Barber as well. When Barber showed him the reduction of the standing-eagle model done the previous fall, Hering informed him that it was a pretty poor reduction and he thought that Barber could do better. Hering asked about the reducing lathe that Barber had used on the standing-eagle model. Barber showed Hering the old machine but was not forthcoming about the recently installed Janvier machine.[10]

Hering returned to Philadelphia during the week of February 10.[11] He joined Charles Barber in the pressroom, and the coin now known to numismatists as the Ultra High Relief $20 gold piece was created from the Saint-Gaudens obverse and reverse models.

Using a medal press with a hydraulic pressure of 150 tons, the first blow was struck on the gold planchet. The resulting impression showed little more than half of the design elements. It was only after seven blows that all the details of the die emerged.[12] Before each striking, the coin underwent an annealing process. The coin was heated red-hot and then cooled in a diluted solution of nitric acid. This process removed the copper alloy on the surface of the coin, leaving a thin film of pure, malleable gold.[13]

The result—more medal than coin—was a beauty. Saint-Gaudens had followed all of his basic rules for a successful composition. He used the simple verticals formed by the folds in Liberty's skirt to impart a sense of tallness and beauty to the figure. The acute angles of the folds at the base of the skirt as well as Liberty's hair blowing in the wind gave an overall feeling of motion.[14] In the background, rays emanated from a rising sun with the Capitol in silhouette on the left. In a theme from the Washington Inauguration Centennial medal, 46 stars for the states of the Union encircled the coin's rim. Saint-Gaudens would admonish his students and assistants, "Remember that your background is your atmosphere, and part of the composition, and that the composition should extend from edge to edge of the frame."[15] On the reverse, the flying eagle was adorned with a style of feathers that was unique to Saint-Gaudens. A sunburst in low relief radiated in the background. The fields on both sides of the coin were kept clean by placing the motto, E PLURIBUS UNUM, on the edge of the coin. No one had communicated the style of this lettering to Barber so at some point he pressed into service collars that he had used on his own trial $20 design. The inscription, with a star between each letter, was not serifed or located in any particular manner in relation to the other design elements.[16]

This design confirmed Saint-Gaudens's best artistic skills. There was one question: Saint-Gaudens felt that a full face in a medallion was too much for the gods. Now he was violating his own rule with a full frontal standing figure, which had never been employed on an American coin. He was never one for technical explanations, composing more often than not on intuition. If pressed, he would simply say that the face was frontal because that was what was meant to be.[17]

As beautiful as this piece was, the impracticality of its ultra high relief was apparent to all. A second production experiment was then undertaken, using a planchet the size of a $10 gold piece, expecting that the extreme relief would be easier to strike on the smaller area. To meet the gold-content requirements, the thickness of the planchet was increased to approximately the size of a checker. It was subsequently discovered that the revisions to the 1890 coinage statutes fixed the size for all coins at their then-existing diameters, making this experiment illegal.[18]

This phase of the work complete, Hering returned to Cornish empty-handed but knowing that the design would have to be modified. He had suggested while in Philadelphia that certain casts be made to document the degree of success of each strike on the planchet. Saint-Gaudens immediately followed up, requesting Roberts order casts of the planchets with one, two, five, and seven strikes—a process set—so that he could judge for himself the problems encountered with this relief. In addition he wanted actual finished specimens struck in both gold and lead, as well as a checker-sized coin in lead only. He also wanted a cast of the finished steel hub from which future dies would be made. Finally, he wanted his original models back. With these pieces in hand, Gus would be able to inspect the quality of Barber's work and successfully modify the relief in his next effort.[19]

Nearly completed first (or "Ultra High Relief") model for the gold-coins design, in the negative. E PLURIBUS UNUM appears on the rock under Liberty's foot. There is no sunburst in the field.

Final model for the Ultra High Relief $20 gold piece submitted to Theodore Roosevelt for his approval in December 1906. E PLURIBUS UNUM has been removed from the rock and the sunburst has been restored.

An Ultra High Relief $20 gold piece originally from the Roosevelt family. A comparison to the final model of the obverse above shows a certain loss of detail in the translation of the design to the hub. (1.5x actual size)

Experimental strike of the Ultra High Relief design on the smaller, extra-thick planchet. (actual size, set over the normal-sized 34 mm planchet)

George B. Cortelyou. As President Roosevelt's secretary, he modernized White House protocols and procedures. Later he would serve as secretary of commerce and labor, postmaster general, and secretary of the Treasury, all during Roosevelt's presidency.

Meanwhile, Roberts ordered four of the experimental pieces sent to Washington for his examination. When he subsequently instructed the Mint to comply with Saint-Gaudens's request, he learned that the dies were broken. All they could do was to provide what was on hand: first, second, and third strikes and a finished piece in gold. They could also provide lead impressions of the finished design in both the regular and small sizes. No lettering was on the edges of these pieces. Barber, in response to this request, flatly stated that the finished coin was the best impression of the steel hub and he would make no cast.[20]

Gus, when he had finished his work, returned these pieces to Philadelphia. The finished ultra high relief double eagle with no lettering did not languish there long. Henry Hering, whose memory could be suspect, later related that this coin ended up in the possession of Theodore Roosevelt.[21]

Finally, on March 4, George Roberts, with the Treasury secretary's approval, ordered two of these ultra high relief coins for the Mint's cabinet.[22] The order contained no authority to make replacement dies.

After Henry Hering's return from Philadelphia, it was apparent to Gus that additional modifications in the form of a second model would be needed. Roberts asked that Saint-Gaudens in his next modification include a well-rounded rim that would better withstand abrasion. Expecting a successful conclusion with the next set of models, Roberts ordered on February 23 that none of the double eagles of the old design for 1907 be placed in circulation.[23]

On March 12, Gus sent to Roberts plaster casts of the second model. While the basic design concept was unchanged, there were modifications and enhancements. A fold was added to Liberty's skirt to further emphasize the beauty and sense of motion of the figure and to smooth the transition from the high relief of the central figure to the surrounding field. The Capitol silhouette was made more prominent and Liberty's torch was slimmed down. All were adjustments that would have been apparent to the practiced eye of Saint-Gaudens. This second model would result in a coin artistically superior to the ultra high relief version.

Gus had a second point to make in this letter to Roberts. He sent separately three plaster models of the first obverse. He requested that these be compared to the plaster casts taken from the ultra high relief $20 gold piece. Saint-Gaudens would be satisfied with nothing less than perfection. He said he was "convinced that the die, or hub, is not as successful as it could be" and that the coating of the plaster with stearine (which protected the model and allowed the runner of the lathe to glide smoothly over its surface) might be the cause of this problem. He was making the plaster casts for the second model in a lighter and weaker plaster in accordance with the practice of Monsieur Janvier in Paris. This softer plaster allowed the stearine to be absorbed without leaving a surface coating on the plaster, which was the case with harder models.[24]

This last comment stemmed from a developing disagreement with Barber. Of his own accord, Roberts had wired the Philadelphia Mint on February 16 to inquire as to the status of the plaster casts of the successive strikes in the first trial for Saint-Gaudens.[25] Barber first said that he could not have them ready before the 19th or 20th. On the 20th Barber sent only electrotypes—surface impressions electrodeposited and backed up with lead. His excuse was that plaster had proved "not suitable for the purpose and quite unsatisfactory." Since he understood the request to be urgent, he had turned to electrotypes, which he maintained could have been better if he had had more time.[26]

On the 24th Gus wrote politely to Roberts, again saying that he had only received the electrotypes and was waiting for the gold impressions and the cast of his original models. On the 26th Superintendent Landis complied.[27] It was the condition of this plaster cast when it arrived in Cornish that upset Saint-Gaudens and resulted in his comments to Roberts concerning the success of the first reduction.

Charles Barber's rebuttal to Saint-Gaudens came on March 25. He reminded Roberts that the reduction had been done by Henri Weil. Barber claimed that stearine was not the cause of the injury to the plaster cast; it was the tracer point of the reducing machine.[28]

Was the stearine the cause? Improper application would have blurred the fine detail, making it impossible to obtain an accurate reduction. Was the machine incapable of reproducing the detail required in the Saint-Gaudens design? Was unfamiliarity with the machine the cause? It must be remembered that Weil had requested "Keene cement" or a very hard plaster to facilitate reducing the Franklin reverse the second time around. While softer plaster was the rule in France, skill in working with it had not come across the ocean with Henri Weil. For Gus, a comparison of this work with the reductions he had received of his standing-eagle design from Paris put the problem squarely in Philadelphia.

One thing was sure: Saint-Gaudens had not forgotten that Weil's direct reduction from his plaster model for the Roosevelt inaugural medal had been a failure. A bronze cast would be needed for the next reduction.

At the same time, a changing of the guard was underway at the Treasury Department. Shaw resigned effective March 4.[29] Roosevelt, wanting changes at the Treasury, chose George B. Cortelyou as Shaw's replacement. Over the years, Cortelyou had gained Theodore's confidence, serving in several Cabinet positions and as his campaign manager in the 1904 election.

Meanwhile, Saint-Gaudens had proceeded to rework his one-cent model eliminating the eagle.[30] The finished work bears an exact resemblance to his earlier uniface medal of *Nikh-Eiphnh* or Victory-Peace. Gus really had no choice in the matter. Given his greatly weakened physical state, he had to turn to a design that was tried and acceptable in his eyes; there was no time for the endless experimentation that a new design would entail. The *Nikh-Eiphnh* filled this bill perfectly. Over Liberty's head, he symbolically arranged 13 stars in an arc. It was as chaste and noble a thing as the best Greek coins. Gus sent the completed models to the president on February 5. Up came the Indian headdress issue again. Gus was resistant,[31] but Roosevelt's affinity for all things Western was unwavering. In a letter to Gus written on February 8, Theodore pleaded his case, asking for just one coin with the headdress.

> It seems dreadful to look such a gift horse in the mouth, but I feel very strongly that on at least one coin we ought to have the Indian feather head-dress. It is distinctly American, and very picturesque. Couldn't you have just such a head as you have now, but with the feather head-dress?[32]

Saying no to the president was not an option. Gus offered to begin a trial with the utmost dispatch. The model followed promptly. Still there was reluctance on the part of the sculptor concerning the headdress. Although the model turned out well, Gus did not prefer it and struggled over what to say to the president. Deferentially, as he had been with Root over the Franklin medal in 1906, he would leave the decision to Roosevelt.[33]

So it seemed that steady, if slow, progress was now being made on the gold coins' design. Yet this was misleading. Witter Bynner, a professional writer who was a friend and former classmate of Homer's at Harvard,[34] was spending the winter at Cornish. He arrived in mid-January and set up a work area for himself in the studio. The second day there, Bynner found Gus looking so ill he lost his composure and Gus saw it. He described Saint-Gaudens's face as pinched and grey, his hands as long and thin, with little bones as limp as spaghetti. There were hot-water bottles between his knees and between his shins. The touching of one toe to another was torture to his nerves. In such pain, Gus had great difficulty holding onto a thought.

On January 30, Bynner noted that the "Saint" was carried out to the studio for ten minutes to criticize and direct the work of his assistants on the Phillips Brooks Monument and the cent model. Bynner called these sessions pathetic little visits in which eight or ten sentences would totally exhaust the man.

Bynner went on to say that Gus had been having setbacks. The sculptor thought that his family and the doctors were drugging him, but the family said the sculptor was on very few drugs. Gus believed that he was mortally ill and not being told. Even Bynner began to doubt.[35]

Throughout the fall and early winter Saint-Gaudens had been given morphine as a painkiller. Morphine dependency in combination with the large dosages of bromidia had proved disastrous. A cycle of pain followed by morphine followed by sleep took over his need to eat, and the resulting malnutrition led to a vitamin deficiency that in turn caused his neuropathy. The doctors had recognized the symptoms and eliminated the morphine in October. In January they had taken away the bromidia.

Thus by the end of January, Saint-Gaudens, as Witter Bynner described him, was in a living hell from the withdrawal of these medications. Still, as the withdrawal symptoms began to abate, the sculptor gained some weight. However, during one severe attack of pain he suffered a slight paralysis of his right leg that was no doubt from the neuropathy. Then in February lumps were discovered in his rectum and the pain treatment had to be resumed.[36] To concentrate on the gold coins' design, not to mention making any decisions at all on his other projects, now took a will of iron.

On February 18, with the one-cent model in hand, President Roosevelt pretty much preempted the decision in regard to the feather headdress.

> I wonder if I am one of those people of low appreciation of artistic things, against whom I have been inveighing? I like that feather head-dress so much that I have accepted that design of yours. Of course all the designs are conventional, as far as head-dresses go, because Liberty herself is conventional when embodied in a woman's head; and I don't see why we should not have a conventional head-dress of purely American type for the Liberty figure.[37]

By Roosevelt's own admission, art was the one subject about which he felt some uncertainty, but he did have some ideas of his own on the subject.[38] It still rankled that he had not stood his ground regarding the bison heads on the State Dining Room fireplace. During the White House renovation, McKim, wanting to maintain a classical look, insisted upon lions' heads. Theodore had appealed to Edith but she sneered at the idea. Just weeks before he left the White House in 1909, without telling Edith of his intentions, he would have Phimister Procter replace them with buffalo heads.[39] This time he felt Saint-Gaudens, by doing the model, was on his side. There were no Edith and McKim to gang up on him. He liked the feather headdress and approved the model.

Gus forwarded the approved cent models to the Mint on March 12 with his second models for the gold coins. Again the issue of relief came to the forefront, this time as a valid objection: there was too little metal in a one-cent planchet to strike up high relief. Gus acquiesced readily, and the model came back to his studio for revision.[40]

On the 1st of March, Roosevelt was still having second thoughts about the motto "In God We Trust." Roberts told him that the revised statutes of 1874 mandated the required devices and inscriptions. At the time the Mint director, Dr. Henry Linderman, had objected that the additional motto would overcrowd the coins and mar the artistic effect. When the dollar design was revised in 1878, President Hayes had insisted that the motto be retained. Hayes's authority for such action was unclear. The solicitor of the Treasury Department held that the decision to include or omit this motto lay with the executive branch of the government.[41] This explanation was reassuring enough for Roosevelt to allow the process to proceed without the motto.

On the day he shipped the cent and gold-coin models to the Mint, Saint-Gaudens updated the president. He told Roosevelt that there had been no change in the design that would be used on the $20 gold piece (which was an overgeneralization). He had made changes necessary for the coin to strike up in one blow. These addressed the thickness of the gold in certain places and the weight of the pressure when the blow was struck. Saint-Gaudens's position in this matter without another trial was speculative.

Homer later said that his father had warmed to the idea of the headdress.[42] Gus wrote that he was pleased that Roosevelt had suggested doing it, and now he wanted to see how this head would look in place of the proposed standing Liberty on the double eagle. He admitted to being apprehensive about using the full figure on Liberty and that he had probably lost sight of whatever had been the merits or demerits of that design. His fear now was that the standing Liberty design did not "tell" enough in contrast to the eagle on the other side. He was sure, however, that this would not be the case using the head of Liberty with the feathered headdress, and he asked Roosevelt's permission to have a trial strike using this Liberty paired with the flying-eagle reverse.[43]

Saint-Gaudens was seeking perfection once more. His eye was searching for the right pairing. Roosevelt quickly encouraged him, writing on March 14, having no idea of the consequences.[44]

This project was now in its third year. Had the president known Gus's physical state, would he have hesitated? Gus had limited time left. Or did he now realize in the back of his mind a need for a fallback position, should this second version of the standing Liberty design not strike up satisfactorily?

With spring had come some improvement in Gus's condition. His mind was clear and active, and he could put about two hours daily into his work. He was even trying to walk now and then. He had once advised a friend that work could be of some comfort in the presence of the great and awful mystery of death.[45] Again Witter Bynner described the situation.

> I grew used to his gaunt face, the everlasting, painful shifting of his sore bones, his fear, his melancholy, his crying and his look of being hunted by death and knowing it but turning at bay with sheer will and self-creation. When they would carry him out to the studios and place him in front of his work, the dejection, the grim unhappy will, the constant looking over his shoulder, so to speak, as if death were there, would vanish in an illumination of beauty and the creation of beauty; his eyes would burn again in the moment's victory.[46]

Meanwhile, at the president's directive, a trial strike was made using Liberty with a headdress on the obverse of the $20 gold piece with the flying eagle for the reverse, and the result was impressive. Below the "Americanized" *Head of Victory* was the word LIBERTY in bold letters. The date, in roman numerals, had been moved to the reverse and superimposed on the rising sun.[47]

Still there was no real progress. Charles Barber could not delegate the reduction work as he had the first time. He found himself unable to make a reduction from the models and complained that the soft plaster that Saint-Gaudens had used hampered the reduction process. It was at this point that Roberts was forced to reveal to Saint-Gaudens that it was not Barber who actually made the reductions from the first model.[48] Gus, having anticipated Barber's problem and based upon his experience with the Roosevelt Inaugural and Franklin medals, had had bronze casts made. Not happy with his cast, he suggested that the Mint do likewise using the founder "so warmly recommended to Mr. Hering by Mr. Barber," using the better of the two. That founder happened to be the same Keller Mechanical Engraving Company who had failed with their reducing lathe.[49]

Roberts met Roosevelt at the White House on Saturday, March 22 and reported to Gus on Sunday, March 23 that he was authorizing Charles Barber to have the bronze casts made—but the plasters that Gus had provided were too soft from which to make bronze casts. Roberts also that day had to deal with Cortelyou, who had passed on the request for an update on the project. The Mint director now committed in writing that second models were in hand and work was being pushed with all possible expedition.[50]

Meanwhile Charles Barber had gone with the soft plaster model to New York and had a successful bronze casting made. The harder plaster models from Saint-Gaudens would not be necessary. On April 12 the Mint received Saint-Gaudens's bronze casting. Roberts cautioned Saint-Gaudens that he could not assume that no additional modifications of the design or models would be required until the Mint had made a test of the hubs in process. On the 13th a surly Barber answered an inquiry by Roberts that it was impossible for him to state when the hubs from the second model would be ready. He was working day and night.[51]

All was not well with the Mint people. Barber's technical knowledge told him that this second model was almost as unacceptable as the first. There was no way it would strike up with full details with one blow of the coin press, even with the help of a forming die. Bluntly, he told Hering that he wanted nothing to do with it.[52] With Barber's

First model version from January and February 1907 for the obverse of the one-cent piece. The design comes directly from the uniface Victory-Peace medal.

One-cent model modified to add the Indian headdress requested by Theodore Roosevelt.

Three proposed designs for the reverse of the one-cent piece.

Indian Head pattern $20 gold piece. (actual size)

Obverse of the second model for the $20 gold piece, which was modified at John Landis's suggestion to lower the relief. This version ultimately became the High Relief $20 gold coin issued in December 1907.

John Landis, superintendent of the Philadelphia Mint. He was keenly interested in the quality and design of the new $20 gold coins.

observations in hand, Roberts now began contacting mint officials in Britain and France. He had to have substantial evidence on his side if he was going to convince the president of the impracticality of striking high-relief coins.

The only prompt reply came from the Department of Coins and Medals of the British Museum, and gave little or no real support to the Mint's opposition to high relief. Any position in the response was compromised by the opening statement that they had not much experience in the matter. Roberts then queried the Royal Mint but heard nothing. Finally on April 29 he wrote the French mint, which had the most practical experience with striking high relief. The French did not reply until July 2, too late for events that were about to occur.[53]

Roberts also turned again to his old friend Frank Leach, forwarding to him an ultra high relief double eagle. Leach's reply revealed the Mint's concerns. A heavier rim was imperative. No part of the relief must rise above the rim; otherwise the coins would not stack, making them unacceptable to bankers. Leach was not concerned about counterfeiting or other fraud, in particular the practice of "sweating," the use of abrasion to remove particles of gold from the coin. He also dismissed the concern that the coin would gather dirt. Finally Roberts asked Leach to comment upon the public's acceptance of the design. Leach would never personally like the flying eagle of the reverse. The man had a hard time balancing his real-world knowledge of eagles with Saint-Gaudens's artistic interpretations. However, he did have a valid point when he said the design was bad because of the "peculiarities of the piece." By this, he meant it would prove difficult to strike fully when the obverse design was matched with that of the reverse. Leach was the first person in this project to verbalize the potential pitfalls of Saint-Gaudens's design. He did regard the coin as a beautiful piece of work.[54]

Meanwhile in Cornish, Gus seemed a little better. He was able to take bread and milk without indigestion—but he put off Anders Zorn, who wanted to visit, and he was not signing his correspondence.[55] Augusta, whom Bynner described as snappish, left in May for a short rest in Richmond. A full-time nurse was required in her absence. His decline that winter had been hard on her. Her frustrations were not directed so much at Gus but against the Fates that brought on this tragedy.[56]

By the first week of May, the situation had come to a head in Philadelphia and Washington. In typical manner, Charles Barber kicked it off in a May 4 letter to Landis. The dies were completed and he had attempted to strike some pieces, which he was enclosing for examination. He had subjected the planchets to 150 tons of pressure, which was the practical limit of endurance for a die with the diameter of a $20 gold piece. He had encountered immediate difficulties. The convexity of the die was so pronounced in order to yield the desired high relief that the pressure of the medal press was in effect concentrated upon a much smaller area. The resulting die wear was excessive, with one of the dies sinking or losing its convexity.[57] The conclusion from these disappointing tests was that the relief of both the first and second models was quite similar. What changes Saint-Gaudens had made to the design to facilitate striking a high relief had fallen short.

Eight pieces were sent for Roberts's inspection. On May 6, when Roosevelt had his secretary inquire of Cortelyou on the progress of the double eagle, Mint personnel were ready.[58] In their view, significant changes were going to be required in order for this coin project to be successful.

Roberts spelled out the test results to Saint-Gaudens and enclosed the eight trial strikes. Two had been given one impression, two had been given two impressions, two had been given three impressions, and two had been given ten impressions—a double process set. Because a single blow in February had accomplished so much, they had been misled into thinking that minor modifications would turn the trick.

The results were clearly unsatisfactory and went far toward convincing Roberts that a radical modification of the designs would be required. While a single blow accomplished much, subsequent blows did not produce commensurate results. Roberts felt that the relief must be reduced and strongly wanted Saint-Gaudens to come to the Mint. He could not possibly have had any idea of Gus's failing health.[59]

It was a discouraged, almost defeated, Theodore Roosevelt who wrote to Gus on May 8.

> I am sorry to say I am having some real difficulties with the striking of those gold coins. It has proved hitherto impossible to strike them by one blow, which is necessary under the conditions of making coins at the present day. . . . I am afraid it is not practicable to have coins made if they are struck with more than one blow. Of course I can have a few hundreds of these beautiful coins made, but they will be merely souvenirs and medals, and not part of the true coinage of the country. Would it be possible for you to come to the mint? I am sure that the mint authorities now really desire to do whatever they can, and if it would be possible for you to go there I could arrange to have some of the Tiffany people there at the same time to see if there was anything practicable to be done.

Roberts and company had presented their case most effectively. That the president reiterated the Mint director's request that Saint-Gaudens come to the Mint indicated that Roosevelt had no idea how ill Gus was. The president assured Gus that the Mint authorities desired to do whatever they could to help. In a handwritten note at the bottom of the page, a more upbeat Roosevelt said he believed that either a slightly altered or low relief, or possibly a profile figure of Liberty, might yet do the trick.[60]

The gold-coin project now hung in the balance. Gus knew there was not time to start over again with a standing Liberty in profile. Besides, it was his intent that she be striding forward. He would not give in on this point. In spite of his physical condition, Gus was not quitting. Still, he was willing to compromise to get an acceptable design. He summoned all his strength and replied to Theodore on May 11. He was too proud to tell the president just how sick he was, simply saying that it was wholly impossible for him to leave Cornish at the present time. Hering would go in his place to Philadelphia the following week.[61]

> After all the question is fairly simple, and I have not the slightest doubt that making the coins in low relief will settle the matter satisfactorily. Greatly as I should like to please you, I feel that I cannot now model another design in profile for the Twenty Dollar gold piece. Indeed, as far as I am concerned, I should prefer seeing the head of Liberty in place of any figure of Liberty on the Twenty Dollar coin as well

as on the One Cent. If the idea appeals to you, I would refine the modeling of the head now that I have seen it struck in the small, so as to bring it in scale with the eagle. I am grieved that the striking of the die did not bring better results. Evidently it is no trifling matter to make Greek art conform with modern numismatics.[62]

Theodore was heartened by this letter that offered a fallback plan; if the figure of Liberty was not successful for a general-circulation $20 gold piece, a Liberty head in profile with a feather headdress would more than suffice. However, he still preferred the standing Liberty figure for this largest of the American gold coins. If the design must be discarded as impractical, he would insist upon a small issue anyway. Gus was to refine the Liberty-in-headdress design. Roosevelt also wanted to see Hering after his meeting in Philadelphia.[63]

Theodore was back on top of his game. Had he not stood firm here, the design project would have died.

As this letter exchange was transpiring, there was a softening of opinions at the Mint. Landis, essentially a bystander up to this point, wrote to Roberts subtly casting doubt on Barber's opinion that the design was unworkable. By asking for permission to strike the coin with a one-fifth reduction in relief, he effectively undercut the engraver's position and supported the position of Roosevelt and Saint-Gaudens. This lowering of the relief could be accomplished with the Janvier lathe. Landis closed with the prescient observation that he very much regretted the exclusion of the motto "In God We Trust."[64] This communication was out of character for Landis, whom Roberts had considered replacing the prior year. That he would stick his neck out indicated that some at Philadelphia felt the Saint-Gaudens design could be coined.

On May 17 Hering was at the Mint along with Roberts and a manufacturing superintendent from Tiffany's. Roberts wanted the Tiffany's man there to confirm the opinions of the Mint for Saint-Gaudens and Roosevelt.[65] They examined both the standing Liberty and Liberty-in-headdress reductions. They also inspected the reduction made at Landis's suggestion. Nothing was revealed as to the coinability of this last modification. That a third model would be needed could be inferred from Gus's subsequent note to Landis. He asked for lead impressions of the standing Liberty and Liberty-with-feather-headdress models as well as an impression or cast of Barber's lower-relief reduction of the standing Liberty. From Philadelphia, Hering went to the White House the next day to give Roosevelt a full progress report.[66]

Faced with the inevitable reduction in relief for the next set of models, Gus tried one more time, on May 23, to sway the president to his thinking for the $20 gold piece.

Now that this business of the coinage is coming to an end and we understand how much relief can be practically stamped, I have been looking over the other models that I have made and there is no question in my mind that the standing eagle is the best. You have seen only the large model, and probably on seeing it in the small will have a different impression. The artists all prefer it, as I do, to the flying eagle.

First, in that it is more on a scale with the figure of Liberty on the other side.

Second, it eliminates the sunburst which is on both sides of the coin as it will be if adopted as settled up to now.

Third, it is more dignified and less inclined toward sensational.

Fourth, it will occupy no more time to use this model than it will to do the other work that will be necessary, and I think it is a little more favorable for stamping.

The majority of the people that I show the work to evidently prefer with you the figure of Liberty to the head of Liberty and that I shall not consider any further on the Twenty Dollar gold coin.[67]

Gus was correct in stating that the standing eagle in combination with the standing Liberty would strike up better on the $20 gold piece. As far back as early February, Saint-Gaudens had written the Mint requesting the return of his standing-eagle model.[68] He had always favored this design. Now that he felt the project was nearing its completion, he was making one last plea to return to the designs that most approximated his original conceptions. Yet in the end, he would once again defer to the president.

This letter also shed some light on the feasibility of employing a relief reduced by 20%, as suggested by Landis. Clearly, Hering had returned from the Mint optimistic that Landis's modification was all that was needed to successfully strike an acceptable high-relief coin. He was overly optimistic in this regard. Barber had not mastered the option of reducing relief mechanically with the Janvier machine. His reduction from the second model had lost much detail, which he then had attempted to restore by hand directly on the hub.[69]

Roosevelt asked Roberts to meet with him on May 25 to discuss Gus's new position on the gold-coin design. Roberts supported Saint-Gaudens's views, advocating the standing Liberty in combination with the standing eagle as the primary design for use on the $20 gold piece. Theodore stood firm. He wanted the full figure of Liberty in combination with the flying-eagle reverse. Having been briefed the previous week on the probable success of a 20% reduction in relief, there was no moving him. The president agreed that the relief should be reduced to a degree that would make it practical without further experiments. This was to be "the last word on the subject."[70]

Roberts asked Roosevelt to give him a brief handwritten memorandum summarizing the decisions of the meeting to be placed in his private file "as a memento of the coinage."[71] Gus readily accepted the president's decision. He promised models to follow in two reliefs: one in a form that Henry Hering believed would be practical, and another in ordinary flat relief. Once again the parties involved thought that decisions had been made that would bring the project to a satisfactory conclusion. They were wrong.

At the end of May, Barber prepared an electrotype of his reduced relief on the $20 gold piece and forwarded it to Saint-Gaudens. Gus could not have been happy with what he saw. The electrotype had lost much detail in the standing figure of Liberty in Barber's first attempt at lowering the relief mechanically with the Janvier lathe.[72]

During June activity at Cornish slowed down. Hering was inexplicably away for ten days. Concurrently Gus went into decline. The last week of June, another snag developed. The annual Philadelphia Mint maintenance shutdown scheduled for July had been advanced to June 22 to accommodate tours for an Elks convention starting on July 15.[73] Essentially six weeks were going to pass with little or nothing accomplished from the Mint's standpoint on the design project.

As July commenced, the models for the $20 coin in reduced relief were not ready. Promised models in flat relief had not even been addressed yet. Gus was now confined to his bed. Homer's wife did not see how he could last.[74] This coin design project that he had initially so wanted, even if it did scare him blue, had become a burden.

Another blow to the project came from an unexpected quarter. On July 8, George Roberts announced his resignation as director of the Mint. He had a lucrative offer to become president of the Commercial National Bank in Chicago. Still, there may have been more to it; he had turned down a similar job offer in St. Louis in 1902.[75] The gold-coin project was not the issue, although its contentiousness may have contributed. For almost a year, Roberts had been attempting to remove the coiner at the new Denver Mint due to problems maintaining the required fineness of the branch mint's gold-coin production. In June, thanks to the state's governor, the matter had hit the president's desk. Roberts did not like the resulting compromise that removed the man.[76]

One thing was certain about the resignation: it was not forced. Theodore Roosevelt said in a kind note that Roberts's leaving was a loss to the government and he felt it personally as well. Roosevelt respected George Roberts. He had kept some of the Mint director's economic writings near at hand for ready reference. Roosevelt would certainly miss Roberts, and in the final months of his presidency appointed him to the 1909 Assay Commission.[77]

Still, Theodore Roosevelt was keeping the pressure on. From the summer White House he sent requests for updates with maddening frequency to Cortelyou. The secretary's answers were vague. Roberts had promised Cortelyou that before he retired at the end of the month he would visit Philadelphia and "give further attention to the matter."[78]

Meanwhile, July in Cornish was proving to be unseasonably hot, punctuated by rolling thunderstorms, causing Gus to suffer even more. He was having fevers of 104 degrees. Mercifully, however, the pain had abated.[79]

George Roberts wound up his term as Mint director with a letter to Secretary Cortelyou. He addressed President Roosevelt's desire to have a special issue of the first model ultra high relief $20 gold pieces, saying there was no law prohibiting this action. He suggested that several hundred pieces, enough to eliminate any numismatic premium, be coined and distributed only after the regular issue of the new Saint-Gaudens design in low relief for the $20 coin was generally available.[80]

As a follow-up to his recommendation for the ultra high relief production, he ordered new dies to replace the ones broken in February to facilitate a limited production run. In a last act of appreciation, he asked that two of these beautiful coins be given to his longtime secretary, Margaret Kelly.[81] A very limited number of these coins would be struck with distinctively serifed edge lettering. E PLURIBUS UNUM would be positioned over the top of Liberty in a move taken from one of Saint-Gaudens's early sketches, followed by a string of stars. These gold coins, in combination with the first strikes in February, would become one of the great American numismatic treasures of the 20th century.[82]

Roberts returned to the Mint two of the checker-sized gold pieces that he had obtained from Philadelphia at the conclusion of the first strikings in February. He retained two of the ultra high relief double eagles, reimbursing the Mint for their cost. He noted as justification for keeping the remaining two $20 gold pieces that the rule requiring experimental issues be melted was to be waived by the president anticipating the intended special striking.[83]

One of these two gold pieces with the original edge lettering appeared at auction at Sotheby's in 1992, without provenance. The second appeared at another auction three years later, again at Sotheby's. This one was offered simply as the "property of a gentleman." At the age of 102, George Roberts's son passed away in New York City in 1996. These coins must have stayed in Roberts's family as heirlooms for almost 90 years.[84]

Once again, Theodore Roosevelt weighed in on the coin designs. He agreed with Roberts to have a few hundred of the ultra high relief $20 gold pieces struck for the benefit of collectors after the general release of the new design. In a handwritten addition at the end of the letter, he stated that this design should be preserved as the work of a great American artist.[85] Little did Roosevelt know at the time how appropriate that statement was to be.

It was now the end of July 1907. Bynner had returned to Cornish, and he and Gus sat on the terrace at Aspet looking at Mount Ascutney on the western horizon. So many times before, Gus had taken his meals among friends on that terrace with the mountain providing a spectacular backdrop. This time, storm clouds had advanced eastward over and past the mountain. In their place, stretching on both flanks of the peak, was an orange band of light as the sky cleared in the west to make way for the last rays of a setting sun. Bynner exclaimed over the beauty of the sunset and called it "chaos pacified." At this point Gus looked to Bynner and said there were too many city people coming to Cornish and if he could, he would move again.[86]

As the two men sat quietly talking, Gus's mind must have wandered back to the time of that special masque in the early summer of 1905. It had been ostensibly to commemorate the 20-year existence of the art colony that flourished around Saint-Gaudens. But it was really about Saint-Gaudens. The masque's theme was easily chosen, given Gus's adoration of Greek art. The storyline went that the ancient gods and goddesses of Greek mythology lived in the mountains and foothills surrounding Cornish. They had suffered an invasion of mortals and, having found one worthy to rule in their place, they wished to move on to a new realm. A golden bowl revealed the name of the mortal selected to take their places: Augustus Saint-Gaudens. Gus had been touched. He had called it extraordinary; he had never seen anything more beautiful and impressive.[87] Afterward, Gus designed a plaque commemorating the event as a memento for each guest.

Gus had also worked in these last months on a bas-relief of Gussie holding that golden bowl. Now, it seemed so long ago. His body was tired, much too tired. He sensed that the end was near. He was telling Bynner in his own way that he was ready to follow in the footsteps of those mythological Greek gods of the masque. Now, what mortal would succeed Saint-Gaudens?

He never finished that portrait relief. On his last day of consciousness, he shooed Witter Bynner away, saying, "Go away. Don't look at me. It's too humiliating."[88]

He slipped into a coma on August 2 and died the following evening. The autopsy would reveal that the cancer had spread to his liver.[89] The great sculptor Augustus Saint-Gaudens was gone, and Theodore Roosevelt's design project for the gold coins was once more hanging in the balance.

Part 5

Carry a Big Stick— Cast a Long Shadow

Chapter 20

A Cameo in Gold

As Saint-Gaudens lay dying, there was a gold coin from the Mint in his possession. But it was not the $20 gold piece that he had been struggling with since the preceding fall. It was a $10 gold piece. Its origin that spring had caught him by complete surprise.

When George Roberts reported to Saint-Gaudens the outcome of his meeting with Roosevelt at the White House on Saturday, March 22, 1907, the sculptor was puzzled that Roberts had stated that "the obverse of the one-cent design is now wanting with a view to the use upon a gold coin. I think we will now devote ourselves at present to making a success of the gold coinage."[1] Here was the heart of what had transpired at the White House. The one-cent design was off the table. The profile *Head of Victory* in Indian headdress was going to be appropriated for a second gold-coin design. Here the matter sat for the next two months while the Mint prepared dies for the second model of the $20 gold piece.

This matter came back to the front burner in the meeting of Roosevelt and Roberts on May 25 to discuss Gus's position that Liberty with the headdress be considered for the obverse of the $20 gold coin. The president rejected this idea, but he was willing to compromise by employing the feathered head of Liberty in combination with the standing eagle for the $10 gold piece. Gus had never considered this pairing. Left open was whether this design would also be applied to the smaller gold coins, although Roberts expected that it would.[2]

During the first week of June, Gus sent to the Mint models for the obverse and reverse of the $10 gold coin. The adaptation had not been difficult, centering primarily on the inscriptions. The date on the obverse model was in roman numerals. Saint-Gaudens had set the relief to what Charles Barber had told Henry Hering could probably be struck. If the models did not strike up successfully, Barber had assured Hering that the relief could be lowered very simply on the Janvier reducing machine.[3] Second models in coin relief would follow.

Charles Barber was cornered again. His lack of proficiency in reducing the relief would be there for all to see. Defensively he sat down and penned another of his letters, saying Saint-Gaudens was mistaken. Barber had never said anything other than standard coin relief was acceptable. The current models sent were not coin relief although Barber would not unconditionally call them unacceptable. He also strongly took issue with the statement that the Janvier machine could adequately reduce the model both in size and in relief. Barber claimed the machine lost design details when used to reduce relief.

Finally Barber raised the issue of roman numerals versus arabic. The quantity of roman numerals and hence space requirements for a date such as 1928 were far different from those of 1907. On the smaller gold coin, spacing for roman numerals was a legitimate issue. Barber preferred arabic notation. He wanted official decisions made on the application of mechanical reduction to gain satisfactory relief and the use of an arabic date before contracting for bronze intermediate casts.[4] Bronze castings cost the Mint all of $35 apiece.

Roberts had just missed Hering at the Philadelphia Mint when he wrote Saint-Gaudens on June 11. He set forth Barber's reasons for using arabic notation. He also supported Charles Barber's position that too great a reduction in relief using the Janvier machine would result in loss of the finer details in the design. This loss, he felt, would facilitate counterfeiting. Matters concerning the new $10 gold coin were now on hold. Roberts wrote again on the 18th for Gus's approval of the use of arabic notation before the bronze castings were authorized. Gus had been waiting for Hering to return from his meeting at the Mint. He was expected on the 21st.[5]

In the meantime, Gus confirmed that he was willing to use arabic numbers on the $10 gold piece, forwarding a new model on the 24th. On the 25th Gus wrote to Roberts that after consulting with Hering he did not believe the problem of loss of the finer details during the reduction process would occur. Enhanced sharpness of the design elements compared to the standing eagle model reduced in Paris would be enough to overcome the problem.[6]

When the Mint came back into operation, Barber completed hubs for the new $10 gold-piece design. Two new gold coins were put in Roberts's hands and he forwarded one to Cortelyou on July 22. Work was not quite complete. Lacking the necessary segmented collars, the 46 stars representing the states of the Union were not yet on the edge of the coin as intended. Roberts was not happy with the new coin. Its finish was smooth without the sharply cut details that he had desired to guard against counterfeiting. Herein lay a conflict. One of Gus's basic tenets was that the outline of the face must not be too sharply cut against the background so as to give a look of having been shaved off and pasted against the field.[7] Roberts did state that he felt the relief was now perfectly feasible to coin but there was a defect on the reverse: the standing eagle was a shade too high compared to the rim. Two coins placed back to back would rock, a clearly unacceptable situation.[8]

Saint-Gaudens from the very beginning of the project knew that the rim of the coin had to be higher than its design elements. His model would never have left Cornish with this defect, no matter how sick the man. Barber, preparing the hubs, had reduced the relief from the models as much as the lathe would allow.[9] The problem had to be somewhere in Barber's work. Still there was more; the sharp triangular points that Saint-Gaudens used before and after the legends on the reverse model were reduced in some cases to mere blobs. On the obverse, the points of the stars were fuzzy and weak. If nothing else, this episode corroborated Hering's observations concerning Barber's inexperience with the Janvier reducing machine.[10]

Sick or not, Gus asked the Mint director on that same July 22 for the results obtained from the new $10 gold-coin dies.[11] Roberts complied immediately, forwarding his remaining strike of the new gold coin. He also set forth frankly his objections

A Cameo in Gold

concerning the coin's finish and the problem with the eagle on the reverse. In closing, Roberts informed Gus of his resignation and his sincere regret at not seeing the new designs through to their implementation. He thought that Saint-Gaudens would find his successor, Frank Leach, a thoroughly practical man and one who would take great interest in the project. On July 25 Saint-Gaudens requested of Roberts a plaster cast of the new die.[12] This information would confirm what he already suspected about Barber's latest engraving effort.

Once again, Theodore Roosevelt weighed in on the coin designs. Cortelyou had forwarded the $10 gold coin he had received from Roberts to the president. Roosevelt liked the smooth finish. He recognized the Mint's concern over counterfeiting but asked if a few thousand pieces could be struck and then the rest minted in sharp detail, consistent with existing practice.[13]

So the $10 gold piece at Saint-Gaudens's death stood very close to fruition. On August 7, 1907, Roosevelt impatiently demanded progress on the project by September 1. He was specific in his instructions, saying that if dies of a sharper cutting were required, the Mint should contact Hering. Barber responded that dies for the $10 gold piece had been waiting approval since July 22. No instructions had been received from either the Mint director or Saint-Gaudens. With presidential instructions "to go ahead with the dies as they now are," Barber begged to say that the dies were ready. He made no mention of the perceived need for a sharper image or the problem with the reverse from the initial strike.[14] Acting Superintendent Norris did note that the Mint had encountered difficulties coming up with a collar that would impress the stars on the edge. They had sought help from authorities in Paris, to no avail. Finally they had turned to their machine shop to devise the necessary sectional collar. Norris now put a work crew on overtime to complete the collars.[15]

Seemingly not comprehending that Roosevelt was demanding results, Charles Barber on August 26 raised the issue of the lack of an acceptable edge on the existing $10 model. When the coin was struck, the metal, not having a border area into which to flow, would be forced between the die and the collar, forming a fin or wire edge. This fin would soon disappear, leaving an underweight and therefore unacceptable coin for commercial purposes. He again brought up the stacking issue due to the high point on the shoulder of the standing eagle on the reverse. However, he now no longer blamed the problem on Saint-Gaudens. It was due to the convexity of the die, which had a tendency to change during the tempering of the steel and in the striking process itself. His solution was to turn a border in the die. There would be a delay, but only a minor one. In his opinion the border did not detract from the artistic merits of the coin and added to its appearance.[16] From this statement it is clear that Barber understood that he was still under the stricture not to alter the Saint-Gaudens designs in any manner whatsoever. As a result, while he had presented a valid solution to the problem, he had sat upon it for a month doing nothing. On August 27 Acting Director Preston, responding to Cortelyou's orders, had no option but to instruct the Mint to strike 500 of the $10 coins.[17]

At this point, matters concerning the $10 coin took a different turn. On August 27, Augusta Saint-Gaudens sent the promised second set of models.[18] Homer, who was knowledgeable about the efforts to bring his father's designs to life, was being pushed aside by his mother, who was not. Preston's reply was not forthcoming as to events transpiring with the $10 gold coin at that point. He wanted to know when the third model of the $20 gold piece would be ready. He also told Augusta that he was forwarding her letter to Philadelphia so that the engraver could address more fully the issue of raising the rims.[19] Barber did not reply.

The models themselves appeared to be quite satisfactory. A rim had been added, and the relief was now coinable. The engraver was pressed to complete these dies as soon as possible.[20] Again he made paraffin reductions that he took to New York to have bronze castings prepared to facilitate the reduction in steel for the hub necessary for die preparation. Barber's satisfaction with this model's relief was even relayed to the estate by Norris.[21]

Meanwhile on August 30, Preston amended his authorization, ordering the $10 gold pieces from the first model struck on the medal press. He instructed that they be kept on hand, as he was expecting that Roosevelt would want some of them. He wanted no delays should that request materialize. Ultimately, 542 of these coins with a wire rim would be struck.[22] The stars at the borders exhibited weakness although the central devices, Liberty and the eagle, struck up well.

Even prior to these $10 coins being struck from Saint-Gaudens's first model, Charles Barber had completed his modifications turning the border in the hub to correct the faults he first raised over the sculptor's work. On August 27 he sent a strike from the modified hub to Preston. The raised stars adjacent to the rim still needed perfecting. However, Preston viewed this coin as superior to those now being struck and did not expect the president to object to this modification.[23]

On September 9, Preston after consulting with the engraver authorized coinage from the Barber-modified dies from the first model of the $10 gold piece to commence. Starting September 13, a total of 31,500 were struck on the coin presses. Another 50 were produced on the medal press. Then production just as suddenly was halted on the 18th. The decision had come down to Preston that none would go into circulation until the new $20 gold pieces were ready, making their continued striking unnecessary.[24]

Meanwhile Charles Barber had completed the hub for the second model for the new $10 coin. The coinability of this gold piece was much improved. Details were much sharper, particularly the feather ends on the obverse. However, the bullet points separating the motto E PLURIBUS UNUM were gone. Also the relief was virtually eliminated. Henry Hering with Homer Saint-Gaudens's implicit approval had most likely made these changes to insure a successful trial striking. Barber would not have deviated by eliminating the bullet points, considering all the heat he was receiving from the White House. Also, had Barber reduced the relief mechanically, the design would have no doubt suffered a loss of the required sharpness.

On September 23 Augusta Saint-Gaudens relayed Hering's request that it would be well to see a sample striking of the $10 gold piece from the second model. It fell to Norris to answer Augusta. Dies had been cut from the second model for the $10 coin and some experimental pieces struck. The matter had been referred to Washington on the 25th. The request for a sample strike was ignored.[25]

$10 gold piece struck from the first model by Augustus Saint-Gaudens.

$10 gold piece struck from the first model as modified by Charles Barber, with a "rolled rim."

Second model of the reverse for the $10 gold piece submitted by Henry Hering, showing the removal of the bullet points.

$10 gold piece struck from the second and officially adopted model prepared by Henry Hering.

Striking Change

"Referred to Washington" meant that Superintendent Landis had sent new $10 coins from both the modified first model and second model to Robert Preston for his review. Landis pointed out in his letter that the detail on the eagle was much improved on the gold coin from the second model. Overall this coin gave a well-detailed appearance. Its prominent, broad border allowed the coin to stack perfectly. Landis recommended that coins from the modified first model not be released into circulation. Ignoring the Saint-Gaudens estate, Preston made the decision, selecting the second model. With his limited strikes of the first model in hand, Roosevelt was satisfied and signed off October 3.[26]

The design for the $10 gold piece was now accepted. The rolled-edge variety from the first model was ordered to the melting pot on November 9. However, about 50 of these coins survived.[27] The wire-rim variety was held in abeyance. In December, assistant secretary of the Treasury J. H. Edwards ordered these gold pieces transferred to the Treasury for the president. They were subsequently distributed to friends of Roosevelt and administration officials. The whole situation in August and September had bordered on chaotic. Samples of the various strikes had been requested within and through the Treasury for viewing that had not been returned. Preston, in frustration, would later lament that he hoped to get all the pieces back before he died.[28] He was unsuccessful.

Chapter 21

A Man for the Occasion

It was Friday, November 22, 1907. Thanksgiving was just around the corner. The day was cloudy and cold with some light rain that chilled to the bone as Frank Leach walked into the president's office. As the newly appointed director of the United States Mint, he was hardly settled into his job, much less ready for a face-to-face encounter with the president of the United States. It had been nearly four months since Saint-Gaudens had passed away. Yet from his first days in office, Leach had been dealing with the new gold-coin designs. He was aware that this project had the attention of a number of prominent people in New York City and Boston, as well as the president himself.[1] Decisions had been made on the $10 coin, but the $20 coin was still mired in problems.

Theodore Roosevelt lost no time in warming to his subject. From the very beginning of this project, his interest had been with the $20 gold piece. The project was languishing. His patience was at an end. Saint-Gaudens was gone and his beautiful $20 coin design might never see the light of day.

Theodore would have no more of the bureaucratic excuses. In Frank Leach's words, he set out what he wanted, the striking of the new $20 gold pieces. He went on to describe the problems and failures that had been encountered to date with the high-relief design by Saint-Gaudens. Finally he told Leach what he needed to accomplish. But it was more colorful than that. Theodore would typically hammer his desk with his fist to emphasize his anger. He also had a habit of thrusting his head forward aggressively when making a point. He suggested, in Leach's tempered words, "some details of action of a drastic character." That was an understatement. Roosevelt's anger and denunciations could be truly blasting when he turned on his full voltage, a tropic blaze of heat.[2] All of the frustration of almost three years of futile effort in dealing with the Mint came flooding out.

The news of Gus's death on August 3, 1907, had profoundly saddened Theodore and Edith Roosevelt; they had lost a friend.[3] Edith was moved to write a personal note of condolence to Gussie.

> The President I know has written but I must also tell you of my sympathy, and regret at the loss which has come not only to you but to all Americans in the death of your

305

husband. He was so intensely vital that I can scarcely realize it. So much work seemed to be before him. I hope that someday I may see you to say many things which I can not write.[4]

So much lay before him! Indeed. Edith knew exactly where the gold-coin design project stood. It was stopped dead in its tracks. Now there was no one but her husband to push it through to completion.

Storm clouds gathered almost at once. George Roberts, on his last day in his position, communicated to Cortelyou that his successor, Frank Leach, would not be ready to assume his post in Washington for an indefinite period. There had been difficulties finding a replacement for him at the San Francisco Mint. Roberts assured Cortelyou that the Mint would be in capable hands under Robert Preston. He went on to report that in spite of the Mint's best efforts, there remained problems with the models submitted by Saint-Gaudens—they were too large, resulting in a loss of detail when reduced to the size of a die. That statement was absolutely wrong. Barber had not been fully forthcoming with his superior. Even now, Roberts did not understand that the problem involved reducing the relief mechanically, which Barber still had not mastered. The retiring director went on to state that the continual delays had been due to the experimenting to achieve a coinable high relief. Roberts believed that the project should be delayed until dies that fully met coinage standards were obtained.

In closing, Roberts mentioned that he had rejected a quote by the United States Express Company to move gold bullion from the West Coast to Philadelphia. He dismissed the exposure of having large amounts of gold at San Francisco and could not foresee a financial situation in the East that could not be met with the gold stocks at hand. He did concede that it was more desirable to have gold coins accumulated in the East, but not at the expense of the transfer at what he deemed an exorbitant rate.[5]

When Secretary Cortelyou forwarded this letter to Roosevelt, the president lost no time. It was in his letter of August 7 demanding that work move forward on the $10 gold piece that he went much further with Cortelyou. He wanted the Mint to move ahead with the dies for the new $20 gold piece just as they were. He acknowledged the goodwill on the part of Mint authorities. However, he could not help but feel "there has been a certain cumbersomeness of mind and inability to do the speediest modern work." With Saint-Gaudens's death, the Mint should get in touch with Henry Hering to address any concerns. Roosevelt wanted both gold pieces issued by September 1. In case Cortelyou and the Mint missed the point, Roosevelt closed by saying again that there had been too much delay and he wanted the project finished immediately. Cortelyou passed the letter on with a directive that Roosevelt's instructions be carried out and the work expedited.[6]

Roosevelt's order that the Mint commence immediately with the new designs created a stir. Preston was not adequately up to speed after one week as acting director. He queried Roberts in Chicago as to the exact status of the project at the time of his departure, with both Saint-Gaudens and the president. Roberts's reply left much unanswered.[7] At the same time Preston forwarded Roosevelt's letter to Philadelphia. He trusted that every effort would be made to expedite this coinage. Using a skill that had served him well throughout his career, Preston was passing the buck.

Both Landis and Barber were on vacation. The acting superintendent, A.A. Norris, telephoned Barber at the beach in New Jersey. The engraver returned and made arrangements for the striking of new gold coins during the following week.[8] Up to that point, the response was all positive.

While Barber could proceed with the $10 gold piece, the double eagle was an entirely different matter. Barber had no model that could be used for general coinage. He was waiting for a new model that would remove the objectionable high-relief features. He had heard nothing from the Saint-Gaudens people regarding this model. Left unanswered was why he had not taken the initiative to contact Henry Hering directly. Barber went on to conclude that the delays on the $20 coin were not in any sense the fault of the Engraving Department. He even pointed out that the appliances used in the engraving process were of the most improved type. The department had worked nights and Sundays on the Saint-Gaudens designs. In the case of the first reduction, he had completed the work in one month while it took Saint-Gaudens six months to have the equivalent work done in Paris. Not noted, of course, was that there was no comparison in quality of work. Also, he failed to point out that he had had help in preparing the first hub. Until the Saint-Gaudens people supplied him with a model in low enough relief that it could be reduced on the new Janvier machine, his hands were tied. It would be utterly impossible to meet the September 1 deadline for the new $20 gold piece, even if the models had been now in hand.[9] It was pure Barber.

Barber's letter was forwarded to Preston. However, Norris felt the need to defend Barber and drafted his own reply. It had not been lost on Norris who the president was accusing. He took issue, defending Barber. The Mint had tried twice to strike a suitable double eagle from the Saint-Gaudens models. The results were unsuccessful. The second model would not work in a coin press. They were now waiting on a third model. Without a satisfactory hub, how could they comply with the president's directive to begin striking the new coin?

Charles Barber had offered to take the Saint-Gaudens designs and make workable models from them. No authority to do so had been forthcoming. Of course, Barber had objected that Saint-Gaudens's design would not meet modern coinage requirements. However, he had not allowed this observation to interfere with his preparation of the necessary hubs and dies. Norris repeated verbatim Barber's assertion of the long hours he had put into the project in order to push through the die preparation rapidly. The engraver was still perfecting the edge collar needed to place the stars on the rim of the $10 coin. In fact, Norris asserted, the delays were due to Saint-Gaudens. Finally, taking a classic bureaucratic position, Norris questioned the legality of striking the two gold-coin designs as they now were and then making changes later as events warranted. Would not that be a change in design, requiring an act of Congress?[10] Roosevelt's message was not getting through to the people in Philadelphia.

These two letters bring to mind Saint-Gaudens's observation that one person would still be standing in the rubble of the Mint. No doubt that person would be waiting for someone to provide a "suitable" model for the new $20 gold-piece design. Acting Director Preston did ask Landis on August 15 to wire Homer Saint-Gaudens to inquire about the status of the third $20 coin model. Homer replied that a finished model for the $10 coin, one that had been promised with "flat relief" from the end of

May, would be sent during the following week to the Mint. He was silent on the status of the third model for the $20 gold coin. A second query brought forth the reply that the new $20 model would be ready in one month.[11] Henry Hering was waiting for the results of the latest model for the $10 coin, which was at a relief slightly lower than the French 20-franc piece designed by Chaplain. Barber had assured Hering that the Mint could produce this relief. Far be it from Barber to say that the U.S. Mint could not duplicate what was being accomplished in Europe. Also Hering knew that this relief was the lowest that Saint-Gaudens would accept. This second model for the $10 gold piece would be ready in four days. Until the results on this coin were known, it would be fruitless to begin work on another $20 model.[12]

Roosevelt, hearing nothing, wrote Cortelyou again on August 22. He would accept no additional delays. He wanted to know exactly when the new coins would be issued. He reminded Cortelyou that a few thousand of the ultra high relief coins were to be struck after the first of the regular-issue $20 gold pieces. If there were delays, he was going to ask Kunz from Tiffany's to take over the project.[13] The president was not to be trifled with. However, his letter added confusion on one point. At the end of July he had anticipated that only a few hundred of the ultra high relief $20 gold pieces would be made available for collectors. Perhaps in the heat of the moment he had become confused in his intentions, forgetting that it was the $10 coin from the first model of which he had originally desired to have a few thousand struck. Regardless, his letter must have raised serious concerns at the Mint that a large issue of the ultra high relief gold coins would have to be struck.

The following day, Roosevelt received a letter from W.D. Sohier, a Boston attorney and an old friend. Under any circumstances, its contents would have been unsettling. Sohier had talked to Daniel French, who remained close to the Saint-Gaudens family. French was aware that Saint-Gaudens's work was in jeopardy. He felt it was a pity. His concern that Saint-Gaudens's designs would be lost was heightened by his and others' perceptions that the Mint would never approve or use an outside design. French went on to say that there existed a machine that would reduce the relief absolutely proportionally. If resistance at the Mint continued, he recommended bringing in outside experts and suggested Victor D. Brenner as the only trained medalist in the country capable of assisting in the work.[14]

Angry, Roosevelt immediately fired off a curt letter to Cortelyou. He enclosed Sohier's letter for the benefit of the Mint officials. He again wanted to know when both the new gold coins would appear—within a fortnight, he hoped. Then he leveled a threat: if there were any further delays, he would call in Kunz, French, and Brenner to supervise the new coinage. Roosevelt's missive was a wrecking ball aimed directly at the Mint. It was a self-satisfied president who penned a reply to Sohier saying that now he would get the coins.[15]

Preston had never faced a situation such as this one. On the one side, he had a rebellious Mint staff in Philadelphia. On the other side, he had a very angry president. The acting director was caught in the middle. On August 27 Preston instructed the Mint to strike 500 of the $20 gold pieces from the second model. Cortelyou had ordered it done.[16] The Treasury secretary knew that Roosevelt was not bluffing about bringing Tiffany's into the picture.

Theodore Roosevelt in a moment of emotion, by James Earle Fraser. This plaque was commissioned by the Roosevelt Association immediately after the president's death. The caption reads: "Aggressive fighting for the right is the noblest sport the world affords."

Frank A. Leach. As superintendent of the San Francisco Mint, he was the first person to verbalize the potential pitfalls in Saint-Gaudens's design, though he did consider it a beautiful work of art. As director of the U.S. Mint he would have to deal with those pitfalls.

Flat-rim High Relief $20 gold piece from the second model by Augustus Saint-Gaudens (as modified by Charles Barber).

Third model, in the negative, of the obverse of the $20 gold piece by Henry Hering (before modifications at the Mint to facilitate striking for general circulation). The sun rays have been sharpened, but the details on Liberty's gown remain. On the reverse of this plaster is the notation VICTORY, which would have been Saint-Gaudens's nomenclature for this design.

A circulation-strike $20 gold piece from the oficially adopted "modified" third model.

Barber was now faced with pressing into service the dies using the 20% reduction in relief that he had prepared in May. These coins were the first emission of what was to be known by coin collectors as the High Relief $20 gold piece. Barber had no choice. He needed to buy time. The second models for the $10 gold piece had proved satisfactory. He even optimistically ventured that if the new $20 models arrived with the same relief, acceptable coinage dies could be made.[17] This judgment was even communicated to the Saint-Gaudens estate by Norris. On September 10 five of these high-relief coins were delivered to Assistant Treasury Secretary Edwards.[18] Roosevelt's order had been met.

As the Mint struggled to comply with the president's directive, Preston, on September 18, instructed the Philadelphia Mint to begin striking $20 gold pieces from the old design. Free gold stocks were getting low and the U.S. treasurer was requesting an increased output of gold coins. The situation that former director Roberts had dismissed concerning gold stocks in July was developing. Preston told Philadelphia to go on this coinage until told otherwise.[19]

In spite of the minting of a few high-relief pieces, the issue of the coinability of the design for the $20 gold coin remained. With the beginning of September Augusta Saint-Gaudens entered the picture, as she had with the $10 gold piece. She had devoted her time in August to more pressing concerns of the estate, seeing that the unfinished commissions were going to be completed and assuring clients and committees who thought they were acquiring works from the master's hands that the end products would still reflect his creative genius. There also was the entanglement of the Boston Public Library groups, which threatened to turn into a significant liability.

Above all, money matters were now paramount for Gussie. As she gathered the financial reins and pushed Homer to the sidelines, a certain amount of confusion regarding the coin models from the family's end took place. On September 3, Augusta sent the models for the one-cent coin to the Mint. Was she not aware that work on that coin had stopped? Was she merely fulfilling the terms of the original engagement letter in order to ensure full payment from Treasury? Had Hering wasted time in August on these models?

In reply to Preston's inquiry at the end of August about the third models for the double eagle, Augusta in turn on September 11 relayed that work had been ongoing for a month and two more weeks would be required.[20]

On Saturday the 28th, Hering appeared at the Philadelphia Mint with the third model for the $20 gold piece. In Hering's words, Barber rejected it out of hand. While it had the lowest relief, Barber insisted that it was still much too high. Hering was surprised at this rejection. Nevertheless, Barber knew that he had no choice but to proceed. Norris, acting in Landis's place, duly reported to Preston that Barber would begin work on this third model on the following Monday.[21]

By now Barber had come to expect pressure from above, and he promptly got it.[22] His response was a long-winded letter of explanation to Landis on October 10. Homer Saint-Gaudens had promised to send both models created to the relief being achieved on French gold coins. In Barber's opinion, the second model of the $10 coin had arrived with too high a relief, although it was useable. The relief of this third $20 model was actually higher than the relief of the second $10 model. The relief on the $20 gold piece had to be lower than the $10 gold piece because of its increased diameter, which

Striking Change

made it more difficult to strike. Barber concluded that it would be a waste of time to make reductions from this model because it would be quite impossible to coin using one strike of the coin press. He was left with no choice but to try to use the Janvier lathe to mechanically reduce the relief. The plaster models, however, were too large. Barber had just received the bronze intermediate castings that day and was starting immediately to make the steel reductions.

He went on to make no promises as to the success of this approach, reminding Landis that the results for the first model of the $10 gold piece had been unsatisfactory. He called it a worn out, dull, or blind look. It was, in his opinion, unavoidable when relief was reduced mechanically with the Janvier machine. He also had special concerns for the $20 gold-coin design. While he could reduce the relief on many of the steep high points, detail on the low-relief portions of the coin would be lost.

Ever the pessimist, Barber had grave doubts that this design would ever strike up satisfactorily in the coin press. He had tried to impress upon Henry Hering from the very beginning the absolute necessity for low relief. Until those models were provided, Barber could not be assured of successful results.

At this point, Barber could not resist complaining. What they were doing still was in the nature of an experiment. Models should have been made with the full knowledge of the requirements for modern coinage. That had not been done. Barber unjustly accused Saint-Gaudens of furnishing models without the least knowledge of minting coins. The result had been simply a failure and an unparalleled waste of time. "Dies enough to have coined millions had been made had the models exhibited the least rudimentary knowledge of coinage." Nevertheless the Mint was doing all that it could to solve the problem.

Barber couldn't keep from reminding Landis that each time high-relief models had been delivered, he had pointed out their impossibility. Each time the trials had proved him right. In no case, had there been enough reduction in the relief to guarantee success. As soon as he could see the effects of the reducing lathe, he would report what prospect there was of using these dies.[23]

In this diatribe by Barber, there is one fact in support of the engraver. Hering had not delivered the relief anticipated by Barber in this last $20 coin model. Neither Homer Saint-Gaudens nor Henry Hering had promised the Mint that this third model would comply with the parameters set for the relief of the $10 coin. Saint-Gaudens himself set the restrictions on how low the relief could be for the $20 gold piece when he told Roosevelt in May that he then understood what could be practically stamped, the 20% reduction from the ultra high relief. Had Hering exercised some discretion in the matter, the reduction might have been acceptable. However, in defense of Hering, the Mint had not complied with his request to provide a strike from the second model of the $10 gold coin, leaving him in the dark as to the suitability of its relief. Now Barber would have to reduce the relief mechanically, a process he had not mastered.

On October 22, Barber came back with the results of his work. It was just as he had predicted. The dies from the third model had been completed and trial strikes in the coin press made. Reducing the relief from the model with the Janvier lathe had, as expected, caused a considerable loss of detail. The coin had an old and worn look. One specimen was forwarded to Washington and ended up in the hands of

312

Assistant Treasury Secretary Edwards.[24] Barber recommended that he start with a model with much lower relief so that such loss of detail on the figure of Liberty and the eagle would not occur with the reducing lathe. The modeling technique would now have to eliminate all steep changes in relief in order to facilitate coining with only one blow from the press. What was Barber recommending? He was asking for a fourth model for the $20 gold coin. This letter earned Barber an immediate trip to Washington.[25]

Barber's line of reasoning was not the only one being put forth in Philadelphia. The coiner, Rhine R. Freed, had specific ideas about how to improve the coining characteristics of this third model. He suggested to Landis reducing the relief on the foot, knee, and chest of Liberty. Metal-flow requirements would then be lessened, allowing the other portions of the die to impress more sharply on the planchet.[26] This report was not forwarded to Preston.

The meeting in Washington did not advance Barber's cause. With the specimen from the third model in hand, Assistant Secretary Edwards had a different reaction to the problems encountered. He attended the meeting with his own agenda, a set of questions that he wanted answered immediately. Barber's reply to his questions gives good insight into the thinking outside the confines of the Bureau of the Mint. That thinking had to be driven by Roosevelt's desires. How many $20 gold pieces of the new design could be coined by operating the existing medal presses around the clock? What would be the cost compared to that for the present design? How long before additional presses could be built?

Barber's answers were not reassuring. The Mint could strike 400 pieces per day. The cost would be 6¢ per coin compared to 1/20 mil for the present $20 coin design, which could be struck on the automatic coining press. To coin the same number of pieces as the regular coining presses, 144 new medal presses would need to be added at an estimated cost of $450,000, not counting the associated manpower. There was not room enough in the existing building to add these machines, and there was no adjacent ground upon which to expand in order to accommodate them. Additional medal presses were out of the question.

These numbers were so distorted as to be almost ridiculous. They could only have been based upon medal production numbers or the experience of the trial strikes at the end of August and therefore gave no allowance for a learning curve. Barber closed by saying that the only solution for the gold coinage was models that would produce dies that could strike up the design with one blow, as was done in all the civilized countries of the world at that time.[27]

Where were the other players? Frank Leach was still not effectively in charge. George Roberts's idea of using a forming die to prepare the planchet in advance of the actual die for the $20 gold piece had fallen by the wayside. Neither Charles Barber nor Robert Preston was an advocate.

Meanwhile the Saint-Gaudens family was totally in the dark. The Mint had previously cut them out of the decision-making process on the $10 gold piece. Now Augusta was again writing to Preston, on October 25, saying that she had received no reply to her inquiry as to the status of the project. She still did not realize that the cent had been dropped. Preston replied with an almost perfunctory letter and left it to Landis to convey to her that the models for the $20 gold piece still exhibited too great a relief. Landis's remedy was to echo Barber's request for a fourth model.[28]

Innocently, Frank Leach took full control of the Mint at the beginning of November and walked into a hornet's nest. The country had been lingering in a recession for some six months. A slumping stock market was contributing to a liquidity crunch, with tight money conditions now starting to bite. The first problem occurred on October 31. Edwards, serving as acting secretary of the Treasury, in an unexpected move, authorized Preston to begin paying out the new $10 gold coins. The Treasury Department had been under the impression that once Roosevelt had signed off, coining of the new $10 gold pieces had begun. Washington did not realize that the Mint had never commenced coining the new $10 gold pieces, due to the order to delay public release until the new $20 gold pieces were ready.[29]

As Leach took over, the unforeseeable had happened. The suspension of coinage of double eagles from February until September and the postponing of the decision to move gold bullion and coin east in August now appeared regrettable. All personnel in Philadelphia were focused on striking the new $10 coin. Enough working dies had to be prepared to support the mass production of this new coin.

No prior experience could have prepared Gussie for dealing with the United States Mint. However, she knew that Landis's answering letter of October 29 spelled trouble for the $20 gold-piece design.[30] Now she turned to Charles O. Brewster, the estate attorney, for help. However, her concerns, no doubt exacerbated by the plunging value of her stock portfolio, were as much about payment as they were about successful implementation of the $20 gold-piece design. Brewster requested a meeting with Leach and Edwards in Philadelphia. Hering and Homer Saint-Gaudens would also be present. Barber was sick, so the meeting was postponed until November 14.[31]

For Leach, the education about the $20 gold piece was beginning. Hering had not seen a trial strike from the third model for the big gold coin. A specimen was provided to him, but it had been struck in the medal press, which was of no real benefit: Hering needed to see how the coin struck up in the coin press using the maximum allowable pressure. At the very least, he wanted to see plaster casts of the dies that Barber had prepared from the last model. Leach in turn wanted a fourth model from Hering. If Hering would exaggerate the detail in a certain manner, he felt, the resulting sharpness would not be lost in the reduction process and the chances for a successful design were quite good. However, Hering wanted to wait until he could see the business strikes from the third model. He also needed the large plaster cast returned to help him with his new model.[32] This further delay before a fourth model could be commenced did not suit Leach.

Brewster now raised the issue of compensation. The work that the Saint-Gaudens estate had been required to perform had far exceeded that contemplated in the original contract. Additional moneys should be considered for the estate to cover the expenses of a fourth model. Brewster also sought resolution of the status of the cent design. In all, Brewster walked away from the meeting with a good impression of Leach.[33]

On November 16, Leach met with Charles Barber in Washington. They talked at length about how to make the third model work. The Mint director asked Barber to make another set of dies from this third model. That work would take another two to three weeks. Leach also wanted to conduct some experiments with the coin presses to better determine the maximum pressure the dies would tolerate as well as the die life itself. The nature of that request showed that Leach was going to be a different sort of Mint director. He was knowledgeable of and was going to be involved in the manufacturing operations of the Mint. He also brought a positive attitude to the job. In the discussion, it became apparent to Leach that Hering had enough information to ensure that a fourth model would be successful. Leach wrote expectantly to Brewster asking when he could expect to receive the fourth model. The Mint director had to report that the cent project had been abandoned in favor of the $10 gold piece. He had also written the secretary of the Treasury regarding additional compensation. There was no more money available at that time to compensate the estate for the extra work, but Leach acknowledged that their request was justified and said he inferred that the secretary had not closed the door on a future reconsideration. Pressure from the ongoing financial crisis in the country precluded any consideration of additional funds for the present. Leach had also approached Assistant Secretary Edwards over the matter of the payment but had gotten nowhere.[34] This frugality on the part of the government was misguided, and Leach knew it.

Brewster came back with a disheartening reply to the Mint director: Hering would require three weeks on the reverse model and seven weeks on the obverse model. Ten weeks in total was a ridiculous amount of time. Hering had spent 174 hours in August and another 85 hours in September preparing the most recent $10 and $20 models.[35] In fact, the correspondence argued that Hering only worked on the $20 model in September. Nothing from August or September would have supported Hering's estimate of ten weeks. In addition to more time, Hering urgently needed the strike at full pressure from the coin presses.

Brewster was very firm concerning the payment of more money to the estate. He wanted to impress upon both Leach and Edwards that a fourth model would cost from $500 to $1,000. Considering the ten-week time estimate, those cost projections might even have been low. It was unfair to expect Augusta Saint-Gaudens to authorize proceeding under such circumstances. Brewster did not see why the secretary of the Treasury could not join Leach in giving assurances that at least $7,500 in total would be paid to the estate at completion of the contract. Otherwise he expected that Augusta would drop the work where it stood and file a claim at a later date for additional compensation.[36]

Matters were threatening to escalate out of control for Frank Leach when William Loeb conveyed to Cortelyou on November 20 President Roosevelt's query as to the whereabouts of the new $20 gold pieces. They were a much more handsome coin than the new $10 gold pieces, and he wanted them distributed at once if possible. Cortelyou answered that he had sent Director Leach to Philadelphia "to look into the matter personally" the preceding day.[37] Theodore Roosevelt was not one to stand on reporting formalities. Frank Leach was on his way to the White House.

On November 22, the Bureau of the Mint's seeming intransigence had finally pushed Theodore Roosevelt over the edge. Now Frank Leach, who had not been on the job a month, sat directly across the desk from the president. Roosevelt had been under intense pressure during the final days of October. The meltdown of the New York financial markets was casting a pall over his presidency. Bank failures were threatening to spread out of New York into the heartland of the country. When it came to finances and economics, Theodore was largely clueless.[38] To stem the tide, Cortelyou had been forced to turn to J. Pierpont Morgan to bail the administration out of the situation. This action was particularly difficult for Theodore to swallow. Morgan was perhaps the leading financier and capitalist in the country. Theodore had expended much energy in his administration trying to curb what he felt was the undue power exerted by these people in the American marketplace. While the direction was positive, matters still hung in the balance some four weeks later. Just the previous Saturday night Roosevelt had huddled with Cortelyou, Root, and his postmaster general, deciding to issue $100 million in bonds to prop up the markets.[39] All the frustrations of the past month now had boiled over. There was fire in his eyes and he had very well meant to explode.

However, the fires that had tempered Frank Leach were far hotter than anything that President Roosevelt could muster that day.

Leach had been brought up in frontier California with limited schooling. He had spent his adult life as a California newspaperman. Over time, he became involved in Republican politics. Out of the blue in 1897 came the notification that he was the choice of the California congressional delegation to be the superintendent of the San Francisco Mint.[40]

Leach immediately immersed himself in the nuts and bolts of its manufacturing operations. He presided over the conversion from steam to electric power. He studied in great detail the workings of the refining department. By 1906, Frank Leach had become the longest-serving superintendent in the history of the San Francisco Mint.

The story might have ended there but for one event.

The earthquake that hit San Francisco on April 18, 1906, was terrible enough. However, the ensuing fires created the horror that destroyed the city. Ultimately the mint would be virtually surrounded by those fires. The situation was a matter of life and death. Fortunately, only ten days previously workmen had finished piping the building for fire control, placing hydrants throughout the structure and tying the system into a water well. Leach organized the successful firefighting effort and took his turn on the hoses to save the "Granite Lady," as the mint became affectionately known after the fire. Leach was also prominent in the recovery operations. With $300 million in the mint's vaults, he greatly assisted in reestablishing the city's financial infrastructure.[41]

When George Roberts announced his retirement as director of the Mint, he recommended Frank Leach as his successor. Leach had the experience and the executive ability for the job. Cortelyou's unqualified endorsement came the next day. The president promptly approved the secretary's recommendation. In Roosevelt's words, he could not do otherwise than appoint Frank Leach. It would have been both unwise and improper to pass the man over. The job required a *special* ability.[42]

Now, however, Leach knew his brief honeymoon was over. He told the president point blank that if he "did not have free rein in the matter he would not attempt the work."

Leach asked for time to assess the situation. He would correct the problem, but he insisted that he be in charge. "All you want, Mr. President, is the production of the coin with the new design, is it not?" Leach asked. "Yes," Roosevelt answered. "Well, that I promise you," Leach replied.

Leach did not think that the president sounded confident at all that he could get the job done. The uncertainties that Leach faced at this point gave Roosevelt the right to be less than confident. However, the president had just given Leach more authority than he had anyone else. Roosevelt and Saint-Gaudens at last had an ally in bringing closure to the "pet crime."

Frank Leach wasted no time. On that same Friday, by order of the president, he instructed the Mint to use every facility at its command to strike high-relief $20 gold pieces using the second model as modified at Landis's suggestion. Never mind that the Mint was straining to pump liquidity into the American financial markets. Never mind that in the previous week they had produced 50,000 $20 gold pieces of the old design in one day at Philadelphia in response to the monetary crisis, and that their production schedule looking forward was just as aggressive. Never mind that the men were regularly staying beyond their normal four o'clock quitting time until ten at night.[43] It was Leach's intention to strike five or six thousand of the new $20 gold coins on the medal press by the first week in December to satisfy Theodore Roosevelt. Additional strikes of the ultra high relief coin were no longer under consideration. Meanwhile Barber was ordered to rush completion of work for a second hub from Hering's third model for use in the standard coin presses.[44]

Leach revealed these decisions and a little more of the meeting with the president in a letter to Charles Brewster on November 23. The fourth model would be postponed while another set of dies from the third model were readied.[45] Brewster replied two days later that he concurred with that decision. Then he raised another point. Mrs. Saint-Gaudens had shown him the obverse of the third model plaster cast returned from the Mint. She then compared it to a second cast taken by Hering from the same mold. The cast returned from the Mint appeared blurred, and all the sharpness of outline was gone. Brewster then asked a very innocent question. Was it necessary to destroy all that sharpness before making the reduction? Of course, he would be glad to forward the two casts for Leach.[46]

Hering no doubt had prompted Brewster that Saint-Gaudens had raised the same issue to no avail in March. However, in raising the issue in this manner, he accomplished his purpose. Without putting the Mint director on the defensive, he had alerted Leach that all was not right with the reduction process at the Mint. If Barber blamed it on the stylus of the reducing lathe this time, Leach would expect the engraver to correct the problem on the spot. Leach was puzzled. Certainly no one at the Mint would have taken the liberty of altering the models. If current efforts ran into problems, he would consider calling in Henry Hering again. It was a diplomatic answer, and it did not dodge the issue of where the responsibility lay. Leach did not need to compare the two plaster casts. He left immediately for Philadelphia.[47]

Meanwhile in Philadelphia, Charles Barber was pulling out all the stops to comply with Frank Leach's directive. He put his people to work around the clock and on Sundays. For the second-model high-relief coin, he needed another set of dies in order to start a second production line. That was no easy process. The die stock for these dies had to be cut to measure, trued up, and annealed to get the steel to flow into all the difficult and high points of the design when hubbed. Only Barber and Morgan had the skill to do this work. Again it was apparent that Barber still had not mastered the essentials of the Janvier lathe.

The engraver wanted the $20 gold pieces struck in 1,000-coin lots. That way, if the dies broke, all would not be lost. A new die would almost surely produce a doubling effect. A collar would be added for the final strike to place the inscription E PLURIBUS UNUM on the edge. With this statement, Barber let the cat out of the bag regarding the coinability of the high-relief double eagles. It took two blows of the medal press to bring up design details and a third blow with the special collar to impress the edge lettering. While still not feasible within the limits of a coin press, these high-relief double eagles came much nearer being coinable than Barber wanted to admit.[48]

On December 2, Leach walked into Roosevelt's office with the new Saint-Gaudens $20 gold piece from the third model. Of course the piece was low relief. Its color was pale compared to the high-relief coins, which exhibited a true gold color as a result of their annealing process. Theodore was nonetheless "delighted."[49] Barber had risen to the occasion. With Leach's authority, Barber could now make the needed modifications to strike up the design on the coin presses. For the sake of the Mint Service, he had put aside his animosity for Saint-Gaudens. He had drawn upon the skills taught by his father. In time-honored fashion, this last of the old-school engravers had deftly made the cuts directly into the hub to restore the detail of the design that he could not capture with the reducing lathe. In doing so, he had saved the Saint-Gaudens design. This was Charles Barber at his best.[50]

Leaving Roosevelt, Leach wrote to Brewster that same day, enclosing the new low-relief coin for his review. If Brewster wished any of the features touched up, it could be done on the master dies. However, the lawyer must not delay, as every moment was precious. Pride exuded from the letter. Leach left the door open for a fourth model, though, if the Saint-Gaudens people felt the coin could be improved. At the same time he could not promise any additional compensation but felt he could achieve that goal after the financial crisis had passed.[51]

Now it was Brewster's turn to communicate with Augusta. He told her that the new high-relief $20 gold piece would give her a sense of pride and joy. It was indeed a beautiful work of art. He sent her both the high-relief coin and the low-relief impression intended for general circulation. As Augusta was suffering from a cold, he knew to remain silent on the troubling topic of a fourth model and additional compensation for work completed.[52]

With the new low-relief dies completed and the high-relief coins in production, Charles Barber seemed to have done a 180-degree turnaround. But it was only an appearance. Leach had instructed that the high-relief gold pieces be placed in bags of 250 coins for shipping purposes. One of these bags was delivered to the secretary of the Treasury on December 6. A considerable number of coins were defective, with excessive fins on the edges. Leach was humiliated. He had specifically ordered that such coins be pulled out in Philadelphia. In a heated letter to Superintendent Landis, Leach left little doubt as to where the blame lay. He had given explicit orders to "the man who

A Man for the Occasion

seemed to have the coins in charge." Leach wanted an investigation to see why his instructions were not carried out.[53]

Production of the high-relief $20 gold pieces continued, coupled with close inspection to throw out the defective pieces, until Leach had an occasion to bring Charles Barber to Washington. Leach believed the problem of striking high-relief coins might be helped with some pre-shaped and pre-milled planchets that he had had prepared at the San Francisco Mint.[54] The pre-shaped pieces yielded no improvements, however, indicating that George Roberts's idea of pre-forming would not work. The pre-milled pieces, on the other hand, showed some potential for rectifying the fin problem. Barber then returned to Philadelphia, where Mint personnel implemented a new design for a milling machine that, when placed in operation, eliminated the fin. It did this by thickening the edges of the planchet and producing a flat rim in advance of striking. Pieces struck prior to this changeover were known as "wire rim" and, afterward, as "flat rim." Naturally Barber was proud of this accomplishment, sending Leach two sample coins. However, he was scared that Roosevelt might like the new coins too well and insist upon their continuance. He was quick to point out to Leach that this modified process still required the same number of blows from the medal press.[55] The engraver was careful, however, to remain mum about how long it now took, given the efficiencies learned, to strike each coin.

This coin is the most beautiful American design to ever reach the general public. It was struck in the relief that the sculptor had found acceptable.[56] Saint-Gaudens had complied fully with the legal requirements for inscriptions on the coin. The word LIBERTY was inscribed above the standing figure. The date, in roman numerals, was unique. The aforementioned 46 stars formed a border on the obverse, and E PLURIBUS UNUM with 13 stars appeared on the edge of the coin. Thus Saint-Gaudens employed all the required devices as well as those of a more traditional nature yet avoided detracting from his design with too many inscriptions.

This new issue was avidly sought. Justice Oliver Wendell Holmes wanted one. Once again William Eleroy Curtis—the smooth operator who had been involved with the Lorenzo Lotto portrait and the Columbian Exposition half dollar—was working for James Ellsworth to acquire this $20 gold piece and the $10 example of the first model. Even Bosbyshell from World's Fair days wanted one.[57] The coins were shipped to the sub-treasuries and then allocated to the banks. Banks and individuals were limited to five coins. Boston received an allocation of 500 coins or two bags, and they were dispersed in a single day. In response to the demand, the Mint continued striking these coins well past Roosevelt's goal of 5,000 to 6,000. Ultimately, upon Leach's instructions, the Mint worked throughout December, striking some 11,000 to 12,000 of these high-relief $20 gold pieces. Of this total, about 3,000 were the flat rim variety. Regardless, a premium for this coin developed that ranged from $5 to $15.[58] Over the years, this coin would continue to command a premium far above other coins of comparable numismatic rarity.

Theodore Roosevelt was more than "delighted" over the new $20 gold coin. When Leach brought him the new low-relief coin for his inspection, he immediately asked for 20 more of the high-relief coins.[59] He would send high-relief coins with notes to many of his close personal friends. Leach himself thought the work a distinct

319

Striking Change

improvement over earlier August trial strikings from the second model. When Leach returned just before Christmas with high-relief coins without the wire edge, Theodore confiscated them and wanted more.[60] He was like a child in a candy store. His "pet crime" had finally been accomplished.

Even as the high-relief gold pieces were being struck, production from the modified low-relief dies of the third model was ready to be set in motion. On December 6 Leach gave authority to commence striking $20 gold coins based on the third model from the coin presses.[61] Still Barber balked at carrying out Leach's orders. Nothing yet had been heard from the Saint-Gaudens estate in regard to the strike from the modified dies of the third model. Barber wrote Landis, questioning the legal status of the new $20 coin design. No formal declaration of approval had been given. All of his work had been of an experimental nature. No provision had been made in the Engraving Department to support a full-scale production of this coin. He needed authority to make the dies for the business strikes from the third model. Leach was miffed. He replied that the formal declaration would be attended to at the proper time. Furthermore, he had assumed when he authorized the striking of the new $20 gold pieces with the coin presses that it included—at least by inference—the making of all necessary dies.[62]

Leach did have approval of sorts from the estate. Henry Hering had replied to Charles Brewster on December 5. The attorney read Hering's letter over the phone to Leach. He then attached Hering's suggestions without substantial comment to his own letter.[63] Hering's letter had no suggestions for touching up the master die. The thing to be done was to get a better reduction. He thought a great improvement could still be made, although the Mint said otherwise. Hering was willing to make another model; he would make any changes Leach wished to sharpen the background detail as long as the relief of the central figures was not changed. Just as he had done with the third model, Hering was unwilling to reduce the basic central relief of the design beyond what Gus had approved in May. Hering closed by saying that softer plaster should be used in combination with the stearine in spite of what Charles Barber had said. Hering had confirmed from other sources that the softer plaster would indeed work. Virtually ignoring Hering's comments, Brewster added in his own letter that he had shown both the high-relief and low-relief examples to Augusta. She was quite naturally disappointed with the low-relief coin. However, she acknowledged that the Mint was doing all within its power to maintain as high a relief as possible in the general-circulation coin.[64]

With Brewster's letter in hand, Leach had closed the door on the prospect of a fourth model with his December 6 order. He had an acceptable work product with presidential approval. Still, Leach had second thoughts. When a required trip to San Francisco fell through, the Mint director ordered Barber to come to Washington. They reviewed Hering's letter and the issue of a fourth model for the better part of a day. Barber took issue with using a softer plaster as Hering had suggested but was willing to try. Leach felt that it was possible with a new model to better bring up the background detail. However, that model must have a lower relief than the third model. While the coin from the modified third model was now ready for production, Leach believed that the Mint was capable of producing a coin with a higher relief than was presently being done.

A Man for the Occasion

He conveyed these thoughts to Charles Brewster. There was just one problem: Leach could not guarantee that the government would pay for another model. If the estate wished to improve the appearance of the coin, they would have to accept the burden of the expense, at least temporarily. Brewster in turn placed the issue of the fourth model to Augusta.[65] Gus would have done the fourth model without a moment's hesitation, but for Gussie it was an issue of money, not art. There would be no fourth model.

On December 19 Frank Leach received official approval for the Saint-Gaudens design for the $20 gold piece. Likewise he belatedly received approval for the $10 coin, already released into circulation.[66] Production delays had been encountered after Leach's first authorization of the 6th. The coin was both new to the pressmen and a very difficult piece to strike. There had been initial troubles getting the lettering on the edge of the coins. However, by the weekend of December 15 that problem was overcome. Over the second half of December, the Mint was coining up to 25,000 of the new low-relief $20 gold pieces a day.[67] Total production would be 362,000 pieces by year's end.

After just one month shy of three years, the new double eagles were released into general circulation. When compared to the high-relief example, changes were evident. Of course, the roman numerals had been replaced—contrary to Saint-Gaudens's desire that no arabic numbers appear on the coin.[68] Hering made this change unilaterally to eliminate the issue first raised with the $10 coin. Liberty's face had been noticeably flattened and made more rounded in appearance. The relief of Liberty's chest, knee, and foot was lowered in apparent accordance with the coiner's suggestions. However, the anchoring of the left leg was lost in the transition. Also, some of the rich detail of Liberty's blouse at the bustline was gone. Most disappointing was the treatment of the sun rays. Hering had made the obverse rays sharper, more rounded, such that they appeared to form a concentric semicircle. While no record of Hering's reverse model exists, it can be assumed that it was the sculptor who again sharpened the rays of the sun to facilitate striking. With the relief that he anticipated on the eagle, this change would have been acceptable. However, Barber's reduced relief now caused the eagle to lose its dominance against Hering's overly sharpened sun rays. The reverse design now suffered from this lack of coordination between Barber and Hering.

The saga of the Saint-Gaudens gold coins was now over. In the end, Roosevelt had gotten his limited issue of high-relief $20 gold pieces. The Mint reverted to low relief for the general-circulation coins. However, even in low relief, the Saint-Gaudens design was a vast improvement over anything that had come before. The "pet crime" was a triumph. One coin was an American art piece.

There are three postscripts to the story. The Mint still had 13 of the experimental $20 coins in "checker" size. In January 1908, the Mint curator wrote Frank Leach asking to put samples of this coin into the Mint Cabinet or coin collection. After that was done the others were destroyed, although not without a hitch. When asked for his specimen, Charles Barber said he would return his when the other pieces had been collected for destruction.[69] This he ultimately did, as the coin was clearly illegal to hold.

Over the years, Barber had retained examples of both coins and medals from his work at the Mint. While subsequent Mint ethical standards discouraged this activity, it was not exceptional in Barber's time. He may have resisted implementing Saint-Gaudens's designs, but he actively added them to his collection. In addition to the Indian Head pattern double eagle, he retained eight of the ultra high relief $20 gold coins and two of the $10 coins, one with the wire rim and one with the rolled rim struck on the medal press. In fact, his records also show that he held four of the World's Columbian Exposition medals with the rejected Saint-Gaudens reverse.[70]

In the third postscript, Leach realized just before Christmas 1907 that the ultra high relief $20 gold pieces could still be had. He ordered three from Philadelphia: one for the Saint-Gaudens estate, one for Secretary Cortelyou, and one for himself. If President Roosevelt did not have one, a fourth would be necessary. However, he would not distribute these coins until after the first of the coming year lest word leak out and others besiege him with requests for this rarity. None were on hand, so Barber struck three more on the last day of the year. Not knowing that only three coins were struck and that a fourth would be needed for the president, Leach on January 2 told Brewster he would try to obtain one of the ultra high relief coins for Augusta.[71] When only three coins arrived, the estate was shorted and Leach was in a fix, since the die by law had to be retired at year's end.

Chapter 22

The Last Words

The $20 gold piece had not even been issued yet when the firestorm over the new designs erupted. Roosevelt had had misgivings for some time about the motto "In God We Trust." However, he never anticipated that omitting the motto would stir up such a stink.

Perhaps it was public frustration over the fallout from the October collapse of the financial markets. That event was now called the Panic of 1907. The president's opponents were quick to dub it the "Roosevelt Panic"[1] although its causes were much more complex. Now came Roosevelt's decision to exclude the motto. This was an issue the general public could easily understand, and they vocally expressed their displeasure.

Diverse groups such as the Grange, the Women's Christian Temperance Union, the Junior Order of the United Mechanics of America, and the Christian Endeavor Union were quick in their denunciation. There was much misinformation about the issue. First, the motto was termed "age old." In fact it was not, having first appeared on circulating coins in 1864. Second, detractors insisted that Roosevelt's removal of the motto by executive order was unconstitutional, because Congress had jurisdiction over coinage matters. The fact was that Congress had not mandated the incorporation of the motto onto the nation's coinage in the revised statutes of 1874. Nevertheless, Roosevelt was blamed; his tampering was perceived as unpatriotic and unchristian.[2]

The proposal for a motto such as "In God We Trust" had originated with a clergyman from Pennsylvania, in the midst of renewed religious sentiment during the Civil War. It was probably appropriate that the leader of the opposition to its removal from the gold pieces was also from Pennsylvania. He was F. Carroll Brewster, a prominent Philadelphia lawyer and Episcopalian layman. He authored a pamphlet and organized a movement across many of the Eastern states to restore the motto.[3]

This grassroots opposition was aided by those who opposed the president for other reasons. The New York *Sun* and the *Wall Street Journal* waded into the fray. The *Sun* had opposed Roosevelt at practically every turn in his political career. The *Journal* was upset that the needs of the commercial interests had been ignored in the drive for high relief on the new coins.[4] More serious in Theodore's mind, his good friend Lyman Abbot, editor of the *Outlook*, was only lukewarm in support of him. Abbot acknowledged that the new $10 gold coin was the more beautiful for the simplicity of its design, helped in part by the omission of the motto. However, the strength of the

323

aesthetic reasons for removing the motto did not adequately compensate for the resulting public misunderstanding. Abbot felt that Roosevelt had shocked the people. He went on to express regret that church assemblies did not show half as much emotion over the burning social abuses of the times as they did over the motto issue.[5]

Abbot's measured criticism was lost in a roar of less restrained commentary. Religious leaders blasted the president from the pulpit. The Episcopal Diocese of New York in convention narrowly passed a resolution seeking the restoration of the motto. J.P. Morgan was reportedly on the floor of that convention, actively working for the resolution's passage.[6] The argument that the motto's removal was evidence of the secular spirit of the age struck a responsive chord. Some accused Roosevelt of a premeditated assault on religion. Others said he was guilty of displaying a reckless and impulsive disregard for the religious sentiments of the majority of Americans. The most strident declared that Roosevelt was an atheist.[7]

The controversy brought out the combative element in the president. He could have laid the blame on the dead Saint-Gaudens. He could have ducked the issue by saying he was merely complying with the law. Instead he chose to argue the issue on its merits and try to marshal opinion to his side. He sought support from his network of influential friends. One, Silas McBee, was editor of the Episcopalian newspaper the *Churchman*. McBee reminded Episcopalians that "the sober second thought of Christian America will surely support the President on this matter. The robust Christian faith of this nation needs no such clinking asseveration."[8] However, McBee later told the president that he had written this editorial before seeing the $10 gold piece. He was no fan of Saint-Gaudens and called it bad art. Roosevelt blithely ignored the criticism and sent him one of the new high-relief $20 gold pieces. McBee liked the obverse of this coin but could not sign on to the reverse.[9]

Other national church organs weighed in on the president's side. They dismissed the motto's omission as an act of little consequence. The *Baptist Commonwealth, Catholic Citizen,* and *American Hebrew* all attached little significance to its removal. Others felt that linking the Deity with money was more sacrilege than piety.[10] This support came only from the nation's intellectual leadership, unfortunately, and was narrow-based, which boded ill for the president.

Roosevelt addressed the issue head-on in a letter to a clergyman on November 11, 1907. He pointed out that he was not required by law to include the motto on the new coins. Here, however, he faced the issue squarely. He stated that he would have included it if he felt its use on coinage was warranted, but he felt that the motto's inclusion on coins was irreverent and came very close to sacrilege. This line of reasoning had been provided to him by his secretary of commerce, Oscar Strauss.[11] "In God We Trust" was a motto that deserved to be put on our most important buildings and monuments, he asserted: its use on money, on the other hand, cheapened it. He went on to say that in his lifetime he had never heard anyone speak reverently of the motto or show any sign that it appealed to their higher emotions. Instead people would twist the phrase's meaning by saying such things as "In God we trust for the short weight." This last comment was a slam against the depreciated bullion value of the nation's coinage from the Free Silver days. He closed by saying that if Congress directed him to restore the motto he would do it promptly.[12]

The Last Words

After waiting a short interval, Roosevelt attempted to shore up his defense by making this letter available to the press. It was a failure. People pounced on his point that the motto inspired irreverence rather than lofty emotions. They suggested replacing the eagle on the coins' reverse with a teddy bear and the inscription "In Theodore We Trust." Roosevelt was losing sleep over the issue.[13] He needed a way out.

An incident that showed Roosevelt, the man, occurred in December of that year. Richard Watson Gilder, although starting to show the strains of a lifetime of hard work, was still very much involved with Saint-Gaudens's new designs. Homer Saint-Gaudens had submitted an article concerning his father's gold coins that defended the omission of the motto. Before publishing the piece, Gilder sent it to Roosevelt for his review, suggesting modifications that would protect Roosevelt.[14] Theodore wrote back and asked that Gilder delete the reference to the motto. He said that Homer was "an awfully nice young man" but that he "simply does not understand the undesirability of arousing the people to attack the coinage which his father had designed." Roosevelt knew he must quell the issue or it would overshadow the coins themselves.[15]

Congress reconvened on December 2, 1907. Congressmen had been inundated by clamors from their constituents to do something about the motto issue, and there was a stampede to introduce legislation restoring the motto.[16] Roosevelt's own Republican Party was in opposition to him. His problem politically went all the way back to the day following his election in 1904. He had impetuously declared that he would consider his time in office from McKinley's assassination to be a first term in office. This would be his second term. He would not break with tradition; therefore he would not stand for reelection in 1908. If anyone doubted his intentions, a letter from Roosevelt to Cortelyou at this time settled the issue. It had come to his attention that "certain office-holders" in the Treasury were working to secure his renomination. That must not be. Such actions would be a serious violation of official propriety and would be dealt with accordingly.[17] It was as diplomatic as Roosevelt could be in telling Cortelyou to back down. He was now a lame-duck president. The Republicans were scrambling to avoid handing the Democrats an issue in an election year.

If Republicans in Congress were not going to stand by Theodore Roosevelt, they would nevertheless give him a way out. A bill introduced by one of their own, Congressman J. Hampton Moore from Pennsylvania, a friend of the president's, would provide that exit. The Republican leadership knew that Roosevelt's dander was up over the issue and they feared a veto. They asked Moore to go to the White House. Moore likened this assignment to going to beard the lion in his den.[18]

There was a set protocol to visiting with the president. Roosevelt received visitors between 10:00 a.m. and 1:30 p.m. For the first two hours, senators and representatives had entrée without going through Secretary William Loeb for an appointment. Sometimes there would be a score of people waiting for the president in the Executive Office. Theodore would go from one to another making a circuit of the room, sometimes half a dozen times, speaking rapidly and gesturing freely.[19]

The Executive Office was crowded that day. In Moore's observation, Roosevelt "was putting them through, senators, congressmen, and citizens in his usual whirlwind fashion." Moore broached the subject of the motto. The president's hackles immediately rose. He did not see the need for legislation to mandate its use on the

325

nation's coinage. Moore argued that the Democrats were pressing the issue and the newspapers were picking up on the story. Roosevelt sneered. Then Moore blundered, starting to mention the New York *Sun*. Roosevelt lost his temper. Moore stood his ground: the president had needlessly shocked the country with this action. More conversation ensued. Finally Roosevelt relented somewhat. The issue was "rot." However, there was potential to misconstrue his motives and stir up a sensation. Therefore if the Senate and House passed such a law, he would not veto it. Moore had survived the lion's den.[20]

The president signed the bill into law on May 19, 1908. The motto was restored effective July 1, 1908. The issue quickly subsided, and the beauty of the new designs by Saint-Gaudens became the intended focal point. Roosevelt had lost the battle over the motto in order to achieve the broader goal of acceptance of the new coins themselves.

Charles Barber was happy to have an opportunity to go back and touch up the designs. His choice of placement of the motto for the $10 gold piece was easy: he put IN GOD WE TRUST in the open field of the reverse, balancing it against the motto E PLURIBUS UNUM. However, his real concern was the $20 gold piece. Here he placed IN GOD WE TRUST on the reverse in an arc between the sun and its rays. It was a nice touch and did not interfere with Saint-Gaudens's masterful composition on the reverse. More importantly for Barber, it gave him an opportunity to refine his take-off from the third model.[21]

As the motto issue moved from full boil to a simmer, comments on the coins themselves began to be heard. The medalist Victor David Brenner called the designs the embryo of a beautiful conception and regretted that Saint-Gaudens had not lived to complete his work. However, it was obvious that the $20 gold piece far surpassed the $10 in beauty. The latter coin came in for criticism of the Indian headdress.[22] The public failed to see the headdress as the unique American symbol of liberty as Theodore Roosevelt had. It mattered little how brilliantly Saint-Gaudens had treated that headdress. The *New York Times* claimed that a woman named Mary Cunningham had posed for some of the later work on the $10 gold piece. She was of Irish heritage, and that would not do. Only a pure American should be on the coinage.[23] The eagle on the reverse of the $10 gold piece was praised in some quarters as bold and strutting while being criticized in others for legs that seemed disproportionately large.

The Saint-Gaudens family became defensive. The headdress was Roosevelt's idea, they asserted. The woman's profile was merely "a suggestion."[24] The style of eagle was common to the sculptor's work and had never drawn criticism before. To Gus, it was not enough to just portray the bird; the eagle needed to say something artistically. In total frustration Homer Saint-Gaudens called Barber's reduction of the second model for the $10 gold piece a villainous reproduction. It was far from it. Frank Leach made the mistake of repeating to Roosevelt the criticism that on the $20 gold piece the eagle was stiff-legged. Leach just could not bring himself to like Saint-Gaudens's artistic eagles. He had no idea that Theodore was a naturalist at heart. His comment earned the Mint director a trip to the presidential woodshed—in this case, the Rock Creek Aviary.[25] Leach returned with a new respect for Theodore Roosevelt, having learned that eagles did indeed fly with their talons extended.

$10 gold piece modified for the mandated IN GOD WE TRUST motto. (2x actual size)

$20 gold piece modified for the mandated motto. (2x actual size)

Ironically, on December 6, 1907, the day Frank Leach ordered production of the $20 gold piece, the British Royal Mint finally addressed George Roberts's questions pertaining to their experience with high relief. It was an informative letter. The deputy master had useful observations. If a line drawn from the point of highest relief on the obverse to the point of highest relief on the reverse passed through the plane of the planchet at a right angle, there would be problems coining that relief at one blow of the press. Put simply, there would not be enough metal to flow into both designs at the same time.[26] He had two corollary points to make on high relief. If the greater portion of the obverse and reverse was in high relief (for example, two busts), difficulties would be encountered. Likewise, a standing figure extending from top to bottom with flat spaces to right and left would impose a limitation upon the degree of relief achievable. Furthermore, the pressure required to bring up the relief was impacted by the degree of convexity of the die. The ratio of the diameter of the coin to its thickness also played a part. Thus a smaller planchet would accept a higher relief at the same coining pressure than a larger planchet. Finally the deputy master pointed out that sharpness of design was really a matter of taste. His preference personally was for sharpness. However, the impressionistic style of the day inclined more toward soft modeling of rounded edges for lettering and details. This letter was certainly a vindication for Charles Barber's frustration during the three-year odyssey. However, this did not excuse his antagonistic actions.[27]

Applying the experience of the Royal Mint, the Saint-Gaudens $20 gold-piece design—with its large diameter, standing figure on the obverse, and relief high points opposite one another on the obverse and reverse—was not workable. There were two crucial decision points that could have altered this situation. In the White House meeting between Roosevelt and Roberts on May 25, the design for the double eagle could have been altered. By May, Saint-Gaudens had come to realize that his standing eagle was a more suitable match for coining purposes to the standing Liberty. While the design was still burdened with an upright figure, the conflicting high points on the obverse and reverse were not as pronounced. By picking the devices for the $20 gold piece that he did, Roosevelt minimized the achievable relief without understanding what he had done. At the same time, it should be recognized that Roosevelt did use the standing eagle in combination with Liberty in headdress for the smaller $10 gold piece. It should have been no surprise to any knowledgeable person that Barber was able to produce a suitable coin from that combination with modest relief on his first attempt.

The second point occurred when Frank Leach ordered the modified third model of the standing Liberty design into production on December 6. The approval that had come from the Saint-Gaudens estate was a stretch at best. Henry Hering was advocating a fourth model that would have achieved some modest degree of relief. There was no doubt from Leach's actions that he was a man in a hurry. Hering had said that the obverse model would take seven weeks. The issue of compensation promised to be very sticky. In Leach's mind, it was time for closure; never mind that the process was then almost three years in the making. The issue of the motto omission had to play a part in his rush to production.

The $10 gold piece had appeared with mixed artistic reviews and much criticism for the omission of "In God We Trust." Congress had come into session on December 2.

The Last Words

If the $20 gold piece did not reach production status quickly, there was a real chance that Congress could act rashly, seeking to block its issue. Subsequently one proposed piece of legislation to restore the motto did just that.[28] Should Congressman Joe Cannon have gotten it into his head to stop the design change, he could easily have done so, given the emotional nature of the motto controversy. There was also the fact that the high-relief coins were costly to mint, which added fuel to the fire. Roosevelt obliquely referred to the fact that Cannon or one of his minions called him to task on this point.[29] The potential was there for a replay of the World's Columbian Exposition award medal. The result would have been disastrous. Leach was right in making the decision to forgo the fourth model. The time for experimenting was over; Saint-Gaudens's double eagle needed to reach the public's hands.

Across the Atlantic, with spring 1908 on the horizon, an old man reached into his pocket. His head was crowned with an almost full mane of white hair; likewise his face was accented with both a white mustache and goatee, stylish for the times. As a newspaperman this individual had recorded firsthand the metamorphosis of his country into a world power. Now he was in England, in the final stages of a distinguished diplomatic career. He pulled out the $20 gold piece that was carefully wrapped so that it would not become worn or scratched. He had insisted that Cortelyou give him a flawless example of this unusual gold coin.[30] Today he was showing it to another of his friends in the British government as a striking example of what the American government under Roosevelt's leadership could do. Few who saw the flashy coin with its stunning high relief failed to speak of it as the most beautiful coin they had ever seen. The old man agreed. After all, as he had uncharacteristically carried on to Cortelyou, he had been there at the beginning, had procured General Sherman's sitting for Saint-Gaudens.[31] He had even been sitting at the dinner table where Roosevelt challenged Saint-Gaudens to redesign America's coinage.

Whitelaw Reid smiled at his English friend and carefully put the shimmering beauty back into his pocket.

Glenn Brown. The secretary of the American Institute of Architects had worked behind the scenes with both the Senate Park Commission and the White House renovation. After Saint-Gaudens's death, Brown would mount an ambitious and successful traveling exhibit of the artist's work.

Chapter 23

A Requiem for Gus

Too little time had passed since the release of the $20 gold piece before the two sides were again squabbling. At issue was the request for additional money to the Saint-Gaudens estate for the extra models and the question of where to obtain an ultra high relief strike for Augusta. This was no way to remember Augustus Saint-Gaudens.

With the start of the new year, Augusta Saint-Gaudens reentered the picture. It was time that she received payment for Gus's designs. On January 14, 1908, she wrote to Treasury Secretary George Cortelyou, asking for payment of $8,000. Her concern was that the preparation of numerous models had pushed out-of-pocket expenses to $3,700. The remaining money was barely adequate to compensate for Saint-Gaudens's time.[1] Estate attorney Charles Brewster followed up with a diplomatic letter to Mint Director Frank Leach. He hoped that if Cortelyou consulted Leach the director would support the increase. Brewster also assumed that the matter would be taken up with the president.[2]

Leach went back to the original letter agreement between Shaw and Saint-Gaudens. The language was clear: Gus would provide two designs or four models to the government for $5,000. Leach did not feel the estate was entitled to additional payments for the work involved in determining a suitable relief. Saint-Gaudens had provided a fifth model, which was ultimately used for the second gold-coin design.[3] That would entitle the estate to an additional $1,250. There was only $6,098 remaining in the account from which moneys were to be taken to pay for this work, and any payment over this amount would require a congressional appropriation. Therefore Leach recommended paying the estate $6,000.[4]

Cortelyou approved. It now fell to the director to inform Brewster that the government was reducing Augusta's request. To his credit, Leach was straightforward in explaining the government's position: a payment beyond $6,000 would require an act of Congress.[5] After the fact, Brewster pressed to learn whether Roosevelt had been involved in the decision. Leach couldn't say for certain but told Brewster that he inferred as much from his discussion with Cortelyou. Gussie was not happy with the government's position. However, on February 21, she cashed the check.[6] For Gussie, with one exception, this affair was finished.

That one exception was an increasingly vexing problem for Frank Leach. He was short one ultra high relief double eagle to provide to Augusta; there were none to be had in Washington. Leach began to hedge. He told Brewster that he had written to

331

Philadelphia to see if any were available. Barber was certainly not going to be forthcoming about his small cache. Leach also told Brewster on January 2 not to say anything to Gussie until he knew definitely that he could acquire a coin for her. Brewster, however, was not letting Leach off the hook. Leach reported on the 7th that he had been unsuccessful but would take the matter up with Secretary Cortelyou.[7]

In conveying Augusta's acceptance of the government's offer for final settlement, Brewster made a subtle linkage. Had Leach been able to secure the ultra high relief $20 gold piece yet? Leach missed the linkage or chose to ignore it, replying that it now looked doubtful.[8]

For Gussie, frustration over the coins was growing. In March Brewster had asked that the estate be involved with the insertion of the motto "In God We Trust" into the gold-coin designs. Leach wrote back that it never occurred to him that the estate would be interested in this matter. Wanting to avoid any delay once the legislation requiring this motto looked certain, Leach had submitted the necessary modifications in February to Roosevelt.[9] Leach was absolutely not about to revisit a decision by the president. Left unaddressed in this exchange was the lost opportunity for a fourth model for the $20 gold piece.

That episode was enough for Gussie. She would stand her ground on the ultra high relief double eagle. She took her case directly to Theodore Roosevelt in April. She got prompt action. Before even inquiring as to the availability of the coin, he penned a brief note to Augusta on the 15th assuring her that she would receive the coin.[10] Frank Leach had just earned another summons to the White House. Roosevelt was very direct: Leach must provide an ultra high relief $20 gold piece to the estate even if they must coin one that by law would bear the date of 1908.

Leach scrambled. There were two ultra high relief double eagles in the Mint Cabinet. It was the Mint's practice to retain two of each piece coined for inclusion in this collection in order to display both the obverse and reverse of the design at the same time. One of these coins could be provided to Augusta to avoid the criticism that would surely arise if it became known that the Mint had struck a single coin for a private individual. On April 20, Leach wrote Brewster that Augusta could obtain one ultra high relief double eagle for $20 plus 12¢ postage.[11] Thus Gussie would receive her additional compensation through the back door.

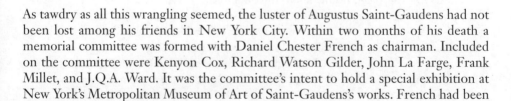

As tawdry as all this wrangling seemed, the luster of Augustus Saint-Gaudens had not been lost among his friends in New York City. Within two months of his death a memorial committee was formed with Daniel Chester French as chairman. Included on the committee were Kenyon Cox, Richard Watson Gilder, John La Farge, Frank Millet, and J.Q.A. Ward. It was the committee's intent to hold a special exhibition at New York's Metropolitan Museum of Art of Saint-Gaudens's works. French had been elected a museum trustee in 1903 and was the de facto curator for American sculpture.

French had his work cut out for him. Under his leadership the committee raised $10,000 to fund the memorial exhibit. Much of this money went to making plaster replicas of Saint-Gaudens's existing monuments. French also appealed to private owners for loans of their pieces. In all, the committee assembled 154 of Saint-Gaudens's works. At French's request Kenyon Cox painted a replica of his 1887 portrait of Saint-Gaudens that had been destroyed in the Cornish fire.[12]

It was French's intent that Saint-Gaudens's monumental and personal works be seen side by side. Initially, Augusta was more than happy to cooperate in this endeavor. The seated Lincoln destined for Chicago would be displayed in bronze for the first time. These pieces would be exhibited in the museum's newly renovated Hall of Sculpture, later known as the Great Hall.[13]

It had not been an easy chore for Daniel Chester French. Besides dealing with the always-difficult Augusta, he had wanted the models for the newly issued gold coins. French went directly to Cortelyou on January 4, 1908, with a loan request for the gold-coin models. French also wanted the dies from the original experimental gold-coin models. In addition, he wanted whatever was in the Mint's possession that pertained to the World's Fair award medal. When queried by Cortelyou, Leach had no problem releasing the plasters from the early models.[14] However, the remainder of French's request was not that simple to satisfy. By custom, the Mint never released the models for circulating coins. Also, Charles Barber had always resisted exhibiting any of his die work.

Matters dragged. French followed up with a second letter and then for good measure had J.P. Morgan write to Elihu Root, the onetime Wall Street lawyer.[15] Now Cortelyou answered. The Mint would provide the first models for the ultra high relief double eagle. They would also loan one of the two coins from this trial strike that had been retained in their Cabinet collection. However, Cortelyou told French that they could not loan out the modified models that had been adopted for the gold-coin designs, as they were in constant use by the Engraving Department in Philadelphia. Also, the experimental dies from the original or first double-eagle model had been destroyed as required by law. Neither of these explanations was correct, however. The Mint did not possess the adopted models for the double eagle, and unbeknownst to either Cortelyou or Leach, the ultra high relief dies had not been destroyed and would not be until 1910.[16]

In the process of dealing with French's request, Leach remembered that he had returned the third models for the $20 gold piece to Cornish. He now had to get them returned. He also wanted the model that had been sent to Paris for the test reduction. It would be March before Saint-Gaudens's assistant Henry Hering delivered these to Philadelphia. Ultimately, four plaster models and two electrotypes (the World's Fair award medal) made it to the showing.[17]

On February 29, two days prior to the opening of the exhibit, a farewell memorial to Augustus Saint-Gaudens was held at New York's Mendelssohn Hall. Gathered were Gus's New York art colleagues as well as the notables and politicians of the city. Daniel Chester French was there. John Flanagan attended. Good friends Richard Watson Gilder and Will Low spoke. The speakers' platform was decorated with garlands of roses and carnations. At the back of the rostrum was one of Saint-Gaudens's trademark angels, loaned by the Metropolitan Museum.

There was heartfelt praise for the artist's achievements. He had taught Americans that beauty in art, as in nature, is not a luxury but a necessity for happiness. Gilder read three stanzas from a poem that he had composed and dedicated to the memory of Saint-Gaudens. Will Low noted Gus's ability in matters of art to render criticism; whether this criticism was frank and merciless or warm and enthusiastic, it was always rendered in the hopes of achieving a more perfect art form.[18] As these words were spoken there was no applause; a hushed, solemn mood settled over the audience. At the completion of the eulogies, a string quartet played Chopin's "Funeral March." Then, on a lighter note, the musicians broke into a medley of Gus's classical favorites so often heard at the Sunday afternoon concerts held at his studio.[19]

The exhibit at the Metropolitan opened on March 2 to great fanfare. Five thousand visitors attended the opening-night celebration. The tribute was fitting. In the words of the museum's bulletin, "Saint-Gaudens occupied such an exceptional and commanding position in American art, being almost universally recognized not only as our foremost sculptor, but as our greatest artist in any branch of the arts of form" that a complete exhibition of his works should be gotten together at this time.[20] As visitors entered the exhibit hall, they immediately encountered the towering standing Lincoln. From there they could turn to *The Puritan* on the one side and the great equestrian Sherman on the other side. Perhaps his greatest monumental work, the Shaw Memorial, was shown only in photograph. His bas-reliefs of friends as well as other portrait commissions and even a cameo brooch from his earliest days were all gathered and displayed under French's watchful eye.[21]

The exhibit was a great popular success, remaining open until May 31, being twice extended. Museum hours were expanded to accommodate the crush of visitors. The exhibition catalog went into a second printing. The museum believed that this exhibition was of the highest importance in the history of fine arts. It had given pleasure to many thousands of visitors and it would remain in memory as a monument to a man of genius. Afterward French was able, through private donations, to have bronzes made from plaster originals of two of Saint-Gaudens's busts and two of his bas-reliefs. French would continue diligently acquiring Saint-Gaudens's sculptures for the museum until his death 23 years later.[22]

As the exhibit closed, Augusta called for delivery of her ultra high relief double eagle, which Leach had promised would come from the exhibit. On June 30 it arrived at Cornish, closing the saga of the gold coins' design for her.[23] She also asked for the electrotype of Gus's rejected World's Fair medal reverse with the nude male. In the ultimate irony, it fell to Robert Preston, still at the Mint, to reject her request for the award-medal reverse. It was government property, duly bought and paid for.[24] It would remain in the Mint Cabinet.

In spite of Daniel Chester French's hard work, Saint-Gaudens's shadow could have slowly faded from the national consciousness. Gussie had squabbled with the Metropolitan's exhibit managers. There would be no more displays of his works if she had her way. It fell to architect Glenn Brown to rectify the situation and leverage French's genuine tribute to his friend into the larger national recognition that Saint-Gaudens's passing deserved.

Brown wanted an exhibition of Saint-Gaudens's works in Washington to be organized and underwritten by the American Institute of Architects. Brown would serve as secretary of the committee in charge. His first task was to travel to New York to look over the Metropolitan's exhibit. There he found Augusta both depressed and in a combative frame of mind. Gussie could be extremely formidable in one of these moods. She felt that French and the committee in their installation had destroyed much of the beauty of her husband's sculpture. They had ignored her criticisms and suggestions. In her mind the pieces were placed without reference to size or character. They had been arranged helter-skelter so that color clashed with color, size with size, and delicacy with boldness. In confirmation of her view, the *New York Tribune* sniffed that all was not perfect with the exhibit: here and there a work in marble would be surrounded by three or four portraits in bronze, each having a different patina.[25] Gussie's greatest complaint was that the Adams memorial had been placed upon a three-foot-high platform when it had been designed to rest upon a slab one foot high. Gussie was so irritated that Brown was scared to ask her about a Washington exhibit. At first she wouldn't even listen to his plea. However, Gussie was no match for Glenn Brown, who had honed his skills dealing with the likes of Congressman Joe Cannon.

Brown had come prepared. He wanted the exhibition in the Corcoran Gallery of Art, and he had brought a plan for how the exhibition should be installed. He explained to Gussie the intent of the American Institute of Architects to gather the top government officials and ambassadors to speak on opening night. She was intrigued. Such an event would further Gus's reputation, which even at this early date she was intensely trying to protect. She did not commit immediately but kept Brown on tenterhooks; she went down to Washington and spent several days going over the plan in detail before assenting to his wishes. To fund the exhibit the Institute sought and easily obtained subscriptions.

The first disappointment came from Theodore Roosevelt, who declined to speak at the opening ceremonies, saying the country would be amply represented by Elihu Root. Root was in turn to line up the ambassadors. Trouble came again when one noted ambassador refused to be associated at the same level on the program with ambassadors from lesser countries. He would withdraw unless the speakers were confined to five or six of the larger countries. Time was drawing short when this glitch occurred. Brown appealed to Root, who for once could not resolve the situation. Not at a loss, Brown went back to Roosevelt and explained the situation. The president volunteered to go on the program, and the difficulty was resolved.

As the opening approached, Brown had one more problem: West Point had refused to loan the bust of Sherman. First they had declined. Then they agreed but imposed such onerous conditions that its display was impossible. Brown understood well the ways of Army bureaucrats and went with Augusta to the White House. President Roosevelt had his secretary, William Loeb, direct the West Point officials to provide the bust for the exhibit with no conditions. Then, a few days before the opening, Theodore and Edith came to the gallery. The president, seeing Brown, asked if they had received the bust yet. No, Brown had not. The Roosevelts walked off to an office. A few minutes later Edith came back and said that Theodore wished to see Brown. Brown followed her back to the office, where Theodore had finished drafting a presidential order to the commandant of West Point:

> Colonel Scott, see to it personally that the Bust of General Sherman is at the Corcoran Gallery within twenty-four hours.

Striking Change

"That will bring it," Roosevelt said, bringing his fist down with a bang on the desk.[26] It did.

There was another clash with F.B. McGuire, the Corcoran director. He wanted to close one gallery where Brown planned to group the low reliefs and small busts. Neither side would budge. Augusta threatened to cancel. Finally Cass Gilbert, the president of the American Institute of Architects, went to the head of the museum corporation; the issue was decided in Brown's favor.

In spite of these rocky moments, the exhibit opened according to plan with the memorial meeting held the night of December 15, 1908. For Glenn Brown it was a highlight of his long association with the Institute. Years later he could still recall beautiful ladies in rich jeweled costumes, charming girls simply but richly dressed, and distinguished men in their formal eveningwear. Brown remembered the plaster cast of the Angel of Victory; she appeared to be moving forward as she welcomed the guests to the imposing display of Saint-Gaudens's work. Opposite the angel and at the same level Brown erected a platform for the speakers: the president, members of his Cabinet, and the foreign ambassadors. Some 2,000 guests passed through the receiving line.[27]

Elihu Root opened the ceremonies. He had known Gus since the sculptor's days in Rome. There, Root had bought what he loosely termed a "pot boiler" from the struggling young artist. He still had that piece and counted it among his most prized possessions. Before introducing the president, Root summed up Saint-Gaudens: "We can help our own people in America to appreciate how honored art should be by showing honor to the artist and we can put heart and hope into artists of the future by honoring this, our leader in their art." Root then introduced Roosevelt.[28]

The president stated that he felt a particular satisfaction in the deeds of every man who added to the sum of worthy national achievement. Within this context Saint-Gaudens was an artist who could hardly be placed too high. Roosevelt justly lavished praise upon Saint-Gaudens's Sherman. For a man who in a few short months would be a private citizen again and would style himself "The Colonel," there had to be a personal affinity here. He praised Saint-Gaudens for showing the soul within his subjects. Saint-Gaudens's sculptures did more than reflect beauty, he asserted: they showed the spirit inside.

Roosevelt's words were to the point. However, within his talk he digressed for more than a moment. First he praised the daring and original imagination shown in the double-eagle design. Then he talked of the head of Liberty on the $10 coin. He had felt the sting from the criticism of their $10 gold coin. Liberty was not strikingly beautiful, but rather characteristically American in that the headdress was one of the few items of "wearing gear" produced independently in North America—a bonnet of eagle plumes.

Most of the criticism that Roosevelt had endured was based upon the assumption that only an Indian could wear a feather headdress and that the head of Liberty ought to have a Phrygian cap, Greek helmet, or some classical equivalent. Roosevelt called this idea nonsense. Why should not the Indian be a symbol of freedom and a life of liberty? It took a great American artist with the boldness of genius to see that Liberty should have something distinctively American about her. Saint-Gaudens put the American Liberty in an American headdress.[29] It was a solid analysis.

"About half of the practice of a decent lawyer is telling would-be clients that they are damned fools and should stop."
—Elihu Root.

Root made his name as a young private-practice attorney in 1860s New York City, where he attracted a distinguished clientele. He served as secretary of war under both William McKinley and Theodore Roosevelt, and in 1905 was named Roosevelt's secretary of state. He won the Nobel Peace Prize in 1912, and later became the first president of the Carnegie Endowment for International Peace.

While Saint-Gaudens had prepared both the obverse and reverse designs, he had never intended that they be combined. That had happened in the White House during Roosevelt's meeting with George Roberts in May 1907. Tellingly, Saint-Gaudens's initials appear nowhere on this gold coin. Even in his extreme illness, Hering would have inserted the sculptor's initials unless Saint-Gaudens had directed otherwise. The omission was deliberate. He was saying the composition was not his alone; it was a collaboration with Roosevelt.

The occasion was a fine and fitting national tribute to the great American artist. Sadly, few of Saint-Gaudens's real friends were there to add to the glitter. In Gilder's place came his longtime assistant at the *Century*, Robert Underwood Johnson. Mead came in McKim's place.[30] Both Gilder and McKim were in failing health. In many respects, this memorial marked a passing of the guard for those who were the creative force behind the World's Columbian Exposition. Upon the exhibit's closing in Washington, a satisfied Augusta, with Glenn Brown's aid, would allow it to embark upon a national tour. However, there would be more spats between her and museum directors over its arrangement and presentation.[31]

Sixty-three years later, the classically trained art historian Cornelius Vermeule summed up the gold-coin designs nicely. He said Saint-Gaudens's $10 gold piece missed being a great design by the addition of the Indian headdress. On the other hand, he noted, the $20 gold piece was perhaps the most majestic to ever come out of the United States Mint. Compared to what had come before, these coins both burst as artistic skyrockets in the horizon of American academic creativity.[32]

Saint-Gaudens, who had struggled so with the allegorical figure in the Shaw Monument and moved on so boldly with the Sherman, now had achieved perfection. The truth of the "American Experience" so boldly proclaimed by the World's Columbian Exposition of 1893 comes striding forward in the beauty of this $20 gold piece. The sculptor had transformed Liberty into the "Spirit of America." Augustus Saint-Gaudens and Theodore Roosevelt had accomplished their "pet crime" and in so doing created a beautiful monument in miniature.

Yet as the men and women filed out of the Corcoran Gallery that night, one question remained unanswered. Who would inherit the golden bowl now that Gus had gone to live with the mythical Greek gods?

Chapter 24

The Legacy

While the Saint-Gaudens gold-coin designs had been a success, Theodore Roosevelt was not done. First and foremost there remained the issue of the design for the smaller gold coins: the half eagle and quarter eagle. The issuance of the larger gold coins had hardly commenced when the president stirred the pot.

Traditionally the design for the $10 gold piece was used for the two smaller issues. The first indication that this tradition was to be bucked came from the president's secretary, William Loeb, at the end of November 1907. Roosevelt wanted the design for the $20 gold piece used on the smaller coins and these dies prepared at once.[1] Perhaps the president was sensitive to the extreme criticism that the $10 coin was encountering that month.

Roosevelt in his rush to complete the "pet crime" overlooked one important consideration. While the design for the $10 gold piece could easily be adapted to the smaller-sized coins (the half eagle being the size of a nickel, and the quarter eagle the size of a dime), would the $20 design do as well? Without considering this point, Mint Director Frank Leach promptly ordered it done with Treasury Secretary Cortelyou's approval.[2] It fell to engraver Charles Barber to raise issues. Would the denominations be spelled out? Could the motto "E Pluribus Unum" be successfully placed on the edges of the smaller coins? The problems were particularly acute for the quarter eagle.[3]

The first issue from Barber's point of view was to control the process. With Leach's approval, he used the third model from the $20 gold-piece design for his reductions. This action cut Saint-Gaudens's assistant Henry Hering out of the process. Then he went to work and a curtain of silence descended upon the engraver's shop in Philadelphia.

President Roosevelt had other ideas. Perhaps it was the issue of how best to show the denomination on the smallest of the gold coins that tipped him to the potential trouble. Maybe Frank Leach expressed doubts. Regardless, he was in a receptive mood when an old friend from Boston, William Sturgis Bigelow, contacted him. Bigelow, a graduate of the Harvard Medical School, had long since quit the practice of medicine, choosing to travel the Far East. He had steeped himself in Japanese culture and amassed a collection of Japanese art that would become the nucleus of an extensive collection at the Museum of Fine Arts, Boston. Roosevelt, when on official business in Boston, would

Striking Change

plot unofficial escapes with his friend for breakfast and a surreptitious trip to a bookstore. Theodore had kept Sturgis apprised of his collaboration with Saint-Gaudens and the problems they were encountering at the Mint. Thus Bigelow was on Roosevelt's distribution list when it came time to pass out samples of the high-relief $20 gold piece. It was Bigelow's reply to that gift (on January 8, 1908) that piqued Theodore's interest and set him off on a different course.

Sturgis Bigelow lauded the Saint-Gaudens $20 gold piece as the best strike in 2,000 years and as the standard for the next 2,000. Also he had an idea that might get around the problems that Roosevelt had encountered with the Saint-Gaudens design at the Mint, and the nation's commercial concerns. His plan might be bad but it was new, and nobody had been able to say that it was not good. He now had two die cutters and the experts at the Museum of Fine Arts wrestling with his idea. Sturgis believed it was possible to strike a coin with high relief in such a manner as to permit stacking. He was waiting to get models that would suit him before approaching the president. Impetuously Roosevelt, without worrying about the ramifications, replied that he was extremely interested in the experiment.[4]

Now it was a footrace to see if Sturgis Bigelow could get his project off the ground before Charles Barber finished the dies. The man putting Bigelow's idea into a practical design and model was the Boston-area sculptor (and former Saint-Gaudens pupil at the Art Students League) Bela Lyon Pratt.

On April 2 Theodore Roosevelt sprang his little surprise on Frank Leach over a simple lunch, devoid of any ceremony.[5] Tellingly, Edith attended. Among the others present was William Sturgis Bigelow. Roosevelt deftly steered the conversation to high-relief coinage, which he believed afforded greater opportunities for artistic expression. Leach was quick to point out that the coins of the ancient Greeks were in high relief on one side only. The president expressed surprise and sent to his rooms for an example he had of a gold coin from the time of Alexander the Great. He quickly learned Leach was right.

After lunch, Bigelow unveiled Pratt's new design for the smaller gold coins. The novel idea that Pratt had implemented in his model was an incused-relief design. In other words, the design was cut intaglio below the surface of the planchet, thus gaining greater relief without impairing the ability of the coins to stack. The art form really was not new. It had been employed by the ancient Egyptians, thus requiring Bigelow to spend some time in the vaults of the Museum of Fine Arts in Boston. Pratt's model was a faithful image of the head of an American Indian. That choice certainly played to Roosevelt's affinity for all things Western. It also blunted the criticism of the headdress on Liberty employed on the $10 coin. The president ended the meeting by authorizing Leach to produce some trial pieces.[6]

It happened that smoothly. If Pratt's design could be coined in this novel approach, Saint-Gaudens's design for the smaller gold coins was dead. Leach should have offered some resistance to this shift proposed by the president. That he did not argues that Barber must have encountered difficulties applying Saint-Gaudens's $20 design to the smallest gold coin, as Frank Leach had anticipated. Mint records would reveal the existence of a pattern $5 gold piece with the Saint-Gaudens design—but no quarter eagle.

As Leach left the White House, the plan was for Pratt to complete the obverse model of the Indian. Barber was instructed to model the reverse based upon the $10 coin

340

in deference to Saint-Gaudens. Pratt was more than pleased with this arrangement in spite of the fact that he was to receive only $300. When contacted by Leach, he told the Mint director he could have the obverse model finished within a few months.[7] Meanwhile Leach conferred with Barber about the reverse model. Barber wanted nothing to do with preparing a standing-eagle design in the incused style, which would undoubtedly be compared to that of Saint-Gaudens. Leach then returned to Pratt and asked that he prepare the reverse design. He told Pratt to take one of the new $10 gold coins for an idea of positioning. However, he might want to consider shortening the legs of the bird, if indeed that was to be his design, to improve and make more realistic its appearance.[8] Frank Leach would finally have his revenge on allegorical eagles.

On June 29 Pratt sent his models to the Philadelphia Mint. He innocently asked that they be followed literally in preparing the dies. If any changes were necessary, Leach should notify him. He also wanted to see the finished coin.[9] Leach assured Pratt that Barber would not take liberties or make changes unless the model was found to be inconsistent with acceptable coinage operations, in which case Pratt would be promptly notified. It would take Barber several months or more to prepare the dies.[10]

From here poor Pratt was left out in the cold. Due to a comedy of errors, he did not see the first pattern strike from the Mint, which Roosevelt had instead sent to Bigelow after having given his approval on September 26. In the meantime Barber was to proceed with making a new die of the obverse, incorporating changes that Leach had discussed with the president. Details were to be sharpened and the relief strengthened.[11] Bigelow, however, could not be immediately reached. By the time the pattern strike caught up to Bigelow, the Mint had completed work on the new dies that restored detail that had been lost in reducing the design from the model. It was the same old story; Barber still had not mastered the Janvier lathe.

Finally, at the end of October, Pratt saw his first production strike from his now modified models. They were to be known as the Bigelow-Pratt design. Pratt was not at all happy with the retouching. He told Leach that he was shocked at the liberties taken by Barber.[12] However, it was too late. The new half- and quarter-eagle coins were already being released into circulation.

Immediately there were problems with this incused style that Leach and Barber had not anticipated. The planchets warped in the striking process. Also, given equal masses of metal, the incused design called for a raised field, resulting in a thinner coin when compared to a standard design raised over a recessed field. Thus, it was impossible for a commercial establishment to count mixed quantities of the old and new designs by using stacks of equal height. There was also resistance from the public to the design: the head of the Indian was said to be without artistic merit; the eagle resembled more closely a golden eagle than the national bird; dirt would collect in the design's recesses.

The designs did not deserve this criticism. Pratt's depiction on the obverse of an American Indian was the first of its kind to grace the coinage, and it foreshadowed a trend toward more naturalistic depictions in the future.

Roosevelt was not done; he still had the one-cent design to replace. Time was running out. Facts concerning the genesis of Roosevelt's final effort are lacking. Some time in the summer of 1908 the president was sitting for Victor D. Brenner (for the preparation of a Panama Canal service medal), and the topic came up. Brenner, who had just finished a plaque of Abraham Lincoln, was enthusiastic to adapt this work to a coin design. He had aggressively written to the Mint director as word leaked of new designs in early 1907. The 100th anniversary of the birth of Lincoln would be in 1909. Whether Brenner initiated the discussion or not, Roosevelt was receptive.[13] As with Bigelow, this work would proceed outside official channels.

On December 14, 1908, Brenner brought models to the White House.[14] From this point forward, he would work within the system. For the obverse, Brenner had employed a version of his own Lincoln in profile. For the reverse he apparently submitted two alternatives straight from current French coinage. Brenner was also fishing to provide designs for the subsidiary silver coinage as well. It took Leach to rein him in, saying they would concentrate on the one-cent piece; his current submittals for the reverse were unacceptable and Brenner must come up with his own design.

In February 1909 the sculptor submitted models that reflected the Lincoln cent with the wheat-ear reverse as it was finalized, with two exceptions. On the obverse the head of Lincoln extended to the upper border of the coin. On the reverse, Brenner had used "V" for "U" in the inscriptions, a style very much in vogue at that time. This was a pet peeve of the president's. While Saint-Gaudens could get away with it on his inaugural medal, Brenner could not. It had to go. Otherwise the design had Roosevelt's approval. Now it was time for Brenner to interface with Charles Barber.

Of course there would be issues when Barber saw the model. The engraver objected to Brenner's use of multiple radii when developing the field of the coin. The engraver wanted only one. Brenner stood his ground; the models would have multiple radii.

Brenner also stood his ground over review of Barber's reductions. This time Barber was conciliatory. He had received much criticism over the modifications made to both Saint-Gaudens's and Pratt's gold-coin designs. It was well that Brenner insisted: when he saw the hubs he was not pleased, particularly with the obverse. Barber in turn suggested that Brenner be allowed to supply his own hubs. After much posturing, Brenner went to Henri Weil in New York City.

Up to this point the proposed Lincoln cent did not incorporate the motto "In God We Trust," as it was not required on minor coins in the law change of 1908. Leach was not happy over the design; the head was too near the rim, resulting in difficulties striking up Lincoln's features. Leach had Barber recenter the Lincoln profile, which resulted in an unseemly gap between the top of Lincoln's head and the coin's rim. Into this void went the motto. After one minor blowup over the coin's thickness, which was causing it to jam in vending machines, the new secretary of the Treasury, Franklin MacVeagh, approved the design on July 14, 1909. Roosevelt was now gone from the White House, but his coin redesign project was finally completed.

Frank Leach resigned August 1, 1909. He had struggled with Roosevelt's successor, William Howard Taft, whose management style was too easygoing.[15] In addition, Taft was gradually rooting out the Roosevelt people. Leach and his family missed the West Coast, so when an opportunity came for him to return, he jumped at it. In less

The so-called Bigelow-Pratt $5 gold piece was the result of William Sturgis Bigelow's theory that an incused-relief design would permit stackable high-relief coins. Bela Lyon Pratt, a former student of Saint-Gaudens, was given the task of putting Bigelow's theory into practical form. (shown enlarged 2x)

Victor David Brenner's Lincoln cent. (shown enlarged 2x)

James Earle Fraser at work in his studio. A student of Saint-Gaudens, the artist went on to a highly successful career in his own right.

than two years he had successfully managed the most radical changes in design to United States coinage in 50 years.

Brenner's success was now marred by a slight at the hands of the Treasury Department. He had previously been given permission to add his initials, V.D.B., in the reverse field next to the rim at the base. MacVeagh objected, saying the initials were too prominent. The engraver could remove all three initials from the reverse master die, but replacing them with a single "B" would take 14 days and require a new master die. That delay would be unacceptable given the need to mint massive quantities of these coins to meet public demand. Besides, confusion with Barber's work would result. Barber regarded the Lincoln one-cent piece as a failure and wanted no mistaken association with it. Barber also felt that placing the "B" on Lincoln's shoulder would be next to impossible given the limited area in which to work. During the long, contentious process with Saint-Gaudens, one could at times sympathize with Charles Barber. Not this time; this was pettiness on Barber's part. However, he carried the day.[16]

If Brenner thought Saint-Gaudens's designs to be an "embryo of a beautiful conception," his work did not begin to compare. The ultimate condemnation came years later from James Earle Fraser.

> However your thought made me realize that a Lincoln coin should be adequate. Whereas the penny is criticised [sic] because the words "one cent" are three times the size of the words "United States of America"; "E Pluribus Unum" is hardly readable. Yet it was so vital to Lincoln. The other wording is equally tiny and the portrait is so small in the circle that it seems entirely inadequate.[17]

One of Theodore Roosevelt's last acts in his waning administration was in support of the arts. The consultative board that he had established as the successor to the Senate Park Commission in 1905 had proved too weak. Working with Glenn Brown and the American Institute of Architects, Roosevelt corrected this situation with a second executive order on January 19, 1909.[18] Thereafter, all Executive Department heads had to submit all plans for buildings, treatment of grounds, and site selection for statues to a Council of Fine Arts for their approval, unless overridden by the president. This order had teeth. The 1902 Senate Park Commission could not have hoped for more.

Before leaving the Mint directorship, Frank Leach directed Charles Barber to prepare some pattern nickel pieces portraying George Washington on the obverse. These played out over 1909 and 1910. While this effort lost much of its impetus as Leach left office, public agitation for a change was building. Here the matter stood until 1911, when Treasury Secretary MacVeagh instructed the Mint director to seek a replacement for Barber's old nickel design. The Mint director by this time was a familiar face, George Roberts. Secretary MacVeagh had been a director of the Commercial National

Bank that Roberts joined as president in 1907. When that bank merged with Continental Bank in Chicago, MacVeagh brought Roberts back to the Mint.

It seemed a natural progression for Roberts to turn to James Earle Fraser for the nickel design. Fraser had executed the commission, upon Saint-Gaudens's recommendation, for a portrait bust of Theodore Roosevelt. It had been an amazing experience for the young sculptor. Roosevelt had been skeptical of his youth but reckoned that if Saint-Gaudens said Fraser could do it, Fraser would do it. Roosevelt believed in taking the advice of people he trusted.[19] What came out defined the image of Theodore Roosevelt for all time. Fraser had gotten his man even better than Saint-Gaudens and Weinman had that same year. The commission also brought to the attention of those in Washington that Fraser was an artist of real merit.

Roberts initially wanted Fraser to prepare a design using the profile of Lincoln. Why he wanted another Lincoln for the five-cent piece with the new penny already in circulation is open to conjecture. Perhaps there was latent dissatisfaction with Brenner's one-cent design. Fraser proceeded to execute the requested sketch, but he had ideas of his own. He wanted a design to do more than glorify an individual: he wanted his design to tell a story of America.[20] Fraser had several Indian portraits in the round. Ultimately he used the likenesses of three individual Indians to prepare a composite sketch. He employed both the traditional feather headdress and, in a departure from past practice, feathers attached to the scalp lock, much more typical for an American Indian. For the reverse he sketched the American bison (commonly called a buffalo) "Black Diamond."[21]

As Fraser and Roberts started down this road, there was some concern within the Treasury Department that a competition be held. Who would oversee the competition? What of Roosevelt's Fine Arts Council? It did not exist any more. Joe Cannon refused to fund it, and President Taft had issued an executive order revoking Roosevelt's previous one. It was not that Taft was opposed; rather, his style of government centered on consensus. With now-senator Elihu Root's help, Taft pushed for congressional action to establish a Commission of Fine Arts. The proposal became law on May 17, 1910. However, this body had only the power of advice.[22] One year later the commission's authority was hardly defined, particularly as it might extend to coinage designs.

Fraser wanted no part of a competition. He argued that a competition tied the Mint to the particular design chosen, with little or no chance to make subsequent modifications, because such changes would subvert the competition process. Instead Fraser proposed to work with the Mint and let the design evolve through modifications and improvements. Fraser did offer to go before the commission and satisfy their concerns. This argument was enough for Roberts, and he allowed the process to continue.

By September 1911, Fraser had moved well beyond where he should have, considering that he did not have a commission. His enthusiasm for the project had gotten the better of him. With George Roberts's encouragement he submitted to MacVeagh electrotypes for his various sketches, including an Indian with feathers from the scalp lock. This design, combined with the buffalo on the reverse, made for a truly American coin.

In January 1912 MacVeagh signed off on the Indian-head-and-buffalo sketch submitted by Fraser. The inscriptions still needed to be added. In approving the design,

Teddy Roosevelt as the Rough Rider, by James Earle Fraser (1910).

Fraser's Buffalo nickel (the original design and the modified reverse by Charles Barber).

Panama-Pacific $50 gold piece, by Robert Aitken. Striking of such a large commemorative coin had first been considered for the World's Columbian Exposition.

Winged Liberty dime, by Adolph Weinman.

Liberty Walking half dollar, by Adolph Weinman.

348

Standing Liberty quarter, by Hermon MacNeil.

The Standing Liberty quarter, as modified in 1917. Liberty's previously exposed breast was covered with chain-mail armor. This was not in response to a public outcry against the indecency of her exposure (as popular numismatic legend has it). Her armor had more to do with the war in Europe, and America's commitment to protecting its own interests.

High-relief Peace dollar of 1921, by Anthony de Francisci, patterned in part after Augustus Saint-Gauden's *Head of Victory*.

349

MacVeagh ordered only those inscriptions required by law, so as not to mar the beauty of the design and to avoid crowding. As with the cent, the nickel was a minor coin not requiring "In God We Trust."

Fraser then labored to refine the models, inserting the required inscriptions and reducing them to several reliefs. Relief certainly remained an issue with the Mint, requiring Fraser's presence in Washington in June of 1912 to resolve the matter. At that point the Treasury Department released notice of the existence of the design to the press. This announcement was premature and would cause both Fraser and the Mint difficulties.

Even at this advanced stage, MacVeagh was uneasy about the process. He insisted that three members of the Commission of Fine Arts (Daniel Chester French, Edwin Blashfield, and Cass Gilbert) be allowed to evaluate Fraser's work. French summed up this ad hoc committee's reaction nicely. He congratulated Fraser; he called the models very fine in both design and execution. Gilbert brought up the relief and wished that the design could be struck with the higher relief that was exhibited in one of Fraser's models. Fraser had told Gilbert that practical objections were being raised at the Mint. With these comments in hand, MacVeagh told Roberts that Fraser's design essentially had the approval of the Commission of Fine Arts and that the Mint should not delay in implementing this design.

Now the premature press release came back to haunt the Treasury. The nickel five-cent piece was used extensively in vending machines. There had been discussion in Congress in 1911 of changing its alloy and reissuing a three-cent piece due to inflationary pressures that had put the vending industry in a defensive mode. Now, facing another specter of change, they rose up in protest. At issue was the counterfeit-detecting mechanism used to reject slugs. An arrangement of needles was set so that they would only unlock when they touched the surface of the coin at a certain number of places.[23] There were also rings that fit between the rim of the coin and the inscriptions. Under consideration, Fraser's nickel relief was greater than that of the old nickel, negating the function of the detection needles. The issue dragged throughout the remainder of 1912 with Fraser resisting any material changes to his design and George Roberts seeking a compromise that would please all parties.

Finally it came down to one man from the vending industry who would not be satisfied: Clarence Hobbs of Hobbs Company and the American Stamp and Ticket Vending Machine Company. This man was adamant in his opposition to the new design. Fraser provided Hobbs with electrotype shells that Henri Weil had produced to test.[24] Hobbs then proceeded to demand that Fraser modify his design, including reducing the size of the buffalo and moving the inscriptions away from the rim of the coin. Fraser complained to Roberts that Hobbs had gone too far. His point was that the government should not be forced to accept an inferior design when the detecting machines could be altered at the manufacturer's expense without hindering their effectiveness. Fraser was willing to help Hobbs except to the extent of making a bad design. He felt that Hobbs was trying to gain everything at Fraser's expense while refusing to expend moneys on his own part.

Meanwhile MacVeagh had a problem of his own. He wanted President Taft's approval for the new design. MacVeagh had first shown the letters of French, Blashfield,

The Legacy

and Gilbert to Taft in September. Taft wanted to see the "thing," but MacVeagh, embarrassingly, had not brought Fraser's models with him. The Treasury secretary then arranged for Fraser and French to meet with Taft at his little White House in Beverly, Massachusetts, in October. At the last minute, though, the president postponed the meeting. It was just one month short of the election, and Taft was fighting for his political life against Roosevelt and the Democratic nominee, Woodrow Wilson. Ultimately, MacVeagh arranged for Fraser and himself to meet Taft at the White House. As the two men waited outside the president's office, they heard gales of laughter coming from inside. The loudest was Taft's.[25] It unnerved Fraser. Having had an intimate inside look at the high-energy Roosevelt White House while he modeled the president, the sculptor was not prepared for the informal approach of this president. Regardless, Taft's approval was gained.

With the presidential hurdle cleared, MacVeagh now had no problem putting the vending-machine issues to rest. He urged Roberts to give Fraser final approval for his designs. Now it was time for the hubs to be prepared. Charles Barber, facing higher relief than he desired and an unfamiliar design, wanted nothing to do with this function. Consequently Fraser retained Henri Weil to again do the work. Fraser wanted to be present at the trial striking, which occurred in early January 1913. Now Hobbs came back, and Roberts tried once more to accommodate the man. The result was another set of hubs from Weil. Hobbs protested again. The changes that had been promised had not translated from the model to the hub. Fraser threw up his hands. The time and effort of the sculptor to please this man over the preceding six months had been immeasurable. The situation was now so bad that Fraser brought an attorney friend with him when the two sides met in Washington in February to try to resolve differences. This meeting revealed that no other vending-machine company was insisting on changes to the new design. MacVeagh put his foot down and ordered business strikes to commence. The coins were released on March 4, 1913—Inauguration Day for Woodrow Wilson.

Fraser was pleased with his new coin. He felt that the engraving at the Mint to make the two sides of the coin fit exactly, the reduction of the coin's edge, and the simplifying of the background under the buffalo's head were beautifully done. He could not tell the difference between his surface and the surface worked over at the Mint. Overall he was delighted with their work. Even though he had submitted his models without an initial, fearing the reaction that Brenner had suffered, the Mint had inserted an "F" below the date.[26]

Early that year James Earle Fraser wed Laura Gardin. She had been his student at the Art Students League from 1907 to 1910, and was an accomplished sculptor in her own right. When they left the church, the newly wedded couple took a bus to the Metropolitan Museum of Art, their favorite haunt. "Jimmie" gave a quarter to the conductor and in change received his first Buffalo nickel. The Frasers were elated.[27]

That elation, however, did not last long. Charles Barber had been afraid from the inception of this design that it would be easy to counterfeit. Fraser had placed the coin's denomination on the raised ground upon which the buffalo was standing, the highest point on the reverse. It became evident to Barber that even the slightest wear would be enough to obliterate the inscription. He even went so far as to gild a coin to test

351

whether it could be passed as a $5 gold piece. His own painful experience in this regard no doubt drove this action. Fraser approved Barber's solution, which was to recess the area where the inscription had been placed, removing it from virtually any wear. Now the buffalo appeared to be standing upon a plain. One is left to wonder why Barber didn't simply incuse the term FIVE CENTS into the mound. Fraser was not aware of Barber's other action: he polished out all of the texture in the fields of the coin, giving it a smooth finish. It attempting to reduce the risk of counterfeiting, he had exceeded his authority. However, no one called his hand, and the change was allowed to stand.[28]

Years later, Fraser revealed what he thought about this action. He had had a change of heart. The diesinkers at the Mint during that period were against outside artists' making designs, he stated. They had mutilated his model to a great extent, trying to aid the vending-machine interests and claiming that the coin would not strike easily—meaning the relief was too great—and would not stack. To his frustration, he later verified from the coiners that these coins were easier to strike than the old nickels.[29]

Yes, the second version was decidedly inferior to the first version. However, either version of this coin was a splendid example of Americana. Over the following century it would become an American icon. James Earle Fraser had jumped the bar set by Augustus Saint-Gaudens.

As 1915 drew to a close, Woodrow Wilson's Treasury secretary, William Gibbs McAdoo, chose to treat the coinage law as a mandate to change designs every 25 years. As a result, the Barber coins (the dime, quarter, and half dollar) would be up for replacement in 1916. On December 3, 1915, Mint Director Robert Woolley met with the Commission of Fine Arts to talk about changes. He brought along Charles Barber. Before going outside the Mint for designs, he wanted the Commission to review some designs that Barber had developed. It was the Mint's intent to use three different designs this time around. The Commission formed a committee composed of Edwin Blashfield and Herbert Adams, who now held the Commission seat for sculpture. It fell to Adams to reject Barber's sketches and to recommend three artists to prepare sketches for the coins. They were Adolph Weinman, Hermon MacNeil, and Albin Polasek.[30]

It was the committee's intent that each artist be asked to devote his work to one coin. When Woolley interviewed each of the artists at the end of December in New York City, they came away with differing ideas of what was being asked of them. One thing was clear: they were being asked to submit several designs that could be used for one, two, or even three of the coins. In effect it would be a competition. Adams was agitated. Each of these men was skilled and open to suggestions, and would work with the Mint to obtain the best designs possible. A competition would be no incentive to them and would hinder the process.[31] Charles Moore, by now chairman of the Commission of Fine Arts, calmed Adams down. It was not the Mint's intention to have a competition. However, Woolley wanted to retain the option to use an artist on more than one coin if his designs were superior. The Mint director would discuss the designs with the Commission of Fine Arts. That was a fine distinction—he was not going to seek the Commission's approval.[32]

Augustus Saint-Gaudens: as depicted by Kenyon Cox at work at his easel; and pictured third from left with the Sherman Victory at Cornish. James Earle Fraser stands on Saint-Gaudens's right.

Unofficial Roosevelt inaugural medal of 1905, by Augustus Saint-Gaudens and Adolph Weinman. This is the specimen given by Roosevelt to his son Archie. (medal shown actual size)

The president was impressed by the bold, high-relief coins of the ancient Greeks—his inspiration for a renaissance in American coinage. (1.5x actual size)

The original Franklin medal obverse with the laurel wreath. (.75x actual size)

Obverse and reverse of the Franklin medal as approved by Secretary of State Elihu Root. (.75x actual size)

Charles Barber's 1901 Lafayette commemorative dollar, and his 1906 pattern for the $20 gold coin. (2x actual size)

Indian Head $10 gold coin designed by Saint-Gaudens. Top: Wire Rim variety; bottom: regular circulation strike. (2x actual size)

Saint-Gaudens's Ultra High Relief $20 gold double eagle originally owned by Theodore Roosevelt. (2x actual size)

Top: the High Relief version. (1.5x actual size) Bottom: the regular circulation strike. (1.5x actual size)

Fraser's Buffalo nickel (the original design, top and lower left, and the modified reverse by Charles Barber, lower right). (3x actual size)

Winged Liberty dime, by Adolph Weinman. (3x actual size)

Commemorative coins of the 1915 Panama-Pacific Exposition. Top to bottom: $1 gold piece, by Charles Keck; $2.50 gold piece, by Charles Barber (obverse) and George Morgan (reverse); half dollar, by Barber (obverse) and Morgan (reverse); $50 gold piece, by Robert Aitken. (1.5x actual size)

Standing Liberty quarter, by Hermon MacNeil. (3x actual size)

MacNeil's Standing Liberty quarter, as modified in 1917. (3x actual size)

Top: Lincoln cent, designed by Victor David Brenner. Bottom: Walking Liberty half dollar, by Adolph Weinman. (2x actual size)

Top: incuse Indian Head $5 gold coin designed by Bela Lyon Pratt. Bottom: high-relief Peace dollar of 1921, by Anthony de Francisci. (2x actual size)

Illinois Centennial commemorative half dollar, featuring an unbearded portrait of Abraham Lincoln. Obverse by George Morgan; reverse by John R. Sinnock. (2x actual size)

Oregon Trail Memorial commemorative half dollar, by James Earle Fraser and Laura Gardin Fraser. (2x actual size)

George Washington's death bicentennial $5 gold piece, from the design by Laura Gardin Fraser. (2x actual size)

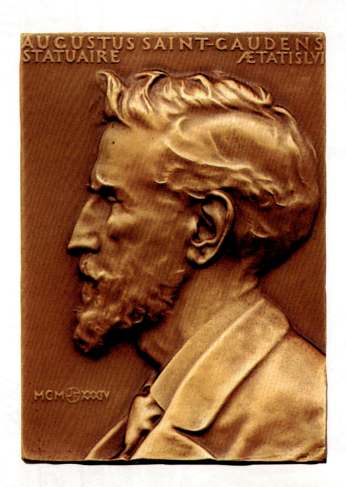

A commemorative portrait plaque of Augustus Saint-Gaudens, by James Earle Fraser (1934).

Theodore Roosevelt in a portrait projecting vigorous self-confidence, by Gari Melchers (1908).

Augustus Saint-Gaudens's last work, showing his wife Augusta with the golden bowl from the June 1905 masque at Cornish. (actual size 350.8 x 590.6 mm (13.8125 x 23.25 inches))

C32

The Legacy

Moore knew that the Commission needed to tread lightly. The Treasury was empowered to choose the designs on United States coinage. The Commission's involvement was purely a courtesy on the Treasury Department's part. Besides, the Commission had just suffered at the hands of the Treasury the preceding year.

As part of an exposition in San Francisco celebrating the opening of the Panama Canal, as well as the city's rebirth after its 1906 earthquake, four commemorative coins were to be struck. There would be a silver half dollar, a gold dollar, a gold quarter eagle, and a $50 piece (or quintuple eagle), also struck in gold. The $50 coin was reminiscent of the assay coins struck during the Gold Rush and would be in both round and octagonal forms. George Roberts was still at the helm of the Mint. Contrary to his actions in 1911 in dealing with James Earle Fraser, Roberts recommended going to the Commission of Fine Arts in advance. Treasury Secretary McAdoo approved, and the Commission designated four sculptors to design the pieces. The sketches were submitted, and McAdoo, at the urging of his assistant secretary, William Malburn, rejected all four. Immediately upon the rejections, Barber was instructed to begin preparing alternatives.[33] Only after much prodding did the Treasury Department give their objections, and these only for the gold dollar and $50 coins. Time was of the essence. Charles Keck, a former Saint-Gaudens assistant, redesigned his $1 gold piece. Robert Aitken, designer of the $50 gold coin, only modified his, addressing the objections specifically. Ironically, it was Henri Weil again who assisted Aitken in making his bronze reductions.[34] The Treasury then accepted these changes and substituted work by Morgan and Barber for the other two pieces. Commission chairman Daniel Chester French, who had informally approved the original designs, was upset but could effectively do nothing. However, one good thing came from the process: Robert Aitken, taking Minerva from the California state seal and pairing her with the owl sacred to the goddess on the reverse, had designed a spectacular piece, particularly in its octagonal form.[35]

Adams finally acquiesced to the Mint's insistence on multiple designs from the artists.[36] By the end of February 1916, the three artists had submitted about two dozen designs for consideration. Woolley informed the Commission that there were six designs that he and McAdoo liked: five by Weinman and one by MacNeil. It was Woolley's intent to combine one of Weinman's designs with the single approved work of MacNeil for the quarter. Weinman would get the dime and half dollar. Woolley carefully pointed out that the Treasury had made these selections. The Commission of Fine Arts was welcome to look at what was done, but that there would be no formal submission to the Commission. The Commission was disappointed, but pleased that the designs were not being done within the Philadelphia Mint.[37]

In March Adams met Woolley in New York and recommended that MacNeil be given an opportunity to design a reverse to pair with his approved obverse. Adams feared that a certain monotony of designs would exist if five of the six came from Weinman.[38] That was all the Commission could do at this point. Woolley accepted Adams's recommendation and the work now was in the hands of Weinman and MacNeil. Completed models were due May 1. Afterward, Adams groused that it seemed the Mint's approach was to make the Commission of Fine Arts almost irrelevant.[39]

The choice of Weinman and MacNeil was a good one. While these men had been associated with Saint-Gaudens, they had cut their teeth under Philip Martiny at the

Striking Change

World's Columbian Exposition. Weinman had also worked as an assistant to Daniel Chester French.[40]

Both men submitted their models close to the deadline. Weinman's dime design consisted of a head of Liberty with a winged cap on the obverse. The head was meant to be simple and firm in form, the profile forceful. The reverse design featured a fasces, symbolic of unity, the nation's strength. Surrounding the fasces was a fully foliaged branch of olive, representing peace. Weinman's half dollar obverse featured a full-length figure of Liberty enveloped in folds of the national flag, progressing in full stride toward the dawn of a new day, carrying branches of laurel and oak, symbolic of civil and military glory. Liberty's right hand was outstretched in bestowal of the spirit of freedom on America. On the reverse an eagle perched on a high mountain crag, fearless in spirit and conscious of his power. Springing from a rift in the rock was a sapling of mountain pine, representing America.[41]

MacNeil's design for the quarter was intended to typify the awakening interest of the country in its own defense. On the obverse of the quarter, a full-figured Liberty was shown in a front view, head turned to the left, breast exposed, stepping forward to the gateway of the country. Her left arm was upraised and bore a shield in the attitude of protection from which the covering was being withdrawn. Her right hand held an olive branch of peace. The reverse depicted an eagle in full flight sweeping across the coin. Connecting the inscriptions on the outer circle of the reverse were olive branches.[42] Both men's designs reflected the war raging in Europe.

Now began the difficult and seemingly endless rounds of modifications as the sculptors and the Mint attempted to settle upon coinable designs. While the dime was all right, the Mint director felt the obverses of the quarter and half dollar would need to be redone.[43] The dime would be put on the fast track to production.

In July 1916, Weinman forwarded to the Mint new bronze intermediate reductions made by Henri Weil for the dime. He had taken the opportunity to refine his olive branch on the reverse, greatly simplifying it. He also began experimenting with the placement of inscriptions on the obverse of the half dollar. He took the time to instruct the Mint not to polish the dies used in the trial strikings for either of his coins; he felt it made them look cheap.[44]

Weinman was staying on top of the process. In a letter conveying photographs of changes in the reverse of his fifty-cent piece to Secretary McAdoo, he complained that the dies made from the first set of models for the dime were weak, the relief being less than his models called for. He again brought up the rubbed fields of the dies. He requested that McAdoo instruct Barber to use the strongest possible relief for both his coins and not to rub or burnish any part of the dime die.[45]

Progress was seemingly made. McAdoo approved the new dime design on August 10, 1916. He instructed that the burnishing be corrected. He also approved the reverse for the half dollar. Weinman still wanted to experiment with the inscriptions on the obverse of this coin.[46]

McAdoo's order for the dime set the wheels in motion at the Mint. Production of Barber's old design was halted, and dies for the new design were sent to San Francisco and Denver. At this point a problem developed from a not-unexpected location. The vending industry had requested some of the new dimes to test in their machines.

The Legacy

Clarence Hobbs of Buffalo nickel fame was in the mix again. Hobbs's company now supplied vending machines for dispensing stamp books in U.S. post offices. This time he had an ally in American Telephone and Telegraph. AT&T operated 60,000 to 70,000 pay phones. Technology had advanced a long way from the time of the World's Fair and even since Fraser's experience in 1912. Now the public would be inconvenienced if there were a problem.

At the same time, the Bureau of the Mint acquired a new director, F.J.H. von Engelken. Woolley had resigned to work in President Wilson's reelection campaign. Von Engelken on September 6 instructed the Philadelphia Mint to release no more information on the dime. Obviously there was a problem. Actually, there were two. Hobbs was asking that the inscription of LIBERTY be moved slightly away from the rim to facilitate the detection ring in the stamp-vending machine. Just as serious, AT&T found that the new dimes were jamming in their pay phones, because the dime's rim had a slight fin.[47]

With the election at hand, McAdoo was all over this potentially embarrassing situation. He even considered having Barber take over the design process. However, the engraver would require six to eight months to complete the project, and with expectations of new designs, that was an unacceptable delay.[48] Changes were going to have to be made on Weinman's work at the Mint. The inscription was moved to accommodate Hobbs, and the rim was rounded, with the relief lowered slightly to eliminate the fin. The end result was the delay of issuance of the new dimes until October.[49]

Meanwhile Weinman had made progress on the fifty-cent piece. After consultation at Philadelphia, he had reduced the figure of Liberty on the obverse and rearranged the inscriptions. Difficulties had been encountered in striking the trial pieces from the earlier model. A fin had developed at the juncture of the rim and the edge, and the thickness of the coin at the rim was uneven. Weinman, however, had misgivings and stayed on top of the Philadelphia superintendent, A.M. Joyce. He was concerned that Liberty not be unduly reduced in size and height of relief.[50]

Still there remained problems with the uneven rim thickness. Barber tried a beaded border. That move required a reduction in the size of the design devices on both sides, but Weinman kept quiet. Von Engelken opted Weinman's way and authorized production from his last models, without the beaded border. Weinman was relieved as he offered a New Year's greeting to Superintendent Joyce: "With very good wishes to you for every day of the New Year and with thanks to the Almighty and yourself that the beads are not on the border of the new half dollar."[51]

Charles Barber had once again tried to dictate the situation. He had complained that the half dollar design had been made with only the artistic character in mind. An effort to urge conformance to mechanical restrictions had been met with objections. Barber had argued that the uneven rim could not be fixed without shrinking the design toward the center of the tondo.[52] He even complained that the new dime and the Buffalo nickel had the same problem, and said the only solution was to change the design and lower the relief. This argument failed when the Denver Mint began striking the new half dollars and encountered no difficulty with an uneven rim.[53]

Throughout this process little was heard from Hermon MacNeil. The sculptor modified both his obverse and his reverse during the summer months. Dolphins had

355

Striking Change

been added to either side at the base of the gate on the obverse. He learned from Barber that the quarter would be minted from these last designs, which McAdoo had approved. On September 1, 1916, MacNeil received permission from McAdoo to place his initials under the head of the dolphin on the right side of the gate. He was urged to hasten the preparation of the cast for the obverse.[54] From the tenor of communications, there was no reason for MacNeil to believe that any problems were developing at the Mint.

MacNeil would have been wrong to come to that conclusion, however. Difficulties were developing around the design's relief. Von Engelken ordered that final decisions be brought to him after consulting with MacNeil. Lead impressions of the proposed quarter now shuffled between Philadelphia and Washington in October. Von Engelken was clearly making design decisions based upon trials from the Engraving Department.[55] To compound matters, von Engelken told Joyce that it would be inexpedient to authorize MacNeil to come to Philadelphia to consult. In November the quarter design reached closure at the Mint. McAdoo wanted Liberty in the last version cut more sharply. Von Engelken told the secretary that it could not be done without going over all of their past work. McAdoo shelved his objection. Von Engelken said that the Mint intended to sharpen the design of the shield. Dies would then be prepared.[56]

It was a naive MacNeil who wrote to Superintendent Joyce on January 6, 1917, saying that he saw in the newspapers that the new quarter was being issued. He hoped that the last models had been workable. Having heard nothing, he presumed that this was indeed true. He would like to see the new coins.[57] Was he in for a surprise when this happened!

The Mint had used a modification from his first submitted version for the obverse. They had discarded the approved second design. The reverse was only a semblance of his original work. MacNeil immediately went to the Mint. Here he saw many variations that had been tried and discarded. He was frustrated at having been shut out of the process, since he himself had tried some of these variations in arriving at his final designs. Still he saw good in what had been done; yet more could be done in the form of modest changes to improve the design. The figure of Liberty needed to be reworked to bring it more in line with the second model. This and other changes were absolutely essential. On the reverse the eagle needed badly to be raised in the field.[58] MacNeil was reasonable in his communication with von Engelken over the liberty taken with his design.

MacNeil went further. He brought Herbert Adams back into the equation. Adams was a strong advocate, stating that it was unacceptable that the Mint had made changes without consulting MacNeil. Adams felt it was important to accommodate MacNeil in view of future relations between artists and the Mint. MacNeil helped himself in this situation as well by expressing a desire to work with the Mint, making only modifications to the existing design rather than insisting upon a return to his second models. McAdoo wanted no embarrassment for the Treasury and ordered the Engraving Department's full cooperation in making the sculptor's modifications.[59]

There was one problem: the law would have to be specifically amended to allow for the modification. To von Engelken's credit, he knew he was in the wrong. He followed up McAdoo's orders with Joyce and told him to see to it that Barber kept his objections to himself.⁶⁰ MacNeil then began working directly with George Morgan, still the assistant engraver. The reverse was quickly fixed. The eagle was raised and three of the 13 stars were moved into the field to better balance and space the inscriptions. The obverse was another story. MacNeil and Morgan went through an exercise to substitute the figure of Liberty from the second model into the final design; this action met with failure.⁶¹

Concurrent to this effort, war fever was building in the United States. Patriotism was the order of the day. In this atmosphere, MacNeil completely revamped the figure of Liberty, covering her exposed breast in chain mail. The stars in the field on the reverse were moved beneath the eagle. When the enabling legislation passed on July 9, 1917, the new design was placed into circulation and MacNeil's ordeal was over.⁶²

The three new designs were all good, MacNeil's less so. They measured up well artistically. It had been the Treasury Department's intent that the design for the half dollar be well received by the public in hopes that its circulation, which had been lagging, would pick up. Reviews of the half dollar were very favorable. The dime was largely overlooked. Years later James Earle Fraser in a tribute to Adolph Weinman said it best: "[T]he dime, infinitesimal in size compared with most of his other work, is considered a beautiful coin—one of the best done in any nation, at this period."⁶³

Charles Barber did not live to see the quarter revised and placed into circulation. He died February 18, 1917. He had been in the employ of the United States Mint for 48 years, 37 of them as chief engraver. Barber's engraving skills were unquestionable. He was a master craftsman. His subsidiary silver-coin designs, while not embraced as artistic, were highly functional. They retained enough details and inscriptions, even with heavy wear, to be recognizable. The designs that followed in almost every case did not withstand wear as well as his. That is why he kept referring to failed designs in the 1909–1916 period. Barber, however, got himself into trouble when he stepped out of familiar territory into the field of artistic designs.

In retrospect Charles Barber seemed at his worst when Roosevelt and Saint-Gaudens insisted that the Mint implement the latest technology in reducing lathes. Taken out of his comfort zone, Barber both failed to adapt and became combative. Yet the man had the respect of George Roberts and Frank Leach, two excellent Mint directors. For the good of the Mint Service, he "made" the third model for the $20 gold piece work.

Subsequently historians have been harsh with Barber. They have sided with Saint-Gaudens—who wrongly blamed Barber for his World's Fair award-medal mess—and overlook the public embarrassment that Saint-Gaudens visited upon Barber at the New York City coin-design exhibition in May 1895. Charles Barber deserved better.

The nomination of George T. Morgan to succeed Charles Barber was sent to the Senate on March 12, 1917.⁶⁴ Morgan, who had stood in Barber's shadow for all these years, was finally going to get his turn at the job. Interestingly, Adolph Weinman took the time to send a letter of recommendation to Secretary McAdoo supporting Morgan. This act would clearly indicate that Weinman was pleased with whatever work Morgan had undertaken with his designs the preceding year.

In 1918, Morgan returned Brenner's initials to the cent at the base of Lincoln's shoulder. A wrong was righted.

The final act in the redesign of circulating United States coins actually started with the World War. In financial support of Great Britain, the United States melted huge quantities of silver dollars kept in storage at the Mint to be shipped as bullion to that country's colonies. With the war successfully concluded, there was a need to replace these silver dollars, which were required as backing for circulating Silver Certificates. Concurrently the American Numismatic Association began lobbying Congress at the end of 1920 to issue a circulating silver dollar commemorating the peace. This move was a bit premature, since the United States and Germany would not conclude a peace agreement until July 2, 1921. The legislation calling for a commemorative Peace dollar with an appropriate design was introduced on May 9, 1921.

At this point the Commission of Fine Arts entered the picture. Charles Moore and James Earle Fraser met with Mint Director Raymond Baker on May 26. Baker wanted a design that was distinctly American, while commemorating the World War and celebrating peace. He would leave the matter of securing the design up to the Commission. Moore noted that the designs called for in the legislation might conflict with existing laws. Baker's reply was to quote the existing statutes for coin designs.[65] That he did not address the possible exemption for this coin as contained in the legislation was not a good sign.

With another coin-design project likely, the Commission of Fine Arts now moved to reinforce their position with the Mint. The Wilson administration had turned a tin ear to the arts. Now, with Warren Harding, there was hope for something better. On July 22, 1921, the president issued an executive order extending the Commission's authority to include review of coin designs. Immediately Charles Moore related to Baker their resolve to retain the head of Liberty on the obverse and to try for a really fine head. In regard to the reverse, they asked whether the present law would allow them to change it and solicited Baker's suggestions for a new design.[66]

Concurrently, a move was made to enact the enabling legislation by having it placed on the House's unanimous-consent calendar. When the title of the bill was read before the House on August 1, there was one objection and the bill died.[67] The simple fact remained that the old Morgan dollar design, having been pressed into production again at the beginning of the year, could be replaced at any time. The only hitch was that the Peace dollar must meet existing design mandates. Here the matter sat.

James Earle Fraser, now a Commission member, and Director Baker met on November 12 to talk it over. The decision was made to seek designs under existing authority. Baker would leave it up to the Commission as to the mechanics of obtaining sketches. Reductions of the chosen models and dies would be made at the Mint.[68]

The commission moved rapidly, desiring that the issuance of the coin commence in the year that peace had been reached with Germany—these coins must be issued before year's end. James Earle Fraser along with Herbert Adams and Daniel Chester French would judge the sketches.[69] Eight artists would be asked to submit proposals:

Robert Aitken, Chester Beach, Victor D. Brenner, Anthony de Francisci, John Flanagan, Henry Hering, Hermon MacNeil, and Adolph Weinman. Sketches were to be delivered to Fraser in New York not later than December 12.[70]

On December 14 the Commission notified Baker that the obverse and reverse by Anthony de Francisci had been chosen. De Francisci was a former pupil of James Earle Fraser's. He had also worked for Weinman and MacNeil.[71] It appears that all three men on the jury were particularly taken by de Francisci's head of Liberty. Afterward, Moore said he was particularly happy over the head; it was exactly what he had been longing for and expecting for some time to see realized.[72] What the three men saw was a rendition strikingly similar to Saint-Gaudens's aborted one-cent design that ended up on the $10 gold piece with the Indian headdress. After the meeting, Fraser gave de Francisci his cast of the *Head of Victory* from which to make improvements upon his model before submitting it to the director for approval.[73] De Francisci had submitted two reverse models from which the committee chose the standing eagle on a mountain crag facing a rising sun, the dawn of a new era. The rejected option showed an eagle tearing at a sword, representing disarmament.

The rush was on to make the production deadline. Somewhere in the process a broken sword was added to the standing-eagle model. Moore told Fraser on December 20 that Baker was depending upon him and de Francisci to get a perfect coin. Baker would back the two men all the way at Philadelphia. James Earle Fraser was going to have free rein. That same day, with the necessary approvals in hand, a beaming Director Baker went public with the new designs.[74] The broken sword was explained as representing the likely outcome of the ongoing arms conference.

Then the firestorm hit. A broken sword symbolized only one thing in the public's mind: defeat. It had to go. The Janvier lathe was useless in this situation. There simply was not time to do a new model. De Francisci went to the Philadelphia Mint on December 23 and watched while George Morgan with his old-time engraving skills cut the sword out of the die.[75] The Mint press release of December 24 glibly stated that the new silver dollars would be issued December 30. The sword that appeared on the model would not be on the coin. For the Commission of Fine Arts, however, this issue was not over. Under Secretary of the Treasury S.P. Gilbert Jr. requested a memorandum from the Commission speaking to the issue of the broken sword. This document would of course not be for publication but only for the Treasury Department's official record.[76] There was frustration at the top of the Treasury with the Commission.

The coin that reached the public bearing the date 1921 was in strong relief. With allowance for the fact that the eagle was now naturalistic, this silver-dollar design approximated what Saint-Gaudens's $10 gold piece would have looked like without a headdress. Of course it was still de Francisci's work, but Fraser's influence is there. Unfortunately this high-relief coin was a one-year issue. Die life was entirely unacceptable. Given the volume of silver that the Mint had to monetize in 1922 to support the issuance of Silver Certificates, it was an unacceptable situation. Fraser and de Francisci tried, but in the end the design finished the rest of its life in coin relief.

The designs of the $10 and $20 gold pieces both had their roots in the greatest monumental works of Saint-Gaudens. His interminable project delays and his struggles with money restrained what could have been for this man. McKim observed that as his commissions grew, his incapacity to meet the demands on his time brought on the habit of a procrastinator, not of a lazy man, for he worked and worried himself in his efforts to catch up.[77] Yet what he did was so good. Writing after his death to his widow, Daniel Chester French praised the sculptor.

> Perhaps it cannot be stated too often however how valuable was the example he set by his absolute fidelity to his ideas of perfection. . . . The art of Saint-Gaudens is a thing by itself. While it has the qualities of composition and mass, of truth to nature and respect for traditions that are common to all great or even good art, the style of it is so personal, the technique is so entirely his own and his conceptions are so original. . . . Saint-Gaudens was a master, future generations will proclaim as does the present one.[78]

From 1907 to 1921, every circulating United States coin was redesigned. Gilder's dream from so long ago was finally realized. Saint-Gaudens set the standard. While some designs, particularly the Buffalo nickel's, were better than others, all were good. Each designer with the exception of Victor D. Brenner had some tie back to Saint-Gaudens. It was an admirable accomplishment made possible by the partnership of Augustus Saint-Gaudens and Theodore Roosevelt.

Postscript

Chapter 25

Striking Change

Theodore Roosevelt left office on March 4, 1909. He had accomplished his "pet crime" although the effort had been far greater than he had ever contemplated.

As the years passed, Roosevelt grew to regret his statement that he would consider his years succeeding the assassinated McKinley as a first term. He easily could have been reelected in 1908. When Roosevelt bolted the Republican Party after failing to receive its presidential nomination under questionable circumstances in 1912 to lead the Progressive Party, he opened the way for Democratic control of the presidency for the first time since Grover Cleveland. Roosevelt spent the next several years in the political doghouse. Still, by 1918 the country was tiring of Woodrow Wilson, and Theodore Roosevelt began mounting another run at the White House. He visited Washington that January to gauge support and speak at the Press Club. Edith came along. She joined her stepdaughter for one last lunch with Henry Adams, now a month shy of his 80th birthday. Alice noted that Henry looked sadly little and old.[1] He would pass away quietly the night of March 26–27.

That run at the presidency in 1920 was not to be. John Hay once said that Roosevelt would surely outlive him but would not die an old man. Hay was right. On January 6, 1919, Theodore Roosevelt died of an embolism at age 60 and historians were left to speculate on what might have been with a Roosevelt presidency instead of Warren Harding. Edith Kermit Roosevelt had no choice but to soldier on alone, carefully staying out of the public limelight except to endorse Herbert Hoover against Franklin Delano Roosevelt in 1932. She rejoined Theodore on September 30, 1948, having lived 87 years.

The establishment of a Lincoln Memorial that extended the Mall beyond the Washington Monument to the banks of the Potomac River had been a major recommendation of the Senate Park Commission in January 1902. The following March, McKim and Saint-Gaudens had traveled from New York and, together with Charles Moore, staked out its proposed location in the Potomac River bottoms at the west end of the Mall.[2] For years nothing happened with this project. Joe Cannon had opposed the Senate Park

Commission and everything for which it stood. When the push was finally made to build the Lincoln Memorial, it came as no surprise that Speaker Cannon was opposed.

The Lincoln Memorial Commission was established on February 9, 1911. Its chairman was President Taft; its remaining six members were equally divided between House and Senate, Democrat and Republican. Joe Cannon was included. Their first tasks were to select a site and choose an architect. Under this umbrella a memorial to President Lincoln would be built. The Potomac River site was mandated in January 1913. Completion of this building would be the final peg needed, to use Elihu Root's words, to preserve the Mall.

Henry Bacon, who had designed several of the last pedestals for Saint-Gaudens's monuments, was to be the architect. Had McKim and Saint-Gaudens lived, this commission most likely would have been theirs. Even so Augusta Saint-Gaudens attempted to horn in. In Bacon's words, she opened fire about using a replica of Saint-Gaudens's standing Lincoln in Chicago for this new memorial. Bacon not only refused, he told Augusta that it would be an outrage to enlarge Saint-Gaudens's important work for this memorial. Furthermore, if Saint-Gaudens knew about it, he would be turning in his grave. Augusta asked if he would step aside from his responsibility over the statue. Bacon refused.[3]

French resigned his position as chairman of the Commission of Fine Arts to avoid a conflict to do the Lincoln Memorial. In the sculpture contract of June 1915, French and Bacon proposed a 12-foot bronze in a granite chair. After four design enlargements, including a full-sized model erected on site in May 1917, it was obvious that the two men had failed. The statue would have to be enlarged to 19 feet and now would be carved in Georgia marble with a Tennessee marble base. The finished work of French and Bacon was dedicated on May 30, 1922, and hailed as one of the great American monuments.[4]

Joe Cannon was in his last term as a congressman when the Lincoln Memorial was completed. Glenn Brown saw him seated alone on a streetcar. Never one to shy away from an adversary, Brown took a seat next to Cannon. He told Cannon that he had been both a feared and respected opponent for years. Brown then asked, "Now that the Lincoln Memorial is completed are you now pleased with it?" Cannon replied that he had been in many battles. Some he had lost and some he had won. It might have been better if he had lost more battles. In the case of the Lincoln Memorial, he was pleased that he had lost.[5]

With designs set for 25 years on all the circulating coins, affairs at the Mint should have slowed down a bit. However, the commemorative-coin boom hit with the end of the First World War. In 1918 George Morgan collaborated with a young assistant engraver, John Sinnock, to produce a very respectable Illinois State centennial coin with modest relief, featuring a bust of the young Abraham Lincoln on the obverse and the state seal on the reverse.

Much of the potential for the commemorative program was diluted in the 1920s by either awkward themes or unwieldy inscriptions mandated for the coin designs. One notable exception was the Oregon Trail Memorial half dollar of 1926. Freed from the design requirements for circulating coinage, James Earle and Laura Fraser teamed up to provide an outstanding coin. On the obverse was a Conestoga wagon drawn by a team of oxen trekking west toward a setting sun. On the reverse an American Indian, set against the backdrop of an outline of the United States, held out his hand in a gesture that seemed to be saying, "Stop."

The next real challenge to the Mint came in 1931. Congress approved legislation that called for a new circulating commemorative quarter celebrating the bicentennial of George Washington's birth. The Commission of Fine Arts, working with the George Washington Bicentennial Commission, had mistakenly gotten ahead of this process by calling for a competition for the design of a commemorative half dollar. Laura Gardin Fraser had won this competition.[6]

When the secretary of the Treasury contacted Charles Moore at the Commission for a list of sculptors for a competition for the new quarter, Moore attempted to preserve the winning design of the Washington Bicentennial Commission. He recommended that Laura Fraser's design be retained and that she receive a $300 commission from the Treasury. Moore was attempting to honor the spirit of the original competition. All he did was inflame the secretary of the Treasury. Andrew Mellon had now served under three presidents starting with Harding and was a fixture in the Washington political establishment. He no doubt still remembered the near public-relations disaster of the broken-sword issue with the Peace dollar. Mellon replied testily that the Treasury Department had not been a party to the Washington Bicentennial Commission project. Jurisdiction over coinage was confined by law to the Treasury. Furthermore no other agency was empowered to interfere with this duty by negotiating for designs or setting commissions.[7]

Matters were off to a rocky start. This time there would be no limited competition: 100 models were submitted from 98 competitors in October 1931. Charles Moore, Adolph Weinman (now holding the sculptors' chair), and H.P. Caemmerer, Commission secretary, reviewed the models and found only six acceptable. In Weinman's opinion one set of models was far superior to all the others.[8] At this point no one outside of the Treasury knew the identity of the sculptors. A week later the full Commission was unanimous in their selection of the obverse and reverse models of entry #56. The Commission found the designs of #56 simple, direct, and permanent in character, yet elegant. The models were also technically correct in terms of spacing, balance, and lettering. They recommended that the sculptor be given an opportunity to restudy certain elements of the design before a final acceptance.[9]

Mellon's reply was not what the Commission was expecting. He had looked over the models and wanted to give the sculptors of three other sets an equal opportunity. The Commission had no choice but to acquiesce and send Mellon design critiques of all four sets. They noted that each of the three chosen by Mellon had fundamental problems that pertained to the essence of the design. On the other hand they pointed out the positive attributes of #56. At this point the Commission did learn that two of the sculptors under consideration were Laura Fraser and John Flanagan. However, they still did not know who had done which models.[10]

The revised models came back in mid-January. Again the Commission felt #56 was the winner. The bust of Washington based upon the work of Houdon showed strength. On the reverse the eagle was well rendered, retaining a vigor while being presented in a truly heraldic fashion. The Commission also considered recommending Saint-Gaudens's flying eagle from the reverse of the $20 gold piece as a substitute. That idea was rejected. The Commission believed using the design from another coin would be unfortunate and subject to criticism. Furthermore, the eagle as it currently appeared on the $20 gold piece had lost the essential quality that Saint-Gaudens had given it.[11]

Nothing of this recommendation carried weight with Andrew Mellon. Before he left office on February 12, 1932, he chose the clearly inferior work of John Flanagan. Charles Moore was astounded. He even approached Mellon's successor, Ogden Mills, to reverse the decision. Mills would not. He bluntly reminded Moore that the responsibility for the selection fell to the secretary of the Treasury and not to the Commission of Fine Arts. The Commission's function in the process was purely advisory.[12] Mellon had put the Commission of Fine Arts in its place—and the losers were Laura Fraser, the designer of #56, and the American public. However, the Frasers were gracious losers. Jimmy wrote his friend John Flanagan a warm letter of congratulations upon learning that his design had carried the competition.[13]

Ground had been lost. In a speech to the Franklin Institute in 1948, the director of the Mint, Nellie Tayloe Ross, showed that attitudes had not changed.

> The mere fact of one's having attained fame as a sculptor gives no assurance that he can produce a design satisfactory for use on metal, in bas-relief. Some famous artists are shown, by Mint records, to have made dismal failures in that direction. Best results, I mention in passing, are to be expected from Mint sculptors who know something of the exigencies of the coinage process. A design may be perfectly beautiful in a clay model, the size of a dinner plate, and may have been executed by an eminent sculptor, but when reduced to the size of a coin, be lacking in distinction, or be unadaptable to coinage.

This statement was not allowed to stand uncontested. The president of the National Sculpture Society, Sidney Waugh, wrote the rebuttal.

> It was only through the combined wisdom and efforts of President Roosevelt and of Augustus Saint-Gaudens which first caused practicing sculptors to be employed by the Unites States Mint, and I think you will agree that since the issuance of the Lincoln penny our coinage has steadily improved in quality. Such, at least, is the opinion of the great majority of competent critics.[14]

The golden bowl of the masque.

Left: Illinois Centennial commemorative half dollar, featuring an unbearded portrait of Abraham Lincoln. This is a superb example of what could be accomplished at the mint. (Obverse by George T. Morgan; reverse by John R. Sinnock.)

Right: Oregon Trail Memorial commemorative half dollar. Freed from the design requirements for general-circulation coins, this commemorative demonstrates the height of artistic achievement by the Frasers.

George Washington's death bicentennial $5 gold piece. Though reduced to the size of a nickel, the superiority of Laura Gardin Fraser's design for the quarter is apparent.

Left: Plaster model of James Earle Fraser's proposal for the Lincoln cent. Middle: Fraser's sketch for the reverse. Right: Model for the reverse.

The artistic issues remained the same. In other ways the Mint was no longer the same as it was in the time of Saint-Gaudens. With the creation of the Federal Reserve Board in 1913, fiscal policy was removed from the control of the Treasury Department. Decisions regarding coin production were effectively removed from the Mint's control. When the United States abandoned the gold standard in 1933, the Mint's role in fiscal policy was diminished even further. Without gold-coin production, the Mint's ability to contribute to money supply was marginal. After World War II the ravages of inflation further eroded the real value of the Mint's output. By 1950 it was a pure cost-driven manufacturing operation.

In 1951, after a conversation with Mint Director Ross, James Earle Fraser gave a proposed new Lincoln cent design to the Mint for consideration. Ross called the models beautiful. The Lincoln on the obverse was, in her opinion, far better than Brenner's. The reverse depicted an oak tree, symbolic of strength and long life. Fraser also intended it to recall Lincoln as the rail-splitter.[15] Ross cautioned Fraser that the timing might not be right as the Mint was currently under intense pressure for uninterrupted production. Nevertheless, dies were made and pattern pieces struck by May 1952. This trial indicated that the figures taking up more surface area on the coin's faces would require greater striking pressure, causing a shorter die life. Modifications would have to be made, including lowering the relief and strengthening the inscriptions.[16] Could Fraser come to Philadelphia to help? No, his arthritis was too bad to travel; but he would work with the Mint if they could come to him. It never happened. Production demands increased and Ross could spare neither the personnel nor the facilities to continue the tests. With the change of administrations in 1953 and Fraser's death in October, the project ended. In 1959, the Mint did replace the reverse of the Lincoln cent with a rendition of the Lincoln Memorial that looked like "a streak across the face of the coin."[17]

All artistic expression has not been lost at the Mint. The commemorative-coin program, shut down in 1954 due to promotional and political excesses, was reinstituted in 1982, offering new opportunities. In 1999 the Mint revived Laura Fraser's beautiful quarter design, this time using it on a $5 gold piece commemorating the 200th anniversary of Washington's death.

The golden bowl from that long-ago masque still sits on the dining-room table at the Saint-Gaudens National Historic Site at Cornish, New Hampshire. Yet its symbolism extends beyond the physical. For a time certainly Adolph Weinman inherited the bowl. So did James Earle and Laura Fraser. Daniel Chester French deserved the golden bowl. Each of them figuratively grasped it for a moment and then passed it on for the benefit of those in succeeding generations. Thus the spirit of Augustus Saint-Gaudens, sitting in residence with those mythic Greek gods, lives on.

Resources

Notes, Bibliography, and Index

Notes

Abbreviations in Notes

ASG	Augustus Saint-Gaudens
ASG Papers	Augustus Saint-Gaudens Papers, Dartmouth College, Rauner Special Collections Library
ASG LibCong Papers	Augustus Saint-Gaudens Papers, Manuscript Division, Library of Congress
Atkinson Papers	Edward Atkinson Papers, Massachusetts Historical Society
Award Committee Letters	Records of Various Divisions Within the Office of the Secretary of the Treasury, Letters Sent by the Executive Committee on Awards 1892–1896
Board President's Letterbook	Board of Lady Managers: President's Letterbook, Chicago Historical Society
CFA Files	Commission of Fine Arts project files 1910–1952
Gilder Papers	Richard Watson Gilder Papers, New York Public Library, Manuscripts and Archives Division
J.E. Fraser Papers	James Earle Fraser Papers, Syracuse University
McKim Papers	Charles Follen McKim Papers, Manuscript Division, Library of Congress
Mint Archives	Box 45, Archives, Record Group 104, NC 152, Entry 330, Folder 232
Mint Director Correspondence	Correspondence of the Director of the Mint, Records of the Bureau of the Mint, National Archives
Mint Director Letters Received	Letters Received by the Director of the Mint, Records of the Bureau of the Mint, National Archives
Mint Documents: Eagle	U.S. Mint Documents: New Designs for Eagle and Double Eagle, 1906–1909, Philadelphia Regional Archives
Mint Documents: Subsidiary Coins	U.S. Mint Documents: Designs for New Subsidiary Coins 1916–1917, Philadelphia Regional Archives
Mint General Correspondence	Records of the U.S. Mint at Philadelphia, Mint Documents, General Correspondence
Mint Letters Sent	Records of the U.S. Mint at Philadelphia, Mint Documents, Letters Sent by the Director and Superintendent of the Mint 1866–1900
Morris Papers	Harrison Morris Papers, Princeton University Library
NYCAC Sherman	Archives of the New York City Art Commission, Sherman folder
TR	Theodore Roosevelt
TR Papers	Theodore Roosevelt Papers, Manuscript Division, Library of Congress
Treasury Secretary Letters	General Records of the Department of the Treasury, Correspondence of the Office of the Secretary of the Treasury, Letters Sent 1878–1917, Letters Sent by the Division of Mail and Files (L Series) 1878–1902
White House Functions	The White House 1904–1905, Official Functions, National Archives

Prologue: "All Ye Need to Know"

1. ASG to Augusta Homer Saint-Gaudens, 21 December 1904, reel 21, Augustus Saint-Gaudens Papers, Dartmouth College, Rauner Special Collections Library (hereafter cited as ASG Papers).
2. ASG to Augusta Homer Saint-Gaudens, 16 December 1904, reel 21, ASG Papers.
3. Charles Follen McKim to ASG, 24 December 1904, reel 10, ASG Papers.
4. John W. Reps, *Washington on View: The Nation's Capital Since 1790* (Chapel Hill: University of North Carolina Press, 1991), 195.
5. *gave needed color:* Glenn Brown notes, reel 1096, Francis Millet Rogers Papers, Archives of American Artists, Smithsonian Institution; *75 dignitaries:* Charles Moore, compiler, *The Promise of American Architecture: Addresses at the Annual Dinner of the American Institute of Architects, 1905* (Washington, DC: AIA, 1905), 3.
6. Augustus Saint-Gaudens, *The Reminiscences of Augustus Saint-Gaudens,* edited and amplified by Homer Saint-Gaudens (New York: The Century Company, 1913), 2:281.
7. *"Charles the Charmer":* Charles Moore, *The Life and Times of Charles Follen McKim* (New York: Houghton Mifflin, 1929), 55; *in New York City:* Saint-Gaudens, *Reminiscences,* 1:160.
8. Frances Duncan to ASG, 5 June 1906, reel 5, ASG Papers.
9. C. Moore, *The Life and Times of Charles Follen McKim,* 182–183.
10. Reps, *Washington on View,* 241.
11. Glenn Brown, *1860–1930 Memories: A Winning Crusade to Revive George Washington's Vision of a Capital City* (Washington, DC: W.F. Roberts, 1931), 343.
12. Glenn Brown notes, reel 1096, Francis Millet Rogers Papers.
13. ASG to John Hay, 13 December 1904, reel 8, ASG Papers.
14. *Porcupinus Angelicus:* John H. Dryfhout, *The Work of Augustus Saint-Gaudens* (Hanover, NH: University Press of New England, 1981), 265; *under diplomatic seal:* Patricia O'Toole, *The Five of Hearts: An Intimate Portrait of Henry Adams and His Friends, 1880–1919* (New York: Clarkson N. Potter, 1990), 376.
15. ASG to Charles Follen McKim, 24 May 1905, Michael Richman Papers, private collection.
16. Brown, *1860–1930 Memories,* 434.
17. *"Old Folks at Home":* C. Moore, *The Promise of American Architecture,* 3; *16-year-old Pommard:* AIA menu, 11 January 1905, reel 45, ASG Papers.
18. C. Moore, *The Promise of American Architecture,* 3.
19. C. Moore, *The Life and Times of Charles Follen McKim,* 208.
20. Charles Follen McKim to ASG, 29 December 1904, Charles Follen McKim Papers, Manuscript Division, Library of Congress (hereafter cited as McKim Papers).
21. C. Moore, *The Life and Times of Charles Follen McKim,* 242.
22. *two days before:* Brown, *1860–1930 Memories,* 478. The man was under a doctor's care. He had been operated on for a malignant tumor in his throat and would die before the end of the year; *as foolproof as possible:* C. Moore, *The Life and Times of Charles Follen McKim,* 244.
23. C. Moore, *The Promise of American Architecture,* 19.
24. Ibid., 22.
25. *planning to attend:* Charles Follen McKim to Glenn Brown, 4 January 1905, McKim Papers; *to this effect:* McKim to William Loeb, 3 January 1905, McKim Papers.
26. Charles Follen McKim to Elihu Root, 9 January 1905, McKim Papers.
27. *The American Architect and Building News* 87, no. 1517 (21 January 1905): 19.
28. Ibid.
29. C. Moore, *The Life and Times of Charles Follen McKim,* 244.
30. C. Moore, *The Promise of American Architecture,* 43.
31. Louise Hall Tharp, *Saint-Gaudens and the Gilded Era* (Boston: Little, Brown, 1969), 344.
32. *garbled this one too:* Charles Follen McKim to ASG, 28 May 1905, McKim Papers; *the toastmaster was drunk:* ASG to Augusta Homer Saint-Gaudens (draft), 12 January 1905, reel 21, ASG Papers.
33. Ibid.
34. C. Moore, *The Promise of American Architecture,* 51; ASG speech to AIA, 11 January 1905, reel 45, ASG Papers.
35. ASG to Augusta Homer Saint-Gaudens, 8 January 1905, reel 21, ASG Papers.
36. *wealth could buy:* Brown, *1860–1930 Memories,* 58; *for monetary support:* ibid., 99.
37. ASG to Rose Nichols, 12 January 1905, reel 11, ASG Papers.

38. *the American Academy:* Charles Follen McKim to Daniel Newhall, 14 January 1905, McKim Papers; *back on board:* McKim to ASG, 14 March 1905, McKim Papers.

Chapter 1: New York City

1. Edwin G. Burrows and Mike Wallace, *Gotham: A History of New York City to 1898* (New York: Oxford University Press, 1999), 735.
2. Saint-Gaudens, *Reminiscences*, 1:11.
3. *for the families to survive:* Burrows and Wallace, *Gotham*, 742; *for anything French:* ibid., 714.
4. Saint-Gaudens, *Reminiscences*, 1:12.
5. Ibid., 1:20.
6. Ibid., 1:21–22.
7. *as a consequence:* ibid., 1:27; *a career in art:* Burke Wilkinson, *The Life and Works of Augustus Saint-Gaudens* (New York: Dover Publications, 1992), 12.
8. Burrows and Wallace, *Gotham*, 726 and 736.
9. Fourth Avenue later became Park Avenue.
10. Saint-Gaudens, *Reminiscences*, 1:27.
11. David McCullough, *Mornings on Horseback: The Story of an Extraordinary Family, a Vanished Way of Life, and the Unique Child Who Became Theodore Roosevelt* (New York: Simon & Schuster, 1981), 20.
12. *on Fifth Avenue:* Burrows and Wallace, *Gotham*, 715; *erected as storefronts:* ibid., 660; *promenading window shoppers:* ibid., 668.
13. *emphasis on the fine arts: The Century, 1847–1946* (New York: Century Association, 1947), 3; *its original precepts:* Burrows and Wallace, *Gotham*, 713; *a member in 1864: The Century, 1847–1947*, 401.
14. McCullough, *Mornings on Horseback*, 28.
15. Burrows and Wallace, *Gotham*, 782.
16. Ibid., 842.
17. Ibid., 850.
18. McCullough, *Mornings on Horseback*, 28.
19. Saint-Gaudens, *Reminiscences*, 1:38.
20. Ibid., 1:39–41.
21. Ibid., 1:45.
22. Tharp, *Saint-Gaudens and the Gilded Era*, 21.
23. Burrows and Wallace, *Gotham*, 888–890.
24. Saint-Gaudens, *Reminiscences*, 1:44.
25. *regrets over this decision:* McCullough, *Mornings on Horseback*, 57; *at Long Branch, New Jersey:* ibid., 58.
26. Ibid., 91–92.
27. This action was exactly the wrong thing to do. Asthma diminishes the ability of the lungs to exhale, not inhale.
28. Saint-Gaudens, *Reminiscences*, 1:51.
29. Burrows and Wallace, *Gotham*, 904–905.
30. Kathleen Dalton, *Theodore Roosevelt: A Strenuous Life* (New York: Random House, 2002), 34.
31. Saint-Gaudens, *Reminiscences*, 1:50.
32. Ibid., 1:63–68.
33. Edmund Morris, *The Rise of Theodore Roosevelt* (New York: Random House, 2001), 14.
34. Ibid., 27–28.
35. Ibid., 34–35.
36. Theodore Roosevelt, *Theodore Roosevelt: An Autobiography* (New York: Charles Scribner's Sons, 1913), 30.
37. E. Morris, *The Rise of Theodore Roosevelt*, 45.
38. TR to Richard Watson Gilder, 20 August 1903, Theodore Roosevelt Papers, Library of Congress (hereafter cited as TR Papers), reel 331, vol. 41, p. 413.

Chapter 2: Making Their Way

1. Richard Watson Gilder, *The Letters of Richard Watson Gilder*, ed. Rosamond Gilder (Boston: Houghton Mifflin, 1916), 107.
2. Ibid., 57.
3. Ibid., 62.
4. Will H. Low, *A Chronicle of Friendships, 1873–1900* (New York: Charles Scribner's Sons, 1908), 239.

5. Saint-Gaudens, *Reminiscences*, 1:161–162.
6. ASG to J.Q.A. Ward, 26 June 1876, ASG Papers and Michael Richman Papers.
7. Saint-Gaudens, *Reminiscences*, 1:170–171.
8. *beauty to the client:* C. Moore, *The Life and Times of Charles Follen McKim*, 69; "*. . . my life ever since*": Saint-Gaudens, *Reminiscences*, 1:159.
9. C. Moore, *The Life and Times of Charles Follen McKim*, 38.
10. Paul R. Baker, *Stanny: The Gilded Life of Stanford White* (New York: Macmillan, 1989), 22–23.
11. *winter of 1876–1877:* ASG to Rev. Winchester Donald, 21 May 1893, reel 5, ASG Papers; *Henry Adams:* Baker, *Stanny*, 25.
12. *the Academy's library:* Marchal E. Landgren, *Years of Art: The Story of the Art Students League of New York* (New York: Robert M. McBride, 1940), 17; *League in reaction:* Gilder, *Letters*, 79.
13. *his days in Rome:* Tharp, *Saint-Gaudens and the Gilded Era*, 113; *space was indeed available:* Saint-Gaudens, *Reminiscences*, 1:188–189.
14. Gilder, *Letters*, 81–82.
15. Tharp, *Saint-Gaudens and the Gilded Era*, 106.
16. *come to Europe:* Baker, *Stanny*, 43; *come to Paris:* Saint-Gaudens, *Reminiscences*, 1:220.
17. Baker, *Stanny*, 48.
18. *the legs on Farragut:* Augusta Homer Saint-Gaudens to Mrs. Thomas J. Homer, 30 May 1879, reel 20, ASG Papers; *conventional monument:* ASG to John A. Dix, 12 February 1879, reel 6, ASG Papers.
19. C. Moore, *The Life and Times of Charles Follen McKim*, 44.
20. Maitland Armstrong, *Day Before Yesterday: Reminiscences of a Varied Life*, ed. Margaret Armstrong (New York: Scribner's, 1920), 266.
21. Gilder, *Letters*, 89.
22. Augusta Homer Saint-Gaudens to Helena de Kay Gilder, n.d., box 15, Richard Watson Gilder Papers, New York Public Library, Manuscripts and Archives Division (hereafter cited as Gilder Papers).
23. Tharp, *Saint-Gaudens and the Gilded Era*, 157.
24. *as he neared completion:* Baker, *Stanny*, 61; "*. . . nothing but that statue*": ASG to Richard Watson Gilder, 29 December 1879, box 15, Gilder Papers.
25. Saint-Gaudens, *Reminiscences*, 1:216.
26. ASG to John J. Cisco, 23 August 1879, reel 5, ASG Papers.
27. C. Moore, *The Life and Times of Charles Follen McKim*, 56.
28. Augusta Homer Saint-Gaudens to Mrs. Thomas J. Homer Saint-Gaudens, 6 February 1880, reel 20, ASG Papers.
29. *side by side:* Tharp, *Saint-Gaudens and the Gilded Era*, 109; *contribution to the statue:* ibid., 157.
30. Ibid., 140–143.
31. ASG to Stanford White, 6 November 1879, reel 14, ASG Papers; Donald Martin Reynolds, *The Architecture of New York City: Histories and Views of Important Structures, Sites, and Symbols* (New York: Wiley, 1994), 329–331.
32. James Earle Fraser, "Augustus Saint-Gaudens" draft, n.d., box 61, Writings, James Earle Fraser Papers, Syracuse University (hereafter cited as J.E. Fraser Papers).
33. Saint-Gaudens, *Reminiscences*, 1:240.
34. Reynolds, *The Architecture of New York City*, 329–331.
35. *in the ceremonies:* Baker, *Stanny*, 64; *not be recognized:* Tharp, *Saint-Gaudens and the Gilded Era*, 139.
36. *into his work:* "The Farragut Monument," *Scribner's Monthly*, June 1881, 164; *on American coinage:* ibid., 166.
37. M.G. Van Rensselaer, "Mr. St. Gaudens's Statue of Admiral Farragut in New York," *American Architect and Building News* 10, no. 298 (1881): 119.
38. H.H. Richardson to ASG, 24 February 1881, reel 12, ASG Papers.
39. H.H. Richardson to ASG, 29 November 1881, box 3, Edward Atkinson Papers, Massachusetts Historical Society (hereafter cited as Atkinson Papers); Edward Atkinson, "The History of the Shaw Monument" (draft), 8 March 1897, box 9, Atkinson Papers.
40. Sarah Shaw to Edward Atkinson, 10 April 1883, box 4, Atkinson Papers.
41. *the rest of the work:* Edward Atkinson to M.P. Kennard, 11 April 1883, box 18, Atkinson Papers; *the contract for 1886:* Atkinson to ASG, 28 February 1884, box 18, Atkinson Papers.
42. O'Toole, *The Five of Hearts*, 102.

43. *next door to Gilder's home:* Arthur John, *The Best Years of the Century: Richard Watson Gilder, Scribner's Monthly, and the Century Magazine, 1870–1909* (Urbana: University of Illinois Press, 1981), 108; *membership in 1880: The Century, 1847–1946,* 380.
44. John, *The Best Years of the Century,* 181.
45. Ibid., 190.
46. Herbert F. Smith, *Richard Watson Gilder* (New York: Twayne, 1970), 13.
47. E. Morris, *The Rise of Theodore Roosevelt,* 108.
48. Roosevelt, *An Autobiography,* 56–57.
49. E. Morris, *The Rise of Theodore Roosevelt,* 154.
50. *the national level:* ibid., 172; *through the Assembly:* ibid., 180.
51. Ibid., 229.
52. Ibid., 249.
53. Robert Underwood Johnson, *Remembered Yesterdays* (Boston: Little, Brown, 1923), 385.
54. Gilder, *Letters,* 35.
55. Richard Watson Gilder to TR, 10 June 1884 and 4 June 1898, box 1, p. 300, Gilder Papers.
56. Richard Watson Gilder to TR, 16 December 1885, box 1, p. 481, Gilder Papers.
57. Wilkinson, *The Life and Works of Augustus Saint-Gaudens,* 114.
58. *The Century, 1847–1946,* 401.
59. Tharp, *Saint-Gaudens and the Gilded Era,* 145–146.
60. Ibid., 149–152.
61. Ibid., 145–146.
62. ASG to Eugenie Homer, n.d., reel 17, ASG Papers.
63. Tharp, *Saint-Gaudens and the Gilded Era,* 107.
64. Ibid., 152.
65. ASG to Stanford White, 3 June 1886, box 4, Atkinson Papers.
66. Edward Atkinson to ASG, 5 November 1886, Atkinson Papers.
67. C. Moore, *The Life and Times of Charles Follen McKim,* 62.
68. *at Harvard in her name:* Lucia Valentine and Alan Valentine, *The American Academy in Rome 1894–1969* (Charlottesville: University Press of Virginia, 1973), 4; *promoted his idea further:* C. Moore, *The Life and Times of Charles Follen McKim,* 130.
69. Ibid., 136.
70. Ibid., 140.
71. Ibid., 147.
72. *the school's startup:* ibid., 149; *four-year curriculum:* ibid., 153.
73. Ibid., 151–152.

Chapter 3: Gilder's Dream

1. "Nebulae," *The Galaxy* 21, no. 6 (June 1876): 866.
2. George G. Evans, *U.S. Mint Centennial 1792–1892* (Philadelphia: George G. Evans, 1892), 100.
3. Johnson, *Remembered Yesterdays,* 101–102.
4. Evans, *U.S. Mint Centennial,* 93–94. He had attended Harvard's scientific school and finished his education in Germany, achieving a master of arts and doctor of philosophy. Also while in Germany he had taken courses in mining and metallurgy. He maintained a consulting business in New York City.
5. William J. Stillman, "The Coinage of the Greeks," *The Century,* March 1887, 788–799.
6. Richard Watson Gilder, "Topics of the Time," *The Century,* March 1887, 808–809.
7. James P. Kimball to Charles S. Fairchild, 2 April 1887, vol. 46, Correspondence of the Director of the Mint, entry 235, record group 104, NC 152, Records of the Bureau of the Mint, National Archives (hereafter cited as Mint Director Correspondence).
8. James P. Kimball to Richard Watson Gilder, 6 April 1887, vol. 46, Mint Director Correspondence.
9. Charles S. Fairchild to James P. Kimball, 5 April 1887, box 3, Letters Received by the Director of the Mint, entry 229, record group 104, NC 152, Records of the Bureau of the Mint, National Archives (hereafter cited as Mint Director Letters Received).
10. James P. Kimball, draft of circular, April 1887, box 3, Mint Director Letters Received. In cases in which two designs were combined, the award would be split, with $400 going to the obverse designer and $100 to the reverse designer.

11. *circular in the process:* James P. Kimball to Tiffany & Co., 9 April 1887, vol. 46, Mint Director Correspondence; *such sweeping changes:* Kimball to Justin S. Morrill, 13 April 1887, vol. 46, Mint Director Correspondence.
12. Speech of Hon. Justin S. Morrill of Vermont, 5 December 1883, Congressional Record, Manuscript Division, Library of Congress.
13. James P. Kimball to Charles S. Fairchild, 9 April 1887, vol. 46, Mint Director Correspondence.
14. *from the attorney general:* James P. Kimball to Charles S. Fairchild, 19 April 1887, vol. 46, Mint Director Correspondence; *Treasury's legal counsel:* Fairchild to Kimball, 9 May 1887, and Department of Justice to Fairchild, 6 May 1887, box 3, Mint Director Letters Received. The finding of the attorney general was that Section 3510 provided the necessary authority for the engraver to prepare the devices, models, and original dies for coins newly authorized by Congress; however, it only allowed the engraver to prepare dies from the original dies for existing coins.
15. 2 April 1884, Congressional Record.
16. Annual Report of the Director of the Mint, 1887, 124–130, Manuscript Division, Library of Congress.
17. *a number of other papers:* Richard Watson Gilder to James P. Kimball, 3 April 1888, vol. 49, Mint Director Correspondence; *June of 1888:* undated list, box 3, Mint Director Letters Received.
18. Mrs. Schuyler Van Rensselaer, *The Independent*, 5 April 1888, 7. This change fell through the cracks.
19. James P. Kimball to Richard P. Bland, 16 March 1888, vol. 49, Mint Director Correspondence.
20. Annual Report of the Director of the Mint, 1888, 76–77.
21. Ibid.
22. James A. Barnes, *John G. Carlisle: Financial Statesman* (New York: Dodd, Mead & Co., 1931), 114–150. Revenues well in excess of expenditures were piling up in the federal treasury. Opponents were pushing increased federal spending to get excess moneys back into circulation. Ultimately, tariff reform failed and the Republicans swept the 1888 fall elections, regaining control of the House and putting Cleveland out of the White House.
23. Gilder, *Letters*, 189.
24. Clarence Winthrop Bowen, editor, *The History of the Centennial Celebration of the Inauguration of George Washington as the First President of the United States* (New York: D. Appleton, 1892), 138–139.
25. William A. Coffin, reminiscences of Augustus Saint-Gaudens, reel 36, p. 5, ASG Papers.
26. *his disposal for this work:* Richard Watson Gilder to ASG, 11 February 1889, box, 3, p. 100, Gilder Papers; *effort by Martiny:* Cornelius Vermeule, *Numismatic Art in America: Aesthetics of the United States Coinage* (Cambridge, MA: Belknap Press, 1971), 96.
27. Bowen, *History of the Centennial Celebration*, 139.
28. Ibid.
29. Kimball to Richard Watson Gilder, 22 February 1889, vol. 52, Mint Director Correspondence.
30. William A. Coffin, reminiscences of Augustus Saint-Gaudens, reel 36, pp. 5–6, ASG Papers.
31. Vermeule, *Numismatic Art in America*, 96–97.
32. Richard Watson Gilder to ASG, 4 March 1889, box 3, p. 113, Gilder Papers.
33. Stack's, *The Americana Sale, January 16–17, 2007*, 304–305.
34. *effect upon the coinage:* Gilder, *Letters*, 188; Tharp, *Saint-Gaudens and the Gilded Era*, 235; *were widely distributed:* Bowen, *History of the Centennial Celebration*, 139. There were 2,000 copies of this medal cast. It was the desire of the committee to put this work within the reach of those with modest means. As a result, the medals were sold for $2 apiece in neat paper boxes lined with blue plush.
35. *revived in the House:* 24 February 1890, Congressional Record; *on September 26:* E.I. Renick to Richard Watson Gilder, 3 October 1890, box 82, *Century* Papers, Manuscript Division, New York Public Library. In retrospect it was fortunate that the legislation passed when it did. The Democrats swept the House elections in the fall of 1890, and the tariff issue—and gridlock—returned to that chamber. In addition, there were severe financial clouds on the horizon that would soon occupy the legislative focus.

Chapter 4: A Mountain of Labor

1. Gloria Peters and Cynthia Mohon, *The Complete Guide to Shield and Liberty Nickels* (Virginia Beach: DLRC Press, 1995), 6.
2. Don Taxay, *The U.S. Mint and Coinage: An Illustrated History From 1776 to the Present* (New York: Arco, 1966), 259. With the formation of the modern German state at the conclusion of the Franco-Prussian War, the new nation adopted an exclusive gold standard. Enormous stocks of silver were

Notes

dumped into the export markets. This action caused silver prices to drop. In a chain reaction, neighboring countries suspended silver coinage, worsening the situation.

3. C.W. Fremantle to Horatio C. Burchard, 1 October 1879, box 4, Mint Director Letters Received.
4. Taxay, *The U.S. Mint and Coinage*, 285.
5. Burchard to A. Louden Snowden, 6 September 1879, vol. 20, Mint Director Correspondence.
6. C.W. Fremantle to Horatio C. Burchard, 1 October 1879, box 4, Mint Director Letters Received.
7. Horatio C. Burchard to C.W. Fremantle, 22 October 1879, vol. 20, Mint Director Correspondence.
8. Burchard to A. Louden Snowden, 3 December 1879, vol. 20, Mint Director Correspondence.
9. Horatio C. Burchard to John Sherman, 6 December 1879, vol. 20, Mint Director Correspondence.
10. Snowden to Burchard, 29 November 1881, box 5, Mint Director Letters Received. He made his case that the design of the existing nickel, using an ornamental shield representing the Union, did not conform to the coinage laws requiring a device emblematic of liberty. On this basis, Snowden believed that the director of the Mint had the authority to authorize a change without going to Congress. He also had a problem with the diameter of the piece, which was not great enough to efficiently support the required weight. As a result the planchets—the round blanks upon which the coin designs were stamped—were too thick, causing difficulties in the coining process. Because weight and composition changes would be required on the one- and three-cent pieces, requiring legislative approval, Snowden reasoned that they could wait upon the completion of the work on the nickel.
11. Taxay, *The U.S. Mint and Coinage*, 285.
12. R.S. Yeoman, *A Guide Book of United States Coins*, 52nd ed., edited by Kenneth Bressett (New York: Golden Books, 1998).
13. Evans, *U.S. Mint Centennial*, 96–97.
14. Charles Barber to Oliver Bosbyshell, 23 September 1890, box 4, Mint Director Letters Received.
15. Saint-Gaudens, *Reminiscences*, 1:174. At the time of Saint-Gaudens's return from Rome, he had participated in a competition only to have the rules changed after all work had been submitted, and the commission was awarded to another. At that point, he swore never to enter another competition. He would not even submit a conceptual sketch until he had the commission in hand.
16. T.O. Conaut to Edward O. Leech, 3 April 1891, box 4, Mint Director Letters Received.
17. Andrew Mason to Edward O. Leech, 3 April 1891, box 4, Mint Director Letters Received.
18. Charles E. Barber to Edward O. Leech, 2 April 1891, box 4, Mint Director Letters Received.
19. Edward O. Leech to Charles Foster, 4 April 1891, vol. 267, Mint Director Correspondence.
20. "New Designs for Coins," *New York Tribune*, 7 April 1891, 5.
21. "The Design for United States Coins," *Harper's Weekly*, 4 July 1891, 507–508.
22. "Choosing Their Own Terms," *New York Times*, 23 May 1894, 8. Ward and Warner were out of town.
23. Ibid.
24. ASG to Edward O. Leech, 19 May 1891, box 4, Mint Director Letters Received.
25. Edward O. Leech to Daniel Chester French, 21 May 1891, vol. 251, Mint Director Correspondence.
26. Edward O. Leech to ASG, Henry Mitchell and Charles Barber, 27–29 May 1891, vol. 251, Mint Director Correspondence.
27. Obituary of Henry Mitchell, *Boston Evening Transcript*, 2 August 1909.
28. *political connections:* Edward O. Leech to Henry Mitchell, n.d., vol. 56, Mint Director Correspondence; *as early as 1890:* Leech to Mitchell, 5 July 1890, vol. 57, Mint Director Correspondence.
29. *reported in the press:* Edward O. Leech to Henry Mitchell and Charles Barber, 27–29 May 1891, vol. 251, Mint Director Correspondence Archives; *all out of hand:* A.A. Norris to George E. Roberts, 24 August 1905, box 234, Mint Director Letters Received.
30. "The Design for United States Coins," *Harper's Weekly*, 4 July 1891, 507–508.
31. R.W. Julian, *Medals of the United States Mint: The First Century, 1792–1892* (El Cajon, CA: Token and Medal Society, 1977), 330.
32. "The New Designs for Our Silver Coinage," *American Journal of Numismatics* 26 (July 1891): 1–3.
33. ASG, Henry Mitchell, and Charles Barber to Edward O. Leech, 3 June 1891, box 4, Mint Director Letters Received.
34. Edward O. Leech to Oliver C. Bosbyshell, 11 June 1891, vol. 261, Mint Director Correspondence.
35. Henry Mitchell to Edward O. Leech, 11 June 1891, box 4, Mint Director Letters Received.
36. Edward O. Leech to Henry Mitchell, 12 June 1891, vol. 251, Mint Director Correspondence.
37. "The Design for United States Coins," *Harper's Weekly*, 4 July 1891, 507–508.
38. This Morning's News, *Boston Evening Transcript*, 20 July 1891, 7.
39. "The New Designs for Our Silver Coinage," *American Journal of Numismatics* 26 (July 1891): 1–3.

Striking Change

40. Richard Watson Gilder to the editor of the *New York Tribune*, 20 July 1891, box 19, letterbook 5, Gilder Papers.
41. Edward O. Leech to Richard Watson Gilder, 8 August 1891, vol. 262, Mint Director Correspondence.
42. J. Hewitt Judd, *United States Pattern Coins: Experimental and Trial Pieces*, 8th ed., edited by Q. David Bowers (Atlanta: Whitman Publishing, 2003), 207.
43. *emanating from France:* Vermeule, *Numismatic Art in America*, 88; *the inclusion of the wreath:* David Lawrence, *The Complete Guide to Barber Halves* (Virginia Beach, VA: DLRC Press, 1991), 4.
44. Edward O. Leech to Charles E. Barber, 28 September 1891, vol. 261, Mint Director Correspondence.
45. Charles E. Barber to Oliver C. Bosbyshell, 2 October 1891, box 4, Mint Director Letters Received. He described in great detail the medallic history from which he prepared his reverse design of the Great Seal. If there was too much filling up of the design, it was not Barber's fault. He formed his design and adapted it to the requirements of the coin. Leech had also objected to the placement of the scroll bearing the motto E PLURIBUS UNUM across the neck of the eagle as being contrary to artistic principles. Barber asked rhetorically that if it were wrong to have the scroll pass before the eagle, it being wrong to have one surface pass over another, would it not also be wrong to pass the shield over the eagle's breast.
46. Oliver C. Bosbyshell to Edward O. Leech, 3 October 1891 box 4, Mint Director Letters Received.
47. Edward O. Leech to Oliver C. Bosbyshell, 5 October 1891, vol. 261, Mint Director Correspondence. Leech wanted the work on the dies to continue. He wanted to see experimental pieces with the reverse as originally presented and with the design for the reverse omitting the wreath. The criticisms offered had been for the purpose of evaluating these experimental pieces when struck and were not to be brushed lightly aside. His instructions in this regard to the engraver had been clear and could not have been misunderstood. He had received no other instructions. In regard to the stars, it mattered very much to Leech how many points were used. The count of the leaves and the olive branch and the issue of the scroll needed to be carefully considered. He was holding to his original opinions but would leave these issues in the hands of Barber.
48. Cobb to Edward O. Leech, 6 October 1891, box 4, Mint Director Letters Received.
49. Charles E. Barber to Oliver C. Bosbyshell, 6 October 1891, box 4, Mint Director Letters Received. Barber was willing to turn to nature pertaining to the leaves. If Leech could quote him the appropriate authority for nine leaves, he would be satisfied. He was obstinate about the scroll passing in front of the eagle. His preference was for five points on the stars. Given that the design would appear on not only the half dollar but also the quarter, six-point stars would be harder to distinguish. The closest Barber came to acknowledging Leech's anger was when he stated that he had no intention of brushing aside lightly the criticisms of Leech in regard to the olive leaves and the stars.
50. *his next correspondence:* Leech to Bosbyshell, 9 October 1891, vol. 261, Mint Director Correspondence; *with Secretary Foster:* Leech to Bosbyshell, 16 October 1891, vol. 261, Mint Director Correspondence. Barber proceeded to prepare two plaster models, with the scroll passing in front and behind the eagle. Leech took the issue up with the secretary of the Treasury. Between them, they decided that the scroll passing behind the eagle gave a more powerful appearance. Leech had bested Barber on this issue by invoking higher authority. On the issue of the olive branches, Leech was not satisfied. He sent an olive branch from the Agricultural Department to Philadelphia for Barber's benefit.
51. Charles E. Barber to Oliver C. Bosbyshell, 24 October 1891, vol. 261, Mint Director Correspondence. On October 23, Barber submitted three alternative patterns to Superintendent Bosbyshell for consideration that addressed the major concerns of the Mint director. The rays around the eagle were gone. In one variation, the eagle was enlarged and the clouds were made more prominent. On the obverse the stars were five-pointed. The second version removed the wreath, allowing the eagle to be further enlarged. The ribbon bearing the motto E PLURIBUS UNUM was positioned in front of the eagle. On the obverse the stars were six-pointed. In the third version the clouds were modified slightly and the ribbon was positioned behind the eagle. The obverse was identical to the second version. In each of the three versions, the olive branch had 13 leaves. As to the wreath on the reverse, Leech was undecided. However, he noted that the secretary of the Treasury objected to the wreath. Leech wanted a second opinion from the secretary before committing. On October 31, he wired the Philadelphia superintendent to prepare dies using the third pattern.
52. David Lawrence, *The Complete Guide to Barber Quarters* (Virginia Beach, VA: DLRC Press, 1995), 5–7; Lawrence, *The Complete Guide to Barber Halves*, 5. The second version also moved the ribbon behind the eagle.
53. Edward O. Leech to Oliver C. Bosbyshell, 7 November 1891, vol. 261, Mint Director Correspondence.

Notes

54. "The Design for the New Silver Coins," *Harper's Weekly*, 21 November 1891, 919.
55. Ibid.

Chapter 5: The World's Columbian Exposition

1. Nathan Eglit, *Columbiana: The Medallic History of Christopher Columbus and the Columbian Exposition of 1893* (Chicago: Hewitt Brothers, 1965), 10.
2. Rossiter Johnson, ed., *A History of the World's Columbian Exposition* (New York: D. Appleton, 1897), 16.
3. Brown, *1860–1930 Memories*, 344.
4. Norman Bolotin and Christine Laing, *The World's Columbian Exposition: The Chicago World's Fair of 1893* (Urbana: University of Illinois Press, 2002), 73.
5. *two immense beer casks:* ibid., 76. It required 569 cow hides; *weighing 5,176 pounds:* ibid., 88, and Archives, Record Group 56, General Records of the Treasury Department, Records Relating to Expositions, World's Columbian Exposition, entry 518, vol. 13, p. 12, awards 553 and 553 1/2.
6. *18,000 lamps:* Bolotin and Laing, *The World's Columbian Exposition*, 80; *allowed to be struck:* ibid., 98.
7. Quoted in Tharp, *Saint-Gaudens and the Gilded Era*, 250.
8. Henry Adams, *The Education of Henry Adams: An Autobiography* (1918; repr., Boston: Houghto Mifflin, 2000), 341.
9. Isabelle K. Savell, *The Tonetti Years at Snedens Landing* (New York: Historical Society of Rockland County, 1977), 52.
10. To translate monetary amounts from the late 19th century into early 21st-century dollars, one must use a multiplier of approximately 30 based upon equivalent prices for an ounce of gold.
11. *including Burnham:* Johnson, *History of the World's Columbian Exposition*, 1:135; *Court of Honor at the fair:* ASG to Daniel H. Burnham, 17 June 1891, reel 35, ASG Papers.
12. *his direct supervision:* Savell, *The Tonetti Years*, 54; *Art Students League:* Barry Faulkner, *Sketches From an Artist's Life* (Dublin: William L Bauhan, 1973), 145.
13. *take a pay cut:* "Souvenir Coin Bill Hangs Fire," *Chicago Daily Tribune*, 24 May 1892, 6; *$2.5 million:* Johnson, *History of the World's Columbian Exposition*, 63–64.
14. "Fair Souvenirs," *Chicago Daily Tribune*, 21 August 1892, 29.
15. "To Sell at a Dollar," *Chicago Daily Tribune*, 7 August 1892, 8.
16. "Dockery's Report Approved," *Chicago Daily Tribune*, 20 May 1892, 9.
17. National Americana Society, *James William Ellsworth: His Life and Ancestry*, vol. 1 of *The Ellsworth Family* (New York: National Americana Society, 1930), 45–46; Ellsworth to Frank D. Millet, 6 January 1892, box 1, file 10, Outgoing Correspondence, James W. Ellsworth Collection, Chicago Public Library; "World's Fair Coins," *Chicago Daily Tribune*, 17 January 1892, 11. The idea was even floated in the press of issuing an octagonal $50 gold piece in the manner of those assay pieces coined during the California gold rush.
18. "Coins for the Fair," *Chicago Daily Tribune*, 28 April 1892, 13.
19. ". . . *cause of the Exposition*": "What It Will Say," *Chicago Daily Tribune*, 6 May 1892, 9; *process under control:* William Edmond Curtis to James W. Ellsworth, 21 May 1892, box 3, file 54, Incoming Correspondence, Ellsworth Collection.
20. *Who Was Who in America, Volume I: 1897–1942* (Chicago: Marquis Who's Who, 1981).
21. William Edmond Curtis to James W. Ellsworth, 14 May 1892, box 3, file 53, Incoming Correspondence, Ellsworth Collection.
22. Burnham to Ellsworth, 13 June 1892, box 3, file 3, Incoming Correspondence, Ellsworth Collection.
23. William Edmond Curtis to James W. Ellsworth, 21 May 1892, box 3, file 54, Incoming Correspondence, Ellsworth Collection.
24. William Edmond Curtis to James W. Ellsworth, 30 June 1892, box 3, file 55, Incoming Correspondence, Ellsworth Collection.
25. "For a Sunday Close," *Chicago Daily Tribune*, 13 July 1892, 1.
26. *painting in his possession:* William H. Meredith to James W. Ellsworth, 15 July 1892, box 7, file 51, Incoming Correspondence, Ellsworth Collection. Ellsworth had lent the Lotto portrait to the Bureau of Engraving and Printing to have a picture taken that would then serve as the basis for a stamp to be issued using the Lotto likeness of Columbus. Curtis had coordinated the logistics; *based upon the Lotto portrait:* William Edmond Curtis to Ellsworth, 22 July 1892, box 4, file 33, Incoming Correspondence, Ellsworth Collection.
27. *Exposition on the reverse:* "Designs for the Souvenir Coins," *New York Tribune*, 7 August 1893, 5; *engraving of the dies:* "Chose Lotto's Portrait," *Chicago Daily Tribune*, 7 August 1892, 8; *to Leech on*

379

August 4: W.E. Curtis to Leech, 4 August 1892, Records of the U.S. Mint at Philadelphia, Mint Documents, entry 1, General Correspondence, G-03-10-08-1 to G-04-03-03-2 (hereafter cited as Mint General Correspondence), box 177.

28. "Offers $1.50 for Each Souvenir," *Chicago Daily Tribune*, 12 August 1892, 8.

29. *his proposed design:* "Design for the Souvenir Coins," *Chicago Daily Tribune*, 16 August 1892, 8; *caravel in the background:* "Pictures of the Half Dollar," *Chicago Daily Tribune*, 20 August 1892, 13.

30. *the numbers 14 and 92:* National Americana Society, *James William Ellsworth*, 45–46; sketch by Charles Barber of his proposed design, box 1:13, Ephemera, Ellsworth Collection; *designs were finalized:* Robert E. Preston to George R. Davis, 17 August 1892, vol. 269, Mint Director Correspondence.

31. "Col. Davis Is Not Pleased," August 1892, reel 1, John Boyd Thacher Scrapbooks, NYS Library.

32. *and Olin Warner:* National Americana Society, *James William Ellsworth*, 1:45–46; *the face in the sketch:* "Design for the Souvenir Coins," *Chicago Daily Tribune*, 16 August 1892, 8.

33. "Cannot Use the Lotto Portrait," *Chicago Daily Tribune*, 26 August 1892, 8.

34. Edward O. Leech to George R. Davis, 26 August 1892, vol. 269, Mint Director Correspondence.

35. Robert E. Preston to William M. Meredith, 4, 13, and 15 August 1892, vol. 269, Mint Director Correspondence.

36. Olin Warner Papers, quoted in George Gurney, "Olin Levi Warner (1844–1896): A Catalogue Raisonné of His Sculpture and Graphic Works" (Ph.D. diss., University of Delaware, 1978).

37. Gurney, "Olin Levi Warner," 775.

38. "Approves the Design," *Chicago Daily Tribune*, 31 August 1892, 8.

39. Edward O. Leech to John W. Foster, 7 September 1892, vol. 269, Mint Director Correspondence.

40. R.U. Johnson to James W. Ellsworth, 6 September 1892, box 6, file 51, Incoming Correspondence, Ellsworth Collection. In this letter, Johnson as associate editor of *The Century* asked if their article on the Lotto portrait, to be published in the October issue, could include the fact that its likeness would be used on the souvenir coin. The article never made mention of the fact.

41. "Design for Souvenir Coins," *Chicago Daily Tribune*, 3 September 1892, 19.

42. Edward O. Leech to Russell B. Harrison, 3 September 1892, vol. 269, Mint Director Correspondence.

43. Sketch by Charles Barber of his proposed design, box 1:13, Ephemera, Ellsworth Collection.

44. E.O. Leech to F.W. Peck, 9 September 1892, box 6:45, Incoming Correspondence, Ellsworth Collection.

45. *animation to the design:* Eglit, *Columbiana*, 94; *souvenir half dollar:* Gurney, "Olin Levi Warner," 776; Frank D. Millett to James W. Ellsworth, 24 October 1892, box 1:16, Incoming Correspondence, Ellsworth Collection.

46. Edward O. Leech to Oliver C. Bosbyshell, 17 September 1892, vol. 269, Mint Director Correspondence.

47. Edward O. Leech to Oliver C. Bosbyshell, 21 September 1892, vol. 269, Mint Director Correspondence.

48. Howard O. Edmonds to James W. Ellsworth, 23 September 1892, box 4, file 43, Incoming Correspondence, Ellsworth Collection.

49. "Will Use the 'Lotto' Portrait," *Chicago Daily Tribune*, 24 September 1892, 10.

50. Edward O. Leech to George R. Davis, 28 September 1892, vol. 269, Mint Director Correspondence.

51. Roger Welles Jr. to James W. Ellsworth, 26 September 1892, box 10, file 55, Incoming Correspondence, Ellsworth Collection. This letter telling of Welles's meeting with Leech on the subject came on the letterhead of W.E. Curtis.

52. J.C. Van Dyke to James W. Ellsworth, 26 September 1892, box 10, file 50, Incoming Correspondence, Ellsworth Collection.

53. Charles Barber to James W. Ellsworth, 29 September 1892, box 1:28, Incoming Correspondence, Ellsworth Collection.

54. "Art Notes," *New York Times*, 30 September 1892, 4.

55. Frank D. Millett to James W. Ellsworth, 24 October 1892, box 1:16, Incoming Correspondence, Ellsworth Collection.

56. Charles Barber to James W. Ellsworth, 30 September 1892, box 1:29, Incoming Correspondence, Ellsworth Collection.

57. Charles Barber to James W. Ellsworth, 11 October 1892, box 1:30, Incoming Correspondence, Ellsworth Collection.

58. "Souvenir Coins Are Being Pushed," *Chicago Daily Tribune*, 28 October 1892, 8.

59. *cardboard impressions:* Cardboard impressions or proofs were quickly made impressions from a soft die to observe the state of the die. They were made in place of lead proofs, which would require placing the die in a press, or splasher proofs, in which the soft die would be pressed into slightly molten tin or lead and allowed to harden; *the hair of Columbus:* Charles Barber to James W. Ellsworth, 31 October 1892, box 1:33, Incoming Correspondence, Ellsworth Collection.

60. *the end of the year:* Edward O. Leech to Davis, 28 September 1892, vol. 65, Mint Director Correspondence. Leech had previously estimated that the Mint could strike 250,000 of the coins per week; *officers of the Exposition:* Leech to Davis, 3 November 1892, vol. 66, Mint Director Correspondence; *secretary of the Treasury:* Leech to Bosbyshell, 10 January 1893, vol. 271, Mint Director Correspondence.

61. Charles Barber to James W. Ellsworth, 10 November 1892, box 1:34, Incoming Correspondence, Ellsworth Collection.

62. Gurney, "Olin Levi Warner," 779.

63. *Ellsworth was present:* Charles Barber to James W. Ellsworth, 16 November 1892, box 1:35, Incoming Correspondence, Ellsworth Collection; *below Leech's estimate:* Robert E. Preston to Ferdinand W. Peck, 19 November 1892, vol. 269, Mint Director Correspondence.

64. Yeoman, *A Complete Guide Book of United States Coins,* 68.

65. Ellsworth to Barber, 19 January 1893, Outgoing Correspondence, Ellsworth Collection.

66. "Mint Busy at Work," *Chicago Daily Tribune,* 4 December 1892, 12; "Half Dollar Here," *Chicago Daily Tribune,* 19 December 1892, 1.

67. *at the celebratory event:* "Into Their Pockets," *Chicago Daily Tribune,* 20 December 1892, parts 3–4; *quickly developed:* "Coins Go Quickly," *Chicago Daily Tribune,* 21 December 1892, 9.

68. Charles Barber to James W. Ellsworth, 22 December 1892, box 1:36, Incoming Correspondence, Ellsworth Collection.

69. Olin L. Warner to James W. Ellsworth, 2 January 1893, box 10, file 50, Incoming Correspondence, Ellsworth Collection.

70. "The Columbian Half Dollar," *American Journal of Numismatics* 22, no. 3 (3 January 1893): 9.

71. Charles Barber to James W. Ellsworth, 24 January 1893, box 1:39, Incoming Correspondence, Ellsworth Collection.

72. James W. Ellsworth to Charles E. Barber, 19 January 1893, box 1, file 29, Outgoing Correspondence, Ellsworth Collection. Ellsworth complained in this letter that President Higinbotham of the Exposition Company had taken these special strikes for his own use in spite of an agreement between the two men. Ellsworth had previously gotten Higinbotham's agreement that these coins would be for Ellsworth to distribute. He then promised them to the wives of Exposition dignitaries, Barber and Bosbyshell, and executives of certain railroads who had been large purchasers of Exposition Company bonds that would not have been sold otherwise. Higinbotham subsequently changed his mind and appropriated the issue for his own use, much to Ellsworth's anger and embarrassment.

73. Edward O. Leech to Oliver C. Bosbyshell, 9–10 January 1893, vol. 271, Mint Director Correspondence. As part of this exchange, Leech asked for three or four of the coins struck on polished planchets to be forwarded to him.

74. Johnson, *History of the World's Columbian Exposition,* 70–71.

75. Ibid., 68–69.

Chapter 6: Ladies Rebuffed

1. Bertha Honoré Potter to George Kunz, 31 October 1892, George Kunz Papers, New-York Historical Society.

2. ". . . *of the United States*": Jeanne Madeline Weimann, *The Fair Women: The Story of the Woman's Building at the World's Columbian Exposition of 1893* (Chicago: Academy Chicago, 1981), 479; *from Kenyon Cox:* "Ready for Distribution by May 1," *Chicago Daily Tribune,* 11 March 1893, 9.

3. Weimann, *The Fair Women,* 42, 182, and 188.

4. Bertha H. Palmer to Sara T. Hallowell, 24 February 1893, vol. 15, Board of Lady Managers: President's Letterbook, Chicago Historical Society (hereafter cited as Board President's Letterbook).

5. ". . . *down to the ground*": ASG to Stanford White, 31 December 1905, Stanford White Papers, Avery Library, Columbia University; *to be made immediately:* Bertha Palmer to Sara Hallowell, 27 February 1893, vol. 15, Board President's Letterbook; *his former students:* "Jersey Sculptress," 10 July 1909, clipping from Philadelphia paper, reel 35, ASG Papers.

6. Edward O. Leech to Bertha H. Palmer, 14 March 1893, vol. 270, Mint Director Correspondence.

7. Edward O. Leech to Oliver C. Bosbyshell, 17 March 1893, vol. 271, Mint Director Correspondence.

Striking Change

8. Bertha H. Palmer to Edward O. Leech, 15 March 1893, vol. 15, Board President's Letterbook.

9. Edward O. Leech to Bertha H. Palmer, 17 March 1893, vol. 270, Mint Director Correspondence.

10. Bertha H. Palmer to Alan C. Durborow, 23 March 1893, vol. 15, Board President's Letterbook.

11. "Miss Carrie Peddle," *Indianapolis Journal*, 1 April 1893.

12. Bertha H. Palmer to Caroline C. Peddle, 22 March 1893, vol. 15, Board President's Letterbook.

13. Bertha H. Palmer to John G. Carlisle, 4 April 1893, vol. 15, Board President's Letterbook.

14. Weimann, *The Fair Women*, 480.

15. Edward O. Leech to Oliver C. Bosbyshell, 27 March 1893, vol. 271, Mint Director Correspondence.

16. Edward O. Leech to Bertha H. Palmer, 31 March 1893, vol. 270, Mint Director Correspondence.

17. *proceed at once:* Edward O. Leech to Caroline C. Peddle, 31 March 1893, vol. 270, Mint Director Correspondence; *the reverse after all:* Leech to Oliver C. Bosbyshell, 29 March 1893, vol. 271, Mint Director Correspondence.

18. Bertha H. Palmer to John G. Carlisle, 4 April 1893, vol. 15, Board President's Letterbook.

19. Caroline C. Peddle to Oliver C. Bosbyshell, 3 April 1893, box 5, Mint Director Letters Received.

20. Edward O. Leech to Oliver C. Bosbyshell, 31 March 1893, box 180, Mint General Correspondence.

21. Caroline C. Peddle to Oliver C. Bosbyshell, 3 April 1893, box 5, Mint Director Letters Received.

22. Edward O. Leech to Oliver C. Bosbyshell, 3 April 1893, vol. 271, Mint Director Correspondence.

23. Edward O. Leech to Oliver C. Bosbyshell, 8 April 1893, vol. 271, Mint Director Correspondence.

24. Charles E. Barber to Oliver C. Bosbyshell, 3 April 1893, box 5, Mint Director Letters Received.

25. Oliver C. Bosbyshell to Edward O. Leech, 4 April 1893, box 5, Mint Director Letters Received.

26. Edward O. Leech to Oliver C. Bosbyshell, 6 April 1893, vol. 271, Mint Director Correspondence.

27. Edward O. Leech to Caroline C. Peddle, 4 April 1893, vol. 270, Mint Director Correspondence.

28. Bertha H. Palmer to Caroline C. Peddle, 6 April 1893, vol. 15, Board President's Letterbook.

29. Caroline C. Peddle to Edward O. Leech, date illegible, box 5, Mint Director Letters Received.

30. Edward O. Leech to Caroline C. Peddle, 7 April 1893, vol. 270, Mint Director Correspondence.

31. Oliver C. Bosbyshell to Caroline C. Peddle, 7 April 1893, box 5, Mint Director Letters Received.

32. Edward O. Leech to Bertha H. Palmer, 7 April 1893, vol. 270, Mint Director Correspondence.

33. Bertha H. Palmer to Edward O. Leech, n.d. [8 April 1893], vol. 15, Board President's Letterbook.

34. Edward O. Leech to Bertha H. Palmer, 10 April 1893, vol. 270, Mint Director Correspondence.

35. Charles E. Barber to Oliver C. Bosbyshell, 8 April 1893, box 5, Mint Director Letters Received.

36. Edward O. Leech to Bertha H. Palmer, 10 April 1893, vol. 270, Mint Director Correspondence.

37. Edward O. Leech to Bertha H. Palmer, 13 April 1893, vol. 270, Mint Director Correspondence.

38. ASG to Bertha H. Palmer, 18 April 1893, Bertha Honoré Palmer Correspondence, Ryerson and Burnham Archives, the Art Institute of Chicago. Leech added that he had had the intention to allow the sculptor to prepare the obverse and model the reverse from Mint sketches. However, it had been his experience that artists with no previous experience preparing models for coinage purposes did work of little value beyond the design process. This fact had been demonstrated in the design of the Columbian half dollar by Olin Warner. That work had been clearly unsuitable for the low relief demanded for coinage purposes and had had to be modified by the Mint engravers.

39. Edward O. Leech to Oliver C. Bosbyshell, 8 April 1893, vol. 271, Mint Director Correspondence.

40. Edward O. Leech to Oliver C. Bosbyshell, 11 April 1893, vol. 271, Mint Director Correspondence.

41. Oliver C. Bosbyshell to Edward O. Leech, 12 April 1893, box 5, Mint Director Letters Received. Barber had complied with Leech's instructions. However, his two alternatives hardly fell within the category of original designs. One contained the oak wreath surrounding a shield with a heraldic eagle superimposed. The second was of an eagle atop a shield surrounded by two laurel sprigs.

42. Edward O. Leech to Bertha H. Palmer, 12 April 1893, vol. 270, Mint Director Correspondence.

43. *used by Peddle:* ibid.; *supplied her model:* Edward O. Leech to Bertha H. Palmer, 13 April 1893, vol. 270, Mint Director Correspondence.

44. Oliver C. Bosbyshell to Edward O. Leech, 13 April 1893, box 5, Mint Director Letters Received.

45. Edward O. Leech to Bertha H. Palmer, 14 April 1893, vol. 270, Mint Director Correspondence.

46. Edward O. Leech to Mary E. Trautman et al., 22 April 1893, vol. 270, Mint Director Correspondence.

47. Edward O. Leech to Bertha H. Palmer, 21 April 1893, vol. 270, Mint Director Correspondence.

48. Oliver C. Bosbyshell to Edward O. Leech, 22 April 1893, Records of the U.S. Mint at Philadelphia, Mint Documents, entry 6, Letters Sent by the Director and Superintendent of the Mint 1866–1900, G-04-03-06-1 to G-04-03-09-3, box 24 (hereafter cited as Mint Letters Sent), book 59.

49. *"Board of Lady Managers"*: Edward O. Leech to Bertha H. Palmer, 24 April 1893, vol. 270, Mint Director Correspondence; *their ordeal was over*: board meeting minutes, 5 May 1893, vol. 5, box 1, folder 5, Board of Lady Managers Minute Book, Chicago Historical Society.

50. "The 'Isabella' Quarter Dollar," *American Journal of Numismatics*, October 1893, 40.

51. *on June 13*: Charles Barber to James W. Ellsworth, 23 June 1893, box 1:40, Ellsworth Collection; *in Proof format*: Walter Breen, *Walter Breen's Complete Encyclopedia of U.S. and Colonial Coins* (New York: Bantam Doubleday Dell, 1988), 582.

52. *American forest regions*: Edmond Morris, *The Rise of Theodore Roosevelt*, 388; *known as the "shack"*: Valentine and Valentine, *The American Academy in Rome*, 1.

53. John G. Carlisle to Senator Hoke Smith, 14 August 1894, quoted in Barnes, *John G. Carlisle*, 351.

54. Barnes, *John G. Carlisle*, 221–226.

55. Ibid., 315.

56. Ibid., 236.

57. Ibid., 256.

Chapter 7: Thacher's Gambit

1. "An Act in Aid of the Columbian Exposition," 52nd Cong., 1st sess., ch. 381, 5 August 1892, box 290, Mint Director Letters Received; "Goes to the House," *Chicago Daily Tribune*, 18 June 1892, 13.

2. By early 1893 the subcommittee would assume the more grandiose title of Executive Committee on Awards.

3. John Boyd Thacher to John G. Carlisle, 11 March 1893, Award Committee Letters.

4. Charles Foster to George R. Davis, 26 August 1892, vol. 269, Mint Director Correspondence.

5. *the best talent available*: Edward O. Leech to James Boyd Thacher, 15 September 1892, vol. 269, Mint Director Correspondence; *". . . a fine design"*: Charles Barber to James W. Ellsworth, 17 October 1892, box 1:31, Ellsworth Collection.

6. "Wants Everyone to Compete," *Chicago Daily Tribune*, 21 January 1892.

7. "By St. Gaudens and Lowe," *Chicago Daily Tribune*, 6 October 1892, 5.

8. John Boyd Thacher to Charles Foster, 7 October 1892, box 4, Mint Director Letters Received.

9. Acting secretary of the Treasury to ASG, 11 October 1892, record group 56, General Records of the Department of the Treasury, Correspondence of the Office of the Secretary of the Treasury, Letters Sent 1878–1917, entry 73, Letters Sent by the Division of Mail and Files (L Series) 1878–1902, vol. 18 (hereafter cited as Treasury Secretary Letters).

10. ASG to Edward Atkinson, 10 November 1892, Lee Family Papers 1535–1957, Massachusetts Historical Society.

11. "Souvenir Coins Are Being Pushed," *Chicago Daily Tribune*, 28 October 1892, 8.

12. *working on it*: "Edward Atkinson, The Shaw Memorial and the Sculptor St. Gaudens," *The Century* 54 (June 1897): 179; *completion of the work*: John Murray Forbes to Edward Atkinson, 16 November 1892, Atkinson Papers.

13. ASG to J.M. Forbes, 14 November 1891, reel 5, ASG Papers.

14. ASG to Edward Atkinson, 20 January 1891, Atkinson Papers.

15. John Murray Forbes to Edward Atkinson, 15 June 1891, Atkinson Papers.

16. Augusta Homer Saint-Gaudens to Edward Atkinson, 21 February 1892, Atkinson Papers.

17. ASG to J.M. Forbes, 14 November 1891, reel 5, ASG Papers.

18. Edward Atkinson to ASG, 9 December 1891, Atkinson Papers.

19. Edward Atkinson to ASG, 24 December 1891, Atkinson Papers.

20. Augusta Homer Saint-Gaudens to Edward Atkinson, 6 January 1892, Atkinson Papers.

21. Augusta Homer Saint-Gaudens to Edward Atkinson, 13 January 1892, Atkinson Papers.

22. *goals were met*: ASG to Edward Atkinson, 23 June 1892, Atkinson Papers; *finishing was imminent*: Atkinson to John Murray Forbes, 18 June 1892, Atkinson Papers; *inscriptions for the memorial*: Colonel Henry Lee to Atkinson, 3 October 1892, Atkinson Papers.

23. John Murray Forbes to Edward Atkinson, 16 November 1892, Atkinson Papers.

24. John Boyd Thacher to Edward O. Leech, 31 October 1892, entry 509, vol. 1, Records of Various Divisions Within the Office of the Secretary of the Treasury, Letters Sent by the Executive Committee on Awards 1892–1896 (hereafter cited as Award Committee Letters).

25. *temporary release*: Thacher to Leech, 1 November 1892, Award Committee Letters; *Foster promptly did*: Leech to Thacher, 1 November 1892, vol. 269, Mint Director Correspondence; *Saint-Gaudens be released*: I.I. Minturn to Edward Atkinson, 10 November 1892, Atkinson Papers.

Striking Change

26. John Boyd Thacher to ASG, 3 November 1892, Award Committee Letters.
27. Edward Atkinson to ASG, 9 November 1892, Atkinson Papers.
28. ASG to Edward Atkinson, 10 November 1892, Lee Family Papers.
29. John Boyd Thacher to John DuFais, 3 November 1892, Award Committee Letters.
30. *for Saint-Gaudens's release:* John Boyd Thacher to J.M. Forbes, 10 November 1892, Lee Family Papers; *had done its duty:* Thacher to John DuFais, 29 October 1892, Award Committee Letters.
31. John Murray Forbes to Col. Henry Lee, 21 October 1892, Lee Family Papers.
32. John Boyd Thacher to Edward O. Leech, 4 November 1892, Award Committee Letters.
33. Edward Atkinson to ASG, 11 November 1892, Atkinson Papers.
34. John Murray Forbes to Edward Atkinson, 16 November 1892, Atkinson Papers.
35. Edward Atkinson to John Foord, 18 November 1892, Atkinson Papers.
36. John Boyd Thacher to ASG, 30 November 1892, Award Committee Letters.
37. *with much satisfaction:* "Mint Busy at Work," *Chicago Daily Tribune*, 4 December 1892, 12; *if not distinctively better:* "Art at the Big Fair," *Chicago Daily Tribune*, 20 December 1892, 16.
38. *recourse to the last:* John Boyd Thacher to Daniel Gilman, 5 December 1892, Award Committee Letters; *in detail personally:* Thacher to John W. Woodside, 7 December 1892, Award Committee Letters.
39. Colonel Henry Lee to Edward Atkinson, 15 December 1892, Atkinson Papers.
40. Edward Atkinson to John Murray Forbes, 21 December 1892, Atkinson Papers.
41. *breach of contract:* Edward Atkinson to ASG, 4 February 1893, Atkinson Papers; *his artistic prerogatives:* ASG to Rev. Winchester Donald, 1 March 1893, reel 5, ASG Papers; *at home or with friends:* Augusta Homer Saint-Gaudens to Edward Atkinson, 11 February 1893, Atkinson Papers.
42. John Boyd Thacher to Charles Foster, 23 December 1892, Award Committee Letters.
43. Augusta Homer Saint-Gaudens to Edward Atkinson, 29 January 1893, Atkinson Papers.
44. Edward Atkinson to ASG, 16 March 1893, Atkinson Papers.
45. *payments in the offing:* ASG to Richard Watson Gilder, 1893, box 15, Augustus Saint-Gaudens folder, Gilder Papers; *tide the sculptor over:* Augusta Homer Saint-Gaudens to Mrs. Thomas J. Homer, n.d. [1893], reel 20, ASG Papers.
46. ASG to Edward Atkinson, 20 March 1893, Atkinson Papers.
47. Edward Atkinson to ASG, 13 April 1893, Atkinson Papers.
48. Augusta Homer Saint-Gaudens to Edward Atkinson, 28 April 1893, Atkinson Papers.
49. *suited to this task:* Neil MacNeil, *The President's Medal 1789–1977*, 42; *help in the matter:* John Boyd Thacher to ASG, 15 April 1893, Award Committee Letters.
50. Oliver C. Bosbyshell to Edward O. Leech, 26 April 1893, book 59, Mint Letters Sent.
51. Charles S. Hamlin to John Boyd Thacher, 5 May 1893, vol. 19, Treasury Secretary Letters.
52. *three and one-half inches:* John Boyd Thacher to Charles S. Hamlin, 8 May 1893, box 5, Mint Director Letters Received; *the proper size:* Edward O. Leech to Thacher, 8 November 1892, vol. 269, Mint Director Correspondence.
53. Charles S. Hamlin to ASG, 26 May 1893, Treasury Secretary Letters, vol. 19.
54. ASG to John Boyd Thacher, 2 June 1893, box 5, Mint Director Letters Received.
55. John Boyd Thacher to John G. Carlisle, 5 June 1893, box 5, Mint Director Letters Received.
56. Robert E. Preston to Edward O. Leech, 7 June 1893, vol. 270, Mint Director Correspondence.
57. John G. Carlisle to ASG, 10 June 1893, Treasury Secretary Letters, vol. 19.
58. Edward Atkinson to ASG, 20 June 1893, vol. 49, Atkinson Papers.
59. *was at stake:* Edward Atkinson to Augusta Homer Saint-Gaudens, 30 June 1893, vol. 49, Atkinson Papers; *work were complete:* Atkinson to ASG, 27 July 1893, vol. 49, Atkinson Papers.
60. *brought this upon himself:* Edward Atkinson to ASG, 17 August 1893, vol. 49, Atkinson Papers; *as long as he could:* Atkinson to ASG, 23 September 1893, vol. 49, Atkinson Papers.

Chapter 8: Embarrassment Enough for All

1. "Eighteen Feet of Coins," *Chicago Daily Tribune*, 28 June 1893, 9. They were stacked in the Manufacturing Building. The replica was 18 feet high and 2-1/2 feet wide at the base. There were still plenty of coins left over to go around.
2. Robert E. Preston to Eugene Townsend, 12 October 1894, vol. 273, Mint Director Correspondence.
3. Anthony Swiatek, *Commemorative Coins of the United States: Identification and Price Guide* (Sidney, OH: Coin World, 1993), 9–15.
4. Robert E. Preston to John W. Woodside, 28 September 1893, vol. 275, Mint Director Correspondence.
5. Robert E. Preston to Peter Krider, 31 October 1893, vol. 275, Mint Director Correspondence.

Notes

6. Vermeule, *Numismatic Art in America*, 95.
7. Barnes, *John G. Carlisle*, 304. Preston's reasons were not an excuse to avoid attendance. His annual report would contribute to Treasury Secretary Carlisle's report of the country's finances being prepared for Congress. With the country then in the clutches of a depression, special attention to the report's preparation was needed.
8. Robert E. Preston to John W. Woodside, 21 October 1893, vol. 275, Mint Director Correspondence.
9. Robert E. Preston to Oliver C. Bosbyshell, 25 October 1893, vol. 271, Mint Director Correspondence.
10. Robert E. Preston to ASG, 4 November 1893, vol. 275, Mint Director Correspondence.
11. Barber to Landis, 11 May 1910, box 290, Mint Director Letters Received. Saint-Gaudens called them 10-inch models. However, Barber would much later state that the diameter was actually 8 inches. Since these reductions were still in his possession at the time of this statement, it is assumed correct.
12. ASG to Robert E. Preston, 17 November 1893, reel 5, ASG Papers.
13. "Fair Medal Casts Go to the Mint," *Chicago Daily Tribune*, 8 November 1893, 8.
14. Robert E. Preston to Oliver C. Bosbyshell, 7 November 1893, vol. 271, Mint Director Correspondence.
15. Oliver C. Bosbyshell to Robert C, Preston, 8 November 1893, book 61, Mint Letters Sent.
16. Robert E. Preston to ASG, 13 November 1893, vol. 275, Mint Director Correspondence.
17. Robert E. Preston to John W. Woodside, 13 November 1893, vol. 275, Mint Director Correspondence.
18. Robert E. Preston to Oliver C. Bosbyshell, 22 November 1893, box 184, Mint General Correspondence.
19. *to bear the names:* Charles E. Barber to John H. Landis, 11 May 1910, box 290, Mint Director Letters Received; *could be accomplished:* The Awards Subcommittee had insisted upon raised lettering on the surface of the medals for the recipient inscription instead of hand-engraved incised lettering. Such raised lettering required a design with a cartouche panel and a die with an aperture cut into it where the panel was located. A separate plug of metal called an insert die was made to fit snugly into that aperture. This insert die was engraved with the required lettering for each individual medal. The striking process was highly labor-intensive. The insert die would have to be engraved, proof-read and placed in the aperture while the die was on the press. The medal would be struck and annealed and returned to the press for a final striking. Fins would inevitably be squeezed out around the insert die, which would have to be removed.
20. Oliver C. Bosbyshell to Robert C Preston, 2 December 1893, book 61, Mint Letters Sent.
21. Robert E. Preston to John W. Woodside, 2 December 1893, vol. 275, Mint Director Correspondence.
22. ASG to Oliver C. Bosbyshell, 10 December 1893, box 184, Mint General Correspondence.
23. This observation is based upon a red paint mark appearing on Columbus's left leg that still remains on this medal, now in the possession of the American Numismatic Society.
24. Robert E. Preston to ASG, 17 December 1893, vol. 275, Mint Director Correspondence.
25. Eglit, *Columbiana*, 16–17. At the time aluminum was still an exotic metal. It required tremendous electric current in its manufacture, impacting its commercial viability. Only in the 1880s had its cost and availability become more reasonable.
26. Robert E. Preston to C.P. Goss, 6 January 1894, vol. 277, Mint Director Correspondence.
27. "Bronze Medal for Exhibitors," *Chicago Daily Tribune*, 28 December 1893, 5.
28. Augusta Homer Saint-Gaudens to Thomas Homer, 4 February 1894, reel 17, ASG Papers. The story of the medal controversy, as told by the family and quoted extensively in the New York papers, centered on a leak of the design at the Mint. Senator Chandler of New Hampshire wrote a letter of introduction to the director of the Mint for an employee of the Page Belting Company. Page Belting was one of the world's leading suppliers of power-transmission leather belting, operating from a substantial industrial complex in Concord, New Hampshire. The company representative, a skilled draftsman claiming an interest in art, asked to see the medal. Upon returning to the company, he reproduced from memory a very crude copy. These drawings were given to the Brooks Bank Note and Circular Engraving Company to be struck off as letterhead. Page Belting Company then used these letterheads on an advertising circular proclaiming it had won this medal as an exhibitor at the Exposition and was the only belt manufacturer authorized to publish it. Their claim was in fact correct. However, their motive was questionable. This version of the leak was told by Homer Saint-Gaudens in Gus's autobiography which Homer amplified and published in 1913. Homer was only 13 at the time the controversy erupted. Therefore, his version is essentially not firsthand. In other parts of the autobiography, Homer, with the help of Augusta and the urging of his editor, omitted facts that were not positive or reinforcing of Gus's reputation. Therefore, the family's version of this story is subject to strong question.
29. Taxay, *The U.S. Mint and Coinage*, 386.

30. "Mr. St. Gaudens Is Angry," *New York Tribune*, 20 January 1894, 3.

31. "Defends the Medal," *Chicago Daily Tribune*, 4 February 1894, 34.

32. *business from the Mint:* George A. Pierce to Eugene Townsend, 22 May 1894, box 185, Mint General Correspondence; *an advertising circular: New York Times*, 13 February 1894, 5; "What St. Gaudens Must Do," *Boston Herald*, 8 February 1894, 5.

33. "By Governor's Consent," *Concord Evening Monitor*, 20 September 1893, 4. George Page was both civic-minded and an accomplished businessman. He had been appointed to the New Hampshire World's Fair Board by the governor. He had resigned in August 1893 in disgust when state funds appropriated for New Hampshire exhibits at the fair were deposited, against his advice, by the board's treasurer in a bank in which that individual was a director. The bank succumbed to the panic and failed two weeks later, losing the funds and preventing additional exhibits at the New Hampshire building for the fair. Anger over this affair very likely clouded Page's judgment.

34. Pete Smith, *American Numismatic Biographies*, 33–34.

35. O.C. Bosbyshell to James W. Ellsworth, 13 March 1893, box 1, file 70, Ellsworth Collection.

36. O.C. Bosbyshell to James W. Ellsworth, 3 November 1893, box 1, file 72, Ellsworth Collection.

37. O.C. Bosbyshell to James W. Ellsworth, 13 November 1893, box 2, file 16, Ellsworth Collection.

38. E.W. Eckman to Oliver C. Bosbyshell, 22 November 1893, box 184, Mint General Correspondence.

39. *on December 14:* Oliver C. Bosbyshell to Robert C. Preston, 15 December 1893, book 61, Mint Letters Sent; *found to be short:* "Official Waives Vault Check," *Coin World*, 24 April 2006; *confessed to embezzlement:* "Startling Disclosures," *Concord Evening Monitor*, 20 September 1893.

40. *"boys without pants":* Tharp, *Saint-Gaudens and the Gilded Era*, 254; *the award-medal affair:* "Art Appreciation in Boston," *New York Tribune*, 10 February 1894, 4.

41. "Fair Medal Is Cheap," *Chicago Daily Tribune*, 13 January 1894, 8.

42. George R. Davis to James W. Ellsworth, 15 January 1894, box 4:10, Ellsworth Collection.

43. Summary, *The American Architect and Building News* 43, no. 945 (3 February 1894): 49–50.

44. *the medal was issued:* Augusta Homer Saint-Gaudens to Thomas Homer, 4 February 1894, reel 17, ASG Papers; *Evarts, Choate & Beaman:* "Mr. St. Gaudens Is Angry," *New York Tribune*, 20 January 1894, 3; *sent to Page Belting:* Evarts, Choate & Beaman to Page Belting Company, 16 January 1894, reel 6, ASG Papers; *New Hampshire farmers:* Augusta Homer Saint-Gaudens to Thomas Homer, 4 February 1894, reel 17, ASG Papers. Beaman was a close friend who sold the Aspet summer house at Cornish to Saint-Gaudens.

45. *to Vilas's attention:* Senator Edward O. Wolcott to Charles C. Beaman, 29 January 1894, reel 1, ASG Papers; *on January 18:* Charles Gross to Robert E. Preston, 17 January 1894, vol. 276, Mint Director Correspondence.

46. Oliver C. Bosbyshell to Robert C Preston, 20 January 1894, book 61, Mint Letters Sent.

47. Oliver C. Bosbyshell to Robert C. Preston, 26 January 1894, book 61, Mint Letters Sent.

48. "That St. Gaudens Medal," *New York Tribune*, 26 March 1894, 2.

49. John Boyd Thacher to Charles Foster, 22 March 1893, Award Committee Letters.

50. "Fair Medal Is Cheap," *Chicago Daily Tribune*, 13 January 1894, 8.

51. *the figure's genitals:* John G. Carlisle to ASG, 23 January 1894, reel 15, ASG Papers, Manuscript Division, Library of Congress (hereafter cited as ASG LibCong Papers); *a conversation with Vilas:* Carlisle had moved over to the Senate when his party lost the majority status in the House and with it his Speakership during the Harrison Administration.

52. *". . . vulgarity in art" appears:* John G. Carlisle to William F. Vilas, 19 January 1894, vol. 19, Treasury Secretary Letters; *the design be changed:* Carlisle to John Boyd Thacher, 19 January 1894, vol. 19, Treasury Secretary Letters.

53. "The Figure Must Be Draped," *New York Tribune*, 26 January 1894, 8.

54. Barnes, *John G. Carlisle*, 308–315.

55. ASG to John G. Carlisle, 25 January 1894, reel 15, ASG LibCong Papers.

56. *conclusions in writing:* John G. Carlisle to William F. Vilas, 27 January 1894, vol. 19, Treasury Secretary Letters; *the medal's design:* "St-Gaudens and His Fair Medal," *Chicago Daily Tribune*, 28 January 1894, 4.

57. *the world had ever seen:* "May Not Change St. Gaudens' Medal," *Chicago Daily Tribune*, 1 February 1894, 2; *buddies of long standing:* Barnes, *John G. Carlisle*, 205; *that of condemnation:* Senator Edward O. Wolcott to Charles C. Beaman, 29 January 1894, reel 1, ASG Papers.

58. *the artist was unwilling:* "St. Gaudens Defends His Medal," *New York Tribune*, 29 January 1894, 2; *deteriorating American economy:* Barnes, *John G. Carlisle*, 314–319. On that same January 29 Carlisle was forced to go to New York himself to salvage the bond issue. His meeting with the bankers was

satisfactory. On the 31st the success of the issue was assured. However, Carlisle paid a huge price personally. He had never been comfortable with the New York financial community. Now he was driven to ally himself with a group he had avoided. His power over Congress, where he had invested so many years, had been compromised by the silver interests. The laboring man, in whose service he had dedicated his life, was now aligned against him. There were calls for his impeachment. The Knights of Labor were suing to stop the bond issue.

59. "Mr. St. Gaudens' Medal to Be Altered," *New York Tribune*, 2 February 1894, 1.
60. Robert C. Preston to Oliver C. Bosbyshell, 2 February 1894, vol. 273, Mint Director Correspondence.
61. *the company a thief:* "Mr. St. Gaudens May Be Sued," *New York Tribune*, 6 February 1894, 4; *on their own merits:* "The St. Gaudens World's Fair Medal," *Chicago Daily Tribune*, 21 January 1894, 28; *the National Sculpture Society:* F. Wellington Ruckstuhl to Richard Watson Gilder, n.d., box 15, Gilder Papers.
62. Ibid.
63. "That St. Gaudens Medal," *New York Tribune*, 26 March 1894, 2.
64. "Asks St. Gaudens to Change His Medal," *New York Times*, 14 February 1894, 1. The first communication of the Senate Quadro-Centennial Committee's decision was actually conveyed by W.E. Curtis on February 13, 1894, to Saint-Gaudens.
65. John G. Carlisle to ASG, 21 February 1894, reel 15, vol. 19, ASG LibCong Papers, and Treasury Secretary Letters.
66. Richard Watson Gilder to ASG, 27 February 1894, reel 9, Gilder Papers.
67. *a suggestion from Gilder:* Richard Watson Gilder to ASG, 27 February 1894, box 19, letterbook 9, p. 76, Gilder Papers; *Ellsworth in Chicago:* ASG to John G. Carlisle, 15 March 1894, reel 15, ASG LibCong Papers.
68. John G. Carlisle to ASG, 17 March 1894, vol. 19, Treasury Secretary Letters.
69. "Mr. St. Gaudens Submits New Designs," *New York Tribune*, 28 March 1894, 3.
70. John G. Carlisle to William F. Vilas, 4 April 1894, vol. 19, Treasury Secretary Letters.
71. "Augustus Saint-Gaudens," *Newark (Ohio) Daily Advocate*, 4 April 1894, 2.
72. Charles E. Barber to John H. Landis, 11 May 1910, box 290, Mint Director Letters Received.
73. *immediately take action:* John Boyd Thacher to Edward O. Leech, 8 March 1893, and Thacher to John G. Carlisle, 11 March 1893, Award Committee Letters; *purchased bonds from him:* Thacher to James W. Ellsworth, 13 March 1893, Award Committee Letters.
74. *exhibits from the judging:* "Awards of the World's Fair," *New York Times*, 15 January 1894, 4; *had alienated everybody:* Thacher memorandum, n.d., reel 1, John Boyd Thacher Scrapbooks.
75. Richard Watson Gilder to W.E. Curtis, 11 July 1894, series 3, reel 9, letterbook 9, Gilder Papers; John G. Carlisle to Daniel E. Burnham, 12 March 1894, vol. 19, Treasury Secretary Letters. Carlisle had found Burnham's correspondence offensive and ungentlemanly and had stated that the Treasury Department would have no further correspondence with Burnham on the subject at hand—or any subject. The blowup occurred over the secretary's refusal to implement the Tarsney Act, which mandated that outside architects be allowed to compete in the design of government buildings.
76. Robert E. Preston to ASG, 26 April 1894, vol. 277, Mint Director Correspondence.
77. Saint-Gaudens, *Reminiscences*, 1:179.
78. J.M. Forbes to Edward Atkinson, 4 November 1893, vol. 51, p. 512, Atkinson Papers.
79. *mistake of a lifetime:* Edward Atkinson to ASG, 1 February 1894, vol. 25, Atkinson Papers; *distracting Saint-Gaudens:* Atkinson to ASG, 6 February 1894, vol. 51, p. 175, Atkinson Papers; *his modeling work:* Atkinson to J.M. Forbes, March 29, 1894, vol. 51, p. 512, Atkinson Papers.
80. *visited him in New York:* ASG appointment calendar April–May 1894, 18 May 1894, reel 44, ASG Papers; *still nothing happened:* "St. Gaudens Medal Trouble Ended," *Chicago Daily Tribune*, 1 May 1894, 2.
81. ASG to Richard Watson Gilder, 22 May 1894, box 15, Gilder Papers.
82. *model for the reverse:* Robert E. Preston to ASG, 18 May 1894, vol. 277, Mint Director Correspondence; *studies as alternatives:* Stanford White to ASG, 17 May 1894, Stanford White Papers, Avery Library; *in the profession:* ASG to Robert E. Preston, 17 May 1894, reel 15, ASG Papers.
83. "Medals to Be Ready About July 1," *Chicago Daily Tribune*, 20 May 1894, 1.
84. Paul Bion to ASG, 1 May 1894, reel 15, ASG Papers. The works considered the best in an exhibition were placed at eye level, while lesser pieces migrated toward the ceiling in a practice called skying. Thus skying had negative connotations and was an artist's worst fear.
85. ASG to Robert E. Preston, 23 June 1894, reel 15, ASG LibCong Papers.

Striking Change

86. *short of cash:* Stanford White to ASG, 17 May 1894, letterbook 9, p. 437, Stanford White Papers, Avery Library; *he lamented:* ASG to White, 14 May 1894, reel 14, ASG Papers.
87. Robert E. Preston to ASG, 23 June 1894, vol. 277, Mint Director Correspondence.
88. John G. Carlisle to Charles E. Barber, 27 June 1894, vol. 19, Treasury Secretary Letters.
89. Robert E. Preston to Eugene Townsend, 28 June 1894, vol. 273, Mint Director Correspondence.
90. "St. Gaudens's Design Rejected," undated newspaper clipping, reel 15, ASG LibCong Papers.
91. ASG to John G. Carlisle, 3 July 1894, reel 15, ASG LibCong Papers.
92. ASG to Richard Watson Gilder, 3 July 1894, box 15, Gilder Papers.
93. Gilder, *The Letters of Richard Watson Gilder,* 243–248.
94. *Cleveland to intercede:* George F. Kunz to Richard Watson Gilder, n.d., box 15, Gilder Papers; *John Boyd Thacher:* calling card of John Boyd Thacher to Gilder asking that he telegraph President Cleveland, n.d., reel 7, ASG Papers; *exactly this action:* "For a New Silver Dollar," *The (New York) Sun,* 21 August 1894, 8.
95. Gilder to William Edmond Curtis, 3 July 1894, series 3, reel 9, letterbook 9, Gilder Papers.
96. Gilder to F. Wellington Ruckstuhl, 5 July 1894, series 3, reel 9, letterbook 9, Gilder Papers.
97. Richard Watson Gilder to Charles Miller, 2 July 1894, series 3, reel 9, letterbook 9, Gilder Papers.
98. Gilder to William Edmond Curtis, 11 July 1894, series 3, reel 9, letterbook 9, Gilder Papers.
99. Richard Watson Gilder to ASG, 28 July 1894, box 19, letterbook 9, p. 456, Gilder Papers.
100. W.E. Curtis to his mother, 7–8 July 1894, William Edmond Curtis Papers, Library of Congress.
101. ASG to Richard Watson Gilder, 30 July 1894, box 15, Gilder Papers.
102. Saint-Gaudens was counting the two variations with a ribbon covering the offending body part as one revision.
103. ASG to John G. Carlisle, 11, 13, and 17 August (drafts), and 20 August 1894, reel 15, ASG LibCong Papers.
104. "For a New Silver Dollar," *The (New York) Sun,* 21 August 1894, 8.
105. Stanford White to ASG, 18 August 1894, letterbook 10, p. 227, Stanford White Papers, Avery Library.
106. *Mead was supportive:* Stanford White to ASG, 20 August 1894, letterbook 10, p. 227, Stanford White Papers, Avery Library; *"thing" in the newspaper:* White to ASG, 24 August 1894, letterbook 10, p. 227, Stanford White Papers, Avery Library; *without a protest:* White to ASG, 27 August 1894, letterbook 10, p. 227, Stanford White Papers, Avery Library.
107. Reel 15, ASG LibCong Papers. The contents of the letter are as follows:

> Sir:
>
> It occurs to me that the following résumé of my relations with the Washington authorities in charge of the commission for the Columbian Exposition Medal, may not be without a pleasant moral to others moved to entertain government proposals. I therefore send it, for insertion to your influential Journal.
>
> On the twenty-seventh of June (1894), I received notification of the rejection of my third design for the reverse of the Columbian medal. At the same time it was publicly announced that a design by Mr. Barber of the United States Mint, had been adopted in its stead.
>
> I had myself undertaken the execution of this medal only after earnest solicitation by those then in authority to the detriment of other and important interests.
>
> My first design, although it had been formally accepted by the Honorable J.G. Carlisle, was immediately afterwards rejected because its composition included a nude figure, to which impertinent attention was drawn by an incorrect and offensive copy, made and published by private parties.
>
> I regret to admit that, subsequently, at the urgent request of Mr. Carlisle, and upon his representations, I foolishly altered my design to flatter the sensitiveness of the rampant "pure."
>
> This second design, in which neither my feelings nor my draperies were spared, was again refused, and I was formally requested through Mr. Preston, Director of the Mint, to furnish an entirely new model "at an early date." Unpardonably as it now appears, I complied, producing once more the required model, which was again in due course of time set aside.
>
> The rejection of this third and last model is the more curious to explain, in that with excessive care for the sensitive acuteness of the Hon. Secretary of Treasury, I had this time in my composition scrupulously turned from classic thought of humanity, draped or undraped surely avoided all erotic insinuation by the substitution for the offending figure of "The Bird," whose fair fame is beyond suggestive possibilities.

I have reserved in this mortifying confession of criminal naïveté the final letter of vast persuasion that undid me. Let me print it, that others may judge the frank tone and incredible bonhomie that may be dangerously imported into government communications and that also I may find in their opinion "extenuating circumstances."

"From Mr. Preston, Director of the Mint, to Augustus St. Gaudens, N.Y.

"Philadelphia, May 18th, 1894

"Dear Sir: I am very much gratified by the receipt of your letter yesterday, stating that you would prepare and submit another design for the reverse of the World's Columbian Exposition Medal. As soon as the reverse is received, preparation will be made to have it engraved immediately, and to make a faithful reproduction of the same. I feel sure that the Mint has made a success in the engraving of the obverse and will be equally as successful in engraving the reverse.

"Very truly, etc., etc."

On the receipt of this guarantee to accept my further work, accompanied as it was by expressions of interest in its completeness and an assurance that every care would be bestowed upon its reproduction, it was, for me, impossible to hesitate. Never was commission clearer or more kindly thoughtful in detail. In the face of this promise, that as soon as the Reverse is received, preparations will be made to have it engraved immediately, and to make a faithful reproduction of the same, to harbor further uncertainty would have implied unmannerly doubt of the word of the gentleman who had written it. I may be excused if, in my simplicity, the idea ever of such possibility never occurred to me.

And now I am willing to confess that the condition of good faith common among gentlemen which could contemplate an engagement with another man to produce this same reverse at the very moment of holding out to me as an encouragement in my work that the "Mint has made a success in the engraving of the obverse and will be equally successful in engraving the reverse" does suggest a complication of bureaucratic conscience and Machiavellian subtlety with which I have found myself utterly unable to cope.

I shall in all humility, await from these official gentlemen their own explanation.

And I have, sir, the honor to be, Very truly yours,

[unsigned]

P.S. Mr. Carlisle's may be the legal right to combine my work with that of another on the same medal, but the rare shamelessness of such offense will be appreciated by all my confreres at home and abroad, and it is as much in their interest as in my own unbridled astonishment that I make this protest public.

108. Vermeule, *Numismatic Art in America*, 94.

Chapter 9: Aftermath

1. C.P. Goss to Robert E. Preston, 7 January 1895, box 6, Mint Director Letters Received.
2. ASG to Charles E. Barber, 3 April 1894, box 290, Mint Director Letters Received.
3. *probably three months:* Robert E. Preston to W.H. Eckman, 17 July 1894, vol. 277, Mint Director Correspondence; *in the bid circular:* Preston to Charles E. Barber, 23 July 1894, vol. 277, Mint Director Correspondence.
4. *was not completed:* Robert E. Preston to Hollander and Company, 4 August 1894, vol. 277, Mint Director Correspondence; *having a sketch:* Preston to Charles E. Barber, 23 August 1894, vol. 277, Mint Director Correspondence.
5. *the end of August:* Robert E. Preston to Fred W. Kelcey, 24 August 1894, vol. 277, Mint Director Correspondence; *versions to Saint-Gaudens:* Preston to ASG, 30 August 1894, vol. 277, Mint Director Correspondence.
6. Robert E. Preston to Charles E. Barber, 27 August 1894, vol. 277, Mint Director Correspondence.
7. *$0.926 per medal:* Preston to Carlisle, 6 September 1894, vol. 276, Mint Director Correspondence; *blanks since 1859:* Preston to Herman Kretz, 26 March 1896, vol. 283, Mint Director Correspondence.
8. *January 1, 1895:* Robert E. Preston to H.B. Battle, 24 September 1894, vol. 277, Mint Director Correspondence; *until June 1895:* Preston to Henry Bennatelli, 26 November 1894, vol. 277, Mint Director Correspondence.
9. *a master list:* Robert E. Preston to John Boyd Thacher, 24 September 1894, vol. 277, Mint Director Correspondence; *$0.30 per medal:* C.P. Goss to Preston, 10 January 1895, box 6, Mint Director Letters Received.

10. *in July and August:* C.P. Goss to Robert E. Preston, 28 January 1895, box 7, Mint Director Letters Received; *wanted Preston's help:* Goss to Preston, 1 February 1895, box 7, Mint Director Letters Received.
11. George F. Kunz to Robert E. Preston, 13 March 1895, box 9, Mint Director Letters Received.
12. *World's Fair award medal:* George F. Kunz to Robert E. Preston, 26 April 1895, box 11, Mint Director Letters Received; *for the fair award medal:* Charles E. Barber to Preston, 26 March 1895, box 9, Mint Director Letters Received.
13. "Mr. St. Gaudens Talks About His Medal," *New York Tribune*, 10 May 1895, 1.
14. Ibid.
15. "The Story of an Artist's Model—A New York 'Trilby,'" *The World*, 13 October 1895, 29.
16. Charles E. Barber to Robert E. Preston, 18 May 1895, box 12, Mint Director Letters Received.
17. Robert E. Preston to Eugene Townsend, 10 May 1895, vol. 280, Mint Director Correspondence.
18. *on this account:* Charles E. Barber to Robert E. Preston, 18 May 1895, box 12, Mint Director Letters Received; *in early June:* C.P. Goss to Preston, 6 June 1895, box 14, box 12, Mint Director Letters Received; *great commercial value:* John W. Woodside to Preston, 20 August 1895, box 17, box 12, Mint Director Letters Received.
19. *after the bronzing:* C.P. Goss to Robert E. Preston, 12 September 1895, box 18, Mint Director Letters Received; *required of Charles Barber:* Preston to Herman Kretz, 20 September 1895 and 17 October 1895, vol. 280, Mint Director Correspondence; *ready for distribution:* Goss to Preston, 5 November 1895, box 21, Mint Director Letters Received.
20. Charles E. Barber to Robert E. Preston, 11 January 1896, box 24, Mint Director Letters Received.
21. "The Columbian Exposition Medal," *American Journal of Numismatics*, April 1896, 119–120; "The Saint-Gaudens Columbian," *American Journal of Numismatics*, July 1896, 28.
22. George E. Roberts to C.P. Goss, 19 January 1900, vol. 316, Mint Director Correspondence.
23. Barnes, *John G. Carlisle*, 483.
24. William R. Boyd, "Eminent Iowan Series," *Annals of Iowa* 29, no. 6 (October 1948): 417.
25. *Statue of Liberty:* Thomas P. Somma, "'The Son by the Side of the Father': David d'Angers' Busts of Washington and Lafayette in the Rotunda of the U.S. Capitol," in *Paris on the Potomac: The French Influence on the Architecture and Art of Washington, DC*, ed. Cynthia R. Field, Isabelle Gournay, and Thomas P. Somma (Athens: Ohio University Press, 2007), 56–76; *surrender at Yorktown:* "In Memory of Lafayette," *Chicago Daily Tribune*, 15 September 1898, 3.
26. *Lafayette Memorial Commission:* "The Lafayette Memorial," *New York Times*, 20 February 1899, 2; *secretary to Peck:* "Row Over Lafayette Design," *Chicago Daily Tribune*, 20 November 1899, 5.
27. "To Ask Lafayette Coins," *Chicago Daily Tribune*, 25 January 1899, 19.
28. Auditor to A. Piatt Andrew, 21 April 1910, box 290, Mint Director Letters Received.
29. *some preliminary sketches:* George E. Roberts to Henry K. Boyer, 21 March 1899, vol. 306, Mint Director Correspondence; *a monument design:* Robert J. Thompson to Roberts, 22 March 1899, box 88, Mint Director Letters Received.
30. *drawing of the monument:* Charles E. Barber to Henry K. Boyer, 25 March 1899, box 88, Mint Director Letters Received; *one side of the coin:* George E. Roberts to Boyer, 24 March 1899, vol, 306, Mint Director Correspondence.
31. George E. Roberts to Charles E. Barber, 5 April 1899, vol. 305, Mint Director Correspondence.
32. Charles E. Barber to George E. Roberts, 12 April 1899, box 89, Mint Director Letters Received.
33. Ibid.
34. Robert J. Thompson to Charles E. Barber, 14 April 1899, box 89, Mint Director Letters Received.
35. Charles E. Barber to Henry K. Boyer, 17 April 1899, box 89, Mint Director Letters Received.
36. George E. Roberts to Robert J. Thompson, 22 April 1899, vol. 305, Mint Director Correspondence.
37. *by July 1:* "Lafayette Memorial Dollar," *Chicago Daily Tribune*, 7 May 1899, 4; *with Roberts's approval:* Robert J. Thompson to George E. Roberts, 9 May 1899, box 91, Mint Director Letters Received; *the date to be used:* Henry K. Boyer to Roberts, 12 May 1899, box 91, Mint Director Letters Received.
38. Robert J. Thompson to George E. Roberts, 15 May 1899, box 91, Mint Director Letters Received; Charles E. Barber to Roberts, 23 May 1899, box 92, Mint Director Letters Received. For the obverse Barber was proposing to model Washington's head from the Washington Before Boston medal by Du Vivier, which had used Houdon for its source. For Lafayette's likeness he intended to use the French medal engraved in 1824 by Caunois.

39. *into the dedication:* George E. Roberts to Henry K. Boyer, 29 May 1899, vol. 306, Mint Director Correspondence; "*. . . Lafayette, Paris 1900*": Boyer to Roberts, 31 May 1899, box 92, Mint Director Letters Received; *this finessed inscription:* Roberts to Robert J. Thompson, 2 June 1899, vol. 305, Mint Director Correspondence.
40. Robert J. Thompson to George E. Roberts, 5 June 1899, box 93, Mint Director Letters Received.
41. *to their likeness:* Charles E. Barber to George E. Roberts, 8 June 1899, box 93, Mint Director Letters Received; *of this proposal:* Roberts to Robert J. Thompson, 10 June 1899, vol. 305, Mint Director Correspondence; *with the engraver:* Roberts to Barber, 12 June 1899, vol. 305, Mint Director Correspondence.
42. Charles E. Barber to George E. Roberts, 16 June 1899, box 93, Mint Director Letters Received.
43. *designs sent to Thompson:* Ferdinand W. Peck to Charles E. Barber, 17 June 1899, box 94, Mint Director Letters Received; *pending Roberts's approval:* Barber to George E. Roberts, 20 June 1899, box 94, Mint Director Letters Received; *including the prayer:* Robert J. Thompson to B.F. Butler, 24 June 1899, box 94, Mint Director Letters Received; *sent them to Thompson:* Butler to Thompson, 21 June 1899, vol. 305, Mint Director Correspondence.
44. *the jugate busts:* Robert J. Thompson to George E. Roberts, 24 June 1899, box 94, Mint Director Letters Received; *approved or not:* Charles E. Barber to Roberts, 27 June 1899, box 94, Mint Director Letters Received; *await Roberts's return:* Robert E. Preston to Barber, 29 June 1899, vol. 305, Mint Director Correspondence; *designs for the coin:* Thompson to Roberts, 29 June 1899, box 94, Mint Director Letters Received; *rest with the commission:* Preston to Barber, 1 July 1899, vol. 305, Mint Director Correspondence.
45. Charles E. Barber to George E. Roberts, 6 July 1899, box 95, Mint Director Letters Received.
46. Thompson to Roberts, 16 October 1899, box 102, Mint Director Letters Received.
47. Roberts to Thompson, 18 October 1899, vol. 305, Mint Director Correspondence.
48. *to Roberts from Philadelphia:* Henry K. Boyer to George E. Roberts, 23 November 1899, box 104, Mint Director Letters Received; *to Ferdinand Peck:* Roberts to Robert J. Thompson, 2 December 1899, vol. 305, Mint Director Correspondence; *exposition as well:* Frank Millet biography notes, reel 1095, Francis Millet Rogers Papers; *the regular dollar coin:* Ferdinand W. Peck to Lyman Gage, 5 December 1899, box 105, Mint Director Letters Received; *in Millet's praise:* "Souvenir Coins Nearly Ready," *Chicago Daily Tribune,* 9 December 1899, 2.
49. *the first strike:* Henry K. Boyer to George E. Roberts, 27 November 1899, box 105, Mint Director Letters Received; *the death of George Washington:* Roberts to Boyer, 12 December 1899, vol, 306, Mint Director Correspondence; *the day before:* Roberts to Boyer, 13 December 1899, vol. 306, Mint Director Correspondence; *the Republic of France:* Roberts to Robert J. Thompson, 27 December 1899, vol. 305, Mint Director Correspondence; Swiatek, *Commemorative Coins of the United States,* 17–18.
50. George E. Roberts to Charles E. Barber, 2 January 1900, vol. 316, Mint Director Correspondence.
51. Swiatek, *Commemorative Coins of the United States,* 16.
52. Vermeule, *Numismatic Art in America,* 100–102.
53. Truman Bartlett ms., box 47, Paul Wayland Bartlett Papers, Manuscript Division, Library of Congress.

Chapter 10: A Sherman Connection

1. Saint-Gaudens, *Reminiscences,* 1:378.
2. *on his behalf:* [indecipherable] to Stanford White, 1886, Stanford White Papers, New-York Historical Society; *as a spendthrift:* Rachel Sherman to William T. Sherman, 3 September 1888, CSHR 2/172, William T. Sherman Family Papers, University of Notre Dame Archives.
3. Royal Cortissoz, *The Life of Whitelaw Reid* (New York: Charles Scribner's Sons, 1921), 379.
4. Arline Boucher Tehan, *Henry Adams in Love: The Pursuit of Elizabeth Sherman Cameron* (New York: Universe, 1983), 74.
5. Ibid., 183.
6. Edward Chalfant, *Better in Darkness: A Biography of Henry Adams; His Second Life, 1862–1891* (Hamden, CT: Archon Books, 1994), 449.
7. Tehan, *Henry Adams in Love,* 115.
8. Lloyd Lewis, *Sherman: Fighting Prophet* (New York: Harcourt, Brace and Co., 1932), 643.
9. *longtime managing editor:* Baker, *Stanny,* 108; *start of that battle:* Lewis, *Sherman: Fighting Prophet,* 233.

10. Reid to Cortelyou, 5 March 1908, George B. Cortelyou Papers, Library of Congress.
11. *a two-hour sitting:* William T. Sherman diaries, 3 January 1888, CSHR 5/09, William T. Sherman Family Papers; *his head turned too:* Saint-Gaudens, *Reminiscences,* 1:381.
12. ASG to Henry Adams, 25 January 1888, reel 6, Henry Adams Papers, Massachusetts Historical Society.
13. R. Cleveland Coxe, "Coxe Reminisces Today: Gay Anecdotes of Brilliant Men," *Santa Barbara Morning Press,* 21 December 1924.
14. *the portrait was complete:* William T. Sherman to Colonel John C. Tourtellotte, 6 March 1888, CSHR 1/76, William T. Sherman Family Papers; *to stop the sittings:* Tehan, *Henry Adams in Love,* 183; *when the work was done:* W.T. Sherman to Tourtellotte, 6 March 1888, CSHR 1/76, William T. Sherman Family Papers.
15. Saint-Gaudens, *Reminiscences,* 1:381.
16. *the proper left:* Dryfhout, *The Work of Augustus-Saint-Gaudens,* 168; *turned-over collar:* Coxe, "Coxe Reminisces Today."
17. ASG to Adams, 25 January 1888, reel 6, Henry Adams Papers.
18. Tehan, *Henry Adams in Love,* 183.
19. Wilkinson, *The Life and Works of Augustus Saint-Gaudens,* 234.
20. Tehan, *Henry Adams in Love,* 184.
21. Wilkinson, *The Life and Works of Augustus Saint-Gaudens,* 236–238.
22. *his first cousin:* Thomas E. Sherman to William T. Sherman, 22 June 1890, CSHR 3/93, William T. Sherman Family Papers; *he was recovering:* T.E. Sherman to W.T. Sherman, 26 May 1888, CSHR 3/88, William T. Sherman Family Papers.
23. *centered upon an angel:* Thomas E. Sherman material, 1863–1891, CSHR 3/91, William T. Sherman Family Papers; *Louis Saint-Gaudens in 1887:* Dryfhout, *The Work of Augustus Saint-Gaudens,* 254–255. Davida posed for this work of Gus's, requiring that he have Louis sign it to maintain discretion.
24. Lewis, *Sherman: Fighting Prophet,* 651.
25. Charles C. Beaman to Philemon Tecumseh Sherman, 15 February 1891, New-York Historical Society; oral history from Miss E. Sherman Fitch, 11 November 1943; Tehan, *Henry Adams in Love,* 115.
26. Tehan, *Henry Adams in Love,* 112.
27. *to design the statue:* "St. Gaudens Selected," *New York Times,* 10 April 1891, 8; *a figure of "Victory":* Samuel D. Babcock to ASG, 21 May 1891, reel 12, ASG Papers.
28. "St. Gaudens Selected," *New York Times,* 10 April 1891, 8.
29. *". . . of great value":* ASG to Philemon T. Sherman, 15 April 1891, CSHR 3/151, William T. Sherman Family Papers; *a rough model:* Sherman contract, 21 March 1892, reel 36, ASG Papers. A photograph of this model was attached to a patent application of February 2, 1892, which has since been lost.
30. Stanford White to Henry Adams, 13 August 1888, reel 6, Henry Adams Papers.

Chapter 11: In Search of an Angel

1. Edward Atkinson to ASG, 9 December 1891, Atkinson Papers.
2. Edward Atkinson to Shaw Committee, 28 September 1893, Atkinson Papers.
3. Ibid.
4. Edward Atkinson to Shaw Committee, 6 October 1893, Atkinson Papers.
5. John Murray Forbes to Edward Atkinson, 9 October 1893, Atkinson Papers.
6. *conveying greater severity:* Charles Follen McKim to ASG, 7 March 1894, reel 1, McKim Papers; *to complete the memorial:* Edward Atkinson to John Murray Forbes, 10 October 1894, Atkinson Papers.
7. John M. Forbes to Henry Lee, 20 December 1894, Lee Family Papers.
8. Edward Atkinson to Shaw Committee, 20 April 1895, Atkinson Papers.
9. Edward Atkinson to Shaw Committee, 12 July 1895, Atkinson Papers.
10. *changes on the angel:* Edward Atkinson to *Boston Transcript,* 22 May 1896, Atkinson Papers; *should be smaller:* ASG to Atkinson, undated, 1895, Atkinson Papers.
11. Weinman Speech to the National Arts Club, 13 April 1948, reel 5887, Adolph Weinman Papers, Archives of American Artists.
12. Edward Atkinson to Shaw Committee, 11 May 1896, Atkinson Papers.
13. Edward Atkinson to Shaw Committee, 21 May 1896, Atkinson Papers.
14. Edward Atkinson to ASG, 5 June 1896, Atkinson Papers.
15. George Von Lengerke Meyer had served on the Boston City Board of Aldermen for one term, 1891–1892, and was instrumental in obtaining the appropriation for the Shaw terrace. He was

Charles Follen McKim's former brother-in-law and would help acquire the Villa Mirafiori for the American Academy in Rome in 1904 while serving as ambassador to Italy.

16. Edward Atkinson to ASG, 6 June 1896, Atkinson Papers.

17. Edward Atkinson to Shaw Committee, 9 June 1896, Atkinson Papers.

18. John Murray Forbes to Edward Atkinson, 25 June 1896, Atkinson Papers.

19. Edward Atkinson to Shaw Committee, 26 August 1896, Lee Family Papers.

20. ASG to Edward Atkinson, 24 September 1896, Atkinson Papers.

21. Edward Atkinson to John Murray Forbes, 8 October 1896, Atkinson Papers.

22. Edward Atkinson to Henry Lee, 19 October 1896, Atkinson Papers. Asking for a personal mortgage was an extraordinary step. It was most likely taken because of the mysterious circumstances surrounding a fire at the Morgan mausoleum of August 22, 1884, in Hartford, Connecticut. Saint-Gaudens had designed the mausoleum for former governor E.D. Morgan. The stonework was surrounded by scaffolding and a wooden building. Within the building were three nearly complete marble carvings of angels for the tomb. Given the time of year and the intensity of the fire, it was clearly viewed as arson. There was no insurance. Saint-Gaudens lost all but a small portion of the commission which was gained in a settlement with the estate. Afterward Saint-Gaudens told his friend, Paul Bion, that enemies of Governor Morgan set the fire. However, Saint-Gaudens's nemesis, Truman Bartlett, alleged that the sculptor himself set the fire. The committee may or may not have known of the differing accusations but they certainly would have been aware of the tragedy and were therefore taking steps to protect themselves.

23. Rose Standish Nichols, "Familiar Letters of Augustus Saint-Gaudens," *McClure's Magazine* 31, no. 6 (October 1908): 603–616.

24. *Columbia, South Carolina:* William E. Hagans, "Saint-Gaudens, Zorn and the Goddesslike Miss Anderson," *Archives of American Art* 16, no. 2 (Summer 2002), 93; *two years previously:* ASG to Stanford White, 27 March 1895, letterbook 13 (March 15, 1895–July 11, 1895), p. 39, Stanford White Papers, Avery Library; *the figure of a goddess:* Nichols, "Familiar Letters of Augustus Saint-Gaudens."

25. James Earle Fraser, "Augustus Saint-Gaudens" draft, n.d., box 61, Writings, J.E. Fraser Papers; Nichols, "Familiar Letters of Augustus Saint-Gaudens."

26. Nichols, "Familiar Letters of Augustus Saint-Gaudens."

27. Tehan, *Henry Adams in Love*, 147–156.

28. *the final product:* ASG to Augusta Homer Saint-Gaudens, 26 February 1898, reel 21, ASG Papers; *inner sanctum:* Wilkinson, *The Life and Works of Augustus Saint-Gaudens*, 291; *his enthusiasm:* Saint-Gaudens, *Reminiscences*, 2:123–124.

29. ASG to Augusta Homer Saint-Gaudens, 26 February 1898, reel 21, ASG Papers.

30. *assistant in Paris:* ASG to Charles Keck, 19 July 1898, reel 8, ASG Papers; *Art Students League:* Saint-Gaudens, *Reminiscences*, 2:133; *came and went:* Tharp, *Saint-Gaudens and the Gilded Era*, 300.

31. Wilkinson, *The Life and Works of Augustus Saint-Gaudens*, 304; Dryfhout, *The Work of Augustus-Saint-Gaudens*, 316.

32. Fred L. Reed III, "Famous But Unknown," *Coin World*, 15 May 2000, 82.

33. James Earle Fraser, "Augustus Saint-Gaudens" draft, n.d., box 61, Writings, J.E. Fraser Papers.

34. Saint-Gaudens, *Reminiscences*, 2:133 and 135.

35. *as he proceeded:* ASG to Abbott Thayer, 5 September 1905, reel 13, ASG Papers; *model of the angel:* Saint-Gaudens, *Reminiscences*, 2:133.

36. ASG to Stanford White, 21 October 1898, Stanford White Papers, New-York Historical Society.

37. Saint-Gaudens, *Reminiscences*, 2:133–134.

38. ". . . *so things go*": ASG to Homer Saint-Gaudens, n.d., reel 23, ASG Papers; *the offending garment:* Saint-Gaudens, *Reminiscences*, 2:135.

39. Wilkinson, *The Life and Works of Augustus Saint-Gaudens*, 297–298.

40. Saint-Gaudens, *Reminiscences*, 2:137.

41. Henry Adams to Elizabeth Cameron, 13 July 1899, *The Letters of Henry Adams*, edited by Worthington Chauncey Ford (Cambridge, MA: Harvard University Press), vol. 4.

42. *July in 1899:* ASG to Augusta Homer Saint-Gaudens, June [undated] 1899, reel 21, ASG Papers; *the French countryside:* Nichols, "Familiar Letters of Augustus Saint-Gaudens," 603–616.

43. Wilkinson, *The Life and Works of Augustus Saint-Gaudens*, 309. Neurasthenia is a condition brought on by fatigue, worry, and lack of zest.

44. ASG to Homer Saint-Gaudens, 2 May 1899, reel 22, ASG Papers.

45. *could feel cocky:* ASG to Homer Saint-Gaudens, 2 May 1899, reel 22, ASG Papers; *10 in the morning:* James Earle Fraser, "Augustus Saint-Gaudens" draft, n.d., box 61, Writings, J.E. Fraser Papers; *the colossal work:* Adams, *The Education of Henry Adams,* 385; *so earnestly sought:* Wilkinson, *The Life and Works of Augustus Saint-Gaudens,* 291–292.
46. *long since completed:* Augusta Homer Saint-Gaudens to Homer Saint-Gaudens, 16 November 1899, reel 22, ASG Papers, and ASG to Augusta Homer Saint-Gaudens, 4 September 1899, reel 21; *accomplishing nothing:* Henry Adams to Elizabeth Cameron, 4 August 1899, *The Letters of Henry Adams,* vol. 5.
47. *youthful, soft, and sweet:* Dryfhout, *The Work of Augustus-Saint-Gaudens,* 291; *very stunning:* Tharp, *Saint-Gaudens and the Gilded Era,* 303; *horse and rider:* Wilkinson, *The Life and Works of Augustus Saint-Gaudens,* 305; *straight nose:* Tehan, *Henry Adams in Love,* 184.
48. Saint-Gaudens, *Reminiscences,* 2:332.
49. Wilkinson, *The Life and Works of Augustus Saint-Gaudens,* 305.
50. *studio gossip:* Tehan, *Henry Adams in Love,* 158; *etching to Lizzie:* ibid., 184.
51. Ibid.
52. Ibid., 282.
53. Rachel Sherman Thorndike to ASG, 28 October 1902, reel 13, ASG Papers.
54. ASG to Helen Mears, 28 January 1900, reel 10, ASG Papers.
55. ASG to Helen Mears, 16 March 1900, reel 10, ASG Papers.
56. ASG to Louis Saint-Gaudens, 15 May 1900, reel 25, ASG Papers.
57. Saint-Gaudens, *Reminiscences,* 2:185.
58. *all used up:* Augusta Homer Saint-Gaudens to Homer Saint-Gaudens, 11 May 1900, reel 23, ASG Papers; *a heart condition:* ASG to Homer Saint-Gaudens, 10 May 1900, reel 23, ASG Papers.
59. James Earle Fraser, "Augustus Saint-Gaudens" draft, n.d., box 61, Writings, J.E. Fraser Papers.
60. *do away with himself:* James Earle Fraser, memoir notes on Saint-Gaudens for unpublished autobiography, box 64, J.E. Fraser Papers; *the United States:* Baker, *Stanny,* 269.
61. Saint-Gaudens, *Reminiscences,* 2:128.
62. Philippe Julian, *The Triumph of Art Nouveau: Paris Exposition 1900* (London: Phaidon Press, 1974), 206.

Chapter 12: Edith

1. E. Morris, *The Rise of Theodore Roosevelt,* 566.
2. S. Morris, *Edith Kermit Roosevelt,* 17–18.
3. *spelling her name:* ibid., 23; *usually won out:* ibid., 27.
4. Ibid., 52.
5. Ibid., 53.
6. Ibid., 55–56.
7. Ibid., 58–59.
8. Ibid., 62 and 64.
9. Ibid., 65.
10. Ibid., 71.
11. Ibid., 78.
12. Ibid., 79–83.
13. E. Morris, *The Rise of Theodore Roosevelt,* 357.
14. Ibid., 375.
15. Ibid., 405.
16. S. Morris, *Edith Kermit Roosevelt,* 124–125.
17. Ibid., 124.
18. Tehan, *Henry Adams in Love,* 97.
19. S. Morris, *Edith Kermit Roosevelt,* 126.
20. Henry Adams to Richard Watson Gilder, 14 October 1896, reel 1, ASG Papers.
21. Henry Adams to Elizabeth Cameron, 6 May 1892, *The Letters of Henry Adams,* vol. 4.
22. S. Morris, *Edith Kermit Roosevelt,* 148–149.
23. Ibid., 152–154.
24. Ibid., 154.
25. Ibid., 165.

Chapter 13: Homeless

1. *near 80 degrees:* The Weather, *New York Times,* 23 July 1900, 3; *expected it to be:* Tharp, *Saint-Gaudens and the Gilded Era,* 307.
2. Wilkinson, *The Life and Works of Augustus Saint-Gaudens,* 311.
3. *on July 28:* Augusta Homer Saint-Gaudens to Louis Saint-Gaudens, 2 August 1900, reel 25, ASG Papers; *a colostomy was performed:* undated notes in Augusta Saint-Gaudens's handwriting, reel 11, ASG Papers; *in five to seven years:* Tharp, *Saint-Gaudens and the Gilded Era,* 307.
4. *recuperating at the hospital:* Tom Homer to Augusta Homer Saint-Gaudens, 28 August 1900, reel 5, ASG Papers; *as porous plaster:* ASG to Stanford White, 27 September 1900, reel 14, ASG Papers.
5. *not a success:* Augusta Homer Saint-Gaudens to Charles O. Brewster, 4 July 1901, reel 2, ASG Papers; *the need for the colostomy:* Dr. W.M. Polk to Augusta Homer Saint-Gaudens, 27 March 1901, reel 11, ASG Papers.
6. Wilkinson, *The Life and Works of Augustus Saint-Gaudens,* 312.
7. ASG to Henry Adams, 29 May 1904, reel 5, ASG Papers.
8. Saint-Gaudens, *Reminiscences,* 2:228–231.
9. Wilkinson, *The Life and Works of Augustus Saint-Gaudens,* 312.
10. E. Morris, *The Rise of Theodore Roosevelt,* 629.
11. Ibid., 797.
12. Ibid., 699.
13. *November 21, 1899:* ibid., 746; *vice presidential nomination:* ibid., 755.
14. Ibid., 747.
15. *would not violate:* Alice Roosevelt Longworth, *Crowded Hours,* 34; *make herself conspicuous:* Isabella Hagner James, "Chieftess of the Roosevelt Clan," *New York Herald Tribune Magazine,* 30 October 1932, section XI, 5 and 14.
16. *Augustus Saint-Gaudens:* Tiffany & Co. to ASG, 17 January 1901, reel 13, ASG Papers; *"tense with religious fervor":* James Earle Fraser, "Augustus Saint-Gaudens" draft, n.d., box 61, Writings, J.E. Fraser Papers.
17. E. Morris, *The Rise of Theodore Roosevelt,* 775.
18. James Earle Fraser autobiography draft, ASG Papers, reel 6.
19. *days making modifications:* Saint-Gaudens, *Reminiscences,* 2:227; *a classical Greek gown:* Tharp, *Saint-Gaudens and the Gilded Era,* 316.
20. *siting the Sherman:* Charles Follen McKim to ASG, 18 June 1897, reel 10, ASG Papers; *Gus left for Paris:* McKim to ASG, 12 December 1897, reel 10, ASG Papers.
21. *but no action taken:* ASG to Samuel D. Babcock, 22 April 1898, reel 12, ASG Papers; *causing McKim to hesitate:* Stanford White to ASG, 2 March 1898, letterbook 19 (September 7, 1897, to April 2, 1898), Stanford White Papers, Avery Library.
22. Charles Follen McKim to ASG, 12 December 1899, reel 2, ASG Papers.
23. ASG to Augusta Homer Saint-Gaudens, 8 July 1899 and 6 October 1899, reel 21, ASG Papers.
24. ASG to Charles Follen McKim, 1 January 1900, reel 2, ASG Papers.
25. Samuel Parsons, *Samuel Parsons and the Central Park of New York,* edited by Mabel Parsons (New York: G.P. Putnam's Sons, 1926), 100–101.
26. "Statues in the Parks," *New York Times,* 30 March 1900, 14.
27. "Artistic Vandals," *New York Times,* 10 April 1900, 6.
28. William E. Dodge to Charles Follen McKim, 25 April 1900, McKim Papers.
29. *the* Times *and the* Tribune: Parsons, *Samuel Parsons and the Central Park of New York,* 30; *had not consulted Parsons:* ibid., 100.
30. ASG to Charles Follen McKim, 2 June 1900, ASG Papers, reel 10.
31. Charles Follen McKim to ASG, 1 May 1900, McKim Papers.
32. Horace Porter to ASG, 29 March 1899, reel 12, ASG Papers.
33. ASG to Charles Follen McKim, 24 June 1900, reel 10, ASG Papers.
34. Wilkinson, *The Life and Works of Augustus Saint-Gaudens,* 324.
35. Charles Follen McKim to ASG, 29 December 1900, McKim Papers.
36. Ibid.
37. ASG to Charles Follen McKim, 5 January 1901, reel 12, ASG Papers.

38. *to sort things out:* Charles Follen McKim to ASG, 4 February 1901, McKim Papers; *architectural firm's efforts:* Stanford White to ASG, 9 September 1901, letterbook 26, p. 43, Stanford White Papers, Avery Library.

39. Charles Curran to ASG, 13 February 1901, and William A. Coffin to ASG, 22 March 1901, reel 11, ASG Papers.

40. Saint-Gaudens, *Reminiscences,* 2:299–300.

41. *the Monroe Doctrine:* "America as a Unit: The Master Thought on Dedication Day," *Harper's Weekly,* 1 June 1901, 554; *provide for the Exposition:* TR to Richard Watson Gilder, 7 May 1901, reel 326, vol. 28, p. 829, TR Papers; *so much taffy:* Gilder, *The Letters of Richard Watson Gilder,* 339.

42. *trotting into a barn:* Tharp, *Saint-Gaudens and the Gilded Era,* 317; *taken by the Sherman:* S. Morris, *Edith Kermit Roosevelt,* 210; *its arresting beauty:* "Pictures at the Pan-American Exposition," *Harper's Weekly,* 13 July 1901, 707–708.

43. Theodore Roosevelt Sr. to TR, 31 May 1901, reel 326, vol. 29, p. 20, TR Papers.

44. Ibid.

45. TR to ASG, 31 May 1901, reel 326, vol. 29, p. 45, TR Papers.

46. TR to Elihu Root, 1 June 1901, reel 326, vol. 29, p. 70, TR Papers.

47. TR to ASG, 6 June 1901, reel 326, vol. 29, p. 129, TR Papers.

48. Elihu Root to TR, 4 June 1901, reel 15, TR Papers.

49. *"nervous snap":* Saint-Gaudens, *Reminiscences,* 2:289; *destruction of Georgia:* ibid., 2:227.

50. *his prolonged recovery:* Charles Follen McKim to ASG, 7 June 1901, McKim Papers; *and the melancholia:* Wilkinson, *The Life and Works of Augustus Saint-Gaudens,* 321.

51. Saint-Gaudens, *Reminiscences,* 2:237.

52. *by the Sherman:* Herbert Adams to ASG, 28 July 1901, reel 1, ASG Papers; *James Earle Fraser:* ASG to William Coffin, 11 August 1901, reel 2, ASG Papers.

53. Charles Follen McKim to Charles T. Barney, 31 December 1901, McKim Papers.

54. Annual Report and Minutes of the Art Commission for 1902, Astor, Lenox and Tilden Foundation, 696854A, New York Public Library.

55. Charles T. Barney to George C. Clausen, 26 December 1901, Archives of the New York City Art Commission, Sherman folder (hereafter cited as NYCAC Sherman).

56. *the original plan:* George C. Clausen to Charles T. Barney, 30 December 1901, NYCAC Sherman; *was vetoed:* Charles Follen McKim to Barney, 31 December 1901, McKim Papers.

57. *discuss his endorsement:* ASG to Frederic Law Olmsted, 13 January 1902, reel 25, file 502, Central Park, Frederic Law Olmsted Papers, Manuscript Division, Library of Congress; *lukewarm toward the project:* ASG to Augusta Homer Saint-Gaudens, 17 February 1902, reel 21, ASG Papers.

58. *the mall was lacking:* ASG unaddressed letter, 14 March 1902, reel 12, ASG Papers; *he was hopeful:* ASG to Augusta Homer Saint-Gaudens, 14 March 1902, reel 21, ASG Papers.

59. Charles Follen McKim to ASG, 14 March 1902, McKim Papers.

60. Ibid.

61. *to these modifications:* ASG to Frederic Law Olmsted, 19 March 1902, reel 25, file 502, Central Park, Frederic Law Olmsted Papers; *a final determination:* Charles Follen McKim to William E. Dodge, 18 March 1902, McKim Papers.

62. *strongly against it:* ASG handwritten notes, n.d., reel 12, ASG Papers; *only one option:* William E. Dodge to ASG, 20 March 1902, reel 12, ASG Papers.

63. *for the Sherman:* William R. Willcox to John De Witt Warner, 26 May 1902, NYCAC Sherman; *65 feet away:* unaddressed letter by ASG, 17 March 1902, reel 12, ASG Papers. Gus noted a similar viewing arrangement for Thomas Ball's statue of Washington, of the same approximate size, in the Boston Public Garden; *the trees surrounding the circle:* ASG to Daniel Chester French, 19 March 1902, reel 2, ASG Papers.

64. William R. Willcox to John De Witt Warner, 26 May 1902, NYCAC Sherman.

65. *serving as its chairperson:* Annual Report and Minutes of the Art Commission for 1902, Astor, Lenox and Tilden Foundation, 696854A; *approved by the Art Commission:* Minutes and Documents of the Board of Commissioners of the Parks Department, 26 June 1902, New York Public Library.

66. ASG notation, n.d., reel 21, ASG Papers.

67. *gild the Sherman entirely:* ASG to William E. Dodge, 3 September 1902, reel 12, ASG Papers; *looked like stovepipes:* Saint-Gaudens, *Reminiscences,* 2:293–294.

68. *the surrounding scenery:* Samuel Parsons Jr. to William R. Willcox, 24 May 1902, NYCAC Sherman; *better with the gilding:* ASG to Charles Follen McKim, undated, 1902, ASG Papers, reel 10.

69. Brown, *1860–1930 Memories*, 337.
70. *to cast the lettering:* Charles Follen McKim to ASG, 30 December 1902, McKim Papers; *day and night:* Tharp, *Saint-Gaudens and the Gilded Era*, 331.
71. *from the year before:* "The Sacredness of the Trees," *New York Evening Post*, 7 March 1903, 4; *and remove the trees:* ASG to William R. Willcox, 17 March 1903, reel 12, ASG Papers.
72. William R. Willcox to ASG, 20 March 1903, reel 12, ASG Papers.
73. Parsons, *Samuel Parsons and the Central Park of New York*, 149–150.
74. *20 inches in diameter:* "Artist, Spare That Tree," *New York Times*, 30 May 1903, 6; *the Parks Department:* John De Witt Warner to Daniel Chester French, 12 May 1903, NYCAC Sherman.
75. Saint-Gaudens, *Reminiscences*, 2:296.
76. *the fight over the trees:* ibid.; *his forceful support:* Daniel Chester French to John De Witt Warner, 8 May 1903, Michael Richman Papers.
77. *Sherman from Fifth Avenue:* "Decoration Day Events," *New York Times*, 31 May 1903, 6; *looking into the situation:* Report of the Proctor Committee, 25 May 1903, NYCAC Sherman; *the reviewers' stand:* "Artist, Spare That Tree," *New York Times*, 30 May 1903, 6.
78. "Statue of Sherman Unveiled," *New York Tribune*, 31 May 1903, 1.
79. *Victory pointed the way:* "Equestrian Statue of General Sherman Unveiled by Hero's Grandson," *New York Herald*, 31 May 1903, 3–4; *effect of the gilding:* "Gold Against Bronze," *New York Times*, 21 June 1903, 8.
80. *spirits remained undampened:* "Statue of Sherman Unveiled," *New York Tribune*, 31 May 1903, 1–2; *the previous day:* "Statue Is Revealed as Thousands Gaze," *New York Herald*, 31 May 1903, 4.
81. "Statue of Sherman Unveiled," 1–2.
82. *also at the luncheon:* luncheon arrangement of guests, 30 May 1903, reel 13, ASG Papers; *John G. Carlisle:* "Pay Tribute to Fame of Sherman," *New York Herald*, 31 May 1903, 4.
83. Whitelaw Reid to George B. Cortelyou, 5 March 1908, George B. Cortelyou Papers.
84. Daniel Chester French to ASG, 4 July 1903, reel 7, ASG Papers.
85. TR to ASG, 3 August 1903, reel 331, vol. 41, p. 210, TR Papers.
86. ASG to TR, 15 August 1903, reel 12, ASG Papers.

Chapter 14: The Confident Years

1. *reigning supreme:* Saint-Gaudens, *Reminiscences*, 2:227–228; *an annual event:* ASG to Henry Adams, 29 May 1904, reel 1, ASG Papers.
2. *David Jayne Hill:* Saint-Gaudens, *Reminiscences*, 2:280–281; *to get together:* C.F. McKim to ASG, 17 April 1901, McKim Papers.
3. Pamela J. Scott, "A City Designed as a Work of Art: The Emergence of the Senate Park Commission's Monumental Core," in *Designing the Nation's Capital: The 1901 Plan for Washington, DC*, ed. Sue Kohler and Pamela Scott (Washington, DC: U.S. Commission of Fine Arts, 2007), 4.
4. Brown, *1860–1930 Memories*, 359–363.
5. Scott, "A City Designed," 15. Excluded from War Department control were the Smithsonian grounds stretching from 7th to 12th streets and the Department of Agriculture from 12th to 14th streets.
6. C. Moore, *The Life and Times of Charles Follen McKim*, 184.
7. *a great people:* Frederick Law Olmsted Jr., "Landscape in Connection with Public Buildings in Washington," *American Architect and Building News*, 19 January 1901, 19; *the L'Enfant plan:* C. Moore, *The Life and Times of Charles Follen McKim*, 183.
8. *Detroit Park Commission:* Brown, *1860–1930 Memories*, 76; *the federal Treasury:* ibid., 97.
9. Reps, *Washington on View*, 237–240.
10. *went to work for him:* H.P. Caemmerer to James Earle Fraser, 24 November 1942, box 6, Fraser Papers; *to the senator:* Charles Moore, *Daniel H. Burnham* (New York: Da Capo Press, 1968), 1:137.
11. C. Moore, *The Life and Times of Charles Follen McKim*, 182.
12. *into the Mall:* Brown, *1860–1930 Memories*, 79; *most of the Mall:* Scott, *A City Designed*, 12; *endorsed the work:* C. Moore, *The Life and Times of Charles Follen McKim*, 185.
13. Ibid., 204.
14. C. Moore, *Daniel H. Burnham*, 147–148.
15. Charles Follen McKim to Rev. Winchester Donald, 1 December 1901, McKim Papers.
16. Scott, *A City Designed*, 37.
17. Ibid., 53.
18. Ibid., 57.

19. *was now resolved:* ibid., 61–62; *for the president:* Charles Follen McKim to Charles Moore, 21 November 1901, Charles Moore Papers.
20. *around outside walls:* Charles Follen McKim to Charles Moore, 11 December 1901, Charles Moore Papers; *from January 1 to the 15th:* McKim to Moore, 23 December 1901, Charles Moore Papers; *an extension to February 1:* McKim to Moore, 28 December 1901, Charles Moore Papers.
21. Brown, *1860–1930 Memories,* 269.
22. C. Moore, *The Life and Times of Charles Follen McKim,* 200–201.
23. C. Moore, *Daniel H. Burnham,* 1:154 and 158.
24. Reps, *Washington on View,* 241.
25. *and liked it:* C. Moore, *The Life and Times of Charles Follen McKim,* 201–203; *near the Immortals:* Brown, *1860–1930 Memories,* 258.
26. Henry Adams to Elizabeth Cameron, 19 January 1902, *The Letters of Henry Adams,* vol. 5.
27. *St. Louis:* Charles Follen McKim to ASG, 2 February 1902, McKim Papers; *by this affront:* McKim to TR, 10 February 1904, reel 13, ASG Papers; *Library of Congress:* McKim to Jules Guerin, 24 March 1903, McKim Papers.
28. *between Theodore's meetings:* S. Morris, *Edith Kermit Roosevelt,* 224; *". . . all the politicians":* Isabella Hagner James, draft memoirs, Isabella Hagner James Papers, White House Collection, White House Historical Association, 11.
29. Gilder, *The Letters of Richard Watson Gilder,* 341.
30. C. Moore, *The Life and Times of Charles Follen McKim,* 208.
31. "Social Duties of Mrs. Roosevelt," *Pearson's Magazine* 10, no. 6 (December 1903): 532.
32. *the evening of April 3:* White House invitation to Mr. and Mrs. Augustus Saint-Gaudens, 3 April 1902, reel 12, ASG Papers; *his wife were present:* Beaux, *Background With Figures,* 231.
33. *freely with the guests:* "Social Duties of Mrs. Roosevelt," *Pearson's Magazine* 10, no. 6 (December 1903), 532; *brilliant evening for all:* S. Morris, *Edith Kermit Roosevelt,* 235–236. There would be many more musicales, with Edith bringing in the Vienna Male Choir and Pablo Casals.
34. *the* Century *magazine:* Richard Watson Gilder to TR, 15 April 1902, reel 26, TR Papers; *the painting stayed:* Edith Roosevelt to Emily Carow, n.d., Theodore Roosevelt Collection, Houghton Library, Harvard University, quoted in S. Morris, *Edith Kermit Roosevelt,* 237; *got his permission:* TR to Richard Watson Gilder, 18 April 1902, reel 328, vol. 34, p. 107, TR Papers.
35. *proposition for its alteration:* William B. Bushong, "Glenn Brown, the White House and the Urban Renaissance of Washington, DC," *White House History,* no. 11 (Summer 2002): 311; *its present location:* C. Moore, *The Life and Times of Charles Follen McKim,* 204–205.
36. *an office space:* ibid.; *soon become permanent:* ibid., 206–207.
37. *Tuesday, April 22:* McKim to Charles Moore, 19 April 1902, Charles Moore Papers; *to Edith both days:* McKim to ASG, 24 April 1902, McKim Papers; *a colonnaded terrace:* Charles Moore, "The Restoration of the White House," *The Century Magazine* 65, no. 6 (April 1903): 807–831.
38. *the fire of 1814:* C. Moore, *The Life and Times of Charles Follen McKim,* 207; *conflicting design schemes:* William B. Bushong, "Glenn Brown, the White House and the Urban Renaissance of Washington, DC," 317; *to fall into place:* Charles Follen McKim to Moore, 19 April 1902, Charles Moore Papers.
39. *regard to the renovation:* Charles Follen McKim to ASG, 24 April 1902, McKim Papers; *presented them to the president:* ibid.
40. *leave the country:* ASG to E.B. Green, 15 September 1905, reel 8, ASG Papers; *sent them to the White House:* C. Moore, *The Life and Times of Charles Follen McKim,* 208.
41. Ibid.
42. *right and appropriate:* Archibald Butt, *The Letters of Archie Butt* (Garden City, NY: Doubleday, Page & Co., 1924), 127; *he paid for it:* S. Morris, *Edith Kermit Roosevelt,* 5; *free from impulse:* James, "Chieftess of the Roosevelt Clan," 5 and 14; *invisible governance:* Owen Wister, *Roosevelt: The Story of a Friendship, 1880–1919* (New York: Macmillan, 1930), 89.
43. *forced to interrupt them:* *The Letters of Archie Butt,* 241; *afraid of his "Edie":* Mrs. Winthrop Chanler, *Roman Spring: Memoirs* (Boston: Little, Brown, 1934), 203.
44. Quoted in C. Moore, *The Life and Times of Charles Follen McKim,* 208–209.
45. Charles Follen McKim to Charles Moore, 20 May 1902, Charles Moore Papers.
46. *when Congress reconvened:* TR to Charles Follen McKim, 10 May 1902, reel 328, vol. 34, p. 286, TR Papers; *"confronting the lion":* Brown, *1860–1930 Memories,* 445.
47. C. Moore, *The Life and Times of Charles Follen McKim,* 210.

48. Cost estimate from the offices of McKim, Mead, and White, 27 May 1902, Charles Moore Papers.
49. C. Moore, *The Life and Times of Charles Follen McKim*, 211.
50. Ibid., 209–210.
51. Edith Kermit Roosevelt to Charles Follen McKim, 2 June 1902, Charles Moore Papers.
52. *never carried out:* Senate Committee on the District of Columbia, memorandum in regard to the White House, 5 June 1902, Charles Moore Papers; *the White House:* Charles Follen McKim to Charles Moore, 10 June 1902, Charles Moore Papers.
53. C. Moore, *The Life and Times of Charles Follen McKim*, 213.
54. Elihu Root to James McMillan, 11 April 1902, Charles Moore Papers.
55. Charles Follen McKim to Charles Moore, 3 June 1902, Charles Moore Papers.
56. Charles Follen McKim to Charles Moore, 10 June 1902, Charles Moore Papers.
57. Charles Follen McKim to Charles Moore, 18 June 1902, Charles Moore Papers.
58. C. Moore, *The Life and Times of Charles Follen McKim*, 214–215.
59. TR to Charles Follen McKim, 28 June 1902, reel 329, vol. 35, p. 252, TR Papers.
60. Treaty of Oyster Bay, 2 July 1902, Charles Moore Papers.
61. C. Moore, *The Life and Times of Charles Follen McKim*, 215–217.
62. James, "Chieftess of the Roosevelt Clan," 5 and 14.
63. C. Moore, *The Life and Times of Charles Follen McKim*, 217–218.
64. Ibid., 222.
65. *he was transferred:* TR to Theodore A. Bingham, 23 March 1903, reel 329, vol. 39, p. 198, TR Papers; *exit gracefully:* Isabella Hagner James, draft memoirs, 46.
66. *Bingham's departure:* Isabella Hagner James, draft memoirs, 48; *brigadier general and retired:* TR to Theodore A. Bingham, 1 July 1904, reel 334, vol. 48, p. 172, TR Papers.
67. Chanler, *Roman Spring*, 196 and 203.
68. Charles Follen McKim to ASG, 5 November 1902, McKim Papers.
69. Isabella Hagner James, draft memoirs, 18.
70. Brown, *1860–1930 Memories*, 121.
71. ASG to TR, 15 August 1903, reel 12, ASG Papers.
72. *easier to accomplish:* Daniel H. Burnham to L.M. Shaw, 16 July 1903, reel 35, TR Papers; *had ever run across:* L.M. Shaw to TR, 18 July 1903, reel 35, TR Papers.
73. L.M. Shaw to Daniel H. Burnham, 18 July 1903, reel 35, TR Papers.
74. C. Moore, *Daniel H. Burnham*, 1:206–214.
75. Ibid., 1:217.
76. Brown, *1860–1930 Memories*, 97.
77. Ibid., 275.
78. C. Moore, *Daniel H. Burnham*, 1:218.
79. ASG to TR, 10 February 1904, reel 13, ASG Papers.
80. *Roosevelt would intervene:* Brown, *1860–1930 Memories*, 276; *broad straight malls:* TR to Charles Follen McKim, 11 February 1904, reel 333, vol. 45, p. 312, TR Papers; *given his approval:* McKim to ASG, 19 February 1904, McKim Papers.
81. C. Moore, *Daniel H. Burnham*, 1:219.
82. *a fatal mistake:* ibid., 1:226; *without opposition:* ibid., 1:227; *Senate Park Commission report:* Brown, *1860–1930 Memories*, 179.
83. Saint-Gaudens, *Reminiscences*, 2:222.
84. ASG to E.B. Green, 4 July 1904, reel 8, ASG Papers.
85. *break engagements to attend:* Edith Kermit Roosevelt to Augustus and Augusta Homer Saint-Gaudens, undated correspondence of 1902 and 1903, reel 12, ASG Papers; *legitimacy of the Academy:* Charles Follen McKim to ASG, 6 February 1904, McKim Papers.
86. ASG to Charles Follen McKim, 12 October 1903, Maloney Collection, New York Public Library.
87. *to help him:* Tharp, *Saint-Gaudens and the Gilded Era*, 395; *Victory-Peace:* Dryfhout, *The Work of Augustus Saint-Gaudens*, 256.
88. *go to Tiffany's:* Faulkner, *Sketches From an Artist's Life*, 56; *Head of Victory:* Dryfhout, *The Work of Augustus Saint-Gaudens*, 288.
89. *an attack of pain:* Dr. Frances B. Herrington to Dr. John D. Brewster, 24 September 1904, reel 8, ASG Papers; *plagued by these attacks:* ASG handwritten note, n.d., reel 11, ASG Papers.
90. Faulkner, *Sketches From an Artist's Life*, 57–59.

91. *articles for his attention:* Isabella Hagner James, draft memoirs, 57; *wanted him to see:* James, "Chieftess of the Roosevelt Clan," 5 and 14.
92. Gilder, *The Letters of Richard Watson Gilder,* 348.

Chapter 15: The Stage Is Set

1. "Social Duties of Mrs. Roosevelt," *Pearson's Magazine* 10, no. 6 (December 1903), 531.
2. Edith Roosevelt diaries, 12 January 1905, Theodore Roosevelt Collection, Houghton Library, Harvard University; ASG to Augusta Homer Saint-Gaudens (draft), 12 January 1905, reel 21, ASG Papers.
3. Vol. 4, The White House 1904–1905, entry 159, record group 42, Official Functions, National Archives (hereafter cited as White House Functions).
4. "At the White House," *The (Washington, DC) Evening Star,* 13 January 1905 (clipping in White House Functions).
5. *whom he caricatured:* Low, *A Chronicle of Friendships,* 506; *promptly at 10:45:* "White House Guests," *Washington Post,* 13 January 1905 (clipping in White House Functions).
6. *for the affair:* Edith Roosevelt to Emily Carow, 15 January 1905, Edith K.C. Roosevelt Papers, Theodore Roosevelt Collection, Houghton Library, Harvard University (87M-101); *among others:* White House Functions; *feeling cocky:* ASG unaddressed notes, 13 January 1905, reel 14, ASG Papers.
7. *the Legion of Honor:* Tharp, *Saint-Gaudens and the Gilded Era,* 306 and 308; *Theodore's approval: The Letters of Archie Butt,* 219.
8. ASG to Augusta Homer Saint-Gaudens, 27 November 1904, reel 21, ASG Papers.
9. Tehan, *Henry Adams in Love,* 223.
10. *in early December:* Richard Watson Gilder to TR, 5 December 1904, reel 50, TR Papers; *on December 9:* desk diaries, 9 December 1904, reel 430, TR Papers.
11. TR to Leslie M. Shaw, 27 December 1904, reel 336, vol. 53, p. 22, TR Papers.
12. The law in question was even broader. A close reading would have told him that he could also change the design of the nickel and silver dollar as well. However, minting of the silver dollar had been discontinued in 1904.
13. *the Mint produce it:* Henry Hering, "History of the $10 and $20 Gold Coins of 1907 Issue," *The Numismatist* 62, no. 8 (August 1949), 455–458; *". . . my pet crime":* Saint-Gaudens, *Reminiscences,* 2:329.
14. Presentation by Archibald Roosevelt at the December 14, 1934, meeting of the New York Numismatic Club, *The Numismatist* 48, no. 2 (February 1935): 103.
15. ASG to Louis Saint-Gaudens (draft), 14 January 1905, reel 25, ASG Papers.
16. *"life is a tug":* Gilder, *The Letters of Richard Watson Gilder,* 261; *no more commissions:* Wilkinson, *The Life and Works of Augustus Saint-Gaudens,* 351.
17. Roosevelt, *An Autobiography,* 434.
18. *functions at the Mint:* Boyd, "Eminent Iowan Series," 417; *who reported to him:* Frank A. Leach, *Recollections of a Newspaper Man: A Record of Life and Events in California* (San Francisco, CA: Samuel Levinson, 1917), 401.
19. George E. Roberts to ASG, 13 January 1905, reel 14, ASG Papers.
20. ASG to George E. Roberts, 20 January 1905, reel 12, ASG Papers.
21. George E. Roberts to Leslie M. Shaw, 16 January 1905, vol. 347, Mint Director Correspondence.

Chapter 16: A Medal for Edith

1. J.R. Carmody to George E. Roberts, 31 December 1904, and Roberts to John H. Landis, 6 January 1905, box 224, Mint Director Letters Received.
2. Charles E. Barber to John H. Landis, 10 January 1905, box 224, Mint Director Letters Received.
3. "Complete History of the United States Stamped on Silver Medals," *New York Herald,* 4 December 1904, magazine section, 11.
4. F.D. Millet to Edith Kermit Roosevelt, 13 January 1905, reel 52, TR Papers.
5. George E. Roberts to Leslie M. Shaw, 16 January 1905, and H.A. Taylor to TR, 16 January 1905, vol. 347, Mint Director Correspondence.
6. TR to Leslie M. Shaw, 16 January 1905, reel 337, vol. 53, p. 261, TR Papers.
7. Presentation by Archibald Roosevelt at the December 14, 1934, meeting of the New York Numismatic Club, *The Numismatist* 48, no. 2 (February 1935): 103.
8. Saint-Gaudens, *Reminiscences,* 2:254.
9. Augusta Homer Saint-Gaudens to ASG, 23 January 1905, reel 20, ASG Papers.

10. TR Papers, 17 January 1905, reel 337.
11. Ibid.
12. General John M. Wilson to ASG, 19 January 1905, reel 14, ASG Papers.
13. *striking the medals:* 20 January 1905, reel 12, ASG LibCong Papers; *in supporting him:* ASG to Louis Saint-Gaudens (draft), 14 January 1905, reel 25, ASG Papers. Saint-Gaudens always used capital letters in his correspondence to express strong emotion.
14. Saint-Gaudens, *Reminiscences*, 2:254 and 257.
15. General John M. Wilson to ASG, 23 January 1905, reel 14, ASG Papers.
16. Adolph A. Weinman to General John M. Wilson, 1 February 1905, reel 13, ASG Papers.
17. *forwarded them to Wilson:* ASG to TR, 28 January 1905, reel 337, TR Papers; *quotes were too high:* General John M. Wilson to ASG, 30 January 1905, reel 14, ASG Papers.
18. Adolph A. Weinman to General John M. Wilson, 1 February 1905, reel 13, ASG Papers.
19. TR to General John M. Wilson, 28 January 1905, reel 337, TR Papers.
20. ASG to J.J. Albright, 1 February 1905, reel 2, ASG Papers.
21. *"A Square Deal for Every Man":* Neil MacNeil, *The President's Medal, 1789–1977*, 59; *too colloquial for a medal:* TR to ASG, 2 February 1905, reel 337, TR Papers.
22. *"The Right and Fear Not":* ASG to William Loeb, 10 February 1905, reel 14, ASG Papers; *his campaign slogan:* William Loeb to ASG, 14 February 1905, reel 14, ASG Papers.
23. ASG to General John M. Wilson, 19 February 1905, reel 14, ASG Papers.
24. *a letter the next day:* Adolph A. Weinman to ASG, 21 February 1905, reel 14, ASG Papers; *strike the medal:* Weinman to George E. Roberts, 21 February 1905, box 225, Mint Director Letters Received.
25. *no silver casts:* General John M. Wilson to ASG, 23 February 1905, reel 14, ASG Papers; *the medal at cost:* George E. Roberts to Adolph A. Weinman, 23 February 1905, vol. 353, Mint Director Correspondence.
26. Adolph A. Weinman to ASG, 4 March 1905, reel 13, ASG Papers.
27. *the potential trouble:* Tiffany & Co. to ASG, 7 March 1905, reel 13, ASG Papers; *ten days or a fortnight:* ASG to Tiffany & Co., n.d., reel 13, ASG Papers.
28. Adolph A. Weinman to ASG, 7 March 1905, reel 13, ASG Papers.
29. Adolph A. Weinman to ASG, 10 March 1905, reel 13, ASG Papers.
30. Adolph A. Weinman to ASG, 13 March 1905, reel 13, ASG Papers.
31. Quoted in Neil MacNeil, *The President's Medal, 1789–1977*, 61.
32. ASG to Tiffany & Co., 9 March 1905, reel 13, ASG Papers.
33. *ready in two days:* Adolph A. Weinman to ASG, 20 March 1905, reel 13, ASG Papers; *a slight gold tint:* Tiffany & Co. to ASG, 21 March 1905, reel 13, ASG Papers.
34. Adolph A. Weinman to ASG, 3 April 1905, reel 13, ASG Papers.
35. Adolph A. Weinman to ASG, 10 March 1905, reel 13, ASG Papers.
36. Adolph A. Weinman to ASG, 5 April 1905, reel 13, ASG Papers.
37. ASG to Adolph A. Weinman, 7 April 1905, reel 13, ASG Papers.
38. Charles Follen McKim to ASG, 9 March 1905, reel 2, ASG Papers.
39. Adolph A. Weinman to ASG, 3 May 1905, reel 13, ASG Papers.
40. Tiffany & Co. to Adolph A. Weinman, 3 May 1905, reel 13, ASG Papers.
41. Adolph A. Weinman to ASG, 21 May 1905, reel 13, ASG Papers.
42. *which he found pleasing:* Adolph A. Weinman to ASG, 15 June 1905, reel 13, ASG Papers; *sent to Cornish:* Weinman to ASG, 17 May 1905, reel 13, ASG Papers.
43. Fred L. Reed III, "Sculpturing TR," *Coin World*, 22 July 2002, 66.
44. ASG to Homer Saint-Gaudens, fall 1905, reel 23, ASG Papers.
45. *close friends and family:* General John M. Wilson to TR, 7 July 1905, TR Papers; *his personal use:* Wilson to ASG, 28 July 1905, reel 14, ASG Papers.
46. ASG to TR, 6 July 1905, reel 56, TR Papers.
47. Homer Saint-Gaudens, *The Century*, April 1920, 721–736.
48. TR to Henri Cabot Lodge, 11 July 1905, *The Letters of Theodore Roosevelt*, ed. Elting E. Morison (Cambridge, MA: Harvard University Press, 1951), vol. 4.
49. Edith Kermit Roosevelt to ASG, 19 July 1905, reel 12, ASG Papers.
50. *". . . like thirty cents?":* Frank Millet to TR, 20 July 1905, reel 57, TR Papers; *the Renaissance style:* Vermeule, *Numismatic Art in America*, 110.
51. ASG to TR, 6 July 1905, reel 56, TR Papers.

Chapter 17: An Unwanted Headache

1. George E. Roberts to ASG, 10 July 1905, box 229, Mint Director Letters Received.
2. TR to Leslie M. Shaw, 12 July 1905, reel 338, vol. 56, p. 351, TR Papers.
3. *reverse of the cent:* Leslie M. Shaw to ASG, 29 July 1905, vol. 347, Mint Director Correspondence; *stacking of the coins:* ASG to Leslie M. Shaw, 11 August 1905, box 233, Mint Director Letters Received.
4. ASG to Richard Watson Gilder, 8 January 1905, Gilder Papers; Wilkinson, *The Life and Works of Augustus Saint-Gaudens,* 331–332.
5. Charles E. Barber to George E. Roberts, 27 July 1905, box 232, Mint Director Letters Received.
6. Frank A. Leach to George E. Roberts, 17 August 1905, box 234, Mint Director Letters Received.
7. *morphine for his pain:* note in Augusta Homer Saint-Gaudens's handwriting, n.d., reel 11, ASG Papers; *also being continued:* 31 July–5 August 1905, ASG LibCong Papers.
8. *beloved ice cream:* Calendar May 29, 1905–January 16, 1906, ASG LibCong Papers; *constructed at Aspet:* Calendar May 29, 1905–January 16, 1906, ASG LibCong Papers.
9. Weir Mitchell to ASG, 10 August 1904, reel 6, ASG Papers.
10. *The Franklin Bicentennial Celebration: A Record of the Proceedings* (Philadelphia: American Philosophical Society, 1906), vii.
11. Harrison Morris, *Confessions in Art* (New York: Sears Publishing, 1930), 124–125.
12. *a moving spirit:* Francis Loomis to Harrison Morris, 6 March 1905, reel 6, ASG Papers; *a member that April:* "Scientific Body Elects Roosevelt," *Philadelphia Inquirer,* 9 April 1904, 3.
13. *the medal's preparation:* John Hay to ASG, 8 August 1904, reel 6, ASG Papers; *Gus refused:* ASG to Harrison Morris, n.d., reel 6, ASG Papers; *de facto chairman:* Hay to Morris, 8 August 1904, box 146, folder 1, Harrison Morris Papers, Princeton University Library (hereafter cited as Morris Papers).
14. Remembrances of Augustus Saint-Gaudens by Frances Grimes, n.d., reel 36, ASG Papers.
15. *September 1904:* Harrison Morris to ASG, 16 September 1904, reel 6, ASG Papers; *because of sciatica:* Morris to ASG, 24 September 1904, reel 6, ASG Papers; *October 21:* Morris to ASG, 19 October 1904, Morris Papers.
16. ASG to Harrison Morris, 2 November 1904, Morris Papers.
17. *preparation of the dies:* Harrison Morris to ASG, 17 November 1904, reel 6, ASG Papers; *a second time:* Morris to John Hay, 31 October 1904, Morris Papers.
18. *"officialism and courtesy":* Harrison Morris to ASG, 16 August 1905, reel 6, ASG Papers; *the beginning of 1905:* ASG to George E. Roberts, 18 February 1905, reel 14, ASG Papers.
19. ASG to George E. Roberts, 18 February 1905, reel 14, ASG Papers.
20. *slow to start:* Weir Mitchell to Harrison S. Morris, 5 August 1904, Morris Papers; *that pleased no one:* Morris to Louis Saint-Gaudens, 13 March 1905, Morris Papers.
21. *the bust by Houdon:* ASG to Harrison Morris, 23 November 1905, Morris Papers; *above the figures:* sketch in ASG's hand, n.d., reel 6, ASG Papers.
22. *at Gus's suggestion:* Harrison Morris to Louis Saint-Gaudens, 13 March 1905, Morris Papers; *die for the medal:* Morris to John Hay, 5 March 1905, Morris Papers; *struck at the Mint:* Francis Loomis to Morris, 6 March 1905, reel 6, ASG Papers.
23. Deitsch Brothers to ASG, 28 March 1905, reel 5, ASG Papers.
24. Harrison Morris to Louis Saint-Gaudens, 7 April 1905, Morris Papers.
25. *recommend Deitsch Brothers:* ASG to Louis Saint-Gaudens, 11 April 1905, Morris Papers; *permission to proceed:* Herbert H.D. Peirce to Harrison Morris, 3 July 1905, Morris Papers.
26. Louis Saint-Gaudens to Harrison Morris, 10 July 1905, Morris Papers.
27. Louis Saint-Gaudens to Harrison Morris, 23 July 1905, Morris Papers.
28. *did not materialize:* ASG to Harrison Morris, 22 July 1905, Morris Papers; *addressed to Gus:* ibid.
29. *completion of both models:* Harrison Morris to ASG, 16 August 1905, reel 6, ASG Papers; *strike the medals:* ASG to Leslie M. Shaw, 14 August 1905, box 233, Mint Director Letters Received; *visit the Mint:* A.A. Norris to George E. Roberts, 19 August 1905, box 229, Mint Director Letters Received.
30. *strike the medals:* Barber to Landis, 16 August 1905, box 233, Mint Director Letters Received; *to be conservative:* Adolph A. Weinman to ASG, 11 September 1905, reel 6, ASG Papers; *acknowledged their letters:* ASG to Leslie M. Shaw, 15 September 1905, box 235, Mint Director Letters Received.
31. ASG to Harrison Morris, 14 August 1905, Morris Papers.

32. *cut the die directly:* Henri Weil to ASG, 7 September 1905, reel 5, ASG Papers; *positive and negative:* Weil to ASG, 11 September 1905, reel 5, ASG Papers.
33. *the organization's name:* Harrison Morris to ASG, 13 September 1905, reel 6, ASG Papers; *". . . Society in Philadelphia":* early photograph of the obverse model of the Franklin medal, n.d., reel 47, ASG Papers.
34. *supply the inscriptions:* Edgar Smith to Weir Mitchell, 16 September 1905, reel 6, ASG Papers; *that man's death:* Mitchell to Harrison Morris, 16 September 1905, Morris Papers; *the Philosophical Society:* Morris to ASG, 19 September 1905, reel 6, ASG Papers.
35. *the end of September:* Harrison Morris to ASG, 11 October 1905, reel 6, ASG Papers; *ready to start:* Henri Weil to ASG, 11 October 1905, reel 5, ASG Papers.
36. Harrison Morris to ASG, 11 October 1905, reel 6, ASG Papers.
37. *the dies were cut:* Harrison Morris to ASG, 16 October 1905, reel 6, ASG Papers; *to Secretary Root:* ASG to Morris, 18 October 1905, Morris Papers.
38. Henri Weil to ASG, 16 October 1905, reel 5, ASG Papers.
39. *to cut the die:* Henri Weil to ASG, 21 October 1905, reel 5, ASG Papers; *additional pay:* Weil to ASG, 28 October 1905, reel 5, ASG Papers; *the time being:* ASG to Deitsch Brothers, 29 October 1905, reel 6, ASG Papers.
40. *strike the medals:* Harrison Morris to ASG, 6 November 1905, reel 6, ASG Papers; *model to Deitsch:* Deitsch Brothers to ASG, 9 November 1905, reel 5, ASG Papers.
41. Calendar May 29, 1905–January 16, 1906, ASG LibCong Papers.
42. ASG to Harrison Morris, 11 November 1905, Morris Papers.
43. *the casts to Root:* Harrison Morris to ASG, 11 November 1905, reel 6, ASG Papers; *a mere formality:* Morris to ASG, 13 November 1905, reel 6, ASG Papers.
44. ASG to Harrison Morris, 13 November 1905, Morris Papers.
45. ASG to Harrison Morris, 14 November 1905, Morris Papers.
46. Adolph A. Weinman to ASG, 16 November 1905, reel 6, ASG Papers.
47. *had signed off:* Harrison Morris to ASG, 21 November 1905, reel 6, ASG Papers; *January 1, 1906:* ibid.
48. *in four sections:* Henri Weil to ASG, 23 November 1905, reel 5, ASG Papers; *bronze casting:* Weil to ASG, 4 December 1905, reel 5, ASG Papers. Several lines appeared on the 13-inch paraffin reduction that Weil sent to Saint-Gaudens. If time had not been so short, Weil would have preferred to redo the reduction. However, Weinman suggested sending it as it was. Weil recommended that a plaster mold be taken. In this manner the lines would be raised, allowing the sculptor to retouch them so that Weil could proceed with the reduction. Gus agreed to the procedure.
49. Tiffany & Co. to ASG, 6 December 1905, reel 6, ASG Papers.
50. Charles E. Barber to John H. Landis, 12 December 1905, reel 6, ASG Papers.
51. *". . . and approve of it":* ASG to Harrison Morris, 19 December 1905, reel 6, ASG Papers. He understood (from what source he did not reveal) that the ceremonial gold medal was to be transported to France on January 4. He laid out for Morris his timeline. Deitsch would deliver the dies to Tiffany's in time for them to begin striking the medals on the 27th or 28th; *presentation of the medal:* Morris to ASG, 20 December 1905, reel 6, ASG Papers.
52. Harrison Morris to ASG, 23 December 1905, reel 6, ASG Papers.
53. ASG to Adolph A. Weinman, 20 December 1905, reel 6, ASG Papers.
54. Harrison Morris to ASG, 23 December 1905, reel 6, ASG Papers.
55. Saint-Gaudens had his date wrong. Franklin's birthday is January 17.
56. ASG to Harrison S. Morris, 25 December 1905, Morris Papers.
57. ASG to Harrison Morris, 25 December 1905, reel 6, ASG Papers.
58. Harrison Morris to ASG, 26 December 1905, reel 6, ASG Papers.
59. ASG to Harrison S. Morris, 28 December 1905, Morris Papers.
60. ASG to Stanford White, 31 December 1905, letterbook 15, p. 1, Stanford White Papers, Avery Library.
61. *Deitsch Brothers:* Deitsch Brothers to ASG, 30 December 1905, reel 5, ASG Papers; *proceed with the striking:* ASG to Adolph A. Weinman, 2 January 1906, reel 6, ASG Papers; *opium to subdue:* Augusta Homer Saint-Gaudens to Homer Saint-Gaudens, 5 January 1906, reel 122, ASG Papers.
62. ASG to Deitsch Brothers, 2 January 1906, reel 6, ASG Papers. Saint-Gaudens felt that the added costs really should have been considered as included in the original quote. The only increase in the

scope of work in his opinion was his requirement that paraffin reductions be made for his review and approval.

63. Deitsch Brothers to ASG, 4 January 1906, reel 5, ASG Papers.

64. Harrison Morris to ASG, 6 January 1906, reel 6, ASG Papers.

65. ASG to Deitsch Brothers, 9 January 1906, reel 6, ASG Papers.

66. *an effort to placate him:* Deitsch Brothers to ASG, 12 January 1906, reel 5, ASG Papers; *very hard plaster:* Deitsch Brothers to ASG, 16 January 1906, reel 5, ASG Papers.

67. Tiffany & Co. to ASG, 24 January 1906, reel 6, ASG Papers.

68. Dr. Henri Baldwin to ASG, 28 December 1905, reel 1, ASG Papers.

69. *depression and crying:* calendar May 29, 1905–January 16, 1906, ASG LibCong Papers; *that day in despair:* Dr. Henri Baldwin to ASG, 28 January 1906, reel 1, ASG Papers.

70. Tiffany & Co. to ASG, 30 January 1906, reel 6, ASG Papers. This price was significantly below the Deitsches' quote. During the period Tiffany's was subcontracting the die work to Henri Weil. He most likely recut the reverse die anyway. Tiffany's strategy could have been to underquote the die work to ensure they got the contract to strike the medals.

71. *now sending them:* ASG to Harrison Morris, 6 February 1906, reel 6, ASG Papers; *on February 6:* ASG to Tiffany & Co., 6 February 1906, reel 6, ASG Papers.

72. Herbert H.D. Peirce to Harrison Morris, 5 February 1906, Morris Papers.

73. *pleading for the casts:* Herbert H.D. Peirce to Harrison Morris, 10 February 1906, Morris Papers; *making a new one:* ASG to Morris, 11 February 1906, reel 6, ASG Papers; *released the reverse:* ASG to Tiffany & Co., 16 February 1906, reel 6, ASG Papers.

74. *schedule for completion:* Harrison Morris to ASG, 9 February 1906, reel 6, ASG Papers; *little time to spare:* ASG to Morris, 11 February 1906, reel 6, ASG Papers.

75. Memorandum from Elihu Root, n.d., reel 6, ASG Papers.

76. *would disconcert Gus:* Harrison Morris to ASG, 19 February 1906, reel 6, ASG Papers; *sick and bedridden:* ASG to George F. Kunz, 21 February 1906, reel 6, ASG Papers.

77. *had been particularly valuable:* ibid.; *still be done in time:* ASG to Harrison Morris, 21 February 1906, reel 6, ASG Papers.

78. Ida Metz Reed to Harrison Morris, 25 February 1906, reel 6, ASG Papers.

79. *by Augusta's secretary:* Ida Metz Reed to George F. Kunz, 27 February 1906, reel 6, ASG Papers; *of little matter to Saint-Gaudens:* Tiffany & Co. to ASG, 1 March 1906, reel 6, ASG Papers.

80. Augusta Homer Saint-Gaudens to Homer Saint-Gaudens, 7 March 1906, reel 22, ASG Papers.

81. Augusta Homer Saint-Gaudens to Homer Saint-Gaudens, 18 March 1906, reel 22, ASG Papers.

82. *the presentation piece:* Tiffany & Co. to ASG, 16 March 1906, reel 6, ASG Papers; *Morris and Weinman:* ASG to Tiffany & Co., 17 March 1906, reel 6, ASG Papers.

83. *she found touching:* Augusta Homer Saint-Gaudens to Homer Saint-Gaudens, [March 1906,] reel 22, ASG Papers; *until March 28:* Augusta Homer Saint-Gaudens to Homer Saint-Gaudens, 29 March 1906, reel 22, ASG Papers; *an "ugly time":* ASG to Richard Watson Gilder, 13 April 1906, Gilder Papers.

84. Harrison Morris to ASG, 4 April 1906, reel 6, ASG Papers.

85. ASG to Tiffany & Co., 5 April 1906, reel 6, ASG Papers.

86. Tiffany & Co. to ASG, 5 April 1906, reel 6, ASG Papers.

87. ASG to Harrison Morris, 6 April 1906, reel 6, ASG Papers.

88. ASG to Harrison Morris, April 1906 [date missing], reel 6, ASG Papers.

89. Herbert H.D. Peirce to Tiffany & Co., 19 April 1906, reel 6, ASG Papers.

90. *consistency across the medals:* Harrison Morris to ASG, 23 April 1906, reel 6, ASG Papers; *completed on time:* ASG to Morris, 20 April 1906, reel 6, ASG Papers.

91. "A Gold Medal for French Ambassador," *Philadelphia Inquirer,* 21 April 1906, 4.

92. George F. Kunz to ASG, 23 April 1906, reel 6, ASG Papers.

93. ASG to Herbert H.D. Peirce, 25 April 1906, reel 6, ASG Papers.

94. ASG to Harrison Morris, 29 April 1906, reel 6, ASG Papers.

95. Harrison Morris to ASG, 1 May 1906, reel 6, ASG Papers.

96. Herbert H.D. Peirce to ASG, 4 May 1906, reel 6, ASG Papers.

97. Tiffany & Co. to ASG, 1 June 1906, reel 6, ASG Papers.

98. *the State Department:* Harrison Morris to ASG, 2 June 1906, reel 6, ASG Papers; *in February 1907:* Elihu Root to Leslie M. Shaw, 6 February 1907, box 250, Mint Director Letters Received.

Notes

99. *rejected wreath medal:* Tiffany & Co. to ASG, 26 May 1906, reel 6, ASG Papers; *as recently as 2006:* Presidential Coin and Antique Company, *The Benj Fauver Collections*, 15 July 2006, no. 399.
100. ASG to Harrison Morris, 3 May 1906, reel 6, ASG Papers.
101. George F. Kunz to ASG, 26 April 1906, reel 6, ASG Papers.

Chapter 18: Engagement

1. *models such as these:* Saint-Gaudens, *Reminiscences*, 2:22; *friends and guests:* Wilkinson, *The Life and Works of Augustus Saint-Gaudens*, 351; *33-3/4 inches:* ASG Papers, reel 5, Henri Weil to ASG, 14 September 1905.
2. TR to ASG, 6 November 1905, reel 339, TR Papers, quoted in Homer Saint-Gaudens, "Roosevelt and Our Coin Designs," *The Century*, April 1920, 725.
3. 11 November 1905, reel 60, TR Papers, quoted in H. Saint-Gaudens, "Roosevelt and Our Coin Designs," 725.
4. Miscellaneous sketches, reel 38, ASG Papers.
5. Roger Collom, *Coin World*, 28 October 2002, 70. The book was most likely a catalog of the British Museum's collection entitled *Coins of the Ancients*. Gus had purchased a copy of this book from Richard Watson Gilder's brother-in-law in 1885.
6. 14 November 1905, reel 339, TR Papers, quoted in H. Saint-Gaudens, "Roosevelt and Our Coin Designs," 726.
7. TR to H.C. Hoskier, 19 December 1905, reel 326, vol. 29, p. 20, TR Papers.
8. George E. Roberts to John H. Landis, 21 November 1905, vol. 348, Mint Director Correspondence.
9. ASG to TR, 22 November 1905, reel 61, TR Papers, quoted in H. Saint-Gaudens, "Roosevelt and Our Coin Designs," 726–727.
10. ASG to Leslie M. Shaw, 22 November 1905, reel 61, TR Papers, quoted in H. Saint-Gaudens, "Roosevelt and Our Coin Designs," 727.
11. TR to ASG, 24 November 1905, reel 339, TR Papers, quoted in H. Saint-Gaudens, "Roosevelt and Our Coin Designs," 727.
12. *"In God We Trust":* Leslie M. Shaw to TR, 24 November 1905, *The Letters of Theodore Roosevelt*, vol. 4; *". . . if St. Gaudens desires":* TR to Shaw, 27 November 1905, box 45, folder 232, entry 330, record group 104, NC 152, Records of the Bureau of the Mint, National Archives (hereafter cited as Mint Archives).
13. *was getting along:* TR to ASG, 20 December 1905, reel 340, vol. 60, p. 131, TR Papers; *ready in a month:* ASG to TR, 24 December 1905, reel 12, ASG Papers.
14. ASG to H.C. Hoskier, 24 December 1905, reel 8, ASG Papers.
15. *couple or three days:* ASG to Adolph A. Weinman, 2 January 1906, reel 6, ASG Papers; *set eyes upon her:* Weinman to ASG, 1 January 1900, reel 6, ASG Papers; "Reminiscences of an Idiot," reel 36, ASG Papers.
16. ASG to Leslie M. Shaw, 2 January 1906, reel 62, record group 104, folder 232, box 45, TR Papers.
17. Ibid.
18. TR to ASG, 6 January 1906, reel 340, TR Papers, quoted in H. Saint-Gaudens, "Roosevelt and Our Coin Designs," 728.
19. *Indian headdress:* ASG to Adolph A. Weinman, 7 January 1906, reel 6, ASG Papers; *John Flanagan:* Weinman to ASG, 11 January 1906, reel 13, ASG Papers.
20. 9 January 1906, reel 62, TR Papers, qtd. in H. Saint-Gaudens, "Roosevelt and Our Coin Designs," 728.
21. Calendar May 29, 1905–January 16, 1906, ASG LibCong Papers.
22. George E. Roberts to Leslie M. Shaw, 13 January 1906, Mint Archives.
23. Leslie M. Shaw to ASG, 16 January 1906, Mint Archives.
24. *visited Henry Adams:* William Loeb to ASG, 1 February 1906, reel 362, vol. 109, p. 253, TR Papers; *at the White House:* attendance roster for the congressional reception, 1 February 1906, reel 435, TR Papers. This was the last time that Theodore Roosevelt and Augustus Saint-Gaudens saw each other in person; *could not eat:* Olivia Rodham to Elizabeth Dolley, 3 February 1906, reel 34, ASG Papers.
25. *Head of Victory:* S. Morris, *Edith Kermit Roosevelt*, 303; *overcome by the gift:* Edith K. Roosevelt to Augusta and Augustus Saint-Gaudens, 16 February 1906, reel 12, ASG Papers.
26. *too severe for travel:* ASG to John La Farge, 13 June 1906, reel 9, ASG Papers; *a real concern:* note in Augusta Homer Saint-Gaudens's handwriting, n.d., reel 11, ASG Papers; also ASG to Rose Nichols, 29 April 1906, reel 17; *playing some golf:* ASG to J.J. Albright, 28 April 1906, reel 2, ASG Papers.

27. *"auld lang syne"*: Charles Follen McKim to ASG, 13 April 1906, McKim Papers; *a couple of weeks:* McKim to ASG, 20 April 1906, McKim Papers.
28. Stanford White to ASG, 11 May 1906, Richman files, ASG Papers.
29. ASG to Augusta Homer Saint-Gaudens, 26 December 1904, reel 21, ASG Papers.
30. ASG to Leslie M. Shaw, 23 May 1906, Mint Archives.
31. *take it up with Roosevelt:* Leslie M. Shaw to ASG, 25 May 1906, Mint Archives; *give him his head about it:* TR to ASG, 26 May 1906, reel 341, TR Papers, quoted in H. Saint-Gaudens, "Roosevelt and Our Coin Designs," 729.
32. ASG to TR, 29 May 1906, quoted in H. Saint-Gaudens, "Roosevelt and Our Coin Designs," 729.
33. *$20 gold coin:* George E. Roberts to ASG, 29 May 1906, box 244, Mint Director Letters Received; *letter of introduction:* ASG to the Mint, 10 May 1906, record group 104, series II, entry 628, U.S. Mint Documents: New Designs for Eagle and Double Eagle, 1906–1909, G-12-08-03-1, box 71, Philadelphia Regional Archives (hereafter cited as Mint Documents: Eagle).
34. *to year's end:* Homer Saint-Gaudens to Charles S. Dolley, 27 June 1906, reel 35, ASG Papers; *denial or concealment:* Low, *A Chronicle of Friendships*, 506.
35. *small-sized cent:* ASG to George E. Roberts, 16 June 1906, Mint Archives; *the old design:* Roberts to ASG, 20 June 1906, Mint Archives.
36. TR to ASG, 22 June 1906, reel 62, TR Papers, quoted in H. Saint-Gaudens, "Roosevelt and Our Coin Designs," 729.
37. ASG to TR, 28 June 1906, reel 62, TR Papers, quoted in H. Saint-Gaudens, "Roosevelt and Our Coin Designs," 730.
38. *". . . would settle it":* ASG to Richard Watson Gilder, n.d., Gilder Papers; *the* Century: TR to Gilder, 26 May 1906, reel 341, vol. 64, p. 128, TR Papers.
39. Janvier et Duval to ASG, 29 June 1906, reel 8, ASG Papers.
40. *Gus's support too:* Charles Follen McKim to ASG, 11 July 1906, McKim Papers; *what to say:* Baker, *Stanny*, 380.
41. Saint-Gaudens, *Reminiscences*, 2:252.
42. *days at a time:* Saint-Gaudens, *Reminiscences*, 2:246; *slowness of his recovery:* Charles Follen McKim to ASG, 19 July 1906, McKim Papers; *dying by inches:* Carlota Dolley Saint-Gaudens to Dr. Charles Sumner Dolley, 15 August 1906, reel 23, ASG Papers.
43. Homer Saint-Gaudens to TR, 2 August 1906, reel 66, TR Papers.
44. *March, in 1907:* TR to ASG, 6 August 1906, quoted in H. Saint-Gaudens, "Roosevelt and Our Coin Designs," 730; *could not stand the shock:* Homer Saint-Gaudens to Dr. Margaret Abigail Cleaves, 26 September 1906, reel 4, ASG Papers.
45. *met with the president:* H. Saint-Gaudens, "Roosevelt and Our Coin Designs," 732; TR to ASG, 1 October 1906, reel 343, TR Papers; *in New York City:* ASG to Homer Saint-Gaudens, 8 May 1906, reel 22, ASG Papers.
46. *a writer in the process:* Homer Saint-Gaudens to Charles S. Dolley, 15 and 22 May 1906, reel 35, ASG Papers; *a clear indication:* White House diary, 10 September 1906, reel 430, TR Papers.
47. TR to Leslie M. Shaw, 11 September 1906, reel 342, vol. 66, p. 382, TR Papers.
48. *on September 25:* Leslie M. Shaw to C.H. Keep, 18 September 1906, Mint Archives; *to Oyster Bay:* George E. Roberts to John H. Landis, 24 September 1906, Mint Archives; Keep to Leslie M. Shaw, 26 September 1906, vol. 356, Mint Director Correspondence.
49. George E. Roberts to Leslie M. Shaw, 26 September 1906, Mint Archives.
50. *40 years old:* Hering, "History of the $10 and $20 Gold Coins," 456. The machine had been acquired in September 1867 from William Wyon in London, who had purchased all rights to the machine the year before from C.J. Hill for its use in his family's medallic business; *difficult to find:* Charles E. Barber to John H. Landis, 11 April 1904, box 212, Mint Director Letters Received.
51. *delivery in nine months:* Charles E. Barber to John H. Landis, 25 September 1906, box 245, Mint Director Letters Received; *had been unsatisfactory:* Barber to Landis, 13 June 1906, box 245, Mint Director Letters Received; *in June 1906:* George E. Roberts to Landis, 25 June 1906, Mint Archives.
52. Charles E. Barber to George E. Roberts, 5 October 1906, box 248, Mint Director Letters Received.
53. TR to ASG, 1 October 1906, reel 343, TR Papers, quoted in H. Saint-Gaudens, "Roosevelt and Our Coin Designs," 732.
54. ASG to Adolph A. Weinman, 8 March 1905, reel 14, ASG Papers.
55. Homer Saint-Gaudens to TR, 6 October 1906, ASG LibCong Papers.

Notes

56. TR to George E. Roberts, 10 October 1906, reel 343, vol. 67, p. 240, TR Papers.
57. *to show what it could do:* Charles E. Barber to John H. Landis, 8 October 1906, box 248, Mint Director Letters Received; *the purchase be expedited:* William Loeb to George E. Roberts, 9 October 1906, vol. 357, Mint Director Correspondence; *at Deitsch Brothers:* Roberts to Barber, 9 October 1906, vol. 357, Mint Director Correspondence.
58. George E. Roberts to ASG, 10 October 1906, Mint Archives.
59. ASG per Homer Saint-Gaudens to George E. Roberts, 6 October 1906, Mint Archives.
60. *this new treatment:* Augusta Saint-Gaudens to Charles Freer, 18 October 1906, reel 7, ASG Papers; *to cross Mrs. Saint-Gaudens:* Elizabeth Dolley to Dr. Charles Sumner Dolley, 16 October 1906, reel 30, ASG Papers.
61. *considering layoffs:* Augusta Homer Saint-Gaudens to Homer Saint-Gaudens, 14 October 1906, reel 23, ASG Papers; *spending it all on assistants:* Louis Saint-Gaudens to Annette Saint-Gaudens, 8 June 1901, reel 25, ASG Papers; *one of Gus's clients:* Augusta Saint-Gaudens to Charles Freer, 18 October 1906, reel 7, ASG Papers. The moneys were advanced by Charles Freer.
62. *model for the other side:* Charles E. Barber to George E. Roberts, 6 November 1906, box 248, Mint Director Letters Received; *waiting for the other model:* Robert E. Preston to Roberts, 7 November 1906, Mint Archives; *$20 gold piece:* Leslie M. Shaw to ASG, 10 November 1906, Mint Archives.
63. Homer Saint-Gaudens to Leslie M. Shaw, 14 November 1906, Mint Archives.
64. Charles E. Barber to John H. Landis, 26 November 1906, Mint Archives.
65. Homer Saint-Gaudens to Leslie M. Shaw, 21 November 1906, Mint Archives.
66. Charles E. Barber to Robert E. Preston, 26 November 1906, Mint Archives.
67. *the $20 gold piece:* Report of Destruction of Dies and Hubs, 24 May 1910, box 290, Mint Director Letters Received; *the Saint-Gaudens designs:* Charles E. Barber to George E. Roberts, 5 October 1906, box 228, Mint Director Letters Received.
68. Judd, *United States Pattern Coins,* 268.
69. George E. Roberts to George F. Kunz, 28 November 1906, Mint Archives. The Mint director also asked if Kunz would like to serve as a member on the annual Assay Commission that would meet the next February.
70. Charles E. Barber to George E. Roberts, 30 November 1906, box 250, Mint Director Letters Received.
71. *the standing eagle:* George E. Roberts to ASG, 28 November 1906, vol. 357, Mint Director Correspondence; *this lead impression:* John H. Landis to Roberts, 26 November 1906, box 249, Mint Director Letters Received.
72. ASG to George E. Roberts, 8 December 1906, Mint Documents: Eagle.
73. George E. Roberts to Homer Saint-Gaudens, 11 December 1906, vol. 357, Mint Director Correspondence.
74. Charles E. Barber to George E. Roberts, 12 December 1906, box 249, Mint Director Letters Received.
75. Charles E. Barber to George E. Roberts, 11 December 1906, box 249, Mint Director Letters Received.
76. TR to ASG, 11 December 1906, reel 344, TR Papers, quoted in H. Saint-Gaudens, "Roosevelt and Our Coin Designs," 732.
77. C. Moore, *Daniel H. Burnham,* 2:13. Three days later an old friend came to Cornish. There was snow on the ground. Augusta took the sleigh to pick Daniel Burnham up at a hotel in Windsor that morning. McKim had written in November that reports of Gus's condition were less and less hopeful. Augusta had written McKim that the sculptor spent much of his time in bed. Just before noon that day Burnham said goodbye to Gus and left for the train station. Burnham did not record in his diary his impressions of the visit.
78. ASG to TR, quoted in H. Saint-Gaudens, "Roosevelt and Our Coin Designs," 732.
79. TR to ASG, 20 December 1906, reel 344, TR Papers, quoted in H. Saint-Gaudens, "Roosevelt and Our Coin Designs," 732.
80. George E. Roberts to TR, 27 December 1906, vol. 357, Mint Director Correspondence.

Chapter 19: An End of Sorts

1. Tharp, *Saint-Gaudens and the Gilded Era,* 363.
2. TR to George E. Roberts, 26 December 1906, reel 344, vol. 69, p. 282, TR Papers.
3. *on December 6:* William Howard Taft to Leslie M. Shaw, 6 December 1906, box 249, Mint Director Letters Received; *about six weeks:* George E. Roberts to TR, 27 December 1906, vol. 357, Mint Director Correspondence.

Striking Change

4. George E. Roberts to John Landis, 27 December 1906, Mint Documents: Eagle.
5. Charles E. Barber to John H. Landis, 28 December 1906, Mint Archives.
6. *casts of these reductions:* Charles Deitsch to John H. Landis, 8 August 1907, box 256, Mint Director Letters Received; *the machine and its capabilities:* Charles E. Barber to George E. Roberts, 25 March 1907, box 251, Mint Director Letters Received.
7. Frank A. Leach to George E. Roberts, 4 January 1907, box 251, Mint Director Letters Received.
8. George E. Roberts to William Loeb, 6 February 1907, vol. 367, Mint Director Correspondence.
9. Hering, "History of the $10 and $20 Gold Coins," 455.
10. Minutes for New York Numismatic Club meeting of 14 December 1934, *The Numismatist* 48, no. 2 (February 1935): 103–106.
11. George E. Roberts to William Loeb, 8 February 1907, Mint Archives.
12. *on the gold planchet:* Charles E. Barber to John Landis, 4 May 1907, Mint Documents: Eagle; *details of the die emerged:* Hering, "History of the $10 and $20 Gold Coins," 455–456. In Hering's narrative, he recalls that nine blows were required. However, in a letter written to George Roberts from ASG on February 21, 1907, Saint-Gaudens states that seven blows were required. On the basis that Saint-Gaudens's letter is concurrent to the event, I am assuming his count is accurate.
13. Leach, *Recollections of a Newspaper Man,* 374.
14. *beauty to the figure:* Saint-Gaudens, *Reminiscences,* 2:21–22; *feeling of motion:* ibid.
15. *encircled the coin's rim:* Oklahoma would be admitted later in the year, bringing the total number of states to 46; *". . . edge to edge of the frame":* quoted in Saint-Gaudens, *Reminiscences,* 2:23.
16. Judd, *United States Pattern Coins,* 270.
17. *too much for the gods:* Saint-Gaudens, *Reminiscences,* 2:24; *what was meant to be:* ibid., 2:23. Was it really? Some speculation is called for here. On both the obverse and reverse of the first design for the World's Fair medal, Saint-Gaudens's figures are not in full frontal position. In both instances the left leg of the figure is angled or cocked at an awkward angle. The same is true, only much less so, with the nude figure on the reverse of the Franklin medal. One can speculate that this was Saint-Gaudens's modeling blind spot. The obvious way to avoid it would be to design the figure full frontal with a liberal use of drapery.
18. J. Hewitt Judd, *United States Pattern, Experimental, and Trial Pieces,* 5th ed. (Racine, WI: Western Publishing, 1974), 213. The total number struck was 13.
19. ASG to George E. Roberts, 21 February 1907, Mint Documents: Eagle.
20. Charles E. Barber to John Landis, 25 February 1907, Mint Documents: Eagle.
21. *pieces to Philadelphia:* ASG to John Landis, 13 March 1907, Mint Documents: Eagle; *Theodore Roosevelt:* Hering, "History of the $10 and $20 Gold Coins," 456.
22. George E. Roberts to John H. Landis, 4 March 1907, vol. 366, Mint Director Correspondence.
23. *second model would be needed:* ASG to George E. Roberts, 24 February 1907, Mint Archives; *better withstand abrasion:* Roberts to ASG, 26 February 1907, Mint Archives. While all of the efforts to date from the Mint's standpoint were of an experimental nature to establish the limits of high relief, there is evidence that someone in the Saint-Gaudens camp did not consider it so. With the completion of the first set of models, a bill, likely sent by Gussie (as she and the family attorney were taking over the sculptor's financial affairs) went to George Roberts. Then, with the results of the test striking in hand, Saint-Gaudens asked that Roberts hold the bill in abeyance; *placed in circulation:* Roberts to John H. Landis, 23 February 1907, vol. 366, Mint Director Correspondence.
24. *Monsieur Janvier in Paris:* ASG to George E. Roberts, 12 March 1907, Mint Archives; *with harder models:* ibid.
25. A.A. Norris to George E. Roberts, 16 February 1907, box 251, Mint Director Letters Received.
26. Charles E. Barber to John H. Landis, 20 February 1907, Mint Archives.
27. *his original models:* ASG to George E. Roberts, 24 February 1907, Mint Archives; *Landis complied:* John H. Landis to Roberts, 26 February 1907, box 251, Mint Director Letters Received.
28. *Henri Weil:* Charles E. Barber to John H. Landis, 8 April 1905, box 248, Mint Director Letters Received; George E. Roberts to Barber, 8 April 1905, vol. 366, Mint Director Correspondence; *the reducing machine:* Barber to Roberts, 25 March 1907, box 251, Mint Director Letters Received. Barber had taken the step of having Henri Weil do the reduction to avoid any such complaint as had arisen from Saint-Gaudens. Now Saint-Gaudens had sent him another plaster cast from the same mold as the original cast for the first model to show him the difference between one that had had stearine applied and one that had not. Barber in turn applied stearine to the second cast with the intent of returning it to Saint-Gaudens so that the sculptor could see that stearine was not the

cause of the injury to the plaster cast. Had Barber known the issues that had arisen with the Franklin medal, he might not have extolled Weil's virtues so strongly. Weil had certainly done an adequate job of the obverse bust of Franklin. However, he had fallen down when faced with the intricate reverse details. In terms of difficulty, the gold-coin design was much closer to the Franklin medal reverse.

29. *New York Times*, 4 March 1907, 2; Edmund Morris, *Theodore Rex* (New York: Random House, 2001), 327. He was to become president of Carnegie Trust in New York City, though it was widely understood that he had presidential ambitions in 1908.
30. George E. Roberts to William Loeb, 8 February 1907, Mint Archives.
31. *the best Greek coins:* Witter Bynner, *Selected Letters*, edited by James Kraft (New York: Farrar Straus Giroux, 1981), 14–18; *on February 5:* ASG to TR, 5 February 1907, reel 12, ASG Papers; *Gus was resistant:* H. Saint-Gaudens, "Roosevelt and Our Coin Designs," 733.
32. TR to ASG, 8 February 1907, reel 344, TR Papers.
33. *the utmost dispatch:* ASG to TR, 11 February 1907, quoted in H. Saint-Gaudens, "Roosevelt and Our Coin Designs," 733; *decision to Roosevelt:* note, n.d., reel 13, ASG Papers.
34. In 1911 Homer Saint-Gaudens had run into difficulties with *The Reminiscences of Augustus Saint-Gaudens.* He had the structure pretty well built but little or none of the finished work. He turned to Witter Bynner for help. In his self-deprecating way, Bynner said he played the role of literary interior decorator in each of the book's 25 chambers (Bynner, *Selected Letters*, 35).
35. Bynner, *Selected Letters*, 14–18.
36. Note in Augusta Saint-Gaudens's handwriting, n.d., reel 11, ASG Papers.
37. TR to ASG, 18 February 1907, reel 344, TR Papers, quoted in H. Saint-Gaudens, "Roosevelt and Our Coin Designs," 733.
38. *The Letters of Archie Butt*, 355–356.
39. Ibid.
40. George E. Roberts to ASG, 8 March 1907, vol. 367, Mint Director Correspondence.
41. George E. Roberts to William Loeb, 1 March 1907, vol. 367, Mint Director Correspondence.
42. H. Saint-Gaudens, "Roosevelt and Our Coin Designs," 733.
43. ASG to TR, 12 March 1907, reel 11, ASG LibCong Papers, quoted in H. Saint-Gaudens, "Roosevelt and Our Coin Designs," 733–734.
44. TR to ASG, 14 March 1907, reel 345, TR Papers, quoted in H. Saint-Gaudens, "Roosevelt and Our Coin Designs," 734.
45. *Gus's condition:* Saint-Gaudens, *Reminiscences*, 2:246; *into his work:* notes in Augusta Saint-Gaudens's handwriting, n.d., reel 11, ASG Papers; *mystery of death:* ASG to Helen F. Mears, 16 March 1900, reel 2, ASG Papers.
46. Witter Bynner to Barry Faulkner, 27 July 1907, Witter Bynner Letters, Houghton Library, bMS AM 1891 (266), and ASG Papers, reel 36.
47. *the result was impressive:* Charles E. Barber to George E. Roberts, 25 March 1907, box 251, Mint Director Letters Received; *the rising sun:* Charles Barber personal notebooks, "Coins and Patterns Barber Owned," American Numismatic Association Library. This pattern coin somehow subsequently ended up in Charles Barber's possession.
48. George E. Roberts to ASG, 26 March 1907, vol. 367, Mint Director Correspondence; George E. Roberts to Charles E. Barber, 23 March 1907, Mint Archives.
49. *happy with his cast:* ASG to John Landis, 11 April 1907, Mint Documents: Eagle; *better of the two:* George E. Roberts to John H. Landis, 23 March 1907, Mint Archives; *reducing lathe:* Roberts to ASG, 26 March 1907, vol. 367, Mint Director Correspondence.
50. *Saturday, March 22:* George B. Cortelyou to William Loeb, 23 March 1907, Mint Archives; *to make bronze casts:* George E. Roberts to ASG, 25 March 1907, Mint Archives; *all possible expedition:* Cortelyou to Loeb, 23 March 1907, Mint Archives.
51. *would not be necessary:* George E. Roberts to ASG, 26 March 1907, vol. 367, Mint Director Correspondence; *Saint-Gaudens's bronze casting:* ASG to John H. Landis, 12 April 1907, box 252, Mint Director Letters Received; *the hubs in process:* Roberts to ASG, 12 April 1907, vol. 367, Mint Director Correspondence. Someone within the Saint-Gaudens camp again presented a bill for payment; *working day and night:* A.A. Norris to Roberts, 13 April 1907, box 252, Mint Director Letters Received.
52. Hering, "History of the $10 and $20 Gold Coins," 455.
53. *experience in the matter:* British Museum Dept. of Coins and Medals to George E. Roberts, 8 April 1907, Mint Archives; *striking high relief:* George E. Roberts to M.A. Arnauné, 29 April 1907, Mint

Archives; *about to occur:* Arnauné to Roberts, 2 July 1907, Mint Archives. The French had a different take on the situation. Their engravers sought the highest relief possible that could be obtained with one blow of the coin press, giving consideration that die wear not be excessive. They encountered no difficulties from stacking, abrasive wear, or buildup of dirt in the recesses of the coin. They raised only one point in opposition to the Saint-Gaudens design. A full face was difficult to strike sufficiently to bring up the tip of the nose. This tip then became the high point and the coin would take on a bad appearance when wear obliterated the nose. As a result, the French expressed a preference for faces in profile. The breadth of the face in profile tended to retain its essential design elements even with heavy wear.

54. Frank A. Leach to George E. Roberts, 22 April 1907, Mint Archives.
55. Dr. John Brewster to Augusta Homer Saint-Gaudens, 3 May 1907, reel 2, ASG Papers; ASG to Charles Deering and Charles Deering to ASG, 3 May 1907, reel 5, ASG Papers.
56. *rest in Richmond:* Charles O. Brewster to Homer Saint-Gaudens, 2 May 1907, reel 8, ASG Papers; *required in her absence:* Tharp, *Saint-Gaudens and the Gilded Era,* 359; *brought on this tragedy:* Bynner, *Selected Letters,* 15.
57. Charles E. Barber to John H. Landis, 4 May 1907, Mint Archives.
58. *for Roberts's inspection:* A.A. Norris to George E. Roberts, 4 May 1907, box 253, Mint Director Letters Received; *personnel were ready:* William Loeb to George B. Cortelyou, 6 May 1907, Mint Archives.
59. George E. Roberts to ASG, 7 May 1907, vol. 367, Mint Director Correspondence.
60. TR to ASG, 8 May 1907, reel 345, TR Papers, quoted in H. Saint-Gaudens, "Roosevelt and Our Coin Designs," 734.
61. Augusta Saint-Gaudens to George E. Roberts, 13 May 1907, box 254, Mint Director Letters Received.
62. ASG to TR, 11 May 1907, quoted in H. Saint-Gaudens, "Roosevelt and Our Coin Designs," 734–735.
63. TR to ASG, 12 May 1907, quoted in H. Saint-Gaudens, "Roosevelt and Our Coin Designs," 735.
64. John H. Landis to George E. Roberts, 9 May 1907, Mint Archives.
65. George E. Roberts to George F. Kunz, 14 May 1907, Mint Archives.
66. *reduction of the standing Liberty:* ASG to John Landis, 22 May 1907, Mint Documents: Eagle; *a full progress report:* ASG to TR, 12 May 1907, reel 12, ASG Papers.
67. ASG to TR, 23 May 1907, reel 74, TR Papers, quoted in H. Saint-Gaudens, "Roosevelt and Our Coin Designs," 735–736.
68. George E. Roberts to John H. Landis, 7 February 1907, Mint Archives.
69. Report on Destruction of Hubs and Dies, 24 May 1910, box 290, Mint Director Letters Received.
70. George E. Roberts to ASG, 25 May 1907, Mint Archives.
71. George E. Roberts to Robert E. Preston, 12 August 1907, Mint Archives. The whereabouts of this letter are unknown.
72. *forwarded it to Saint-Gaudens:* ASG to John Landis, 31 May 1907, Mint Documents: Eagle; *the Janvier lathe:* Charles E. Barber to Landis, 27 May 1907, Mint Documents: Eagle.
73. *went into decline:* Dr. John D. Brewster to Dr. Charles Sumner Dolley, 5 July 1907, reel 29, ASG Papers; *starting on July 15:* George E. Roberts to John H. Landis, 18 June 1907, vol. 366, Mint Director Correspondence.
74. *confined to his bed:* Saint-Gaudens, *Reminiscences,* 2:246; *see how he could last:* Carlota Dolley Saint-Gaudens to Dr. Charles Sumner Dolley, 9 July 1907, reel 26, ASG Papers.
75. *director of the Mint:* George E. Roberts to TR, 8 July 1907, vol. 367, Mint Director Correspondence; *Commercial National Bank in Chicago:* George B. Cortelyou to TR, 9 July 1907, reel 75, TR Papers; *in St. Louis in 1902:* "Fort Dodge Men Refuse Big Salaries," *Fort Dodge Messenger,* 5 March 1902.
76. *the president's desk:* J.B. Reynolds to Henry A. Buchtel, 14 June 1907, box 255, Mint Director Letters Received; *that removed the man:* George E. Roberts to J.B. Baldwin, 1 July 1907, vol. 367, Mint Director Correspondence.
77. *felt it personally as well:* TR to George E. Roberts, 11 July 1907, reel 346, TR Papers; *for ready reference:* TR to Roberts, 1 January 1907, reel 344, vol. 69, p. 328, TR Papers; *the 1909 Assay Commission:* TR to George B. Cortelyou, 23 January 1909, reel 353, vol. 90, p. 272, TR Papers.
78. *frequency to Cortelyou:* William Loeb to George B. Cortelyou, 12 July 1907, Mint Archives; ". . . attention to the matter":* Cortelyou to Loeb, 15 July 1907, Mint Archives.

79. Dr. John D. Brewster to Dr. Charles Sumner Dolley, 19 July 1907, reel 29, ASG Papers.
80. George E. Roberts to George B. Cortelyou, 23 July 1907, Mint Archives.
81. George E. Roberts to John Landis, 31 July 1907, Mint Documents: Eagle.
82. Mint Archives. Mint records are murky on this subject. They do not distinguish between the two differing rim-lettering schemes. Frank Leach in a report to the secretary of the Treasury on February 5, 1908, gave the number minted as 13. Six were distributed to Mint Bureau officials and the president. Five were in the hands of Mint officials and two were in the Mint Cabinet. In addition Charles Barber at his death had in his possession eight pieces. Whether any of these were included in the count given here is unknown.
83. *first strikings in February:* Frank A. Leach to John H. Landis, 8 February 1908, vol. 368, Mint Director Correspondence; *intended special striking:* George E. Roberts to Landis, 25 July 1907, Mint Archives.
84. *"property of a gentleman":* "Rare 1907 Gold $20 Pattern Realizes $488,750 Top Price," *Coin World,* 11 April 2005, 3; *almost 90 years:* Efforts to contact direct descendants of George Roberts were not successful.
85. TR to George B. Cortelyou, 29 July 1907, Mint Archives.
86. Witter Bynner to Barry Faulkner, 27 July 1907, reel 36, ASG Papers, and Witter Bynner Letters, bMS AM 1891 (266), Houghton Library.
87. *Augustus Saint-Gaudens:* Dr. Henri Duffy, *A Masque of "Ours" or the Gods and the Golden Bowl,* Friends of the Saint-Gaudens Memorial, Spring 2005, 1–4; *beautiful and impressive:* ASG to James Earle Fraser, 27 June 1905, box 1, J.E. Fraser Papers.
88. Bynner, *Selected Letters,* 80.
89. *the following evening:* Tharp, *Saint-Gaudens and the Gilded Era,* 365; *had spread to his liver:* Dr. John D. Brewster to Dr. Charles Sumner Dolley, 6 August 1907, reel 29, ASG Papers.

Chapter 20: A Cameo in Gold

1. *March 22, 1907:* George B. Cortelyou to William Loeb, 23 March 1907, Mint Archives; *". . . success of the gold coinage":* George E. Roberts to ASG, 25 March 1907, Mint Archives.
2. George E. Roberts to Robert E. Preston, 12 August 1907, Mint Archives.
3. ASG to George E. Roberts, 3 June 1907, Mint Archives.
4. Charles E. Barber to John H. Landis, 7 June 1907, Mint Archives.
5. *details in the design:* George E. Roberts to ASG, 11 June 1907, Mint Archives; *castings were authorized:* Roberts to ASG, 18 June 1907, vol. 367, Mint Director Correspondence; *expected on the 21st:* ASG to Roberts, 20 June 1907, Mint Archives.
6. ASG to George E. Roberts, 24 June 1907, Mint Archives; ASG to Roberts, 25 June 1907, Mint Archives.
7. Saint-Gaudens, *Reminiscences,* 2:24.
8. George E. Roberts to George B. Cortelyou, 22 July 1907, Mint Archives.
9. ASG to George Roberts, 25 July 1907, with handwritten notation by Barber, Mint Documents: Eagle.
10. Hering, "History of the $10 and $20 Gold Coins," 456.
11. ASG to George E. Roberts, 22 July 1907, Mint Archives.
12. *interest in the project:* George E. Roberts to ASG, 22 July 1907, Mint Archives; *cast of the new die:* ASG to George E. Roberts, 25 July 1907, Mint Archives.
13. TR to George B. Cortelyou, 29 July 1907, Mint Archives.
14. TR to George B. Cortelyou, 7 August 1907, quoted in Taxay, *The U. S. Mint and Coinage,* 315.
15. A.A. Norris to Robert E. Preston, 14 August 1907, box 256, Mint Director Letters Received.
16. Charles E. Barber to John H. Landis, 26 August 1907, Mint Archives.
17. Robert E. Preston to John H. Landis, 27 August 1907, vol. 366, Mint Director Correspondence.
18. Augusta Saint-Gaudens to Robert E. Preston, 27 August 1907, Mint Archives.
19. Robert E. Preston to Augusta Saint-Gaudens, 5 September 1907, vol. 367, Mint Director Correspondence.
20. *relief was now coinable:* Robert E. Preston to John H. Landis, 27 August 1907, Mint Documents: Eagle; *as soon as possible:* Preston to Landis, 30 August 1907, vol. 366, Mint Director Correspondence.
21. *necessary for die preparation:* ibid.; *the estate by Norris:* Albert A. Norris to Augusta Homer Saint-Gaudens, 29 August 1907, reel 41, estate letter register, ASG Papers.
22. *struck on the medal press:* Robert E. Preston to John H. Landis, 30 August 1907, vol. 366, Mint Director Correspondence; *should that request materialize:* Preston to A.A. Norris, 30 August 1907, Mint Documents: Eagle; *a wire rim would be struck:* Mint Archives. This figure is drawn from a

report by Frank Leach to the secretary of the Treasury on February 5, 1908. Five hundred were reported to have been distributed generally. Mint Bureau personnel and Assistant Treasury Secretary Edwards retained twenty-nine. Mint officials in Philadelphia kept eight. Two coins went to the Mint cabinet, and two coins went to the Metropolitan Museum's Saint-Gaudens exhibition. The remaining coin was sent to an individual in Connecticut.

23. Robert E. Preston to John H. Landis, 27 August 1907, Mint Documents: Eagle.

24. *gold piece to commence:* Robert E. Preston to John H. Landis, 9 September 1907, Mint Documents: Eagle; *produced on the medal press:* Landis to Preston, 25 September 1907, box 257, Mint Director Letters Received; *halted on the 18th:* Preston to Landis, 18 September 1907, vol. 366, Mint Director Correspondence; *continued striking unnecessary:* Preston to Landis, 18 September 1907, Mint Documents: Eagle.

25. A.A. Norris to Augusta Saint-Gaudens, 28 September 1907, box 257, Mint Director Letters Received.

26. *released into circulation:* John H. Landis to Robert E. Preston, 25 September 1907, box 257, Mint Director Letters Received; *signed off October 3:* Preston to Landis, 3 October 1907, vol. 366, Mint Director Correspondence.

27. Mint Archives. This figure is drawn from a report by Frank Leach to the secretary of the Treasury on February 5, 1908. A total of 31,450 pieces were reported as melted. Ten pieces were in the hands of Mint Bureau personnel. Mint officials in Philadelphia retained eight pieces. Two pieces were in the Metropolitan Museum's Saint-Gaudens exhibition, and thirty pieces remained on hand. The report is silent on the fifty pieces authorized to be struck on the medal press.

28. *and administration officials:* Frank A. Leach to John H. Landis, 14 December 1907, vol. 366, Mint Director Correspondence; *before he died:* Robert E. Preston to A.A. Norris, 25 November 1907, Mint Documents: Eagle.

Chapter 21: A Man for the Occasion

1. Leach, *Recollections of a Newspaper Man*, 373.

2. "*. . . a drastic character*": ibid., 375; *blaze of heat:* Wister, *Roosevelt: A Story of a Friendship*, 47.

3. TR to Augusta Saint-Gaudens, 5 August 1907, reel 345, TR Papers.

4. Edith Kermit Roosevelt to Augusta Saint-Gaudens, 7 August 1907, reel 16, ASG Papers.

5. George E. Roberts to George B. Cortelyou, 31 July 1907, Mint Archives.

6. *finished immediately:* TR to George B. Cortelyou, 7 August 1907, quoted in Taxay, *The U.S. Mint and Coinage*, 315; *the work expedited:* Cortelyou to [indecipherable] Weaver, 9 August 1907, Mint Archives.

7. George E. Roberts to Robert E. Preston, 9 August 1907, Mint Archives.

8. A.A. Norris to Robert E. Preston, 14 August 1907, box 256, Mint Director Letters Received.

9. Charles E. Barber to John H. Landis, 14 August 1907, box 256, Mint Director Letters Received.

10. A.A. Norris to Robert E. Preston, 14 August 1907, Mint Archives.

11. *the third $20 coin model:* Robert E. Preston to John H. Landis, 15 August 1907, vol. 366, Mint Director Correspondence; *the $20 gold coin:* Homer Saint-Gaudens to A.A. Norris, 16 August 1907, Mint Documents: Eagle; *ready in one month:* Robert E. Preston to Homer Saint-Gaudens, 19 August 1907, reel 41, estate letter register, ASG Papers.

12. Homer Saint-Gaudens to Robert E. Preston, 20 August 1907, Mint Documents: Eagle.

13. TR to George B. Cortelyou, 22 August 1907, Mint Archives; reel 346, TR Papers.

14. William D. Sohier to TR, 23 August 1907, Mint Archives.

15. *supervise the new coinage:* TR to George B. Cortelyou, 24 August 1907, reel 346, TR Papers; *he would get the coins:* TR to William D. Sohier, 24 August 1907, reel 346, vol. 74, p. 468, TR Papers.

16. Robert E. Preston to John H. Landis, 27 August 1907, vol. 366, Mint Director Correspondence. This is the same order that authorized 500 $10 gold pieces from the first Saint-Gaudens model.

17. *had proved satisfactory:* Albert A. Norris to Augusta Homer Saint-Gaudens, 29 August 1907, reel 41, estate letter register, ASG Papers; *dies could be made:* Charles E. Barber to John Landis, 27 August 1907, Mint Documents: Eagle.

18. *estate by Norris:* Albert A. Norris to Augusta Homer Saint-Gaudens, 29 August 1907, reel 41, estate letter register, ASG Papers; *Assistant Treasury Secretary Edwards:* John H. Landis to Robert E. Preston, 9 September 1907, Mint Archives.

19. Robert E. Preston to John Landis, 18 September 1907, Mint Documents: Eagle.

20. Augusta Saint-Gaudens to Robert E. Preston, 11 September 1907, box 257, Mint Director Letters Received.

Notes

21. *surprised at this rejection:* Hering, "History of the $10 and $20 Gold Coins," 456; *the following Monday:* A.A. Norris to Robert E. Preston, 28 September 1907, box 257, Mint Director Letters Received.
22. Robert E. Preston to John Landis, 8 October 1907, Mint Documents: Eagle.
23. Charles E. Barber to John H. Landis, 10 October 1907, box 258, Mint Director Letters Received.
24. A.A. Norris to Augusta Saint-Gaudens, 30 October 1907, box 258, Mint Director Letters Received.
25. *one blow from the press:* Charles E. Barber to John H. Landis, 22 October 1907, Mint Archives; *an immediate trip to Washington:* A.A. Norris to Robert E. Preston, 23 October 1907, vol. 366, Mint Director Correspondence.
26. Rhine R. Freed to John Landis, 22 October 1907, Mint Documents: Eagle.
27. Charles E. Barber to John H. Landis, 25 October 1907, box 258, Mint Director Letters Received.
28. *had been dropped:* Augusta Saint-Gaudens to Robert E. Preston, 25 October 1907, Mint Archives; *too great a relief:* Preston to Augusta Saint-Gaudens, 29 October 1907, Mint Archives; *a fourth model:* John H. Landis to Augusta Saint-Gaudens, 30 October 1907, box 258, Mint Director Letters Received.
29. Robert E. Preston to John H. Landis, 31 October 1907, vol. 366, Mint Director Correspondence.
30. Robert E. Preston to Augusta Saint-Gaudens, 29 October 1907, vol. 367, Mint Director Correspondence.
31. *$20 gold-piece design:* Charles O. Brewster to Augusta Homer Saint-Gaudens, 19 November 1907, reel 3, ASG Papers; *would also be present:* entries from Register of Charles O. Brewster, reel 40, estate Augustus Saint-Gaudens, ASG Papers; *until November 14:* Frank A. Leach to Charles O. Brewster, 11 November 1907, vol. 367, Mint Director Correspondence.
32. Frank A. Leach to Charles O. Brewster, 16 November 1907, vol. 367, Mint Director Correspondence; Charles O. Brewster to Frank A. Leach, 15 November 1907, box 259, Mint Director Letters Received.
33. *a fourth medal:* ibid.; *good impression of Leach:* Charles O. Brewster to Augusta Homer Saint-Gaudens, 3 December 1907, reel 3, ASG Papers.
34. Frank A. Leach to Charles O. Brewster (two letters), 16 November 1907, vol. 367, Mint Director Correspondence.
35. Estate payroll journal, 5 September 1907, p. 29, and 17 October 1907, p. 48, reel 41, ASG Papers.
36. Charles O. Brewster to Frank A. Leach, 19 November 1907, box 259, Mint Director Letters Received.
37. *at once if possible:* William Loeb to George B. Cortelyou, 20 November 1907, Mint Archives; *the preceding day:* George B. Cortelyou to William Loeb, Mint Archives.
38. Roosevelt had lost a large part of his inheritance in a cattle-ranching venture in the Dakota Territory in the mid-1880s. The industry had overexpanded, and it collapsed when the blizzard of 1887 hit. When he returned east permanently after his marriage to Edith, she controlled the family finances totally. She would give him a daily allowance of $20 in the morning, and he would return home at night unable to tell her where it had been spent.
39. "All Records Broken in the Making of Money," *New York Times,* 24 November 1907, 2.
40. Leach, *Recollections of a Newspaper Man,* 287–289.
41. *after the fire:* ibid., 323; *the city's financial infrastructure:* ibid., 336–339.
42. *Leach as his successor:* George E. Roberts to George B. Cortelyou, 9 July 1907, box 19, George B. Cortelyou Papers; *came the next day:* Cortelyou to TR, 9 July 1907, reel 75, TR Papers; *a special ability:* Roberts to Cortelyou, 8 July 1907, and Cortelyou to TR, 9 July 1907, box 19, George B. Cortelyou Papers.
43. "All Records Broken in the Making of Money," *New York Times,* 24 November 1907, 2.
44. Frank A. Leach to John H. Landis, 22 November 1907, vol. 366, Mint Director Correspondence.
45. Frank A. Leach to Charles O. Brewster, 23 November 1907, vol. 367, Mint Director Correspondence.
46. Charles O. Brewster to Frank A. Leach, 25 November 1907, box 259, Mint Director Letters Received.
47. *Henry Hering again:* Frank A. Leach to Charles O. Brewster, 27 November 1907, vol. 367, Mint Director Correspondence; *immediately for Philadelphia:* Frank A. Leach to Charles O. Brewster, 2 December 1907, vol. 367, Mint Director Correspondence.
48. Charles E. Barber to Frank A. Leach, 23 November 1907, box 259, Mint Director Letters Received.
49. *On December 2:* Frank A. Leach to Charles O. Brewster, 2 December 1907, vol. 366, Mint Director Correspondence; *nonetheless "delighted":* Leach, *Recollections of a Newspaper Man,* 376.
50. Report of Charles E. Barber, 24 May 1910, box 290, Mint Director Letters Received.
51. Frank A. Leach to Charles O. Brewster, 2 December 1907, vol. 367, Mint Director Correspondence.
52. *for general circulation:* Charles O. Brewster to Augusta Homer Saint-Gaudens, 3 December 1907, reel 3, ASG Papers; *for work completed:* Charles O. Brewster to Augusta Homer Saint-Gaudens, 29 November and 2 December 1907, reel 3, ASG Papers.

53. Frank A. Leach to Charles O. Brewster, 6 December 1907, vol. 366, Mint Director Correspondence.
54. Frank A. Leach to John Landis, 21 December 1907, vol. 366, Mint Director Correspondence.
55. Charles E. Barber to Frank A. Leach, 20 December 1907, box 260, Mint Director Letters Received.
56. Homer Saint-Gaudens to Richard Watson Gilder, 7 December 1907, reel 24, ASG Papers.
57. *Holmes wanted one:* William Loeb Jr. to Frank A. Leach, 30 November 1907, Mint Documents: Eagle; *example of the first model:* William E. Curtis to Leach, 17 February 1908, Mint Documents: Eagle; *World's Fair days wanted one:* O.C. Bosbyshell to A.A. Norris, 10 December 1907, Mint Documents: Eagle.
58. *11,000 to 12,000:* Mint Archives. Frank Leach in a report to the secretary of the Treasury on February 5, 1908, gave the number minted as 12,153. However, the coiner at Philadelphia in a letter written on July 13, 1908, gave the number as 11,250; *$20 gold pieces:* Leach to John H. Landis, 14 December 1907, vol. 366, Mint Director Correspondence; *from $5 to $15:* "Side Notes on the New Double Eagle," *The Numismatist,* January 1908, 10–11.
59. Frank A. Leach to John H. Landis, 2 December 1907, vol. 366, Mint Director Correspondence.
60. *from the second model:* ibid.; *and wanted more:* Frank A. Leach to John H. Landis, 23 December 1907, vol. 366, Mint Director Correspondence.
61. Frank A. Leach to John H. Landis, 10 December 1907, vol. 366, Mint Director Correspondence.
62. *from the third model:* A.A. Norris to Leach, 9 December 1907, box 259, Mint Director Letters Received. There was also the issue of whether this design was to be used on the smaller gold coins. If so, there was a problem of space constraints for the denomination on the quarter eagle. In addition, applying the motto E PLURIBUS UNUM on the rim of this thinner coin posed a problem; *all necessary dies:* Leach to Landis, 10 December 1907, vol. 366, Mint Director Correspondence.
63. Charles O. Brewster to Augusta Homer Saint-Gaudens, 7 December 1907, reel 3, ASG Papers. Brewster apparently had little respect for Hering. When Gussie asked for more high-relief $20 gold pieces in this same timeframe, Brewster sought her assurance that none of these coins would end up in Hering's hands to give to his friends.
64. Henry Hering to Charles O. Brewster, 5 December 1907, box 260, Mint Director Letters Received.
65. *at least temporarily:* Frank A. Leach to Charles O. Brewster, 17 December 1907, vol. 367, Mint Director Correspondence; *model to Augusta:* Charles O. Brewster to Frank A. Leach, 18 December 1907, box 260, Mint Director Letters Received.
66. Frank A. Leach to George B. Cortelyou, 19 December 1907, box 260, Mint Director Letters Received.
67. Frank A. Leach to Charles O. Brewster, 17 December 1907, vol. 367, Mint Director Correspondence.
68. Henry Hering to Frank A. Leach, 21 December 1907, box 260, Mint Director Letters Received.
69. Taxay, *The U.S. Mint and Coinage,* 325.
70. Charles Barber personal notebooks, "Coins and Patterns Barber Owned," American Numismatic Association Library.
71. *requests for this rarity:* Frank A. Leach to John H. Landis, 23 December 1907, Mint Documents: Eagle; *last day of the year:* A.A. Norris to Leach, 8 January 1908, box 260, Mint Director Letters Received; *coins for Augusta:* Charles O. Brewster to Leach, 4 January 1908, box 260, Mint Director Letters Received.

Chapter 22: The Last Words

1. "All Records Broken in the Making of Money," *New York Times,* 24 November 1907, 2.
2. Willard B. Gatewood Jr., *Theodore Roosevelt and the Art of Controversy* (Baton Rouge: Louisiana State University Press, 1970), 222–223.
3. Ibid., 222.
4. Ibid., 224.
5. Lyman Abbot, Editorial, *The Outlook,* 30 November 1907, 707–708.
6. *restoration of the motto:* "Put Back 'In God We Trust,'" *The (New York) Sun,* 14 November 1907, 1; *the resolution's passage:* Gatewood, *Theodore Roosevelt and the Art of Controversy,* 225.
7. Ibid., 223.
8. Silas McBee, "The Motto on the Coins," *Churchman,* 23 November 1907, 3.
9. *called it bad art:* Silas McBee to TR, 6 December 1907, reel 79, TR Papers; *$20 gold pieces:* TR to Silas McBee, 7 December 1907, reel 347, vol. 76, p. 468, TR Papers; *sign on to the reverse:* Silas McBee to TR, 21 December 1907, reel 80, TR Papers.
10. Gatewood, *Theodore Roosevelt and the Art of Controversy,* 224–225.

11. Diary entries for 1907, 123–124, Oscar Strauss Papers, Library of Congress.
12. TR to Rev. Roland C. Dryer, 11 November 1907, reel 347, vol. 76, p. 200, TR Papers.
13. *available to the press:* "Put Back 'In God We Trust,'" 1; *losing sleep over the issue:* Gatewood, *Theodore Roosevelt and the Art of Controversy,* 227.
14. Richard Watson Gilder to TR, 16 December 1907, TR Papers.
15. TR to Richard Watson Gilder, 18 December 1907, reel 347, vol. 77, p. 38, TR Papers.
16. Gatewood, *Theodore Roosevelt and the Art of Controversy,* 230.
17. TR to George B. Cortelyou, 19 November 1907, reel 347, TR Papers.
18. *provide that exit:* J. Hampton Moore, *Roosevelt and the Old Guard* (Philadelphia: MacRae Smith Co., 1925), 199. The bill had been drafted by the same Carroll Brewster, a constituent of Moore's, who had done so much to whip up support for the motto's restoration; *the lion in his den:* ibid., 200.
19. S. Morris, *Edith Kermit Roosevelt,* 248.
20. J. Moore, *Roosevelt and the Old Guard,* 201–203.
21. David W. Akers, *A Handbook of 20th-Century United States Gold Coins 1907–1933* (Wolfeboro, NH: Bowers and Merena Galleries, 1988), 101.
22. *to complete his work:* "Saint-Gaudens Coins," *New York Tribune,* 17 December 1907, 7; *the Indian headdress:* Farran Zerbe, "A Consideration of Our New Gold Coins," *The Numismatist,* January 1908, 7–8.
23. Saint-Gaudens, *Reminiscences,* 2:331–332.
24. Charles O. Brewster to Augusta Homer Saint-Gaudens, 23 September 1907, reel 3, ASG Papers.
25. *a villainous reproduction:* Homer Saint-Gaudens to Richard Watson Gilder, 7 December 1907, reel 24, ASG Papers; *Rock Creek Aviary:* Leach, *Recollections of a Newspaper Man,* 378.
26. The term *congruent mass* is also used.
27. *lettering and details:* William Ellison-McCartney to Frank A. Leach, 6 December 1907, box 260, Mint Director Letters Received; *his antagonistic actions:* This antagonism started with the replacement of the Hill lathe. Barber was taken out of his comfort zone when faced with the unfamiliar Janvier lathe.
28. Frank A. Leach to Representative George A. Pearce, 18 January 1908, vol. 369, Mint Director Correspondence.
29. TR to William Sturgis Bigelow, 10 January 1908, reel 347, vol. 77, p. 340, TR Papers.
30. Whitelaw Reid to George B. Cortelyou, 18 February 1908, George B. Cortelyou Papers.
31. Whitelaw Reid to George B. Cortelyou, 5 March 1908, George B. Cortelyou Papers.

Chapter 23: A Requiem for Gus

1. Augusta Homer Saint-Gaudens to George B. Cortelyou, 14 January 1908, box 261, Mint Director Letters Received.
2. Charles O. Brewster to Frank A. Leach, 15 January 1908, box 261, Mint Director Letters Received.
3. Saint-Gaudens prepared two models for the $20 gold piece and two models for the one-cent piece. The obverse model of the one-cent piece was used as the obverse model for the $10 gold piece. The fifth model became the standing-eagle model for the reverse of the $10 gold piece.
4. Frank A. Leach to George B. Cortelyou, 23 January 1908, vol. 369, Mint Director Correspondence.
5. Frank A. Leach to Charles O. Brewster, 21 January 1908, vol. 370, Mint Director Correspondence.
6. *discussion with Cortelyou:* Frank A. Leach to Charles O. Brewster, 2 March 1908, vol. 370, Mint Director Correspondence; *cashed the check:* cash receipts ledger, entry for 21 February 1908, reel 42, ASG Papers.
7. *acquire a coin for her:* Frank A. Leach to Charles O. Brewster, 2 January 1908, vol. 370, Mint Director Correspondence; *Leach off the hook:* Brewster to Leach, 4 January 1908, box 260, Mint Director Letters Received ; *Secretary Cortelyou:* Leach to Brewster, 7 January 1908, vol. 370, Mint Director Correspondence.
8. *$20 gold piece yet:* Charles O. Brewster to Frank A. Leach, 3 February 1908, box 261, Mint Director Letters Received; *now looked doubtful:* Leach to Brewster, 4 February 1908, vol. 370, Mint Director Correspondence.
9. Frank A. Leach to John H. Landis, 20 February 1908, Mint Archives.
10. TR to Augusta Homer Saint-Gaudens, 15 April 1908, reel 349, vol. 80, p. 150, TR Papers.
11. *for a private individual:* Frank A. Leach to William Loeb, 18 April 1908, vol. 370, Mint Director Correspondence; *plus 12¢ postage:* Frank A. Leach to Charles O. Brewster, 20 April 1908, vol. 370, Mint Director Correspondence.

Striking Change

12. Thayer Tolles, "Daniel Chester French and the Sculpture of Augustus Saint-Gaudens," *Antiques Magazine*, January 2000.
13. "The Saint-Gaudens Memorial Exhibition," *Bulletin of the Metropolitan Museum of Art* 3, no. 2 (February 1908).
14. Frank A. Leach to George B. Cortelyou, 15 January 1908, vol. 369, Mint Director Correspondence.
15. George B. Cortelyou to Elihu Root, 5 February 1908, vol. 369, Mint Director Correspondence.
16. *as required by law:* George B. Cortelyou to Daniel Chester French, 1 February 1908, vol. 369, Mint Director Correspondence; *not be until 1910:* Report of Destruction of Dies and Hubs, 24 May 1910, box 290, Mint Director Letters Received.
17. *for the test reduction:* Frank A. Leach to Charles O. Brewster, 15 January 1908, vol. 370, Mint Director Correspondence; *to Philadelphia:* Leach to Brewster, 2 March 1908, vol. 370, Mint Director Correspondence; *made it to the showing:* P.H. Reynolds to John Landis, 12 June 1906, Mint Documents: Eagle.
18. "Art Pays Tribute to Saint-Gaudens," *New York Times*, 1 March 1908, 7.
19. C. Lewis Hind, *Augustus Saint-Gaudens* (New York: John Lane, 1908), 15–16.
20. *the opening-night celebration:* "Five Thousand Persons Visit the Metropolitan Museum of Art," *New York Tribune*, 3 March 1908, 7; *gotten together at this time:* "The Saint-Gaudens Memorial Exhibition," *Bulletin of the Metropolitan Museum of Art* 3, no. 2 (February 1908).
21. "Saint-Gaudens Memorial," *New York Times*, 3 March 1908, 3; Hind, *Augustus Saint-Gaudens*, 32–33.
22. *a man of genius:* form letter by Daniel Chester French and Robert Deforest to those who loaned pieces to the exhibit, 3 June 1908, Daniel Chester French Papers, Library of Congress; *23 years later:* Tolles, "Daniel Chester French and the Sculpture of Augustus Saint-Gaudens."
23. *from the exhibit:* Frank A. Leach to Charles O. Brewster, 9 May 1908, vol. 370, Mint Director Correspondence; *design for her:* Augusta H. Saint-Gaudens to John H. Landis, 30 June 1908, Mint Documents: Eagle.
24. Robert E. Preston to Augusta and Homer Saint-Gaudens, 8 June 1908, vol. 370, Mint Director Correspondence.
25. "The Works of Augustus Saint-Gaudens at the Museum," *New York Tribune*, 3 March 1908, 7.
26. Brown, *1860–1930 Memories*, 507.
27. Ibid., 503–512.
28. American Institute of Architects, Journal of Proceedings, third session, 15 December 1908, 97–98.
29. Ibid., 98–101.
30. Ibid., 122–125.
31. William M.R. French to Daniel Chester French, 11 August 1909, Daniel Chester French Papers. W.M.R. French (Daniel French's brother) was director of the Art Institute of Chicago, where the exhibit went on display in 1909. He called Augusta Saint-Gaudens the most ill-tempered, unreasonable person he had ever had extended dealings with.
32. Vermeule, *Numismatic Art in America*, 115–116.

Chapter 24: The Legacy

1. William Loeb to Frank A. Leach, 29 November 1907, Mint Archives.
2. Frank A. Leach to John H. Landis, 2 December 1907, Mint Documents: Eagle.
3. Charles E. Barber to John H. Landis, 9 December 1907, Mint Documents: Eagle.
4. *approaching the president:* William Sturgis Bigelow to TR, 8 January 1908, reel 80, TR Papers; *interested in the experiment:* TR to Bigelow, 10 January 1908, reel 347, vol. 77, p. 340, TR Papers.
5. Desk diaries, 2 April 1908, reel 431, TR Papers.
6. Leach, *Recollections of a Newspaper Man*, 381–382.
7. *deference to Saint-Gaudens:* Frank A. Leach to John H. Landis, 4 November 1908, Mint Director Correspondence; *only $300:* Leach to Landis, 22 May 1908, vol. 368, Mint Director Correspondence; *within a few months:* Bela Lyon Pratt to Leach, 27 April 1908, box 264, Mint Director Letters Received.
8. Frank A. Leach to Bela Lyon Pratt, 5 May 1908, vol. 370, Mint Director Correspondence.
9. Bela Lyon Pratt to Frank A. Leach, 29 June 1908, box 265, Mint Director Letters Received.
10. *promptly notified:* Frank A. Leach to Bela Lyon Pratt, 15 July 1908, vol. 370, Mint Director Correspondence; *prepare the dies:* Leach to Pratt, 27 May 1908, vol. 370, Mint Director Correspondence.
11. *on September 26:* TR to William Sturgis Bigelow, 26 September 1908, reel 351, vol. 85, p. 307, TR Papers; *the relief strengthened:* Barber to Landis, 9 October 1908, Mint Documents: Eagle.
12. Leach to Bigelow, 31 October 1908, vol. 370, Mint Director Correspondence.
13. "The Lincoln Plaque," 23 July 1947, folder 7, Mint Director Correspondence.

Notes

14. Desk diaries, 14 December 1908, reel 431, series 9, TR Papers.
15. Leach, *Recollections of a Newspaper Man*, 400.
16. Taxay, *The U.S. Mint and Coinage*, 330–338.
17. James Earle Fraser to Nellie Tayloe Ross, 19 November 1951, folder 9, Mint Director Correspondence.
18. Brown, *1860–1930 Memories*, 378.
19. James Earle Fraser, notes on modeling the bust of Roosevelt, box 64, J.E. Fraser Papers.
20. Paul H. Brown to Laura Gardin Fraser, 24 October 1961, box 9, J.E. Fraser Papers.
21. *an American Indian:* James Earle Fraser to Charles Hamilton, 11 October 1949, box 7, J.E. Fraser Papers; *"Black Diamond":* Fraser to Fairchild Osborne, 16 January 1950, box 7, J.E. Fraser Papers. In this letter Fraser states that the bison was located at the Bronx Zoo. Black Diamond was not at this location, however, having been kept at the smaller Central Park Menagerie instead. After nearly 40 years, Fraser must have confused the location in his mind.
22. Brown, *1860–1930 Memories*, 379–383.
23. Writings of J.E. Fraser on the Buffalo nickel, box 61, J.E. Fraser Papers.
24. Felix Weil, "History of Medallic Art Company," 48, ms. in the possession of D. Wayne Johnson. Fraser also had Weil produce copper galvanos or intermediate reductions of his oversize models electroplated in nickel to inspect the coins' ultimate color and finish.
25. Writings of J.E. Fraser on the Buffalo nickel, box 61, J.E. Fraser Papers.
26. James Earle Fraser to Howland Wood, 21 April 1936, box 5, J.E. Fraser Papers.
27. *from 1907 to 1910:* Laura Gardin Fraser biographical notes, n.d., box 52, J.E. Fraser Papers; *the Frasers were elated:* Laura Gardin Fraser to F.M. Tate, 17 April 1964, box 9, J.E. Fraser Papers.
28. Taxay, *The U.S. Mint and Coinage*, 340–346.
29. Writings of J.E. Fraser on the Buffalo nickel, box 61, J.E. Fraser Papers.
30. *seat for sculpture:* Commission of Fine Arts, minutes for the meeting of 3 December 1915; *Albin Polasek:* ibid., exhibit D, Herbert Adams to R.W. Woolley, 8 December 1915.
31. Herbert Adams to Colonel William W. Harts, 28 December 1915, box 13 (Design of Coins), record group 66, entry 17, Commission of Fine Arts project files 1910–1952 (hereafter cited as CFA Files).
32. Charles Moore to Herbert Adams, 29 December 1915, box 13, CFA Files.
33. *Fine Arts in advance:* memorandum of George E. Roberts, 24 July 1914, box 140, CFA Files; *to design the pieces:* Colonel William W. Harts to Roberts, 27 July 1914, box 140, CFA Files; *rejected all four:* Harts to Daniel Chester French, 9 February 1915, box 140, CFA Files; *preparing alternatives:* T.P. Dewey to A.M. Joyce, 13 February 1915, entry 660, box 120, U.S. Mint Documents: Panama Medal, Panama-Pacific Exposition 1913–1917, G-12-09-02-2.
34. *gold dollar and $50 coins:* William Gibbs McAdoo to Colonel William W. Harts, 13 February 1915, box 140, CFA Files; *his bronze reductions:* Robert I. Aitken to Charles E. Barber, 17 April 1915, entry 660, box 120, U.S. Mint Documents: Panama Medal, Panama-Pacific Exposition 1913–1917, G-12-09-02-2.
35. *effectively do nothing:* Daniel Chester French to William S. Malburn, 1 February 1915, box 140, CFA Files; *in its octagonal form:* Robert Aitken to T.P. Dewey, 23 January 1915, box 140, CFA Files.
36. Herbert Adams to Colonel William W. Harts, 9 January 1916, box 13, CFA Files.
37. Colonel William W. Harts to Herbert Adams, 28 February 1916, box 13, CFA Files.
38. Herbert Adams to Colonel William W. Harts, 4 March 1916, box 13, CFA Files.
39. Herbert Adams to Colonel William W. Harts, n.d., box 13, CFA Files.
40. Speech to Architectural League, n.d., reel 5887, Adolph Weinman Papers.
41. Weinman coin descriptions, May 1916, entry 617, box 57, U.S. Mint Documents: Designs for New Subsidiary Coins 1916–1917, G-12-08-01-1, Philadelphia Regional Archives (hereafter cited as Mint Documents: Subsidiary Coins).
42. MacNeil coin descriptions, May 1916, Mint Documents: Subsidiary Coins.
43. R.W. Woolley to A.M. Joyce, 24 June 1916, Mint Documents: Subsidiary Coins.
44. *obverse of the half dollar:* Adolph A. Weinman to Charles E. Barber, 26 July 1916, Mint Documents: Subsidiary Coins; *made them look cheap:* Weinman to A.M. Joyce, 18 July 1916, Mint Documents: Subsidiary Coins.
45. Adolph A. Weinman to William G. McAdoo, 7 August 1916, Mint Documents: Subsidiary Coins.
46. *burnishing be corrected:* William G. McAdoo to Robert W. Woolley, 10 August 1916, Mint Documents: Subsidiary Coins; *reverse for the half dollar:* McAdoo to Adolph A. Weinman, 14 August 1916, Mint Documents: Subsidiary Coins; *obverse of this coin:* Weinman to A.M. Joyce, 19 August 1916, Mint Documents: Subsidiary Coins.

47. *information on the dime:* F.J.H. von Engelken to A.M. Joyce, 6 September 1916, Mint Documents: Subsidiary Coins; *the stamp-vending machines:* C.W. Hobbs to F.L. Fishback, 6 September 1916, Mint Documents: Subsidiary Coins; *jamming in their pay phones:* George K. Thompson to Joyce, 7 September 1916, Mint Documents: Subsidiary Coins.
48. F.J.H. von Engelken to William G. McAdoo, 11 December 1906, vol. 415, Mint Director Correspondence.
49. F.J.H. von Engelken to A.M. Joyce, 6 October 1916, Mint Documents: Subsidiary Coins.
50. *rearranged the inscriptions:* Adolph A. Weinman to A.M. Joyce, 19 September 1916, Mint Documents: Subsidiary Coins; *rim was uneven:* F.J.H. von Engelken to Joyce, 7 September 1916, Mint Documents: Subsidiary Coins; *height of relief:* Weinman to Joyce, 21 October 1916, Mint Documents: Subsidiary Coins.
51. *a beaded border:* Weinman to George F. Kunz, 24 November 1916, Mint Documents: Subsidiary Coins; *". . . of the new half dollar":* Weinman to A.M. Joyce, 2 January 1917, Mint Documents: Subsidiary Coins.
52. Charles E. Barber to A.M. Joyce, 28 November 1916, Mint Documents: Subsidiary Coins.
53. *lower the relief:* Barber to A.M. Joyce, 9 December 1916, Mint Documents: Subsidiary Coins; *with an uneven rim:* F.J.H. von Engelken to Joyce, 29 December 1916, Mint Documents: Subsidiary Coins.
54. *from these last designs:* Hermon A. MacNeil to A.M. Joyce, 14 August 1916, Mint Documents: Subsidiary Coins; *McAdoo had approved:* William G. McAdoo to MacNeil, 19 August 1916, Mint Documents: Subsidiary Coins; *cast for the obverse:* F.J.H. von Engelken to Joyce, 1 September 1916, Mint Documents: Subsidiary Coins.
55. *consulting with MacNeil:* F.J.H. von Engelken to A.M. Joyce, 7 September 1916, Mint Documents: Subsidiary Coins; *Washington in October:* von Engelken to Joyce, 17 October 1916, Mint Documents: Subsidiary Coins; *the Engraving Department:* von Engelken to Joyce, 22 October 1916, Mint Documents: Subsidiary Coins.
56. *design of the shield:* F.J.H. von Engelken to A.M. Joyce, 11 November 1916, Mint Documents: Subsidiary Coins; *then be prepared:* von Engelken to Joyce, 16 November 1916, Mint Documents: Subsidiary Coins.
57. Hermon A. MacNeil to A.M. Joyce, 6 January 1917, Mint Documents: Subsidiary Coins.
58. Hermon A. MacNeil to F.J.H. von Engelken, 11 January 1917, Mint Documents: Subsidiary Coins.
59. *between artists and the Mint:* Herbert Adams to F.J.H. von Engelken, 30 January 1917, box 13, CFA Files; *his second models:* Taxay, *The U.S. Mint and Coinage*, 349; *making his modifications:* F.J.H. von Engelken to William G. McAdoo, 17 January 1917, box 173, McAdoo Papers.
60. *allow for the modification:* Herbert Adams to Colonel William W. Harts, 2 April 1917, box 13, CFA Files; *objections to himself:* Hermon A. MacNeil to A.M. Joyce, 30 January 1917, Mint Documents: Subsidiary Coins.
61. *space the inscriptions:* Hermon A. MacNeil to A.M. Joyce, 2 February 1917, Mint Documents: Subsidiary Coins; *met with failure:* MacNeil to Joyce, 9 February 1917, Mint Documents: Subsidiary Coins.
62. *in chain mail:* MacNeil to A.M. Joyce, 18 February 1917, Mint Documents: Subsidiary Coins; *ordeal was over:* Raymond T. Baker to Joyce, 6 January 1917, Mint Documents: Subsidiary Coins.
63. Speech by James Earle Fraser, n.d., box 64, J.E. Fraser Papers.
64. William G. McAdoo to Adolph A. Weinman, 14 March 1917, reel 5884, Adolph Weinman Papers.
65. Extract from minutes of meeting of 9 June 1921, box 144, CFA Files.
66. *tin ear to the arts:* Brown, *1860–1930 Memories*, 194; *review of coin designs:* executive order of 22 July 1921, entry 8, box 1, Commission of Fine Arts, General Records: General Correspondence of the Secretary/Executive Officer 1910–1922; *suggestions for a new design:* Charles Moore to Raymond T. Baker, 26 July 1921, box 144, CFA Files.
67. 1 August 1921, Congressional Record.
68. Charles Moore to Raymond T. Baker, 14 November 1921, box 144, CFA Files.
69. Daniel Chester French to Lt. Col. C.O. Sherrill, 30 November 1921, box 144, CFA Files; Herbert Adams to Lt. Col. C.O. Sherrill, 2 December 1921, box 144, CFA Files.
70. Program of Competition, box 144, CFA Files.
71. Vermeule, *Numismatic Art in America*, 149.
72. Charles Moore to James Earle Fraser, 20 December 1921, box 144, CFA Files.
73. James Earle Fraser to Charles Moore, 17 December 1921, box 144, CFA Files.
74. *at Philadelphia:* Charles Moore to James Earle Fraser, 20 December 1921, box 144, CFA Files; *with the new designs:* "New U.S. Silver Dollar Shows Dawn of Era of World Peace," *Washington Post*, 20 December 1921.

75. Freas Styer to Raymond T. Baker, 30 January 1922, Mint Director Correspondence, entry A1 328N, box 4.
76. *not be on the coin:* statement by the director of the Mint (press release), 24 December 1921, box 144, CFA Files; *official record:* S.P. Gilbert Jr. to Charles Moore, 29 December 1921, box 144, CFA Files.
77. Charles Follen McKim to E. Winchester Donald, 8 May 1901, Charles Moore Papers.
78. Daniel Chester French to Augusta and Homer Saint-Gaudens, 26 November 1914, Daniel Chester French Papers.

Chapter 25: Striking Change

1. Alice Roosevelt Longworth, *Crowded Hours*, 269.
2. C. Moore, *The Life and Times of Charles Follen McKim*, 201–203.
3. Michael Richman, *Daniel Chester French: An American Sculptor*, 173–175.
4. Ibid., 171–184.
5. Brown, *1860–1930 Memories*, 102. Brown remembers this conversation as having taken place just after Cannon returned to Congress from having been defeated for a term. That would have been 1915 and most surely is wrong, since the Lincoln Memorial was completed in 1922 and Brown was clear in the story that the memorial was finished.
6. Charles Moore to Mary M. O'Reilly, 17 April 1931, box 197, CFA Files.
7. Andrew W. Mellon to Charles Moore, 21 April 1931, box 197, CFA Files.
8. *only six acceptable:* H.P. Caemmerer memorandum to the Commission of Fine Arts, 27 October 1931, box 197, CFA Files; *all the others:* Caemmerer to Adolph A. Weinman, 6 November 1931, box 197, CFA Files.
9. Charles Moore to Andrew W. Mellon, 4 November 1931, box 197, CFA Files.
10. *positive attributes of #56:* Charles Moore to Andrew W. Mellon, 10 November 1931, box 197, CFA Files; *who had done which models:* Moore to Mellon, 17 November 1931, box 197, CFA Files.
11. Charles Moore to Andrew W. Mellon, 19 January 1932, box 197, CFA Files.
12. Ogden L. Mills to Charles Moore, 11 April 1932, box 197, CFA Files.
13. James Earle Fraser to John Flanagan, 26 April 1932, box 5, J.E. Fraser Papers.
14. Sidney Waugh to Nellie Tayloe Ross, 1 September 1948, reel 5886, Adolph Weinman Papers.
15. *Mint for consideration:* James Earle Fraser to Nellie Tayloe Ross, 19 November 1951, folder 9, Mint Director Correspondence; *better than Brenner's:* Ross to Fraser, 25 January 1952, folder 9, Mint Director Correspondence; *the rail-splitter:* Fraser to Ross, 31 January 1952, folder 9, Mint Director Correspondence.
16. *uninterrupted production:* Nellie Tayloe Ross to James Earle Fraser, 25 January 1952, folder 9, Mint Director Correspondence; *a shorter die life:* Paul Heckman to Ross, 7 May 1952, folder 9, Mint Director Correspondence; *strengthening the inscriptions:* Edwin Dressel to Ross, 20 June 1952, folder 9, Mint Director Correspondence.
17. *continue the tests:* Nellie Tayloe Ross to James Earle Fraser, 3 March 1953, folder 9, Mint Director Correspondence; *". . . the face of the coin":* Charles E. Barber to Oliver C. Bosbyshell, 8 April 1893, box 5, Mint Director Letters Received.

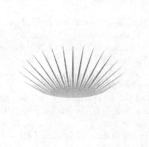

Bibliography

Archival Materials

Henry Adams Papers, Massachusetts Historical Society.

Art Commission of 1902, Annual Report and Minutes of the, New York Public Library.

Edward Atkinson Papers, Massachusetts Historical Society.

Charles Barber Personal Notebooks, American Numismatic Association.

Paul Wayland Bartlett Papers, Manuscript Division, Library of Congress.

Board of Commissioners of the Parks Department, Minutes and Documents of the, New York Public Library.

Board of Lady Managers, President's Letterbook and Minute Book, Chicago History Museum.

Century Papers, Manuscript Division, New York Public Library.

Commission of Fine Arts, General Records: General Correspondence of the Secretary/Executive Officer 1910–1922, record group 66, entry 8, box 1, National Archives and Records Administration, Washington, DC.

Commission of Fine Arts, Meeting Minutes, Archives of the Commission of Fine Arts.

Commission of Fine Arts, Project Files 1910–1952: Design of Coins, record group 66, entry 17, box 13; Panama Pacific Exposition, record group 66, entry 17, box 140; George Washington Coin, record group 66, entry 17, box 197; National Archives and Records Administration, Washington, DC.

Congressional Record, Manuscript Division, Library of Congress.

George B. Cortelyou Papers, Manuscript Division, Library of Congress.

William Edmond Curtis Papers, Manuscript Division, Library of Congress.

James W. Ellsworth Collection, Chicago Public Library.

James Earle Fraser Papers, Syracuse University.

Daniel Chester French Papers, Manuscript Division, Library of Congress.

Richard Watson Gilder Papers, Manuscripts and Archives Division, New York Public Library.

Isabella Hagner James Papers, the White House Collection, White House Historical Association.

George Kunz Papers, New-York Historical Society.

Lee Family Papers 1535–1957, Massachusetts Historical Society.

Maloney Collection, New York Public Library.

Charles Follen McKim Papers, Manuscript Division, Library of Congress.

Charles Moore Papers, Manuscript Division, Library of Congress.

Harrison Morris Papers, Manuscript Division, Princeton University Library.

Frederic Law Olmsted Papers, Manuscript Division, Library of Congress.

Bertha Palmer Correspondence, Ryerson and Burnham Library, Art Institute of Chicago.

Michael Richman Papers, private collection.

Francis Millet Rogers Papers, Archives of American Artists, Smithsonian Institution.

Theodore Roosevelt Collection, Houghton Library, Harvard University.

Theodore Roosevelt Papers, Manuscript Division, Library of Congress.

Augustus Saint-Gaudens Papers, Manuscript Division, Library of Congress.

Augustus Saint-Gaudens Papers, Rauner Special Collections Library, Dartmouth College.

Sherman Folder, Archives of the New York Art Commission.

Sherman Family Papers, New-York Historical Society.

William T. Sherman Family Papers, University of Notre Dame Archives.

John Boyd Thacher Scrapbooks, New York State Library.

U.S. Department of the Treasury, record group 56, General Records of the Treasury Department: Correspondence of the Office of the Secretary of the Treasury, Letters Sent 1878–1917, L series, Letters Sent by the Division of Mail and Files, entry 73 (abbreviated as Treasury Secretary Letters); Letters Sent by the Executive Committee on Awards 1892–1896, entry 509 (abbreviated as Award Committee Letters); Records Relating to Expositions, World's Columbian Exposition, entry 518; National Archives and Records Administration, College Park, MD.

U.S. Mint, Annual Report of the Director of the Mint, Manuscript Division, Library of Congress.

U.S. Mint Documents: Designs for New Subsidiary Coins 1916–1917, G-12-08-01-1, Philadelphia Regional Archives (abbreviated as Mint Documents: Subsidiary Coins); General Correspondence, record group 104 (abbreviated as Mint General Correspondence); Letters Sent by the Director and Superintendent of the Mint 1866–1900, record group 104 (abbreviated as Mint Letters Sent); New Designs for Eagle and Double Eagle 1906–1909, G-12-08-03-1, record group 104, series II, entry 628, box 71, Philadelphia Regional Archives (abbreviated as Mint Documents: Eagle); Panama Medal, Panama Pacific Exposition, record group 104; National Archives and Records Administration, Philadelphia.

U.S. Mint, Records of the Bureau of the Mint: box 45, folder 232, entry 330, record group 104, NC 152 (abbreviated as Mint Archives); Correspondence of the Director of the Mint, vol. 46, entry 235, record group 104, NC 152 (abbreviated as Mint Director Correspondence); Gold Coins Design, entry 330, record group 104; Letters Received by the Director of the Mint, entry 229, record group 104, NC 152 (abbreviated as Mint Director Letters Received); National Archives and Records Administration, College Park, MD.

Adolph Weinman Papers, Archives of American Artists, Smithsonian Institution.

Stanford White Papers, Avery Library, Columbia University.

Stanford White Papers, New-York Historical Society.

The White House 1904–1905, Official Functions, National Archives and Records Administration.

Books and Articles

Adams, Henry. *The Education of Henry Adams: An Autobiography*. 1918. Reprint, Boston: Houghton Mifflin, 2000.

———. *The Letters of Henry Adams*. Edited by Worthington Chauncey Ford. Cambridge, MA: Harvard University Press, 1930.

Akers, David W. *A Handbook of 20th-Century United States Gold Coins 1907–1933*. Wolfeboro, NH: Bowers and Merena Galleries, 1988.

Armstrong, Maitland. *Day Before Yesterday: Reminiscences of a Varied Life*. Edited by Margaret Armstrong. New York: Charles Scribner's Sons, 1920.

Baker, Paul R. *Stanny: The Gilded Life of Stanford White*. New York: Macmillan, 1989.

Barnes, James A. *John G. Carlisle: Financial Statesman*. New York: Dodd, Mead, 1931.

Beaux, Cecilia. *Background With Figures: Autobiography of Cecilia Beaux*. Boston: Houghton Mifflin, 1930.

Bolotin, Norman, and Christine Laing. *The World's Columbian Exposition*. Urbana: University of Illinois Press, 2002.

Bowen, Clarence Winthrop, ed. *The History of the Centennial Celebration of the Inauguration of George Washington as the First President of the United States*. New York: D. Appleton, 1892.

Boyd, William R. "Eminent Iowan Series." *Annals of Iowa* 29, no. 6 (October 1948).

Breen, Walter. *Walter Breen's Complete Encyclopedia of U.S. and Colonial Coins*. New York: Bantam Doubleday Dell, 1988.

Brown, Glenn. *1860–1930 Memories: A Winning Crusade to Revive George Washington's Vision of a Capital City*. Washington, DC: W.F. Roberts, 1931.

———, ed. *Proceedings of the 43rd Annual Convention of the American Institute of Architects*. Washington, DC: American Institute of Architects, 1908.

Burrows, Edwin G., and Mike Wallace. *Gotham: A History of New York City to 1898*. New York: Oxford University Press, 1999.

Bushong, William B. "Glenn Brown, the White House, and the Urban Renaissance of Washington, DC." *White House History*, no. 11 (2002).

Butt, Archibald. *The Letters of Archie Butt*. Edited by Lawrence F. Abbott. Garden City, NY: Doubleday, Page, 1924.

Bynner, Witter. *Selected Letters*. Edited by James Kraft. New York: Farrar Straus Giroux, 1981.

The Century, 1847–1946. New York: Century Association, 1947.

Chalfant, Edward. *Better in Darkness: A Biography of Henry Adams; His Second Life, 1862–1891*. Hamden, CT: Archon Books, 1994.

Chanler, Mrs. Winthrop [Margaret Terry]. *Roman Spring: Memoirs*. Boston: Little, Brown, 1934.

Cortissoz, Royal. *The Life of Whitelaw Reid*. 2 vols. New York: Charles Scribner's Sons, 1921.

Coxe, R. Cleveland. "Coxe Reminisces Today: Gay Anecdotes of Brilliant Men." *Santa Barbara Morning Press*, 21 December 1924.

Dalton, Kathleen. *Theodore Roosevelt: A Strenuous Life*. New York: Random House, 2002.

Dryfhout, John H. *The Work of Augustus Saint-Gaudens*. Hanover, NH: University Press of New England, 1981.

Eglit, Nathan N. *Columbiana: The Medallic History of Christopher Columbus and the Columbian Exposition of 1893*. Chicago: Hewitt Brothers, 1965.

Evans, George G., ed. *U.S. Mint Centennial 1792–1892*. Philadelphia: George G. Evans, 1892.

Faulkner, Barry. *Sketches From an Artist's Life*. Dublin, NH: William L Bauhan, 1973.

The Franklin Bicentennial Celebration: A Record of the Proceedings. Philadelphia: American Philosophical Society, 1906.

Gatewood, Willard B., Jr. *Theodore Roosevelt and the Art of Controversy*. Baton Rouge: Louisiana State University Press, 1970.

Gilder, Richard Watson. *The Letters of Richard Watson Gilder*. Edited by Rosamond Gilder. Boston: Houghton Mifflin, 1916.

Gurney, George. "Olin Levi Warner (1844–1896): A Catalogue Raisonné of his Sculpture and Graphic Works." Ph.D. diss., University of Delaware, 1978.

Hagans, William E. "Saint-Gaudens, Zorn and the Goddesslike Miss Anderson." *Archives of American Art* 16, no. 2 (Summer 2002): 66–89.

Hering, Henry. "History of the $10 and $20 Gold Coins of 1907 Issue." *The Numismatist* 62, no. 8 (August 1949).

Hind, C. Lewis. *Augustus Saint-Gaudens*. New York: John Lane, 1908.

Illustrated History of the United States Mint. Philadelphia: George G. Evans, 1892.

James, Isabella Hagner. "Chieftess of the Roosevelt Clan." *New York Herald Tribune Magazine*, 30 October 1932, section XI, 5 and 14.

John, Arthur. *The Best Years of the Century: Richard Watson Gilder, Scribner's Monthly, and the Century Magazine, 1870–1909*. Urbana: University of Illinois Press, 1981.

Johnson, Robert Underwood. *Remembered Yesterdays*. Boston: Little, Brown, 1923.

Johnson, Rossiter, ed. *A History of the World's Columbian Exposition*. Vol. 1. New York: D. Appleton, 1897.

Judd, J. Hewitt. *United States Pattern Coins: Experimental and Trial Pieces*. 8th ed. Edited by Q. David Bowers. Atlanta: Whitman Publishing, 2003.

———. *United States Pattern, Experimental, and Trial Pieces*. 5th ed. Racine, WI: Western Publishing, 1974.

Julian, Philippe. *The Triumph of Art Nouveau: Paris Exposition 1900*. London: Phaidon Press, 1974.

Julian, R.W. *Medals of the United States Mint: The First Century, 1792–1892*. El Cajon, CA: Token and Medal Society, 1977.

Landgren, Marchal E. *Years of Art: The Story of the Art Students League of New York*. New York: Robert M. McBride, 1940.

Lawrence, David. *The Complete Guide to Barber Halves*. Virginia Beach, VA: DLRC Press, 1991.

———. *The Complete Guide to Barber Quarters*. Virginia Beach, VA: DLRC Press, 1995.

Leach, Frank A. *Recollections of a Newspaper Man: A Record of Life and Events in California*. San Francisco, CA: Samuel Levinson, 1917.

Lewis, Lloyd. *Sherman: Fighting Prophet*. New York: Harcourt, Brace, 1932.

Longworth, Alice Roosevelt. *Crowded Hours*. New York: Charles Scribner's Sons, 1933.

Low, Will H. *A Chronicle of Friendships, 1873–1900*. New York: Charles Scribner's Sons, 1908.

McCullough, David. *Mornings on Horseback: The Story of an Extraordinary Family, a Vanished Way of Life, and the Unique Child Who Became Theodore Roosevelt*. New York: Simon & Schuster, 1981.

McNeil, Neil. *The President's Medal 1787–1977*. New York: Clarkson N. Potter, 1977.

Moore, Charles. *Daniel H. Burnham*. 2 vols. New York: Da Capo, 1968.

———. *The Life and Times of Charles Follen McKim*. New York: Houghton Mifflin, 1929.

———, compiler. *The Promise of American Architecture: Addresses at the Annual Dinner of the American Institute of Architects, 1905*. Washington, DC: AIA, 1905.

Moore, J. Hampton. *Roosevelt and the Old Guard*. Philadelphia: MacRae Smith, 1925.

Morris, Edmund. *The Rise of Theodore Roosevelt*. 1979. Reprint, New York: Modern Library, 2001.

———. *Theodore Rex*. New York: Random House, 2001.

Morris, Harrison S. *Confessions in Art*. New York: Sears Publishing, 1930.

Morris, Sylvia Jukes. *Edith Kermit Roosevelt: Portrait of a First Lady*. New York: Coward, McCann & Geoghegan, 1980.

National Americana Society. *James William Ellsworth: His Life and Ancestry*. Vol. 1 of *The Ellsworth Family*. New York: National Americana Society, 1930.

"New U.S. Silver Dollar Shows Dawn of Era of World Peace." *Washington Post*, 20 December 1921.

Nichols, Rose Standish. "Familiar Letters of Augustus Saint-Gaudens." *McClure's Magazine* 31, no. 6 (October 1908), 603–616.

O'Toole, Patricia. *The Five of Hearts: An Intimate Portrait of Henry Adams and His Friends, 1880–1919*. New York: Clarkson N. Potter, 1990.

Parsons, Samuel. *Samuel Parsons and the Central Park of New York*. Edited by Mabel Parsons. New York: G.P. Putnam's Sons, 1926.

Peters, Gloria, and Cynthia Mohon. *The Complete Guide to Shield and Liberty Nickels*. Virginia Beach, VA: DLRC Press, 1995.

Reps, John W. *Washington on View: The Nation's Capital Since 1790*. Chapel Hill: University of North Carolina Press, 1991.

Reynolds, Donald Martin. *The Architecture of New York City: Histories and Views of Important Structures, Sites, and Symbols*. New York: Wiley, 1994.

Richman, Michael. *Daniel Chester French: An American Sculptor*. 1976. Reprint, Washington, DC: Preservation Press, 1983.

Roosevelt, Theodore. *The Letters of Theodore Roosevelt*. Vol. 4. Edited by Elting E. Morison. Cambridge, MA: Harvard University Press, 1951.

———. *Theodore Roosevelt: An Autobiography*. New York: Charles Scribner's Sons, 1913.

Saint-Gaudens, Augustus. *The Reminiscences of Augustus Saint-Gaudens*. 2 vols. Edited and amplified by Homer Saint-Gaudens. New York: The Century Company, 1913.

Saint-Gaudens, Homer. "Roosevelt and Our Coin Designs." *The Century*, April 1920, 721–736.

Savell, Isabelle K. *The Tonetti Years at Snedens Landing*. New York: Historical Society of Rockland County, 1977.

Scott, Pamela J. "A City Designed as a Work of Art: The Emergence of the Senate Park Commission's Monumental Core." In *Designing the Nation's Capital: The 1901 Plan for Washington, DC*, ed. Sue Kohler and Pamela Scott. Washington, DC: U.S. Commission of Fine Arts, 2007.

Smith, Herbert F. *Richard Watson Gilder*. New York: Twayne Publishers, 1970.

Smith, Pete. *American Numismatic Biographies*. Rocky River, OH: Gold Leaf Press, 1992.

Somma, Thomas P. "'The Son by the Side of the Father': David d'Angers' Busts of Washington and Lafayette in the Rotunda of the U.S. Capitol." In *Paris on the Potomac: The French Influence on the Architecture and Art of Washington, DC*, edited by Cynthia R. Field, Isabelle Gourmay, and Thomas P. Somma, 56–76. Athens: Ohio University Press, 2007.

Swiatek, Anthony. *Commemorative Coins of the United States: Identification and Price Guide*. Sidney, OH: Coin World, 1993.

Taxay, Don. *The U.S. Mint and Coinage: An Illustrated History From 1776 to the Present Day*. New York: Arco, 1966.

Tehan, Arline Boucher. *Henry Adams in Love: The Pursuit of Elizabeth Sherman Cameron*. New York: Universe Books, 1983.

Tharp, Louise Hall. *Saint-Gaudens and the Gilded Era*. Boston: Little, Brown, 1969.

Valentine, Lucia, and Alan Valentine. *The American Academy in Rome, 1894–1969*. Charlottesville: University Press of Virginia, 1973.

Vermeule, Cornelius. *Numismatic Art in America: Aesthetics of the United States Coinage*. Cambridge, MA: Harvard University Press, 1971.

Weil, Felix. "History of Medallic Art Company." Unpublished ms. in collection of D. Wayne Johnson.

Weimann, Jeanne Madeline. *The Fair Women: The Story of the Woman's Building at the World's Columbian Exposition of 1893*. Chicago: Academy Chicago, 1981.

Who Was Who in America, Volume I: 1897–1942. Chicago: Marquis Who's Who, 1981.

Wilkinson, Burke. *The Life and Works of Augustus Saint Gaudens*. New York: Dover, 1992.

Wister, Owen. *Roosevelt: The Story of a Friendship, 1880–1919*. New York: Macmillan, 1930.

Yeoman, R.S. *A Guide Book of United States Coins*. 52nd ed. Edited by Kenneth Bressett. New York: Golden Books, 1998.

Index

Italic page numbers refer to images.

$5 gold piece, 339–41, *343*, *367*, 368

$10 gold piece: ASG's models for, 301–2, *303*; Barber's opposition to design of, 299–300, 301; compensation for Saint-Gaudens estate, 315; criticism of, 324, 326; defects in, 300–301; detail in, 300; eagle on, 326; head-dress on, 326, 336; inscriptions on, 326, *327*; Landis and, 304; modified for motto, *327*; numerals on, 299, 300; omission of ASG's initials, 338; origin of, 299; reductions for, 300; relief of, 299, 300; Roberts's objections to, 300–301; roots of design, 360; sharpness of, 300; striking of from first model, 302, *303*; striking of from second model, *303*; suspension of coinage of, 314; TR and, 299, 301, 328, 336, 338; use of *Head of Victory*, 299; varieties of final design of, 304; views of, 338. *See also* coinage, gold

$20 gold piece: approval for production, 328; attempts to use third model, 314; Barber and, 306, 307, 311–12, 313; changes in low relief pieces, 321; coinability of, 313, 318, 328; compensation for Saint-Gaudens estate, 314, 331; criticism of, 324; defective pieces, 318–19; delays in striking, 307; destruction of experimental coins, 321; excessive fins, 318–19; exclusion of Saint-Gaudens family from decisions, 313; expedited production of, 317–18, 328–29; Gussie's interference with, 311; High Relief pieces, *310*, 311, 317, 319–20; Indian Head pattern, 288; inscriptions, 323–26, *327*, 332; lack of for Gussie, 331–32; Leach and, 279, 314, 316–17, 318–19, 326, 329; loss of sharpness, 317; models for, 288, 307–8, *310*, 311, 312, 314, 315, 333; number produced, 319; omission of "In God We Trust," 323–26; popularity of, 318–19; production of high relief pieces, 318; production of low relief pieces, 320–21; reception of, 318–19, 326, 338; reductions, 306, 317; release into circulation, 321; relief of, 311–13, 320; rims, 318–19; roots of design, 360; suggestion of using outside experts, 308; TR and, 306, 308, 319–20, 328; Ultra High Relief piece, 279–80, *281*, 294–95, 322. *See also* coinage, gold

$50 Panama-Pacific gold piece, *348*, 353

Abbot, Lyman, 323–24

Adams, Clover, 154, 174

Adams, Henry: friendship with Edith Roosevelt, 174; memorial for wife, 154–55; on plans for Mall's renovation, 198; relationship with Lizzie Cameron, 151, 154, 162

Adams, Herbert, 352, 353, 356

Aitken, Robert, 353

American Institute of Architects, 193, 209, 334–36

American Numismatic and Archeological Society, 138

American Philosophical Society, 241. *See also* Franklin medal

American School of Architecture in Rome, 41

Anderson, Harriette Eugenia, 161, *163*, 164, 261

Angel of Victory, 210, 261, 264. *See also* Head of Victory; Sherman Monument

Annual Diplomatic Reception (1905), 215–16

Ardisson, Gaetan, 190

art, American, Gilder's promotion of, 37

Art Students League, 29

Atkinson, Edward, 34, 102, *104*, 105, 159–60

AT&T, 355

award medal, World's Columbian Exposition: ASG and, 102, 106, 107, 108, 109, 113–14, 123, 131, 139; attempts to circumvent Mint, 110, 113; Carlisle and, 112; cutting of dies for, 111, 112, 114, 117, 137, 140; delays in distribution, 140; descriptions of in press, 114, 118–19; facsimile of, *122*; French judgment of, 131; Gilder's support of ASG, 132–34; insertion of names on, 117–18, 138, 140; Krider's alternative designs, 124; lack of formal approval procedure, 124; leak of design to press, 119–20, 123; manufacturing bids, 114, 117, 118; manufacturing of, 140; misspelled names on, 143; nudity on, 123, 126; opposition to design of, 123, 124, 125; photograph of, *116*, *122*, *129*; reception of, 143; reduction of models, 110; rejection of ASG's design, 125–27, 128, 135; rejection of redesigned reverse, 131–32, 134; requests to show in silver dollar exhibit, 138–39; reverse,

128, *129*, 131–32, 134, 136, 137; Thacher's plans for, 101–2; trial medal, *116*

Babcock, Samuel D., 188
Bacon, Henry, 364
Baker, Raymond, 358
Barber, Charles: and $10 gold piece (*see* $10 gold piece); and $20 gold piece (*see* $20 gold piece); appointment as chief engraver, 54, 57; ASG's opinion of ability, 106; and award medal (*see* award medal, World's Columbian Exposition); career of, 53, 54; changes to Fraser's nickel design, 351–52; and Columbian half dollar, 79, 80, 81, 82–84, 86; and Columbian quarter, 87–88, 92, 93–94; death of, 357; and design of smaller gold coins, 339, 341; and half dollar design, 355; inability to use Janvier lathe, 269, 270, 278, 299, 300; and Lafayette dollar, 144–45; opinion of ASG's abilities, 272; opposition to hiring assistant, 61; portrait of, *55*; redesign of nickel, 57; and redesign of silver coinage, 62, 65–68; report on European minting practices, 238; retention of work samples, 322; view of high-relief, 61; visit to silver dollar exhibit, 140
Bartlett, Paul, 148
Bartlett, Truman, 148
bas-relief, ASG and, 33, 37
Bigelow, William Sturgis, 339–40
Bigelow-Pratt $5 gold piece, 339–41, *343*
Bingham, Theodore, 203–4, 206
Blaine, James G., 38
Bosbyshell, Oliver, 66, 93, 120, *121*, 124
Boston Public Library commission, 40
Brenner, Victor D., 308, 342, 345, 358
Brewster, Charles, 314, 317, 331
Brewster, F. Carroll, 323
British Royal Mint, 328
Brown, Glenn, 193, 194, 208, *330*, 334–36, 364
Buffalo nickel, 346, *348*, 350–52
Burchard, Horatio, *45*, 54
Burnham, Daniel, 71, *73*, 194, 208
Bynner, Witter, 285, 287, 295

Cabot Lodge, Henry. *See* Lodge, Henry Cabot
cameo cutting, ASG's training in, 17, 18
Cameron, Elizabeth Sherman (Lizzie): as possible model for Sherman angel, 165, 166; relationship with ASG, 151, 165; relationship with Henry Adams, 151, 154, 162
Cannon, Joe, 201–2, 208, 363–64
Carlisle, John G.: appointment as secretary of Treasury, 88; and Columbian award medal, 112, 124, 126–28; life after Mint, 192; portrait of, *96;* and United States economy, 99
Carow, Edith Kermit. *See* Roosevelt, Edith

Central Park, 181, 187
Century Club, 39
Century Illustrated Monthly Magazine, 37, 44
charity, need for, 16
Civil War, 17–18, 21
Clark, Davida, 41, 109, 164, 166, 209
Clausen, George, 180–81, 187
Coffin, William, 182–83
coinage, American: ASG's criticisms of Barber's designs, 67–68; authority to change design, 47, 58; Barber's redesign of, 57, 62, *64*, 65–68; change in design, 352; competition for redesign of, 47, 58–61; copper (*see* one-cent piece); criticism of, 147; diameters of, 283; dollar coin (*see* dollar coin); eagle on, 264, *265*, as fine art, 43; Gilder's desire to improve design of, 43, 48; gold (*see* coinage, gold); half dollar (*see* half dollar); inscriptions on (*see* inscriptions); Kimball's attempts to change design of, 44, 47–48; Liberty on (*see* Liberty); nickel (*see* nickel); public dissatisfaction with design, 54; redesign of, 58–62, 65–68; ASG and redesign of, 58, 59–60, 61, 62; Roberts's dislike of design, 220; statutes regarding design of, 217, 257, 260, 264, 283, 323, 352; TR's desire to change design of, 216–17; TR's opinion of, 216, 217; viewed as ugly, 43
coinage, copper. *See* one-cent piece
coinage, gold: $5 gold piece, 339–41, *343*; $10 gold piece (*see* $10 gold piece); $20 gold piece (*see* $20 gold piece); $50 gold piece, *348*, 353; ASG's alternative for, 291–92; ASG's delays in designing, 255; ASG's design proposals for, 255–56, *258*, *259*; ASG's designs for, 261, *266*, 277 (*see also* $10 gold piece; $20 gold piece); ASG's signature on, 277; attempts to circumvent Mint, 235, 267, 269; attempts to have dies made abroad, 267; Barber's alternative design for, 272, *273*, 274; Barber's rejection of ASG's models, 279, 287; bronze casts for, 287; commercial requirements, 257; costs of, 278, 283–84; cutting of dies for, 264, 267, 268–69, 274; delays in production of, 293–94; description of ASG's, 280; eagle on, 278–79, 290, 292–93; edge of, 274; experimental pieces, 280, 283; headdress, 264, 286, 287; Hering and, 263, 264, 279, 312, 314, 315, 320; and high relief, 255, 261, 262, 269, 274 (*see also* $10 gold piece; $20 gold piece; Indian on, 256, 257; Indian Princess, *265;* inscriptions, 256, 257, 260–61, 275, 279, 280; Landis's modification of, 292, 293; Leach's help in striking, 279; Liberty on, 256, 257, 261, 264, *266*, 286, 291–92, 293; Mint's experiments with models, 271–72; model preparation, 274–75;

modifications to design, 283, 286, 287; offer to strike limited number of ASG's design, 262; omission of "In God We Trust," 279, 323–26; Panama-Pacific $50 piece, *348*, 353; reductions for, 264, 267, 269, 279, 284, 287, 292, 293; relief of, 257, 264, 279, 280, 290, 292; rims, 255, 261; in Saint-Gaudens memorial exhibit, 333; Shaw's objection to design, 263; smaller coins, 339–41; striking of, 279–80, 290–91; sun rays, 275; TR and, 222, 255, 256–57, 260, 270, 275–76, 277–78, 291, 293; use of Liberty head, 291–92. *See also* $10 gold piece; $20 gold piece

coinage, Greek, 44, *C18*

Columbian award medal. *See* award medal, World's Columbian Exposition

Columbian half dollar. *See* half dollar, World's Columbian Exposition

Columbian quarter dollar. *See* quarter, World's Columbian Exposition

commemorative coins, 364–65. *See also individual coins*

Commission of Fine Arts, 346, 350, 352, 353, 358–59

Cortelyou, George B., *281*, 316, 325

counterfeiting, 57, 300, 351–52

Curtis, William Edmund, 124, 133–34

Curtis, William Eleroy, 76

Davis, George, 81, 123

de Francisci, Anthony, 359

Deitsch Brothers, 243–44, 249, 269. *See also* Weil, Henri

depression, ASG's bouts with, 165, 167, 168

dime, 353, 354–55

dollar coin: Bland dollar, *46;* competition for new designs for, 138–39; Indian Princess, *265;* Lafayette dollar, *142*, 144–48; Peace dollar, *349*, 358–59; silver dollar exhibit, 140; size of, 144

double eagle. *See* $20 gold piece

Drake, Alexander, 37

Durborow, Alan, 88

economy of United States: fears of going on silver standard, 99; and gold standard, 54, 98, 125, 367; Panic of 1857, 16; Panic of 1907, 315–16; Republican mismanagement of, 98

Ellsworth, James, 76, 77, 79, 80, 82, 84

Exposition Universelle. *See* Paris Exposition of 1900

Farragut Monument, 26, 30, 33–34, *35*

Flanagan, John, 366

Foord, John, 106

Joseph Francis medal, 61, *63*

Franklin medal: additional medals, 253; appropriation for, 241; approval of design for, 247,

248, 249, 250; approved design for, *246;* ASG's design proposal for, 242; attempts to circumvent Mint, 242–43, 247, 248; bronze used in patina, 252; cost of, 249–50; Cox's design proposal for, *245;* deadline, 248–49; dies for, 242, 243–44, 249–50, 252–53; gold used in, 251, 252; inscriptions, 244; and Louis Saint-Gaudens, 241–42, 252; model, *245;* payment of fees for, 253; portrayal of Franklin, 243, *246,* 247–48, 251; presentation date, 248, 249; quotes on striking of, 248; reductions for, 244; Root's rejection of, 250–51

Fraser, James Earle: bust of TR, 346; new Lincoln cent design proposal, 367; nickel design, 346, 350–52; and Peace dollar, 358, 359; portraits of, *344*

Fraser, Laura Gardin, 351, 365–366, 367, 368

Freed, Rhine R., 313

French, Daniel Chester: concern for $20 gold piece, 308; and Lincoln Memorial, 364; memorial exhibit for ASG, 332–33; and Panama-Pacific commemorative coins, 353; praise of ASG, 360; and Sherman Monument, 187, 188, 192

Gilder, Helena de Kay, 25, 29

Gilder, Richard Watson: bas-relief of, *32;* and coin redesign, 43, 44, 48; early career of, 25; establishment of *Century Illustrated Monthly Magazine,* 37; as model for Farragut's legs, 30; and opening of Pan-American Exposition, 183; portrait of, *130;* praise of Farragut Monument, 34; and redesign of gold coinage, 267; relationship with TR, 38–39, 210, 212; salon of, 25; service in Civil War, 39; speech at Saint-Gaudens memorial exhibit, 333–34; support of ASG in award medal affair, 132–34; on use of Barber to redesign silver coinage, 65

"Girl in the Pie" incident, 139, *142*

gold coinage. *See* coinage, gold

gold standard, 54, 98, 125, 367

Grant Memorial, 196, 197

half dollar: Barber and, *64*, 355; Illinois State centennial, 364, *368;* Liberty Walking, *348*, 354; Oregon Trail Memorial, 365, *368;* rim, 355; Washington Bicentennial, 365; Weinman's design of, 353, 354, 355; World's Columbian Exposition (*see* half dollar, World's Columbian Exposition)

half dollar, World's Columbian Exposition: Barber and, 81, 82–84; criticism of, 79, 84, 86; date on, 75, 81; design for, 76, 79–83; failure of, 113; as means of financing construction, 75–76; photograph of, *85;* portrayal of

Columbus, 76, 79–81, 82; Proof strikes, 84, 86; reverse of, 80–81; sales of, 84, 86; use of low-relief, 84, 86; Warner's design for, 80, 82

Hallowell, Sara, 87

Hamlin, Charles, 110

Hastings, Thomas, 203

Hay, John, 241

Head of Victory, 210, *211*, 299

headdress: on gold coins, 264, 286, 287, 326, 336; on one-cent piece, 284–85

Hering, Henry, 263, 264, 279, 312, 314, 315, 320

High Relief $20 gold piece, *310*, 311, 317, 319–20

Hill reducing machine, 269

Hobbs, Clarence, 350, 351, 355

Homer, Augusta. *See* Saint-Gaudens, Augusta Homer (Gussie)

Illinois State centennial half dollar, 364, *368*

Indian Princess, *265*

inscriptions: on American coins, 257, 260, 285, 286, 323, 350; on Columbian quarter, 91–92, 97; on gold coins, 256, 257, 260–61, 275, 279, 280, 323–26, *327*, 332

Janvier reducing lathe, 227, 238, 269, 270, 278, 299, 300

Kimball, James P.: attempts to change coin design, 44, 47–48; medal for, *46*

Krider, Peter, 124

Kunz, George, 138, 252

La Farge, John, 26, 29

Lafayette dollar: Barber and design of, 144–45, 146, 148; date on, 145; delays in, 147; design of, 144; desire to include prayer on, 144–45, 146, 148; inclusion of Bartlett's name, 148; objections to design of, 146; photograph of, *142;* reception of, 147–48; size of, 144

Lafayette Memorial, 144

Landis, John, *289*, 292, 293, 304

Leach, Frank: and $20 gold piece, 278–79, 290, 314, 316–17, 318–19, 326, 329; and design of smaller gold coins, 339, 340–41; knowledge of Mint operations, 315, 316; as Mint director, 301, 314, 315, 316; and one-cent piece design, 342; portrait of, *309;* resignation of, 342; and San Francisco earthquake, 316; views on relief, 238

LeBrethon, Jules, 18, 22

Lee, Alice. *See* Roosevelt, Alice Lee

Leech, Edward O.: and Columbian half dollar, 80, 81, 82, 83; and Columbian quarter, 87–88, 91, 92, 93, 94, 97; criticism of Barber's designs, 65–67; portrait of, *56;* and redesign of silver coinage, 58–62, 65–68

Liberty: on American coins, 43, *45*, 257, 260; on gold coins, 256, 257, 261, 264, *266*, 286, 291–92, 293; on half dollar, *348*, 354; with headdress, 264; on nickel, *55*, 57; on one-cent piece, 285; on Peace dollar, 359; on quarter, *349*, 354, 357

lifesaving medal, 61

Lincoln cent, 342, *343*, 345, 358, 367

Lincoln funeral procession, *20*, 21

Lincoln Memorial: location of, 198; on one-cent piece, 367; proposal for, 363–64

Lincoln Memorial Commission, 364

Linderman, Henry, 54

Lodge, Henry Cabot, 38–39, 173

Logan Monument, 158

Low, Will, 334

MacNeil, Hermon, 41, 352, 353, 354, 355–57

MacVeagh, Franklin, 345, 346, 350–51

Mall. *See* National Mall

Martiny, Philip, 49, 50, 76

McAdoo, William Gibbs, 352, 353, 356

McKim, Charles: bas-relief of, *28;* Boston Public Library commission, 40; defense of plans for National Mall, 208; early career of, 26; establishment of American School of Architecture in Rome, 41; pedestal for Sherman Monument, 180, 189, 191; portrait of, *195;* relationship with ASG, 26, 40–41; and renovation of White House, 200–204, 286; on Senate Park Commission, 194, 196–98; and siting of Sherman Monument, 180–82, 186–88

McMillan, James, 194

medals, 221–22. *See also individual medals*

Mellon, Andrew, 365

memorial exhibits: at Corcoran Gallery of Art, 335–36, 338; at Metropolitan Museum of Art, 332–34

Millet, Frank: approval of Lafayette dollar, 147; criticism of coin design, 147; desire for better medals, 221–22; views of inaugural medal, 233

Mint, San Francisco. *See* Leach, Frank

Mint, United States: chief engraver position, 53, 54, 57 (*see also* Barber, Charles; Morgan, George T.); and coinage for Philippines, 278; culture of, 49, 50, 220, 366–67; die production, 269; director of, *see under names of directors;* engraving department, 53, 54 (*see also* Barber, Charles; Morgan, George T.); and gold coinage (*see* coinage, gold); lack of attention to medal work, 221–22; loss of influence, 367; organization of, 53; output of, 58; use of Hill reducing machine, 269. *See also individual projects*

Mint Act of 1873, 53

minting practices, European vs. American, 238

429

Mitchell, Henry, 60–61
Mitchell, Weir, 241, 244
monetary system, 53–54
money. *See* coinage, American
Moore, Charles: and renovation of White House, 200, 201; and Senate Park Commission, 194; and silver coin design, 352; and Washington Bicentennial quarter, 365
Moore, J. Hampton, 325–26
Morgan, George T.: bid for cutting of die for Franklin medal, 243; as chief engraver, 357–58; design for Columbian quarter, 94; early career, 54; Illinois State centennial half dollar, 364; and Peace dollar, 359; reduced to assistant engraver, 57
Morrill, Justin S., 47
Morris, Harrison S., 240, 241, 242, 244, 247
mottos. *See* inscriptions

National Academy of Design, 21, 29
National Mall: defense of plans for, 208–9; Lincoln Memorial, 363–64; opposition to plans for, 206, 208; photograph of, *195*; plans for renovation of, 193, 196–98 (*see also* Senate Park Commission)
Newlands, Francis G., 209
nickel: Barber's changes to Fraser's design, 351–52; Barber's redesign of, 55, 57; Buffalo nickel, 346, *348*, 350–52; counterfeiting of, 57, 351–52; design of, 35; desire for change, 345; Fraser's design for, 346, 350–52; hubs for, 351; Indian portrait on, 346; inscriptions on, 350; Liberty Head, 55, 57; relief, 350; use in vending machines, 350, 351
Nike-Eiphnh, 210, *211*, 284

Olmsted, Frederic, Jr., 187, 194
one-cent piece: abandonment of ASG's design, 315; ASG's designs for, 264, *266*, 284–86; attempts to circumvent Mint, 235; Flying Eagle, *265*; Gussie's interference with, 311; headdress on, 284–85; inscriptions on, 285; Liberty on, 285; Lincoln on (*see* Lincoln cent); models for, *288*; proposed designs for, 235, *288*; TR and, 222, *288*, 285, 342
Oregon Trail Memorial half dollar, 365, *368*

Page, George F., 119
Page Belting Company, 119, 123
Palmer, Bertha Honoré, 87, 88, *89*, 91, 92, 97
Pan-American Exposition, 182–83, *185*
Panama-Pacific Exposition commemorative coins, *348*, 353
Panic of 1857, 16
Panic of 1907, 315–16, 323
Paris Exposition of 1900, 144, 162, 167
Paris Salon, 161, 164, 165

Parsons, Samuel, 181, 188, 189, 190
Peace dollar, *349*, 358–59
Peck, Ferdinand, 143
Peddle, Caroline, 88, *90*, 91–93
Peirce, Herbert, 252–53
penny. *See* Lincoln cent; one-cent piece
philanthropy, 16–17
plaster, 284, 287
Porter, Horace, 182, 184
Pratt, Bela Lyon, 340–41
Preston, Robert E.: and $10 gold piece, 304; and Columbian award medal, 114, 117, 118, 135, 137, 138; medal for, *115*
Proctor, Phimister, 158
Public Art League, 193–94

quarter: Liberty on, *349*, 354, 357; MacNeil's design for, 355–57; Mint's modification of design, 356–57; relief on, 356; Washington Bicentennial, 365–366
quarter, World's Columbian Exposition: ASG and, 94; Barber and, 87–88, 92, 93–94; control of design, 88; design of, 91–93; failure of, 113; inscriptions, 91–92, 97; Leech and, 87–88, 92, 93, 94, 97; Morgan's design of, 97; obverse of, 97; Peddle and, 88, 91–93; photographs of, *95*, *96*; portrayal of Isabella, 91; representation of Board of Lady Managers, 97; reverse of, 94, 98

Reid, Whitelaw, 152
Richardson, Henry Hobson, 26, 34
Roberts, George: and gold coins, 257, 269, 274, 291, 300–301; and nickel design, 346; objections to high relief, 262; opinions of coin design, 220; portrait of, *239*; relationship with TR, 294; resignation of, 294; return to Mint, 345–46
Roman Bronze Works, 232
Roosevelt, Alice Lee: death of, 38; marriage to TR, 37, 171; photograph of, *36*; relationship with Edith, 171
Roosevelt, Edith: agenda as First Lady, 199; childhood, 170; condolences to Gussie, 305; death of, 363; early relationship with TR, 169–71; entertainment in White House, 199; in family portrait, *230*; friendship with Henry Adams, 174; marriage to TR, 172; preference for Washington, 176; relationship with Alice, 171; and social protocol, 179; views of inaugural medal, 233; in Washington society, 173–74; White House interior decorating, 286; and White House renovation, 200–201, 202, 204
Roosevelt, Theodore, Jr.: ambitions for United States, 217; as assistant secretary of the Navy, 178; asthma, development of, 21;

belief in philanthropy, 17; blamed for Panic of 1907, 323; bust of, *347;* as civil service commissioner, 173; creation of Council of Fine Arts, 345; death of, 363; and death of Alice, 171; defense of $10 gold coin, 336, 338; early friendship with ASG, 183–84; early life, 15; early relationship with Edith, 169–71; education of, 22, 23; election to New York State Assembly, 38; European tours of, 22, 23; experience in West, 171; financial circumstances, 173; and gold coinage (*see* $10 gold piece; $20 gold piece; coinage, gold); as governor of New York, 178; and "In God We Trust" motto, 323, 324–25; and inaugural medal (*see* Roosevelt inaugural medal); inauguration, 229 (*see also* Roosevelt inaugural medal); interest in politics, 37–38; lack of artistic knowledge, 285; as lame duck president, 325; marriage to Alice, 37, 171; marriage to Edith, 172; and memorial exhibit, 335–36; nomination for mayor of New York City, 172; and omission of "In God We Trust," 323; and one-cent piece design, 222, 284–85, 342; and opening of Pan-American Exposition, 183; opinion of coinage, 216, 217, 277; opposition to, 323; partnership with ASG, 256; physical activity of, 22–23; and plans for National Mall, 208–9; plaque, *309;* as police commissioner, 176; portraits of, *19, 36, 223, 230;* presidency, ascension to, 186; presidency, election to, 210, 212; reentry into politics, 173; rejection of mayoral nomination, 176; relationship with Gilder, 38–39, 210, 212; relationship with Roberts, 294; reputation as reformer, 173; return to New York, 176; Rough Riders, 178; and Sherman Monument, 184, 192; solicitation of ASG to redesign coinage, 217, 220; and vice presidency, 178–79; views of plans for National Mall, 198

Roosevelt, Theodore, Sr., 16, 18

Roosevelt inaugural medal: ASG and, 222, 225, 228, 232; approval of, 231, 232; cost of, 226–27; criticism of, 221; description of, 232; funding for unofficial medal, 225; inscriptions, 226, 228; Mint's neglect of, 221; photographs of, *223, 230;* quotes for manufacturing of, 226; reductions, 227, 228, 231; size of, 225, 226–27; striking of, 226, 227, 228, 231, 232; TR and, 222, 223; views of, 233–34

Root, Elihu: and Franklin medal, 247, 250–52, 263; jurisdiction over federal parklands, 196; and memorial exhibit, 335, 336; and plans for renovation of Mall, 203; portrait of, *337;* and siting of Sherman Monument, 184

Ross, Nellie Tayloe, 366, 367

Rough Riders, 178

Saint-Gaudens, Augusta Homer (Gussie): and ASG's estate, 311, 331; and ASG's health, 270–71, 290; contributions to Farragut Monument, 33; death of father, 40; demand for compensation for gold-coin designs, 331; disappointment in low-relief gold coins, 320–21; and financial management, 40, 271; health of, 40, 41; interference with Lincoln Memorial, 364; involvement in gold coins, 311, 314; letters written for ASG, 109; meeting of ASG, 26; and ASG memorial exhibits, 334, 335; portraits of, *31, 111;* promised Ultra High Relief gold piece, 322, 334

Saint-Gaudens, Augustus: apprenticeship of, 17, 18; attempts to establish self as sculptor, 26; attempts to take care of Louis, 242; backlog of commissions, 157, 158; Cornish, permanent move to, 177; criticism of by Paris Salon, 161; death of, 295; depression, 165, 167–68; early friendship with TR, 183–84; early life, 13–15; at École des Beaux-Arts, 22; education, 14, 15, 17, 21; financial circumstances, 109, 131; health, 167–68, 177, 186, 189, 209, 226, 238, 241, 247, 250, 251, 263, 264, 267, 268, 270–71, 285, 286–87, 290, 291; loss of studio, 210; masque in honor of, *236–37,* 295, 367, *368;* medication, 285; Paris, first trip to, 21–22; portraits of, *19, 27, 141;* procrastination of, 360; recognition in France, 165, 166; on Senate Park Commission, 196; sketch of, *163. See also individual projects*

Saint-Gaudens, Homer, 33, 40, 248, 267, 268, 271, 325

Saint-Gaudens, Louis, 61, 241–42, 243, 252

Saltonstall, Rose, *36*

San Francisco: earthquake, 316; exposition, 353

San Francisco Mint. *See* Leach, Frank

Scovill Manufacturing Company, 118, 137–38, 140

Senate Park Commission: ASG added to, 196; ASG's support of plans, 206; creation of, 194, 196; and Lincoln Memorial, 363–64; plans for renovation of Mall, 196–98; Shaw's opposition to plans, 206

Shaw, Leslie: comments on White House renovation, 206; opposition to Senate Park Commission Plan, 206; portrait of, *207;* and redesign of gold coinage, 235, 257, 260, 261–62, 263; and redesign of one-cent piece, 235

Shaw Monument: angel, *32,* 37, 157, 158, 159, 161; ASG's breach of contract, 108; Atkinson's exasperation with ASG, 159–60; commissioning of, 34, 37; Committee's threat to engage new sculptor, 157; dedication of, 161; delays in, 40, 102, 105–6, 109, 112, 128, 157, 159–60; payment for, 160; photograph of, *163;* reception of, 161; site of, 157; Thacher's attempts to have ASG released from, 106, 107

Sherman, Elizabeth. *See* Cameron, Elizabeth Sherman (Lizzie)

Sherman, Rachel, 166, 182

Sherman, William Tecumseh: ASG's admiration for, 151; ASG's attempts to secure sessions with, 151, 152; ASG's bust of, 154, 335–36; ASG's memorial for (*see* Sherman Monument); death of, 155; sittings for ASG, 154

Sherman Monument: angel, 161, 164, 165, 166, *185* (*see also* Angel of Victory); casting of, 178; dedication, *185,* 190–91; display of in Paris, 162, 164, 165, 167; gilding of, 188–89, 191; horse, 158; inscriptions, 189; models for, 161; in Pan-American Exposition, 182–83; pedestal, 180, 189, 191; Proctor's assistance, 158; reception of, 186, 192; selection of ASG to create, 155–56; shed for, 179; siting of, 180–82, 184, 186–88; trees at site of, 188, 189–90; work on in Paris, 162, 164

Sherman Silver Purchase Act of 1890, 98

silver, 53, 54, 98

Snowden, A. Loudon, 54

Sohier, W.D., 308

Spanish-American War, 178

Spring-Rice, Cecil, 172

statuary, rules for in New York City, 181

stearine, 283, 284

Stillman, William J., 44

Taft, William Howard, 342, 346

Thacher, John Boyd: attempts to secure ASG's release from Shaw Commission, 106, 107; plans for Columbian award medal, 101–2; portrait of, *103;* securing of ASG for award medal, 108

Thorndike, Paul, 182

Thorndike, Rachel Sherman, 166, 182

Tiffany's: and Columbian award medal, 117; and Franklin medal, 248, 250, 252; and Roosevelt inaugural medal, 225, 226, 227, 228, 231, 232; and striking of gold coinage, 274

Treasury Department. *See* Cortelyou, George B.; MacVeagh, Franklin; Shaw, Leslie

Ultra High Relief $20 gold piece, 279–80, *281,* 294–95, 322, 331–32. *See also* $20 gold piece; coinage, gold

United States Mint. *See* Mint, United States

vending machines, 350, 351, 354–55

Victory-Peace, 210, *211,* 284

von Engelken, F.J.H., 355, 356

Warner, Olin, 80, 81, 82, 84

Washington, DC. *See* National Mall; White House

Washington Bicentennial quarter, 365–66

Washington Inauguration Centennial: badge, 50, *51;* medal, 48–50, *51, 52*

Washington's death bicentennial $5 gold piece, *367,* 368

Waugh, Sydney, 366

Weil, Henri: and Franklin medal, 243–44; portrait of, *224;* preparation of hubs for nickel, 351; and Roosevelt inaugural medal, 227, 228, 231; use of Janvier lathe, 278; use of work on gold coins, 278

Weinman, Adolph A.: ASG's opinion of, 232; and Franklin medal, 247, 248; portrait of, *224;* redesign of dime, 353, 354; redesign of half dollar, 353, 354, 355; and Roosevelt inaugural medal, 225–26, 228; and silver coin designs, 352; support of Morgan, 357

White, Stanford, 30, 33–34, 263, 267

White House: condition of, 198–99; entertainment in, 199; greenhouses, *195,* 201, 204; interior decorating, 204, 286; renovation of, 199–206, *205*

Wilkinson, Burke, 166

Willcox, William R., 188, 189–90

Wilson, John, 225, 226, 228

Woodside, John, 114, 117

Woolley, Robert, 352, 353

World War I, 357, 358–59

World's Columbian Exposition: acclaim of, 98; ASG's involvement in, 72, 75, 76; award medal (*see* award medal, World's Columbian Exposition); commemorative coins (*see* half dollar, World's Columbian Exposition; quarter, World's Columbian Exposition); Court of Honor, *74;* directory badge, 81, *85;* exhibits, 72; failure of commemorative coins, 113; financing, 71, 75–76, 86 (*see also* half dollar, World's Columbian Exposition; quarter, World's Columbian Exposition); sculptural pieces, 75

Zorn, Anders, 161; sketch of ASG, *163*